British Library Resources

A Bibliographical Guide

Robert B. Downs
Assisted by Elizabeth C. Downs

American Library Association, Chicago

Mansell Information/Publishing Ltd., London   1973

Library of Congress Cataloging in Publication Data

Downs, Robert Bingham, 1903–
  British library resources.

    1. Bibliography--Bibliography. 2. Library
resources--Great Britain. I. Downs, Elizabeth (Crooks)
II. Title.
Z1002.D63   016.016   73-1598
ISBN 0-8389-0150-6

Printed in the United States of America by the
American Library Association and in Great Britain by
Balding & Mansell Ltd.

Mansell Information/Publishing Ltd.
3 Bloomsbury Place, London WC1A 2QA, England

Contents

CONTENTS

CONTENTS

Individual Bibliography, Biography and Criticism

CONTENTS

CONTENTS

Preface

Grateful acknowledgment is made to many persons and institutions for aid and encouragement in the conception and preparation of the present work. Without such generous assistance, the aim of describing British library resources bibliographically could hardly have been carried to a successful conclusion.

The undertaking was made possible in the first place by a fellowship granted by the John Simon Guggenheim Memorial Foundation.

Indebtedness to British librarians extends to a list too long for individual mention. Friendly interest and full co-operation were received from librarians throughout the United Kingdom. Many persons in the British Museum, the National Libraries, university and college libraries, large public libraries, and society and association libraries expended time and effort to assure comprehensive listing of their collections. The results, it is hoped, will justify their strong support.

Valuable help in establishing a basic list of references was provided at the outset by Cathleen C. Flanagan.

The preparation of the manuscript for publication was in the highly competent and experienced hands of Clarabelle Gunning and Deloris Holiman.

Robert B. Downs

Introduction

The purpose of the present work is to offer a bibliographical guide to the resources for advanced study and research in the libraries of the United Kingdom and Eire. The intention is to record all published library catalogs—general and special; all check-lists of specialized collections in libraries; calendars of manuscripts and archives; exhibition catalogs; articles descriptive of library collections; guides to individual libraries and their holdings; directories of libraries—both general and in specialized fields; union lists of periodicals, newspapers, and other serials; and any other records, descriptive, analytical, or critical, that may guide the scholar, research worker, or advanced student in finding significant materials to meet his needs.

In general, annual reports, histories of libraries, and administrative studies are omitted unless, as in some instances, they shed light on the nature and development of particular collections. Further, articles discussing or describing single works, printed or manuscript, are rarely included, except for items of extraordinary importance or uniqueness.

The present compilation is designed to be inclusive of all types of libraries, all subject fields, and all categories of library materials, current and retrospective. Some entries are partly or entirely of historical interest, e.g., 19th-century catalogs of public libraries, which may be of value from several points of view: indicating the state of the bibliographical art at a given period, indicating the cultural level of the book collections available in a particular community, and tracing scarce items not found elsewhere. It is significant, too, that some bibliographical records are timeless. Evidence of this is the recent reprinting of various British Museum, Bodleian, and other catalogs and calendars which made their first appearance a century or more ago.

It is noteworthy that numerous entries are international in scope, extending beyond Britain to include libraries on the Continent, in America, and occasionally in other regions of the world. Especially common are lists which locate copies of rare books in both the British Isles and the United States, showing the extensive migration of this type of material across the Atlantic. Thus, resources for research are widely distributed internationally and may turn up practically anywhere, though the primary aim here, of course, is to identify collections in British and Irish libraries.

In the compilation of references recorded herein, heavy reliance was placed on the British Museum, which theoretically should receive all copyrighted and most other publications originating in Britain. In addition, the bibliographical resources of the University of London (especially the Middlesex Library North), the Library Association Library, the National Central Library, the Aslib Library, and the Bibliographical Society Library proved to be rich sources of information. Visits to the Bodleian Library at Oxford, the Cambridge University Library, and the university libraries of Aberdeen, Edinburgh, Glasgow, Birmingham, Leeds, Manchester, Newcastle upon Tyne, and Sheffield; the John Rylands Library; the National Libraries of Scotland and Wales; the public libraries of Aberdeen, Edinburgh, Glasgow, Birmingham, Manchester, Leeds, Newcastle upon Tyne, and Sheffield; and to scores of society and other special libraries in London helped to complete and to round out the record. Within the time available for the project it was naturally unfeasible to visit in person hundreds of other libraries of potential importance for bibliographical material. Fortunately, information on the collections in numerous libraries was received through widely scattered published sources and by correspondence.

The picture of British library resources presented here is necessarily uneven, since it does not reflect the strength of libraries from which publications are lacking. In particular, important collections newly acquired may not yet have been covered by catalogs, guides, or other descriptive material. For example, British universities have proliferated since about 1900, and their library collections have grown rapidly in recent years. With few exceptions, however, the holdings of newer university libraries have not been publicized, because their energies and funds have been spent in acquisition activities and in providing library service to rapidly expanding student enrollments and teaching faculties.

Several points relating to the format and general arrangement of the guide may be helpful to users. Specifically, it should be noted that:

1. The arrangement is broadly by the Dewey Decimal Classification, though with occasional variations. For example, language is grouped with literature, and most references relating to individuals are placed together at the end of the subject groupings.
2. Each entry is numbered separately and is intended to be listed only once, under what appears to be the most appropriate heading. It is probable, however, that a few duplications may have occurred inadvertently. The disadvantages of this scheme are believed to have been counterbalanced by the detailed index of authors, editors, compilers, institutions, subjects, and occasional titles. All items are entered in the index by individual numbers, rather than by page references.
3. Except for periodical articles and chapters in books, libraries are preferred to persons for main entries, on the assumption that names of institutions are more important for reference and research purposes. Again, any shortcomings in this plan are corrected by index listings of personal names.

Because this is a pioneer work, the first of its kind for the British Isles, it has the defects of a first edition. If its users regard it as reasonably successful in achieving its objectives, despite omissions and some inevitable errors, there may be further editions presenting fuller data, adding new titles, and updating the record. Addenda and corrigenda will be highly welcome.

General

General Bibliography and Reference Books

1. Aslib. Thesauri held in the Aslib Library: January 1971. London, Aslib Library, 1971. 9*l*.

2. Association of Assistant Librarians, East Midland Division. East Midlands union list of bibliographies, a selection of bibliographies with locations in libraries of the East Midlands, ed. by W. E. French. Peterborough, Hunts.: The Association, 1954. 27p.
    Locates copies in 33 libraries.

3. ———, Greater London Division, Reference books and bibliographies; a union list, by L. M. Payne and Joan M. Harries. (A combined revision of the Union list of bibliographies and the Union list of reference books) London: The Association, 1957. 92p.
    Locations in numerous libraries.

4. ——— ———. Union list of bibliographies; a selection of four hundred bibliographies with locations in some metropolitan and Greater London libraries, ed. by Joan M. Harries. London, 1950. 53p.
    Locates copies in 80 libraries.

5. ——— ———. Union list of reference books; a selection of four hundred reference books, with locations in some metropolitan and Greater London libraries, ed. by A. J. Walford. London, 1954. 76p.
    Classified arrangement; locations in 80 libraries.

6. Aston, University, Library. Subject guide to abstracts and indexes, by Emma Cusworth. Birmingham, 1972. 19p.

7. Beddington and Wallington Public Libraries. Catalogue of bibliographical material contained in the stock of the Beddington and Wallington Public Libraries. n.p., 1957. 89p.

8. Bibliographical Society Library. Handlist of books in the Library of the Bibliographical Society, March 1935, ed. by J. V. Scholderer. London: Oxford Univ. Pr., 1935. 67p.

9. British Museum, Dept. of Printed Books. A handlist of bibliographies, classified catalogues, and indexes, placed in the Reading Room of the British Museum for reference, by G. W. Porter. London: The Museum, 1881. 105p.

10. ———. List of bibliographical works in the Reading Room of the British Museum, 2d ed. London: The Museum, 1889. 103p.

11. ———. List of books forming the Reference Library in the Reading Room of the British Museum, 4th ed. London: The Museum, 1910. 2v.
    v.1, authors; v.2, index of subjects.

12. ———. List of catalogues of English book sales, 1676-1900, now in the British Museum. London: The Museum, 1915. 523p.
    Copies of catalogs in various libraries shown in annotated copy of the list in British Museum; 8,000 items listed.

13. ———. List of the books of reference in the Reading Room of the British Museum, 3d ed. London: The Museum, 1889. 475p.

14. Cambridge, University, Library. List of books in class "Ref" (reading room, south end), 2d ed. Cambridge: Univ. Pr., 1937. 138p.

15. ———. Subject guide to class "Ref"—current reference books—in the University Library. Cambridge, 1968. 106*l*.

16. Deakin, Terence J. Catalogi librorum eroticorum; a critical bibliography of erotic bibliographies and book-catalogues. London: Cecil & Amelia Woolf, 1964. 28p.
    Detailed bibliographical descriptions; copies located in 5 libraries, British, American, and French.

17. Doyle, Anthony Ian H. "More sale catalogues." Durham philobiblon, 2 (1958-62), 9-14, 52-54.

Checklists of catalogs in King's College Library (Newcastle upon Tyne) and in Durham University Library.

18. Hamlin, Arthur T. "The book collections of British university libraries; an American reaction." International library review, 2 (1970), 135-73.

Survey of libraries' holdings of general bibliographies, periodical indexes, encyclopedias, and general reference works.

19. Keele, University, Library. Subjects and methods; a list of a hundred books and articles in Keele University Library that touch on the methodology of subjects or the possibility of overlaps between disciplines, by Francis Celoria. Keele, 1966. Unpaged.

20. Scottish Central Library. A classified list of catalogues and bibliographies in the Library, comp. by S. T. H. Wright and others. Edinburgh, 1955. 63p.

Records 665 titles, classified with author index.

21. Sheffield, University, Library. Current French national bibliographies, a short guide, by W. John Hutchins. Sheffield, 1966. 5p.

22. ————. Current German national bibliographies; a short guide, by W. J. Hutchins. Sheffield, 1966. 9p.

23. ————. Current Russian national bibliographies, a short guide, by W. John Hutchins. Sheffield, 1966. 6p.

24. ————. Current Spanish, Portuguese & Latin American national bibliographies, a short guide, by W. John Hutchins. Sheffield, 1967. 8p.

Government Publications

25. Birmingham, University, Library. A directory of British government publications. Birmingham, 1966. 16p.

General guide, based on Birmingham University Library's holdings.

26. British Museum. Index-catalogue of Indian official publications in the Library, British Museum, comp. by Frank Campbell. London: Library Supply Co., 1900. 314 + 72p.

Arranged by areas of Asia and India.

27. ————, State Paper Room. A brief checklist of American state government serials currently received by the British Museum State Paper Room. London: Institute of United States Studies, 1970. 5p.

28. ———— ————. Checklist of British official serial publications, 5th ed. to June 1971. London: The Museum, 1971. 62p.

29. Cambridge, University, Centre of South Asian Studies. Union catalogue of the central government of India publications held by libraries in London, Oxford and Cambridge, by Rajeshwari Datta. London: Mansell, 1970. 471 cols.

Serial and nonserial publications located in 12 libraries.

30. ———— ————. Union catalogue of the government of Ceylon publications held by libraries in London, Oxford and Cambridge, by Teresa Macdonald. Cambridge: Mansell, 1970. 75 cols.

Locates copies in 18 libraries.

31. ———— ————. Union catalogue of the government of Pakistan publications held by libraries in London, Oxford, and Cambridge, by Rajeshwari Datta. London: Mansell Information Publishing, 1967. 116 cols.

Locations in 11 libraries.

32. ————, Library. A guide to official publications in the University Library, Cambridge, with special reference to material relating to the British Commonwealth and Empire, by K. A. C. Parsons and R. C. G. Vickery. Cambridge, 1960. 115*l*.

33. Lancaster, University, Library. Serials list: supplement; British government and international organisations serials. Lancaster, 1969. 37p.

Lists library's holdings.

34. London Library. List of Parliamentary papers, comp. by C. T. Hagberg Wright. Westminster: P. S. King, 1903. 124p.

Subject list of papers in London Library.

35. London, University, Library. British government publications in the University Library. Typescript undated and unpaged.

Lists 392 items chronologically, 1839-1966.

36. Newcastle upon Tyne City Libraries. Index catalogue of the Parliamentary papers in the Public Reference Library (second-third-Index Catalogue of the Parliamentary Papers . . . describing those added 1915-1922-1923-33), by Joseph Walton. Newcastle upon Tyne, 1915-33. 3pts.

Subject index to Parliamentary papers.

37. Royal Institute of International Affairs. Index to United Nations' documents to December 1947. London, 1947. 93p. Supplements 1-3. London, 1948-49. 3pts.

38. Southampton University Library. British government publications; a mainly alphabetical guide to what they are, what the Library has and how to find them, by Diana Marshallsay. Southampton, 1970. 14p. (Occasional paper, no.2)

39. Sussex, University, Library. British government publications, 2d ed., comp. by D. V. Kennelly. Brighton, 1971. 37p.

40. Waterloo, University, Dana Porter Arts Library. A guide to the content and use of government publications in the Dana Porter Arts Library. Waterloo, 1969. 46l.

Introduction to Canadian, British, U.S., and other government publications, with notes on library's holdings.

41. York, University, Library. British government publications. York, 1969. 25p. (Library guide, no.4)

Dissertations

42. Cant, Ronald Gordon. "The St. Andrews University theses, 1579-1747; a bibliographical introduction." Edinburgh Bibliographical Society transactions, 2 (1941), 105-50.

Detailed descriptions of 51 theses, with locations of copies.

43. ———. "The St. Andrews University theses, 1579-1747, a bibliographical introduction; supplement." Edinburgh Bibliographical Society transactions, 2 (1946), 263-72.

44. Library Association. A survey of thesis literature in British libraries, by P. D. Record. London, 1950. 21p.

Notes availability and lists British university theses and availability of foreign theses in British libraries.

45. London University. A list of English, Scandinavian, and German theses in the University of London, by A. H. Smith and A. T. Hatto. London, 1939. 40p. (London mediaeval studies, monograph, no.2)

46. Oxford, University, Bodleian Library. Catalogus dissertationum academicarum quibus nuper aucta est Bibliotheca Bodleian MDCCCXXXII. Oxford: E. Typographeo Academico, 1834. 448p. + index.

47. Standing Conference of National and University Libraries. Foreign theses in British libraries, comp. by R. S. Johnson. Cardiff: Univ. College, 1971. 27p.

Locates theses of 160 universities in 38 libraries.

Library Science

48. Association of Assistant Librarians. Bristol and District Division. Union list of professional periodicals; of librarianship and bibliography in libraries in Cornwall, Devon, Gloucestershire, Somerset, and Wiltshire, comp. by D. M. Laverick. Bristol: The Association, 1961. 9p.

Locates files in 19 libraries.

49. ——— ———. Union list of professional textbooks, books on librarianship and allied subjects in libraries in Gloucestershire, Somerset and Wiltshire, comp. by David J. Bryant and Roger J. Crudge. Bristol: The Association, 1958. 56p.

Copies located in 12 libraries.

50. ———, North-Eastern Division. Union list of professional periodicals in northern libraries, comp. by Norman W. Wood and Alan G. Thompson. London: The Association, 1963. 17p.

Locations in numerous libraries.

51. ———, South Wales and Monmouthshire Division. Union list of library periodicals. n.p., 1956. 10l.

Entries for 62 titles; holdings recorded for 23 libraries.

52. ———, Sussex Division. Union list of textbooks available in libraries of the Sussex Division. Chichester, 1955. 48p.

Locates copies in 8 libraries.

53. ———, West of Scotland Division. Periodicals on librarianship held by special libraries in Scotland, ed. by H. A. Whatley. London, 1963. 6p.

54. ——— ———. Union list of professional periodicals; periodicals on librarianship held by Scottish libraries, ed. by F. J. Guthrie. London, 1962. 19p.

Locations in numerous libraries.

55. Bermondsey Public Libraries. Bibliography and librarianship; a select list. London, 1954. 6 pts.

56. Birmingham Public Libraries. Select list of books on librarianship available in Birmingham Reference Library, comp. by A. J. Illes and B. G. Staples. Birmingham, 1958. 20p.

57. Calvert, Drusilla. "Periodicals received by the L.A. Library." Library Association library and information bulletin, no.9 (1970), 6-28. Supplement, no.16 (1971), 2-6.

Alphabetical list.

58. College of Librarianship Wales Library. Annual reports. Aberystwyth, 1971. 22p.

List of library annual reports held by library.

59. ———. Library link. Aberystwyth, no.1- . April 1970- .

Fortnightly list of library's current accessions.

60. ———. List of current periodicals, November 1970. Aberystwyth: College of Librarianship Wales, 24p.

61. ———. Serials holdings. Aberystwyth, 1971. Unpaged.

Alphabetical list.

62. Ealing Public Libraries. Librarianship and allied subjects; a catalogue of books and periodicals in the Reference Library of interest to students of librarianship, 3d ed. Ealing, 1961. 81p.

63. Library Association. Catalogue of the Library. London, 1958. 519p.

Lists more than 19,000 books, pamphlets, and periodicals in Association Library on 1 March 1956.

64. ———, North Midland Branch. Union list of periodicals on librarianship in the North Midlands area. Nottingham, 1958. 15p.

Locates files in 36 libraries.

65. North Western Polytechnic Library. A bibliography of librarianship; being a select list of books available to students in the Library, 1956. London: North Western Polytechnic, Dept. of Printing, 1957. 24p.

Library Catalogs and Surveys

GENERAL

66. Aslib. Aslib directory, 3d ed., ed. by Brian J. Wilson. London, 1968-70. 2v.

v.1, information sources in science, technology, and commerce; v.2, information sources in medicine, the social sciences, and the humanities. About 5,200 entries, including all types of libraries, associations, and societies; government departments; and commercial firms.

67. Association of Assistant Librarians, Midland Division. Students' guide; methods and resources of libraries in the area of the Midland Division of the Association of Assistant Librarians, ed. by H. A. Whatley. Birmingham, 1952. 20p.

68. Association of London Chief Librarians. Directory of London public libraries, 4th ed., ed. by K. R. McColvin. London, 1970. 142 p.

Data on resources and services, arranged by institutions.

69. Besterman, Theodore. British sources of reference and information; a guide to societies, works of reference and libraries. London: Pub. for the British Council by Aslib, 1947. 56p.

Analysis of resources of all types of libraries.

70. Burkett, J. Special library and information services in the United Kingdom, 2d ed. London: Library Association, 1965. 366p.

Reviews resources of national, governmental, society, industrial, and other types of libraries.

71. CADIG Liaison Centre Reference Library. Directory of membership and resources. Coventry, 1967. 40l.

Directory with selected data on resources of Coventry and District Information Group.

72. Collison, R. L. W. "The B.B.C. libraries." Library review, 137 (Spring 1961), 18-21.

Description of resources and services of libraries serving the BBC's radio and television programs.

73. Donaldson, Robert. "Some private collections in three Scottish libraries." Books (May-June 1964), 85-89.

In National Library of Scotland and Edinburgh and Glasgow university libraries.

74. Durkan, John, and Ross, Anthony. Early Scottish libraries. Glasgow: John S. Burns & Sons, 1961. 196p.

Present locations of books from early collections in Scottish and other libraries.

75. Freedland, Vernon D. "Special libraries of the Manchester area." Aslib proceedings, 7 (1955), 143-52.

Descriptions of resources of individual libraries in technical and scientific fields.

76. Great Britain, Ministry of Defence. Guide to government department and other libraries and information bureaux, 20th ed. London, 1971. 114p.

Data for 390 general and special libraries.

77. ———, Treasury, Organization and Methods Division. A guide to government libraries, 2d ed. London: H. M. Stationery Office, 1958. 139p.

Data on resources and services of individual libraries.

78. Hampshire Technical Research Industrial Commercial Service (HATRICS). Directory of resources. Southampton: Central Library, 1970. 63p.

Directory of libraries and other organizations, with data on holdings and services, followed by index of special subject interests.

79. Harrison, Kenneth Cecil. Libraries in Britain, 4th ed. London: Pub. for the British Council by Longmans, 1968. 41p.

80. Harrod, L. M. The libraries of Greater London. London: G. Bell & Sons, 1951. 252p.

Guide to public and special libraries; includes details of general and special collections and special services available; subject index.

81. Hepburn, A. G. Guide to Glasgow libraries. Glasgow: R. D. Macleod Trust, 1965. 23p.

Notes on special collections, number of volumes, etc.

82. Hepworth, P. "Archives and manuscripts in libraries, 1961." Library Association record, 64 (1962), 269-83.

Comprehensive summary of archival collections in all types of British libraries, large and small.

83. ———. Archives and manuscripts in libraries, 2d ed. London: Library Association, 1964. 69p. (Library Association pamphlet, no.18)

Deals with archives and manuscripts in libraries and catalogs and guides to manuscripts in libraries in England, Scotland, Wales, Northern Ireland, and Eire.

84. Hobson, Anthony. Great libraries. London: Weidenfeld and Nicolson, 1970. 320p.

Reviews history and describes collections of notable European and American libraries, including 6 British and Irish institutions.

85. Jones, Philip Henry. Books in Leicester and Rutland: a research report on the holdings of academic and public libraries in two Midland counties. Leicester: County Library, 1969. 32p. (Thesis, College of Librarianship Wales)

86. Kent, F. L. "Library resources of Bristol and the South-west." Aslib proceedings, 2 (1950), 187-94.

Descriptions of collections held by various types of libraries comprised in the 9 counties in the South-Western Regional Library System.

87. Laban, W. H. "Bibliotheken in Engelands Noord-Western" [Libraries in Northwestern England]. Bibliotheekleven, 51 (1966), 80-94, 215-23.

Description of resources and services of Manchester Public Library, John Rylands Library, etc.

88. Lewanski, Richard Casimir. European library directory: a geographical and bibliographical guide. Florence: Olschki, 1968. 774p.

p.283-375 list British libraries, with notes on volume holdings and special collections.

89. ———. Subject collections in European libraries; a directory and bibliographical guide. N. Y.: R. R. Bowker, 1965. 789p.

Lists some 6,000 libraries, arranged by Dewey Decimal Classification; for each collection notes statistics of holdings, list of catalogs, etc.

90. Libraries, museums and art galleries year book, 1971, comp. and ed. by Edmund V. Corbett and Enid W. Corbett. Cambridge and London: James Clarke, 1971. 694p.

Grouped by types of libraries, with brief data on their resources and services; first published in 1923.

91. Library Association. Investigation into information provision in town and country planning; pilot survey of library resources. [London?] 1968. 30l. + appendixes.

Report on resources of various types of libraries.

92. ———. Libraries in the United Kingdom and the Republic of Ireland; a complete list of public library services and a select list of academic and other library addresses. London, 1971. 60p. + index.

Directory of 916 institutions.

93. ———. Libraries of London, 2d. ed., ed. by Raymond Irwin and Ronald Staveley. London, 1964. 332p.

Descriptions of governmental, university, special, and other types of libraries in London and their resources.

94. ———. Survey of libraries: reports on a survey made by the Library Association during 1936-1937; general editor, L. R. McColvin. London, 1938. 719p.

Partial contents: 1. Great Britain: Northern Scotland, by D. Gray. 2. Great Britain: North-west England, South-west Scotland, and Northern Ireland, by A. S. Cooke. 3. Great Britain: North-east England and South-east Scotland, by R. W. Lynn. 4. Great Britain: Lancashire, excluding Furness, by W. Pollitt. 5. Great Britain: West Riding of Yorkshire, by E. Sydney. 6. Great Britain: Cheshire, Shropshire, and North Wales, by F. S. Smith. 7. Great Britain: West Midlands, by J. W. Forsyth. 8. Great Britain: East Midlands, by J. E. Walker. 9. Great Britain: South Wales and South-west England, by H. Woodbine. 10. Great Britain: South Midlands and central south coast, by F. E. Sandry. 11. Great Britain: London (north of the Thames), Herts, and Essex, by H. P. Marshall. 12. Great Britain: London (south of the Thames), Kent, Middlesex, and Surrey, by H. Fostall.

95. ——, North Western Branch. Libraries in the North West. Manchester, 1971. 39p. (Special issue of North Western newsletter, no.116)

Includes reviews of public, academic, and industrial libraries in area.

96. ——, Northern Ireland Branch. Directory of Northern Ireland libraries. Belfast, 1967. 22p.

Entries for 69 public, academic, and special libraries; includes index of special collections.

97. ——, Reference and Special Libraries Section, North-western Group. The libraries of Greater Manchester: a guide to resources and special collections, ed. by Harold Smith. Manchester, 1956. 92p.

Brief notes on 140 libraries.

98. —— ——, South Eastern Group. Library resources in the Greater London area, no.3: sources of illustrations, by J. L. Howgego. London: The Association, 1955. 18p.

Description of resources of libraries, museums, art galleries, commercial organizations, and other collections.

99. ——, Reference, Special, and Information Section. Library resources in the East Midlands, ed. by L. F. Craik. London, 1969. 63p.

Directory of 218 libraries with data on resources.

100. —— ——, Northern Group. Directory of northern library resources, 3d ed., comp. by G. R. Stephenson. Ashington: Northumberland County Technical College, Northern Circle of College Librarians, 1966. 30p.

101. —— ——, North Western Group. Library resources in Greater Manchester, 2d ed., ed. by Kenneth Whittaker. London: The Section, 1966. 87p.

Contains 256 entries with data on collections and services.

102. —— —— ——. Library resources on Merseyside, ed. by Frank Gibbons. London: The Section, 1967. 66p.

213 numbered items, with limited data on resources.

103. —— ——, South Eastern Group. Library resources in London and South East England, ed. by Selwyn Eagle. London: The Section, 1969. 380p.

Brief data on 1,123 institutions: volume holdings, main and special subjects, etc.

104. —— ——, West Midlands Group. Library resources in the West Midlands, 2d ed., ed. by B. G. Staples. London, 1963. 90p. First ed, 1958.

Contains 283 entries for Hereford, Shropshire, Staffordshire, Warwickshire, and Worcestershire; describes main subjects, special collections, and services.

105. —— ——, Western Group. Library resources in South-west England and the Channel Islands, ed. by V. A. Woodman and J. E. Spink. London, 1965. 86p.

Directory of 282 public, academic, and special libraries in Cornwall, Devon, Dorset, Gloucestershire, Hampshire, Somerset, Wiltshire, and Channel Islands.

106. —— —— ——. Library resources in Wales and Monmouthshire, ed. by Barbara Burton and J. M. Wood. London, 1967. 61p.

Directory, with data on resources, of 198 public, academic, industrial, research, government, and society libraries.

107. —— ——, Yorkshire Group. Directory of Yorkshire library resources, 1961, 2d ed. London, 1961. 119p. First ed. 1953.

Lists 369 institutions, with brief data on resources.

108. —— —— ——. Library resources in Yorkshire, ed. by Janet Bromley, 3d ed. London: The Section, 1968. 79p. First ed, 1953.

Directory of 237 libraries, with data on resources.

109. McDonald, William R. "Circulating libraries in the north-east of Scotland in the eighteenth-century." Bibliotheck, 5 (1968), 119-37.

Notes location of extant library catalogs.

110. Newcombe, Luxmoore. The university & college libraries of Great Britain and Ireland; a guide to the material available for the research student. London: John & Edward Bumpus, 1927. 220p.

Reviews subjects covered, special collections, incunabula, periodicals, catalogs, and other features of 310 institutions.

111. Northern Circle of College Librarians. Directory of northern libraries, 5th ed., ed. by G. R. Stephenson. Ashington: Northumberland County Technical College, 1969. 45p.

Contains about 130 entries, with details of holdings and special collections.

112. O'Neill, Thomas P., and Clarke, Desmond J. "Libraries in Ireland; an historical outline." Library Association record, 58 (1956), 47-57.

Historical background and present status of principal types of Irish libraries.

113. Philip, Alexander John. An index to the special collections in libraries, museums, and art galleries (public, private, and official) in Great Britain and Ireland. London: Pub. for the author by F. G. Brown, 1949. 190p.

Arranged alphabetically by subjects; little detail.

114. Plant, Marjorie. The supply of foreign books and periodicals to the libraries of the United Kingdom; report of a survey made under the auspices of the Rockefeller Foundation. London: Library Association, 1949. 60p.

Statistical report on holdings of British libraries in books published abroad.

115. Rye, Reginald Arthur. The students' guide to the libraries of London, with an account of the most important archives and other aids to study, 3d ed. London: Univ, of London Pr. 1928. 581p.

Historical introduction, p.1-72; British Museum, Public Record Office and general libraries, p.73-248; special libraries, arranged by subjects, p.249-451; detailed index.

116. Scottish Library Association and Library Association, Reference, Special and Information Section. Library resources in Scotland, ed. by Colin Smith and John S. Walker. Glasgow: Scottish Library Association, 1968. 107p.

Directory of 347 libraries with selected data on resources.

117. Sheffield Interchange Organization (SINTO). SINTO information resources: directory and guide, ed. by John Bebbington. Sheffield, 1971. 20p.

Data on resources and services of 58 special libraries; subject index.

118. Sheffield, University, Library, Information Service. Computerized information services available in the United Kingdom. Sheffield, 1971. 27p.

119. Society of Sussex Librarians. Library resources in Sussex. Chichester, 1967. 37p.

Directory of 165 libraries with data on collections.

120. South-Eastern Regional Library System. Subject specialisation: list of subjects arranged in order of Dewey decimal classification showing the library authority responsible for purchase together with index of co-operating libraries with their code numbers and subjects of specialisation. London, 1952. 22p.

Notes subject specializations of some 85 libraries.

121. Sutton, Charles William. Special collections of books in Lancashire and Cheshire; a paper read before the Library Association, Manchester, 5th September, 1899. Aberdeen: Univ. Pr., 1900. 61p.

General discussion, followed by appendix listing, under names of libraries, specialized collections.

122. Wales, A. P. International library directory: a world directory of libraries, 1969-70, 3d ed. London: A. P. Wales Organization, 1968. 1,222p.

Largest general work of its type; about 40,000 entries for libraries in more than 150 countries.

123. Walker, T. MacCallum. "Libraries and librarianship in Northern Ireland." Libri, 4 (1954), 315-29. Also appeared in Leabharlann, 13 (March 1955), 19-32.

General history, review of types of libraries, and comments on resources.

124. World guide to libraries, 3d ed. N.Y.: Bowker, 1970. 4v.

Lists 25,000 special, university, and public libraries in 157 countries; contains subject index to collections.

GENERAL AND SPECIAL LIBRARIES

125. Advocates Library. Catalogue of the printed books in the Library of the Faculty of Advocates, commenced by S. Halkett and completed by J. A. Hjaltalin. (Supplementary volume) Edinburgh and London: William Blackwood, 1867-79. 7v.

Library transferred in 1925 to National Library of Scotland, except for law collection.

126. Athenaeum Library. Catalogue of the Library of the Athenaeum, Liverpool. London: Chiswick Pr. for the Athenaeum, Liverpool, 1864. 589p.

127. Baillies' Library. Catalogue of the Library of Baillie's Institution. Glasgow: Strathern & Freeman, 1887. 313p.

Dictionary catalog.

128. Bath Royal Literary and Scientific Institution. Catalogue of the Library of the Bath Royal Literary and Scientific Institution, comp. by C. P. Russell, to which is appended a catalogue of books belonging to the Bath and West of England Society . . . deposited in the library of the Institution. Bath: W. and F. Dawson, 1879. 2pts.

129. Bedford Literary and Scientific Institute and General Library. Catalogue of the Circulating and Reference Libraries, and of the Old Library . . . together with a history of the different institutions, which have been amalgamated to form the present Society, by T. G. Elger. Bedford, 1892, 320p.

130. Belfast Library and Society for Promoting Knowledge. General catalogue, comp. by George Smith, etc. Belfast, 1896. 355p.

131. Bibliotheca Lindesiana. Catalogue of the printed books. Aberdeen: Univ. Pr., 1910. 4v.

132. Birmingham Library. Catalogue of the Birmingham Library, by Charles E. Scarse. Birmingham, 1883-86. 2v.

    pt.1, authors; pt.2, subjects.

133. ———. Catalogue of the Birmingham Library, supplement, 1883-1902, comp. by Charles E. Scarse. Birmingham, 1904. 578p.

134. ———. A catalogue of the books in the Birmingham Library, with a copy of the laws, etc. Birmingham, 1863. 500p. Earlier eds., Birmingham, 1781. 32p.; Birmingham: Thomas Pearson, 1795. 199p.; Birmingham: T. A. Pearson, 1798. 175p.; Birmingham: Thomas Knott, 1838. 315p.

    Library founded in 1779 by Joseph Priestley.

135. Bishopsgate Foundation and Institute. Bishopsgate Institute; descriptive catalogue of books contained in the Lending Library, comp. by C. W. F. Goss. London, 1901. 639p.

    Dictionary arrangement.

136. ——— Library. Descriptive catalogue of books contained in the Lending Library; supplementary catalogue of additions. London, 1911. 306p.

137. Brighton and Sussex Students' Library and Educational Foundation Library. Library catalogue. Brighton, 1955. 23p.

138. British Museum. Books in print and forthcoming publications. London: Director Publications, British Museum, 1971. 71p.

    Arranged by groups: printed books, manuscripts, Oriental printed books and manuscripts, etc.

139. ———, Dept. of Printed Books. Bibliothecae Regiae catalogus; a catalogue of the library of George III, acquired by the British Museum in 1823, comp. by F. A. Barnard. London: Bulmer and Nicol, 1820-29. 10v.

    King's library catalog; collection of George III.

140. ——— ———. Catalogue of printed books: Academies. London: Clowes, 1885-86. 1,018,100 cols.

    Catalogue of publications of learned societies.

141. ——— ———. Catalogue of printed books: England, Scotland, Ireland. London, 1891-1900. 3pts.

142. ——— ———. General catalogue of printed books, ed. from 1881-1889 by R. Garnett, and from 1890-1900 by A. W. K. Miller. London, 1881-1900. 393pts. in 95v. Reprinted, 1946. 58v.

143. ——— ———. General catalogue of printed books; supplement, ed. by A. W. K. Miller. London: The Museum, 1900-5. 44pts. in 15v. Reprinted, 1950. 10v.

    Contains titles of all books added to library during years 1882-99 which were not incorporated in the General catalogue during process of printing.

144. ——— ———. General catalogue of printed books, ed. by Wilfrid A. Marsden and Henry Thomas. London, 1931-54. 51v. No more published.

145. ——— ———. General catalogue of printed books. London: Trustees of the British Museum, 1959-66. 263v.

    Complete to end of 1955.

146. ——— ———. General catalogue of printed books; ten-year supplement, 1956-1965. London: The Museum, 1968. 50v.

147. ——— ———. General catalogue of printed books; five-year supplement, 1966-1970. London: The Museum, 1971- . v.1- . (In progress)

148. ——— ———. Subject index of the modern works added to the Library . . . 1881-1900, comp. by G. K. Fortescue. London: The Museum, 1902-3. 3v.

    Supersedes 3 5-year indexes covering 1880-95. Contains about 155,000 entries. Supplemented by 5-year cumulations, 1901- . London: The Museum, 1906- .

149. The British National Bibliography. London: Council of the British National Bibliography, 1950- . Weekly with cumulations for varying periods up to 5 years.

    Based upon books received by the agent for the Copyright Libraries; arranged by Dewey classification with full indexes.

150. Candie Library. Catalogue of the books in the Candie Library, Guernsey, comp. by G. E. Lee. Guernsey: Frederick Clarke, 1895. 211p.

151. Carlton Club Library. Catalogue of the Library of the Carlton Club, London, by Henry Thomas Cox. London, 1901. 524p.

    Dictionary catalog.

152. Chetham's Library. Catalogue of the John Radcliffe collection, comp. by Charles T. E. Phillips. Manchester; 1937. 100p.

Collection received by bequest by Cheetham's Library in 1918; listed alphabetically by authors and subjects.

153. City Liberal Club Library. Catalogue of the Library of the City Liberal Club. London: Unwin Bros., 1887. 244p.

154. Devon and Exeter Institution Library. Catalogue of the Devon and Exeter Institution Library. Exeter: W. Balle, 1863. 358p.
Library comprehensive of all major fields.

155. Dr. Williams's Library. Bibliothecae quam vir Doctus & admodum Reverendus Daniel Williams, S.T.P., Bono publico legavit, catalogus. London: Jacobi Bettenham, 1727. 414p. + index. 2d ed. London, 1801. 377p.
First and 2d editions of catalog of Dr. Williams's Library, devoted to religion, philosophy, and related fields, founded in 1715.

156. ———. Bulletin of Dr. Williams's Library, no.1- .1921- .
Contains selected lists of current accessions.

157. ———. Catalogue of the Library. London: Richard and John E. Taylor, 1841. 2v. v.3, London: Woodfall and Kinder, 1870. 149p. v.3, supplement. London: C. Green and Son, 1885. 204p. Catalogue of accessions, 1900-1950. London: Dr. Williams's Trust, 1955. 776p. + Supplement, periodicals, publications of societies, connected series, etc. cxlvp. Catalogue of accessions, 1951-1960. London: Dr. Williams's Trust, 1961. 181p.
Library founded in 1715; holds 100,000 volumes in religion, philosophy, and related fields.

158. Dudley Library. Laws and catalogue of the Dudley Library, established December 19th, 1805. Dudley, W. Maurice, 1826. 214p.

159. Great Britain, Colonial Office Library. Catalogue of the Colonial Office Library, London. Boston, Mass.: G. K. Hall, 1964. 15v. First supplement, 1963-67. 894p.
v.1-2, pre-1950 accessions; v.3-6, post-1950 accessions; v.7-8, subject catalogue, pre-1950 accessions; v.9-13, subject catalogue, post-1950 accessions; v.14-15, classified catalogue.

160. ———, Commonwealth Relations Office. Selective list of accessions to the library. London, 1966- .
Issued jointly by the Colonial Office, the Commonwealth Relations Office, and the Ministry of Overseas Development.

161. ———, Foreign Office Library. Catalogue of the Foreign Office Library, 1926-1968. London: H. M. Stationery Office. 8v. Announced for publication by G. K. Hall, Boston, Mass., 1973.

162. ———, Home Office Library. Catalogue Home Office Library. London: H. M. Stationery Office, 1876, 107p.

163. Greenock Library. Catalogue of the Greenock Library, Watt Monument. Edinburgh: Darien, 1897. 336p.

164. Huguenot Society of London. A rough hand-list, of the Library of the Huguenot Society of London, 1892. Lymington: Chas. T. King, 1892. 21p.
Collection now deposited in University College Library, University of London.

165. Jayne, Sears. Library catalogues of the English Renaissance. Berkeley: Univ. of Calif. Pr., 1956. 225p.
Locates copies in various libraries, in manuscript and printed form.

166. Kelso Library. A catalogue of the books in the Kelso Library. Kelso: Alex. Elliot, 1857. 92p.

167. Leighton Library. Catalogue of selected volumes from the Leighton Library, Dunblane, Scotland, comp. by Godfrey Davidson. Dunblane, 1960. 36p.
Library of 1,200 books once belonging to Robert Leighton (1611-84), strong in classical and Hebrew literature and theology.

168. Literary and Philosophical Society of Liverpool. A hand list of the books of the Literary and Philosophical Society of Liverpool. Liverpool: D. Marples, 1899. 76p.

169. Literary and Philosophical Society of Newcastle upon Tyne. Catalogue of the Library of the Literary and Philosophical Society of Newcastle upon Tyne, established 1793. Newcastle upon Tyne: Andrew Reid, 1903. 1,046p.
General library, arranged by Dewey classification, with author and subject indexes.

170. Liverpool Athenaeum. Catalogue of the Athenaeum Library. Liverpool, 1864. 589p. Supplement. 1892. 190p.
Includes special collections in field of local history.

171. ———. Catalogue of the Library of the Athenaeum, in Liverpool. Liverpool: J. M'Creery, 1902. 174p.

172. Liverpool Library. Catalogue of the Liverpool Library. London: William Clowes and Sons, 1889. 590p.

173. London Institution Library. A catalogue of the Library of the London Institution: systematically classed. London, 1835-52. 4v.

Collection broken up and distributed among University of London libraries.

174. London Library. Catalogue of the London Library, new ed. London, 1913-14. 2v. Supplements. 1913-20. London, 1920, 1920-28. London, 1929; 1928-50. London, 1953.

First published in 1847.

175. ———. Subject index of the London Library, by C. T. H. Wright. London: Williams & Norgate, 1909. 1,254p. Supplements. 1909-22. London, 1923, 1923-38. London, 1938, 1938-53. London, 1955.

176. Malvern Federated Library. Catalogue of the Malvern Federated Library. Malvern, Stevens & Co., 1896. 138p.

177. Manchester Literary and Philosophical Society. Catalogue of the books in the Library of the Manchester Literary and Philosophical Society. Manchester: T. Sowler, 1875. 173p.

178. Maxim, Gordon Eric. A history of library publishing 1600 to the present day. London, 1965. 597l. (Library Association Fellowship Thesis)

Appexdix A: "A list of catalogues published between 1600 and 1825, arranged in chronological order,' a total of 220.

179. National Lending Library for Science and Technology. Index curiositatum. Boston Spa, 1964. 22p.

A list of works held by the library but outside its field.

180. National Liberal Club, Gladstone Linrary. Catalogue of books and pamphlets. London, 1908. 953p.

181. National Library of Scotland. Accessions of printed books, 1959-1964. Edinburgh, 1965. 44p.

Records 300 individual items and 33 collections received.

182. ———. Principal accessions, 1965-1970: printed books. Edinburgh, 1971. 48p. + 8 plates.

Contains 394 selected items.

183. ———. The Roseberry collections. Edinburgh: H. M. Stationery Office, 1958. 15p.

Survey of gifts and bequests to National Library of Scotland from the Primrose family, notably from Barnbougle Castle and the Durdans.

184. Newcastle upon Tyne Literary and Philosophical Society. Catalogue of the Library of the Literary and Philosophical Society of Newcastle upon Tyne, with author and subject indexes. Newcastle upon Tyne, 1903. 1,046p.

185. North Devon Athenaeum. Catalogue of the Circulating and Reference Department of the Library. Barnstaple: Percival Hunter, 1898. 350p.

186. Oxford and Cambridge Club Library. Catalogue of the Library of the Oxford and Cambridge Club. Aberdeen: Univ. Pr., 1887-1909. 2pts.

187. Oxford, University, Bodleian Library. "Index to Duke Humphrey's gifts to the old library of the University in 1439, 1441, and 1444." Bodleian quarterly record, 1 (1914-16), 131-35.

188. ———. "Lists of books presented by the Earl of Essex in 1600, still in the Bodleian." Bodleian quarterly record, 3 (1922), 241-44.

189. Plume Library. Catalogue of the Plume Library at Maldon, Essex, comp. by S. G. Deed and Jane Francis. Maldon, 1959. 192p.

Library of 6,000-7,000 volumes assembled in 17th century by Thomas Plume, Archdeacon of Rochester; emphasis on theology and philosophy, but general in scope.

190. Rationalist Press Association Library. Catalogue of the Library of the Rationalist Press Association. London: Watts & Co., 1937. 146p.

Classified catalog recording over 2,000 volumes relating mainly to anthropology, psychology, philosophy, and theology.

191. Reform Club. Catalogue of Panizzi pamphlets. London: Library Committee, 1920. 58p.

Collection assembled by Anthony Panizzi and presented to Reform Club.

192. Royal Colonial Institute Library. Catalogue of the Library of the Royal Colonial Institute. London, 1895. 543p. First supplementary catalogue, comp. by James R. Boosé. London, 1901. 793p.

Geographical arrangement with index of colonies and subjects.

193. Royal Commonwealth Society. Subject catalogue of the Royal Commonwealth Society (London). Boston, Mass.: G. K. Hall, 1971. 7v.

Supplements Subject catalogue of the Royal Empire Society, 1930-37.

194. Royal Empire Society. Subject catalogue of the Library of the Royal Empire Society, by Evans Lewin. London, 1930-37. 4v. Reprinted, London: Dawsons Pall Mall Pr., 1967.

Now Royal Commonwealth Society. Catalog arranged geographically.

195. Royal Institution of Great Britain Library. A new classified catalogue of the Library of the Royal Institution of Great Britain, with indexes of authors and subjects, and a list of historical pamphlets, chronologically arranged, by Benjamin Vincent. London, 1857-1914. 3v.

196. Royal Society Library. Catalogue of miscellaneous literature in the Library of the Royal Society. London: Richard and John E. Taylor, 1841. 265p.

197. ———. Catalogue of the Library of the Royal Society. London: William Nicol, 1825. 608p.
Alphabetical by authors.

198. Scottish Central Library. Out of print books and mss. on microfilm held in the Scottish Central Library, 3d ed., by S. E. Pringle. Lawnmarket, Edinburgh, 1969. 66p.
Records printed books, mainly 18th- and 19th-century, of Scottish interest; manuscripts drawn from local archives.

199. Sheffield Literary & Philosophical Society. Catalogue of the books in the Library of the Sheffield Literary & Philosophical Society. Sheffield, 1908. 2pts.
pt.1, authors; pt.2, subjects.

200. Sir John Soane's Museum. Catalogue of the Library in Sir John Soane's Museum. London, 1878. 414p.

201. Society of Writers to the Signet Library. Catalogue of the printed books in the Library of the Society of Writers to H. M. Signet in Scotland. [A-O ed. by D. Laing and P-Z by T. G. Law.] (Supplement and list of manuscripts) Edinburgh, 1871-82. 2 pts.

202. ———. List of books added to the Library of the Society in the years 1888-1935. Edinburgh: Neill & Co., Wm. Blackwood, 1889-1936, 5v.

203. ———. A second supplement to the catalogue of books in the Signet Library 1882-1887, with a subject index to the whole catalogue. Edinburgh, 1891. 610p.

204. Victoria and Albert Museum, Science and Art Dept. Dyce collection; a catalogue of the printed books and manuscripts bequeathed by the Reverend Alexander Dyce. London: Eyre and Spottiswoode, 1875. 2v.
Emphasis on classical and theological works and dramatic literature.

PUBLIC LIBRARIES

205. Aberdeen Public Library. Catalogue of the Lending Department, by A. W. Robertson. Aberdeen: Univ. Pr., 1886. 584p.

206. ———. Catalogue of the Lending Department. Aberdeen: Univ. Pr., 1898. 603p.

207. ———, Lending Dept. Indicator list of books of philology, ancient classics, theology, sociology, poetry, mental science. Aberdeen, 1892-95. 11pts.

208. ———. Subject index-catalogue of Lending Department. Aberdeen: Univ. Pr., 1926. 217p.

209. ———. Supplementary catalogue. Aberdeen: W. Jolly, 1901. 164p. Supplementary catalogue. Aberdeen: George Leslie, 1906. 386p.

210. Barrow-in-Furness Free Public Library. Catalogue of the books in the reference and lending departments, comp. by John Frowde. Barrow-in-Furness: S. S. Lord, 1885. 252p.

211. Battersea Public Libraries, Central Library. Catalogue of the Lending Department, comp. and ed. by Lawrence Inkster, 3d ed. London, 1898. 344p.

212. Belfast Public Libraries. Catalogue of the Reference Department, comp. by George Hall Elliott. Belfast: M. Ward, 1896. 480p.

213. Bermondsey Public Libraries. Catalogue of books in the Lending and Reference Departments of the Central Library, comp. by John Frowde. London, 1905. 193p.

214. Bethnal Green Public Libraries. A classified catalogue of the books in the Reference and Adult Lending Departments on social science, economics, political science, law, commerce, history, geography, travel, and biography. London, 1927. 529p.

215. Birkenhead Public Libraries. Catalogue of the Central Lending Library, Hamilton Street, including some of the more important works contained in the Reference Library. Birkenhead: Willmer Bros., 1898. 487p.
Classified by subjects with indexes.

216. Birmingham Public Libraries, Central Reference Library. Catalogue of the Reference Library, by J. D. Mullins. 1883-1890. Birmingham: George Jones, 1890. 1,284p.

217. Blackburn County Public Library. Catalogue of the books in the Reference Department. Blackburn, 1907. 228p.

218. Bolton Public Libraries. Catalogue of books in the Central Lending and Reference Libraries; philosophy and religion, comp. by Archibald Sparke. Bolton, 1913. 387p.

219. ———. Catalogue of books in the Central Lending and Reference Libraries, 2d ed. Bolton: Libraries Committee, 1926. 11pts.

Each part covers section of Dewey Decimal Classification.

220. Brighton Public Library. Catalogue of the Victoria Lending Library, with an appendix of some books of reference. Brighton, [1890]. 375p.

221. Bristol Public Library. Catalogue of additions (non-fiction and fiction) to the adult libraries (Reference Library, Library of Commerce, Central Lending Library, branch libraries), 1953. Bristol, 1954. 420p.

222. ———. Catalogue of additions (non-fiction and fiction) to the adult libraries (Reference Library, Library of Commerce, Central Lending Library, branch libraries). Bristol, 1960. 579p.

Covers year 1959.

223. ———. Catalogue of non-fiction additions to the lending libraries. Bristol, 1962. 511p.

Additions for 1961.

224. ———. Catalogue of non-fiction additions to the lending libraries. Bristol, 1964-65. 2v.

Covers additions for 1963-64.

225. ———, Central Library. Catalogue of non-fiction published prior to 1955 available in the reserve collection. Bristol, 1962. 5v.

226. Cambridge Public Free Library. Catalogue of the books in the Cambridge Free Library, Reference Department, comp. by J. Pink. Cambridge, 1874-99. 4pts.

pt.1, p.54-84, contains "catalogue of Cambridge books, maps & prints, in the Reference Department of the Free Library."

227. ———. The second index-catalogue of the Central Lending Department . . . containing a complete list of the books added since 1893, a new catalogue of music and musical publications and a selection of Braille publications, comp. by J. Pink. Cambridge, 1904. 148p.

228. Cardiff Public Libraries. Catalogue of books in the Central Lending Library, author section. Cardiff: S. Glossop and Sons, 1916. 522p.

229. Carlisle Public Library. Catalogue of books in the Lending Department. Carlisle, 1895. 117p.

230. Chelsea Public Libraries. Catalogue of the Lending Department . . . except fiction, music, & children's books, 5th ed. London, 1928. 578p.

231. Darlington Public Library, Museum, and Art Gallery. Catalogue of the books in the Lending Department, new edition, comp. by B. Rowland Hill. Darlington: Oliver Bros., 1892. 517p.

232. Dorset County Library. Classified catalogue of non-fiction books contained in the Central Library in Dorchester, comp. by H. W. Elliott. Dorsetshire: Dorset County Education Committee, 1936. 474p.

233. ———. Subject index. Dorset, 1965. 221p.

Alphabetical arrangement of subjects with class numbers for books held by library.

234. Dunfermline Carnegie Public Libraries. Catalogue of the books in the Lending and Reference Departments. Dunfermline, 1883. 313p.

235. Edinburgh Public Libraries. Subject and name index of books contained in the libraries; cumulated supplement to third edition, 1949-1965. Edinburgh, 1966. 189p.

236. Edinburgh Public Library. Catalogue of books in the Lending Library. Edinburgh: Public Library Committee, 1890. 538p.

237. ———. Catalogue of books in the Reference Library, including technical section. Edinburgh: Public Library Committee, 1891. 317p.

238. ———. Catalogue of books in the technical section of the Reference Library, together with a subject index of books on technical subjects in the Lending Department. Edinburgh: Public Library Committee, 1913. 172p.

239. Ewart Public Library. Catalogue of the Lending Library, comp. by G. W. Shirley. Dumfries: Public Library Committee, 1904. 553p.

240. Fife County Library. Catalogue of books in Fife County Library. Cupar: Fife Education Authority, printed by J. & G. Innes, 1928. 462p.

Dictionary catalog.

241. Finsbury Public Libraries. Classified catalogue . . . Part I. General works. (Part II. Philosophy), comp. by H. G. T. Cannons. London, 1915. 2pts.

242. ——— Clerkenwell Public Library. Class guide, pt.1, to fiction and juvenile literature; pt.2, to the historical, geographical, and biographical literature; pt.3, to the books on science; fine, recreative, and

useful arts, in the Lending Department, comp. by James D. Brown. London, 1895-98. 294p.

243. ———— ————. Clerkenwell Free Public Library; catalogue of the Lending Department, comp. by J. D. Brown. London, 1889. 308p.

244. Fulham Public Libraries. Catalogue of the Central Libraries (Lending and Reference), comp. with a preface by F. T. Barrett. London, 1899. 437p.

245. Gateshead Public Libraries. A list of the government publications and other pamphlets and the atlases, directories, gazeteers, newspapers and magazines and year books in the Reference Department of the Central Public Library. Gateshead, 1946. 38p.

246. Glasgow Corporation Public Libraries. Catalogue of additions, 1915-1949. Glasgow, 1959-60. 2v.
    pt.1, classified by subjects; pt.2, index. Books added to reference collection of Glasgow Public Libraries.

247. ————. A list of books and manuscripts comprising the collections of I. James Drummond, Bishop of Brechin, and II. The Earls of Erroll, formerly in the possession of the Earls of Erroll, Slains Castle, Aberdeenshire. Glasgow, n.d. 44p.
    Now in Mitchell Library, Glasgow Corporation Public Libraries; 873 items.

248. Glasgow Public Libraries. Union catalogue of additions: classified, annotated and indexed; pt.5: 1939-1944. Glasgow: Mitchell Library, 1952. 1,024p.

249. ————. Union catalogue of additions, classified, annotated and indexed. Glasgow: Mitchell Library, 1955. 1,096p.
    pt.6, 1945-49.

250. Gravesend Public Library. Catalogue of books in the Lending Library, with descriptive notes and cross-references, comp. by Alex. J. Philip. Gravesend, 1906. 137p.

251. Guille-Alles Library and Museum. Encyclopaedic catalogue of the Lending Department, comp. by Alfred Cotgreave and Henri Boland. Guernsey: Guille-Alles Library, 1891. 1,220 + 273p.
    In 2 sections: English and French.

252. Hackney Public Libraries. Catalogue of the books in the Central Public Library, Mare Street, Hackney. Hackney, 1908. 248p.

253. Haddington Public Library. Catalogue of the library of John Gray Haddington, by W. Forbes Gray.

Edinburgh: Printed for Haddington Town Council by Turnbull & Spears, 1929. 96p.
    Catalog of 17th-century library bequeathed to Royal Burgh at Haddington in 1729.

254. Hammersmith Public Libraries. Catalogue of the books contained in the Lending Department of the Carnegie (Central) Library, comp. by Samuel Martin. London, 1905. 237p.

255. ————. Catalogue of the Public Library, Ravenscourt Park (Lending and Reference), comp. by Samuel Martin. London, 1899. 495p.

256. Hampstead Public Libraries. Author catalogue of the works in the Reference Department at the Central Library, Finchley Road, N.W., ed. by W. E. Doubleday. London, 1903. 218p.

257. ————. Catalogue of the books in the Lending Department at the Central Library, comp. by W. E. Doubleday. London, 1899. 324p.

258. Harris Public Library, Museum and Art Gallery. Catalogue of the Free Public Library, Preston. Preston: C. W. Whitehead, 1889. 600p.

259. Harsnett Library at Colchester. A catalogue of the Harsnett Library at Colchester in which are included a few books presented to the town by various donors since 1631, comp. by Gordon Goodwin, London: Richard Amer, 1888. 170p.
    Now part of Colchester Public Library.

260. Hereford Free Public Library and Museum. Catalogue of the Reference Department. Worcester: Ebenezer Baylis, 1901. 460p.

261. Holborn Public Library. General catalogue of the Lending and Reference Departments, 2d ed., 1899, comp. by Henry Hawkes, Librarian. London: N. P. Vallentine, 1899. 467p.

262. Hull Public Libraries. Catalogue of the Central Lending Library, 4th ed. Hull: A. Brown, 1911. 1,001p.
    Classified by subjects with author list.

263. ————. The James Reckitt Public Library for Eastern Hull. Catalogue of the Lending and Reference Library. Hull, 1889. 435p.

264. Inverness Public Library. Catalogue of books in the Lending Department. Inverness: Robert Carruthers, 1901. 252p. Supplementary catalogue. Inverness, 1906. 99p.

265. ————. Catalogue of books in the Reference Department. Inverness, 1903. 106p.

266. Ipswich Public Library. Catalogue of the books in the Reference Department, comp. by Henry Ogle. Ipswich, 1906. 134p.

267. Islington Public Libraries. Select catalogue and guide; classified list of the best books on all subjects in the Central, North, and West Libraries. London: Public Libraries Committee, 1910. 827p.

268. Kent County Library. County Library catalogue; non-fiction (excluding music and drama). Maidstone: Kent Education Committee, 1928. 390p.

269. Lambeth Public Libraries. Catalogue of the books in the Tate Central Library, Brixton, S.W. Lending Department, comp. by F. J. Burgoyne. London: Truslove & Bray, 1893. 270p.

270. ———. Index-catalogue of the books in the Durning Lending Library, Kennington Cross, comp. by Frank J. Burgoyne. London: W. H. Truslove, 1889. 116p.

271. Lancashire County Library. A catalogue of English and foreign literature in the Lancashire County Library, August, 1929. Preston: Lancashire Education Committee, 1929. 127p.

272. Leicester, Old Town Hall Library. A catalogue, with introduction, glossary of the names of places, notices of authors, notes, and list of missing books, compiled for the Corporation of Leicester by Cecil Deedes, J. E. Stocks and J. L. Stocks. Oxford: Corporation of Leicester, 1919. 228p.
    Library established about 1632 in Leicester.

273. Liverpool Public Libraries. Catalogue of works of non-fiction added to the lending libraries, 1925-1935, 1935-1950. Liverpool: Libraries, Museums and Arts Committee, 1935-52. 2v.

274. ———. Catalogue of works of non-fiction (excluding music and foreign literature) added from August 1952 to December 1955. Liverpool: Central Public Library, 1957. 2v. in 1.

275. ———. Catalogue of works of non-fiction (excluding music and foreign literature). Liverpool, 1962. 733p.
    Works added 1956 to 1959.

276. ———. Catalogue of works of non-fiction (excluding music and foreign literature). Liverpool, 1968. 1,031p.
    Records works added 1960 to 1963.

277. Manchester Circulating Library. A catalogue of the present collection of books, in the Manchester Circulating Library. Manchester: G. Nicholson, 1794. 86p.

278. Manchester Public Libraries. Catalogue of the books in the Manchester Free Library, Reference Department, prep. by A. Crestadoro. London: Sampson Low, Son, & Marston, 1864. 975p.

279. Manchester Public Library, Reference Dept. Catalogue of the books in the Manchester Public Free Library. Manchester: Charles Sever, 1864-81. 3v.

280. Newcastle upon Tyne City Libraries. Catalogue of the books in the Central Lending Library, comp. by W. T. Haggerston. Newcastle upon Tyne, 1880. 331p.

281. Plymouth Public Library. Index-catalogue of the Reference Department, including the Devon and Cornwall Library and the Library of the Plymouth Medical Society, comp. by W. H. K. Wright. Plymouth: W. F. Westcott, 1892. 536p.

282. Poplar Public Library. Catalogue of the books in the Lending and Reference Departments, comp. by H. Rowlatt. London, 1894. 317p.

283. Reading Public Library, Museum, and Art Gallery. Catalogue of the Central Lending Library, by Wm. H. Greenhough. Reading, 1912. 695p.

284. St. Helens Free Public Library. Catalogue of the Central Lending Library at the Gamble Institute. St. Helens: Library Committee, 1896. 572p.

285. St. Pancras Public Libraries. Catalogue of the books in the lending department of the Highgate Library. London, 1907. 353p.

286. Sandeman Public Library. Catalogue of the lending department, comp. by John Minto. Perth: Wood & Son, 1898. 360p. Supplement. Perth, 1901. 55p.

287. Sheffield City Libraries. Catalogue of the Central Library, Reference Department. Sheffield: Robertshaw, 1890. 204p.

288. ———. Catalogue of the Sheffield Free Library. Sheffield: Ridge, 1858. 168p.; 1866 ed., 270p.; supplement, 1874. 170p.

289. Skipton Public Library. A catalogue of the Petyt Library at Skipton, Yorkshire. Gargrave: Coulthurst Trust, 1965. 417p.
    Library founded in early 18th century; contains about 5,500 entries for 4,000 works, predominantly English. Majority relate to 17th-century theological controversies, but geography, history, science, etc., are represented. Now housed in Skipton Public Library.

290. Southampton Public Libraries. A catalogue of the Pitt collection. Southampton, 1964. 133p.

Collection of 1,100 books from 3 private collections, the first 300 years old, presented to Southampton Public Libraries.

291. Stoke Newington Public Libraries. Catalogue of the Lending & Reference Departments, comp. by G. Preece. Stoke Newington, 1897. 341p.

292. Swindon Public Libraries. A catalogue of the books in the Richard Jefferies collection of the Swindon Public Libraries, comp. by Harold Jolliffe. Swindon: Libraries, Museum, Arts and Music Committee, 1948. 16p.

293. Twickenham Free Public Library. Catalogue of the books in the Twickenham Free Public Library, comp. by E. Maynard. Oldbury: Midland Printing Co., 1902. 348p.

294. Wandsworth Public Libraries. Catalogue, comp. by C. T. Davis. London, 1896. 423p.

295. Welshpool Free Public Library. Catalogue of books of the Lending Department, June, 1929. Welshpool, 1929. 94p.

296. Westminster Public Libraries. Catalogue of books in the Lending Department of the Public Library, Buckingham Palace Road, S.W., 2d ed. London, 1905. 751p.

297. ———. Classified catalogue of non-fiction books added to stock. London: Westminster Public Libraries, 1952-64. 13v.

298. ———. Classified catalogue of non-fiction books added to stock [1964]. London, 1965. 377p.

299. Wigan Public Library, Reference Dept. Catalogue of books, by Henry T. Folkard. Wigan: R. Platt, 1890-1916. 6v.

300. Woolwich Public Libraries. Catalogue of books in the Lending Department of the Plumstead Library, comp. by W. G. Chambers. Woolwich, 1904. 302p.

COLLEGE AND UNIVERSITY LIBRARIES

301. Aberdeen, University, Library. Catalogue of books added to the General Library of the University of Aberdeen, 1887-9. Aberdeen: Univ. Pr., 1889-97. 6pts.

302. ———. Catalogue of books which have been added to the University Library, Aberdeen, from the 1st Jan. 1857 to the 20th of Aug. 1862 (1876-82, 1887-91). Aberdeen, 1862-91. 5pts.

303. ———. Catalogue of pamphlets in the King, the Thomson, and the Herald collections, comp. by Peter J. Anderson. Aberdeen: Rosemount, 1927. 691p. (Aberdeen University studies, no.104)

Dictionary arrangement: author-title-subject for extensive collection relating to various fields.

304. ———. Catalogue of the books added to the libraries in King's and Marischal Colleges, March 1897 to March 1907. Aberdeen: Univ. Pr., 1898-1907. 10pts.

305. ———. Catalogue of the books added to the library in Marischal College, 1874-1896, by P. J. Anderson. Aberdeen: For the University, 1897. 286p.

306. ———. Catalogue of the General Library of the University of Aberdeen. Aberdeen, 1873-74. 2v. Supplement . . . works added 1875-87. Aberdeen: Univ. Pr., 1887. 544p.

307. ———. List of additions to the Library of the University of Aberdeen. August, 1935, to July, 1936. Aberdeen: Univ. Pr., 1937. 173p.

308. Barnes, Ann P. Bibliography of "Festschriften" composed by members of the University of Cambridge between the dates 1587 and 1640, based on the examination of copies held by the British Museum. London, 1948. Unpaged. (Diploma in Librarianship, Univ. of London)

309. Birmingham, University, Library. A catalogue of the books bequeathed by the Rev. Thomas Wigan for the use of the inhabitants of Bewdley and neighbourhood in 1819. Deposited in the Library of the University of Birmingham, 1950. [With biographical notes and a history of the collection by P. Morgan.] Birmingham, 1955. Unpaged.

About 2,000 volumes, predominantly concerned with theology and with classical and English literature.

310. Cambridge, University, Library. A catalogue of adversaria and printed books containing ms. notes preserved in the Library of the University of Cambridge. Cambridge: Univ. Pr., 1864. 100p.

311. ———, Queen's College Library. A catalogue of the Library of the College of St. Margaret and St. Bernard, commonly called Queen's College in the University of Cambridge, arr. by Thomas Hartwell Horne. London: Bentley, 1827. 2v.

312. ———, St. Catherine's College Library. A catalogue of the books which were given to the Library and Chapel of St. Catherine's Hall, Cambridge, by Dr.

Woodlark, the founder of the college, by G. E. Corrie. Cambridge: Univ. Pr., 1840. 11p. (Cambridge Antiquarian Society, publications, no.1)

313. College of Preceptors. Catalogue of the Library of the College. London, 1904. 160p.

Arranged by subjects: education, geography, history, language and literature, science, etc.

314. Dublin, University, Trinity College Library. Catalogus librorum impressorum qui in Bibliotheca Collegii sacrosanctae et individuae Trinitatis, Reginae Elizabethae, juxta Dublin, adservantur. Dublinii: E Typographeo Academico, 1864-87. 9v.

315. Dulwich College Library. Catalogue of the Library of Alleyn's College of God's Gift at Dulwich, comp. by Arthur W. K. Miller. London: Spottiswoode, & Co., 1880. 586p.

316. Edinburgh, University, Library. Catalogue of the printed books in the Library of the University of Edinburgh. Edinburgh: Univ. Pr., 1918-23. 3v.

Author catalog.

317. ———. Hand catalogue of the Edinburgh University Library, containing a selection of books in all departments. Edinburgh: T. & A. Constable, 1906. 240p.

A "dictionary" catalog.

318. Free Church College Library. Catalogue of books in the Library of the Free Church College, Aberdeen. Aberdeen: G. Rennie, 1862. 102p.

Institution now affiliated with University of Aberdeen.

319. ———. Catalogue of the principal books added to the Library of the Free Church College, Aberdeen, 1862-1878. Aberdeen: Free Pr., Office, 1878. 90p.

Institution now affiliated with University of Aberdeen.

320. Glasgow, University, Library. Catalogus impressorum librorum in Bibliotheca Universitatis Glasguensis. Glasgow, 1791. 496p.

Oldest of Glasgow University Library's catalogs.

321. Liverpool, University, Library. In memoriam Thomas Glazebrook Rylands; a catalogue of the books, printed and in manuscript, bequeathed by the late Thomas Glazebrook Rylands ... to the Library of University College, Liverpool, comp. by J. Sampson. Liverpool: Univ. Pr., 1900. 113p.

In 3 sections: manuscripts (12th to 19th century); early printed books (15th and 16th century); and general catalog.

322. London, University, King's College Library. Catalogue of the Library of King's College, London. London: Clay and Taylor, 1874. 115p.

Classified by subjects.

323. ———, Libraries. Accessions to the Library, 1876-1895. London, 1886-1895. 2v.

324. ——— ———. Catalogue of accessions, 1914-1952. London, 1915-53. 17v.

325. ———, Library. Catalogue of the Library of the University of London, including the libraries of George Grote and Augustus DeMorgan. London: Taylor and Francis, 1876. 795p.

Dictionary arrangement.

326. ——— ———. The Sterling Library; a catalogue of the printed books and literary manuscripts collected by Sir Louis Sterling ... and presented by him to the University of London, comp. by Margaret Canney. Cambridge: Univ. Pr., 1954. 614p. + 8 plates.

In 5 parts: printed books, 15th to 19th century (1,032 entries); printed books, 20th century (610 entries); private presses and limited editions (532 entries); illustrated and extra-illustrated books (258 entries); literary manuscripts (83 entries).

327. ———, University College. Catalogue of books in the General Library and in the South Library at University College, with an appendix. London: Taylor & Francis, 1879. 3v. Supplement. 1897. London, 1897. 485p.

328. ———, Warburg Institute Library. Catalog of the Warburg Institute Library, 2d ed. Boston, Mass.: G. K. Hall, 1967. 12v. 1st ed., 1961. 2v.

Reproduces about 109,000 catalog cards relating to art and archeology, history and symbolism of religions, and general history of the classical tradition.

329. Manchester, University, Library. Catalogue of the Christie collection, comprising the printed books and manuscripts bequeathed to the Library of the University of Manchester by the late Richard Copley Christie, comp. by Charles W. E. Leigh. Manchester: Univ. Pr., 1915. 536p.

An 8,000-volume collection, including over 200 incunabula, works of classical authors, etc., emphasizing Renaissance period in Italy and France.

330. New College of the Free Church of Scotland Library. Catalogue of the printed books and manuscripts in the Library of the New College, Edinburgh (Catalogue of the Library in connection with the chair of Natural Science in the New College, Edinburgh), by John Laing. Edinburgh: William Paterson, 1878. 939p.

331. Newcastle upon Tyne, University, Library. Catalogue of the Gertrude Bell collection in the Library of King's College, Newcastle upon Tyne, by Winifred C. Dunkin. Newcastle upon Tyne, 1960. 64p. (Univ. of Newcastle upon Tyne publications, no.1)

Lists about 2,000 volumes relating to architecture, archeology, literature, and history of East.

332. ———. Catalogue of the Library at Wallington Hall, Northumberland, comp. by Christopher John Hunt. Newcastle upon Tyne, 1968. 137p. (Library publications, extra series, no.9)

Library largely assembled by Sir George Otto Trevelyan, English historian; includes books once belonging to Lord Macauley.

333. ———. Short-title list of the Sandes Library (Kendal Grammar School) deposited in Newcastle University Library, comp. by Alistair Elliot and John Bagnall. Newcastle upon Tyne, 1969. 16p.

334. North Staffordshire Technical College Library. Library catalogue. Stoke on Trent, 1960. 227p.

335. Owens College Library. A catalogue of the books and pamphlets in the Library, arranged according to subjects and authors, by William E. Hoyle. Manchester: J. E. Cornish, 1895. 302p.

Relates primarily to scientific subjects; includes collection formed by Manchester Natural History Society, now part of Manchester University Library.

336. ———. Catalogue of the mss. and printed books, bequeathed to Owens College, Manchester, by the late Right Rev. James Prince Lee, Lord Bishop of Manchester. Manchester: Thos. Sowler and Sons, 1870. 212p. Addenda. 1876. 8p.

Collection now part of University of Manchester Library.

337. ———. Catalogue of the Owens College Library. Manchester: T. Sowler & Co., 1894-99. 5pts.

Arranged by classes: theology, language and literature, and legal sciences; now owned by Manchester University Library.

338. Oxford, University, Balliol College Library. Catalogue of printed books in Balliol College Library. Oxford, 1871. 459p.

339. ———, Bodleian Library. Catalogue of the printed books and manuscripts bequeathed by Francis Douce to the Bodleian Library. Oxford, 1840. 311p.

340. ——— ———. Notable accessions; guide to an exhibition held in 1958. Oxford, 1958. 64p.

341. ———, Hertford College Library. Catalogue of books in the Library of Hertford College, 1888. Oxford, 1888. 258p.

342. ———, Magdalen College. Catalogus librorum impressorum Bibliothecae Collegii B. Mariae Magdalenae in Academia Oxoniensi. (Appendix. catalogus operum ab illustribus alumnis Collegii . . . scriptorum rel colitorum, quibus aucta est Bibliotheca diligentia maxime Joannis Rouse Bloxam.) Oxonii: E Typographeo Academico, 1860-62. 3v.

343. ———, Merton College Library. Catalogue of the printed books in the Library of Merton College. Oxford: E. P. Hall & J. H. Stacy, 1880. 605p. Supplement. Oxford, 1890. 119p.

344. ———, New College. Catalogue of books bequeathed by Thomas Fowler, D.D., President of Corpus Christi College, Oxford . . . to the Wykeham Chair of Logic and kept at New College, prep. by G. G. Berry. Oxford: Hart, 1906. 36p.

345. ———, St. John's College Library. A catalogue of a portion of the Library of H. Butler Clarke . . . now in the Library of St. John's College, by F. de Arteaga y Pereira. Oxford, 1906. 30p.

346. ———, Taylor Institution Library. A catalogue of the books in the Finch collection, Oxford. Oxford, 1874. 318p.

347. ——— ———. Catalogue of the Library of the Taylor Institution. Oxford, 1861. 192p. Addenda, 1879-1920.

348. ———, Trinity College Library. Catalogue of books in the new library. Oxford, 1892. 56p. Supplements, 1892-1901. 3pts.

349. Queen's University Library. Catalogue of books in the Library of Queen's College, Belfast. Belfast, 1897. 975p.

350. St. Andrews, University, Library. Catalogue of books added to the University Library, St. Andrews. 1925-1926, 1926-1927, 1928, 1929-1931, 1932-1933. St. Andrews: Univ. Pr., 5pts.

SURVEYS OF INDIVIDUAL LIBRARIES

351. Alderson, Frederick. "Unfamiliar libraries XIV: Cashel Cathedral." Book collector, 17 (1968), 322-30.

A 12,000-volume collection, about one-half works of theology, the remainder embracing science, medicine, politics, history, Irish imprints, belles lettres, and Americana; includes examples of printing for past 500 years, with emphasis on 16th- and 17th-century culture.

352. Ballantyne, George H. "Scotland's special libraries: the Signet Library." SLA news, no.91 (1969), 299-301.

Description of the Library of the Society of Writers to Her Majesty's Signet, 250 years old in 1972; collection of about 100,000 books, law, history and topography, literature, biography, etc.

353. ———. "The Signet Library, Edinburgh." Law librarian, 2 (April-July 1971), 3-5, 15.

History and description of resources.

354. Barr, K. P. "Non-standard material at the NLL." Aslib proceedings, 17 (Aug. 1965), 240-45.

Describes National Lending Library's collections of preprints, conference proceedings and reports, and translations.

355. Birley, Robert. "The Storer collection in Eton College Library." Book collector, 5 (1956), 115-26.

Describes collection of 2,700 volumes brought together in 18th century by Anthony Storer, consisting of Greek and Latin classics, Italian literature, early English plays, books of Horace Walpole, etc.

356. Black, Hester M., and Gaskell, Philip. "Special collections in Glasgow University Library." Book collector, 16 (1967), 161-68.

Brief descriptions of most noteworthy specialized collections.

357. Blakiston, J. M. G. "Unfamiliar libraries XI: Winchester College." Book collector, 16 (1967), 297-304.

Description of library dating from 14th century; its collections include 40 medieval manuscripts, about 40 incunabula, and between 8,000 and 9,000 books of later periods.

358. ———. "Winchester College Library in the eighteenth and early nineteenth centuries." Library, ser.5, 17 (1962), 23-45.

Traces history and development of library's collections.

359. British Museum. The British Museum Library, 1753-1953; special exhibition, July, 1953. London, 1953. 67p.

Catalog of exhibition.

360. ———, Dept. of Manuscripts. The library of Sir Simonds D'Ewes, by A. G. Watson. London, 1966. 379p.

The library of D'Ewes (1602-50) acquired by British Museum.

361. Bushnell, George H. "Unfamiliar libraries III: St. Andrews University." Book collector, 7 (1958), 128-38.

History and description of contents of library of Scotland's oldest university, founded in 1410.

362. Cambridge, University, Library. Cambridge college libraries; aids for research students, comp. by A. N. L. Munby, 2d ed. Cambridge: Heffer, 1962. 56p.

363. ———. A chronological list of the graces, documents, and other papers in the University Registry which concern the University Library, by H. R. Luard. Cambridge: Univ. Pr., 1870. 76p.

364. ———. Guide to libraries of the University of Cambridge. Cambridge, 1969. 84p.

Includes faculty, departmental, institute, and other libraries in Cambridge; outlines collections, services, history, etc.

365. Dickson, William P. The Glasgow University Library: notes on its history, arrangements, and aims. Glasgow: James Maclehose, 1888. 87p.

"Notes of the Euing collection of Bibles." p.72-87, summarizes most important works in library.

366. Doyle, A. I. "Unfamiliar libraries IV: the Bamburgh Library." Book collector, 8 (1959), 14-24.

Bamburgh Castle Library, dating from 17th century, transferred in 1958 on indefinite loan to Durham University Library, except music section, deposited in Durham Cathedral Library.

367. Drummond, H. J. H. "Aberdeen University Library special collections (printed books)." Bibliotheck, 3 (1959), 35-40.

Descriptions of 14 collections in various fields.

368. Edinburgh, University, Library. "Benefactors of the Library in five centuries," an exhibition of books and manuscripts selected from donations to the library from the 16th to the 20th century. Edinburgh, 1963. Unpaged. (Exhibition catalogue, no.3)

Annotated listing of 137 items.

369. ———. The Edinburgh University Library; an account of its origin, with a description of its rarer books and manuscripts, by David Cuthbertson. Edinburgh: Otto Schulze, 1910. 45p.

Contains numerous facsimiles and illustrations.

370. ———. Guide to the Library. Edinburgh: Univ. Pr., 1931. 26p.

p.12-15, "chief collections" described.

371. Edmondston, Elizabeth. "Unfamiliar libraries IX: Sion College." Book collector, 14 (1965), 165-77.

Institution established in early 17th century in London; library is important repository of early books in theology and humanities, including medieval manuscripts and incunabula.

372. Fordyce, C. J., and Knox, T. M. "The Library of Jesus College, Oxford, with an appendix on the books bequeathed thereto by Lord Herbert of Cherbury." Oxford Bibliographical Society, Proceedings and papers, 5 (1936-1939), 49-115.

History of the college and its collections, followed by catalog of Herbert books received in 1648-49.

373. Fraser, Kenneth C. "The Beveridge collection in St. Andrews University Library." Bibliotheck, 5 (1969), 211-12.

Collections relating to Esperanto, beekeeping, and Norway.

374. Glasgow Corporation Public Libraries. Glasgow Public Libraries 1874-1966. Glasgow, 1966. 56p.

Includes history of development of Mitchell and other collections.

375. Graham, Rigby. "The manacled books of Wimborne Minster." Private library, 7 (1966), 61-64.

Description of small chained library.

376. Hallam, H. A. N. "Unfamiliar libraries XII: Lamport Hall revisited." Book collector, 16 (1967), 439-49.

Library near Northampton of interest for rare volumes of Elizabethan period.

377. Henchy, Patrick. "The National Library of Ireland." Leabharlann, 26 (June 1968), 45-49.

Review of collections and history of library.

378. Hutton, Muriel. "Unfamiliar libraries XIII: The George MacDonald collection, Brander Library, Huntly." Book collector, 17 (1968), 13-25.

Originally a subscription library, but in 1934 incorporated in Aberdeen County Library system; of interest for 19th- and 20th-century literary manuscripts and first editions.

379. India Office Library. East India House to Orbit House; an exhibition of watercolours, prints, manuscripts, and other material illustrating the buildings, East India House, the India Office, Orbit House, which have housed the East India Company and the India Office, and their records, Museum and Library, etc. London, 1969. 32p.

380. John Rylands Library. The John Rylands Library: 1899-1924; a record of its history, with brief descriptions of the building and its contents; in com-memoration of the twenty-fifth anniversary of its inauguration, by Henry Guppy. Manchester, 1924. 144p. + 62 facsimiles and plates.

381. ———. The John Rylands Library, Manchester, a brief descriptive account, with 14 illustrations, by Edward Robertson. Manchester: Univ. Pr., 1954. 32p.

382. ———. The John Rylands Library, Manchester, a brief historical description of the Library and its contents, with catalogue of a selection of manuscripts and printed books exhibited on the occasion of the visit of the Congregational Union of England and Wales in October, MCMXII, by Henry Guppy, with illustrations. Manchester: Univ. Pr., 1912. 143p. + 21 plates.

383. Lambeth Palace Library. Lambeth Palace Library, 1958-1963. London, 1963. 32p.

384. Leeds, University, Brotherton Library. A descriptive guide to the Libraries of the University of Leeds, by Richard Offor. Leeds, 1947, 134p.

Review of holdings in various fields.

385. ———. A descriptive guide to the Libraries of the University of Leeds, supplement, by Richard Offor. Leeds, 1949. 39p.

Includes descriptions of special collections.

386. Lofthouse, Hilda. "Unfamiliar libraries I: Chetham's Library." Book collector, 5 (1956), 323-30.

Description of library founded in 1653 in Manchester; collection is of varied character: medieval and oriental manuscripts, local history, English literature, theology, etc. Collection totals more than 65,000 volumes.

387. Macdonald, Robert H. The library of Drummond of Hawthornden. Edinburgh: Univ. Pr., 1971. 243p.

Reconstruction of notable private library collected early in 17th century by William Drummond of Hawthornden; copies of surviving books located in Edinburgh University Library or in other British and American collections.

388. Mackay, Hugh. "Scotland's special libraries, pt. 5: Baillie's Library, Glasgow." Scottish Library Association news, no.93 (1969), 376-79.

General description of reference library particularly strong in Scottish and Glasgow holdings.

389. Malvern Public Library. Malvern Public Library; the story of its foundation, with a short survey of its present resources, by J. W. Lucas. Malvern, 1940. 45p.

390. National Library of Wales. Charter of incorporation and report on the progress of the library. Oswestry: Woodall, Minshall, Thomas & Co., 1909. 72p.

Includes descriptions of special collections in library.

391. ———. The National Library of Wales; a survey of its history, its contents, and its activities, by W. Ll. Davies. Aberystwyth, 1937. 212p.

Reviews resources of Departments of Manuscripts and Records, Printed Books, and Maps, Prints, and Drawings.

392. Newcastle upon Tyne, University, Library. Special collections in the University Library, 3d ed. Newcastle upon Tyne, 1968. 6p.

Brief descriptive data.

393. Nicholson, F. C. Edinburgh University Library; a lecture. Edinburgh: Heriot-Watt College, 1937. 18p.

History, with notes on development of collections.

394. Nottingham, University, Library. The Library. (Special collections of manuscripts and books) Nottingham, 1950. 21p.

395. Oldham, J. Basil. "Shrewsbury School Library: its history and contents." Transactions of the Salop Archaeological Society, 51 (1943), 53-81.

General description of 7,000-volume collection, which includes 75 incunabula, other early books, and manuscripts.

396. Oxford, University, All Souls College Library. Records of All Souls College Library, 1437-1600, by N. R. Ker. Oxford: Oxford Bibliographical Society by Oxford Univ. Pr., 1971. 223p.

Detailed listing under various categories.

397. ———, Bodleian Library. The Bodleian Library at Oxford, by Falconer Madan. London: Duckworth, 1919. 68p.

History and description.

398. ——— ———. The Bodleian Library in the seventeenth century; guide to an exhibition held during the Festival of Britain, 1951. Oxford, 1951. 53p. + 21 plates.

399. ——— ———. Oxford College libraries in 1556; guide to an exhibition held in 1956, by Neil Ker. Oxford, 1956. 56p.

400. Skeat, T. C., Rendall, F. G., and Nixon, H. M. "Manuscripts and printed books from the Holkham Hall Library." British Museum quarterly, 17 (1952), 23-40 + 8 plates.

Describing library, manuscripts, printed books, and bindings in the Earl of Leicester Library at Holkham Hall (founded by Chief Justice Sir Edward Coke), purchased for British Museum.

401. Stych, F. S. "The Thomas Bray Library from Sheldon in the Birmingham Reference Library." Open access, 12 (Jan. 1964), 1-4.

Bray (1656-1730) was founder of some 39 parish libraries in the American colonies.

402. York, University, Library. Generalia. York, 1968. 49p. (Library guide, no.2)

Select bibliographical guide to materials held by library.

Periodicals and Newspapers

GENERAL

403. Aberdeen, University, Library. List of periodicals [in the Library of the University of Aberdeen], comp. by R. N. Smart. Aberdeen, 1959. 170p.

Alphabetical list showing exact holdings.

404. ———. Rough list of the periodicals in the library. Aberdeen: Univ. Pr., 1896. 59p.

Later editions: List of current serials in the library. Aberdeen: Univ. Pr., 1917. 88p.; List of current serials in the library. Aberdeen: Univ. Pr., 1925. 79p.

405. Acton Public Libraries CICRIS (West London Commercial and Technical Library Service). Select list of periodicals held by members, comp. by Acton Public Libraries, 2d ed. London: Acton Central Library, 1962. 231p.

Locates files in about 170 libraries.

406. Aston, University, Library, and College of Commerce Library, Birmingham. Catalogue of periodicals. Birmingham, 1966. Unpaged.

Comprises holdings of University of Aston in Birmingham and College of Commerce, Birmingham, Libraries.

407. Bedford Public Library. Bedford area list of periodicals, prep. by A. B. Jackson. Bedford, n.d. 52p.

Holdings for about 1,600 titles shown for 24 libraries in Bedford area.

408. Belfast Public Library. Union list of current periodicals and serials in Northern Ireland libraries, ed. by A. K. Megaw. Belfast, 1966. 297p.

Compiled for Northern Ireland Library Advisory Council; notes holdings of numerous libraries.

409. Bradford, University, Library. Periodicals in stock. Bradford, 1969. 212p.
Alphabetical list showing holdings.

410. Bristol Public Libraries. Periodicals and newspapers in the Bristol Public Libraries. Bristol, 1963. 76p.

411. Bristol, University, Libraries. Catalogue of the periodical publications in the libraries of the University of Bristol, comp. by J. Shum Cox. Bristol: The University, 1940. 149*l*.
Lists 2,686 titles alphabetically; holdings shown.

412. British union-catalogue of periodicals; a record of the periodicals of the world, from the seventeenth century to the present day, in British libraries, ed. by James D. Stewart and others. London: Butterworth Scientific Publications, 1955-58. 4v. Supplement to 1960. 1962. 991p. New periodical titles, 1960-1968. 1970. 603 + 128 + 9p. New periodical titles, 1969-1970. 1969-70. 2v. Quarterly supplements.
Records 140,000 titles in 441 libraries.

413. Brunel University Library. Serial holdings of libraries in the London Borough of Hillingdon; a union list. Hillingdon, 1969. Unpaged.
Lists holdings of 3 libraries: Brunel University, Hillingdon Borough Libraries, and Central Library, E.M.I. Electronics, Ltd.

414. Burkett, J. Hawker Siddeley Group Libraries. Union list of periodicals. Slough: Hawker Siddeley Nuclear Power Co., 1959. 34p.

415. CADIG, Coventry and District Information Group. Computer location list of periodical resources. Coventry: Cadig Liaison Centre Reference Library, 1971. 335p.
Locates holdings in 55 libraries.

416. Cambridge, University, Library. Classified list of current serials available in the University Library, with an index of subjects, 4th ed. Cambridge, 1971. 452p.

417. ———. Current periodicals available in the University Library and in other libraries connected with the university, 1966. Cambridge, 1967. 662p.
Locations in numerous colleges, departments, and other divisions of university; holdings shown.

418. ———. Current serials. Cambridge, 1971. 1,014p.
Union list of serials received currently by the Cambridge University Library and the faculty, departmental, and college libraries of the university. List totals about 27,000 titles, British and foreign.

419. ———. List of current English periodicals, 1950, with a subject index. Cambridge, 1950. 179p.
Extent of holdings is shown for the university and 51 departmental libraries.

420. ———. List of current foreign and colonial periodicals, 1934. Cambridge, 1934. Unpaged.
Locates files in 40 libraries.

421. ———. List of current foreign (including colonial) periodicals to be found in the various libraries of the university, 1921. Cambridge: Univ. Pr., 1921. 91p.

422. ———. List of current foreign periodicals, including those published in countries of the British Commonwealth overseas, 1950. Cambridge, 1950. 282p.
Holdings shown for University Library and 61 college and departmental libraries.

423. Co-operative filing of periodicals in Bridgwater, Taunton, Weston-super-Mare and Yeovil Public Libraries. n.p., 1953. Unpaged.
Contains entries for 200 periodicals.

424. Couper, William J. The Edinburgh periodical press; being a bibliographical account of the newspapers, journals, and magazines issued in Edinburgh from the earliest times to 1800. Stirling: Mackay, 1908. 2v.
Locations given in 13 public and private collections in England and Scotland.

425. ———. "The Glasgow periodical press in the eighteenth century." Glasgow Bibliographical Society records, 8 (1930), 99-135.
Entries for 25 newspapers and periodicals located in Scottish and English libraries and in a private collection.

426. Coventry Public Libraries. Periodical publications currently displayed in the Coventry Public Libraries, a classified catalogue with index to subjects and a complete alphabetical list, comp. by Lydia A. Beasley. Coventry: Public Libraries Committee, 1925. 67p.
Locates 623 periodicals in 7 collections and 3 branch libraries.

427. Craig, Mary Elizabeth. The Scottish periodical press, 1750-1789. Edinburgh and London: Oliver & Boyd, 1931. 113p.
Files located in various British and American libraries.

428. Darlow, G. S. A union list of periodicals in the learned libraries of Durham. Newcastle upon Tyne: Kings College Printing Section for Durham Univ. Library, 1962. 137p.
Locations in 12 college and university libraries.

429. Dundee Public Libraries. List of magazines, newspapers, etc. in Dundee Public Libraries. Class index to List of magazines, periodicals, etc. in Dundee Public Libraries. Dundee, 1970. 2pts.

430. Durham County Library. Periodicals. Durham, 1968. 47*l*.
Records periodicals received in Durham County by branch libraries, associated libraries of education, special and technical colleges, county council departments, and hospitals served by County Library.

431. Ealing Public Libraries. Periodicals and newspapers. Ealing, 1962. 13p.
Listing of files available in central and branch libraries.

432. East Anglia, University, Library. List of periodical holdings. Norwich, 1966. 57p.

433. ———. Periodicals in libraries of the Norwich area, a finding list. Norwich, 1970. 100p.
pt.2, humanities and social sciences.

434. Edinburgh Committee for Library Co-operation. Union list of current periodicals in Edinburgh libraries, 2d ed., comp. and ed. by H. Phillips. Edinburgh, 1955. 112p.
Lists 6,250 titles; holdings given for 36 libraries.

435. Edinburgh, University, Dept. of English Literature. A check list of Victorian periodicals in Edinburgh, ed. by K. J. Fielding. Edinburgh, 1970. 30p.

436. ———, Library. Current serials; union list of serials currently received in the University Library in April, 1971. Edinburgh, 1971. 196p.
Includes locations in sectional and departmental libraries; exact holdings shown; frequently revised.

437. Essex County Library. Union list of serial holdings. Essex. County Council, 1971. 214p.
Locates holdings in 42 libraries.

438. Essex, University, Library. Current serials, October 1965. Colchester, 1965. 58p.
Alphabetical list, without record of holdings.

439. ———. Periodicals. Colchester, 1970. Unpaged.
Alphabetical list of holdings.

440. Exeter, University, Library. Periodicals holdings. Exeter, 1970. 130p.
Alphabetical list of holdings.

441. Glasgow Corporation Public Libraries, Mitchell Library. Catalogue of periodicals, comp. by John Gemmell. Glasgow, 1962. 289p.
Alphabetical list showing exact holdings.

442. Glasgow, University, Library. List of current periodicals. Glasgow: Jackson, Wylie & Co., 1932. xxvii, 35p.
In 2 pts.: alphabetical list, classified list.

443. Gloucester Technical Information Service. Union list of serials held in libraries co-operating in the Gloucestershire Technical Information Service, North Gloucestershire Technical College, ed. by Patricia Symons. Cheltenham, 1970. 92*l*.

444. Guildhall Library. Periodicals; a list of the trade, financial & professional periodicals taken currently in the Commercial Reference Room, Guildhall Library, London, 4th ed. London, 1964. 24p.

445. Hertis College Libraries. List of journal holdings. Hertford, 1971. 120p.
Includes holdings of libraries of colleges of technology and further education in Hertfordshire, Hatfield Polytechnic Library, and branches of the County Library.

446. Huddersfield and District Information Service. Union list of periodical holdings. Huddersfield: HADIS, 1964. 62p.
Locates files in 40 libraries.

447. Irish Association for Documentation. Union list of current periodicals and serials in Dublin libraries, 1959. Dublin: National Library of Ireland, 1960. 155*l*.
About 5,400 titles; 13 contributing libraries.

448. ———. Union list of current periodicals and serials in Dublin libraries, 1965. Dublin: National Library of Ireland, 1966. 206*l*.
Locates holdings in 18 libraries.

449. John Rylands Library. List of current periodical publications, including transactions of learned societies, in the John Rylands Library, comp. by T. Murgatroyd. Manchester, 1932. 71p. (Reprinted from the Bulletin of the John Rylands Library)

450. Kingston upon Hull City Libraries, Hull Technical Interloan Scheme, HULTIS. A checklist of members' periodicals, 3d ed. Kingston upon Hull: Library of Science, Technology and Commerce, Central Library, 1964. 90*l*.
Locates files in 44 libraries.

451. Lambeth Public Libraries. List of periodicals. London, 1955. Unpaged.

Records "all the periodicals and newspapers available in Lambeth Public Libraries."

452. Lancaster, County. A union list of periodicals filed in the public and special libraries of North East Lancashire, 2d ed. Lancaster: Rockdale Corp., 1959. 24*l*.

Alphabetical list of holdings in 18 libraries.

453. Lancaster, University, Library. List of serial titles in stock. Lancaster, 1966- .

Serials list issued periodically.

454. ———. Serials list. Lancaster, 1970. 110p.

Alphabetical list of holdings.

455. ———. Ulserplan: a union list of serial publications held by libraries within the City of Lancaster. Lancaster, 1965. 63p.

Locates holdings of 8 libraries.

456. Leeds Polytechnic Library. List of periodicals. Leeds, 1970. Unpaged.

Locations in 8 branch libraries.

457. Leeds, University, Brotherton Library. Current periodicals in the University Libraries. Leeds, 1971. 128p.

Alphabetical list of holdings.

458. Leicester, University, Victorian Studies Centre. Victorian periodicals in Leicester, comp. by Lionel Madden. Leicester, 1969. 34*l*.

Alphabetical list, with holdings.

459. Library Association, London and Home Counties Branch. The London union list of periodicals; holdings of the municipal and county libraries of Greater London. London, 1969. 102p.

Reports holdings of 18 libraries.

460. ——— ———, Kent Sub-Branch. Kent union list of periodicals, ed. by B. Bishop and C. Earl. London: The Association, 1969. 125p.

Locates holdings in numerous libraries.

461. ——— ———, Reference Group. The London union list of periodicals; holdings of the municipal and county libraries of Greater London, 2d ed., ed. by Owen W. Keen and Kathleen Hancock. London: The Association, 1958. 221p.

Lists 225 libraries' holdings.

462. ———, North-Western Branch. Periodicals currently received in the libraries of the North-west. Manchester: The Association, 1952. 69p.

Nearly 3,000 titles listed in 129 libraries; extent of holdings is not shown.

463. ——— ———. Union list of 7,000 periodicals in 112 libraries of the North-West, comp. and ed. by J. C. Hartas, 2d ed. n.p., The Association, 1958. 117p.

Extent of holdings is shown.

464. ———, Reference and Special Libraries Section, Yorkshire Group. A select list of periodicals in Yorkshire libraries; locations in Yorkshire libraries of those periodicals indexed in the Library Association "Subject index to periodicals." Bradford, 1958. 23*l*.

Holdings noted for numerous libraries.

465. ———, Reference, Special and Information Section, North Midlands Group. Union list of current abstracting, indexing and review serials in the libraries of the North and East Midlands, ed. by A. C. Foskett. London, The Association, 1964. 42p.

Locates files in numerous libraries.

466. ——— ——— ———. Union list of current commercial, scientific and technical periodicals in the North and East Midlands, 2d ed., ed. by Audrey A. Buttery and Geoffrey L. Hayhurst. London: The Association, 1969. 55p.

Locates holdings in numerous libraries.

467. ——— ———, Western Group. Union list of current commercial periodicals, ed. by Anthony Baker. London: The Association, 1968. 43p.

Locates holdings in 52 libraries.

468. LINOSCO, Libraries of North Staffordshire in Co-operation. Union list of current periodicals, 3d ed., ed. by N. Emery. Stoke-on-Trent: Horace Barks Reference Library, 1961. 70*l*.

Locates about 1,400 titles, not holdings, in 11 libraries.

469. Liverpool, University, Library. Finding list of periodicals, excluding the humanities. Liverpool, 1971. 251p.

Alphabetical list of holdings.

470. ———. A hand-list of academies and periodical publications in the university libraries, including the departmental libraries of the Faculties of Science, Medicine and Engineering, the class libraries of the Faculty of Arts, the Institute of Archaeology, and the School of Tropical Medicine. Liverpool: Univ. Pr., 1913. 97, 46p.

Arranged alphabetically by place of publication or headquarters of societies; holdings of 21 collections.

471. ———. List of periodicals and other serial publications currently received by the University Library, the City of Liverpool Central and Commercial, Reference Libraries, the Liverpool Medical Institution, the

Liverpool School of Tropical Medicine. Liverpool: Univ. Pr., 1949. 93p. Supplement. 1952. 44p.

Lists 2,717 titles; supplement adds 980 titles.

472. London Chamber of Commerce Library. Periodicals. London, 1970. 42p.

Grouped geographically and by types, with alphabetical and subject lists.

473. London, University, Chelsea College Library. Guide to the abstracting and indexing services available in the College Library, comp. by Tessa White and Jon E. North. London: Chelsea College, 1969. 116p. + subject index.

474. ———, Library. Colonial periodicals in London libraries. London, 1954. 25p.

Files located in 32 libraries.

475. ——— ———. Hand-catalogue of the Library, brought down to the end of 1897. London: H. M. Stationery Office, 1900. 398p.

476. ——— ———. List of current periodicals, 2d ed. London, 1969. 148p.

Alphabetical list showing holdings.

477. ——— ———. List of periodicals. London: The Univ. 1956. 279p.

All-inclusive list of current and retrospective files, with minor exceptions; specific holdings shown.

478. ——— ———. Select list of periodicals newly received by colleges, schools, and institutes of the University of London, 1950-1959. London: Queen Mary College, 1960. 115l.

Alphabetical list showing exact holdings.

479. ———, Royal Holloway College Library. List of periodicals. Egham, Surrey, 1971. 69p.

Exact holdings noted.

480. ———, Standing Conference of Librarians of Libraries of the University of London (SCOLLUL). A union list of periodicals newly received by the following libraries of the University of London since 1st January, 1955, and compiled to supplement the holdings of these libraries recorded in the British union catalogue of periodicals. London, 1957. 43l,

Records holdings of 9 libraries.

481. ———, University College Library. Catalogue of the periodical publications, including the serial publications of societies and governments, in the Library of University College, London, by L. Newcombe. Oxford: Hart, 1912. 269p.

Records 1,441 titles.

482. Manchester Public Libraries. Periodicals and serials currently received in the Reference, Commercial, Technical and Music Libraries. Manchester, 1931. 50p. (Occasional lists, new series, no.5)

No holdings shown.

483. ———. A short title list of periodical holdings in the Reference Libraries. Manchester, 1955. 371l.

Alphabetical list, with holdings noted.

484. Manchester, University, Library. Select list of non-scientific periodicals currently received in the University Library. Manchester, 1971. 71p.

List without holdings; locations in 30 branch libraries.

485. Mid and South Staffordshire Libraries in Cooperation. Union list of periodicals, 4th ed. Stafford: Staffordshire County Library, 1972. 127p.

486. Middlesex Technical Colleges. Union list of periodicals and annual publications, 3d ed. London: Willesden Technical College, 1960. 58p.

487. MISLIC, Mid-Staffordshire Libraries in Cooperation. Union list of periodicals, 3d ed. Stafford, 1967. 55p.

Covers holdings of 30 libraries in Mid- and South Staffordshire area.

488. National Central Library. List of periodicals held by the National Central Library. London, 1967. 35p.

Alphabetical list, showing holdings.

489. National Library of Scotland. Current periodicals. Edinburgh, 1970. Unpaged.

Alphabetical list showing exact holdings.

490. National University of Ireland. Catalogue of current & discontinued periodicals in the Library of University College, Galway, comp. by Michael J. Fahy. Galway: University College Library, 1956. 64l.

491. Newcastle upon Tyne City Libraries. List of periodicals currently received. Newcastle upon Tyne, 1971. 42l.

492. Northern Ireland Library Advisory Council. Current periodicals; a list of newspapers, periodicals, annual and serial publications currently received in Northern Ireland libraries. n.p., 1957. 140l.

Extent of holdings is shown for 25 libraries.

493. ———. Union list of current periodicals and serials in Northern Ireland libraries, by A. K. Megaw. Belfast: Belfast Public Library, 1966. 297p.

Locates files of about 8,000 titles in 46 libraries.

494. North Western Regional Library Bureau. Union list of periodicals in the libraries of the North West. Manchester: Library Association, North-Western Branch, 1958. 465p. + index.

Contains over 17,800 entries for 150 libraries.

495. North Western Regional Library System. Union list of periodicals in the libraries of the North West, supplement. Manchester, 1961. 44*l.* + index to 168 libraries.

Supplements Union list of periodicals in the libraries of the North West, published in 1958 by Library Association's North Western Branch.

496. ———. Union list of periodicals in the libraries of the North West, new ed. Manchester, 1967. 472p.

Locates files in numerous libraries.

497. Nottingham Public Libraries. List of current periodicals. Nottingham, 1966. 53*l.*

498. Nottingham, University, Library. Humanities and social sciences; list of periodicals and serials. Nottingham, 1969. 90*l.*

Alphabetical list noting holdings.

499. Oxford, University, Bodleian Library. Catalogue of periodicals contained in the Bodleian Library: pt.I, English periodicals (pt.III. Foreign periodicals). Oxford, 1878-80. pt.1, 3. No more published.

500. ———. Current foreign and colonial periodicals in the Bodleian Library and in other Oxford libraries. Oxford: Clarendon, 1925. 135p.

Lists 2,215 titles alphabetically; holdings for Bodleian and 35 college and departmental libraries given; supplement, p.133-135, lists 60 additional titles.

501. ———. Current foreign and Commonwealth periodicals in the Bodleian Library and in other Oxford libraries. Oxford: Univ. Pr., 1953. 267*l.* Supplement no.1. Oxford, 1956. 99p. Supplement no.2. Oxford, 1962. 127p.

Alphabetical lists noting holdings.

502. Paisley College of Technology Library. Periodical holdings list, 4th ed. Paisley, 1971. 87p.

Alphabetical list of holdings, followed by subject listing.

503. Portsmouth Polytechnic Library. Periodicals catalogue, session 1971-72. Portsmouth, 1971. 143p.

Alphabetical list of holdings.

504. Preston Commercial and Technical Information Service. List of periodicals held by members, 3d ed. Preston, 1965. Unpaged.

Records periodical holdings of 26 libraries and firms in Preston and district.

505. Queen's University Library. List of current periodicals & serials in Belfast libraries, 4th ed. Belfast, 1937. 281p.

Titles only, without holdings, for 28 libraries; 1,370 titles listed.

506. Reading, University, Library. Current periodical titles, with locations. Reading, 1967. 72p.

Alphabetical list showing holdings.

507. Rowett Research Institute, Reid Library. List of journals, May-June 1970. Aberdeen, 1970. 49*l.*

Alphabetical list of holdings.

508. Royal Society of London. Catalogue of the periodical publications in the Library of the Royal Society of London, comp. by Luxmoore Newcombe and L. Ellston. London: Oxford Univ. Pr., 1912. 455p.

Alphabetical list of 1,811 titles, with society index.

509. Salford, University, Library. Periodicals currently received. Salford, 1971. Unpaged.

Notes holdings.

510. Scottish College of Commerce. The Library bulletin; an index to periodicals in the college library. Jan.-June, 1955. Glasgow, 1955. 135p. + 21p. index.

Subject headings arranged by Dewey classification.

511. Sheffield City Public Libraries. Interchange of technical publications; union list of scientific, technical, and commercial periodicals in the libraries of members of the group interchange system. Sheffield, 1934. 83p.

512. Sheffield Interchange Organization (SINTO). Union list of periodicals. Sheffield: Sheffield City Council Libraries and Arts Committee, 1970. Unpaged.

Locates holdings in 43 libraries.

513. Sheffield, University, Library. List of journals containing abstracts or indexes of periodical articles held in the main library, together with some in the Applied Science Library and departmental libraries. Sheffield, 1971. 15p.

514. Shirley Institute Library. Catalogue of periodicals in the Shirley Institute Library. Manchester, 1962. 179*l.*

515. Shropshire County Library. Shropshire union list of periodicals. Shrewsbury, 1963. 44p.

Lists holdings of 29 libraries of various types in area.

516. Smoothie Publications. Directory of alternative media periodicals, ed. by John Noyce. Sussex, 1970. 74p.

Locates holdings in 33 libraries.

517. Sper, Felix. The periodical press of London, theatrical and literary (excluding the daily newspaper), 1800-1830. Boston, Mass.: F. W. Faxon, 1937. 58p.

Files located in 4 British and 37 U.S. libraries.

518. Stafford, County, Libraries of North Staffordshire in Co-operation. Union list of current periodicals, 3d ed., ed. by N. Emery. Stoke on Trent, 1961. 70*l.* Supplement, ed. by H. Pemberton. Stoke on Trent, 1963. 50*l.*

Locates titles (not holdings) in 18 libraries.

519. Staffordshire County Library, Mid-Staffordshire Libraries in Co-operation (MISLIC). Union list of periodicals in the fields of science, technology and commerce, 2d ed. Stafford, 1965. 26p.

Lists holdings of 18 libraries.

520. Standing Conference of National and University Libraries. Foreign periodicals bulletin. n.p., Nov. 1956- .

Bulletin of foreign periodicals recently acquired by university libraries to inform members of the location of periodicals listed.

521. Stirling, University, Library. Current periodicals, 3d ed. Stirling, 1971. Unpaged.

Alphabetical list of holdings.

522. Strathclyde, University, Andersonian Library. Serial holdings. Glasgow, 1970. 185p.

Alphabetical list of holdings.

523. Surrey, University, Library. Serial holdings. Surrey, 1970. 193p.

Alphabetical list with holdings.

524. Sussex, University, Library. Current periodicals. Brighton, Dec. 1968- .

Issued periodically.

525. ———. A subject index to abstracting and indexing publications held and currently being received. Brighton, 1972. 15*l.*

526. Swansea, University College, Library. Handlist of current periodicals. Swansea, 1966. 42p.

Alphabetical list noting holdings.

527. Swindon Area Association of Libraries for Industry and Commerce. Periodicals; a preliminary union list. Swindon: Public Libraries, 1962. 9p.

528. ULSERPLAN. A union list of serial publications held by libraries in Lancaster. Lancaster: Univ. of Lancaster, 1967. 63p.

Locates holdings in 9 libraries.

529. Union catalogue of the periodical publications in the university libraries of the British Isles, with their respective holdings, excluding titles in the World list of scientific periodicals, 1934; compiled on behalf of the Joint Standing Committee on Library Cooperation by Marion G. Roupe II. London: Joint Standing Committee on Library Cooperation, National Central Library, 1937. 712p.

Lists 23,115 periodicals, with holdings in 113 libraries.

530. Union list of current periodicals taken in the following libraries in the Aberystwyth area, the libraries of: University College of Wales, Theological College, College of Librarianship Wales, Welsh Plant Breeding Station, Gogerddan, National Agricultural Advisory Service, Trawscoed. Aberystwyth, 1969. Unpaged.

Alphabetical list with holdings.

531. Union list of periodical titles currently received in the libraries of the Polytechnic, the College of Education and the Technical College. Brighton, 1970. 35*l.*

Does not record holdings.

532. "Union list of periodicals." Literary and Philosophical Society of Newcastle upon Tyne, Quarterly record, 1 (1928), 35-80.

Entries for about 1,800 titles, with locations in 11 libraries in Newcastle area.

533. Union list of periodicals filed in the public and special libraries of North-East Lancashire, 2d ed. rev. Rochdale, Lancs.: Central Library, 1959. 24*l.*

Records holdings of 18 libraries.

534. University College Dublin Library. List of current periodicals in the Education Library. Dublin: University College, 1969. 27*l.*

535. University College of South Wales and Monmouthshire. List of periodicals in the library. Cardiff, 1953. 94p.

536. University College of Wales Library. List of current periodicals taken in the college libraries. Aberystwyth, 1968. Unpaged.

537. Ward, William S. Index and finding list of serials published in the British Isles, 1789-1832. Lexington: Univ. of Ky. Pr., 1953. 180p.

Files of 1,080 titles located in numerous British and American libraries.

538. Warwick, University, Library. Periodicals list. Coventry, 1971. 98 + 14 + 49p.

In 3 sections: arts and social sciences, British statistical series, and sciences.

539. West London Commercial and Technical Library Service (CICRIS). Select union list of periodicals held by members, comp. by Acton Public Libraries, 2d ed. London, 1962. 231p.

540. Westminster City Libraries. Union list of periodicals. London, 1970. 137p.

Locations noted in 14 district and branch libraries; holdings shown; alphabetical and subject listings.

541. Wiener, Joel H. A descriptive finding list of unstamped British periodicals, 1830-1836. London: Bibliographical Society, 1970. 74p.

Files located in numerous British and American libraries.

542. Wiggins Teape Group Research Organization, Southern and Northern Base Library. Joint periodical holdings at 1st November, 1959. Beaconsfield, Bucks., 1959. 8p.

543. Wiltshire Association of Libraries of Industry and Commerce. Union list of periodicals received in co-operating libraries. Trowbridge: Wiltshire County Library, 1962. 11p.

544. Worcester City Libraries, Museums and Art Galleries. Union catalogue of periodicals in the South West Midlands; a co-operative scheme listing the holdings of 31 technical and further education college libraries, public and industrial libraries, ed. by K. S. Weyman. Worcester, 1971. Unpaged.

Lists holdings of 31 libraries.

545. Worcestershire Association of Technical Libraries. Union list of periodicals, comp. by K. Laugharne and D. C. Honour. Redditch: College of Further Education, 1968. 22p.

AFRICAN

546. Standing Conference on Library Materials on Africa. "Periodicals added to the collections of member libraries." Library materials on Africa, 3 (May 1966)-7 (March 1970). 10pts.

Files located in Conference's member libraries; arranged by countries.

547. ———. Periodicals published in Africa. London, 1965-68. Various pagings.

Geographical listings, with locations in London, Oxford, Cambridge, and Birmingham libraries.

ARABIC

548. Cambridge, University, Middle East Centre. Arabic periodical literature 1961- . Cambridge, 1966- .

Issued periodically.

549. Oxford, University, Libraries. Arabic periodicals in Oxford; a union list, comp. by Derek Hopwood. Oxford: St. Antony's College, 1968. 19l.

Lists Arabic periodicals held in Middle East Centre, Oriental Institute, and Bodleian Library.

CHINESE

550. Association for Asian Studies. Chinese periodicals; international holdings 1949-1960. Ann Arbor, Mich., 1961. Unpaged. Indexes and supplement, 1961. 107p. (Preliminary data papers, April-June, 1961)

Locates holdings in American, British, and Japanese libraries.

551. British Museum. Chinese periodicals in British libraries; handlist no.2. London, 1965. 102p.

Locates files in 17 libraries.

552. ———, Dept. of Oriental Printed Books and Manuscripts. Chinese periodicals in British libraries, handlist no.3, with a provisional list of Chinese research material on microfilm held by four British libraries, comp. by E. D. Grinstead. London: The Museum, 1969. 80p. (Updates Handlist no.2, 1965)

Locates files in 8 libraries.

553. Chinese periodicals in British libraries. Handlist no.1. London? 1962? 41p.

Extent of holdings is shown for 14 libraries. Appendix A lists holdings of 5 specialized libraries of the British Museum, Natural History; Appendix B lists holdings as of June 1962 of the National Lending Library of Science and Technology, Boston Spa, Yorkshire.

554. Shih, Bernadette P. N., and Snyder, Richard L. International union list of Communist Chinese serials, scientific, technical and medical, with selected social science titles. Cambridge, Mass.: Mass. Institute of Technology Libraries, 1963. Unpaged.

Records holdings of about 600 serials in 28 British, American, Canadian, Japanese, and Hong Kong libraries.

INDIAN

555. India Office Library. Commonwealth Relations Office. Catalogue of periodicals. (Catalogue of European printed books, v.10) Boston, Mass.: G. K. Hall, 1964. 143p.

JAPANESE

556. Sheffield, University, Library. Check-list of Japanese periodicals held in British university and research libraries, by S. M. Manddahl and Peter W. Cornell. Sheffield, Yorkshire, 1968. 2pts.

   pt.1, General periodicals, humanities and social sciences; pt.2, science and technology; locates files of 2,449 titles in 36 libraries.

SLAVIC AND EAST EUROPEAN

557. Birmingham, University, Centre for Russian and East European Studies. List (annual list) of current acquisitions of Soviet periodicals and western periodicals concerned with the Soviet Union (and the East European countries). Birmingham, 1963-

558. Glasgow, University, Institute of Soviet and East European Studies. Annual list of current acquisitions; Soviet, East European and Western periodicals and newspapers dealing with the Soviet Union and the East European countries. Glasgow: The University, 1969. 3pts.

   pt.1, Soviet newspapers and periodicals; pt.2, East European newspapers and periodicals; pt.3, Western periodicals. Locates files in 19 British libraries.

559. Library Association, Reference, Special and Information Section, North Western Group. Russian journals: union list of titles held by four libraries in Manchester and Salford. Manchester: Central Library, 1960. 14p.

   Records holdings of 54 titles.

560. National Reference Library of Science and Invention. Periodical publications in the National Library of Science and Invention. pt.2, List of Slavonic and East European titles in the Bayswater Division. London: British Museum, 1971. 105p.

   Alphabetical list with holdings.

561. Polish Cultural Institute. Polish periodicals held by the Polish Cultural Institute, a selective list. London, 1955. 7p.

562. Polish Library. Catalogue of periodicals in Polish or relating to Poland and other Slavonic coun-tries published outside Poland since September 1st, 1939, comp. by Maria Danilewicz and Genowefa Sadowska. London, 1964. 75p.

   Records 895 titles held by Polish Library, London.

563. ———. Catalogue of periodicals in Polish or relating to Poland and other Slavonic countries, published outside Poland since September 1st, 1939, 2d ed., comp. by Maria Danilewicz and Genowefa Sadowska. London, 1971. 126*l*.

NEWSPAPERS

General

564. British Museum, Newspaper Library. Newspapers and journals in microfilm. London: The Museum 1969. 10p.

565. City Business Library. Newspapers; a list of the British and foreign newspapers taken currently in the City Business Library. London, 1969. 7*l*.

566. ———. Newspapers; a list of the British & overseas newspapers (including stock exchange lists) taken currently in the City Business Library, 2d ed. London: Gillett House, 1970. 7p.

   Grouped by countries.

567, Crick, Bernard R., and Daltrop, Anne. List of American newspapers up to 1940, held by libraries in Great Britain and Ireland. Edinburgh, 1958. 90p. (British Association for American Studies. Bulletin, no.7. Supplement)

   Locates files in 20 libraries; geographical arrangement.

568. Hewitt, A. R., comp. Union list of Commonwealth newspapers in London, Oxford and Cambridge. London: Athlone Pr., for the Institute of Commonwealth Studies, Univ. of London, 1960. 101p.

   Lists files of 2,426 newspapers in 62 libraries and newspaper offices; excludes papers published in the British Isles; includes Anglo-Egyptian Sudan.

569. Library Association, Reference and Special Libraries Section, Northern Group. Union list of newspaper files in Northern area. Middlesbrough, Yorks., 1958. 9*l*.

   Holdings of 23 libraries shown.

570. Newcastle upon Tyne City Libraries. Newspaper holdings. Newcastle upon Tyne, 1970. 15*l*.

571. "Newspapers on microfilm." Library Association record, 62 (Aug. 1960), 256-58.

Lists about 200 microfilmed British newspapers, arranged alphabetically, giving dates covered and locations of copies in British and U.S. libraries and publishers' offices.

572. Oxford, University, Bodleian Library. Catalogue of a collection of early newspapers and essayists, formed by the late John Thomas Hope and presented to the Bodleian Library. Oxford: Clarendon, 1865. 178p.

Lists 764 titles.

573. Royal Colonial Institute. List of newspapers, magazines, and other periodicals taken at the Royal Colonial Institute. London, 1925. 32p.

Publications from all areas of former British Empire.

574. Standing Conference on Library Materials on Africa. A tentative list of African newspapers in some London libraries. London, 1969. Unpaged.

Alphabetical list, with holdings in 25 libraries.

British and Irish

575. Barnes, F., and Hobbs, J. L. Handlist of newspapers published in Cumberland, Westmorland, and North Lancashire. Kendal: Titus Wilson, 1951. 16p. (Cumberland & Westmorland Antiquarian & Archaeological Society, Tract series, no.14)

Files located in 27 public and private collections in northern England, for 152 titles.

576. Bibliotheca Lindesiana. Catalogue of English newspapers, 1641-1666; together with notes of a few papers of earlier date, comp. by John P. Edmond. Aberdeen: Univ. Pr., 1901. 78p. (Collations and notes, no.5)

Contains 142 entries.

577. Bristol Public Libraries. Early Bristol newspapers; a detailed catalogue of Bristol newspapers published up to and including the year 1800 in the Bristol Reference Library. Bristol: Corp. of Bristol, 1956. 32p.

Lists 27 titles, 1704-1800.

578. British Museum, Dept. of Printed Books. Catalogue of printed books in the Library of the British Museum. Supplement: Newspapers published in Great Britain and Ireland, 1801-1900. London: W. Clowes, 1905. 532 cols.

Lists about 75,000 titles by place of publication.

579. Brooke, L. E. J. Somerset newspapers, 1725-1960. Yeovil, Somerset, 1960. 103p.

Locates files of 181 titles in libraries, English and American, and newspaper offices.

580. Bullock, John Malcolm. "Files of the local (Aberdeen) press, past and present." Scottish notes and queries, 9 (1896), 170-71.

Lists 20 newspapers in 8 collections (7 in Aberdeen and 1 in Elgin); notes holdings.

581. Cassedy, James. A guide to old Waterford newspapers, by Séamus O'Casaide. Waterford: Waterford News, 1917. 30p.

Holdings given for 14 libraries and 3 private collections.

582. Chester Public Library. Chester newspaper index. Chester, 1970. 347p.

Covers newspapers with Chester imprints for 1960-64.

583. Collins, Douglas C. A handlist of news pamphlets, 1590-1610. London: South-West Essex Technical College, 1943. 129p.

Records copies in 1 American and 5 British libraries; includes STC numbers; 217 entries.

584. Cranfield, G. A. A handlist of English provincial newspapers and periodicals, 1700-1760, rev. ed. Cambridge: Univ. Pr., 1961. 42p.

Locates files in British libraries.

585. Dahl, Folke. A bibliography of English corantos and periodical newsbooks, 1620-1642. London: Bibliographical Society, 1952. 283p.

Locates 349 issues in 508 copies in 43 European and American libraries in chronological order. Expansion of "Short-title catalogue of English corantos and newsbooks 1620-1640," Library, ser.4, 19 (1938), 44-98.

586. ———. "Short-title catalogue of English corantos and newsbooks, 1620-1642." Library, ser.4, 19 (1938), 44-98. Reprinted, 1938.

Listing of 372 items, with locations in British, American, and European libraries.

587. Dix, Ernest R. M. Irish bibliography; tables relating to some Dublin newspapers of the 18th century, shewing what volumes, etc. of each are extant and where access to them can be had in Dublin. Dublin: Hanna & Neale, 1910. 12p.

Holdings given for 7 libraries.

588. Ferguson, Joan P. S. Scottish newspapers held in Scottish libraries. Edinburgh: Scottish Central Library, 1956. 56p.

About 570 titles in 46 libraries; holdings noted in detail.

589. "Files of the local (Aberdeen) press, past and present." Scottish notes and queries, 9 (1896), 170-71.

Lists about 20 newspapers in 8 collections (7 in Aberdeen and 1 in Elgin); holdings given.

590. Guildhall Library. "A complete list of the seventeenth-century newspapers in the Guildhall Library." Guildhall miscellany, 8 (July, 1957), 33-39.

Alphabetical list, noting holdings in detail; supersedes "Handlist" in Guildhall miscellany, 3 (Feb. 1954), 46-56.

591. ———. "Handlist of seventeenth century newspapers in the Guildhall Library." Guildhall miscellany, 3 (Feb. 1954), 46-56.

592. Hertfordshire Local History Council. Hertfordshire newspapers, 1772-1955; a list compiled for the County bibliography by M. F. Thwaite. Hertford, 1956. 42p.

Locates files of 99 titles in libraries, museums, and newspaper offices.

593. Library Association, Reference, Special and Information Section, North Western Group. Newspapers first published before 1900 in Lancashire, Cheshire and the Isle of Man; a union list of holdings in libraries and newspaper offices within that area, ed. by R. E. G. Smith. London, 1964. 47p.

Locates files of 396 titles in numerous libraries and newspaper offices.

594. ——— Yorkshire Branch. Yorkshire newspapers: a bibliography with locations, by George E. Laughton and Lorna R. Stephen. Leeds, 1960. 61p.

Lists 446 titles; locations in numerous libraries and newspaper offices.

595. Munter, Robert LaVerne. A hand-list of Irish newspapers, 1685-1750. London: Bowes & Bowes, 1960. 36p. (Cambridge Bibliographical Society monograph, no.4)

Records 172 titles; locations in 13 Irish and English libraries.

596. Myson, William. Surrey newspapers: a handlist and tentative bibliography. London: Wimbledon Borough Council for the Surrey Libraries Group, 1961. 36p.

Locates files for 215 titles in libraries and newspaper offices.

597. O'Rourke, D. T. "Early provincial newspapers in Reading University Library." Cambridge Bibliographical Society transactions, 4 (1966), 256.

Records holdings of 8 18th-century titles.

598. Oxford, University, Bodleian Library. A catalogue of English newspapers and periodicals in the Bodleian Library, 1622-1800, by R. T. Milford and D. M. Sutherland. Oxford: Printed for the Oxford Bibliographical Society at the Oxford Univ. Pr., 1936. 184p.

Alphabetical list, showing exact holdings.

599. Press Club Library. Catalogue of an exhibition illustrating the history of the English newspaper through three centuries from the Library of the Press Club, London. London: J. & E. Bumpus, 1932. 58p.

Lists 318 items, 1606 to 20th century.

600. ———. Catalogue of London Press Club Library on journalism. v.III. Collection of the newspapers, magazines, news bulletins, wall newspapers, etc., printed, typed, or handwritten by or for the Forces serving at home and overseas during the 1939-45 War, with explanatory notes, comp. by Andrew Stewart. London, 1948. 63l.

601. ———. The evolution of the English newspaper from its origins to the present day, as illustrated by the catalogue of the Press Club collection, comp. by Andrew Stewart. London, 1935. 161l.

602. ———. An exhibition from the London Press Club's collection of English newspapers of the seventeenth and eighteenth centuries. London: G. W. Jones, 1931. 12p.

Lists 109 items.

603. Scottish Central Library. Scottish newspapers held in Scottish libraries, comp. by Miss J. P. S. Ferguson. Edinburgh, 1956. 57p.

Locates files in 46 libraries; exact holdings shown.

604. Thwaite, Mary F. Hertfordshire newspapers, 1772-1955; a list compiled for the County bibliography. Welwyn: Herts. Local History Council, 1956. 42l.

Entries for 99 papers, with locations in 13 museums and libraries and 10 newspaper offices.

605. Wiles, R. M. Freshest advices; early provincial newspapers in England. Columbus: Ohio State Univ. Pr., 1965. 555p.

Appendix C, "Register of English provincial newspapers, 1701-1760," p.374-519, locates files in British, American, and Canadian libraries.

606. Williams, J. B. A history of English journalism to the foundation of the Gazette. London: Longmans, 1908. 293p.

Contains "Catalogue of the periodicals from 1641 to 1666 inclusive," p.218-65, with locations in British Museum.

DIRECTORIES

607. Black Country Librarians Circle. Check list of annuals, directories, etc., in Black Country libraries. Brierly Hill, Staffs.: Central Library, 1958. 27p.

608. CICRIS Commercial and Technical Library Service (West London). Directories and professional and trade registers and yearbooks for the British Isles, 1959. Harrow: Central Reference Library, 1959. Unpaged.

Material listed is held at Central Reference Library, Middlesex County Libraries, Harrow.

609. Emery, N., and Beard, D. R. Staffordshire directories: a union list of directories relating to the geographical county of Stafford. Stoke on Trent: Public Libraries, 1966. 46l.

Copies located in 12 libraries in area.

610. Goss, Charles W. F. The London directories, 1677-1855; a bibliography with notes on their origin and development. London: Denis Archer, 1932. 147p.

Locations in 9 public and private collections.

611. Guildhall Library. Catalogue of the overseas directories in the commercial reference room. London: Corp. of London, 1950. 18p.

612. Henderson, G. P. and I. G. Current British directories; a guide to the directories published in Great Britain, Ireland, the British Commonwealth and South Africa, ed.6, 1970-71. Beckenham, Kent: CBD Research, Ltd., 1970. 270p.

Introduction lists London and other libraries in which "a large proportion of the directories listed may be consulted."

613. Hertfordshire County Library. Specialised trade directories. Hertford, 1966. 26p.

List of British specialized directories in Stevenage Central Library's reference department.

614. Joint Committee on the Lancashire Bibliography. Lancashire directories, 1684-1957, comp. by G. H. Tupling, rev. by Sidney Horrocks. Manchester, 1968. 78p.

Records 1,052 items, with locations in numerous libraries.

615. London Chamber of Commerce Library. United Kingdom directories. London: 1971. 32p.

Alphabetic and subject listings.

616. Manchester Public Free Libraries, Commercial Library and Information Department. Overseas directories and periodicals. Manchester, 1957- .

Issued periodically.

617. Norton, Jane E. Guide to the national and provincial directories of England and Wales, excluding London, published before 1856. London: Royal Historical Society, 1950. 241p.

Lists 878 titles, geographically arranged; locates copies in 20 public and private collections.

618. Smyth, A. L. "Trades, professional and official directories as historical source material." Manchester review, 11 (1966), 39-58.

Classified checklist of directories in Manchester Public Libraries.

619. Stoke on Trent Public Libraries. Staffordshire directories; a union list of directories relating to Stafford, by N. Emery and D. R. Beard. Stoke on Trent, 1966. 46l.

620. Walker, Benjamin. "Birmingham directories." Birmingham Archaeological Society transactions and proceedings, 58 (1934), 1-36.

General review of early and rare directories, with references to locations.

621. West Ham Public Libraries. Handlist of annuals and directories in the Central Reference Library. West Ham: Central Library, 1963. 38p.

622. Westminster Public Libraries. Directories and annuals: an analytical subject index. London, 1950. 46p.

ALMANACS

623. Bosanquet, Eustace F. English printed almanacks and prognostications, a bibliographical history to 1600. London: Bibliographical Society, 1917. 204p. + 35 facsimiles. (The Society's Illustrated monographs, no.17)

Full descriptions of 187 items, with locations.

624. ———. "English printed almanacks and prognostications: corrigenda and addenda." Library, ser.4, 8 (1928), 456-77. Reprinted.

625. Guildhall Library. "A handlist of almanacs in the Guildhall Library." Guildhall miscellany, 1 (Aug. 1956), 40-46.

626. McDonald, William R. "Scottish seventeenth-century almanacs." Bibliotheck, 4 (1956), 257-322.

"Catalogue of almanacs," p.295-322, describes in bibliographic detail, 100 items, 1623-1700; copies located in 8 libraries.

Manuscripts

GENERAL

627. Archbishop Marsh's Library. Catalogue of the manuscripts remaining in Marsh's Library, Dublin, comp. by John Russell Scott, ed. by Newport J. D. White. Dublin: A. Thom, 1913. 137p.

628. Armagh Public Library. Catalogue of manuscripts in the Armagh Public Library . . . 1928, comp. by James Dean. Dundalk: W. Tempest, 1928. 43p.

629. Birmingham, University, Library. Catalogue of letters additional. Birmingham, 1969-70. 3v.

Calendar of individual letters nos. 1-4,500, in library's collection.

630. ———. Corbett autograph collection. Birmingham, 1969. Unpaged. (Catalogues of the manuscript collections, no.18)

Miscellaneous collection representing many different names.

631. ———. Index of single manuscripts acquired up to August, 1969. Birmingham, 1969. 24l.

Miscellaneous manuscripts, arranged alphabetically by author or title.

632. ———. Michael Tomkinson—Gertrude Dauglish album. Birmingham, 1968. 15p. (Catalogues of the manuscript collections, no.15)

Autographs of notable persons.

633. Bluhm, R. K. "A guide to the archives of the Royal Society and to other manuscripts in its possession." Notes and records of the Royal Society of London, 12 (Aug. 1956), 21-39.

Descriptions of principal groups of material.

634. British Manuscripts Project. A checklist of the microfilms prepared in England and Wales for the American Council of Learned Societies, 1941-1945, comp. by Lester K. Born. Washington, D.C.: Library of Congress, 1955. 179p.

Sources of original manuscripts in Britain listed; microfilms deposited in Library of Congress.

635. British Museum. Catalogue of the manuscripts in the Cottonian Library deposited in the British Museum. London, 1802. 618p. + index.

636. ———. A catalogue of the manuscripts of the King's Library; an appendix to the catalogue of the Cottonian Library, by David Casley. London: The Author, 1734. 360p. + 16 plates and index.

637. ———. The catalogues of the manuscript collections in the British Museum, by T. C. Skeat, rev. ed. London: Trustees of the British Museum, 1962. 45p.

638. ———. Description of the Ashburnham manuscripts, and account of offers of purchase, etc., communicated to the Rt. Hon. the Chancellor of the Exchequer by the Principal Librarian of the British Museum, February 21st, 1883. London, 1883. 12p.

639. ———. The Eric George Millar bequest of manuscripts and drawings, 1967; a commemorative volume. London, 1968. 89p. + 34 plates. (Reprinted from British Museum quarterly, v.33)

640. ———. "The Sloane collection of manuscripts." British Museum quarterly, 18 (1953), 6-10.

Collection of more than 4,000 items, assembled in 18th century, now held by British Museum.

641. ———, Dept. of Manuscripts. The Burney manuscripts. London, 1840. 159p.

Manuscripts collected by Charles Burney (1757-1817), classical scholar.

642. ——— ———. Catalogue of a selection from the Stowe manuscripts exhibited in the King's Library in the British Museum, ed. by E. M. Thompson. London: The King's Library, 1883. 83p. + 15 plates.

Lists and describes 77 items.

643. ——— ———. Catalogue of additions to the manuscripts in the British Museum. London, 1843-1970. 24v.

Index 1783-1835. 1849. 514p. Reprinted, 1967. 1836-40. 1843. 300p. Reprinted, 1964. 1841-45. 1850. 863p. Reprinted, 1964. 1846-47. 1864. 522p. Reprinted, 1964. 1848-53. 1868. 576p. Reprinted, 1965. 1854-60. 1875. 938p. Reprinted, 1966. 1861-75. 1877. 1,050p. Reprinted, 1966. Index, 1854-75. 1880. 2v. Reprinted, 1968. 1876-81. 1882. 617p. Reprinted, 1967. 1882-87. 1889. 1,140p. Reprinted, 1968. 1888-93. 1894. 920p. Reprinted, 1969. 1894-99. 1903. 2v. Reprinted, 1969. 1900-5. 1907. 942p. Reprinted, 1969. 1906-10. 1912. 794p. Reprinted, 1969. 1911-15. 1925. 2v. Reprinted, 1969. 1916-20. 1933. 686p. 1921-25. 1950. 1,400p. 1926-30. 1959. 644p. 1931-35. 1967. 878p. 1936-45. 1970. 2v.

644. ——— ———. A catalogue of manuscripts, formerly in the possession of Francis Hargrave, now deposited in the British Museum. London: G. Woodfall, 1818. 188p.

Legal manuscripts of Francis Hargrave (1741-1821), purchased in 1813.

645. ———— ————. Catalogue of manuscripts in the British Museum. n. s, v.I, pt.I, the Arundel manuscripts; pt.II, the Burney manuscripts; pt.III, index. London: G. Woodfall, 1834-41. 3pts.

Index covers Arundel and Burney collections. Arundel collection assembled by Thomas Howard, Earl of Arundel (1585-1646). Acquired by British Museum, 1831.

646. ———— ————. Catalogue of the fifty manuscripts & printed books bequeathed to the British Museum by Alfred H. Huth. London: The Museum, 1912. 130p.

647. ———— ————. A catalogue of the Harleian collection of manuscripts in the British Museum; with indexes of persons, places, and matters. London, 1808-12. 4v.

Manuscripts collected by Robert (1661-1724) and Edward Harley (1689-1741), 1st and 2d Earls of Oxford, purchased in 1753.

648. ———— ————. Catalogue of the important collection of manuscripts from Stowe. London, 1849. 499p.

649. ———— ————. A catalogue of the Lansdowne manuscripts in the British Museum, with indexes of persons, places, and matters, by H. Ellis and F. Douce. London: R. & A. Taylor, 1819. 3pts.

Manuscripts collected by William Petty, 1st Marquess of Lansdowne (1737-1805); purchased by Parliament, 1807.

650. ———— ————. A catalogue of the manuscripts in the Cottonian Library deposited in the British Museum. London, 1802. 618 + 75p.

Manuscripts collected by Sir Robert Cotton (1571-1631); added to British Museum in 1753.

651. ———— ————. A catalogue of the manuscripts preserved in the British Museum hitherto undescribed: consisting of five thousand volumes; including the collections of Sir Hans Sloane, Bart., the Rev. Thomas Birch, D.D. and about five hundred volumes bequeathed, presented or purchased at various times, by Samuel Ayscough. London, 1782. 2v.

Arranged by subjects.

652. ———— ————. Catalogue of the Stowe manuscripts in the British Museum. London: The Museum, 1895-96. 2v.

Catalog and index of manuscripts purchased by Parliament from Bertram, 5th Earl of Ashburnham (1840-1913), in 1883.

653. ———— ————. Catalogue of Western manuscripts in the Old Royal and King's collections, by George F. Warner and Julius P. Gilson. London: The Museum, 1921. 4 vol. + 125 plates.

654. ———— ————. Early autograph albums in the British Museum, by M. A. E. Nickson. London: The Museum, 1970. 32p. + 20 plates.

655. ———— ————. Facsimiles of royal, historical, literary and other autographs in the Department of Manuscripts, British Museum, ed. by George F. Warner. London; The Museum, 1895-99. 5pts.

656. ———— ————. Fontes Harleiani: a study of the sources of the Harleian collection of manuscripts preserved in the Department of Manuscripts in the British Museum, by Cyril Ernest Wright. London: The Museum, 1972. 480p.

657. ———— ————. A guide to a select exhibition of Cottonian manuscripts, in celebration of the tercentenary of the death of Sir Robert Cotton, 6 May, 1931. London: The Museum, 1931. 35p.

658. ———— ————. A guide to the letters, autograph manuscripts, original charters, and royal, baronial, and ecclesiastical seals, exhibited in the Department of Manuscripts and in the King's Library, ed. by E. M. Thompson. London: The Museum, 1887. 79p.

659. ———— ————. Guide to the exhibited manuscripts. London, 1912. 3pts.

pt.1: "Autographs & documents illustrative chiefly of English history and literature"; pt.2: "Manuscripts (Palaeographical and Biblical series and chronicles) charters and seals"; pt.3: "Illuminated manuscripts and bindings of manuscripts."

660. ———— ————. Guide to the exhibited manuscripts; pt.I: autographs and documents illustrative chiefly of English history and literature, 2d ed. London: The Museum, 1928. 98p. + 20 plates.

661. ———— ————. Guide to the exhibited manuscripts. London: The Museum, 1923-28. 3pts.

pt.1: "Autographs and documents illustrative chiefly of English history and literature"; pt.2: "Manuscripts (palaeographical and Biblical series and chronicles) charters and seals"; pt.3: "Illuminated manuscripts and bindings of manuscripts."

662. ———— ————. A guide to the exhibition of some part of the Egerton collection of manuscripts in the British Museum, 1929. London: The Museum, 1929. 50p.

663. ———— ————. A guide to the manuscripts, autographs, charters, seals, illuminations and bindings exhibited in the Department of Manuscripts and the

Grenville Library. London: The Museum, 1906. 155p. + 30 plates.

664. —— ——. Index to the Additional manuscripts, with those of the Egerton collection, preserved in the British Museum and acquired in the years 1783-1835. London: The Museum, 1849. 514p.

665. —— ——. Index to the charters and rolls in the Department of Manuscripts, British Museum; religious houses and other corporations, and Index locorum for acquisitions from 1882 to 1900, ed. by Henry John Ellis and Francis B. Bickley. London: The Museum, 1900-12. 2v. Reprinted, 1966-67.

666. —— ——. Index to the Sloane manuscripts in the British Museum, by Edward J. L. Scott. London: The Museum, 1904. 583p. Reprinted, 1971.

667. Cambridge, University, Christ's College Library. A descriptive catalogue of the Western manuscripts in the Library of Christ's College, Cambridge, by Montague Rhodes James. Cambridge: Univ. Pr., 1905. 36p.

668. ——, Clare College Library. A descriptive catalogue of the Western manuscripts in the Library of Clare College, Cambridge, described by Montague Rhodes James. Cambridge: Univ. Pr., 1905. 51p.

669. ——, Corpus Christi College Library. "A catalogue of the books bequeathed to Corpus Christi College, Cambridge (A.D. 1439), by Thomas Markaunt, with their prices; transcribed from a contemporary register in the Library of the College, with explanatory and historical observations," by James Orchard Halliwell. Cambridge Antiquarian Society, Quarto publication, 1847, p.15-20.

670. —— ——. A descriptive catalogue of the manuscripts in the Library of Corpus Christi College, Cambridge, by Montague Rhodes James. Cambridge: Univ. Pr., 1912. 2v.

671. —— ——. The sources of Archbishop Parker's collection of mss. at Corpus Christi College, Cambridge; with a reprint of the catalogue of Thomas Markaunt's Library, by Montague Rhodes James. Cambridge: Antiquarian Society, 1899. 84p.

672. ——, Emmanuel College Library. The Western manuscripts in the Library of Emmanuel College; a descriptive catalogue, by Montague Rhodes James. Cambridge: Univ. Pr., 1904. 178p.

673. ——, Fitzwilliam Museum. A descriptive catalogue of the McClean collection of manuscripts in the Fitzwilliam Museum, by Montague Rhodes James. Cambridge: Univ. Pr., 1912. 410p.

674. —— ——. A descriptive catalogue of the manuscripts in the Fitzwilliam Museum, by Montague Rhodes James. Cambridge: Univ. Pr., 1895. 472p.

675. ——, Fitzwilliam Museum Library. "A handlist of the additional manuscripts in the Fitzwilliam Museum," by Francis Wormald and Phyllis M. Giles. Transactions of the Cambridge Bibliographical Society v.1, pt.3 (1951), v.4, pt.3 (1966).

676. ——, Gonville and Caius College Library. A catalogue of the manuscripts in the Library of Gonville and Caius College, Cambridge, by J. J. Smith. Cambridge: John Deighton, 1849. 329p.

677. —— ——. A descriptive catalogue of the manuscripts in the Library of Gonville and Caius College, by Montague Rhodes James. Cambridge: Univ. Pr., 1907-14. 3v.

678. —— ——. Pictorial illustrations of the Catalogue of manuscripts in Gonville and Caius College Library, selected by J. J. Smith. Cambridge: John Deighton, 1853. Unpaged.

679. ——, Jesus College Library. A descriptive catalogue of the manuscripts in the Library of Jesus College, Cambridge, by Montague Rhodes James. London: C. J. Clay, 1895. 122p.

680. ——, King's College Library. A descriptive catalogue of the manuscripts other than Oriental in the Library of King's College, Cambridge, by Montague Rhodes James. Cambridge: Univ. Pr., 1895. 87p.

681. ——, Library. A catalogue of the manuscripts preserved in the Library of the University of Cambridge. Cambridge: Univ. Pr., 1856-67. 5v. and index.
    Excludes Orientalia.

682. —— ——. Hengrave Hall mss. deposited in the University Library, Cambridge, 1952. Cambridge, 1953? 10l.

683. —— ——. Summary guide to accessions of Western manuscripts (other than medieval) since 1867, by A. E. B. Owen. Cambridge, 1966. 48p.

684. ——, Magdalene College Library. A descriptive catalogue of the manuscripts in the College Library of Magdalene College, Cambridge, by Montague Rhodes James. Cambridge: Univ. Pr., 1909, 59p.

685. ——, Pembroke College Library. A descriptive catalogue of the manuscripts in the Library of Pembroke College, Cambridge, by Montague Rhodes

James . . . with a hand list of the printed books to the year 1500, by Ellis H. Minns. Cambridge: Univ. Pr., 1905. 314p.

686. ———, Peterhouse College Library. A descriptive catalogue of the manuscripts in the Library of Peterhouse, by Montague Rhodes James, with an essay on the history of the Library, by J. W. Clark. Cambridge: Univ. Pr., 1899. 389p.

687. ———, Queen's College Library. A descriptive catalogue of the Western manuscripts in the Library of Queen's College, Cambridge, described by Montague Rhodes James. Cambridge: Univ. Pr., 1905. 29p.

688. ———, St. Catharine's College Library. A descriptive catalogue of the manuscripts in the Library of St. Catharine's College, Cambridge, by Montague Rhodes James. Cambridge: Univ. Pr., 1925. 27p.

689. ———, St. John's College Library. A descriptive catalogue of the manuscripts in the Library of St. John's College, Cambridge, by Montague Rhodes James. Cambridge: Univ. Pr., 1913. 389p.

690. ———, Sidney Sussex College Library. A descriptive catalogue of the manuscripts in the Library of Sidney Sussex College, Cambridge, by Montague Rhodes James. Cambridge: Univ. Pr., 1895. 132p.

691. ———, Trinity College, Trinity Hall Library. A descriptive catalogue of the manuscripts in the Library of Trinity Hall, by Montague Rhodes James. Cambridge: Univ. Pr., 1907. 46p.

692. ———, Trinity College Library. The Western manuscripts in the Library of Trinity College, Cambridge; a descriptive catalogue, by Montague Rhodes James. Cambridge: Univ. Pr., 1900-4. 4v.

693. Christ Church, Canterbury, A catalogue of the manuscript books [which are preserved in study X.Y.Z. and in the Howley-Harrison collection] in the Library of Christ Church, Canterbury, comp. by C. Eveleigh Woodruff. Canterbury: Cross & Jackman, 1911. 60p.

694. Craster, H. H. E. The Western manuscripts of the Bodleian Library. London: Society for Promoting Christian Knowledge, 1921. 48p.
Description and partial listing by groups.

695. Dr. Williams's Library. Guide to the manuscripts, by Kenneth Twinn, London, 1969. 32p.
Listing by groups and individual items of manuscripts owned by or on deposit in library, dating from 13th century to modern times.

696. Dublin, University, Trinity College Library. Catalogue of the manuscripts in the Library of Trinity College, Dublin, to which is added a list of the Fagel collection of maps in the same Library, comp. by T. K. Abbott. Dublin: Hodges Figgis, 1900. 606p.

697. ———. The manuscripts of Trinity College, Dublin, a catalogue, by J. T. Gilbert. Presses A-G. 1874-8. 2pts. (Royal Commission on Historical Manuscripts. First [etc.] report. 4th, 8th report. Appendix)

698. Dulwich College. Catalogue of the manuscripts and muniments of Alleyn's College of God's Gift at Dulwich, by George F. Warner. London: Longmans, Green, 1881. 388p.

699. ———. Catalogue of the manuscripts and muniments of Alleyn's College of God's Gift at Dulwich, second series, by F. B. Bickley. London: Pub. by the Governors, 1903. 197p.

700. Durham, University, Library. Summary list of the additional manuscripts accessioned and listed between September 1945 and September 1961, by David Ramage. Durham, 1963. 30p.

701. Edinburgh, University, Library. Index to manuscripts. Boston, Mass.: G. K. Hall, 1965. 2v.
Reproduces 31,000 cards, covering more than 8,000 volumes and 28,000 other pieces of postmedieval Western manuscript material.

702. Eton College Library. A descriptive catalogue of the manuscripts in the Library of Eton College, by Montague Rhodes James. Cambridge: Univ. Pr., 1895. 125p.

703. Glasgow, University, Hunterian Museum. A catalogue of the manuscripts in the Library of the Hunterian Museum in the University of Glasgow, planned and begun by the late John Young . . . continued and completed under the direction of the Young Memorial Committee by P. Henderson Aitken. Glasgow: James Maclehose, 1908. 566p.
Two main sections: non-Oriental manuscripts, p.1-450; Oriental manuscripts, p.451-523. Full indexes.

704. Great Britain, Royal Commission on Historical Manuscripts. List of accessions to repositories in 1968. London: H. M. Stationery Office, 1968. 102p.

705. Hepworth, Philip. Select biographical sources; the Library Association manuscript survey. London: Library Association, 1971. 154p.
Alphabetical list by subjects; manuscript sources recorded in numerous repositories.

706. Hodson, J. H. "A university archive repository: the University of Nottingham Department of Manuscripts." Archives, 5 (1962), 145-50.

Includes description of collections held by department: family records, Newcastle collection, literary manuscripts, and industrial records.

707. Hunt, R. W. "The manuscript collection of University College, Oxford: origins and growth." Bodleian Library record, 3 (1950), 13-34.

708. Hunter, Joseph. Three catalogues describing the contents of the Red Book of the Exchequer, of the Dodsworth manuscripts in the Bodleian Library, and of the manuscripts in the Library of the Honourable Society of Lincoln's Inn. London: Pickering, 1838. 413p.

709. Ipswich Public Library. Description of the ancient manuscripts in the Ipswich Public Library, by Montague Rhodes James. Ipswich, 1934. 18p. (Reprinted from Proceedings of the Suffolk Institute of Archaeology and Natural History, v.22, pt.1)

710. James, M. R. "The Royal manuscripts at the British Museum." Library, ser.4,2 (1921), 193-200.

General summary based on British Museum's Catalogue of Western manuscripts in the old Royal and King's collection (1921).

711. Jeaffreson, John Cordy. An index to the ancient manuscripts of the Borough of Leicester, preserved in the Muniment Room of the Leicester Town Hall. Westminster: Nichols and Sons, 1878. 42p.

712. John Rylands Library. Hand-list of the Crutchley manuscripts in the John Rylands Library, by Frank Taylor. Manchester, 1951. 97p. (Reprinted from the Bulletin of the John Rylands Library)

713. ———. Hand-list of the Mainwaring and Jodrell manuscripts in the John Rylands Library, by Robert Fawtier. Manchester, 1923. 56p. (Reprinted, with additions, from the Bulletin of the John Rylands Library)

Consists of early charters, diaries, household books, literary papers, etc., from medieval times.

714. ———. Supplementary hand-list of Western manuscripts in the John Rylands Library, 1937, by Frank Taylor. Manchester, 1937. 49p.

715. Lambeth Palace Library. The manuscripts in the Library at Lambeth Palace, by M. R. James. Cambridge and London, 1900. 64p. (Cambridge Antiquarian Society publications, Octavo series, no.33)

716. Lansdown, Jennifer Mary. Manuscript facsimiles in the University of London Library: a contribution towards a revised edition of the bibliography published by J. Wilkes and D. A. Lacy in 1921. London, 1957. 80p. (Diploma in Librarianship, Univ. of London)

Lists 191 items grouped by languages.

717. Liverpool, University, Library. A guide to the manuscript collections in Liverpool University Library, comp. by D. F. Cook. Liverpool: Univ. Pr., 1962. 32p. (Univ. of Liverpool Library publication, no.1)

In 3 sections: Western manuscripts, medieval and modern; Oxyrhynchus papyri; and Oriental manuscripts.

718. London, University, Library. Catalogue of the manuscripts and autograph letters in the University Library at the Central Building of the University of London, with a description of the manuscript life of Edward, Prince of Wales, The Black Prince by Chandos the Herald, comp. by Reginald Arthur Rye. London: Univ. of London Pr., 1921. 132p. Supplement, 1921-1930, London, 1930. 47p.

719. ———, University College Library. A descriptive catalogue of manuscripts in the Library of University College, London, by Dorothy K. Coveney. London: The University, 1935. 121p.

Arranged by languages; detailed descriptions.

720. Manchester, University, Library. A general exhibition of books and manuscripts in the Library of the University of Manchester, comp. by Margaret M. Wright. Manchester, 1964. 40p.

Lists 233 items, beginning with European manuscripts before 1500.

721. Murray, Robert H. A short guide to some manuscripts in the Library of Trinity College, Dublin. London: Society for Promoting Christian Knowledge, 1920. 63p.

722. National Library of Scotland. Accessions of manuscripts, 1859-1964. Edinburgh: H. M. Stationery Office, 1964. 51p.

723. ———. Catalogue of manuscripts acquired since 1925. Edinburgh, 1938-66. 2v.

Lists 4,000 manuscripts and 2,634 charters and other formal documents.

724. National Library of Wales. Anglesey manuscripts in the National Library of Wales. Aberystwyth, 1929. 24p. (Reprinted from Transactions of the Anglesey Antiquarian Society and Field Club, 1929)

725. ———. Catalogue of manuscripts, v.I—Additional mss. in the collections of Sir J. Williams, by J. H. Davies. Aberystwyth, 1921. 382p.

726. ———. Catalogue of manuscripts and books from the collections presented by Sir John Williams. Aberystwyth: William Jones Printing Works, 1909. 16p.

727. ———. Catalogue of manuscripts and rare books, exhibited in the Great Hall of the Library, 1916. Aberystwyth, 1916. 84p.

728. ———. Handlist of manuscripts in the National Library of Wales. Aberystwyth, 1943-61. 3v.

729. Ogilvy, J. D. A. Books known to the English, 597-1066. Cambridge, Mass.: Mediaeval Academy of America, 1967. 300p.
   Locations frequently cited.

730. Oxford, University, All Souls' College Library. Catalogue of manuscripts in the Library of All Souls' College, comp. by H. O. Coxe. Oxford, 1842. 99p.

731. ———, Balliol College Library. Catalogue of the manuscripts of Balliol College, Oxford, by R. A. B. Mynors. Oxford: Clarendon Press, 1963. 401p.
   Ranges from a 13th-century Bible to correspondence of George Eliot; describes 450 manuscripts at Balliol and about two dozen Balliol manuscripts in other libraries.

732. ———, Bodleian Library. Catalogi codicum manuscriptorum Bibliothecae Bodleianae. Oxford, 1845-1918. 14pts.

733. ——— ———. A descriptive, analytical, and critical catalogue of the manuscripts bequeathed unto the University of Oxford by Elias Ashmole and others, by W. H. Black. Oxford, 1845-66. 2pts.

734. ——— ———. "Early vellum fragments in the Bodleian Library." Bodleian quarterly record, 3 (1922), 287-88.

735. ——— ———. "Palimpsests in the Bodleian Library." Bodleian quarterly record, 3 (1921), 166-70.

736. ——— ———. A summary catalogue of Western manuscripts in the Bodleian Library, Oxford, by Falconer Madan and others. Oxford: Clarendon, 1895-1953. 6v. in 7 and index.
   Describes all manuscripts received by the Bodleian up to 1915.

737. ———, Merton College Library. The medieval books of Merton College, by F. M. Powicke. Oxford: Clarendon, 1931. 288p.

Identifies about 1,200 books, of which 300 are extant.

738. ———, Rhodes House Library. Manuscript collections, excluding Africana, in Rhodes House Library, Oxford, comp. by Louis B. Frewer. Oxford: Bodleian Library, 1970. 62p.

739. ———, St. John's College Library. Summary catalogue of manuscripts 213-305; a supplement to Coxe's catalogue of 1852 [i.e. "Catalogus codicum mss. qui in collegiis aulisque Oxoniensibus hodie adservantur," by H. O. Coxe]. Oxford, 1956. 41p.

740. ———, Taylor Institution Library. Catalogue of autograph material acquired by the Library during the years 1950-1970. Oxford, 1970. 144p.

741. Reading, University, Library. Accessions of general manuscripts up to June, 1970. Reading, 1970. 27l.
   Calendar of 929 items.

742. Royal Society. Bibliotheca Norfolciana: sive catalogus libb. manuscriptorum & impressorum in omni arte & lingua, quos illustriss. Princeps Henricus Dux Norfolciae, & c. Regiae Societati Londinensi pro scientia naturali promovenda donavit. London, 1681. 174l.
   Duke of Norfolk's library, which formed nucleus of Royal Society Library; since largely dispersed; manuscripts transferred to British Museum.

743. ———. Catalogue of the miscellaneous manuscripts preserved in the Library of the Royal Society. London: Richard and John E. Taylor, 1840. 179p.
   Alphabetically arranged by authors; appended "Catalogue of manuscript letters in the possession of the Royal Society."

MEDIEVAL AND ILLUMINATED

744. Aberdeen, University, Library. A catalogue of the medieval manuscripts in the University Library, Aberdeen, by Montague Rhodes James. Cambridge: Univ. Pr., 1932. 140p. + 27 plates.
   Lists and describes 687 items.

745. Backhouse, Janet. "Two books of hours of Francis I." British Museum quarterly, 31 (1967), 90-96.
   Descriptions of 2 16th-century illuminated manuscripts once owned by King of France, now in British Museum.

746. ———. "A Victorian connoisseur and his manuscripts: the tale of Mr. Jarman and Mr. Wing." British Museum quarterly, 32 (1968), 76-92.

Account of collection assembled by John Boykett Jarman, with listing of medieval manuscripts and locations in British and American libraries.

747. Birch, Walter de Gray, and Jenner, Henry. Early drawings and illuminations; an introduction to the study of illustrated manuscripts, with a dictionary of subjects in the British Museum. London: Samuel Bagster, 1879. 310p.

748. British Museum, Dept. of Manuscripts. Early Gothic illuminated manuscripts in England, by D. H. Hunter. London: The Museum, 1965. 32p. + 20 plates. Reprinted, 1970.
   Based mainly on British Museum's collection.

749. ——— ———. An Exultet roll illuminated in the XIth century at the Abbey of Monte Cassino, reproduced from Add. ms. 30337. London: The Museum, 1929. 12p. + 19 plates.
   Reproduction of 11th-century manuscript acquired by British Museum in 1877.

750. ——— ———. Guide to exhibited manuscripts; pt.III: Illuminated manuscripts and bindings of manuscripts exhibited in the Grenville Library. London: The Museum, 1923. 49p. + 20 plates.

751. ——— ———. Illuminated manuscripts in the British Museum; miniatures, borders, and initials reproduced in gold and colours by William Griggs, with descriptive text by George F. Warner, series 1-4. London: The Museum, 1899-1903. 146p. + 60 plates. 2d ed. London: Longmans, 1904.

752. ——— ———. Reproductions from illuminated manuscripts, 3d ed. London: The Museum, 1923-65. 5pts.

753. ——— ———. Romanesque illuminated manuscripts in the British Museum, by D. H. Turner. London: The Museum, 1966. 31p. + 20 plates.

754. ——— ———. Schools of illumination; reproductions from manuscripts in the British Museum. London: The Museum, 1914-30. 6pts.
   pt.I, Hiberno-Saxon and early English schools, A.D. 700-1100; pt.II, English, 12th and 13th centuries; pt.III, English, A.D. 1300 to 1350; pt.IV, English, A.D. 1350 to 1500; pt.V, Carolingian and French to early 14th century; pt.VI, French, mid-14th to 16th centuries.

755. ———, Dept. of Printed Books. Illuminated manuscripts exhibited in the Grenville Library. London: The Museum, 1967. 56p. + 20 plates.

756. Cambridge, University, Corpus Christi College Library. Anglo-Saxon & other manuscripts; catalogue of an exhibition in the Library of Corpus Christi College, Cambridge. Cambridge, 1966. 16p.

757. ——— ———. Illuminated manuscripts. Cambridge, 1923? 4p.
   Account of 19 manuscripts exhibited.

758. ———, Fitzwilliam Museum. Illuminated manuscripts in the Fitzwilliam Museum; an exhibition, by Francis Wormald & Phyllis M. Giles. Cambridge, 1966. 52p.

759. ——— ———. The illuminated manuscripts in the Library of the Fitzwilliam Museum, Cambridge, catalogued, with descriptions and an introduction, by William George Searle. Cambridge: Univ. Pr., 1876. 195p.

760. ———, Trinity College Library. Fifty manuscripts of the VIII to the XV century exhibited in the Library of Trinity College in Cambridge. Cambridge: Univ. Pr., 1909. 14p.

761. ——— ———. A Glastonbury miscellany of the fifteenth century: a descriptive index of Trinity College, Cambridge, MS. O. 9.38, by A. G. Riggs. London: Oxford Univ. Pr., 1968. 161p.

762. Dublin, University, Trinity College Library. The Book of Kells; a selection of pages reproduced with a description and notes, by G. O. Simms. Dublin: Dolmen Pr. for the Library of Trinity College, Dublin, 1961. 16p. + 20 plates.

763. Durham Cathedral Library. Durham Cathedral manuscripts to the end of the twelfth century: ten plates in colour and forty-seven in monochrome. With an introduction [including a list of all known Durham manuscripts before 1200] by R. A. B. Mynors. Durham, 1939. 91p. + 56 pl.

764. Edinburgh, University, Library. A descriptive catalogue of the Western medieval manuscripts in Edinburgh University Library, by Catherine R. Borland. Edinburgh: T. & A. Constable, 1916. 359p.
   Contains numerous facsimiles.

765. Herbert, J. A. Illuminated manuscripts. London: Methuen, 1911. 356p.
   Contains many references to manuscripts in the British Museum.

766. Hoskins, Edward. Horae beatae Mariae Virginis, or Sarum and York primers, with kindred books. London: Longmans, 1901. 577p.

List of Horae or primers, with locations of copies, p.1-104.

767. Hunt, R. W. "List of Phillipps manuscripts in the Bodleian Library." Bodleian Library record, 6 (1957), 348-69.

Manuscripts from Sir Thomas Phillipps collection acquired by Bodleian; list arranged in order of Phillipps numbers.

768. ———. "The Lyell bequest." Bodleian Library record, 3 (1950), 68-82.

Lists and describes 100 medieval manuscripts in Bodleian Library.

769. John Rylands Library. Catalogue of a selection of mediaeval manuscripts and jewelled bookcovers exhibited in the Main Library. MCMXXXIX; with introduction and facsimiles, comp. by Henry Guppy with the collaboration of Frank Taylor. Manchester: Univ. Pr., John Rylands Library, 1939. 70p. + 17 plates.

770. ———. Catalogue of an exhibition of illuminated manuscripts, principally Biblical and liturgical. Manchester: Univ. Pr., 1908. 62p.

771. ———. Catalogue of an exhibition of mediaeval manuscripts and jewelled book covers, shown in the Main Library from January XII to December MCMXII; including lists of palaeographical works and of historical periodicals in the John Rylands Library, by Henry Guppy. Manchester: Univ. Pr.; London: Bernard Quaritch and Sherratt and Hughes, 1912. 134p.

772. ———. Catalogue of an exhibition of mediaeval and other manuscripts and jewelled book-covers, arranged in the Main Library, with introduction and facsimiles, by Henry Guppy. Manchester: Univ. Pr., 1924. 88p. + 17 plates.

773. Ker, N. R. Catalogue of manuscripts containing Anglo-Saxon. Oxford: Clarendon, 1957. 567p. + 8 plates.

Locations and detailed descriptions.

774. ———. Fragments of medieval manuscripts used as pastedowns in Oxford bindings with a survey of Oxford binding, c.1515-1620. Oxford: Oxford Bibliographical Society, 1954. 278p. + 14 plates. (Oxford Bibliographical Society publications, n.s. v.5, 1951-52)

Listing of 2,017 items, with locations in Oxford and Cambridge libraries.

775. ———. Medieval libraries of Great Britain, a list of surviving books, 2d ed. London: Royal Historical Society, 1964. 424p.

Lists of surviving examples under names of places and institutions; index of manuscripts appended.

776. ———. Medieval manuscripts in British libraries. Oxford: Clarendon, 1969. 437p. v.1.

Records about 700 manuscripts in London collections written in Latin or a Western language before A.D. 1500; locations in 48 collections.

777. Lambeth Palace Library. Art treasures of the Lambeth Library; a description of the illuminated manuscripts, etc., including notes on the Library, by S. W. Kershaw. London: Basil Montagu Pickering, 1873. 108p.

778. Lockwood, W. B. "A manuscript in the Rylands Library and Flemish-Dutch and Low German accounts of the life and miracles of Saint Barbara." Bulletin of the John Rylands Library, 36 (1953), 23-37. Reprinted, 1953. 17p.

779. Millar, Eric G. English illuminated manuscripts from the Xth to the XIIIth century. Paris and Brussels: G. Van Oest, 1926. 146p. + 100 plates.

Copies located in British, Continental and American libraries.

780. ———. English illuminated manuscripts of the XIVth and XVth centuries. Paris and Brussels: G. Van Oest, 1928. 107p. + 100 plates.

Copies located in British, Continental, and American libraries.

781. Okasha, Elizabeth. Hand-list of Anglo-Saxon non-runic inscriptions. Cambridge: Univ. Pr., 1971. 159p. + 158 plates.

Covers period A.D. 450-1100, with present locations.

782. Oxford, University, Bodleian Library. Anglo-Saxon illumination in Oxford libraries. Oxford, 1970. 16 + 36p. (Bodleian picture books, special series, no.1)

783. ———. Byzantine illumination. Oxford, 1952. 10p. + 22 plates. (Bodleian picture books series, no.8)

784. ———. English illumination of the thirteenth and fourteenth centuries. Oxford, 1954. 10p. + 22 plates. (Bodleian picture books, no.10)

Lists and describes 22 manuscripts from Oxford's collection.

785. ———. English romanesque illumination. Oxford, 1951. 12p. + 20 plates. (Bodleian picture books series, no.1)

786. ———. Illuminated manuscripts in the Bodleian Library, Oxford, by Otto Pächt and J. J. G. Alexander. Oxford: Clarendon ,1966-70. 2v.

v.1, German, Dutch, Flemish, French and Spanish schools; v.2, English, Italian.

787. ———. Italian illuminated manuscripts from 1400 to 1500; catalogue of an exhibition held in the Bodleian Library, Oxford, 1948, comp. by Otto Pächt. Oxford, 1948. 32p. + 20 plates.

788. ———. Scenes from the life of Christ in English manuscripts. Oxford, 1951. 6p. + 24 plates. (Bodleian picture books series, no.5)

789. Pickford, Cedric E. "An Arthurian manuscript in the John Rylands Library." Bulletin of the John Rylands Library, 31 (1948), 318-44. Reprinted, 1948. 29p.

Manuscripts of the Old French Arthurian cycle, c. 1300.

790. ———. "The 'Roman de la Rose' and a treatise attributed to Richard de Fournival: two manuscripts in the John Rylands Library." Bulletin of the John Rylands Library, 34 (1952), 333-65. Reprinted.

791. Reeves, Pamela Wynn. "The Guildhall chronicles of the Kings of France." Guildhall miscellany, 2 (Feb. 1953), 3-15.

Illuminated manuscript, c. 1400, in Guildhall Library.

792. Rogers, Ralph V. "The John Rylands Library manuscript of the Eyre of Northampton, 3 Edward III (1329) (Latin ms. 180)." Bulletin of the John Rylands Library, 34 (1952), 388-407. Reprinted.

793. Stratford, Jenny. "A Victorian connoisseur and his manuscripts." British Museum quarterly, 32 (1968), 76-92.

Account of John Boykett Jarman's collecting activities, with listing of "Medieval manuscripts from the Jarman collection," mainly books of hours, and their present locations in British and American libraries.

794. Turner, D. H. "The Eric Millar bequest to the Department of Manuscripts." British Museum quarterly, 33 (1968), 16-37.

Detailed descriptions of medieval and Renaissance manuscripts received by British Museum.

795. ———. "List of the medieval and Renaissance manuscripts owned by Eric Millar." British Museum quarterly, 33 (1968), 9-16.

Lists 67 items, with locations in British Museum and elsewhere.

796. Victoria and Albert Museum. Catalogue of illuminated manuscripts, part II: miniatures, leaves, and cuttings. London: H. M. Stationery Office, 1908. 107p.

Arranged in groups by origin: Netherlandish, German, English, French, Italian, Spanish, and Byzantine; subject index.

797. ———. Catalogue of miniatures, leaves, and cuttings from illuminated manuscripts. London: H. M. Stationery Office, 1923. 101p.

798. ———. Historical introduction to the collection of illuminated letters and borders in the National Art Library, Victoria and Albert Museum, by John W. Bradley. London: H. M. Stationery Office, 1901. 182p.

799. Winchester College Library. Some Winchester books in the British Museum. London, 1936. Unpaged.

Descriptions and illustrations of 5 psalters, 10th to 12th centuries.

800. Wormald, F. "The Yates Thompson manuscripts." British Museum quarterly, 16 (1951), 4-6.

Describes 46 French, English, and Italian illuminated manuscripts of 14th and 15th centuries received by British Museum.

CLASSICAL

801. British Museum, Dept. of Manuscripts. Catalogue of ancient manuscripts in the British Museum; pt.1, Greek; pt.2, Latin, by E. M. Thompson and G. F. Warner. London: The Museum, 1881-84. 2pts.

Detailed descriptions with facsimiles of all Greek manuscripts (acquired up to 1881) and Latin manuscripts (acquired up to 1884) which appear to be earlier than A.D. 900, together with a few from the 10th century.

802. ———. Catalogue of the literary papyri in the British Museum, ed. by H. J. M. Milne. London: The Museum, 1927. 243p.

Greek and Latin documents.

803. ———. Guide to a special exhibition of Greek and Latin papyri presented to the British Museum by the Egypt Exploration Fund, 1900-1914. London: Egypt Exploration Society, 1922. 20p.

804. John Rylands Library. Works upon the study of Greek and Latin palaeography and diplomatic in the John Rylands Library. Manchester, 1903. 15p. (Reprinted from the Bulletin of the John Rylands Library)

805. Oxford, University, Bodleian Library. "Catalogue of classical mss. exhibited in the Bodleian

Library, May-July 1919." Bodleian quarterly record, 2 (1919), 253-57.

Representative showing of Bodleian's major examples.

806. Roberts, C. H. "The Rylands collection of Greek and Latin papyri." Bulletin of the John Rylands Library, 36 (1953), 97-110. Reprinted, 1953. 16p.

General description.

GREEK

807. Aubineau, Michel. Codices chrysostomici Graeci 1: Codices Britanniae et Hiberniae. Paris: Centre National de la Recherche Scientifique, 1968. 311p.

Locations in British Museum, Oxford, Cambridge, Trinity College and Chester Beatty Libraries in Dublin, and National Library of Scotland.

808. Barbour, Ruth. "Summary description of the Greek manuscripts from the Library at Holkham Hall." Bodleian Library record, 6 (1960). 591-613.

Descriptions of 113 items acquired by Bodleian Library.

809. British Museum, Dept. of Manuscripts. Greek papyri in the British Museum; catalogue, with texts, ed. by F. G. Kenyon and H. I. Bell. London: The Museum, 1893-1917. 5v.

v.4 contains an appendix of Coptic papyri, edited by W. E. Crum.

810. ———. Inventaire des manuscrits grecs du British Museum (fonds Sloane, additional, Egerton, Cottonian, et Stowe), par Marcel Richard. Paris, 1952. 123p. (Publications de l'Institut de recherche et d'histoire des textes, no.3)

811. Cambridge, University, Fitzwilliam Museum. "Greek manuscripts in Cambridge: recent acquisitions by College Libraries, the Fitzwilliam Museum and private collectors," by Patricia Elizabeth Easterling. Transactions of the Cambridge Bibliographical Society, 4 (1966), 179-91.

812. ———, Library. "Hand-list of the additional Greek manuscripts in the University Library, Cambridge," by Patricia Elizabeth Easterling. Scriptorum, international review of manuscript studies, 16 (1962), 302-23.

813. ———, Trinity College Library. Greek inscriptions from the marbles in the Library of Trinity College, Cambridge, by Peter Paul Dobree. Cambridge, 1824. 30p.

814. John Rylands Library. Catalogue of the Greek papyri in the John Rylands Library, Manchester, ed. by Arthur S. Hunt. Manchester: Univ. Pr., 1911-15. 2v.

815. Omont, H. "Notes sur les manuscrits grecs du British Museum." Bibliothèque de l'École des chartes, revue d'érudition, 45 (1884), 314-50, 584. Reprinted.

816. Oxford, University, Bodleian Library. "Early Greek Bodleian manuscripts." Bodleian quarterly record, 1 (1914), 73-77.

List of Greek manuscripts (other than papyri) in Bodleian Library written before A.D. 1200.

817. ——— ———. Fragmenta herculanensia; a descriptive catalog of the Oxford copies of the Herculanean rolls together with the texts of several papyri accompanied by facsimiles, ed. by Walter Scott. Oxford: Clarendon, 1885, 325p.

818. ——— ———. Greek manuscripts in the Bodleian Library; an exhibition held in connection with the XIIIth International Congress of Byzantine Studies. Oxford, 1966. 55p + 20 plates.

Lists and describes 104 items.

819. ——— ———. Greek ostraca in the Bodleian Library, at Oxford and various other collections, ed. by John Gavin Tait and Claire Preaux. London, 1930-55. 2v.

820. ——— ———. Quarto catalogues. 1. Greek manuscripts, by H. O. Coxe, reprinted with corrections from the edition of 1853. Oxford, 1969. 962p. + 107 cols.

Grouped by collections, a total of 12, received by Bodleian Library, 1629-1817.

821. ———, Christ Church Library. An account of some Greek manuscripts contained in the Library of Christ Church. London, 1895. 31p.

822. Richard, Marcel, Inventaire des manuscrits grecs du British Museum. Paris: Publications de l'Institut de recherche et d'histoire des textes, 1952. 123p.

Includes Sloane, Egerton, and Stowe collections.

823. ———. Répertoire des bibliothèques et des catalogues de manuscrits grecs, 2d ed. Paris: Centre nationale de la recherche scientifique, 1958. 277p. Supplement 1 (1958-1963). Paris, 1964. 77p.

Lists catalogs in British libraries.

824. Thompson, E. Maunde. "Catalogue of classical manuscripts" [in the British Museum]. Classical review, 2 (1888), 102-4, 171-74; 3 (1899), 149-55, 440-45.

Covers Greek authors only.

LATIN

825. British Museum, Dept. of Manuscripts. Facsimiles of ancient Latin manuscripts in the British Museum. London, 1885. 13p. + 28 plates.

Facsimiles of 13 manuscripts, chiefly of English origin.

826. Craster, H. H. E. "Latin Bodleian manuscript fragments, written before A.D. 1200." Bodleian quarterly record, 3 (1920), 19-22.

827. John Rylands Library. A descriptive catalogue of the Latin manuscripts in the John Rylands Library at Manchester, by Montague Rhodes James. Manchester: Univ. Pr., 1921. 2v.

v.I, nos.1-183, letterpress; v.II, plates.

828. ———. Hand-list of additions to the collection of Latin manuscripts in the John Rylands Library, 1908-1928, by Moses Tyson. Manchester, London, 1928. 31p. (Reprinted from the Bulletin of the John Rylands Library)

829. ———. Hand-list of additions to the collection of Latin manuscripts in the John Rylands Library, 1908-1920, by Robert Fawtier. Aberdeen: Univ. Pr., 1921. 21p. (Reprinted from the Bulletin of the John Rylands Library)

830. Kristeller, P. O. Latin manuscript books before 1600: a list of the printed catalogues and unpublished inventories of extant collections, 3d ed. N.Y.: Fordham Univ. Pr., 1965. 284p.

Concentrates on public collections in Europe and in the U.S.

831. Little, A. G. Initia operum Latinorum quae saeculis XIII. XIV. XV. attribuuntur secundum ordinem alphabeti disposita. Manchester: Univ. Pr., 1904. 275*l*.

About 6,000 manuscripts, 13th-14th centuries, with references to sources.

832. Lowe, E. A. Codices Latini antiquiores; a palaeographical guide to Latin manuscripts prior to the ninth century. Oxford: Clarendon, 1934-63. 10pts.

Arranged by countries; pt.II locates manuscripts in Great Britain and Ireland.

833. Oxford, University, Bodleian Library. "Early Latin Bodleian manuscripts." Bodleian quarterly record, 1 (1914-16), 53-58.

List of Latin manuscripts in Bodleian Library written before A.D. 1100. Revised list appeared in Bodleian quarterly record, 1 (1914-16), 344-49.

834. ———. "Latin Bodleian manuscript fragments (written before A.D. 1200)." Bodleian quarterly record, 3 (1920), 19-22.

Listing by centuries, 8th to 12th.

835. ———. "Twelfth-century Latin Bodleian mss." Bodleian quarterly record, 1 (1914-16), 193-96, 323-26, 350-51.

Detailed listing, with provenances and pressmarks.

836. Watson, Andrew G. Latin manuscripts in the British Museum containing the lives of English saints: a bibliography. London, 1954. 239p. (Diploma in Librarianship, Univ. of London)

Records 1,076 items.

ENGLISH

837. Bartlett, Henrietta C. "Extant autograph material by Shakespeare's fellow dramatists." Library, ser.4, 10 (1929), 308-12.

Locates letters and documents in British libraries.

838. Brooks, E. St. John. "The Piers Plowman manuscripts in Trinity College, Dublin." Library, ser.5, 6 (1951), 141-53.

Detailed discussion of 2 manuscripts of Piers Plowman in Trinity College Library.

839. Cambridge, University, Trinity College Library. Facsimiles of twelve early English manuscripts in the Library of Trinity College, Cambridge (with transcripts and notes by W. W. Greg). Oxford, 1913. 12p. + index.

Examples from 11th to 15th century.

840. John Rylands Library. Hand-list of additions to the collection of English manuscripts in the John Rylands Library, 1928-35, by Moses Tyson. Manchester: Univ. Pr., 1935. 74p. (Reprinted from the Bulletin of the John Rylands Library, 1935)

Adds 356 items to 1929 list.

841. ———. Hand-list of additions to the collection of English manuscripts in the John Rylands Library, 1937-1951, by Frank Taylor. Manchester, 1951. 52p. (Reprinted from the Bulletin of the John Rylands Library, 34 [Sept. 1951])

842. ———. Hand-list of the collection of English manuscripts in the John Rylands Library, 1928, by Moses Tyson. Manchester, 1929. 70p. (Reprinted from the Bulletin of the John Rylands Library)

Lists 508 items, 15th to 20th century.

843. Ker, Neil Ripley. English manuscripts in the century after the Norman Conquest. Oxford: Clarendon, 1960. 67p. + 29 plates.

Locations in British and Continental libraries and collections.

844. Library Association, Birmingham. Exhibition of English mss. in the Library of the University of Birmingham, by Lawrence W. Hodson. Birmingham, 1902. 15p.

845. Roberts, W. Wright. "English autograph letters in the John Rylands Library." Bulletin of the John Rylands Library, 25 (1941), 119-36. Reprinted, 1941. 18p.

General survey; collection belongs predominantly to 18th and 19th centuries.

FRENCH

846. John Rylands Library. Hand-list of the collection of French and Italian manuscripts in the John Rylands Library, by Moses Tyson. Manchester, 1930. 68p. (Reprinted from the Bulletin of the John Rylands Library)

Lists 118 French and 61 Italian manuscripts.

847. Meyer, Paul. "Les manuscrits français de Cambridge. ii. Bibliothèque de l'Université." Romania, 15 (1886), 236-357.

848. Millar, Eric G. Souvenir de l'Exposition de manuscrits français à peintures organisée à la Grenville Library (British Museum) . . . 1932; étude concernant les 65 manuscrits. Paris: Société française de reproductions de manuscrits à peintures, 1933. 43p. + 64 plates.

GERMAN

849. Priebsch, Robert. Deutsche handschriften in England. Erlangen: Verlag von Fr. Junge, 1896-1901. 2v.

v.1, Manuscripts in Ashburnham Place, Cambridge, Cheltenham, Oxford, Wigan; v.2, British Museum.

GLAGOLITIC

850. Tadin, M. "Glagolitic manuscripts in the Bodleian Library." Oxford Slavonic papers, 4 (1953), 151-58; 5 (1954), 133-44.

IRISH

851. British Museum, Dept. of Manuscripts. Catalogue of Irish manuscripts in the British Museum, v.1 ed. by Standish Hayes O'Grady, v.2 by Robin Flower, v.3 by Robin Flower and Myles Dillon. London: The Museum, 1926-53. 3v.

852. Dublin, University, Trinity College Library. Catalogue of the Irish manuscripts in the Library of Trinity College, Dublin, comp. by T. K. Abbott and E. J. Gwynn. Dublin, London, 1921. 445p.

853. ———— ————. Guide to the Irish manuscripts exhibited in the Library of Trinity College, Dublin. Dublin: Univ. Pr., 1953. 26p.

Detailed descriptions of ancient and medieval Irish manuscripts, 6th century to 1697.

854. Franciscan Library. Catalogue of Irish manuscripts in the Franciscan Library, Killiney, by Myles Dillon and others. Dublin: Institute for Advanced Studies, 1969. 185p.

855. Gilbert, John T. National manuscripts of Ireland; account of facsimiles of national manuscripts of Ireland, from the earliest extant specimens to A.D. 1719. London: H. M. Stationery Office, 1884. 356 + LXXp.

Appendix contains "Table of the manuscripts represented in facsimile" with locations of originals.

ITALIAN

856. Angelis, Tommaso de. I mss. Italiani in Inghilterra; serie I. Londra—Il Museo Brittanico. London and Caserta, 1899-1902. 3v.

v.1 covers Sloane collection; v.2, Hargrave, Burney, Arundel, and Stowe collections; v.3, Cotton collection.

857. Cesnola, Alessandro Palma di. Catalogo di manoscritti Italiani esistenti nel Museo Britannico di Londra. Torino: Tipografia L. Roux e. c., 1890. 209p.

Lists 1,679 items.

SCOTTISH

858. National Library of Scotland. Scottish manuscripts. Edinburgh, 1967. 47p.

Annotated list of 318 items, dated 1159-1933.

SPANISH AND SPANISH-AMERICAN

859. Bohigas, Pere. "El repertori de manuscrits catalans." Estudis universitaris Catalans, 12 (1927), 411-57.

Discussion and listing of Catalan manuscripts at British Museum, Cambridge, and Oxford.

860. British Museum, Dept. of Manuscripts. Catalogue of the manuscripts in the Spanish language in the British Museum, by Don Pascual de Gayangos. London: The Museum, 1875-93. 4v.

861. Garau Aunós, M. "Manuscritos españoles de la Biblioteca del Trinity College, de Dublin." Biblioteconomia, 22 (Jan. 1965), 52-58.

List and descriptions of 10 manuscripts for period 1463-1665.

862. John Rylands Library. The Spanish manuscripts in the John Rylands Library, by Moses Tyson. Manchester: Univ. Pr., 1932. 12p. (Reprinted from Bulletin of the John Rylands Library, v.16, no.1)

863. Oxford, University, Bodleian Library. A catalogue of Hispanic manuscripts and books before 1700 from the Bodleian Library and Oxford College Libraries, exhibited at the Taylor Institution. Oxford, 1962. 56p.

Concise bibliographical descriptions of 162 notable manuscripts and printed books, 12th to 17th century.

864. Vargas Ugarte, Rubén. Manuscritos Peruanos en las bibliotecas del extranjero. Lima, 1935. 359p. (Biblioteca peruana, v.1)

Includes locations in British Museum, p.1-30.

Paleography

865. Aberdeen, University, Library. List of books in the Aberdeen University Library bearing upon the study of palaeography and diplomatics, comp. by Margaret C. Salmond. Aberdeen, 1913. 39p.

866. London, University, Libraries. Catalogue of works dealing with the study of Western palaeography in the libraries of the University of London, comp. by John Wilks and Arthur Douglas Lacey. London: Univ. of London Pr., 1921. 105p.

Lists 860 works.

867. London, University, Library. The palaeography collection in the University of London Library: an author and subject catalogue. Boston, Mass.: G. K. Hall, 1968. 2v.

Chiefly concerned with manuscript books in Greek, Latin, and Western European languages.

Handwriting

868. Edinburgh, University, Library. An exhibition of books in manuscript; illustrating the history of handwriting and illumination in Western Europe up to the 16th century, held in Edinburgh University Library. Edinburgh, 1952. Unpaged.

Annotated listing of 89 items.

869. Heal, Ambrose. The English writing-masters and their copy-books, 1570-1800; a biographical dictionary & a bibliography. Cambridge: Univ. Pr., 1931. 197p.

Arranged chronologically by authors; occasional references to locations.

870. Oxford, University, Bodleian Library. Humanistic script of the 15th and 16th centuries, by A. J. Fairbank and R. W. Hunt. Oxford, 1960. 8p. + 24 plates. (Bodleian picture book, no.12)

Reproductions are all from manuscripts in Bodleian Library.

871. Victoria and Albert Museum Library. Four hundred years of English handwriting; an exhibition of manuscripts and copy books, 1543-1943, held at the Victoria and Albert Museum. London; 1965. 18*l*.

Lists 136 specimens, drawn mainly from museum's collections.

Calligraphy

872. Backhouse, Janet. "Pioneers of modern calligraphy and illumination." British Museum quarterly, 33 (1968), 71-79.

Detailed descriptions of items received by British Museum.

873. Morison, Stanley. Calligraphy, 1535-1885; a collection of seventy-two writing books and specimens from the Italian, French, Low Countries and Spanish schools. Milano: La Bibliofila, 1962. 175p.

Locations in 45 British, Continental, and American libraries.

874. Walters Art Gallery. 2,000 years of calligraphy; a three-part exhibition organized by the Baltimore Museum of Art, the Peabody Institute Library and the Walters Art Gallery. Baltimore, Md., 1965. 201p.

Includes 218 items drawn from libraries, museums, and private collections in 7 countries, including Britain.

Printing History

GENERAL

875. Association of Assistant Librarians, East Midland Division. Union list of private press material in the East Midlands, ed. by Norman Evan Binns. Midlands, Nottingham, 1955. 27p.

Imprints arranged by presses.

876. Barber, Giles. French letterpress printing; a list of French printing manuals and other texts in French bearing on the technique of letterpress printing, 1567-

1900. Oxford: Oxford Bibliographical Society, Bodleian Library, 1969. 39p. (Occasional publications, no.5)

Locates copies in British and French libraries.

877. Bristol Public Libraries. List of books on printing and the allied trades in the Bristol Public Libraries, prep. under the direction of James Ross. Bristol: Bristol School of Printing, Merchant Venturers' Technical College, 1936. 30p.

878. British Museum. A guide to the printed books exhibited in the King's Library. London, 1891. 111p.

Principally designed to illustrate the history of printing and book production.

879. ———. A guide to the exhibition in the King's Library illustrating the history of printing, music-printing and bookbinding. London, 1939. 163p.

Illustrative of all periods of printing and binding from about 1450 to modern times; many plates.

880. ———, Dept. of Printed Books. British Museum catalogue of an exhibition of books illustrating British and foreign printing, 1919-29. London, The Museum, 1929. 60p.

Includes 189 examples of fine printing—British, Continental, and American.

881. ——— ———. Facsimiles from early printed books in the British Museum; selected pages from representative specimens of the early printed books of Germany, Italy, France, Holland, and England, exhibited in the King's Library. London: The Museum, 1897. 8p. + 32 plates.

882. ——— ———. Printing and the mind of man; catalogue of the exhibitions at the British Museum and at Earls Court, London. London, 1963. 120p. + 32 plates.

Illustrating the impact of print on the history of ideas and Western civilization.

883. Cambridge, University, Fitzwilliam Museum. Catalogue of an exhibition of printing at the Fitzwilliam Museum. Cambridge: Univ. Pr., 1940, 136p.

Exhibition of about 641 items illustrative of history of printing in all periods.

884. Carter, Harry, and Vervliet, H. D. L. Civilité types. Oxford: Univ. Pr., 1966. 138p. (Oxford Bibliographical Society publications, n.s., v.14)

History of printing in Civilité types, 16th-19th centuries, with locations of 636 titles, in British Museum, Bodleian, etc., in which types were used.

885. ———, and Ricks, Christopher. Edward Rowe Mores; a dissertation upon English typographical

founders and founderies (1778), with a catalogue and specimen of the typefoundry of John James (1782). Oxford: Oxford Bibliographical Society, 1961. 145p. (Oxford Bibliographical Society publications, n.s., v.9)

Appendix I, "List of printed works by Edward Rowe Mores," locates copies.

886. Carter, Harry Graham, and others. "A list of type specimens." Library, ser.4, 22 (1942), 185-204.

Lists pre-1800 examples in British, Continental, and American collections.

887. Davis, Herbert J. "The Strickland Gibson collection." Bodleian Library record, 6 (1961), 645-54.

Collection illustrating all stages in process of making a printed book, with examples from 15th century onward, acquired by Bodleian Library.

888. Fyfe, C. H. "The Sierra Leone press in the nineteenth century." Sierra Leone studies, n.s. no.8 (June 1957), 226-36.

More than 30 newspapers, films, and copies located in 6 collections in London.

889. Glasgow, University, Hunterian Library. Broadsides, 16th-20th century: an exhibition held in the Hunterian Library, University of Glasgow. Glasgow, 1971. 18p.

Records 81 items, annotated.

890. Great Britain, Patent Office Library. Subject list of works on photo-mechanical printing and photography. London: H. M. Stationery Office, 1914. 126p.

891. Guildhall Library. List of medals connected with printers and the art of printing, exhibited at the opening of the new library and museum, Guildhall, by William Blades. London, 1872. 14p.

892. Leicester Public Libraries. Catalogue of works on printing, bookbinding, paper-making and related industries. Leicester: C. H. Gee, 1927. 31p.

893. London College of Printing Library. Library book lists, bookbinding and warehouse work; a guide to the literature available up to 1957; compiled by the staffs of London School of Printing and Graphic Arts Library, National Book League Library, St. Bride Printing Library. London, 1959. 41p.

894. ———. List of periodicals. London, 1971. Unpaged.

Alphabetical list showing holdings.

895. London School of Economics and Political Science. British Library of Political and Economic Science. Classified catalogue of a collection of works on publishing and bookselling in the British Library of Political and Economic Science. London, 1961. 186p.

Lists 3,704 titles, including section on French and German publishing and book trade. First edition, 1936. 194p. 2d ed., 1956. 193p.

896. London School of Printing & Kindred Trades. Library catalogue. London, 1941. 60p. Supplement. 1944. p. 61-80.

897. Manchester Public Libraries. Reference Library subject catalogue: section 655, printing, ed. by G. E. Haslam. Manchester: Libraries Committee, 1961-63. 2pts.

pt.1, general works, history of printing; pt.2, type and typesetting, printing processes, publishing and bookselling, copyright; records over 2,500 entries.

898. National Book Council Library. Catalogue of the Library of the National Book Council; a collection of books, pamphlets and extracts on the history and practice of authorship, libraries, printing, publishing, reviewing and reading of books. London: National Book Council, 1944. 64p.

Classified by subjects; now National Book League Library.

899. National Book League Library. Books about books; catalogue of the Library of the National Book League, 5th ed. London: Cambridge Univ Pr., 1955. 126p. Supplement, Jan. 1954-June 1956. 26p.

Lists about 4,000 books on bibliography, authorship, printing, binding, publishing, bookselling, reading, libraries, and related subjects.

900. Norwich Public Library. Books on printing and some related subjects in the Norwich Public Library, by Geo. A. Stephen. Norwich: Norwich and District Master Printers' Association, 1921. 35p.

901. Oxford, University, Bodleian Library. The John Johnson collection; catalogue of an exhibition. Oxford, 1971. 87p.

Lists 259 printed ephemera drawn from Bodleian's extensive collection of broadsides, posters, advertisements, publishers' catalogs, etc.; arranged by subjects.

902. Pollard, H. G., and Ehrman, Albert. The distribution of books by catalogue from the invention of printing to A.D. 1800; based on material in the Broxbourne Library. Cambridge: Printed for the Roxburge Club, 1965. 427p.

Copies of material located in British, Continental, and American libraries.

903. Printing and Allied Trades Research Association Library. Classified lists of text books, reference books and periodicals. London: Patra House, 1937. 66p.

904. Rhodes, D. E. "Printing at Bangalore, 1840-1850." British Museum quarterly, 34 (1970), 83-86.
Based on British Museum holdings.

905. Roberts, R. Julian. "The Greek press at Constantinople in 1627 and its antecedents." Library, ser.5, 22 (1967), 13-43.
Descriptions of 9 extant books printed by or for Nicodemas Metaxas; copies located in several English libraries.

906. St. Bride Foundation Institute Library. Catalogue of an exhibition in commemoration of the centenary of William Blades, comp. by William T. Berry. London: Blades and Blades, 1924. 39p.
Exhibition on printing history drawn from St. Bride Foundation Library.

907. ———. Catalogue of an exhibition of type specimens, 1918-1930. London: St. Bride Foundation Institute, 1930. 21p.
List of 701 items.

908. ———. Catalogue of the general, lending, and reference library (being a branch of the Cripplegate Foundation Library for the Western portion of the city of London), comp. by F. W. T. Lange, 3d ed. London, 1900. 409p. Supplements 1-2. London, 1904-7. 2v.

909. ———. Catalogue of the Passmore Edwards Library, comp. by John Southward and F. W. T. Lange. London: St Bride Foundation, 1897. 79p.
Concerned with developments in printing arts.

910. ———. Catalogue of the periodicals relating to printing and allied subjects in the Technical Library of the Saint Bride Institute. London: St. Bride Foundation Institute, 1951. 35p.
Alphabetical list, noting holdings; about 750 entries.

911. ———. Catalogue of the slide loan collection. London: St. Bride Foundation Institute [1971]. 74p.
Lists 552 items.

912. ———. Catalogue of the Technical Reference Library of works on printing and the allied trades, comp. by R. A. Peddie. London, 1919. 999p.
Alphabetical listing by author of over 30,000 items.

913. ———. Catalogue of the William Blades Library, comp. by John Southward and F. W. T. Lange. London: St. Bride Foundation, 1899. 186p.
Library consists of books on printing, lithography, bookbinding, papermaking, and related subjects.

914. ———. Catalogue of works on practical printing, processes of illustration & bookbinding, pub-

lished since the year 1900 and now in the St. Bride Foundation Technical Library, comp. by R. A. Peddie. London, 1911. 32p.

915. ———. A classified catalogue of books in the Lending Department of the Library of the St. Bride Foundation Institute, comp. by F. W. T. Lange. London, 1912. 347p.

916. ———. Some books on printing; English and American textbooks published since 1900, comp. by W. T. Berry. London: St. Bride Foundation Printing School, 1919-20. 20p.

917. St. Bride Foundation, Technical Reference Library. A select list of books on practical printing, modern English & American textbooks in the Technical Library, comp. by W. T. Berry. London: Students of Saint Bride Foundation Printing School, 1921. 27p.

918. Sheffield City Libraries. Catalogue of books in the central libraries on the printing and allied trades. Sheffield: J. W. Northend, 1925. 31p.

919. Simmons, J. S. G. "Specimens of printing types before 1850 in the Typographical Library at the University Press, Oxford." Book collector, 8 (1959), 397-410.

Includes "Catalogue of specimens," with locations in various libraries and collections: lists 68 items.

920. Victoria and Albert Museum. Early printers' marks. London: H. M. Stationery Office, 1962. 32p. + 28 illustrations.

921. ——— Library. Printed books: a short introduction to fine typography. London: H. M. Stationery Office, 1957. 14p. + 46 plates.

922. Watford College of Technology. A catalogue of journals relevant to printing held at Watford College of Technology, comp. by Alan Pritchard. Watford, 1963. 16*l*.

923. ———. Computer typesetting 1966-68; a select bibliography, comp. by J. T. Graham. Hatfield, Herts: Hertfordshire County Council Technical Library and Information Service, 1968. 58p.

"Most of the items have been examined in the Library of Watford College of Technology."

924. Watford Public Libraries. Books on printing, paper manufacture & bookbinding. Watford, 1951. 17p.

ENGLISH

925. Barker, J. R. A Liverpool printer; an attempt at a bibliography of works printed in Liverpool 1792-1805 by John M'Creery, with an account of his life and a brief survey of the previous history of printing in Liverpool. London, 1951. 162p. (Diploma in Librarianship, Univ. of London)

Locations noted of copies examined.

926. Bennett, H. S. English books & readers, 1475 to 1557; being a study in the history of the book trade from Caxton to the incorporation of the Stationers' Company. Cambridge: Univ. Pr., 1952. 337p.

Appendix I, "Handlist of publications by Wynkyn de Worde, 1492-1535," lists British and American libraries containing copies; Appendix II, "Trial list of translations into English printed between 1475-1560," adds STC numbers.

927. Berry, William Turner, and Johnson, A. F. Catalogue of specimens of printing types by English and Scottish printers and founders, 1665-1830. London: Oxford Univ. Pr., 1935. 98p. + 21 plates.

Copies located, principally in British Museum and St. Bride Institute.

928. ———. "A note on the literature of British type specimens, with a supplement to the Catalogue of specimens of printing types by English and Scottish printers and founders, 1665-1830." Signature, n.s. 16 (1952), 28-40.

Locates copies.

929. Birmingham, University, Library. John Baskerville printer; an exhibition, comp. by Paul Morgan. Birmingham, 1955. 23p.

Annotated catalogue of 38 exhibits drawn from larger collection in University of Birmingham Library.

930. Blakey, Dorothy. The Minerva Press, 1790-1820. London: Printed for the Bibliographical Society at the University Press, Oxford, 1939 (for 1935). 339p.

Late 18th- early 19th-century London publisher; chronological list of publications locates copies in British and American libraries.

931. Bliss, Carey S. "Joseph Moxon's Mechanick exercises; revised census." Printing & graphic arts, 6 (1958), 35-39.

Locates 50 copies in English and American libraries. Supplemented by "Further notes for the Moxon census," ibid., 7 (1959), 110-11, locating 9 additional items.

932. Borrie, M. A. F. "The Cockerell papers." British Museum quarterly, 30 (1966), 88-93.

Extensive archives of Sir Sydney Carlyle Cockerell, printer and bibliophile, received by British Museum.

933. British Museum. An exhibition of books designed, illustrated, or printed in Great Britain for Mr. George Macy of New York, at the British Museum, July-September, 1952; a catalogue. London, 1952. 15p.

934. Burman, Charles Clark. Alnwick typography 1748-1900. History of the Berwickshire Naturalists' Club, 23 (1916-18), 305-59.

Includes checklist of Alnwick imprints, with locations of copies in public and private collections.

935. Cambridge, University, Corpus Christi College Library. Printing with Anglo-Saxon types, 1566-1715; catalogue of a small exhibition, comp. by Bruce Dickins. Cambridge: Univ. Pr., 1952. 13p.

List of 16 annotated items.

936. ———, Press. Catalogue of an exhibition of Cambridge books and printing held in the old court house, Marylebone Lane. Cambridge, 1931. 59p.

937. Cardiff Public Libraries. List of examples of modern English fine printing exhibited in the reference library. Cardiff: S. Glossop, 1915. 16p.

938. Clarke, William James. Early Nottingham printers and printing, 2d ed. Nottingham: Thos. Forman, 1953. 71p.

Includes complete list of local and other collections of principal Nottingham newspapers up to 1775, locating files in public and private collections.

939. Duff, E. Gordon. The English provincial printers, stationers and bookbinders to 1557. Cambridge: Univ. Pr., 1912. 153p.

Appendix I, "List of books printed by provincial printers or for provincial stationers," locates copies in 32 libraries.

940. Eton College Library. "Some unrecorded Cambridge books in the Library of Eton College." Cambridge Bibliographical Society transactions, 1 (1953), 441-43.

941. Gilberthorpe, Enid C. Books and pamphlets printed at Sheffield before 1801: a checklist. High Wycombe: Univ. Microfilms, 1967. Unpaged. (Library Association Fellowship thesis)

Records 265 items; copies located in 6 libraries.

942. Gray, G. J. "William Pickering, the earliest bookseller on London Bridge, 1556-1571." Bibliographical Society transactions, 4 (1898), 57-102.

Bibliography of Pickering imprints, with locations if they could be found.

943. Hazen, Allen T., and Kirby, J. P. A bibliography of the Strawberry Hill Press, with a record of the prices at which copies have been sold, together with a bibliography and census of detached pieces. New Haven, Conn.: Yale Univ. Pr., 1942. 300p.

"Owners of copies," p.279-92, with references to numbered entries.

944. Hilson, James Lindsay. "Berwick-upon-Tweed typography." History of the Berwickshire Naturalists' Club, 23 (1918), 433-55.

Checklist covers period 1753-1857, with locations of copies.

945. Hyett, F. A. "Notes on the first Bristol and Gloucestershire printers." Transactions of the Bristol and Gloucestershire Archaeological Society, 20 (1895/96), 38-51.

Locates copies of imprints in British Museum and Bodleian Library.

946. Isaac, Frank. English and Scottish printing types, 1501-35. 1508-41. 1535-58. 1552-58. London: Printed for the Author at the Cost of the Bibliographical Society at the Oxford Univ. Pr., 1930-32. 2v.

Includes STC numbers for many items.

947. Isaac, P. C. G. "Books printed by William Bulmer." Manchester review, 9 (1962-63), 344-51.

Checklist of Bulmer imprints in Manchester Reference Libraries.

948. McKenzie, D. F. The Cambridge University Press, 1696-1712, a bibliographical study. Cambridge: Univ. Pr., 1966. 2v.

Fully describes 274 works, locating copies in Cambridge University libraries, Bodleian, and British Museum.

949. ———, and Ross, J. C., eds. A ledger of Charles Ackers, printer of the London magazine. Oxford: Univ. Pr., 1968. 331p. (Oxford Bibliographical Society publications, n.s. v.15)

Business ledger of 18th-century printer; Appendix I lists books printed by Ackers, with copies located in 6 English and 3 foreign libraries.

950. McKerrow, Ronald B. Printers' and publishers' devices in England & Scotland, 1485-1640. London: Printed for the Bibliographical Society at the Chiswick Pr., 1913. 216p.

Locates copies in English libraries; contains numerous facsimiles.

951. ———, and Ferguson, F. S. Title-page borders used in England and Scotland, 1485-1640. London: Printed for the Bibliographical Society at the Oxford Univ. Pr., 1932 (for 1931). 234p.

Locates copies in English libraries; contains numerous facsimiles.

952. Madan, Falconer. A chronological list of Oxford books, 1681-1713. Oxford: Univ. Pr., 1954. 72p.

Checklist with some copies located.

953. ———. ɔɹoɟxO books: a bibliography of printed works relating to the University and City of Oxford or printed or published there with appendixes and illustrations. Oxford: Clarendon, 1895-1931. 3v.

Covers period 1468-1680; 3,297 entries with occasional locations.

954. Manchester Public Libraries. The Manchester press before 1801; a list of books, pamphlets and broadsides printed in Manchester in the 18th century, comp. by Geoffrey R. Axon. Manchester: Libraries Committee, 1931. 30p. (Occasional lists, new series, no.6)

Copies located in Manchester Public Libraries and other libraries; chronological arrangement.

955. ———. Wise after the event; a catalogue of books, pamphlets, manuscripts and letters relating to Thomas James Wise displayed in an exhibition in Manchester Central Library, ed. by G. E. Haslam. Manchester: Libraries Committee, 1964. 86p.

956. Morris, John. Cambridge printing, 1740-1766; a short-title list. London, 1961. 131l. (Diploma in Librarianship, Univ. of London)

Contains 531 entries; copies located in 16 libraries.

957. Oxford, University, Pusey House. Nineteenth century pamphlets at Pusey House; an introduction for the prospective user, by Father Hugh [J. A. Fenwich]. London: Faith Pr., 1961. 98p.

Includes subject and author indexes to 24,000 19th-century pamphlets in Pusey House, Oxford.

958. ———, Worcester College Library. Notes from a catalogue of pamphlets in Worcester College Library, ed. by C. H. O. Daniel. Oxford: Henry Daniel, 1874. 79p.

959. Plomer, Henry R. Robert Wyer, printer and bookseller. London: Printed for the Bibliographical Society by Blades, East & Blades, 1897. 57p. + 10 plates.

Locates copies of 98 books produced by Wyer, 16th-century English printer.

960. Reading, University, Library. Reading printing, 1736-1962; an exhibition. Reading, 1963. 10p.

Checklist of 31 items.

961. Rogers, David Morrison. "Henry Jaye, 15-?-1643." Biographical studies, 1 (1951-52), 86-111, 251-52.

List of 34 Jaye imprints, with locations of copies and STC numbers.

962. Sheffield City Libraries. Book printing at Sheffield in the eighteenth century, by Enid C. Gilberthorpe. Sheffield, 1967. 12p. (Local history leaflets, no.12)

963. Sheldon, Peter. Printing in Derbyshire to 1800. London, 1949. 58l. (Diploma in Librarianship, Univ. of London)

Locations in Derby Public Library, Nottingham University Library, and a private collection.

964. Straus, Ralph. The unspeakable Curll; being some account of Edmund Curll, bookseller. London: Chapman and Hall, 1927. 322p.

Includes list of Curll imprints, 1706-46, with locations of copies in British Museum.

965. Tony Appleton, Bookseller, Brighton. XIXth century colour printing. Brighton: Tony Appleton, n.d. Unpaged. (Catalogue, no.7)

Collection of 300 items acquired en bloc by College of Librarianship Wales Library, Aberystwyth.

966. Ungerer, Gustav. "The printing of Spanish books in Elizabethan England." Library, ser.5, 20 (1965), 177-229.

Records 46 items, including STC numbers if listed.

967. VanDorsten, J. A. Thomas Basson, 1555-1613, English printer at Leiden. Leiden: Published for the Sir Thomas Browne Institute by the Universitaire pers Leiden, 1961. 126p.

Basson imprints located in English and Dutch libraries.

968. Weil, Ernst. "Samuel Browne, printer to the University of Heidelberg, 1655-1662." Library, ser.5, 5 (1950), 14-25.

Lists 22 items, with locations of copies in British Museum and German university libraries.

969. Wright, C. E. "Archives of a printing house." British Museum quarterly, 20 (1955), 30-31.

Archives of Richard Bentley, Chiswick Press, and William Strahan, 18th and 19th centuries, received by British Museum.

IRISH

970. Cassedy, James. "Clonmel printing, 1826-1900." Irish book lover, 25 (1937), 90-98.

Checklist, with locations of copies.

971. ———. "List of works projected or published by Patrick Lynch." Waterford and South East of Ireland Archaeological Society journal, 15 (1912), 107-18.

List of 34 items, 1792-1828, with locations of copies in Irish and British collections.

972. ———. "Waterford printing, 1821-1900." Irish book lover, 26 (1939), 128-33; 27 (1940), 149-55.

Checklist, with locations of copies.

973. Dix, E. R. McC. "The Bonmahon press." Irish book lover, 1 (1910), 97-100.

Checklist of imprints, 1852-58, with locations of copies.

974. ———. Catalogue of early Dublin-printed books, 1601 to 1700. Dublin: T. G. O'Donoghue; London: B. Dobell, 1898-1912. 386p. in 4pts.

Copies located in Irish and English libraries.

975. ———. The earliest Dublin printing, with list of books, proclamations, etc., printed in Dublin prior to 1601. Dublin: O'Donoghue, 1901. 30p.

Copies located.

976. ———. "Earliest printing in the town of Sligo." Irish book lover, 2 (1910), 21-24.

Checklist, 1752-1800, with locations of copies.

977. ———. "Early printing in the south-east of Ireland: Carlow." Waterford and South East of Ireland Archaeological Society journal, 9 (1906), 112-19; "Clonmel," 9 (1906), 217-27; "Carrick-on-Suir," 10 (1907), 140-46; "Cashel," 10 (1907), 317-19; "Roscrea," 11 (1908), 236-37; "Wexford," 12 (1909), 15-19; "Carrick-on-Suir," 13 (1910), 69-70; "Carlow," 14 (1911), 108-12.

Checklists, with locations of copies.

978. ———. "Kilkenny printing in the eighteenth century." Irish book lover, 16 (1928), 6-9, 40-41, 55-58.

Locates copies in Irish and English libraries.

979. ———. "Kilkenny printing in the nineteenth century." Irish book lover, 16 (1928), 89-109.

Checklist, 1747-1900, with locations of copies.

980. ———. "List of all pamphlets, books, etc., printed in Cork during the seventeenth century." Royal Irish Academy proceedings, section C, 30 (1912), 71-82.

List of 40 items, with copies located.

981. ———. List of books and newspapers printed in Drogheda, Co. Louth, in the eighteenth century. Dundalk: Wm. Tempest, 1904. 14p.

Checklist, 1728-1800, with locations of copies.

982. ———. List of books and pamphlets printed in Armagh in the eighteenth century. Dublin, 1901. 12p. (Irish bibliographical pamphlets, no.11)

Copies located in several Irish libraries.

983. ———. List of books and pamphlets printed in Armagh in the 18th century, 2d ed. Dundrum: Cuala, 1910. 27p.

Checklist, 1740-99, with locations of copies.

984. ———. List of books and pamphlets printed in Strabane, Co. Tyrone, in the eighteenth century. 2d ed. Dundrum: Dun Emer, 1908. 27p. (Irish bibliographical pamphlets, no.1)

Copies located in public and private collections.

985. ———. "List of books and tracts printed in Belfast in the seventeenth century." Royal Academy of Ireland proceedings, section C, 33 (1916), 73-80.

List of 18 items, 1694-1700, with locations of copies.

986. ———. "List of books, etc., printed at Cork prior to 1801." Cork Historical and Archaeological Society journal, ser.2, 25 (1919), 107-8.

987. ———. List of books, newspapers and pamphlets printed in Ennis, Co. Clare, in the eighteenth century. Dublin: Cuata, 1912. 31p.

Checklist, 1776-1800, with locations of copies.

988. ———. List of books, pamphlets and newspapers printed in Drogheda, Co. Louth, in the eighteenth century. Dundalk: Wm. Tempest, 1904. 14p. (Irish bibliographical pamphlets, no.3)

Copies located.

989. ———. List of books, pamphlets & newspapers printed in Limerick from the earliest period to 1800. Limerick: Guy, 1907. 32p. (Irish bibliographical pamphlets, no.5)

Copies located in public and private libraries.

990. ———. List of books, pamphlets, and newspapers printed in Limerick from the earliest period to 1800, 2d ed. Limerick: Guy, 1912. 45p.

Checklist, 1690-1800, with locations of copies.

991. ———. List of books, pamphlets, & newspapers printed in Monaghan in the eighteenth century. Dundalk: Wm. Tempest, 1906. 16p. (Irish bibliographical pamphlets, no.4)

Copies located in public and private libraries.

992. ———. List of books, pamphlets, journals, etc., printed in Cork in the 17th and 18th centuries. Cork, 1904. 13pts. (Reprinted from Cork Historical and Archaeological Society journal, 1900)

Copies located.

993. ———. "List of books, pamphlets, newspapers, etc., printed in Drogheda from 1801 to 1825 inclusive." Irish book lover, 4 (1912), 1-3.

Checklist, with locations of copies.

994. ———. List of books, pamphlets, newspapers, etc. printed in Londonderry prior to 1801. Dundalk: Wm. Tempest, 1911. 35p.

Copies located.

995. ———. "List of books, pamphlets, newspapers, etc. printed in Newry from 1764 to 1810." Ulster journal of archaeology, 13 (1907), 116-19, 170-73; 14 (1908), 95-96; 15 (1909), 184-85.

Locates copies.

996. ———. "The ornaments used by John Franckton." Transactions of the Bibliographical Society, 8 (1907), 221-27.

Checklist of 9 works by Dublin printer, 1602-17; copies located in English and Irish libraries.

997. ———. "Printing in Armagh, 1801-24." Irish book lover, 4 (1912), 83-84.

Checklist, with locations of copies.

998. ———. "Printing in Armagh since 1825." Irish book lover, 14 (1924), 7-10, 55-56.

List, with locations of copies.

999. ———. "Printing in Athlone in the nineteenth century." Irish book lover, 6 (1915), 106-8.

Checklist, with locations of copies.

1000. ———. "Printing in Athy to 1900." Irish book lover, 17 (1929), 58-59.

Checklist, 1802-1900, with locations of copies.

1001. ———. "Printing in Ballinasloe, 1828-1900." Irish book lover, 7 (1916), 147-48.

Checklist, with locations of copies.

1002. ———. "Printing in Ballinrobe to 1900." Irish book lover, 17 (1929), 9.

Checklist, 1846-1900, with locations of copies.

1003. ———. "Printing in Ballyshannon to 1900." Irish book lover, 17 (1929), 101-2.

Copies located.

1004. ———. "Printing in Banbridge to 1900." Irish book lover, 17 (1929), 7-8.

Checklist, 1844-94, with locations of copies.

1005. ———. "Printing in Birr, or Parsonstown, 1775-1825." Irish book lover, 3 (1912), 177-79.

Checklist, with locations of copies.

1006. ———. "Printing in Boyle." Irish book lover, 7 (1915), 24-26.

Checklist, 1822-97, with locations of copies.

1007. ———. "Printing in Carlow in the eighteenth century." Irish book lover, 11 (1920), 75-76, 94, 109-11, 126-27; 12 (1920), 11-13.

List, with locations of copies.

1008. ———. "Printing in Cashel in the 19th century." Irish book lover, 6 (1915), 194-97.

Checklist, with locations of copies.

1009. ———. "Printing in Castlebar during the nineteenth century." Irish book lover, 9 (1918), 47-49.

Checklist, with locations of copies.

1010. ———. "Printing in Cavan, 1801-1827." Irish book lover, 4 (1913), 165-67.

Checklist, with locations of copies.

1011. ———. "Printing in Cavan, 1828-1900." Irish book lover, 11 (1919), 6-7, 22-23, 40-41.

Checklist, with locations of copies.

1012. ———. "Printing in Clonmel, 1801-25." Irish book lover, 4 (1912), 42-46.

Checklist with locations of copies.

1013. ———. "Printing in Cookstown to 1900." Irish book lover, 17 (1929), 137-38.

Checklist, 1824-1900, with locations of copies.

1014. ———. "Printing in Cork in the first quarter of the eighteenth century, 1701-1725." Royal Irish Academy proceedings, section C, 36 (1921), 10-15.

Checklist, with locations of copies.

1015. ———. Printing in Dublin prior to 1601. Dublin: C. O. Lochlainn, 1932. 43p.

Copies located.

1016. ———. "Printing in Dundalk, 1801-25." Irish book lover, 5 (1913), 46-47, 58-59, 78-80.

Checklist, with locations of copies.

1017. ———. "Printing in Dundalk, 1825-1900." Irish book lover, 8 (1917), 123-25; 9 (1917), 4.

Checklist, with locations of copies.

1018. ———. "Printing in Dungannon, 1801-1827." Irish book lover, 4 (1913), 188-89.

Checklist, with locations of copies.

1019. ———. "Printing in Enniscorthy to 1900." Irish book lover, 17 (1929), 138-39.

Checklist, 1841-1900, with locations of copies.

1020. ———. "Printing in Enniskillen, 1798-1825." Irish book lover, 2 (1911), 185-86.

Checklist, with locations of copies.

1021. ———. "Printing in Enniskillen, 1830-1900." Irish book lover, 7 (1915), 3-5.

Checklist, with locations of copies.

1022. ———. "Printing in Galway, 1754-1820." Irish book lover, 2 (1910), 50-54.

Checklist, with locations of copies.

1023. ———. "Printing in Galway, 1801-1825." Irish book lover, 4 (1912), 59-61.

Checklist, with locations of copies.

1024. ———. "Printing in Galway, 1828-1853." Irish book lover, 9 (1918), 130-31; 10 (1918), 9-10.

Checklist, 1828-1900, with locations of copies.

1025. ———. "Printing in Gorey." Irish book lover' 14 (1924), 100-1.

Checklist, 1854-93, with locations of copies.

1026. ———. "Printing in Kilrush in 19th century." Irish book lover, 9 (1918), 73-74.

Checklist, 1847-79, with locations of copies.

1027. ———. "Printing in Limerick in the nineteenth century." Irish book lover, 18 (1930), 39-42, 75-76, 101-2, 135-36, 163-64; 19 (1931), 117-20, 134-36, 174; 20 (1932), 84-85, 106-8, 124-26; 21 (1933), 7-9, 30-32, 56, 78-80, 109-10.

Checklists, with locations of copies.

1028. ———. "Printing in Longford in 19th century." Irish book lover, 12 (1920), 53-55.

Checklist, 1828-97, with locations of copies.

1029. ———. "Printing in Loughrea, 1766-1825." Irish book lover, 2 (1911), 151-52.

Checklist, with locations of copies.

1030. ———. "Printing in Loughrea." Irish book lover, 6 (1915), 175-76.

Checklist to 1800, with locations of copies.

1031. ———. "Printing in Lurgan in 19th century." Irish book lover, 13 (1921), 54-56.

Checklist, 1804-98, with locations of copies.

1032. ———. "Printing in Monaghan, 1801-25." Irish book lover, 4 (1913), 200-2; 5 (1913), 2-3, 26-27.

Checklist, with locations of copies.

1033. ———. "Printing in Monaghan, 1825-30." Irish book lover, 10 (1918), 34-35; 10 (1919), 55-56.

Checklist, with locations of copies.

1034. ———. "Printing in Mullingar." Irish book lover, 2 (1911), 120-22; 6 (1915), 127-28, 140-41, 160-61.

Checklist, 1773-1900, with locations of copies.

1035. ———. "Printing in Newtownards in the nineteenth century." Irish book lover, 12 (1921), 101-2.

Checklist, 1845-77, with locations of copies.

1036. ———. "Printing in Portadown." Irish book lover, 7 (1916), 123-24, 164-65.

Checklist, 1851-1900, with locations of copies.

1037. ———. "Printing in Sligo during 19th century." Irish book lover, 6 (1914-15), 52-54, 69-71, 89-90; 7 (1915-16), 47, 139; 8 (1917), 115.

Checklists, with locations of copies.

1038. ———. "Printing in Strabane, 1801-1825, 1825-1900." Irish book lover, 4 (1913), 114-16, 135; 7 (1915), 68-69, 91.

Checklist, with locations of copies.

1039. ———. "Printing in the city of Kilkenny in the seventeenth century." Royal Irish Academy proceedings, section C, 32 (1914), 125-37.

Checklist, with locations of copies.

1040. ———. "Printing in Tralee, 1801-30." Irish book lover, 4 (1913), 149-50.

Checklist, with locations of copies.

1041. ———. "Printing in Tralee, 1828-1900." Irish book lover, 10 (1919), 79-81.

Checklist, with locations of copies.

1042. ———. "Printing in Tuam." Irish book lover, 2 (1910), 101-2; 7 (1915), 40-41.

Checklist, 1774-1888, with locations of copies.

1043. ———. "Printing in Wexford in the 19th century." Irish book lover, 27 (1940), 250-54.

Checklist, 1805-99, with locations of copies.

1044. ———. "Printing in Youghal." Irish book lover, 4 (1912), 24-25.

Checklist, 1770-1826, with locations of copies.

1045. ———. "School books printed in Dublin from the earliest period to 1715." Bibliographical Society of Ireland publications, 3, no. 1 (1926), 5p.

Checklist from 1634, with some locations of copies in Irish and British libraries.

1046. ———. "Ulster bibliography: Coleraine." Ulster journal of archaeology, 13 (1907), 22-23.

Copies located.

1047. ———. "Ulster bibliography: Derry." Ulster journal of archaeology, 7 (1901), 135-36, 174; 8 (1902), 24; 9 (1903), 71.

Checklist, 1689-1797, with copies located.

1048. ———. "Ulster bibliography: Downpatrick, Dungannon, and Hillsborough." Ulster journal of archaeology, 7 (1901), 172-74.

Lists of 18th-century items with locations of copies.

1049. Limerick Public Library and Museum. Limerick printers & printing; part one of the catalog of the local collection in the city of Limerick Public Library, comp. by Robert Herbert. Limerick, 1942. 61p.

Checklist of about 500 items.

1050. Macphail, Ian. A bibliography of the books printed at Trinity College, Dublin, 1734-1875. 97*l*. (Diploma in Librarianship, Univ. of London)

Locations in Trinity College Library, Dublin, and in Bradshaw collection, Cambridge University Library.

1051. Marshall, John J History of Dungannon. Dungannon: Tyrone Printing Co., 1929. 137p.

"Dungannon printing and bibliography," p.129-37, is checklist, 1797-1928, with locations of copies.

1052. O'Kelley, Francis. "Irish book-sale catalogues before 1801." Bibliographical Society of Ireland publications, 6, no.3 (1953), 35-55.

Lists 63 items, with locations of copies.

1053. Peddie, Robert Alexander. "Bibliography of Irish printing." Irish book lover, 3 (1911), 51-53.

List of material held by St. Bride Foundation Institute Library.

1054. Tuite, James, and Crone, J. S. "J. C. Lyons and the Ledeston press." Irish book lover, 1 (1910), 69-71; 4 (1913), 98-99.

Checklist of imprints, with locations of copies.

SCOTTISH

1055. Aldis, H. G. A list of books printed in Scotland before 1700, including those printed furth of the realm for Scottish booksellers, with brief notes on the printers and stationers. Edinburgh: Edinburgh Bibliographical Society, 1904. 153p. (Edinburgh Bibliographical Society publication, no.7) Reprinted, 1970.

Locates copies in English and Scottish libraries; chronological arrangement; contains 3,919 entries.

1056. Beattie, William. The Scottish tradition in printed books. Edinburgh: Thomas Nelson for Saltire Society, 1949. 8p. + 20 plates.

Historical treatise, accompanied by list and illustrations from 20 books, 1540-1863, in National Library of Scotland.

1057. Carnie, R. H. Publishing in Perth before 1807. Dundee: Abertay Historical Society, 1960. 39p. (The Society's publication, no.6)

Locates copies in various public and private collections; chronological arrangement, 1770-1807.

1058. Couper, William James. "Robert Sanders the elder." Glasgow Bibliographical Society records, 3 (1914), 26-88.

Lists 202 items, 1661-94, with locations of copies.

1059. Dickson, Robert, and Edmond, John Philip. Annals of Scottish printing, from the introduction of the art in 1507 to the beginning of the seventeenth century. Cambridge: Macmillan & Bowes, 1890. 530p.

Imprints (333) listed under individual presses; copies located in English and Scottish libraries.

1060. Edmond, J. P. The Aberdeen printers Edward Raban to James Nicol, 1620-1736. Aberdeen: Edmond & Spark, 1884-86. 4pts.

Chronological list, with detailed bibliographical descriptions; copies located in Scottish and English libraries.

1061. Fairley, John A. "Bibliography of the chapbooks attributed to Dougal Graham." Glasgow Bibliographical Society records, 1 (1913), 125-215.

Describes and locates copies of 290 items after 1746.

1062. Festival of Britain, Scottish Committee. Catalogue of an exhibition of 18th-century Scottish books at the Signet Library, Edinburgh. Edinburgh: Published for The Committee and National Book League by Cambridge Univ. Pr., 1951. 187p.

Lists 779 items.

1063. Gaskell, Philip. A bibliography of the Foulis Press. London: Rupert Hart-Davis, 1964. 420p.

Detailed descriptions of 706 entries, 1740-1800; copies located in 12 British and American libraries.

1064. Gillespie, R. A. A list of books printed in Glasgow 1701-1775, with notes on the printers and booksellers. London, 1967. 2pts. (Library Association Fellowship thesis)

Records 1,395 imprints, with locations in 6 libraries.

1065. Glasgow Public Libraries. Catalogue of an exhibition of 20th-century Scottish books in the Mitchell Library, Glasgow, comp. by R. O. Dougan. Glasgow: Scottish Committee of the Festival of Britain, 1951. 310p. + 7 plates.

Comprises about 5,100 entries in 33 sections of books by Scotsmen, about Scotland, or printed or bound in Scotland. Items drawn from various sources; no locations, but most of material listed is in Mitchell Library.

1066. Glasgow, University, Hunterian Library. Three Glasgow book collections: William Euing, 1788-1874, John Ferguson, 1837-1916, David Murray, 1842-1928; an exhibition of books and manuscripts held in the Hunterian Library, University of Glasgow. Glasgow, 1969. 39p.

Records 116 items, annotated.

1067. ———, Library. Books published by James MacLehose from 1838 to 1881, and by James Mac-Lehose and Sons to 1905, presented to the Library of the University of Glasgow. Glasgow: Univ. Pr., 1905. 63p.

Represents 578 volumes published by leading Glasgow firm.

1068. Leith, William Forbes-. Pre-Reformation scholars in Scotland in the XVIth century; their writings and their public services, with a bibliography . . . from 1500 to 1560. Glasgow: James Maclehose, 1915. 155p.

Copies located in British and French libraries.

1069. M'Lean, Hugh A. "Robert Urie, printer in Glasgow." Glasgow Bibliographical Society records, 3 (1914), 89-108.

List of 314 Urie imprints, with locations of copies.

1070. National Library of Scotland. Catalogue of the Blackwood exhibition. Edinburgh, 1953. 13p.

Descriptions of 69 items drawn from files of William Blackwood and Sons publishing house, presented to National Library of Scotland.

1071. ———. The Chapman and Myllar prints; nine tracts from the first Scottish press, Edinburgh, 1508, followed by two other tracts in the same volume in the National Library of Scotland; a facsimile, with a bibliographical note by William Beattie. Edinburgh: Edinburgh Bibliographical Society, 1950. 220p.

1072. ———. 450 years of Scottish printing. Edinburgh, 1958. 20p.

Catalog of exhibition in National Library of Scotland.

1073. Ratcliffe, F. W. "Chapbooks with Scottish imprints in the Robert White collection, the University Library, Newcastle upon Tyne." Bibliotheck, 4 (1964), 88-174.

Lists 671 items with indexes of titles, publishers, printers, and booksellers.

1074. Shirley, George William. Dumfries printers in the eighteenth century; with handlists of their books. Dumfries: T. Hunter, Watson, 1934. 58p.

Includes "Handlist of books printed at Kirkbride and Dumfries by 18th century printers and their successors," 1711-1834, with copies located in Ewart Public Library and private collection.

1075. ———. "Mr. Peter Rae, V.D.M., printer." Glasgow Bibliographical Society records, 1 (1913), 216-35.

Lists Rae press imprints at Kirkbride and Dumfries, with locations of copies.

1076. Society of Writers to the Signet Library. Catalogue of an exhibition of 18th-century Scottish books at the Signet Library, Edinburgh, comp. by R. O. Dougan. London: Cambridge Univ. Pr., 1951. 187p. + 15 plates.

Annotated catalog of 780 books and manuscripts exhibited; copies located in 13 libraries.

1077. Thomson, Frances M. "John Wilson, an Ayrshire printer, publisher and bookseller." Bibliotheck, 5 (1967), 41-61.

List of imprints, 1783-1820, locates copies in 9 libraries.

WELSH

1078. Aberystwyth Public Library. Aberystwyth, A.D. 1909; centenary of the introduction of printing in 1809; exhibition of books, portraits, relics, etc., in the Public Library. Aberystwyth, 1909. 8p.

1079. National Library of Wales. "Short-title list of eighteenth-century Welsh books. Part I: 1701-1710." Welsh Bibliographical Society journal 4 (1933), 123-32. Reprinted, 1933. 22p.

Copies located in National Library of Wales.

1080. Rees, Eiluned. "A catalogue of Welsh books, 1546-1820, and ancillary projects." National Library of Wales journal, 16 (1970), 371-80.

Report of progress on compilation of complete record of Welsh books, project undertaken by National Library of Wales.

1081. Swansea Public Library. Catalogue of Welsh books, with English and other literature relating to Wales & Celtic countries in the Central Lending Library; pt.I, authors, pt.II, subjects, comp. by D. Rhys Phillips. Swansea: C. E. Willing, 1911. 50p.

1082. Thomas, Muriel Michaela Anne Austin. The Gregynog Press, Newton, Montgomeryshire; miscellaneous publications, 1921-1941, in the collection of the National Library of Wales, Aberystwyth. London, 50l. (Diploma in Librarianship, Univ. of London)

NETHERLANDS

1083. Copinger, H. B. The Elzevier Press, a handlist of the products of the Elzevier presses at Leyden, Amsterdam, the Hague, and Utrecht, with references to Willems, Berghman, Rahir and other bibliographers. London: Grafton, 1927. 142p.

Locations include British Museum.

1084. Proctor, Robert. Jan van Doesborgh, printer at Antwerp; an essay in bibliography. London: Printed for the Bibliographical Society at the Chiswick Press, 1894. 101p. + 12 plates.

Detailed descriptions of 32 works, produced from c. 1505-30; copies located in British and Continental libraries.

AMERICAN

1085. British Museum. Catalogue of the American books in the Library of the British Museum at Christmas Mdccclvi, by Henry Stevens. London: Chiswick, 1866. 628p.

Addenda include Canadian, Mexican, and other American imprints, and catalog of American maps in British Museum.

1086. Kimber, Sidney A. Cambridge Press title-pages, 1640-1665; a pictorial representation. Takoma Park, Md., 1954. 123p. + 84 illus.

Reproductions of title pages of all publications of first New England press; copies located in U.S. and in 4 English and 2 Scottish libraries.

1087. Stevens, Henry. Catalogue of Canadian books in the Library of the British Museum, Christmas 1856; including those printed in the other British North American provinces. London: Charles Whittingham, 1859. 14p.

1088. ———. Catalogue of Mexican and other Spanish American and West Indian books in the Library of the British Museum. London: Charles Whittingham, 1859. 62p.

INCUNABULA

General

1089. Abbott, Thomas Kingsmill. Catalogue of fifteenth-century books in the Library of Trinity College, Dublin, and in Marsh's Library, Dublin, with a few from other collections. Dublin: Hodges Figgis, 1905. 225p.

Records 606 titles in alphabetical order.

1090. Aberdeen, University, Library. Catalogue of the incunabula in Aberdeen University Library, comp. by William Smith Mitchell. Edinburgh, London: Oliver & Boyd, 1968. 107p. (Univ. of Aberdeen studies, no.150)

Records 230 works, with references to standard bibliographies and statements on provenances.

1091. ———. A list of fifteenth century books in the University Library of Aberdeen. Aberdeen, 1925. 85p. (Aberdeen University studies, no.98)

Detailed bibliographical descriptions of 200 items in Proctor order.

1092. Advocates Library. "List of fifteenth century books on the Library of the Faculty of Advocates," by William Kirk Dickson and Miss J. M. G. Barclay. Publications of the Edinburgh Bibliographical Society, 9 (1913), 125-46.

Transferred to National Library of Scotland.

1093. Bath Municipal Libraries. Catalogue of icunabula. Bath, 1966. 26p.

1094. Beattie, William. "Supplement to the Hand-list of incunabula in the National Library of Scotland." Edinburgh Bibliographical Society transactions, 2 (1944), 151-251.

Geographically arranged, followed by chronological index, index of authors and texts, index of printers and towns, and 11 facsimiles. "Second supplement," ibid., 2 (1946), 331-44, adds 26 titles.

1095. Brighton Public Libraries. Catalogue of manuscripts and printed books before 1500, comp. by A. W. Ball. Brighton: Royal Pavilion, Museums and Libraries Committee of the County Borough of Brighton, 1962. 22p.

Detailed bibliographical descriptions of 10 manuscripts and 42 printed works.

1096. British Museum. An index to the early printed books in the British Museum, from the invention of printing to the year MD; with notes of those in the Bodleian Library, by Robert Proctor. London: Kegan Paul, 1898-1938. 4v.

1097. ———, Dept. of Printed Books. Catalogue of books printed in the XVth century now in the British Museum. pt.1, Xylographica and books printed with types at Mainz, Strassburg, Hamberg, and Cologne. 1908. p.1-312; pt.2, Germany: Eltvil-Trier. 1912. p.313-620; pt.3, Germany: Leipzig-Pforzheim. German-speaking Switzerland and Austria-Hungary. 1913. p.621-864; pt.4, Italy: Subiaco and Rome. 1916. p.1-146; pt.5, Venice. 1924. p.147-598; pt.6, Italy: Foligno, Ferrara, Florence, Milan, Bologna, Naples, Perugia, and Traviso. 1930. p.599-899; pt.7, Italy: Genoa—Unassigned addenda. 1935. p.900-1213; pt.8, France, French-speaking Switzerland. (Index.) 1949. 441p.; pt.9, Holland and Belgium, 1962. 222p.; pt.10, Spain and Portugal, 1971. 148p. London, 1908-71. 10pts.

1098. ———— ————. Collectors and owners of incunabula in the British Museum: index of provenances for books printed in France, Holland, and Belgium, by Lilian G. Clark. Bath: Harding and Curtis, 1902. 75p.

Preliminary edition of work which will form part of the final volume of the Museum's Catalogue of books printed in the fifteenth century.

1099. Cambridge, University, Clare College Library. The early printed books to the year 1500 in the Library of Clare College, Cambridge. Cambridge: Univ. Pr., 1919. 8p.

List of 35 items in Proctor order.

1100. ————, Emmanuel College Library. Early printed books to the year 1500 in the Library of Emmanuel College, Cambridge, by Philip W. Wood. Cambridge: Univ. Pr., 1911-13. 2pts.

1101. ————, Fitzwilliam Museum. Catalogue of the early printed books bequeathed to the Museum by Frank McClean, by C. E. Sayle. Cambridge: Univ. Pr., 1916. 173p.

List of 338 items in Proctor order. Appendix: Fifteenth century books from sources other than the McClean bequest.

1102. ———— ————. List of the fifteenth-century printed books bequeathed to the Fitzwilliam Museum by F. McLean, by Stephen Gaselee. Cambridge, 1905. 12p.

Lists 176 items by place of publication.

1103. ————, Gonville and Caius College Library. A descriptive catalogue of the incunabula in the Library of Gonville and Caius College, Cambridge, comp. by G. A. Schneider. Cambridge: Univ. Pr., 1928. 45p.

Lists 101 items in Proctor order.

1104. ————, King's College Library. A list of the incunabula in the Library of King's College, Cambridge, ed. by George Chawner. Cambridge: Univ. Pr., 1908. 80p.

Lists 198 items in Proctor order.

1105. ————, Library. A catalogue of the fifteenth-century printed books in the University Library, Cambridge, comp. by J. C. T. Oates. Cambridge: Univ. Pr., 1954. 898p.

Lists total of 4,249 items, including some 500 duplicates; Proctor order.

1106. ————, Peterhouse College Library. Early printed books, to the year 1500, in the Library of Peterhouse, Cambridge. Cambridge: Univ. Pr., 1914. 10p.

List of 54 items in Proctor order.

1107. ————, Queen's College Library. Early printed books to the year 1500 in the Library of Queen's College, Cambridge, comp. by Francis G. Plaistowe. Cambridge, 1910. 8p.

Lists 30 items in Proctor order.

1108. ————, St. John's College Library. Incunabula: in the Library of St. John's College, Cambridge, comp. by Ernest W. Lockhart and Charles E. Sayle. Cambridge, 1911. 27p. (Reprinted from the Eagle magazine)

Short-title catalog of 265 items in Proctor order.

1109. ————, Selwyn College Library. List of incunabula, Selwyn College, Cambridge, comp. by Charles W. Phillips. Cambridge, 1934. 8p.

Lists 35 items, with Hain and Proctor numbers.

1110. ————, Sidney Sussex College Library. Early printed books to the year 1500 in the Library of Sidney Sussex College, Cambridge, comp. by A. H. Cook. Cambridge: Univ. Pr., 1922. 8p.

List of 36 items in Proctor order.

1111. ————, Trinity College Library. A catalogue of the fifteenth-century printed books in the Library of Trinity College, Cambridge, by Robert Sinker. Cambridge: Deighton, Bell, 1876. 174p.

Records 510 titles.

1112. ————, Trinity College, Trinity Hall Library. Early printed books to the year 1500 in the Library of Trinity Hall, Cambridge. Cambridge: Univ. Pr., 1909. 7p.

Lists 28 items in Proctor order.

1113. Dodgson, Campbell. English devotional woodcuts of the late fifteenth century, with special reference to those in the Bodleian Library. Walpole Society, seventeenth volume, 17 (1928-29), 95-108.

1114. Donaldson, Robert. "Nine incunabula in the Cathcart White collection in the Edinburgh University Library." Bibliotheck, 2 (1960), 66-69.

Supplements F. C. Nicholson's List of 15th century books in v.9 of Edinburgh Bibliographical Society's publications, 1913.

1115. ————. "Two block-books in the Hunterian Library, Glasgow University." Bibliotheck, 3 (1961), 103-4.

Describes copies of Biblia Pauperum and Apocalypse and Life of St. John.

1116. Dublin, University, Trinity College Library. Catalogue of fifteenth-century books in the Library of Trinity College, Dublin, and in Marsh's Library, Dublin, with a few other collections, by T. K. Abott. Dublin: Hodges Figgis, 1905. 225p. + 11 plates.

Lists 606 items, with annotations.

1117. Edinburgh Bibliographical Society. Lists of fifteenth century books in Edinburgh libraries, by members of the Edinburgh Bibliographical Society. Edinburgh, 1913. 107p.

Includes separate listings for principal libraries.

1118. Edinburgh, University, Library. "List of fifteenth century books in the University Library, Edinburgh," by Frank C. Nicholson. Publications of the Edinburgh Bibliographical Society, 9 (1913), 93-123.

1119. Gesamtkatalog der Wiegendrucke. Leipzig: Hiersemann, 1925-40. v.1-7, v.8, pt.1. A-Federicis.

Locations for 9,730 entries in British and other European and American libraries.

1120. Glasgow Public Libraries. Catalog of incunables and STC books in the Mitchell Library, Glasgow, by A. G. Hepburn. Glasgow, 1964. 131p.

Lists 44 incunabula, mostly late 15th century, and 589 STC books of later date.

1121. Goldschmidt, E. P. Medieval texts and their first appearance in print. London: Printed for the Bibliographical Society at the Univ. Pr., Oxford, 1943. 143p. (Supplement to the Bibliographical Society transactions, no.16)

Locates copies in British, Continental, and American libraries.

1122. Gore, W. G. A. Ormsby-. "Incunabula at Brogyntyn." National Library of Wales journal, 6 (1950), 329-37.

1123. Guildhall Library. "Fifteenth-century printed books in the Guildhall Library." Guildhall miscellany, no.10 (Sept. 1959), 63-74.

Lists 85 incunabula in Proctor order, with indexes of authors, titles, printers, places, and provenances.

1124. John Rylands Library. Descriptive catalogue of an exhibition of printed book illustrations of the fifteenth century, ed. by Henry Guppy. Manchester: Univ. Pr., 1933. 90p. + 16 plates.

Arranged by country and place of origin.

1125. ———. English incunabula in the John Rylands Library: a catalogue of books printed in England and of English books printed abroad between the years 1475 and 1500 ed. by Henry Guppy. Manchester: Univ. Pr., 1930. 102p.

Includes 16 facsimiles.

1126. ———. Woodcuts of the fifteenth century in the John Rylands Library, Manchester; reproduced in facsimile, with an introduction and notes by Campbell Dodgson. Manchester, 1915. 17p.

1127. Lincoln Cathedral Church Library. Incunabula in the Lincoln Cathedral Library, by James Bell and W. H. Kynaston. Lincoln, 1925. 12p.

Lists 97 items in Proctor order.

1128. Liverpool, University, Library. Hand-list of incunabula in the University Library, by David I. Masson. Liverpool, 1949. 46p. First supplement, 1955. 8p.

Main work contains 230 entries.

1129. London, University, Libraries. Incunabula in the Libraries of the University of London: a hand-list, comp. by Margery F. Wild. London, 1963. 40p.

Records 291 numbered items, representing 288 titles and 177 printers in 10 countries; copies located in 12 libraries in University of London.

1130. Marsh's Library. Short catalogue of incunabula remaining in Marsh's Library, Dublin, comp. by T. K. Abbott. Dublin, 1905. 8p.

1131. Meyer-Baer, Kathi. Liturgical music incunabula, a descriptive catalogue. London: Bibliographical Society, 1962. 63p., 12 plates.

Lists 450 15th-century printed books containing music, with locations in British Museum, Bodleian, Cambridge University Library, etc.

1132. ———. "The liturgical music incunabula in the British Museum; Germany, Italy, and Switzerland." Library, 4th ser., 20 (1939), 272-94.

List of 84 incunabula.

1133. Milltown Park College Library. A catalogue of incunabula in the Library at Milltown Park, Dublin, by Paul Grosjean and Daniel O'Connell. Dublin: At the Sign of the Three Candles, 1932. 53p.

Describes 177 works in Gesamtkatalog order.

1134. National Library of Scotland. "Supplement to the Hand-list of incunabula in the National Library of Scotland," by William Beattie. Edinburgh Bibliographical Society transactions, 2 (1944), 151-230.

Annotated checklist of 326 items in Proctor order. Second supplement, ibid., 2 (1946), 331-44, adds 26 items.

1135. ———. Treasures of the Advocates' Library; an exhibition. Edinburgh, 1960. 12p.

Fifteenth-century books, law books, Scottish books, maps, bindings, etc.

1136. National Library of Wales. Hand-list of incunabula in the National Library of Wales, compiled by Victor Scholderer. Aberystwyth, 1940. 44p. (National Library of Wales journal, supplement, ser.1, no.1) Addenda and corrigenda. Aberystwyth, 1941. 10p. (National Library of Wales journal supplement, ser. 1 no.2)

Records 120 titles; geographical arrangement.

1137. Oxford, University, Ashmolean Museum. Woodcuts of the fifteenth century in the Ashmolean Museum, Oxford, ed. by Campbell Dodgson, with notes on similar prints in the Bodleian Library. Oxford, 1929. 36p.

1138. ———, Oriel College Library. Incunabula in Oriel College Library, by W. D. Ross. Oxford, 1919. 4p.

List of 34 items.

1139. Painter, George D. "Incunabula in Cambridge University Library." Book collector, 4 (1955), 51-57.

History and description of the Cambridge collection.

1140. Pollard, Alfred W. "The building up of the British Museum collection of incunabula." Library, ser.4, 5 (1924), 193-214.

General discussion and history of development of collection.

1141. Proctor, Robert George Collier. An index to the early printed books in the British Museum: from the invention of printing to the year MD, with notes of those in the Bodleian Library. London: Kegan Paul, 1898-1938. 4v. (pt.2, section 2-3, by Frank Isaac; pt.2, section 2-3, published by Bernard Quaritch.) Supplements, 1898-1902. London, 1900-3. 5pts.

Arranged by countries, localities, and printers.

1142. Royal Observatory. "List of fifteenth century books in the Crawford Library of the Royal Observatory, Edinburgh," by George P. Johnston. Publications of the Edinburgh Bibliographical Society, 9 (1904-13), 169-78.

1143. St. Andrews, University, Library. Catalogue of incunabula, comp. by A. G. Scott. St. Andrews: Univ. Court, 1956. 101p. (St. Andrews Univ. publication, no.53)

Contains 138 entries, several unique, a large number of which have been in the library since the 15th century.

1144. St. Bride Foundation Institute Library. List of early printed books, by Robert A. Peddie. London, 1904. 4p.

Geographical arrangement by imprints of incunabula in library; about 100 items in Proctor order.

1145. Society of Writers to the Signet Library. "List of fifteenth century books in the Library of the Society of Writers to his Majesty's Signet," by John Philip Edmond. Publications of the Edinburgh Bibliographical Society, 9 (1912), 147-62.

1146. Stocks, E. V. "Incunabula." Durham University journal, n.s.21 (1918), 472-74; 22 (1918-19), 21-23, 57-59.

Checklist of 258 items in Proctor order; includes books at Durham Cathedral and in several other collections.

1147. United Free Church College Library. "List of fifteenth century books in the United Free Church College Library, Edinburgh," by William Cowan. Publications of the Edinburgh Bibliographical Society, 9 (1913), 163-68.

1148. Vernon, Anne. "Eighteenth-century accessions of incunables to the Advocates Library." Bibliotheck 4 (1965), 238-40.

Lists 22 items.

1149. Victoria and Albert Museum Library. Incunabula: a provisional checklist of pre-1500 books in the Library, comp. by G. D. A. McPherson. London, 1970. 10*l.*

1150. Worcester Cathedral Church Library. Worcester Cathedral Library. Incunabula, comp. by Cosmo Gordon. Cambridge: Univ. Pr., 1910. 8p.

Lists 35 items in Proctor order.

English

1151. Butterworth, Margaret. Select bibliography of works on William Caxton, the first printer at Oxford, the St. Albans printer, and John Siberch of Cambridge. London, 1951. 46p. (Diploma in Librarianship, Univ. of London)

Records 178 items; call numbers included for Cambridge University copies, or, if not there, locations in British Museum.

1152. DeRicci, Seymour. A census of Caxtons. Oxford: Printed for the Bibliographical Society at the Oxford Univ. Pr., 1909. 196p.

Records provenances of 108 works, with past or present locations.

1153. Duff, E. Gordon. "English fifteenth century broadsides." Bibliographical Society transactions, 9 (1906-8), 211-27.

General discussion, with locations of surviving examples.

1154. ———. Fifteenth century English books; a bibliography of books and documents printed in England and of books for the English market printed abroad. Oxford: Univ. Pr., 1917. 136p. + 53 plates. Reprinted, 1965.

Lists 431 works, with full bibliographical details; copies located.

1155. Gaines, Barry. "A forgotten artist: John Harris and the Rylands copy of Caxton's edition of Malory." Bulletin of the John Rylands Library, 52 (1969), 115-28.

Describes 1 of 2 extant copies of Caxton's Malory.

1156. Rhodes, D. E. "Some documents printed by Pynson for St. Botolph's, Boston, Lincs." Library, 15 (1960), 53-57.

Identifies and describes 8 Richard Pynson imprints and locates copies.

1157. Rhodes, Dennis Everard. "The remorse of conscience." Library, ser. 5, 13 (1958), 199-200.

Describes 3 editions of anonymous poem printed by Wynkyn de Worde; copies located in several libraries.

1158. Skeat, T. C. "The Caxton deeds." British Museum quarterly, 28 (1964), 12-15.

Description and list of documents relating to William and other members of Caxton family, now in British Museum.

1159. Smith, George. William de Machlinia; the primer on vellum printed by him in London about 1484. London: Ellis, 1929. 26p. + 9 plates.

Leaves of Machlinia primer located in British Museum, Lincoln Cathedral, Cambridge, and Oxford.

French

1160. Beattie, William. "Two notes on fifteenth-century printing. I. Jacobus Ledelh." Transactions of the Edinburgh Bibliographical Society, 3, pt.1 (1952), 75-77.

Describes 3 works printed in Paris, with locations of copies in National Library of Scotland and Bodleian Library.

1161. Claudin, C. The first Paris press; an account of the books printed for G. Fichet and J. Heynlin in the Sorbonne, 1470-1472. London: Printed for the Bibliographical Society at the Chiswick Pr., February 1898 (for 1897). 100p.

Detailed descriptions of 22 works; copies located in British and Continental libraries.

1162. MacFarlane, John. Antoine Vérard. London: Printed for the Bibliographical Society at the Chiswick Pr., 1900 (for 1899). 143p. + 79 plates.

Detailed descriptions of 268 works printed by Vérard, 1485-1500; copies located in French and British libraries.

German

1163. British Museum, Dept. of Printed Books. Johann Gutenberg, the inventor of printing, by Victor Scholderer. London: The Museum, 1963. 32p. + 16 plates. Reprinted, 1970.

Summaries of original documents and facsimile illustrations of earliest printed books.

1164. Morison, Stanley. German incunabula in the British Museum; facsimile plates of fine book-pages from presses of Germany, German Switzerland and Austria-Hungary, printed in the fifteenth century in gothic letter and derived founts. London: Gollancz, 1928. 152p.

Italian

1165. Peddie, R. A. Printing at Brescia in the fifteenth century; a list of the issues. London: Williams and Norgate, 1905. 30p.

Includes notes on extant copies when available.

1166. Redgrave, Gilbert R. Erhard Ratdolt and his work at Venice. London: Printed for the Bibliographical Society at the Chiswick Pr., 1894. 50p.

Descriptions of 66 works attributed to Ratdolt beginning 1476; locations in British Museum, Bodleian, and Cambridge University Library.

Netherlands

1167. Stevenson, Allan. "The quincentennial of Netherlandish blockbooks." British Museum quarterly, 31 (1967), 83-87.

Account of 15th-century works held by British Museum.

Spanish

1168. Rhodes, D. E. "Two notable acquisitions of Spanish incunabula." British Museum quarterly, 20 (1956), 56-57.

Describes 2 rare works, printed at Barcelona in the 1470s, acquired by British Museum.

1169. Vine, Guthrie. "Around the earliest Spanish version of Aesop's Fables." Bulletin of the John Rylands Library, 25 (1941), 97-118. Reprinted. 1941. 24p.

Description of unique copy of 1488 edition, printed at Toulouse, in John Rylands Library.

EARLY PRINTED BOOKS

General

1170. Bath Municipal Libraries. Printed books, 1476-1640, in Bath Municipal Libraries, catalogue, comp. by V. J. Kite. Bath, 1968. 93p.

Lists all books held by libraries published up to 1640.

1171. Bishop Phillpott's Library. Catalogue of books published before 1800. Truro, n.d. 56p.

1172. Bristol Public Libraries. A catalogue of books in the Bristol Reference Library which were printed abroad in languages other than English during the years 1473 to 1700. Bristol: Corp. of Bristol, 1956. 194p.

Collection totals 935 titles, including 31 incunabula and other rare works.

1173. ———. Early printed books and manuscripts in the City Reference Library, Bristol, by Norris Mathews. Bristol, 1899. 84p.

Incunabula and later books to 1628, principally foreign.

1174. Cambridge, University, Corpus Christi College Library. The early printed books in the Library of Corpus Christi College, Cambridge; a handlist arranged in order of country, town, and press, with short references to Proctor's Index and other bibliographical works, comp. by Stephen Gaselee. Cambridge: Univ. Pr., 1921. 38p.

Records 125 incunabula and about 180 16th-century works.

1175. ———, Fitzwilliam Museum. McClean bequest; catalogue of the early printed books bequeathed to the Museum by Frank McClean, by C. E. Sayle. Cambridge: Univ. Pr., 1916. 142p. + 6 plates and index.

Descriptions of 338 15th- and 16th-century books; geographical arrangement by imprints.

1176. ———, Gonville and Caius College Library. A list of the early printed books; and an index of English books printed before the year MDC in the Library of Gonville, and Caius College, Cambridge, comp. by W. R. Collett. Cambridge: J. Deighton, Macmillan, 1850. 2pts.

Descriptions of 15th- and 16th-century works.

1177. ———, Library. Catalogue of a collection of early printed and other books bequeathed to the Library by John Couch Adams. Cambridge: Univ. Pr., 1902. 203p.

1178. ——— ———. Catalogue of books printed on the continent of Europe, 1501-1600, in Cambridge Libraries, comp. by H. M. Adams. Cambridge: Univ. Pr., 1967. 2v.

Includes holdings of British Museum and 32 Cambridge libraries; lists 30,000 items.

1179. ———, St. Catharine's College Library. Early printed books in the Library of St. Catharine's College, Cambridge, by J. B. Bilderbeck. Cambridge: Univ. Pr., 1911. 38p.

Lists 75 items in Proctor order.

1180. ———, St. John's College Library. Catalogue of early printed classics in the Library of St. John's College, Cambridge. Cambridge, 1887. 11p.

1181. Cardiff Public Libraries. Catalogue of early printed books. Cardiff, 1913. 34p.

1182. Darbyshire, J. B. The Hart collection of early printed books, 1450-1700. London, 1967. 163*l*. (Thesis, Library Association Fellowship)

Catalog of 200 works in Blackburn Public Library.

1183. Day, J. C. A short title catalogue of books (English and Continental) printed before 1701 in the Thomlinson collection, Newcastle upon Tyne Central Library. London, 1970. 460 + 92*l*. (Thesis, Library Association Fellowship)

Records collection of 6,250 titles.

1184. Driver, G. R. "Magdalen College Library; list of books printed before 1641 in the Library of Magdalen College, of which the Bodleian Library has no copy." Proceedings and papers, Oxford Bibliographical Society, 2 (1929), 145-200.

Includes English books printed before 1641 that are in both libraries.

1185. Gibson, Jean. A partial bibliography of mainly seventeenth century pamphlets contained in St. George's Chapter Library, Windsor. London, 1955. 485*l*. (Diploma in Librarianship, Univ. of London)

Locates copies also in other British libraries; includes STC and Wing numbers.

1186. Gilbert, John. "Irish bibliography, two papers." Royal Irish Academy proceedings, section C, 25 (1904-5), 117-42.

Appendix, by E. R. McC. Dix, lists 16th- and 17th-century books printed abroad; copies located in Irish and British libraries.

1187. Glasgow, University, Hunterian Museum Library. The printed book in the Library of the Hunterian Museum in the University of Glasgow; a catalogue, prep. by Mungo Ferguson, with a topographical index by David Baird Smith. Glasgow: Jackson, Wylie & Co., 1930. 396p. (Glasgow Univ. publications, no.18)

Collections representative of many early printers, with 534 incunabula and strength in 16th-century works.

1188. Great Britain, Foreign Office Library. A short-title catalogue of books printed before 1701 in the Foreign Office Library, by Colin L. Robertson. London: H. M. Stationery Office, 1966. 177p.

Records 577 titles or editions; includes STC and Wing numbers.

1189. Harris, James Rendel, and Jones, Stephen K. The Pilgrim press; a bibliographical and historical memorial of the books printed at Leyden by the Pilgrim fathers. Cambridge: Heffer, 1922. 89p. + 38 facsimiles.

Copies located in British, American, and other libraries.

1190. Isaac, Frank. An index to the early printed books in the British Museum, pt.II. MDI-MDXX, section II. Italy, section III. Switzerland and Eastern Europe. London: Bernard Quaritch, 1938. 286p.

Arranged by country, city or town, and printers, with indexes. Continuation of Proctor's Index.

1191. John Rylands Library. Catalogue of the selection of books and broadsides illustrating the early history of printing, exhibited on the occasion of the visit of the Federation of Master Printers and Allied Trades in June, MCMVII, by Henry Guppy. Manchester, 1907. 34p.

1192. Lambeth Palace Library. A list of some of the early printed books in the Archiepiscopal Library at Lambeth, by S. R. Maitland. London, 1843. 464p.

Chronologically arranged, 1466 to 1550; English books, 1520-1550, separately listed and described.

1193. Liverpool Cathedral, Radcliffe Library. Short title catalogue of books printed before 1801, by David Clark. Liverpool, 1968. 60p.

Alphabetical list by authors and subjects.

1194. National Library of Scotland. A short-title catalogue of foreign books printed up to 1600; books printed or published outside the British Isles now in the National Library of Scotland and the Library of the Faculty of Advocates, Edinburgh. Edinburgh: H. M. Stationery Office, 1970. 545p.

1195. Newcastle upon Tyne, University, Library. A list of the post-incunabula in the University Library, Newcastle upon Tyne, comp. by William S. Mitchell. Newcastle upon Tyne, 1965. 70p.

Lists STC books, 1501-1640, and books printed on Continent of Europe to 1600.

1196. Ovenell, R. F. "Brian Twyne's Library." Oxford Bibliographical Society publications, n.s.4 (1950), 1-42.

Catalog of Twyne's library, bequeathed to University of Oxford in 1644; about 750 works dating from 1480 to 1640.

1197. Oxford, University, Constance Meade Memorial Collection. A list of the books, pamphlets . . . and leaflets in the . . . collection, that were printed between 1640 and 1701. Oxford: Univ. Pr., 1966. 32l.

1198. ———, Hertford College Library. Catalogue of books in the Library of Hertford College, printed in the 15th and 16th centuries. Oxford, 1910. 16p.

1199. ——— ———. Catalogue of the old books in Hertford College Library. [Oxford] 1947. 363l.

1200. ———, Magdalen College Library. "List of books before 1641 in Magdalen College Library not in the Bodleian Library." Oxford Bibliographical Society, proceedings and papers, 2 (1929), 145-200.

Alphabetical list of about 1,000 titles.

1201. Painter, George D., Allison, A. F., and Nixon, Howard M. "List of books acquired by the British Museum from Chatworth." Book collector, 7 (1958), 401-6; 8 (1959), 52-59.

pt.1, incunabula; pt.2, English books 1501-1640; pt.3, bindings.

1202. Robertson, Colin L. Short title catalogue of books printed before 1701 in the Foreign Office Printed Library. London, 1964. 178l. (Thesis, Library Association Fellowship)

Records total of 579 titles.

1203. Royal Society Library. Catalogue of a collection of early printed books in the Library of the Royal Society. London, 1910. 120p.

Consists of 396 volumes in 981 works; strength in Reformation tracts, Americana, and incunabula.

1204. St. Andrews, University, Library. Catalogue of some fifteenth and sixteenth century books in the University Library, St. Andrews, with indexes of printers and places, watermarks, autographs and original owners. St. Andrews: W. C. Henderson & Son, 1925. 12p.

1205. Salford, University, Library. Supplement to Early printed books; additions made from 1909 to July 1921. Salford, 1921. 41p.

1206. Sheffield, University, Library. Early-printed books in the Library of the University of Sheffield; English to 1640, foreign to 1600, comp. by G. C. Moore Smith. Cambridge: Univ. Pr., 1909. 32p. Supplement, 1921. 41p.
Lists 191 English books and 4 incunabula.

1207. ———. A short-title list of holdings of Sheffield University Library in sixteenth-century books printed on the continent of Europe (excluding France). Sheffield, 1968. 173*l*.

1208. Sheppard, L. A. "A list of the printed books recently acquired by the British Museum from the Earl of Leicester, Holkham Hall." Book collector, 1 (1952), 120-26, 185-89, 259-63.
Descriptions of rare books, 15th to 17th century, purchased by British Museum.

1209. Society of Writers to the Signet Library. Catalogue of early printed books in the Library of the Society of Writers to His Majesty's Signet, by John P. Edmond, ed. by John Minto. Edinburgh: T. & A. Constable, 1906. 27p.
Lists 119 works by countries, in Proctor order.

1210. Winchester Cathedral Library. Early printed books, 1479-1640, comp. by Francis T. Madge. Winchester, 1902. 28p.

British Isles

1211. Alden, John E. Wing addenda and corrigenda; some notes on materials in the British Museum. Charlottesville: Univ. of Va. Bibliographical Society, 1958. 19p.
Additional titles found in British Museum and corrections to Wing.

1212. Allison, A. F. "Early English books at the London Oratory; a supplement to S.T.C." Library, ser.5, 2 (1947), 95-107.
Describes in detail books unrecorded in STC, also other editions and variants and extremely rare items.

1213. Archbishop Marsh's Library. A short catalogue of English books in Archbishop Marsh's Library, Dublin, printed before MDCXLI, by Newport J. D. White. London: Printed for the Bibliographical Society at the Oxford Univ. Pr., 1905. 90p.

1214. Barr, C. B. L. "Early Scottish editions of 'The seven sages of Rome.'" Bibliotheck, 5 (1967), 62-72.
Discussion of 4 17th-century editions in British and American libraries.

1215. Belfast Library and Society for Promoting Knowledge. Catalogue of early Belfast printed books, 1694-1830, comp. by John Anderson. Belfast, 1890. 85p. Supplement to 3d ed., 1894. 23p. Supplement, 1902. 30p.
Chronological checklists, with locations of copies.

1216. Bibliotheca Lindesiana. Catalogue of English broadsides, 1505-1897, by John P. Edmond. Aberdeen: Univ. Pr., 1898. 526p.
Chronological list of 679 items.

1217. Bloom, James Harvey. English tracts, pamphlets and printed sheets: a bibliography. London: Wallace Gandy, 1922-23. 2v.
v.1, 1473-1650 (Suffolk); v.2, 1473-1650 (Leicestershire, Staffordshire, Warwickshire, and Worcestershire); copies located in various English libraries.

1218. Bristol Public Libraries. A catalogue of books in the Bristol Reference Library printed in England and Ireland up to the year 1640 and of English books printed abroad during the same period. Bristol, 1954. 52p.
Record of about 350 titles of STC period.

1219. ———. A catalogue of books in the Bristol Reference Library printed in England, Scotland and Ireland and of English books printed abroad, 1641-1700. Bristol: Corp. of Bristol, 1958. 208p.
Alphabetical by author or title; Wing numbers added.

1220. British Museum, Dept. of Printed Books. Catalogue of books in the Library of the British Museum printed in England, Scotland, and Ireland, and of books in English printed abroad, to the year, 1640, comp. by George Bullen and G. W. Eccles, London, 1884. 3v.

1221. Butterworth, Charles C. The English primers, 1529-1545; their publication and connection with the English Bible and the Reformation in England. Philadelphia: Univ. of Pa. Pr., 1953. 340p.
Checklists include STC numbers.

1222. Cambridge, University, Emmanuel College Library. A hand-list of English books in the Library of Emmanuel College, Cambridge, printed before MDCXLI, by Philip W. Wood and G. H. Watts. Cambridge: Univ. Pr., 1915. 182p.

Author list with index of printers, stationers, etc.

1223. —— ——. An index to the English books and pamphlets in the Library of Emmanuel College, Cambridge, printed before 1700 A.D., comp. by John B. Pearson. Cambridge: Deighton, Bell, & Co., 1869. 101p.

1224. ——, Library. Early English printed books in the University Library, Cambridge (1475-1640), comp. by C. E. Sayle. Cambridge: Univ. Pr., 1900-7. 4v.

Arranged chronologically under presses and publishers; 4th volume is index of authors, titles, printers, etc.; records 8,083 entries.

1225. ——, Trinity College Library. A catalogue of the English books printed before MDCI now in the Library of Trinity College, Cambridge, by Robert Sinker. Cambridge: Deighton, Bell, & Co., 1885. 488p.

Detailed descriptions of 1,107 titles, in Proctor order.

1226. —— ——. An index of such English books printed before the year 1600, as are now in the Library of Trinity College, Cambridge; to which is added, a list of the plays of Shakespeare, printed before 1623, in the Capell collection. Cambridge, 1847. 68p.

1227. Clarke, D. A. A handlist of books said to have been printed by John Day before 1557. London, 1950. Unpaged (Diploma in Librarianship, Univ. of London)

Lists 120 items; locations in 6 libraries; includes STC numbers.

1228. Clough, E. A. A short-title catalogue arranged geographically of books printed and distributed by printers, publishers and booksellers in the English provincial towns and in Scotland and Ireland up to and including the year 1700. London: Library Association, 1969. 119p.

Includes STC and Wing numbers.

1229. Duff, E. Gordon. English printing on vellum to the end of the year 1600. Aberdeen: Printed for the Bibliographical Society of Lancashire by the Aberdeen Univ. Pr., 1902. 20p.

Copies located in British and Continental libraries.

1230. —— and others. Hand-lists of books printed by London printers, 1501-1556. London: Blades, East & Blades for the Bibliographical Society, 1913. Various pagings.

Imprints arranged under individual presses; copies located; issued originally under title Hand-lists of English printers, 1501-1556. London, 1895-1913. 4pts.

1231. "Early Belfast printed books in Museum Library." Belfast Municipal Museum quarterly, 52 (June 1934), 8.

1232. Guildhall Library. "Additions to a List of books printed in the British Isles and of English books printed abroad before 1701, in Guildhall Library". Guildhall miscellany, 3 (1969), 85-89.

1233. ——. "A handlist of some of the 18th century broadsides in Guildhall Library." Guildhall miscellany, 3 (1970), 147-56.

1234. ——. A list of books printed in the British Isles and of English books printed before 1701 in the Guildhall Library, comp. by Kathleen I. Garrett. London: Library Committee, 1966-67. 2v.

Records 6,564 items.

1235. Hiscock, W. G. Christ Church holdings in Wing's STC 1641-1700 of books of which less than 5 copies are recorded in the United Kingdom. Oxford: Christ Church, 1956. 166p. Typescript.

Records about 6,700 items, exclusive of 1,200 in Hiscock's Supplement.

1236. —— The Christ Church supplement to Wing's Short-title catalogue, 1641-1700. Oxford: Holywell, 1956. 48p.

Contains about 1,200 additional entries.

1237. Hodnett, Edward. English woodcuts, 1480-1535. Oxford: Univ. Pr., 1935. 483p.

Lists 2,500 items with STC numbers and other locations; numerous facsimiles.

1238. John Rylands Library. Catalogue of books in the John Rylands Library, printed in England, Scotland and Ireland, and of books in English printed abroad to the end of the year 1640, comp. by Edward G. Duff. Manchester: Cornish, 1895. 147p.

Lists 159 items, arranged by printers.

1239. Johnson, Alfred Forbes. A catalogue of engraved and etched English title-pages, down to the death of William Faithorne, 1691. Oxford: Univ. Pr., Printed for the Bibliographical Society, 1934 (for 1933). 109p. + numerous facsimiles.

Includes STC numbers and some references to other locations.

1240. Lambeth Palace Library. An index of such English books, printed before the year MDC, as are now in the Archiepiscopal Library at Lambeth, by Samuel Roffey Maitland. London: Francis & John Rivington, 1845. 120p.

1241. Legg, Catherine M. A bibliography of the books printed at Reading during the eighteenth century. London, 1961. 346*l*. (Diploma in Librarianship, Univ. of London)

Lists 160 titles, with detailed bibliographical descriptions; copies located in 7 libraries.

1242. Milligan, Edward H. Darton imprints of the eighteenth century, a preliminary check-list. London, 1950. Unpaged. (Diploma in Librarianship, Univ. of London)

Copies located, chiefly in Friends House Library, London; 118 items.

1243. Oxford, University, Bodleian Library. A chronological list of Oxford books, 1681-1713. Oxford, 1954. 72p.

Based on notebook compiled by Falconer Madan; chronological listing; copies in Bodleian Library unless otherwise noted.

1244. ———, Wadham College Library. A short catalogue of books printed in England and English books printed abroad before 1641, in the Library of Wadham College, Oxford, comp. by H. A. Wheeler, 1918. London: Longmans, 1929. 102p.

1245. Pafort, Eloise. "A group of early Tudor schoolbooks." Library, ser. 4, 26 (1946), 227-61.

Wynkyn de Worde, Pynson, and other 15th- to 16th-century imprints located in British and American libraries.

1246. Pollard, A. W., and Redgrave, G. R. A short-title catalogue of books printed in England, Scotland and Ireland, and of English books printed abroad, 1475-1640. London: Bibliographical Society, 1926. 609p. Reprinted, 1950.

Locates copies in numerous libraries of about 26,500 items; known as "STC."

1247. Ramage, David. A finding-list of English books to 1640 in libraries in the British Isles (excluding the national libraries and the libraries of Oxford and Cambridge); based on the numbers in Pollard & Redgrave's Short-title catalogue of books printed in England, Scotland, and Ireland and English books printed abroad, 1475-1640. Durham: G. Bailes & Sons, 1958. 101p.

Records holdings of 144 libraries—a total of 14,000 items in 37,500 locations.

1248. St. Edmund's College, Old Hall. Catalogue of books in the libraries at St. Edmund's College, Old Hall, printed in England and of the books written by Englishmen printed abroad to the year 1640, comp. by Edwin Burton. Ware: Jennings & Bewley, 1902. 94p.

Lists 235 entries, chronologically.

1249. Shakespeare's Birthplace Library. English books published between 1500 and 1640, with S.T.C. references. Stratford-upon-Avon, 1955. 19*l*.

1250. Wing, Donald G. Short-title catalogue of books printed in England, Scotland, Ireland, Wales and British America, and of English books printed in other countries, 1641-1700. New York: For the Index Society by Columbia Univ. Pr., 1945-51. 3v.

Between 80,000 and 90,000 titles; continues Pollard and Redgrave's Short-title catalogue. Wing's standard practice is to locate 10 known copies—5 in Britain and 5 in America; British locations are principally British Museum, Bodleian, Cambridge, and 1 each in Scotland and Ireland.

French

1251. Archbishop Marsh's Library. A catalogue of books in the French language, printed in or before A.D. 1715, remaining in Archbishop Marsh's Library, Dublin, with an appendix relating to the Cashel Diocesan Library, by Newport J. D. White. Dublin: Univ. Pr., 1918. 184p.

1252. British Museum, Dept. of Printed Books. Short-title catalogue of books printed in France and of French books printed in other countries from 1470 to 1600 now in the British Museum. London: The Museum, 1924. 491p. Reprinted, 1966.

1253. ———. A short title catalogue of French books, 1601-1700, in the Library of the British Museum, by V. F. Goldsmith. Folkestone and London, 1969- . Issued in parts.

1254. Glasgow, University, Hunterian Library. French book art: the sixteenth century; an exhibition held in the Hunterian Library, University of Glasgow. Glasgow, 1966. 23p.

Records 78 items, annotated.

1255. Sheffield, University, Library. A short-title list of sixteenth century French books held in Sheffield University Library, by Sonia Thorley. Sheffield, 1967. 85*l*.

1256. Tilley, Arthur. "The early French books at the British Museum." Library, ser.4, 5 (1924), 161-68.

Summary and discussion based on British Museum's Short-title catalogue of books printed in France and of French books printed in other countries from 1470 to 1600 now in the British Museum (London, 1924).

German

1257. British Museum, Dept. of Printed Books. Short-title catalogue of books printed in the German-speaking countries and German books printed in other countries from 1455 to 1600 now in the British Museum, comp. by A. F. Johnson and Victor Scholderer. London, The Museum, 1962. 1,224p.

Lists about 35,000 items.

1258. Brucker, J. A bibliographical catalogue of seventeenth-century German books published in Holland. The Hague, Paris: Manton, 1971. 552p.

Records 623 works; copies located in numerous British, German, American, and other libraries.

1259. John Rylands Library. Catalogue of an exhibition of manuscripts and early printing originating in Germany, arranged to mark the official opening of the Goethe Institute, a German cultural institute for Northern England, in Manchester, November 1969. Manchester, 1969. 35p. + 9 plates.

1260. Ritchie, J. M. "German books in Glasgow and Edinburgh, 1500-1750." Modern language review, 57 (1962), 523-40.

Review of Edinburgh and Glasgow universities' library holdings.

Italian

1261. British Museum, Dept. of Printed Books. Short-title catalogue of books printed in Italy and of Italian books printed in other countries from 1465 to 1600, now in the British Museum. London: The Museum, 1958. 992p.

18,000 entries, with list of books destroyed during the war, 1939-45.

1262. National Book League. The Italian book, 1465-1900; catalogue of an exhibition held at the National Book League and the Italian Institute, arranged by J. Irving Davis. London, 1953. 117p.

Lists 364 items, with locations in public and private collections, British, Italian, and American.

1263. Oxford, University, Bodleian Library. Biblioteca italica, ossia catalogo de'testi a stampa citati nel vocaboloario degli accademici della Crusca, e di altri libri italiani piegevolie rari, gia posseduti dal C.A.M. ed ora passati in proprietà della Biblioteca Bodleiana. Oxford, 1852. 91p.

1264. Rhodes, D. E. "A rare printer at Rome: Ariottus de Trino." British Museum quarterly, 32 (1968), 74-75.

Description of 1521 work in British Museum.

1265. ———. "Seventeenth-century printing at Scigliano (Cosenza)." British Museum quarterly, 30 (1965), 1-2.

Description of 1614 item acquired by British Museum.

Netherlands

1266. British Museum, Dept. of Printed Books. Short-title catalogue of books printed in the Netherlands and Belgium, and of Dutch and Flemish books printed in other countries from 1470 to 1600, now in the British Museum. London: The Museum, 1965. 274p.

Entries for 5,000 books.

Portuguese

1267. British Museum, Dept. of Printed Books. Short-title catalogue of Portuguese books printed before 1601, now in the British Museum, by Henry Thomas. London, The Museum, 1940. 43p.

1268. ——— ———. "Short-title catalogues of Portuguese books and of Spanish-American books printed before 1601 now in the British Museum," by Henry Thomas. Revue hispanique, 65 (1925), 265-315. Reprinted. 1926. 55p.

Slavonic

1269. Tyrrell, E. P., and Simmons, J. S. G. "Slavonic books before 1700 in Cambridge libraries." Transactions of the Cambridge Bibliographical Society, 3 (1963), 382-400.

Descriptions and catalog of 68 titles and variant editions in the university, departmental, and college libraries at Cambridge.

1270. ——— ———. "Slavonic books of the eighteenth century in Cambridge libraries." Transactions of the Cambridge Bibliographical Society, 4 (1966), 225-45.

Descriptions and a catalog of 269 works in the university, departmental, and college libraries at Cambridge.

Spanish and Spanish-American

1271. British Museum, Dept. of Printed Books. Impresos castellanos del siglo XVI en el British Museum, by Francisco Aguilar Piñal. Madrid: C.S.I.C., 1970. 137p. (Cuadernos bibliográficos, no.24)

1272. ———. Short-title catalogue of books printed in Spain and of Spanish books printed elsewhere in Europe before 1601 now in the British Museum, by Henry Thomas. London: The Museum, 1921. 101p.

1273. ———. Short-title catalogue of Spanish, Spanish-American, and Portuguese books printed before 1601 in the British Museum, by Henry Thomas. London: The Museum, 1966. 169p.

Reprint of 3 catalogs issued in 1921, 1944, and 1940.

1274. ———. Short-title catalogue of Spanish-American books printed before 1601 now in the British Museum, by Henry Thomas. London: The Museum, 1944. 19p.

1275. National Library of Scotland. Spanish printed books. Edinburgh: H. M. Stationery Office, 1964. 16p.

Records 167 items, 1487-1952, drawn from National Library of Scotland's collections.

RARE BOOKS

1276. Anderson's College. La Bibliothèque Euing à Glasgow . . . Catalogue descriptif de quelques-uns de ses ouvrages les plus rares et les plus précieux, comp. by Arthur Hubens. (Extrait de la Rivista Musicale Italiana, tome xxiii, fasc.1) Torino, 1916. 30p.

1277. Birmingham Public Libraries. Centenary exhibition of important acquisitions to the Reference Library, 1861-1961. Birmingham, 1961. 32p.

Listing of 159 items, early, rare, or representative, including 24 incunabula and Shakespeareana.

1278. Black, Hester M. "Archbishop Law's books in Glasgow University Library." Bibliotheck, 3 (1961), 107-21; supplement, 5 (1968), 100-1.

List of 85 early works bequeathed by James Law (1560?-1632).

1279. British Museum, Dept. of Printed Books. Bibliotheca Grenvilliana; or bibliographical notices of rare and curious books, forming part of the library of the Right Hon. Thomas Grenville, by John Thomas Payne and Henry Foss. [pt.3, with a general index, by W. B. Rye. pts.2, 3 published by the British Museum.] London, 1842-72. 3pts.

1280. ———. Some notable books added to the Library of the British Museum during the Principal Keepership of Cecil Bernard Oldman, 1948-1959. Oxford: Univ. Pr., 1959. 44p.

1281. ———. Three hundred notable books added to the Library of the British Museum under the Keepership of Richard Garnett, 1890-1899, ed. by A. W. Pollard and R. G. C. Proctor. London: T. and A. Constable, 1899. 184p.

Detailed bibliographical descriptions of incunabula and later rare books.

1282. Cambridge, University, Library. A catalogue of printed books, manuscripts and University archives exhibited in the University Library, Cambridge . . . to celebrate the coronation of Her Majesty Queen Elizabeth II. Cambridge, 1953. 33p.

1283. ———, Merton Hall. The Rothschild Library; a catalogue of the collection of eighteenth-century printed books and manuscripts formed by Lord Rothschild. Cambridge: Univ. Pr., 1954. 2v.

Collection of rare books and manuscripts broadly representative of English 18th-century literature.

1284. ———, Pembroke College. "A list of books presented to Pembroke College, Cambridge, by different donors, during the 14th and 15th centuries," by G. E. Corrie. Cambridge Antiquarian Society, Antiquarian contributions, 2 (1864), 11-23.

1285. ———, St. John's College Library. A descriptive catalogue of the manuscripts and scarce books in the Library of St. John's College, Cambridge, by Morgan Cowie. Cambridge, 1842-43. 3pts. (Cambridge Antiquarian Society, Publications)

1286. Canterbury Royal Museum and Public Library. Treasures from Kent country houses; an exhibition. Canterbury, 1962. 22p.

1287. Dublin, University, Trinity College. Treasures of Trinity College, Dublin; an exhibition chosen from the College and its Library at Burlington House, London, comp. by F. J. E. Hurst. Dublin, 1961. 34p.

1288. Eton College Library. One hundred books in Eton College Library, by Robert Birley. Eton: The College, 1970. 43p.

Describes some of Eton's greatest treasures, ranging from 10th-century manuscript to modern press books.

1289. Friends of the National Libraries. Anniversary exhibition, 1931-1951, in the King's Library of the British Museum. Oxford: Univ. Pr. for the Friends of the National Libraries, 1951. 45p.

Annotated catalog of 142 famous books and manuscripts drawn from 25 British libraries and museums.

1290. Glasgow, University, Library. Dance of death collection; bequeathed to the Library of the University of Glasgow by William Gemmell; chronological list with full descriptive and bibliographical notes by Dr. William Gemmell, with prefatory notes on the origin of "The Dance of Death" and the Gemmell collection. Glasgow, 1919. 24*l.*

1291. Hove Corporation Public Library and Museum Committee. 123, a catalogue of rare and valuable books in the Hove Public Library, including incunabula, facsimiles, books from modern fine printing presses and fine bindings, comp. by Jack Dove. Hove, 1969. 45p.

Annotated list of 123 items.

1292. John Rylands Library. Catalogue of an exhibition of original editions of the principal English classics, shown in the Main Library from March to October, MCMX, by Henry Guppy. Manchester: Univ. Pr., 1910. 85p.

Detailed descriptions of famous works from c. 1400 to 1807.

1293. ———. Catalogue of the Festival of Britain exhibition. Manchester, 1951. 32p. + 16 plates.

Rare and early items drawn from the John Rylands collections.

1294. ———. Catalogue of the manuscripts, books, and bookbindings exhibited at the opening of the John Rylands Library. Manchester, 1899. 42p.

1295. ———. Catalogue of the printed books and manuscripts in the John Rylands Library, Manchester, ed. by E. Gordon Duff. Manchester: J. E. Cornish, 1899. 3v.

Alphabetical listing.

1296. Leeds, University, Brotherton Library. The Brotherton collection; a brief description. Leeds, 1953. 16p. + 16 plates.

Collection of rare books and manuscripts.

1297. ———. The Brotherton collection of books and manuscripts. Leeds, 1936. 58p.

Account of principal categories of rare works, including illuminated manuscripts, incunabula, and English literature.

1298. ———. A catalogue of ancient manuscripts and early printed books collected by Edward Allen, Baron Brotherton of Wakefield, comp. by John Alexander Symington. Leeds, 1931. 300p.

Collection now held by University of Leeds Library.

1299. Loughborough Technical College. The private press; handbook to an exhibition held in the School of Librarianship. Loughborough, 1968. 30p.

1300. Madan, Francis F. A new bibliography of the Eikon Basilike of King Charles the First, with a note on the authorship. Oxford: Univ. Pr., 1950. 200p. (Oxford Bibliographical Society publications, n.s., v.3, 1949)

Describes 81 editions, 1648-1904, and associated works; copies located in British Museum, Bodleian, Cambridge University Library, and occasionally elsewhere.

1301. Manchester Public Reference Library. Private press books in the Manchester Public Reference Library, ed. by Sidney Horrocks. Manchester: Libraries Committee, 1959-60. 2pts.

Records 743 items, alphabetically under presses, with descriptive notes.

1302. National Book League. Fine books from famous houses; an exhibition of printed books and manuscripts from National Trust Houses, org. by Robert Gathorne-Hardy. London, 1958. 48p.

Annotated catalog of 200 items, with locations in 10 National Trust Houses.

1303. National Library of Scotland. Advocates' Library notable accessions up to 1925, a book of illustrations. Edinburgh, 1965. 125 plates.

1304. ———. Notable accessions since 1925: a book of illustrations. Edinburgh: H. M. Stationery Office, 1965. 120 plates.

1305. ———. Treasures from Scottish libraries: catalogue of an exhibition held in the Library of Trinity College, Dublin. Edinburgh, 1964. 42p. + 16 plates.

Includes descriptions of 2 block books, 39 incunabula, and a number of 16th-century printed books.

1306. National Library of Wales. Catalogue of broadsides, posters, paintings, prints, drawings, maps, manuscripts, books, etc., in the Exhibition Gallery of the National Library. Aberystwyth, 1931. 80p.

1307. ———. Catalogue of drawings, paintings, manuscripts, rare books, fine bindings, etc., in the Exhibition Gallery of the National Library of Wales. Aberystwyth, 1926. 56p.

1308. ———. Catalogue of paintings, drawings, maps, manuscripts, rare books, fine bindings, etc., in the

Exhibition Gallery . . . 1930, 2d ed. Aberystwyth, 1930. 71p.

1309. St. Andrews, University, Library. Catalogue of the exhibition of some historic treasures of the University of St. Andrews, Martinmas Term, 1961, by Robert C. Carnie. Dundee: Queen's College, 1961. 44p.

1310. St. Dunstan's Library. A catalogue of some printed books and manuscripts at St. Dunstan's, Regent's Park, and Aldenham House, Herts., collected by Henry Hucks Gibbs. London, 1888. 199p.

Principally pre-1700 imprints, but includes some privately printed and rare books of later date.

1311. Sandars, Samuel. An annotated list of books printed on vellum to be found in the University and College libraries at Cambridge; with an appendix containing a list of works referring to the bibliography of Cambridge libraries. Cambridge: Cambridge Antiquarian Society, 1878. 80p.

1312. Victoria and Albert Museum. List of accessions to the catalogue of the Library. Supplement: Catalogue of miniature books in the Library, including royal loans, comp. by A. J. Sloggett. London: H. M. Stationery Office, 1971. 11*l*.

1313. Vosper, Robert. "Rare books in redbrick cases." Book collector, 11 (1962), 21-34.

Survey of rare-book collections in British university libraries other than Oxford, Cambridge, and London.

BOOKBINDING

1314. Aberdeen, University, Library. Some early bookbindings in the Aberdeen University Library, by Walter B. Menzies. Aberdeen: Univ. Pr., 1938. 7p. + 13 plates.

Examples range from 1481 to 1545.

1315. Barber, Giles. "Bindings from Oxford libraries; the Vice-Chancellor's official New Testament, Oxford 1721." Bodleian Library record, 8 (1970), 191-95.

1316. ——, and Rogers, David. "Bindings from Oxford libraries; a 'duodo' pastiche binding by Charles Lewis." Bodleian Library record, 8 (1969), 138-44.

1317. —— ——. "Bindings from Oxford libraries; some seventeenth-century straw bindings." Bodleian Library record, 8 (1971), 262-65.

1318. Bibliotheca Lindesiana. List of manuscripts and examples of metal and ivory bindings; exhibited to the

Bibliographical Society. Aberdeen: Univ. Pr., 1898. 46p.

Lists and describes 265 items.

1319. Black, Hester M. "Notes on some bindings in Glasgow University Library." Bibliotheck, 4 (1965), 181-99.

Descriptions of 12 early bindings, 16th-18th centuries.

1320. British Museum. Early stamped book-bindings in the British Museum; descriptions of 385 blind-stamped bindings of the XIIth-XVth centuries in the Departments of Manuscripts and Printed Books, mainly by the late W. H. James Weale. London, 1922. 171p. + 32 prints.

1321. ——. English bookbindings in the British Museum; illustrations of sixty-three examples selected on account of their beauty or historical interest, with introduction and descriptions by William Younger Fletcher. London: Kegan Paul, 1895. 66 plates, unpaged.

1322. ——. Foreign bookbindings in the British Museum; illustrations of sixty-three examples selected on account of their beauty or historical interest, with introduction and descriptions by William Younger Fletcher. London: Regan Paul, 1896. XXIVp. + 65 plates.

1323. ——, Dept. of Printed Books. Bookbindings from the library of Jean Grolier: a loan exhibition. London, The Museum, 1965. 78p. + 149 plates.

1324. —— ——. Royal English bookbindings in the British Museum. London: The Museum, 1957. 8p. + 16 plates.

1325. —— ——, King's Library. Oriental bookbindings and book covers; an exhibition held in the King's Library, 1962. London, The Museum [1962]. 23p.

1326. Cambridge, University, Library. Bindings in Cambridge libraries; seventy-two plates, with notes by G. D. Hobson. Cambridge: Univ. Pr., 1929. 179p. + 72 plates.

Locations noted in various Cambridge University libraries.

1327. Chester Beatty Library. Some early bindings from Egypt in the Chester Beatty Library, by Berthe van Regemorter. Dublin: Hodges Figgis, 1958. 26p. + 13 plates.

Description of 8 wooden boards (or pairs of boards) believed to have been bindings and 3 codices, dating from early in the Christian era.

1328. Craig, Maurice. Irish bookbindings, 1600-1800. London: Cassell & Co., 1954. 47p. + 58 plates.

Locates copies of the 186 examples recorded.

1329. Gibson, Strickland. "Bookbindings in the Buchanan collection." Bodleian Library record, 2 (1941), 6-12.

In Bodleian Library.

1330. ———. "Douce bookbindings." Bodleian quarterly record, 7 (1934), 373-75.

In Bodleian Library.

1331. ———. Early Oxford bindings. Oxford: Printed for the Bibliographical Society at the Oxford Univ. Pr., 1903. 69p. + 40 plates.

Detailed descriptions of 28 bindings c. 1460-c. 1647; locations in Oxford and other libraries.

1332. Glasgow, University, Hunterian Library. British bookbindings, 16th-19th century; an exhibition held in the Hunterian Library, University of Glasgow. Glasgow, 1970. 23p.

Records 108 items, annotated.

1333. Hobson, G. D. Blind-stamped panels in the English book-trade, c. 1485-1555. London: Bibliographical Society, 1944. 111p. + 8 plates.

References to locations of examples described.

1334. ———. English binding before 1500. Cambridge: Univ. Pr., 1929. 58p. + 55 plates.

Copies located in British and French libraries.

1335. John Rylands Library. "Exhibition of library bindings." Bulletin of the John Rylands Library, Manchester, 54 (1972), 241-45.

Description of exhibition illustrating characteristic European styles from 15th to 19th century.

1336. London, University, Library. Historical and armorial bookbindings exhibited in the University Library; descriptive catalogue by Reginald Arthur Rye and Muriel Sinton Quinn. London: Univ., 1937. 48p. + 11 plates.

Lists and describes in detail 83 specimens.

1337. Mitchell, William Smith. "Blairs College bindings." Aberdeen University review, 33 (1949), 23-29.

Includes descriptions of early 16th-century bindings.

1338. ———. "German bindings in Aberdeen University Library: iconographic index, and indices of initials, binders, and dates." Library, ser.5, 17 (1962), 46-55.

1339. ———. A history of Scottish bookbinding, 1432 to 1650. Edinburgh and London: Oliver & Boyd, 1955. 150p. + 48 plates.

Records and describes 113 examples, all in Aberdeen University Library except for 2 in Blairs College Library and 2 in Edinburgh University Library.

1340. ———. "Some German bindings in Aberdeen University Library." In: Festschrift Ernst Kyriss. Stuttgart: Hettler, 1961, p.175-90.

Detailed descriptions, accompanied by 10 plates.

1341. Newcastle upon Tyne, University, Library. British signed bindings in the Library of King's College, Newcastle upon Tyne, by W. S. Mitchell. Newcastle upon Tyne, 1954. 28p. (King's College Library publications, no.1)

Records examples of work of about 150 binders.

1342. Nixon, Howard M. "Bookbindings acquired by the Department of Printed Books, 1952-62." British Museum quarterly, 26 (1962), 11-17.

Descriptions of notable examples in British Museum.

1343. Oldham, J. Basil. Blind panels of English binders. Cambridge: Univ. Pr., 1958. 56p. + 67 plates.

Occasional references to locations of copies.

1344. ———. English blind-stamped bindings. Cambridge: Univ. Pr., 1952. 73p. + 61 plates.

Fifteenth to 17th century; references to locations.

1345. Oxford, University, Bodleian Library. Fine bindings, 1500-1700, from Oxford libraries; catalogue of an exhibition. Oxford, 1968. 144p. + 111 plates.

Includes 240 exhibits representing holdings of Bodleian and College libraries.

1346. ———. Gold-tooled bookbindings. Oxford, 1951. 6p. + 24 plates. (Bodleian picture books, no.2)

Examples drawn from Bodleian Library's collection.

1347. ———. Historic bindings in the Bodleian Library, with reproductions of twenty-four of the finest bindings, by W. S. Brassington. London, 1891. 63p.

1348. ———. Scottish "wheel" and "herring-bone" bindings in the Bodleian Library; an illustrated hand-list, by M. J. Sommerlad. Oxford: Oxford Bibliographical Society, 1967. 10p. + plates. (Occasional publications, no.1)

1349. ———. Some notable Bodleian bindings, 12th to 18th centuries, by S. Gibson. Oxford, 1901-4. 11p. + 31 plates. 3pts.

1350. ———. Textile and embroidered bindings. Oxford, 1971. 30p. (Bodleian picture books, special series, no.2)

1351. Powell, Roger. "Some early bindings from Egypt in the Chester Beatty Library: additional notes." Library, 5th ser., 18 (1963), 218-23.

Supplements Berthe van Regemorter's Some early bindings from Egypt in the Chester Beatty Library.

1352. Shrewsbury School Library. Shrewsbury School Library bindings; catalogue raisonné, by J. Basil Oldham. Oxford: Univ. Pr. for the Librarian of Shrewsbury School, 1943. 183p. + 62 plates.

Examples of fine bindings, 15th to 19th century.

1353. Thomas, Henry. Early Spanish bookbindings, XI-XV centuries. London: Printed for the Bibliographical Society at the Univ. Pr., Oxford, 1939 (for 1936). 65p. + 100 plates.

Locations in Continental, British, and American libraries.

1354. Victoria and Albert Museum. Bookbindings, by John P. Harthan, 2d ed. London: H. M. Stationery Office, 1961. 33p. + 79 plates. (Victoria and Albert Museum, Illustrated booklet, no.2)

Based on the museum's collection.

1355. ———. Bookbindings and rubbings of bindings in the National Art Library, South Kensington Museum, by W. H. James Weale. London: H. M. Stationery Office, 1894-98. 2v.

1356. ———. An ordinary of British armorial bookbindings in the Clements collection, Victoria and Albert Museum, by Denis Woodfield. London, 1958. 192p.

Attempt to provide an index to Clements collection and a guide to British armorial bindings generally.

1357. ——— Library. Armorial bookbindings from the Clements collection in the Library of the Victoria and Albert Museum, by J. P. Harthan. London, 1961. 18p.

1358. Weale, W. H. James. Bookbindings and rubbings in the Victoria and Albert Museum. London: Holland, 1962. 329p.

Briefly describes 325 bindings and 915 rubbings in Museum.

BOOK ILLUSTRATION

1359. British Museum, Dept. of Printed Books. English book illustration 966-1846. London: The Museum, 1965. 23p. + 8 plates.

pt.1, illuminated manuscripts; pt.2, illustrated printed books.

1360. Dodgson, Campbell, "Early woodcuts [from the Willshire collection] in the Guildhall Library." Print collectors quarterly, 23 (1936), 243-59.

1361. Edinburgh, University, Library. The art of illustration; an exhibition of 15th-19th century printed books. Edinburgh, 1971.

Lists 42 works drawn from library's collections.

1362. Ferguson, F. S. "Additions to Title-page borders, 1485-1640." Library, ser.4, 17 (1936), 264-93.

Records 300 items.

1363. Glasgow, University, Hunterian Library. Emblem books: an exhibition of books and manuscripts held in the Hunterian Library. Glasgow, 1965. 38p.

Lists 119 annotated titles, 1488-1694.

1364. ———. Emblems and entrances: an exhibition of woodcut, engraved and etched title pages of English books, 1500-1700, held in the Hunterian Library, University of Glasgow. Glasgow, 1970. 17p.

A catalog of 83 items, annotated.

1365. Harris College. Illustrated books and books on illustration. Preston, 1963. 48p. + index.

1366. Kristeller, Paul. Early Florentine woodcuts, with an annotated list of Florentine illustrated books. London: Kegan Paul, Trench, Trübner, 1897. 184p. + 123p. of plates. Reprinted, 1968.

Locations in 47 Continental and British libraries; describes 439 items.

1367. Morris, J. M. "A check-list of prints made at Cambridge by Peter Spendelowe Lambourn (1722-1774)." Cambridge Bibliographical Society transactions, 3 (1962), 295-312.

Locates copies of 94 items in book illustrations in British Museum and Cambridge libraries.

1368. Thomson, Frances M. "A Newcastle collection of wood blocks." Book collector, 17 (1968), 443-57.

Describes collection of about 1,000 wood block illustrations, mostly belonging to 19th century, in University Library, Newcastle upon Tyne.

1369. Victoria and Albert Museum Library. "Illustrated fables; a catalogue of the Library's holdings; part I, other than Aesop," by A. S. Hobbs. Victoria and Albert Museum Library monthly list, Jan. 1972, p.68-89.

1370. ———. List of accessions to the catalogue of the Library: Victorian books exhibition: illustrated books. (Children's books.) London: H. M. Stationery Office, 1967. 63*l.*

1371. ———. "The remaining uncatalogued portion of the Harrod bequest of illustrated books." Monthly list, April 1969, supplement. 10p.

1372. ———. Victorian books exhibition; illustrated books, series 1; a list comprising exhibited books and additional works. London, 1967. 33*l.*

BOOKPLATES

1373. National Library of Wales. Catalogue (with notes) of the Aneurin Williams collection of book plates, by Herbert Millingchamp Vaughan. Aberystwyth, 1938. 142p.

Contains 854 entries, recording bookplates associated with numerous noted persons.

Philosophy and Psychology

General

1374. Aberdeen, University, Library. Catalogue of the books in the Logic Class Library. Aberdeen: Univ. 1906. 13p.

Works in philosophy and related fields.

1375. Cambridge, University, Gonville and Caius College Library. Catalogue of a collection of books on logic presented to the Library by John Venn. Cambridge, 1889. 125p.

List of 1,124 volumes with index of authors.

1376. Dwyer, R. A. "Old French translations of Boethius' Consolatio philosophiae in the National Library of Wales." National Library of Wales journal, 14 (1966), 486-88.

1377. Gateshead Public Libraries. A classified catalogue of the books in the philosophical sections of the Lending and Reference Departments of the Central Public Library, comp. by Robert Lillie. Gateshead, 1945. 35p.

1378. Glasgow, University, Hunterian Library. An exhibition of books on witch-craft and demonology. Glasgow, 1966. 26p.

Annotated catalog of 76 works drawn mainly from Library's Ferguson collection.

1379. Murphy, Gwendolen. A bibliography of English character-books, 1608-1700. Oxford: Oxford Univ. Pr. for the Bibliographical Society, 1925. 179p.

Chronological arrangement; copies located in British Museum and Bodleian Library.

1380. Oxford, University, Pembroke College Library. Catalogue of the Aristotelian and philosophical portions of the Library of the late Henry William Chandler. Oxford, 1891. 182p.

Contains early editions of Aristotle and other philosophers.

1381. Philosophical Institution. Catalogue of the Library of the Philosophical Institution, Edinburgh. Edinburgh: T. & A. Constable, 1881. 415p. Supplement. 1886. 44p.

1382. Royal Philosophical Society. Catalogue of books in the Library of the Royal Philosophical Society of Glasgow, prep. by John Robertson. Glasgow: Robert Anderson, 1904. 368p.

1383. Speculative Society of Edinburgh. Catalogue of pamphlets, and guide to the manuscripts and printed books, comp. by R. M. Maxtone Graham. Edinburgh, 1957. 50p.

1384. Wiener Library. Prejudice, racist-religious-nationalist. London: Institute of Contemporary History, 1971. 385p. (Catalogue series, no.5)

Arrangement chiefly geographical, preceded by lists of reference books and general works.

1385. York, University, J. B. Morrell Library. Select list of reference and bibliographical material in philosophy, religion, the arts, literature and language. York, 1969. 125p. (Library guides, no.5)

1386. Yorkshire Philosophical Society. Catalogue of books in the Library of the Yorkshire Philosophical Society. York, 1900. 103p.

Psychology

1387. Birkbeck College Library. Occupational psychology; handlist of books in the College Library, comp. by A. E. Cooban. London, 1971. 83p. (Library publication, no.42)

1388. Central Association for Mental Welfare. Library catalogue of the Central Association for Mental Welfare. London, 1925. 28p.

1389. Institute for Research into Mental Retardation. Serials in the Library. London, 1967. 8p.

1390. Scott, J. W., and Smith, F. V. "A handlist of psychology periodicals in the learned libraries of Great Britain." Journal of documentation, 6 (1950), 152-66.

Locates 179 titles in 62 libraries; includes data on holdings.

Psychical Research

1391. London, University, Council for Psychical Investigation Library. Short-title catalogue of the Research Library from 1472 A.D. to the present day. London: The Council, 1935. 112p.

Lists about 2,500 items; supplement to 1929 catalog.

1392. ———— ————. "Short-title catalogue of works on psychical research," comp. by Harry Price. Proceedings of the National Laboratory of Psychical Research, London, 1, pt.2 (April 1929), 67-422.

Lists about 10,000 volumes.

1393. ————, Council for Psychical Investigation Research Library. Exhibition of rare works from the Research Library of the University of London Council for Psychical Investigation from 1490 A.D. to the present day. London, 1934. 48p.

1394. National Laboratory of Psychical Research. Short-title catalogue of works on psychical research, spiritualism, magic, psychology, legerdemain, and other methods of deception, charlatanism, witchcraft, and technical works for the scientific investigati no of alleged abnormal phenomena, from circa 1450 A.D. to 1929 A.D., comp. by Harry Price. London: Society for Psychical Research, 1929. 422p. Supplement. 1935. 112p.

1395. Society for Psychical Research. Library catalogue, comp. by Theodore Besterman. Glasgow: Robert Maclehose, 1927. 368p. (Proceedings of the Society for Psychical Research, v.37) Supplements 1-4. 1927-33.

Religion

General

1396. Boehmer, Edward. Bibliotheca Wiffeniana; Spanish reformers of two centuries from 1520; their lives and writings. Strassburg and London: Trübner, 1874. 3v.

Locates copies in British and German libraries.

1397. Brassey Institute Library. An alphabetical index to the printed sermons in the Reference Library, comp. by Edward H. Marshall. Hastings: F. J. Parsons, 1894. 98p.

1398. Hammersmith Public Libraries. A guide to the religious serials and periodicals held in the Metropolitan special collections by the London Borough of Hammersmith Public Libraries. London: Hammersmith Central Library, 1971. 16p. + index.

1399. Holland, Cedric George. The records of the Corporations of the Sons of the Clergy (deposited in the London County Record Office); a catalogue. London, 1962. 2v.

1400. John Rylands Library. Catalogue of the manuscripts and printed books exhibited on the occasion of the visit of the National Council of the Evangelical Free Churches. Manchester, 1905. 38p.

Lists Biblical manuscripts, early printed Bibles, works of the Reformers, early devotional books, etc.

1401. Kirchberger, C. "Bodleian manuscripts relating to the spiritual life." Bodleian Library record, 3 (1951), 155-64.

Discussion of 16th-18th-century manuscripts in Bodleian collections dealing with spiritual life.

1402. Kraft, Robert A., and Tripolitis, Antonia. "Some uncatalogued papyri of theological and other interest in the John Rylands Library." Bulletin of the John Rylands Library, 51 (1968), 137-63. Reprinted. 27p.

1403. Lambeth Palace Library. Christian unity, the Anglican initiative; catalogue of an exhibition of books and manuscripts held in the Library of Lambeth Palace. London: S.P.C.K., 1966. 23p.

Annotated list of 52 items.

1404. London Spiritualist Alliance Library. Catalogue of the Library of the London Spiritualist Alliance. London, 1931. 209p.

1405. Newcastle upon Tyne, University, Library. Lives of the saints; a description of MS. 1 in the University Library, Newcastle upon Tyne, by Barbara Catherine Raw. Newcastle upon Tyne, 1961. 53p.

Thirteenth-century manuscript once belonging to Benedictine Abbey of St. Mary.

1406. Selly Oak Colleges Library. English theological books 1939-1945, by Leonard Jolley. Birmingham, 1946. 14p.

1407. Southampton, University, Parkes Library. The Parkes Library; its formation and transfer to the University of Southampton. Southampton, 1965. Unpaged.

"A centre for the study of relations between the Jewish and non-Jewish worlds."

1408. Spinney, Gordon H. "Cheap repository tracts: Hazard and Marshall edition." Library, ser.4, 20 (1939), 295-340.

Bibliography of religious tracts, issued 1795-98, by Hannah More and others; copies located in British Museum and public libraries of Bath and Bristol; lists 187 items.

1409. Standing Conference of Theological and Philosophical Libraries in London. A directory of libraries and special collections in London devoted to the subjects of religion and philosophy and allied fields. London, 1951. 20p.

Lists 40 institutions with data on resources and services.

1410. Theosophical Society in England. Lending library catalogue. London, 1929. 158p. Supplement, 1935. 43p. Supplement, 1939. 36p.

1411. Wormald, Francis. "Some illustrated manuscripts of the lives of the saints." Bulletin of the John Rylands Library, 35 (1952), 248-66. Reprinted. 1952. 21p.
   Survey of examples in British, Continental, and American libraries.

1412. Wright, Gillian Mary. A bibliography of a collection of sermons of the seventeenth and early eighteenth centuries in the Chapter Library of St. George's Chapel, Windsor. London, 1960. 251l. (Diploma in Librarianship, Univ. of London)
   Alphabetically arranged by authors; includes STC and Wing numbers.

Theological Library Catalogs

1413. Aberdeen Christian Evidence Library. Rules and catalogue of the Aberdeen Christian Evidence Library. Aberdeen, 1847. 12p.

1414. Aberdeen, University, Library. Catalogue of the books in the Students' Theological Library. [Compiled by Mary Robertson.] Aberdeen: Univ. Pr., 1901. 96p.
   Alphabetical list by authors.

1415. Bangor Cathedral Library. A catalogue of books in the Bangor Cathedral Library, ed. by Charles W. F. Jones. Bangor: Nixon & Jarvis, 1872. 58p.

1416. ———. Catalogue of the Bangor Cathedral Library, comp. by E. Gwynne Jones and J. R. V. Johnston. Bangor, 1961. 172p.
   Now deposited in University College of North Wales. Of 4,500 volumes in collection, 1,100 were printed before 1700; many Welsh imprints included.

1417. Carter, Alan. Catalogue of the George Hay Forbes Library in the Theological College of the Episcopal Church in Scotland. London, 1967. 175l. (Thesis, Library Association Fellowship)
   Primarily a theological collection.

1418. Cartmel Priory Church Library. The ancient library in Cartmel Priory Church; history by Samuel Taylor; catalogue by David Ramage, 2d ed. Durham: Univ. Library, 1959. 37p. (Durham Univ. Library publications, no.3)

Includes 123 English books before 1640 and 48 between 1640 and 1700; adds STC and Wing numbers.

1419. Cathedral Church of Durham. Catalogi veteres librorum Ecclesiae Cathedralis Dunelm . . . including catalogues of the Library of the Abbey of Hulm, and of the mss. preserved in the Library of Bishop Cosin, at Durham, ed. by Beriah Botfield. Durham, 1838. 238p. (Surtees Society publications, v.7)

1420. Church of England, Central Council for the Care of Churches. The parochial libraries of the Church of England; report of a committee appointed by the Central Council for the Care of Churches to investigate the number and condition of parochial libraries belonging to the Church of England; with an historical introduction, notes on early printed books and their care and an alphabetical list of parochial libraries past and present. London: Faith, 1959. 125p.

1421. Colchester Public Library. A catalogue of the Harsnett Library at Colchester in which are included a few books presented to the town by various donors since 1631, comp. by Gordon Goodwin. London: Richard Amer, 1888. 170p.
   Catalog of remains of library of Archbishop Samuel Harsnett (1561-1631), bequeathed to Corporation of Colchester.

1422. Derry and Raphoe, Dioceses. Catalogue of the books in the Library of the United Dioceses of Derry and Raphoe. Londonderry: Sentinel Office, 1880. 43p.

1423. Diocesan Church House Library, Liverpool. Classified catalogue of the Library with full author and subject indexes, ed. by G. Harford. Liverpool, 1903. 131p.

1424. Edinburgh, University, Library. Catalogue of the books in the Library belonging to the students of divinity in the University of Edinburgh. Edinburgh, 1775. 54p. Appendix. 6p.

1425. ———, Theological Library. Constitution of the Theological Library in the University of Edinburgh. Edinburgh: A. Balfour, 1829. 266p. Supplement, 1833. 40p.

1426. Ely Cathedral Library. Catalogue of books contained in the Library belonging to the Dean and Chapter in the Cathedral Church of Ely. Ely: T. A. Hills & Son, 1884.
   Transferred to Cambridge University.

1427. Ely Cathedral Church. Catalogus librorum qui in Bibliotheca Cathedralis Eliensis adservantur. London: B. Macmillan, 1815. 138p.
   Transferred to Cambridge University.

1428. Evangelical Library. Larger representative catalogue. London, 1949. 103p.

Subject arrangement.

1429. Exeter Cathedral Library. The Library of Exeter Cathedral, by L. J. Lloyd, with a description of the archives by A. M. Woodcock. Exeter, 1956. 23p.

1430. General Assembly's College. Catalogue of the books in the Fleming Stevenson Memorial Library of the General Assembly's College, Belfast. Belfast: John A. Murphy, 1887. 240p.

Predominantly relating to religion and theology.

1431. Greenslade, S. L. "The contents of the Library of Durham Cathedral Priory." Transactions of the Architectural and Archaeological Society of Durham and Northumberland, 11 (1965), 347-69.

Descriptive essay.

1432. Hereford All Saints' Church Library. Catalogue of the books in All Saints' Church, Hereford, bequeathed by Dr. William Brewster, 1655-1715, by F. C. Morgan. Hereford, 1964? 92l.

1433. Hereford Cathedral Libraries. Hereford Cathedral libraries; including the chained library and the vicars' choral library, and muniments, by F. C. M. and P. E. Morgan. Hereford, 1970. 40p.

1434. Hereford Cathedral Library. Hereford Cathedral Library (including the "Chained Library"), its history and contents, with appendix of early printed books, by F. C. Morgan, 3d ed. Hereford: The Cathedral, 1958. 32p.

1435. ———. Hereford Cathedral Library . . . and . . . All Saints Church chained library. Hereford, 1963. 78p.

1436. ———. Hereford Cathedral; a short account of the chained library, by James Poulter, rev. ed. Hereford, 1949. Unpaged.

1437. James, Montague Rhodes. The ancient libraries of Canterbury and Dover; the catalogues of the libraries of Christ Church Priory and St. Augustine's Abbey at Canterbury and of St. Martin's Priory at Dover; now first collected and published with an introduction and identifications of the extant remains. Cambridge: Univ. Pr., 1903. 552p.

1438. Ker, N. R. "Cathedral libraries." Library history, 1 (Autumn 1967), 38-45.

Discussion of history and present state of British cathedral libraries.

1439. Lamb, J. A. "Theological and philosophical libraries in Scotland." Library Association record, 61 (1959), 327-33.

Reviews history and describes collections in libraries connected with Church of Scotland, other denominations, and universities.

1440. Lichfield Cathedral Church Library. Catalogue of books in the Cathedral Library, Lichfield. Lichfield: T. G. Lomax, 1871. 88p.

1441. ———. A catalogue of the printed books and manuscripts in the Library of the Cathedral Church of Lichfield. London: Sotheran, 1888. 120p.

1442. Lincoln Cathedral Library. Catalogue of foreign books in the Chapter Library of Lincoln Cathedral, comp. by William Herbert Kynaston. London: Oxford Univ. Pr., 1937. 82p.

Arranged by languages; 16th- and 17th-century books.

1443. ———. A catalogue of the books and manuscripts in the Library of Lincoln Cathedral, by G. F. Apthorp. Lincoln: W. & B. Brooke, 1859. 288p. + index of authors. Supplementary catalogue. 1890. 45p.

1444. Miles, Patricia J. A short-title catalogue of books printed before 1550 in Wells Cathedral Library. London, 1956. 33p. (Diploma in Librarianship, Univ. of London)

Lists 77 titles; composed principally of theological works printed on the Continent.

1445. Newcastle upon Tyne, Cathedral Church, Chapter Library. Catalogue of the Newcastle Chapter Library and of the Churchwardens' or Old Parish Library, at the Cathedral Church of St. Nicholas, Newcastle upon Tyne, by E. B. Hicks and G. E. Richmond. Newcastle upon Tyne: Printed for the Chapter, 1890. 46p.

1446. ———, Church Institute, Archdeacon Sharp's Library. Catalogue of Archdeacon Sharp's Library, by David G. Ramage. Durham: Lord Crewe's Trustees, 1935. 93p.

1447. Norwich Cathedral Library. A catalogue of the Library belonging to the Dean and Chapter of Norwich. Norwich: John Stacy, 1836. 86p.

1448. Read, E. Anne. A checklist of books, catalogues and periodical articles relating to the cathedral libraries of England. Oxford: Oxford Bibliographical Society, Bodleian Society, 1970. 59p. (The Society's Occasional publications, no.6)

1449. Rider, R. C. "The Library of St. Paul's Cathedral, Dundee." SLA news, 42 (July-Aug. 1960), 5-11.

History and description of library's collections.

1450. Ripon Cathedral Church Library. "Ripon Minster Library and its founder," by J. T. Fowler. Yorkshire archaeological and topographical journal, 2 (1873), 371-402.

Contains list of printed books, manuscripts, etc.

1451. Rochester Cathedral Church Library. A catalogue of the books in the Cathedral Library of the Dean and Chapter of Rochester. Rochester: William Wildash, 1839. 58p.

1452. ———. A catalogue of the books in the Cathedral Library of the Dean and Chapter of Rochester. Rochester: Caddel & Son, 1860. 54p.

1453. St. Albans, Cathedral Church, Library. The Cathedral Church of St. Alban; alphabetical catalogue of the Library. St. Alban's, 1903. 17p.

1454. St. Asaph Cathedral Library. A catalogue of books in the St. Asaph Cathedral Library, by William Morton. London: T. Richards, 1878. 87p.

Lists 1,513 titles.

1455. St. Edmund Abbey at Bury. On the Abbey of S. Edmund at Bury: I The Library; II The Church, by Montague Rhodes James. Cambridge: Cambridge Antiquarian Society, 1895. 220p.

Section listing "The extant remains of the Library," p.42-107.

1456. St. Owen Parish Church. Catalogue of books in the Library of the Parish Church of St. Owen, Bromham, Bedfordshire, with some notes thereon, comp. by E. C. Cooper. Bromham: D. Cooper, 1961. 65p.

1457. St. Paul's Cathedral Library. A catalogue of Bibles, rituals, and rare books; works relating to London and especially to St. Paul's Cathedral, including a large collection of Paul's cross sermons; maps, plans, and views of London and of St. Paul's Cathedral, by W. Sparrow Simpson. London: Elliot Stock, 1893. 281p.

1458. St. Peter's Cathedral Library. A catalogue of some of the more rare and interesting books of theology, chiefly of the Elizabethan age, in the Minster Library, Peterborough. Cambridge: J.Thorpe, 1842. 42p.

1459. Salisbury Cathedral Church. A catalogue of the Library of the Cathedral Church of Salisbury. [Manuscripts, by Maunde Thompson; Printed books, by J. M. Lakin.] London: Spottiswoode & Co., 1880. 334p.

In 2pts.: 187 manuscripts listed and described; 3,866 volumes of printed books, in alphabetical order.

1460. Scottish Episcopal Church Library. Catalogue of the Scottish Episcopal Church Library. Edinburgh: Robert Anderson, 1863. 224p.

1461. Shropshire County Library. Catalogue of books from parochial libraries in Shropshire, prepared by the Shropshire County Library with the co-operation of the Diocesan authorities of Hereford and Lichfield and of the Walker Trust. London: Mansell, 1971. 607p.

Books listed alphabetically by author and title; locations in 11 libraries.

1462. Smith, Margaret S. "Printed catalogues of books and manuscripts in cathedral libraries: England and Wales." Library, 5th ser., 2 (1947), 11-13.

List of published catalogs.

1463. Society of Biblical Archaeology. Catalogue of the Library of the Society of Biblical Archaeology. London, 1876. 109p.

1464. Tallon, Maura. Church in Wales Diocesan libraries.Westmeath, Ireland: Athlone Printing Works, 1962. 87p.

Account of history and collections of 5 cathedral libraries (Bangor, Brecon, Llandaff, St. Asaph, St. David's), with short lists of individual printed and manuscript books of importance; collections relate mainly to theology and religious controversy, classical texts, and Welsh and Irish books of 16th and 17th centuries.

1465. ———. Hereford Cathedral Library. Dublin, 1963. 80p.

Bibliographical account of one of most notable English cathedral libraries, of its chained library, 227 manuscripts of 9th to 15th century, and 50 incunabula (including 2 Caxtons).

1466. Worcester Cathedral Library. A catalogue of the printed books in the Worcester Cathedral Library, by Maurice Day. Oxford: Printed by E. Baxter, 1880. 226p.

1467. ———. The Library of printed books in Worcester Cathedral, by Canon J. M. Wilson. London: Alexander Moring, 1911. 33p. (Reprinted from The Library, Jan. 1911)

History of library and discussion of holdings.

1468. World Congress of Faiths. Library catalogue. London, 1957. 28p.

Classified by subjects.

1469. York, Dean and Chapter, Library. A catalogue of the printed books in the Library of the Dean and

Chapter of York, comp. by James Raine. York: John Sampson, 1896. 459p.

Predominantly theological in character.

Church Archives

1470. Addy, John. "The archives of the Archdeaconry of Richmond." Archives, no.33 (1965), 25-33.

Describes records now principally deposited in Leeds Central Library.

1471. Bristol Diocese. A catalogue of the records of the Bishop and Archdeacons and of the Dean and Chapter, comp. by Isabel M. Kirby. Bristol: Bristol Corp., 1970. 217p.

1472. British Records Association. The records of the Established Church in England, excluding parochial records, by Dorothy M. Owen. Cambridge, 1970. 46p.

1473. Buckinghamshire Record Office. Records of the Archdeaconry of Buckingham. Aylesbury, 1961. 28*l.* (Occasional publications, 2)

1474. Canterbury, Diocese. An inventory of the Parish registers and other records of the Diocese of Canterbury, ed. by C. Eveleigh Woodruff. Canterbury: Gibbs & Sons, 1922. 258p.

1475. Capron, Susan Isabella Catherine. A descriptive list of the visitation records (in the York Diocesan Registry). York: Univ. of York, Borthwick Institute of Historical Research, 1960. 71p.

1476. Chanter, J. F., and Troup, F. Rose. "Exeter Cathedral Library." [List of MSS. presented to the Bodleian Library in 1602.] Devon and Cornwall notes & queries, 9 (1917), 139-42, 177-78, 195-96.

1477. Chichester, Diocese. A catalogue of the records of the Bishop, Archdeacons and former exempt jurisdictions, comp. by Francis W. Steer and Isabel M. Kirby. Chichester: West Sussex County Council, 1966. 268p.

1478. Clarke, John Thomas. Records of St. Mark's Chapel in the Parish of Malew, Isle of Man, from its foundation in 1771 to 1864; compiled from original documents and papers of the Rev. J. T. Clarke, by William Harrison. Douglas, 1878. 81p. (Manx Society, Publications, v.28)

1479. Cox, J. Charles. Catalogue of the muniments and manuscript books pertaining to the Dean and Chapter of Lichfield; analysis of the Magnum registrum album; catalogue of the muniments of the Lichfield vicars. London: Harrison and Sons, 1886. 230p. + index.

1480. Davies, James Conway. "Ecclesiastical and palatinate archives at Prior's Kitchen, Durham." Journal of the Society of Archivists, 1 (1958), 185-91.

1481. ———. "Official and private records and manuscript collections in the Prior's Kitchen, Durham." Journal of the Society of Archivists, 1 (1959), 261-70.

Description of more than 7 million church and other records deposited at Prior's Kitchen.

1482. ———. "The records of the Church in Wales." National Library of Wales journal, 4 (1945), 1-34.

Records deposited in National Library of Wales.

1483. Durham Cathedral Library. Durham Cathedral manuscripts to the end of the twelfth century, by R. A. B. Mynors. Durham, 1939. 91p. + 56 plates.

Includes list of all known Durham manuscripts before 1200.

1484. Ely Diocese. Ely records; a handlist of the records of the Bishop and Archdeacon of Ely, by Dorothy M. Owen. Chichester: West Sussex Record Office, 1971. 89p.

1485. Ely Palace. Ely Episcopal records; a calendar and concise view of the Episcopal records preserved in the Muniment Room of the Palace at Ely, by A. Gibbons. Lincoln: James Williamson, 1891. 558p.

1486. Fowler, R. C. Episcopal registers of England & Wales. London: Society for Promoting Christian Knowledge, 1918. 32p.

Describes collections available in various repositories.

1487. Gloucester City Corporation. A catalogue of the records of the Bishop and Archdeacons, comp. by Isabel M. Kirby. Gloucester, 1968. 208p. (Records of the Diocese of Gloucester, v.1)

1488. Gloucestershire County Council. Diocese of Gloucester; a catalogue of the records of the Dean and Chapter, including the former St. Peter's Abbey, comp. by Isabel M. Kirby. Gloucester, 1967. 200p. (Records of the Diocese of Gloucester, v.2)

Covers records from 14th to 20th centuries.

1489. Great Britain, Historical Manuscripts Commission. Calendar of the manuscripts of the Dean and Chapter of Wells. London: H. M. Stationery Office, 1907-14. 2v. (Report, no.12)

1490. Guildhall Library. Churchwardens accounts of parishes within the City of London; a handlist, 2d ed. London, 1969. 31p.

1491. Hereford Cathedral Library. A descriptive catalogue of the manuscripts in the Hereford Cathedral Library, comp. by Arthur Thomas Bannister. Hereford: Wilson & Phillips, 1927. 190p.

Mainly medieval manuscripts, 12th century or later; detailed bibliographical analyses.

1492. Hollaender, Albert E. J. "The muniment room of Manchester Cathedral." Archives, no.5 (1951), 3-10.

Summary of records held.

1493. Lambeth Palace Library. Calendar of the Carew manuscripts preserved in the Archiepiscopal Library at Lambeth, ed. by J. S. Brewer and William Bullen. London: Longmans, 1867-73. 6v.

Covers period 1515-1624.

1494. ———. A calendar of the Shrewsbury and Talbot papers in Lambeth Palace Library and the College of Arms, by Catherine Jamison. London: H. M. Stationery Office, 1966. 288p.

v.I: Shrewsbury mss. in Lambeth Palace Library (mss. 694-710).

1495. ———. Catalogue of an exhibition of recent gifts and accessions, 1950-60, to mark the 350th anniversary of the foundation of Lambeth Palace Library, 1610. Westminster: Church Information Office, 1960. 32p.

1496. ———. Catalogue of ecclesiastical records of the Commonwealth, 1643-1660, in the Lambeth Palace Library, by Jane Houston. Farnborough, Hants.: Gregg, 1968. 338p.

Grouped by types of records, with comprehensive indexes of persons and places.

1497. ———. A catalogue of Lambeth manuscripts, 889 to 901 (Carte antique et miscellanee), by Dorothy M. Owen. London, 1968. 213p.

1498. ———. A catalogue of the Archiepiscopal manuscripts in the Library at Lambeth Palace, with an account of the Archiepiscopal registers and other records there preserved. London: Law and Gilbert, 1812. 270p. + indexes. Reprinted. Farnborough, Hants.: Gregg, 1965.

1499. ———. Charters in Lambeth Palace Library; a catalogue of Lambeth manuscripts 889 to 901, by D. M. Owen. London, 1968. 213p.

1500. ———. Commonwealth ecclesiastical records; A. presentation deeds. London, 1960. 87*l*.

1501. ———. Commonwealth records; B. augmentation books, C. parliamentary surveys. London, 1960. 140*l*.

1502. ———. A descriptive catalogue of the manuscripts in the Library of Lambeth Palace, by Montague Rhodes James and Claude Jenkins. Cambridge: Univ. Pr., 1930-32. 5pts.

Detailed analyses of 1,214 manuscripts restored to Lambeth Palace in 1664.

1503. ———. Faculty Office registers, 1534-1549; a calendar of the first two registers of the Archbishop of Canterbury's Faculty Office, ed. by D. S. Chambers. Oxford: Clarendon, 1966. 394p.

1504. ———. Handlist of the registers, act books and institution act books of the archbishops of Canterbury. London, 1960. 44*l*.

1505. ———. Records of the Church Commissioners for England for the Archiepiscopate of Canterbury. London, 1960. 29 + 11*l*.

1506. Leicester Museums and Art Gallery, Dept. of Archives. Handlist of records of Leicester Archdeaconry. Leicester, 1954. 48p.

1507. Lichfield Joint Record Office. Diocesan, probate and Church Commissioners' records. Stafford: Staffordshire County Council, 1970. 49 + 41p. (Staffordshire Record Office, cumulative hand list, pt.I, Lichfield Joint Record Office)

Materials preserved in the Lichfield Joint Record Office, from 16th century onward.

1508. Lincoln Cathedral Church Library. A catalogue of the manuscripts of Lincoln Cathedral Chapter Library, comp. by Richard Maxwell Woolley. London: Oxford Univ. Pr., 1927. 190p.

1509. Lincoln Cathedral, Friends. The muniments of the Dean and Chapter of Lincoln, by Dorothy M. Williamson. Lincoln, 1956. 40p.

1510. Lincoln Diocesan Record Office. A handlist of the records of the Bishop of Lincoln and of the Archdeacons of Lincoln and Stow, comp. by Kathleen Major. Oxford: Oxford Univ. Pr., 1953. 122p.

Describes principal classes of one of most extensive collections of ecclesiastical records in England.

1511. Newstead Abbey. Newstead Priory Cartulary, 1344, and other archives, translated by Violet W. Walker . . . ed. by Duncan Gray. Nottingham: T. Forman & Sons, 1940. 262p. (Thoroton Society, Record series, v.8)

1512. Oxford, University, Bodleian Library. Cartulary of the medieval archives of Christ Church, by N. Denholm-Young. Oxford: Clarendon, 1931. 266p.

Now in the Bodleian Library.

1513. Philip, I. G. "Short list of chartularies of religious houses in the Bodleian Library." Bodleian quarterly record, 8 (1936-37), 263-68.

1514. St. Albans and Hertfordshire Architectural and Archaeological Society. Records of the old archdeaconry of St. Alban's; a calendar of papers, A.D. 1575 to A.D. 1637. St. Alban's, 1908. 156p.

1515. St. Margaret & St. John Vestry. A catalogue of Westminster records deposited at the Town Hall, Caxton Street, in the custody of the Vestry of St. Margaret & St. John, by John Edward Smith. London: Wightman & Co., 1900. 260p.

Contains 3,398 entries.

1516. St. Martin-in-the-Fields, Royal Parish. Catalogue of books and documents belonging to the Royal Parish of St. Martin-in-the-Fields, in the County of London, comp. by Thomas Mason. London: Harrison & Sons, 1895. 87p.

Churchwardens' accounts, poor rate books, vestry minutes, etc.

1517. Sheffield City Libraries. Catalogue of the Ronksley collection. Sheffield, 1937.

Consists of materials for the history of the chapelry of Bradfield.

1518. Shrewsbury, Royal School Library. The early manuscripts belonging to Shrewsbury School, by Stanley Leighton. Shrewsbury, 1897. 24p. (Reprinted from Transactions of the Shropshire Archaeological Society)

Manuscripts of medieval period, chiefly theological in nature, listed and described.

1519. Shropshire County Council. Shropshire Parish documents; a report, comp. by E. C. Peale and R. S. Clease. Shrewsbury, 1903. 378p.

1520. West Sussex County Council. Diocese of Chichester; a catalogue of the records of the Dean of the Chapter, Vicars Choral, St. Mary's Hospital, colleges and schools, comp. by Francis W. Steer and Isabel M. Kirby. Chichester, 1967. 102p.

1521. West Sussex County Records Committee. Exhibition of records from various ecclesiastical public and private archives in the County of West Sussex. Chichester, 1951. 32p.

Lists and describes 110 items with notes on owners.

1522. Westminster Abbey. The manuscripts of Westminster Abbey, comp. by J. Amitage Robinson and Montague Rhodes James. Cambridge: Univ. Pr., 1909. 108p.

1523. ———. Westminster papers; no.1. The Library and Muniment Room, by Lawrence E. Tanner, 2d ed. London: Oxford Univ. Pr., 1935. 19p.

1524. Winchester, Diocese. Hand list of the Episcopal records of the Diocese of Winchester, prep. by Arthur J. Willis. Folkestone, Kent, 1964. 38l.

1525. Worcester Cathedral Library. Catalogue of manuscripts preserved in the Chapter Library of Worcester Cathedral, comp. by John Kestell Flayer, ed. and rev. by Sidney Graves Hamilton. Oxford: Worcestershire Historical Society, 1906. 196p.

1526. York, Diocese, Parochial Documents Commission of the Archdeaconry of the East Riding. Parochial documents of the Archdeaconry of the East Riding; an inventory, ed. by M. W. Barley. Beverley, 1939. 168p. (Yorkshire Archaeological Society, Record series, v.99)

Bible and Biblical Literature

BIBLE

1527. Aberdeen, University, Library. Catalogue of the Taylor collection of Psalm versions. Aberdeen: Univ. Pr., 1921. 307p. (Aberdeen Univ. studies, no.85)

Sections: complete versions, partial versions, books relating to the Psalms.

1528. Birmingham Public Libraries. Bible centenary celebration, 1538-1938; exhibition in the Birmingham Cathedral of Biblical manuscripts and facsimiles of manuscripts and of old and modern editions of the Bible. Birmingham, 1938. 23l.

Catalog drawn chiefly from Birmingham Reference Library.

1529. Brighton Public Library, Museums and Fine Art Gallery. Catalogue of a collection of rare & valuable Bibles, etc., exhibited. Brighton: Dolphin, 1918. 12p.

1530. Bristol Public Libraries. The fourth centenary of the English Bible, 1538-1938: catalogue of Bibles on exhibition in the Central Public Library, Bristol, June to October, 1938. Bristol, 1938. 30p.

1531. ———. A select catalogue of Bibles in the Bristol Central Public Library; to commemorate the three hundred and fiftieth anniversary of the Authorized Version of the English Bible, 1611-1961. Bristol: The Library, 1961. 28p. + 4 plates.

1532. British and Foreign Bible Society. Catalogue of an exhibition celebrating the 350th anniversary of the Authorized Version of the English Bible, 1611-1961. London, 1961. 32p.

Annotated list of 116 items drawn from society's collection.

1533. ———. Historical catalogue of printed editions of the English Bible: 1525-1961, revised and expanded from the edition of T. H. Darlow and H. F. Moule, 1903, by Arthur Sumner Herbert. London, 1968. 549p.

Revision of v.1 of 1903 edition; locates copies in Britain and United States.

1534. ———. Historical catalogue of the printed editions of Holy Scripture in the Library of the British and Foreign Bible Society, comp. by T. H. Darlow and H. F. Moule. London: Bible House, 1903-11. 4pts. Reprinted, N.Y.: Kraus, 1964.

Includes nearly 10,000 entries.

1535. British Museum. British Museum Bible Exhibition, 1911; guide to the manuscripts and printed books exhibited in celebration of the tercentenary of the Authorized Version, with eight plates. London, 1911. 64p.

1536. ———. The Codex Sinaiticus and the Codex Alexandrinus, by H. J. M. Milne and T. C. Skeat. London, 1963. 41p. + 7 plates.

1537. ———. English Bible exhibition. London, 1938. 8p.

1538. ———. General catalogue of printed books, photographic ed. to 1955. Bible, v.17-19. London, 1965. 3v.

Comprehensive bibliography of Bible, as represented by British Museum's holdings.

1539. ———. The Mount Sinai manuscript of the Bible, 4th ed. Oxford, 1935. 23p.

1540. ——— Dept. of Manuscripts. Facsimiles of Biblical manuscripts in the British Museum, ed. by Frederic G. Kenyon. London: The Museum, 1900. 49p.

1541. ——— ———. Fragments of an unknown gospel and other early Christian papyri, ed. by H. Idris Bell and T. C. Skeat. London: The Museum, 1935. 63p.

1542. ——— ———. Guide to the manuscripts and printed books exhibited in celebration of the tercen-

tenary of the Authorized Version. London: The Museum, 1911. 64p. Reprinted 1927.

Includes 107 items with full descriptions.

1543. ———, Dept. of Printed Books. British Museum general catalogue of printed books: Bible. London: The Museum, 1936-37. 3v. 2,746 cols.

1544. Cardiff Public Libraries. Catalogue of the Bibles exhibited in the Reference Library in celebration of the tercentenary of the Authorized Version. Cardiff: Libraries Committee, 1911. 62p.

1545. ———. Catalogue of Welsh Scriptures exhibited in the Reference Department. Cardiff: W. Lewis, 1904. 34p.

1546. ———. Fourth centenary of the Bible, 1938; handlist of Bibles exhibited in the Lesser City Hall by the Cardiff Public Library. Cardiff: Western Mail and Echo, 1938. 28p.

1547. Dublin, University, Trinity College Library. Catalogue of Bibles added to the Library since the year 1872. Dublin, 1903. p.1,493-1,509.

Section drawn from Trinity College Library's Accessions catalogue.

1548. Glasgow, University, Library. Catalogue of an exhibition of Bibles in commemoration of the tercentenary of the Authorized Version, 1611-1911. Glasgow: James Maclehose, 1911, 39p.

Lists 100 works in chronological order to 1811; p.32-39 record 38 Bibles printed in Scotland.

1549. ———. Catalogue of an exhibition of Bibles in commemoration of the tercentenary of the Authorized Version, 1611-1911. Glasgow: Jackson, Wylie, 1925. 54p.

List of 107 items.

1550. ———. Catalogue of the Bibles and New Testaments contained in the Euing collection and in the General Library. Glasgow, 1891. Unpaged.

Manuscript catalog in Glasgow University Library.

1551. Gottstein, M. H. "A list of some uncatalogued Syriac Biblical manuscripts." Bulletin of the John Rylands Library, 37 (1955), 429-45. Reprinted. 1955. 19p.

Locates items listed in libraries in Manchester, Paris, London, Oxford, and Cambridge.

1552. John Rylands Library. La Bible historiée toute figurée de la John Rylands Library; reproduction intégrale [on 29 plates, numbered XIX-XLVII] du manuscrit French 5 accompangée d'une étude par Robert Fawtier. Paris, 1924. 54p.

Facsimile of a manuscript in the John Rylands Library.

1553. ———. Catalogue of an exhibition of Bibles illustrating the history of the English versions from Wiclif to the present time, including the personal copies of Queen Elizabeth, Elizabeth Fry and others. Manchester: Sherratt and Hughes, 1906. 55p.

1554. ———. Catalogue of an exhibition of Bibles illustrating the history of the English version from Wiclif to the present time, by Henry Guppy. Manchester, 1907. 55p.

1555. ———. Catalogue of an exhibition of manuscript and printed copies of the Scriptures, illustrating the history of the transmission of the Bible; tercentenary of the "Authorized Version" of the English Bible, A.D. 1611-1911, by Henry Guppy. Manchester: Univ. Pr.; London: Bernard Quaritch and Sherratt and Hughes, 1911. 128p.

1556. ———. Catalogue of an exhibition illustrating the history of the transmission of the Bible. Manchester: Univ. Pr.; London: Longmans, 1925. 133p. + 20 plates.

1557. ———. Catalogue of an exhibition illustrating the history of the transmission of the Bible, in commemoration of the 400th anniversary of the publication of the first entire Bible to be printed in the English language, which was translated and edited by Miles Coverdale, and completed on the 4th of October, 1535. Manchester, 1935. 125p. + 20 plates.

1558. ———. Coptic Biblical fragments in the John Rylands Library, ed. by Walter C. Till. Manchester, 1952. 29p. (Reprinted from the Bulletin of the John Rylands Library, v.34)

1559. ———. The English Bible in the John Rylands Library, 1525-1640, by Richard Lovett, with 26 facsimiles and 39 engravings. Manchester, 1899. 275p.

1560. Johnston, William. A bibliography of the Thumb Bibles of John Taylor (the Water Poet). Aberdeen: Univ. Pr., 1910. 13p.

Copies located in public and private collections.

1561. Kahsnitz, Rainer. "The Gospel book of Abbess Svanhild of Essen in the John Rylands Library." Bulletin of the John Rylands Library, 53 (1970), 122-66, 360-96.

Latin manuscript of 11th century containing the 4 Gospels.

1562. Lambeth Palace Library. An account of Greek manuscripts, chiefly Biblical, which had been in the possession of the late Professor Carlyle, the greater part of which are now deposited in the Archiepiscopal Library at Lambeth Palace. London: Richard Gilbert, 1823. 74p.

1563. London, University, King's College Library. Exhibition of Bibles from the collection in the College Library to mark the 350th anniversary of the first printing of the Authorized Version in 1611. London, 1961. 55p.

Annotated catalog of 118 items.

1564. McGurk, Patrick. Latin Gospel books from A.D. 400 to A.D. 800. Amsterdam, etc.: Standard-Boekhandel, 1961. 123p.

Surviving copies described fully under countries and individual libraries where presently located.

1565. National Book League. The Bible in English life; an exhibition, arr. by John Stirling. London: Cambridge Univ. Pr. for the National Book League, 1948. 63p.

Annotated list of 182 items, with locations in public and private collections.

1566. Oxford and Cambridge University Presses. The Bible in Britain; an introduction and list of exhibits. Cambridge: Univ. Pr., 1961. 34p.

Lists 106 items, with locations of copies.

1567. Oxford, University, Bodleian Library. The Kennicott Bible. Oxford, 1957. 10p. + 21 plates. (Bodleian picture books, no.11)

Bible written at Corunna, northwest Spain, completed in 1476; now in Bodleian Library.

1568. St. Mary's Seminary Library. Catalogue of the Bible collections in the Old Library at St. Mary's, Oscott, c. 1472-c. 1850, ed. by G. F. Pullen. Sutton Coldfield: The Seminary, 1971. 208 + 12p.

Lists 1,521 items.

1569. Sheffield City Libraries. Exhibition of the English Bible. Sheffield, 1938. 20p.

A catalog.

1570. University College, Hull, Religious Activities Committee. An exhibition of Bibles in the Assembly Hall of the University College, Hull. Hull: Brown & Sons, 1954. 24p.

1571. Wigan Public Library. Exhibition to commemorate the fourth centenary of the authorization of the Bible; catalogue of the exhibits with historical introduction, by Arthur J. Hawkes. Wigan, 1938. 14p. (Reprinted from the Wigan observer)

BIBLICAL LITERATURE

1572. Evangelical Library. Catalogue of commentaries on the Old and New Testaments. London, n.d. 24p.

1573. Glasgow, University, Library. A catalogue of short titles of the books in the University Court Room, other than Bibles and Testaments; being a finding list to the Psalm books and other portions of Scripture, the Biblical bibliography and commentaries, the hymn books and liturgies in the Euing collection.
Manuscript catalog in Glasgow University Library.

1574. Martin, Susan V. A select bibliography of Biblical encyclopaedias, dictionaries, and concordances in London libraries. London, 1962. 93*l*. (Diploma in Librarianship, Univ. of London)
Copies located in 8 London libraries.

Christian Theology

1575. British Museum, Dept. of Printed Books. Catalogue of an exhibition commemorating the four hundredth anniversary of the introduction of the Book of common prayer. London: The Museum, 1949. 37p.
Lists 52 items.

1576. ———. Catalogue of printed books: liturgies. London: W. Clowes, 1899. 776 cols.

1577. Carruthers, Samuel William. Three centuries of the Westminster shorter catechism. Fredericton, B.B.: Univ. of N. B., 1957. 128p.
Includes bibliography, with locations of copies, in British and American libraries.

1578. Church of Scotland, General Assembly, Committee on Public Worship and Aids to Devotion. Draft of a catalogue of books on psalters, hymns and hymnology in the National Library of Scotland, New College Library, Edinburgh, Trinity College Library Glasgow. Edinburgh, 1939. 352*l*.

1579. Cowan, William. "A bibliography of the Book of Common Prayer and Psalm Book of the Church of Scotland, 1556-1644." Edinburgh Bibliographical Society publications, 10 (1913), 53-100.
Lists 70 items, with locations of copies.

1580. Evangelical Library. Christian doctrine; simplified catalogue, ed. by Gordon R. Sayer. London, n.d. 36p.

1581. Great Britain, Public Record Office. The Prayer Book of 1662; exhibition of records. London, 1962. Unpaged.
Exhibition marking tercentenary of fifth Book of Common Prayer.

1582. McRoberts, David. Catalogue of Scottish mediaeval liturgical books and fragments. Glasgow: J. S. Burns, 1953. 28p.
Lists 156 items, with locations of copies.

1583. O'Donoghue, M. J. "Additions to the collections of liturgies." British Museum quarterly, 36 (1971) 1-4.
In British Museum.

1584. Oxford, University, Bodleian Library. Handlist of the Latin liturgical manuscripts in the Bodleian Library, Oxford, by S. J. P. Van Dijk. [196- ?] 7v.
v.1, mass books; v.2, office books; v.3, rituals and directories; v.4, books of hours; v.5, fragments, mass books; v.6, fragments, office books; v.7, indexes.

1585. ———. Latin liturgical manuscripts and printed books; guide to an exhibition held during 1952. Oxford, 1952. 61p. + 20 plates.

1586. Representative Church Body Library, Church of Ireland. The Watson collection; prayer books and related liturgical works given by Edward John McCartney Watson; catalogue, comp. by Newport B. White. Dublin, 1948. 52p.

1587. Wigan Public Library. Notable editions of the Prayer Book, by J. F. Gerrard. Wigan, 1949. 30p.
Catalog of selected editions of Book of Common Prayer exhibited at Wigan Public Library, 1949.

Missions

1588. Cardiff Public Libraries. Missions: a select list of books in the Central and Reference Libraries on missions (mainly foreign). Cardiff, 1925. 14p.

1589. Church Missionary Society Library. Books and pamphlets. London, 1958-59. 2pts.
pt.1, Christian doctrine; pt.2, Christian missions.

1590. ———. Christian doctrine; books and pamphlets 1958. London, 1958. 24p.
Lists library's holdings.

1591.———.Christian missions, books and pamphlets 1959. London, 1959. 50p.

1592. Cobb, Henry S. "The archives of the Church Missionary Society." Archives, no.14 (1955), 293-99.

Description of records held by society founded in 1799.

1593. Evangelical Library. Catalogue of church history missionary works and works on the Holy Spirit. London, n.d. 58p.

1594. Great Britain, Historical Manuscripts Commission. A survey of the archives of selected missionary societies. London. 1968. Unpaged.

Arranged under names of societies, British and foreign.

1595. Keen, Rosemary, and Woods, Jean M. "Sources for African studies: Church Missionary Society." Library materials on Africa, 6 (March 1969), 86-90.

Review of society's library resources.

1596. London Missionary Society. Catalogue of books contained in the Lockhart Library and in the General Library of the London Missionary Society, by G. Mabbs. London, 1899. 320p.

1597. Marchant, Leslie R. A guide to the archives and records of Protestant Christian missions from the British Isles to China. 1796-1914. Perth: Univ. of Western Australia Pr., 1966. 134p.

List of repositories, societies, and records in Britain, arranged under names of societies.

1598. Newcastle upon Tyne City Libraries. Missions: a list of books in the reference and lending libraries on missions. Newcastle upon Tyne, 1926. 8p.

1599. Society for the Propagation of the Gospel in Foreign Parts. S.P.G. lending library catalogue. London, 1927. 175p. Supplement, 1931. 47p.

Christian Churches and Sects

BAPTIST

1600. [Birmingham Public Libraries.] "Baptist manuscripts in the Birmignham Reference Library." Baptist quarterly, n.s.9 (1939), 436.

1601. London, University, Regent's Park College, Angus Library. Catalogue of the books, pamphlets & manuscripts in the Angus Library at Regent's Park College, London. London: Kingsgate, 1908. 348p.

Collection relating to Baptist history.

1602. Whitley, W. T. A Baptist bibliography; being a register of the chief materials for Baptist history, whether in manuscript or in print, preserved in Great Britain, Ireland, and the Colonies. London: Kingsgate, 1916-22. 2v.

Locations in British and American libraries; covers period 1526-1837.

CONGREGATIONAL

1603. Congregational Union of England and Wales. A catalogue of the Congregational Library. London, 1895-1910. 2v.

1604. Dexter, Henry Martyn. The Congregationalism of the last three hundred years, as seen in its literature. London: Hodder & Stoughton, 1879. 716 + 326p.

Appendix, "Collections toward a bibliography of Congregationalism," 1546-1879, locates copies in 55 British and American libraries.

1605. Tibbutt, H. G. "Sources for Congregational Church history." Transactions of the Congregational Historical Society, 19 (Aug. 1960), 33-38.

Brief summary of holdings of Congregational Library, Dr. Williams's Library, diocesan record offices, etc.

DUTCH

1606. Nederlandse Hervormde Gemeente. A catalogue of books, manuscripts, letters, etc., belonging to the Dutch Church, Austin Friars, London, deposited in the Library of the Corporation of the City of London, comp. by W. H. Overall. London, 1879. 184p.

METHODIST

1607. John Rylands Library. "Wesley exhibition." Bulletin of the John Rylands Library, 53 (1970), 1-2.

Description of exhibition: "Early Methodism, John and Charles Wesley."

1608. Tibbott, Gildas, and Davies, K. M. "The archives of the Calvinistic Methodist or Presbyterian Church of Wales." National Library of Wales journal, 5 (1947), 13-49.

MORAVIAN

1609. Blandford, F. M. Catalogue of the archives of the Bristol Moravian Church. London, 1950. Unpaged.

NONCONFORMIST

1610. Cooper, A. Margaret. Protestant nonconformity in the Town of Reading from the 17th century to the present day; a bibliography. London, 1952. 41l. (Diploma in Librarianship, Univ. of London)

Copies of references located in 10 libraries and private collections.

1611. Crippen, Thomas George. "Early Noncon-formist bibliography." Congregational Historical Society transactions. 1 (1901), 44-57, 99-112, 171-84, 252-65, 410-20; 2 (1906), 61-71, 219-29, 432-44.

Chronological list, with locations of copies.

1612. Dr. Williams's Library. Early nonconformity, 1566-1800; a catalogue of books in Dr. Williams's Library, London, comp. by Miss G. Woodward. Boston, Mass.: G. K. Hall, 1968. 12v.

Author, subject, and chronological catalogs.

1613. ———. Index to the John Evans list of dissenting congregations and ministers, 1715-1729, in Dr. Williams's Library, comp. by John Creasey. London: Dr. Williams's Trust, 1964. 36p. (Occasional paper, no.11)

Indexes of places and persons.

1614. ———. Nonconformist congregations in Great Britain; a short-title list of histories and other material in Dr. Williams's Library; ed. by Kenneth Twinn. London, in press.

1615. Nuttall, Geoffrey F. The beginnings of nonconformity, 1660-1665; a checklist. London: Dr. Williams's Library, 1960. 128l.

Locates copies in 35 British and American libraries.

1616. Powell, W. R., and others. "Protestant nonconformist records." Archives, 5 (1961), 1-12.

Summary of records of Presbyterian Church of England, Congregational, Baptist, and Methodist churches; Society of Friends, and nonconformist records in Wales, and their present locations.

1617. Powell, W. R. "The sources of the history of Protestant nonconformist churches in England." University of London, Institute of Historical Research, Bulletin, 25 (1952), 213-27.

1618. Welch, C. E. "Archives and manuscripts in nonconformist libraries." Archives, no.32 (1964), 235-38.

Includes list of libraries with notes on records held.

PRESBYTERIAN

1619. Albaugh, G. P. "American Presbyterian periodicals and newspapers, 1752-1830, with library locations." Journal of Presbyterian history, 41 (1963), 165-87; 243-62; 42 (1964), 54-67, 124-44.

Locations in British Museum and in American and Canadian libraries; alphabetical listing with exact holdings noted.

PURITAN

1620. Dr. Williams's Library. The seconde parte of a register: being a calendar of manuscripts under that title intended for publication by the Puritans about 1593, and now in Dr. Williams's Library, London, ed. by Albert Peel. Cambridge: Univ. Pr., 1915. 2v.

QUAKER (FRIENDS)

1621. Hutton, Brian Gerald. Records of the Hertford and Hitchin monthly meeting of the Society of Friends. London, 1960. 61l. (Diploma in Archive Administration, Univ. of London)

Records deposited with Hertfordshire County Record Office.

1622. Irish Manuscripts Commission. Guide to Irish Quaker records, 1654-1860, by Olive C. Goodbody, with contribution on Northern Ireland records by B. G. Hutton. Dublin: Stationery Office, 1967. 237p.

ROMAN CATHOLIC

1623. Allison, Antony Francis. "Franciscan books in English, 1559-1640." Biographical studies, 3 (1955-56), 16-65.

Describes 42 titles, with locations of copies in British and American libraries.

1624. ———, and Rogers, David Morrison. A catalogue of Catholic books in English printed abroad or secretly in England 1558-1640. Bognor Regis: Arundel, 1956. 2v. (187p.)

Copies located in numerous British, Irish, American, and other libraries; records 931 titles.

1625. ——— ———. A catalogue of Catholic books in English printed abroad or secretly in England, 1558-1640, new ed. with corrigenda. London: Dawson, 1968. 187p.

1626. ——— ———. [Review of] A. C. Southern, Elizabethan recusant prose 1559-1582. Library, 5th ser., 6 (1951), 48-57.

Article "reinforcing, supplementing, or correcting" the Southern bibliography.

1627. Augustinian Convent. "The catalogue of the Library of the Augustinian Friars at York, now first edited from the manuscript at Trinity College, Dublin," by Montague Rhodes James. In: Clark, John Willis. Fasciculus Ioanni Willis Clark dicatus. Cantabrigiae: Typis Academicis impressus, 1909. 577p.

1628. Bell, H. I. "A list of original papal bulls and briefs in the Department of Manuscripts, British

Museum." English historical review, 36 (1921), 393-419, 556-83.

Listing under names of individual popes, 1088-1846, a total of 427 items.

1629. Bowen, Geraint. "The Jesuit library in Hereford Cathedral." Bulletin of the Association of British Theological and Philosophical Libraries, no.20 (Feb. 1965), 13-34; no.21 (Aug. 1965), 17-27.

pt.1 is history and description; pt.2 is a catalog of books in the Cathedral Library.

1630. British Museum, Dept. of Printed Books. Catalogue of printed books. Accessions. Boase collection [of books relating to the Catholic Apostolic Church founded by Edward Irving]. London, 1913. 75l.

1631. ——— ———. Catalogue of printed books: Jesuits. London: W. Clowes, 1889. 58 cols.

1632. Catholic Apostolic Church, Catherine Street. Catalogue of the Library of the Catholic Apostolic, Church, Catherine Street, Glasgow. Glasgow, 1905. 40p.

1633. Chadwick, Hubert. "Unfamiliar libraries II: Stonyhurst College." Book collector, 6 (1957), 343-49.

Library strong in early printed books and manuscripts, of special Catholic interest.

1634. Dublin, Archbishopric. Calendar of Archbishop Alen's Register, c. 1172-1534; prepared and edited from the original in the Registry of the United Dioceses of Dublin and Glendalough and Kildare, by Charles MacNeill, with an index compiled by Liam Price. Dublin, 1950. 377p. (Extra volume of the Royal Society of Antiquaries of Ireland for 1949)

1635. ——— Cathedral Church of Saint Patrick. Calendar of documents contained in the Chartulary commonly called "Dignitas Decani" of St. Patrick's Cathedral, by J. H. Bernard. Dublin, 1905. (Royal Irish Academy, Proceedings, v. 25, section C, no.9)

1636. Edwards, Francis O. "The archives of the English Province of the Society of Jesus at Farm Street, London." Journal of the Society of Archivists, 3 (1966), 107-15.

Catholic organization dating from 1623; description of records.

1637. Franciscan Convent, Merchants' Quay. Report on Franciscan manuscripts preserved at the Convent, Merchants' Quay, Dublin. [A calendar of the collection transferred in 1872 from the Collegio d. Sant'-Isidoro dei Padri Franciscan Irlandesi at Rome, comp.

by G. D. Burtchaell and J. M. Rigg.] Dublin, 1906. 296p. (Historical Manuscripts Commission, no.65)

1638. Inquisition Tribunal, Canary Islands. Catalogue. of a collection of original manuscripts formerly belonging to the Holy Office of the Inquisition in the Canary Islands . . . with a notice of some unpublished records of the same series in the British Museum, by Walter DeGray Birch. Edinburgh and London: William Blackwood, 1903. 2v.

1639. Lambeth Palace Library. Original Papal documents in the Lambeth Palace Library; a catalogue, by Jane E. Sayers. London: Univ. of London, Athlone Pr., 1967. 59p. (Bulletin of the Institute of Historical Research, Special supplement, no.6, Nov. 1967)

1640. Major, Kathleen. "Original Papal documents in the Bodleian Library." Bodleian Library record, 3 (1951), 242-56.

Descriptions of 44 items.

1641. Queen's College Library. Catalogue of classical books and works relating to patristic literature in the Library of Queen's College, Belfast. Belfast: Alexander Mayne & Boyd, 1887. 107p.

1642. St. Mary's Seminary. Recusant books at St. Mary's, Oscott, comp. by G. F. Pullen, New Oscott, War., 1964-66. 2v.

Covers 1518-1830 period.

1643. Southern, A. C. Elizabethan recusant prose, 1559-1582; a historical and critical account of the books of the Catholic refugees printed and published abroad and at secret presses in England, together with an annotated bibliography of the same. London and Glasgow: Sands & Co., 1950. 553p.

Copies located in British Museum and other collections.

1644. Tallon, Maura. Church of Ireland diocesan libraries. Dublin: Library Association of Ireland, 1959. 30p.

Lists most important holdings.

SWEDENBORGIAN (CHURCH OF THE NEW JERUSALEM)

1645. New Church Society. Catalogue of the Library of the New Church Society, Henry Street, Bath, by Elizak Pitman. Bath, 1889. 152p.

A Swedenborgian church library.

1646. Swedenborg Society. Library catalogue. London: Swedenborg House, 1958-66. 4pts.

pt.I, Swedenborg collection; pt.II, archives; pt.III, collateral works.

UNITARIAN

1647. Unitarian Home Missionary College Library. The story of a Nonconformist library. Manchester: Univ. Pr., 1923. 198p. (Publications of the University of Manchester, Historical series, no.41)

Contains listing of 17th-century Unitarian tracts, earliest Unitarian periodicals, and other Unitarian literature.

Non-Christian Religions

BUDDHISM

1648. India Office Library. The Buddhist Tripitaka, as it is known in China and Japan; a catalogue and compendious report, by Samuel Beal. London: The Office, 1876. 117p.

Collection presented to India Office Library by Japanese Government.

JUDAISM

1649. Fraenkel, Josef. Exhibition of the Jewish press in Great Britain, 1823-1963. London: Narod, 1963. 63p.

Copies of 483 items located in British Museum, Jews' College, University College, and Wiener Library in London, and in 4 U.S. and 2 Jerusalem libraries.

1650. ———. Guide to the Jewish libraries of the world. London: World Jewish Congress, 1959. 64p.

Includes non-Jewish libraries with relevant collections; data on British libraries p.15-19.

1651. Jewish Historical Society of England. Calendar of the Plea Rolls of the Exchequer of the Jews pre-served in the Public Record Office, ed. by J. M. Rigg. London, 1905-29. 3v.

Covers reigns of Henry III and Edward I, 1218-1277.

1652. Jewish Memorial Council, Central Committee for Jewish Education. Catalogue of books in the Mrs. Nathaniel L. Cohen Lending Library and the Reference Library of the Central Committee. London, 1934. 79p.

1653. Jews' College Library. Centenary celebration: 1855/5616, 1955/5716; catalogue of an exhibition of books by members of the academic staff and alumni at the Jews' College Library. London: Jews' College, 1955. 16p.

1654. London, University, University College, Mocatta Library and Museum. List of books added to the Jewish Section of the Mocatta Library from 1905 to September 1911. London: University College, 1909-11. 2pts.

1655. Manchester Public Libraries. Jewish book week and exhibition of art, music and ritual. Manchester, 1938. 20p.

1656. Rabinowicz, Harry Mordka. The Jewish literary treasures of England and America. N.Y., London: Yoseloff, 1962. 166p. + 32 plates.

1657. ———. "Judaica in the British Museum." Times literary supplement, 28 April 1966, p.376.

1658. Rye, R. A. Catalogue of the printed books and manuscripts forming the library of Frederic David Mocatta. London: Harrison & Sons, 1904. 803p.

Collection principally illustrating history of Jews in England; portion destroyed during World War II; remainder in University College, London.

Social Sciences

General

1659. British Museum, Dept. of Printed Books. List of social, political, and economic periodicals received from the USSR, 1933-42. London. 1943. 8p.

1660. Clarke, D. A. "The BLPES and the collection of primary materials." Aslib proceedings, 23 (1971), 201-2.

Brief description of British Library of Political and Economic Science's holdings in the social sciences.

1661. Essex, University, Library. Comparative and social studies; a guide to the bibliographical and reference materials held by the Library, by B. J. C. Wintour. Colchester, 1969. 407p. Supplement, 1970. 122p.

Comprises social sciences and humanities in general.

1662. ———— ————. Soviet materials: a guide for social scientists, by Madeline E. Giles. Colchester, 1971. 53p.

1663, Frewer, Louis B. "Rhodes House Library, its function and resources." Bodleian Library record, 5 (1956), 318-32.

Library at Oxford designed to serve as center for advanced study of social, political, and economic development of British Commonwealth, United States, and Africa.

1664. Great Britain, Central Office of Information, Social Survey Library. Government Social Survey Library; book and journal holdings. London, 1969. 214p.

1665. ————, Public Record Office. Records of interest to social scientists, 1919 to 1939, introduction. London: H. M. Stationery Office, 1971. 280p. (Public Records Office handbooks, no.14)

Arranged under broad subject areas.

1666. London School of Economics & Political Science. A London bibliography of the social sciences; being the Subject Catalogue of the British Library of Political and Economic Science at the School of Economics, the Goldsmiths' Library of Economic Literature at the University of London, the Libraries of the Royal Statistical Society and the Royal Anthropological Institute, and certain special collections at University College, London, and elsewhere, comp. under the direction of B. M. Headicar and C. Fuller. London: London School of Economics & Political Science, 1931-32. 4v. Supplements 1-5, 1929-62. London, 1934-68. 10v. 6th Supplement, 1962-68. London: Mansell, 1970. 6v.

1667. National Lending Library for Science and Technology. Select list of social science serials in the N.L.L. Boston Spa, 1966. 25p.

Lists about 350 titles.

1668. York, University, Library. Social sciences. York, 1968. 57p. (Library guides, no.3)

Select bibliographical guide to materials held by library.

Statistics

1669. Aston, University, Library. Statistics; a subject guide to sources in Aston University Library, 2d ed., by M. A. Barnes. Birmingham, 1971. 62p.

1670. British Museum, Dept. of Printed Books. Handlist of statistical publications and state papers of the countries of Continental Europe (including certain of their colonies) preserved in the Library of the British Museum. London: The Museum, 1910. 44 cols.

1671. Essex, University, Library. British statistics; a select list of sources, University of Essex Library. Colchester, 1972. 60p.

1672. Great Britain, Ministry of Overseas Development Library. List of periodicals currently received in the Library. London, 1968. 32 + 29 + 5p.

Alphabetical list, followed by classified lists of periodicals in "Statistics Library," arranged by country and by subject.

1673. Library Association. Economic statistics collections: a directory of research resources in the United Kingdom for business, industry, and public affairs. London: Library Association, for the Committee of Librarians and Statisticians, the Library Association and Royal Statistical Society, 1970. 62p.

Geographical arrangement.

1674. Royal Statistical Society Library. Catalogue of the Library of the Statistical Society. London: Edward Stanford, 1884-86. 2v.

1675. ———. Catalogue of the Library of the Royal Statistical Society. London: The Society, 1921. 274p.

Dictionary arrangement.

1676. Statistical Society of London Library. Catalogue of the Library of the Statistical Society of London, founded 1834. London: John W. Parker, 1859. 142p.

Name changed to Royal Statistical Society of London, 1887.

1677. Westminster Public Libraries. Statistics: a guide to current material. London, 1951. 16p.

Sociology

1678. Cambridge, University, Institute of Criminology Library. List of annual publications. Cambridge, 1969. 6*l*.

1679. ———. Periodicals currently received. Cambridge, 1968. 6*l*.

1680. Glasgow, University, Hunterian Library. Women and books from the sixteenth century to the Suffragettes: an exhibition held in the Hunterian Library, University of Glasgow. Glasgow, 1971. 25p.

Records 138 items annotated.

1681. Great Britain, Commonwealth Institute Library. Race relations; selected reading lists for advanced study. London, 1968. 11p.

Books listed are held by Library of Commonwealth Institute.

1682. Hawkins, Keith. Deprivation of liberty for young offenders; a select bibliography on approved schools, attendance centres, borstals, detention centres and remand homes, 1940-1965. Cambridge: Univ. of

Cambridge Institute of Criminology, 1966. 48*l*. (Bibliographical series, no.1)

Based on Institute of Criminology's collection.

1683. Institute of Race Relations Library. Coloured immigrants in Britain; a select bibliography based on the holdings of the Library of the Institute of Race Relations. London. 1965. 18p.

1684. ———. List of periodicals—holdings in the Library of the Institute of Race Relations. London, 1970. 30p.

1685. International Planned Parenthood Federation. Periodical & newsletter holdings in the I.P.P.F. Central Office Library, 2d ed. London, 1971. 14*l*.

1686. John Howard Library of Criminal Law and Penology. Catalogue. London: Howard League for Penal Reform, 1931. 51p.

1687. ———. Catalogue. London: Howard League for Penal Reform, 1963. 82p.

Classified list with author index.

1688. London Polytechnic Library. A bibliography of industrial sociology (including the sociology of occupations), comp. by S. R. Parker. London, 1965. 15p.

Classified listing.

1689. Northcroft, D. M. Archives of the woman's movement. Librarian & book world, 25 (1936), 326.

Discussion of collections relating to women's movement in Britain and elsewhere.

1690. Reform Club Library. Catalogue of the Library of the Reform Club, comp. by Charles W. Vincent. London: W. Ridgway, 1883. 623p.

1691. ———. Catalogue of the Library of the Reform Club, comp. by Charles W. Vincent. 2d ed. London: Smith & Elder, 1894. 794p.

1692. ———. The Library of the Reform Club. London, 1927. 7p.

1693. Sheffield, University, Library. Sociology; a guide to sources of information. Sheffield, 1971. Unpaged.

1694. Social Sciences Documentation. Survey of criminological journals; a handlist of periodicals of interest to students of criminology with their locations in certain London libraries. London: Institute of Study and Treatment of Delinquency, 1958. 8p.

Gives locations for 53 periodicals in 4 London libraries and about 200 Commonwealth and foreign official report series in 3 London libraries.

Political Science

GENERAL

1695. Bond, Maurice F. "The manuscripts of the House of Lords." Indian archives, 5 (Jan.-June 1951), 34-41.
Describes holdings of the Record Office of House of Lords.

1696. ———. "The Victoria Tower and its records." Parliamentary affairs, 8 (1955), 482-91.
Describes records of the House of Lords.

1697. British Museum. The political scene, 1901-1914: an exhibition to commemorate the fiftieth anniversary of the Parliament Act, 1911, a catalogue. London, 1961. 32p.

1698. Gateshead Public Libraries. A list of books in the Lending and Reference Departments of the Central Public Library on local government. Gateshead, 1946. 15p.

1699. Glasgow, University, Library. A select list of serials in the field of politics, 1967-68. Glasgow, 1967. 15p.
Exact holdings shown.

1700. Gracey, J. W., and Gracey, Howard P. "Northern Ireland political literature, 1968-1970; a catalogue of the collection in the Linen Hall Library." Irish booklore, 1 (1971), 44-82. (To be continued)

1701. Great Britain, Historical Manuscripts Commission. The manuscripts of the House of Lords, 1678-1714. London: H. M. Stationery Office, 1887-1962. 11v. (Report, no.17)

1702. ———, Ministry of Overseas Development Library. Public administration; a select bibliography. London: The Ministry, 1967. 101p. Supplement, 1968. 31p.
Classified by subject.

1703. ——— ———. Public administration; a select bibliography. London, 1970. 54p.

1704. ———, Parliament, House of Commons Library. A bibliography of parliamentary debates of Great Britain. London: H. M. Stationery Office, 1956. 62p.

1705. ——— ——— ———. Current literature bulletin. London, 1968- .

1706. ——— ——— ———. The Library of the House of Commons, handbook. London, 1966. 56p.

1707. ——— ———, House of Lords Record Office. Guide to the records of Parliament, by Maurice F. Bond. London: H. M. Stationery Office, 1971. 352p.
"Describes the complete range of records preserved within the Palace of Westminster: the records of both Houses of Parliament," etc.

1708. Hampton, John. "Scotland's special libraries: County of Lanark Local Government Library." SLA news, no.90 (1969), 259-61.
Library in Hamilton established in 1964, with stock of more than 20,000 items ranging over all subjects concerning local government.

1709. Kingston upon Hull Public Libraries. Civic index; a monthly guide to local government literature. Kingston upon Hull, 1966- .

1710. London County Council Library. Catalogue of the contents of the Library. London: County Council, 1902. 405p. Supplement. 1905. 317p.
Deals primarily with municipal affairs.

1711. Marx Memorial Library. Catalogue. London. 1971. 2pts.
pt.1, Marx classics; pt.2, social and political theory.

1712. ———. Marx House: its history and traditions. London, 1956. 8p.

1713. Menhennet, David. "The Library of the House of Commons." Law librarian, 1 (Dec. 1970), 31-34.
Description of collections and services.

1714. West Ham Public Libraries. Catalogue of books in all the libraries [of West Ham] on the theory and practice of politics, etc. West Ham, 1935. 126p.

SLAVERY

1715. Birt, Joyce. Catalogue of a collection of anti-slavery tracts and pamphlets in the possession of the Anti-Slavery Society for the Protection of Human Rights [London]. London, 1958. 100p.
Includes section describing resources of "Other libraries containing material on slavery," p97-100.

1716 Manchester Public Libraries Slavery and the slave trade in the British dominions; a select list of books and pamphlets in the Reference Library, prepared in connection with the centenary of the death of William Wilberforce Manchester, 1933. 18p.

1717. Oxford, University, Rhodes House Library. Papers of the British and Foreign Anti-Slavery and Aborigines Protection Society, kept in Rhodes House Library. Oxford, 1956. 52p.

Economics

GENERAL

1718. Allen, C. Geoffrey. "Manuscript collections in the British Library of Political and Economic Science." Journal of the Society of Archivists, 2 (1960), 52-60.

Analysis and description of collections.

1719. Aslib, Economics Group. Union list of periodicals. n.p.: Aslib, 1958. 90p. (Aslib publications, no.81)

Records 1,500 titles with locations in 29 libraries.

1720. Black, R. D. Collison. A catalogue of pamphlets on economic subjects published between 1750 and 1900 and now housed in Irish libraries. Belfast: Queen's University, 1969. 632p.

Lists 10,011 items with locations in 17 libraries; chronological arrangement, with indexes of authors, titles, societies, and institutions.

1721. Cambridge, University, Marshall Library of Economics. Catalogue, comp. by Mary Paley Marshall and D. Barber. Cambridge: Univ. Pr., 1927. 134*l*. Supplementary catalogue, 1931. 32p. Second supplementary catalogue, 1933. 38*l*.

Library assembled by Alfred Marshall, presented to Cambridge University.

1722. Committee on Latin America. Latin American economic & social serials. London: Clive Bingley, 1969. 189p.

Listed by countries; holdings reported for numerous libraries.

1723. Commonwealth Economic Committee Library. List of current periodicals received in the C.E.C. Library. London: The Committee, 1961. 53p.

Geographical arrangement.

1724. Great Britain, Board of Trade, Economics Division. Recent additions to the Economics Division libraries. London, 1967- .

1725. ———, Dept. of the Environment Library. Classified accessions list. London, 1942-72. Bimonthly.

Discontinued; succeeded by listings in Library bulletin of the Department of the Environment, 1972- , biweekly.

1726. Hanson, L. W. Contemporary printed sources for British and Irish economic history, 1701-1750. Cambridge: Univ. Pr., 1963. 978p.

Lists 6,497 items; copies located in numerous British, Irish, American, and Canadian libraries; chronological arrangement.

1727. London School of Economics and Political Science, British Library of Political and Economic Science. Guide to the collections. London, 1948. 136p.

Arranged by subjects and types of material. "The Library is probably the largest of its kind in the world" (Walford).

1728. ——— ———. Monthly list of additions. London, no.128- . 1958- .

1729. ——— ———. Notes for readers, 17th ed. London, 1970. 30p.

Includes discussion of library's resources.

1730. ——— ———. Outline of the resources of the Library. London, 1972. 44p.

Describes library's holdings in various subject fields, types of material, and special collections.

1731. ——— Library. A reader's guide to the British Library of Political and Economic Science, University of London, 3d ed. London, 1945. 76p.

1732. London, University, Goldsmiths' Library. The Goldsmiths' Company Library of economic literature, 1903-1953. London, 1954. 5p.

1733. ——— ———. List of economic books and sracts, acts of Parliament, broadsides, and proclamations from the Library of the Earl of Sheffield, presented to the Goldsmiths' Library by the Worshipful Company of Goldsmiths, November, 1907. London 1908. 16p. Supplement, 1907. 4p.

1734. ——— ———. [Manuscript catalogue of the Foxwell library of economic literature. Transcription copy. London, 1909?] 3v.

Collection assembled by H. S. Foxwell and presented to University of London in 1903.

1735. ———, Library. Catalogue of the collection of broadsides in the University Library (Goldsmiths' Library of Economic Literature). London: Univ. of London Pr., 1930. 201p. Supplement, 1930. 4p.

Lists 679 items, 1641 to 19th century, with annotations.

1736. ——— ———. Catalogue of the Goldsmiths' Library of Economic Literature, comp. by Margaret Canney and David Knott. v.1, printed books to 1800. Cambridge: Univ. Pr. for Univ. of London Library, 1970. 838p.

Listing of 18,113 items; v.2 will cover period 1801-50, and v.3 periodicals, manuscripts, and index.

1737. Reeves, Dorothea D. Resources for the study of economic history; a preliminary guide to pre-twentieth century printed material in collections located in certain American and British libraries. Boston, Mass.: Baker Library, Harvard Graduate School of Business Administration, 1961. 62p.

1738. Sperling, John G. "A bibliographical finding list for the South Sea Company." In his: The South Sea Company; an historical essay and bibliographical finding list. Boston, Mass.: Baker Library, Harvard Univ. 1962. 92p.

 List of 625 18th-century items, with locations in 5 British and American libraries.

1739. Toynbee Hall. Toynbee Hall Students' Library; books on economic and social subjects. [A catalogue, by C. F. Newcombe.] London: Penny & Hull, 1900. 52p.

1740. Wagner, Henry Raup. Irish economics, 1700-1783; a bibliography with notes. London: J. Davy, The Dryden Pr., 1907. 95p.

 Lists 369 items, with locations of copies seen in British and Irish libraries.

LABOR AND INDUSTRIAL RELATIONS

1741. Eberlein, Alfred. Die Presse der Arbeiterklasse und der Sozialen Bewegungen. Berlin: Akademie-Verlag, 1968-69. 4v.

 Contains 22,875 entries, recording 957 libraries' holdings of publications from 1830s to 1967 of German, Austrian, and Swiss worker organizations, trade unions, and occupational groups; British libraries included.

1742. Eccles Public Libraries. Trade unions; a union list of books . . . published on behalf of the libraries of Altrincham, Eccles, Sale, Salford, & Swinton & Pendlebury, comp. and edited by J. Turner. Eccles, 1957. Unpaged.

1743. Great Britain, Ministry of Labour Library. Library list of selected articles; abstracted from current periodicals. London, 1966- .

1744. ———. List of current periodicals at the Ministry of Labour Library. London, 1967. 26p.

1745. Hobsbawm, E. J. "Records of the trade union movement." Archives, 4 (1960), 129-37.

 An attempt to trace locations of surviving records in Britain.

1746. Nottingham, University, Library. Trade union periodicals. Nottingham, 1967. 9l.

 Periodicals included in library's special collection of trade union and co-operative material.

PUBLIC WORKS

1747. Great Britain, Ministry of Public Building and Works. Consolidated accessions lists. 1945- . London, 1945- . no.1- .

 Catalog of Ministry Library's books and pamphlets, compiled every 6 months.

1748. ——— ———, Library. Consolidated building reference, 1946- . London, 1946- . no.1- .

 Annual list of references to selected articles from 500 periodicals in Ministry's library.

1749. ——— ——— ———. List of current periodicals. London, 1970. 48l.

 Locates holdings in headquarters and branch libraries.

Business and Commerce

GENERAL

1750. Birmingham, University, Library. Arden and Cobden Hotels, Ltd. business records, 1874-1948. Birmingham, 1969. Unpaged. (Catalogues of the manuscript collections, no.25)

1751. ——— ———. Cannock Chase Colliery Company, Limited, and Wolverhampton Railway. Birmingham, 1967. Unpaged. (Catalogues of the manuscript collections, no.1)

 Calendar of documents.

1752. Bristol Public Library. A guide to the Library of Commerce, ed. by James Ross. Bristol: Central Public Library, 1937. 80p.

 Analysis of Bristol Central Public Library's resources for study of business and commercial activity.

1753. British Nylon Spinners Limited, Library and Information Service, Economics Library. The Common Market, a select bibliography. London, 1962. Unpaged.

 Records 455 references.

1754. Business Archives Council. Indexed sources for business history in London libraries and museums. London, 1958. 9p.

 Notes on resources of 36 libraries.

1755. City Business Library. Periodicals; a list of the commercial, financial and professional periodicals taken currently in the City Business Library. London, 1969. 28p.

1756. ——. Periodicals; a list of the commercial, financial and professional periodicals taken currently in the City Business Library, London. London, 1971. 42p.

Classified by fields.

1757. College of Estate Management. Library catalogue. St. Albans Grove, Kensington, 1953. 151p.

1758. Great Britain, Board of Trade Library. Catalogue of the Library of the Board of Trade. London: Eyre and Spottiswoode, for H. M. Stationery Office, 1866. 648p.

1759. ——, Labour Department, Board of Trade. Catalogue of Library, 1912. London: H. M. Stationery Office, 1913. 467p.

1760. ——, Ministry of Overseas Development Library. Development index; list of periodical articles indexed by the Ministry of Overseas Development Library. London, 1968- .

Issued periodically.

1761. —— ——. Select bibliography on British aid to developing countries, 2d ed. London, 1969. 20p.

Lists 218 items held by Ministry's library.

1762. ——, Ministry of Overseas Development. Selective list of accessions to the Library. London, 1966- .

Issued periodically.

1763. —— ——, Tropical Products Institute Library. List of current periodicals. London, 1970. 30p.

1764. Guildhall Library. London business house histories: a handlist. London: Corp. of City of London, 1965. 156p.

1765. Hargreaves, E. "The resources of the Leeds Public Libraries for the study of commerce, science and technology." Aslib proceedings, 3 (1951), 123-30.

General review, by subjects and types of material.

1766. Incorporated Society of Auctioneers and Landed Property Agents. Library catalogue, March, 1956. London, 1956. 75p.

1767. Joint Committee on the Lancashire Bibliography. Lancashire business histories, comp. by Sidney Horrocks. Manchester, 1971. 116p.

Locates copies in numerous libraries.

1768. Leeds, University, Brotherton Library. Business archives. Leeds, 1968. 16l.

Calendar of materials held, under names of firms.

1769. ——. Robert Clough (Keighley), established 1800; handlist of the firm's business records deposited in the Brotherton Library. Leeds, 1972. 10l. (Handlist, no.12)

1770. Library Association, Reference, Special, and Information Section, Yorkshire Group. Yorkshire business histories, a bibliography, ed. by Joyce M. Bellamy. London: Bradford Univ. Pr. and Crosby Lockwood, 1970. 457p.

Locates copies in 42 libraries.

1771. London Graduate School of Business Studies. Periodicals in the Library of the London Business School. London, 1971. 26l.

Alphabetical list of holdings.

1772. Manchester Public Libraries, Commercial Library & Information Dept. Commercial information: a guide to the Commercial Library, 3d ed., by A. L. Smyth. Manchester, 1969. 33p.

1773. ——. Quality and reliability; a select bibliography, comp. by J. E. Wild. Manchester, 1966. 16l. (Business bibliographies, no.4)

1774. ——. Sources of business bibliographies. Manchester, 1967. 25p.

1775. Nottingham Public Libraries, Commercial and Technical Library. Productivity and management. Nottingham, 1963. 31p.

Comprehensive list of books relating to productivity and management held by Nottingham Library.

1776. Sheffield City Libraries. Catalogue of business and industrial records, 2d ed. Sheffield, 1971. 42p.

1777. Westminster Public Libraries. The consumer and consumer protection. London, 1964? 13p.

Based on holdings of Westminster's Central Reference Library.

ACCOUNTING

1778. Association of Certified and Corporate Accountants Library. Library catalogue. London, 1956. 106p.

Arranged alphabetically by subjects.

1779. Institute of Chartered Accountants in England and Wales Library. Current accounting literature 1971; the catalogue of the Members' Reference Library, comp. and ed. by M. G. J. Harvey. London: Mansell, 1971. 586p.

Approximately 10,000 entries

1780. ———. Library catalogue. London, 1937. 2v.
v.1, subjects and authors; v.2, bibliography of bookkeeping.

1781. ———. Menbers' Library; short list of books. London: The Institute, 1961. 59p.

1782. Institute of Chartered Accountants of Scotland. Catalogue of printed books and pamphlets on accounting and allied subjects dated 1494 to 1896, forming a collection of antiquarian interest in the Institute's Edinburgh Library. Edinburgh, 1963. 44p.
Lists some 250 titles, about one half preceding 1700.

1783. Institute of Cost and Works Accountants. Library catalogue. London, 1963. 71p.
About 1,000 items relating to economics, business management, accountancy, etc.

1784. Society of Incorporated Accountants and Auditors Library. Catalogue of the Library at Incorporated Accountants' Hall. London, 1939. 487p.
Dictionary arrangement.

1785. Yamey, B. S., and others. Accounting in England and Scotland: 1543-1800. London: Sweet and Maxwell, 1963. 228p. + 16 plates.
Includes "bibliography: books on accounting in English, 1543-1800," with locations in Institute of Chartered Accountants in England and Wales and Institute of Chartered Accountants of Scotland.

ADVERTISING AND MARKETING

1786. Institute of Practitioners in Advertising Library. Catalogue of books. London, 1958-60. 2pts.
pt.1, Lending Section; pt.2, Reference Section.

1787. OXO Library. Buying, marketing and advertising. London, 1970. 12p.
Books in library's stock.

1788. ———. Marketing, 3d ed. London, 1969. 10l. (Subject list no.1.)
Books in library's stock.

1789. Regent Advertising Club. Library catalogue. London, [1936.] 40p.

BANKING AND FINANCE

1790. Bank of England Library and Literary Association. Catalogue of the Bank of England Library and Literary Association, instituted March 1, 1850. London: Bank of England, 1881. 287p.
Classified by types of material and subjects.

1791. Edinburgh, University, Library. Decimal coinage in Britain. Catalogue of an exhibition illustrating the development of the idea of a decimal currency for Britain. Edinburgh, 1971. Unpaged.
Listing of 48 items.

1792. Institute of Bankers Library. Books for bankers (reading list). London, 1962. 40l.

1793. ———. Catalogue of the Library, 4th ed. London: Blades, East & Blades, 1915. 185p.

1794. ———. Institute of Bankers Library guide. pt.I: banking and finance. London, 1956. 63p.

1795. ———. Library catalogue. Section 2. Pamphlets. London, 1949. 2v.

1796. ———. Catalogue. London, 1950. 14pts. Typescript.

1797. Manchester Public Libraries, Commercial Library and Information Department. Finance and investment, some serial publications available in the Commercial Library. Manchester, 1965. 23p.
Holdings shown.

INSURANCE

1798. Faculty of Actuaries in Scotland Library. Catalogue of the Library of the Faculty of Actuaries in Scotland. Edinburgh, 1899. 223p.

1799. Institute of Actuaries Library. Catalogue of the Library of the Institute of Actuaries, London. Edinburgh: R. & R. Clark, 1894. 163p.
Dictionary catalog.

1800. ———. Catalogue of the Library of the Institute of Actuaries. London, 1935. 202p. Additions to the Library, 1935-40. London, 1935-40. 6pts.

MANAGEMENT

1801. British Institute of Management. BIM Library periodical holdings. London, 1970. 46p.

1802. ———. Periodicals & house organs held in the Library at British Institute of Management. London, 1963. 46p.
Lists about 400 titles.

1803. ———. Periodicals holdings list of the British Institute of Management Library. London: The Library, 1967. 80p.

1804. Manchester Public Libraries. Commercial Library. Management periodicals available in the Commercial Library, 2d ed. Manchester, 1971. 19p. (Business bibliographies, no.6)

POSTAL SERVICE

1805. Geographical Association, Postal Reference Library. Subject index and author catalogue of the Postal Reference Library of the Geographical Association now at Marine Terrace, Aberystwyth. Aberystwyth, 1925. 80p. Additions . . . May 1925 to May 1926. 95p.

1806. Great Britain, Post Office Library. Catalogue of the Post Office Library. London: General Post Office, 1937. 182p.

SHORTHAND

1807. Guildhall Library. "A handlist of works on shorthand in the Guildhall Library." Guildhall miscellany, 2 (1960), 39-42.

1808. Institute of Shorthand Writers Library. Catalogue of the books in the Library of the Institute of Shorthand Writers practising in the Supreme Court of Judicature, by Matthias Levy. London, 1900. 93p. Addenda to Catalogue, by M. Levy. [1901, 1903, 1904]. London, 1901-4, 3pts.

1809. Manchester Public Libraries. The short-hand collection in the Free Reference Library. Manchester: H. Blacklock and Co., 1891. 44p. (Occasional lists, no.3)

TRANSPORTATION

1810. Birmingham, University, Library. Canals collection handlist. Birmingham, 1968. 5*l*. (Catalogues of the manuscript collections, no.6)
Printed and manuscript items relating to canals in the Midlands area.

1811. Cambridge Shire Hall. Catalogue of plans, documents, etc. Index. Railway, other undertakings, and miscellaneous records, Shire Hall, Cambridge, Muniments Room, catalogued by F. F. Liddle. Cambridge, 1936. 32*l*.

1812. Fowkes, E. H. "Sources of history in railway records of British Transport Historical Records." Journal of the Society in Archivists, 3 (1969), 476-88.

1813. Great Britain, British Railways Board, Research Department Library. Stocks of periodicals held in the libraries of London Road, Derby, and 222, Marylebone Road, London, N.W.1. London: British Transport Commission, 1960. 26*l*.
500 titles listed.

1814. —— —— ——. Stocks of periodicals held in the Library, Derby. London, 1971. 29p.
Alphabetical list of holdings.

1815. ——, Ministry of Transport Library. Library accessions list, January 1966- . London, 1966- .
Preceded by List of recent accessions, July 1963-Dec. 1965.

1816. —— ——. List of periodicals and newspapers currently received. London: The Ministry, 1968- .
Issued periodically.

1817. Hadfield, George. "Sources for the history of British canals." Journal of transport history, 2 (Nov. 1955), 80-89.
Includes data on canal company records in various repositories.

1818. Johnson, L. C. "British Transport Historical Records Department: the first decade." Archives, 6 (1964), 163-71.
Describes books, papers, and documents collected on history of various forms of transport.

1819. London, University, Goldsmiths' Library. List of manuscripts, maps and plans, and printed books and pamphlets mostly on railways and navigation, from the collection of John Urpeth Rastrick, and his son Henry Rastrick; presented by the Worshipful Company of Goldsmiths to the Goldsmiths' Library. London, 1908. 16p.

1820. Manchester, University, Library. Edmondson railway collection. [Manchester,] n.d. Unpaged.
Listing of ephemera, tickets, etc., beginning with 1831.

1821. National Liberal Club, Gladstone Library. Early railway pamphlets, 1825-1900. London, 1938. 60p.

1822. Ottley, George. A bibliography of British railway history. London: Allen & Unwin, 1965. 683p.
Contains total of 7,950 entries; locations in various British libraries and Library of Congress.

1823. Palmer, J. E. C. Railway periodicals of the nineteenth century published in the British Isles: a bibliographical guide. London, 1959. Unpaged. (Diploma in Librarianship, Univ. of London)
Files located in British Museum, Cambridge, Bodleian, and Patent Office.

1824. Peddie, R. A. Railway literature, 1556-1830; a handlist. London: Grafton, 1931. 79p.
Locations in numerous British, American, and other libraries; chronological arrangement.

1825. Smith, G. C. K. "The O'Dell transport collection and local railway history." Aberdeen University review, 43 (1969), 33-38.

Describes collection of about 1,000 printed works, plus maps and plans, manuscripts, and documents, in Aberdeen University Library.

Law

GENERAL

1826. Aberdeen, University, Library. Some early law books in Aberdeen University Library, by Walter Menzies. Edinburgh, 1932. 16p. + 10 plates. (Reprinted from Publications of the Edinburgh Bibliographical Society, v.15)

Descriptions of selected works, 1477-1585.

1827. ———. Subject catalogue of the Law Library in Marischal College. Aberdeen: Adelphi, 1906. 111p.

Arranged by Dewey classification with index of authors.

1828. ———, Marischal College. Law Library subject catalogue. Aberdeen, Rosemount, 1930. 118p.

Dewey classification arrangement, with subject and author indexes.

1829. Advocates Library. Catalogue of the Library of the Society of Advocates in Aberdeen, 1892. Aberdeen: Univ. Pr., 1892. 165p.

Library transferred in 1925 to National Library of Scotland, except law collection.

1830. ———. Catalogue of the Library of the Society of Advocates in Aberdeen, 1905. Aberdeen: William Mutch, 1905. 144p. Supplement, 1907. 7p.

Library transferred in 1925 to National Library of Scotland, except law collection.

1831. Bristol Incorporated Law Society. Catalogue and Library bye-laws of the Bristol Incorporated Law Society, revised and corrected to 5th January, 1914, by James J. Thomas. Bristol, 1914. 237p. Earlier edition: Bristol, 1900. 168p.

1832. British Museum. A chronological list with press-marks of English, Irish and Scottish law reports in the British Museum. Manuscript.

Grouped under House of Lords, Privy Council, Chancery, King's Bench, Crown cases, etc.

1833. Cowley, John Duncan. "The abridgements of the statutes, 1481?-1551." Library, 4th ser., 12 (1931), 125-73.

Detailed descriptions of editions of the English statutes; includes STC numbers and other locations.

1834. ———. A bibliography of abridgements, digests, dictionaries and indexes of English law to the year 1800. London: Quaritch, 1932. 196p.

List of 330 items, with locations of copies.

1835. Darlington Public Library, Museum, and Art Gallery. Catalogue of the Darlington Law Library. Darlington, 1942. 34p.

1836. Faculty of Procurators Library. Catalogue of the books in the Court-house Library . . . at 31st December, 1923. Glasgow, 1924. 50p.

1837. ———. Catalogue of the books in the Library of the Faculty of Procurators in Glasgow. Glasgow: Robert Maclehose, 1887. 497p.

Alphabetical with index of subjects.

1838. Fox, Kenneth Owen. "The records of the Courts of Great Sessions." Journal of the Society of Archivists, 3 (Oct. 1966), 177-82.

Records presented to National Library of Wales; 17th to 19th centuries.

1839. Glasgow, University, Library. Catalogue of a collection of civil and canon law books in the University of Glasgow. Glasgow, 1949. Unpaged.

Record of 262 volumes, 16th-17th centuries, Italian, etc.

1840. Graham, Howard Jay, and Heckel, John W. "The book that 'made' the common law: the first printing of Fitzherbert's Le graunde abridgement, 1514-1516." Law library journal, 51 (1958), 100-16.

Contains census of copies, p,103, in British, American, and Irish libraries.

1841. Gray's Inn. A catalogue of the ancient manuscripts belonging to the Honourable Society of Gray's Inn. London: Spottiswoode, 1869. 22p.

Describes in detail 24 items, 12th-14th centuries.

1842. ——— Library. Catalogue of the books in the Library of the Honourable Society of Gray's Inn, comp. by W. R. Douthwaite. London: C. F. Roworth, 1888. 720p.

1843. ——— ———. Catalogue of the books in the Library of the Honourable Society of Gray's Inn: with an index of subjects, comp. by James Mulligan and M. D. Severn. London: Witherby & Co., 1906. 959p.

1844. Great Britain, Treasury Solicitor's Department. Catalogue of the legal library of the Treasury Solicitor. London, 1963. 189p.

Many early and rare works; author section contains about 1,400 entries.

1845. —— Treasury, Legal Library. Catalogue of the legal library of the Treasury Solicitor, 2d ed. London: Treasury, 1967. 236p.

1846. —— Treasury Solicitor's Dept. Library. Catalogue of the legal library of the Treasury Solicitor, 3d ed., comp. by R. Toole Stott. London: Treasury Solicitor's Dept., 1971. 246p.

1847. Incorporated Law Society Library. Catalogue of the printed books in the library of the Incorporated Law Society, by Frederic Boase. London: Spottiswoode, 1891. 1,084p.

1848. ——. Supplement to the Catalogue of the Library of the Law Society, 1891-1906, by Walter M. Sinclair. London: Spottiswoode, 1906. 632p.

1849. Inner Temple. A calendar of the Inner Temple records . . . ed. by F. A. Inderwick and R. A. Roberts. London: H. Sotheran & Co., 1896-1936. 5v.

1850. —— Library. A catalogue of the printed books and manuscripts in the Library of the Inner Temple, arranged in classes. London, 1833. 289p.

1851. Jacob, I. H. "Later legal records and the historian." Archives, 6 (1964), 135-46.
Study of British legal records and recordkeeping since 1873.

1852. Leeds Law Library. Catalogue of the Law Library. Leeds: Libraries and Arts Committee, 1954. 73p.

1853. Leeds Libraries and Arts Committee. Catalogue of the Law Library, 3d ed. Leeds, 1960. 71p.
Author catalog, with subject index.

1854. Lincoln's Inn Library. A catalogue of pamphlets, tracts, proclamations, speeches, sermons, trials, petitions from 1506 to 1700 in the Library of the Hon. Society of Lincoln's Inn, comp. by William P. Baildon. London: Chiswick, 1908. 482p.
Contains 2,185 titles in chronological order.

1855. ——. A catalogue of the manuscripts in the Library of the Honourable Society of Lincoln's Inn, by Joseph Hunter. London: Hon. Society of Lincoln's Inn, 1838. 157p.

1856. ——. Catalogue of the printed books in the Library of the Hon. Society of Lincoln's Inn, by William H. Spilsbury. London, 1859. 970p.

1857. ——. Catalogue of the printed books in the Library of the Hon. Society of Lincoln's Inn; supplementary volume, containing the additions from 1859-1890, by John Michalson. London, 1890. 467p.

1858. ——. A guide to Commonwealth and colonial law reports and journals in the Lincoln's Inn Library, comp. by Y. H. McGowan. London, 1965. 21*l.*

1859. ——. Guide to Commonwealth and colonial legislation including overseas legislation issued by the Foreign Office held in Lincoln's Inn Library, comp. by Y. H. McGowan and S. J. Hodges. London, 1964. 48*l.*

1860. ——. A guide to Commonwealth law reports, legislation and journals in the Lincoln's Inn Library, 2d ed., comp. by Y. H. McGowan. London, 1967. 79*l.*
Arranged by country or locality.

1861. London, University, Institute of Advanced Legal Studies. A bibliographical guide to the law of the United Kingdom, the Channel Islands and the Isle of Man, etc. London, 1956. 219p.

1862. ——. The Du Parcq Library of Channel Islands Law. Lists of accessions. 1950- .
Issued periodically.

1863. ——. A survey of legal periodicals held in British libraries. London, 1949. 52p.

1864. ——. A survey of legal periodicals; union catalogue of holdings in British libraries, 2d ed. London, 1957. 82p. (Publication, no.1)

1865. ——. Survey of libraries' holdings of legal periodicals. London, 1949. 41p.

1866. ——. Union list of air law literature in libraries in Oxford, Cambridge, and London. London, 1956. 54p. (Publication, no.4)

1867. ——. Union list of Commonwealth and South African law: a location guide to Commonwealth and South African legislation, law reports and digests held by libraries in the United Kingdom at May 1963. London, 1963. 129p. (Publication, no.2)

1868. ——. Union list of legal periodicals; a location guide to holdings of legal periodicals in libraries in the United Kingdom, 3d ed. London, 1968. 179p.
Locates files in numerous libraries.

1869. ——. Union list of United States legal literature: holdings of legislation, law reports and digests in libraries in Oxford, Cambridge and London; 2d ed. London, 1967. 82p. (Union catalogue, no.3)

1870. ——. Union list of West European legal literature; publications held by libraries in Oxford, Cambridge and London. London, 1966. 426p. (Union catalogue, no.5)

1871. Manchester Incorporated Law Library Society. Catalogue of the books of the Manchester Incorporated Law Library Society. Manchester, 1935. 316p.

1872. Middle Temple. A calendar of the Middle Temple records, ed. by C. H. Hopwood. London, 1903. 268p.

1873. Middle Temple Library. A catalogue of books chiefly on foreign and international law collected by the late Baron Phillimore of Shiplake . . . and presented to the Library of the Honourable Society of the Middle Temple, comp. by H. A. C. Sturgess. Glasgow, 1930. 90p.

1874. ———. Catalogue of the printed books in the Library of the Middle Temple, alphabetically arranged with an index of subjects. London: Phipps & Connor, 1880. 943 + 116p.

1875. ———. A catalogue of the printed books in the Library of the Honourable Society of the Middle Temple, by C. E. A. Bedwell. Glasgow: Univ. Pr., 1914. 3v.
    v.1-2, authors; v.3, subject index. Supplement, 1914-1924. Glasgow, 1925. 2pts.

1876. ———. Catalogus librorum bibliothecae Honorabilis Societatis Medii Templi, Londini. London: Carolo Worsley, 1734. 584p.

1877. Richardson, F. P. "The Law Society Library: a short historical description." Law librarian, 1 (Aug. 1970), 15-19.
    History, description of holdings, and services.

1878. Sheffield City Libraries. Catalogue of law literature in the Assize Courts Library and Reference Libraries. Sheffield: Libraries and Arts Committee, 1964. 56p.
    Author catalog, with subject index.

1879. Society of Writers to the Signet Library. Catalogue of the law books in the library of The Society of Writers to Her Majesty's Signet in Scotland, by William Ivory. Edinburgh, 1856. 266p.

1880. Way, D. J. "The Liverpool University Law Library." Law librarian, 1 (April 1970), 3-4.
    History, services, and outline of collections.

INTERNATIONAL LAW AND RELATIONS

1881. Cardiff Free Public Library and Museum. The peace movement in Wales; list of publications in the Cardiff Public Library. Cardiff, 1936. 7p.

1882. Great Britain, Foreign Office Library. Catalogue of printed books in the Library of the Foreign Office, London. London: H. M. Stationery Office, 1926. 1,587p.
    Dictionary catalog, subjects and authors in one alphabet.

1883. London School of Economics, Edward Fry Library of International Law. Catalogue of the books, pamphlets, and other documents in the Library together with other works bearing on the subject of international law contained in the Library of the London School of Economics, comp. by B. M. Headicar. London: St. Clements, 1923. 174p.

1884. Reconciliation Library. Catalogue 1962-1963. London: International Fellowship of Reconciliation, n.d. 56p.
    Relates to peace movements, antiwar efforts, and similar topics.

1885. Royal Institute of International Affairs Library. Catalogue of periodicals currently received in Chatham House Library. London: The Institute, 1971. 20p.
    Lists 669 titles with holdings.

1886. ———. Index to periodical articles, 1950-1964, in the Library of the Royal Institute of International Affairs, London. Boston: G. K. Hall, 1965. 2v.
    Over 30,000 entries for material published between 1950 and 1964 relating to politics, economics, and jurisprudence.

Military Science and History

GENERAL

1887. Cockle, Maurice J. D. A bibliography of English military books up to 1642 and of contemporary foreign works, ed. by H. D. Cockle. London: Simpkin, Marshall, Hamilton, Kent, 1900. 268p.
    Locations in 5 English libraries for 960 works, 1489-1657.

1888. Dobie, Marryat R. "Military manuscripts in the National Library of Scotland." Journal of the Society for Army Historical Research, 27 (1949), 118-20.

1889. Gibson, Strickland. "The art of war, an exhibition." Bodleian Library record, 2 (1941), 43-50; 2 (1942), 59-62.
    Descriptions of early and rare items, drawn from Bodleian Library collection.

1890. Great Britain, Ministry of Defence Libraries. Accessions to the Ministry of Defence Libraries, Sept.

1964- . London: Ministry of Defence Library (Central and Army), 1964- . Monthly.

Adds about 1,000 entries monthly; grouped under 13 subject areas.

1891. ———, Ministry of Defence (Central and Army) Library. A bibliography of regimental histories of the British Army, comp. by Arthur S. White. London: Society for Army Historical Research, 1965. 265p.

Based on Ministry of Defence Library (formerly War Office Library) holdings.

1892. ——— ———. Index of book lists, 1971. London, 1971. 34p.

The numerous lists issued by the library, and frequently updated, report the library's holdings on specialized subjects; index issued in 2 parts: military and nonmilitary subjects.

1893. ———, Royal Artillery Institution Library. A catalogue of the Library of the Royal Artillery at Woolwich; instituted November 1st, 1809. Woolwich: M. Coleman, 1825. 325p.

1894. ——— ———. Catalogue of the Royal Artillery Institution Library (Military Section). Woolwich: The Institution, 1913. 139p.

1895. ———, War Dept., Chemical Defence Experimental Establishment. Catalogue of periodicals held by the Library of the Technical Information and Reference Section. Porton Down, Wilts.: C.D.E.E., 1960. 13p.

1896. ———, War Office, Director of Education. Army Central Library catalogue. London: War Office, 1952. 567p. Supplements 1-4. 1952-58.

Now Ministry of Defence Library.

1897. ——— ———, Army Central Library. Military history collection. London, n.d. 49p.

Now Ministry of Defence Library.

1898. ———, War Office Library. Catalogue of the War Office Library. London: H. M. Stationery Office, 1906-12. 3pts. Supplements, pts.1-2, 1916; pt.3, 1913-32. pts.1-2, authors; pt.3, subject index.

Now Ministry of Defence Library.

1899. Higham, Robin. A guide to the sources of British military history. Berkeley: Univ. of Calif. Pr., 1971. 630p.

Contains bibliographies and notes on archival and manuscript repositories.

1900. Imperial War Museum Library. Army education. London, n.d. 4l. (Booklist, no.1021)

1901. ———. Bibliography of espionage and treason. London, 1955. 21p. Addenda, 1963. 8p.

1902. ———. Bibliography of selected references to Russian naval, military and air forces in the Imperial War Museum Library. London, 1957. 12p.

1903. ———. British medals and decorations. London, n.d. 2l. (Booklist, no.1026)

1904. ———. Censorship during the First World War. London, n.d. 3l. (Booklist, no.1144)

1905. ———. A list of selected references; books and pamphlets, the New Zealand army. London, 1963. 12p.

1906. ———. New Zealand army journals; newspapers, news-sheets, magazines, etc., in the Imperial War Museum Reference Library. London, 1962. 5p.

1907. ———. The Red Army. London, n.d. 3l. (Booklist, no.1267)

1908. ———. The Royal Flying Corps, Royal Naval Air Service and Royal Air Force, 1912-1918; a list of selected references from the Reference Library. London, 1962. 2pts.

1909. Leslie, John Henry, and Smith, D. A bibliography of works by officers, non-commissioned officers, and men, who have ever served in the Royal Madras, or Bombay Artillery, 2d ed., 1909-20. 9pts.

Locates copies.

1910. Myers, M. A. Regimental histories of the Indian Army. London, 1957. 66p. (Diploma in Librarianship, Univ. of London)

Locations in British Museum, India Office Library, War Office Library, etc.

1911. National Book League. The British soldier; an exhibition of books, manuscripts and prints covering the last 250 years, org. by G. A. Shepperd. London, 1956. 54p.

Locations in public and private collections.

1912. Prince Consort's Library. Catalogue of the books, maps, and plans in the Military Library of His Royal Highness the Prince Consort, Aldershot. London: Taylor and Francis, 1860-61. 2pts.

1913. ———. Prince Consort's Library, Aldershot; centenary exhibition; the book display, etc. Aldershot: 1960. 34p.

Includes Prince Consort's Military Library.

1914. ———. The Prince Consort's Library, Aldershot, 1860-1960. Aldershot, 1960. 39p.

Includes Prince Consort's Military Library.

1915. Royal United Service Institution. Calendar of military manuscripts in the Royal United Service Institution, comp. by Colonel Sir Lonsdale Hale. London, 1914. 42p.

1916. —— Library. Catalogue of the Library of the Royal United Service Institution (to January 1st, 1908). London: Harrison & Sons, 1908. 2pts.

1917. Ruddock, Alwyn A. "The earliest records of the High Court of Admiralty (1515-1558)." University of London. Institute of Historical Research bulletin, 22 (1949), 139-51.

1918. Wigan Public Library. Wars and armaments in former days; an exhibition of rare books and manuscripts in the Wigan Public Library. Wigan, 1942. 12p. (Reprinted from the Wigan observer)

NAVAL SCIENCE AND HISTORY

1919. British Shipbuilding Research Association Library. Library catalogue, December 1947. London, 1948. 201p.

1920. ——. Recent additions to the Library, July 1948-   . London, 1948-   .
Issued periodically.

1921. Broadis, George James. Books on inland navigation in the Goldsmith's Library of the University of London. London, 1962. 318l. (Diploma in Librarianship, Univ. of London)
Lists 490 items in chronological order under each locality.

1922. Cobb, H. S. "Parliamentary records relating to internal navigation." Archives, 9 (1969), 73-79.
Records of both Houses of Parliament deposited in House of Lords Record Office.

1923. Cruising Association Library. The Cruising Association Library catalogue; a collection of books for seamen and students of nautical literature, atlases and charts, gathered by Herbert J. Hanson, 3d ed. London: The Association, 1954. 96p.
Author-title list.

1924. Firth, C. H. "Papers relating to the Navy in the Bodleian Library." Mariner's mirror, 3 (1913), 225-29.

1925. Great Britain, Admiralty, Admiralty Centre for Scientific Information and Liaison Library. Catalogue of books held by the Admiralty Research Organization. London, 1960-   .

1926. —— ——. Publications ordered for supply to the Admiralty research establishments during 1963. London, 1963. 51l.

1927. —— ——. Royal Naval Scientific Service; a bibliography of literature relating to fouling and its prevention. London, 1956. 236p.

1928. ——, Admiralty Library. A catalogue of the books in the Admiralty Library, comp. by Richard Thorburn. London: H. M. Stationery Office, 1875. 369p.

1929. —— ——. Subject catalogue of printed books. pt.1. Historical Section. London: H. M. Stationery Office, 1912. 374p.

1930. ——, Ministry of Defence. Author catalogue of the Naval Library, Ministry of Defence, London. Boston, Mass.: G. K. Hall, 1967. 2v.

1931. —— ——. Subject catalogue of the Naval Library, Ministry of Defence, London. Boston, Mass.: G. K. Hall, 1967. 3v.

1932. ——, Public Record Office. Catalogue of an exhibition of naval records at the Public Record Office. London: H. M. Stationery Office, 1950. 53p.
Describes 71 items, 1212-1882.

1933. Imperial War Museum Library. Bibliography of submarine warfare, submarines, and submarine services; a selected list of books and pamphlets. London, 1957. 25p.

1934. ——. "Bismarck" operation. London, n.d. 4l. (Booklist, no.1122)

1935. Laughton, L. G. Carr. "A bibliography of nautical dictionaries." Mariners mirror, 1 (1911), 84-89, 212-15.
Locates copies in Admiralty Library, British Museum, Patent Office Library, Public Record Office, and Library of the Royal United Service Institution.

1936. Lindsay-MacDougall, K. F. "Manuscripts at the National Maritime Museum," pt.1. Mariner's mirror, 40 (1954), 223-26.

1937. Lloyd's Register of Shipping. Catalogue of books in the Library, by Charles Hocking. London, 1961. 105p.
Dictionary arrangement.

1938. Manwaring, G. E. A bibliography of British naval history; a bibliographical and historical guide to printed and manuscript sources. London: George Routledge, 1930. 163p. Reprinted, 1970.
Locates manuscripts in British Museum, Bodleian, Cambridge, Public Record Office, Admiralty Library, and Royal United Service Institution.

1939. Mathias, P., and Pearsall, A. W. H. Shipping; a survey of historical records, Newton Abbott: David & Charles, 1971. 162p.

Describes and locates collections in libraries, archives, and other repositories.

1940. National Maritime Museum. A guide to the manuscripts at the National Maritime Museum, by K. F. Lindsay-MacDougall. London, 1960. 20p. + 13 plates.

Library's special field is British maritime history.

1941. Royal Cruising Club. A list of books in the Library of the Royal Cruising Club, 2d ed. London, 1909. 16p.

1942. Royal United Service Institution. Catalogue of naval manuscripts in the Library of the Royal United Service Institution, comp. by H. J. G. Garbett. London: Harrison & Sons, 1914. 105p.

1943. Woodbridge, Hensley C. "A tentative bibliography of Spanish and Catalan nautical dictionaries, glossaries and word lists." Mariner's mirror, 37 (Jan. 1951), 63-75.

Lists 142 titles chronologically, with locations in British, American, and Continental libraries.

Welfare and Social Activities

GENERAL

1944. Great Britain, Dept. of Health and Social Security Library. Periodicals currently received. London, 1971. 24p.

Shows holdings.

1945. ———, Ministry of Health Library. Current literature on local authority health and welfare services. London, 1968- .

1946. ——— ———. A list of studies on local authority health and welfare services, 1960-1965. London, 1965. 45p. Supplement, 1966. 15p.

1947. ——— ———. Selected bibliography on the National Health Service. London, 1963. 29p.

1948. ——— ———. Selected bibliography on the National Health Service. London, 1967. 50p.

1949. ———, Ministry of Pensions and National Insurance Library. Catalogue of books, pamphlets, etc., held by the M.P.N.I. library service at 31st December 1956. London, M.P.N.I., 1958. 322p.

SECRET SOCIETIES

1950. Card, Robert A., and Heaton, W. E. Catalogue of rare and early books on Freemasonry from the Wallace Heaton collection presented to the United Grand Lodge of England. Brighton: J. S. North, 1939. 41l.

1951. Freemasons' Hall Library. Catalogue of books in the Library of the Supreme Council 33° of the Ancient and Accepted Rite, comp. by Edward Armitage. London: Spottiswoode & Co., 1900. 111p.

1952. ———. United Grand Lodge of Ancient Free & Accepted Masons of England. Catalogue of books in the Library at Freemasons' Hall, London. London: George Kenning, 1888. 48p.

1953. Freemasons, United Grand Lodge of England. [Catalogues of the collections of the United Grand Lodge preserved at Freemasons' Hall. Compiled and arranged by Sir Algernon Tudor-Craig. With plates.] London, 1938. 3v.

v.1, Catalogue of contents of the museum. 341p.; v.2, Catalogue of portraits and prints. 119p.; v.3, Catalogue of manuscripts and library. 227p.

1954. Manchester Association for Masonic Research. Catalogue of books, comp. by Archibald Sparke. Manchester, 1924. 70p.

1955. Provincial Grand Lodge of Warwickshire. Books for Masonic reading, compiled from the books in the Masonic Library and Museum of the Provincial Grand Lodge of Warwickshire, by Sydney James Fenton. Birmingham: Library and Museum Committee, 1931. 20p. (Publication, no.2)

1956. Provincial Grand Lodge of Worcestershire Library. A catalogue of the Library of the Provincial Grand Lodge of Worcestershire, by Herbert Poole. Kidderminster: G. T. Cheshire, 1934. 197p.

1957. Wigan Public Library. Reference Department. Works relating to Freemasonry; catalogued by Henry Tennyson Folkard, 3d ed. Wigan, 1892. 64p.

Education

GENERAL

1958. Birmingham Public Libraries. Books for the multi-racial classroom. Birmingham, 1972. 15p.

1959. ———, Central Reference Library. Periodicals on education in the Reference Library. Birmingham, 1965. 8p.

1960. Birmingham, University, Institute of Education Library. Catalogue. Birmingham, 1951. 90p. Supplement, no.1. Birmingham, 1952. 83p.

Classified arrangement with author index.

1961. ———. Childhood and adolescence. Birmingham, 1959. 43p. (Booklist, no.3)

1962. ———. Exceptional children. Birmingham, 1958. 22p. (Booklist, no.2) Supplement, 1962.

1963. Bristol Public Libraries. The parent-teacher collection: a catalogue of books. Bristol, 1953. 178p.

1964. Chelsea Public Libraries, Metropolitan Borough of Chelsea, Public Library. Books on the history, theory, and practice of education and on educational questions. London, 1910. 36p. (Occasional list, no.1)

1965. City of Leeds and Carnegie College of Education Library. Catalogue of the Carnegie historical collection of books of physical education, sport and recreation, and health education published before 1946, 2d ed., comp. by Joan Newiss. Leeds, 1971. 93*l.*

1966. College of St. Mark and St. John Library. A union list of the periodicals of the area colleges of the London Institute of Education. London, 1959. 19*l.*

1967. Craigie, James. A bibliography of Scottish education before 1872. London: Univ. of London Pr., 1970. 255p.

Locates copies in 24 libraries, mainly in Scotland.

1968. Education Librarians of the East Midlands. Union catalogue fo periodical holdings, n.p., 1965. Unpaged.

Locates holdings of 12 libraries.

1969. Great Britain, Board of Education Library. Catalogue of the Grenfell collection of books on physical education in the Board of Education Library. London: H. M. Stationery Office, 1935. 97p.

1970. ———, Commonwealth Institute Library. Education in the Commonwealth; selected reading lists for advanced study. London, 1968. 23p.

Based on Institute Library's holdings.

1971. Guildhall Library. "Education in London before 1870; a handlist of selected items in Guildhall Library." Guildhall miscellany, 3 (1970), 218-32.

1972. Guyatt, E. Jacqueline. The training of lay primary teachers in France from the beginning of the seventeenth century to 1815; an annotated bibliography. London: Univ. of London, Institute of Edu-

cation, 1960. 215p. (Education Libraries bulletin, supplement 3)

Locates copies in 14 British and French libraries.

1973. Imperial War Museum Library. Germany since 1933; the youth movement and education. London, n.d. 3*l.* (Booklist, no.1265)

1974. King's School, Norton Library. Calendar of the manuscripts belonging to the King's School, Bruton, 1297-1826, ed. by T. D. Tremlett. Bruton, 1939. 40p.

Lists charters, deeds, land grants, leases, school registers and statutes, and other documents.

1975. Leeds Public Libraries. Choose your career. Leeds, 1971. 27p.

1976. Leeds, University, Institute of Education Library. Developing countries; a select booklist on education and related subjects with particular reference to the Commonwealth. Leeds, 1969. 33p.

Classified by subjects and countries; based on Institute's Library.

1977. ——— ———. Educational administration and school organization; a select booklist with particular reference to the Commonwealth. Leeds, 1969. 30p.

Based on Institute Library's holdings.

1978. ——— ———. Immigrants and education; a book list. Leeds, 1971. 19p.

Based on Institute Library's holdings.

1979. ——— ———. Infant and nursery schools; a book list. Leeds, 1968. 26p.

Based on Institute Library's holdings.

1980. ——— ———. Primary education (7-11); a book list. Leeds, 1971. 32p.

Based on Institute Library's holdings.

1981. ——— ———. Union list of periodicals in education (and related subjects). Leeds, 1969. 59p.

Locates files in 13 libraries.

1982. ———, Language Teaching Information Centre Reference Library. Books and materials for language teachers: contents of the Reference Library, Language Teaching Information Centre. Leeds: Nuffield Foreign Languages Teaching Materials Project, 1967. 129p.

1983. Librarians of Institutes and Schools of Education. Education in France: a union list of stock in Institute of Education libraries, ed. by J. V. Marder. Southampton: Univ. of Southampton Institute of Education, 1964. 59p.

Lists holdings of 19 libraries.

1984. ———. Education in Germany: a union list of stock in Institute of Education libraries, comp. by Miss J. V. Best. Southampton: Univ. of Southampton Institute of Education, 1963. 43p.

1985. ———. List of educational pamphlets of the Board of Education, 1904-1943, with locations in Institute of Education Libraries. Newcastle upon Tyne, 1969. 8*l.*
Lists 119 items with locations in 20 libraries.

1986. ———. Union list of books on education & educational textbooks published, or first published, in the 15th-17th centuries (with a few earlier works), rev. ed. Leicester, 1962. 23p.
Records holdings of 13 libraries.

1987. ———. Union list of books on education & educational textbooks published, or first published, 1701-1800. n.p., n.d. 31p.
Reports holdings of 10 libraries.

1988. ———. Union list of books on education & educational textbooks published 1841-1870. Leicester, 1958. 45p.
Records holdings of 15 libraries.

1989. ———. Union list of government publications relating to education (up to and including 1918). Leicester: Univ. of Leicester Institute of Education, 1959. 47p.
Records holdings of 14 libraries, excluding University of London.

1990. ———. Union list of periodicals held in Institute of Education libraries as at 30th June, 1962. 98p.
Records holdings of 17 libraries.

1991. ———. Union list of periodicals held in Institute of Education Libraries as at 31st July, 1968, ed. by J. M. Smethurst. Newcastle upon Tyne: Oriel, 1968. 217p.
Records holdings of 23 libraries for 1,900 titles.

1992. Library Association. Sources for the history of education; a list of material (including school books) contained in the libraries of the Institutes and Schools of Education, together with works from the libraries of the Universities of Nottingham and Reading, by C. W. J. Higson. London, 1967. 196p.
Locates copies in 17 libraries.

1993. ——— Yorkshire Branch. Yorkshire school history: a bibliography: publications held by Yorkshire libraries, with locations, comp. by Robin Bateman. Leeds, 1969. 81p.

1994. London County Council, Education Library. Catalogue. London: County Council, 1935. 847p. First supplement, 1935-1945. London, 1948. 531p.
Classified listing with author index.

1995. London, University, Institute of Education Library. Bibliography on education and psychology, 1939-1948. London, 1949? 36p.

1996. ———. British commentary on American education: a select and annotated bibliography, the nineteenth and twentieth centuries, by Stewart E. Fraser. London: The Institute, 1970. 140p. (Education Libraries bulletin, supplement 14)

1997. ———. Catalogue of periodicals in the Library. London: Institute of Education, 1968. 112p.
Alphabetical list followed by index to periodical holdings by continent; about 1,500 British and foreign titles.

1998. ———. Catalogue of the collection of education in tropical areas. Boston, Mass.: G. K. Hall, 1963. 3v.
Listing of 7,000 books and 11,000 pamphlets.

1999. ———. Catalogue of the Comparative Education Library. Boston, Mass.: G. K. Hall, 1971. 6v.
v.1-2, author catalog; v.3-4, subject catalog; v.5-6, regional catalog.

2000. ———. Education in Africa; a select bibliography, comp. by Margaret Couch. London, 1962-65. 2pts. (Education Libraries bulletin supplement 5, 9)
Based on catalogue of the library of the Department of Education in Tropical Areas, of the University of London Institute of Education; pt.1, British and former British territories, pt.2, French speaking territories.

2001. ———. Education in British India, 1698-1947; a bibliography and guide to the sources of information in London, by Monica Alice Greaves. London, 1967. 182p. (Education Libraries bulletin, supplement 14)
Lists 1,379 items, with copies located in 13 English libraries.

2002. ———. A guide to the literature of education, rev. ed., by S. K. Kimmance. London, 1961. 86p. (Education Libraries bulletin, supplement 1)

2003. ———. An index to nineteenth century British educational biography, by Ann Christophers. London, 1965, 88p. (Education Libraries bulletin, supplement 10)
Based on holdings of Ministry of Education and University of London's Institute of Education Library and Quick Memorial Library.

2004. ———. A provisional bibliography of the works of Sir Fred Clarke, comp. by Mary Clarke Field. London, 1962. 19p. (Education Libraries bulletin, supplement 4)

2005. ———. A selected annotated bibliography in the economics of education, by M. Blaug. London, 1964. 106p. (Education Libraries bulletin, supplement 8)

2006. ———. The training of lay primary teachers in France from the beginning of the seventeenth century to 1815; an annotated bibliography, comp. by E. Jacqueline Guyatt. London, 1960. 215p. (Education Libraries bulletin, supplement 3)
Based on holdings of 14 libraries in England and France.

2007. Loughborough University of Technology Library. Select bibliography on the education and training of technicians. Loughborough, 1967. 13l.

2008. National Book League. The English at school; an exhibition, arr. by Arnold Muirhead. London: Cambridge Univ. Pr. for the National Book League, 1949. 80p.
Lists 548 items concerned with history of education; locations in public and private collections.

2009. National Froebel Foundation, Education Library. Education Library, 1947, catalogue. London, 1956. 175p.

2010. National Union of Teachers. Library catalogue. London, 1959. 308p.
Includes education and background subjects.

2011. Newcastle upon Tyne City Libraries. Catalogue of books and pamphlets on education in the Central Library (reference and lending) and in the Stephenson and Victoria branches, by Basil Anderton. Newcastle upon Tyne, 1909. 136p.

2012. Nottingham, University, Library. W. G. Briggs collection of early educational literature, handlist. Nottingham, 1970. 42p.
Author-title list.

2013. Nowell, George F. A finding-list of books and pamphlets relating to education in the City of Bradford. London, 1952. 73l. (Diploma in Librarianship, Univ. of London)
Locates copies in 3 local libraries.

2014. Rotherham Public Library. Campaign for education; National education week, 11th-16th November 1963; a list of books on all aspects of education in the stock of the Rotherham Public Library. Rotherham, 1963. 43p.

2015. Scottish Central Film Library. Catalogue of 16mm. silent and sound educational films. Glasgow: Scottish Film Office, 1953. 224p.

2016. ———. Catalogue of silent and sound educational films. Glasgow: Scottish Film Office, 1959. 358p.

2017. ———. Catalogue of silent and sound educational films. Glasgow: Scottish Film Office, 1967. 310p.

2018. South Kensington Museum, Educational Division. Classed catalogue of the Educational Division of the South Kensington Museum. London: H.M. Stationery Office, 1876. 618p. Supplement, 55p.
Collection now part of Science Museum Library.

2019. Spence, B. V. "School Board records in County Durham, 1870-1904." Archives, 45 (1971), 20-27.
Records principally held by Durham County Record Office.

2020. Swindon Public Libraries. Books on education in the Swindon Public Libraries. Swindon, 1957. 40p.
Classified by subject.

2021. Tate, W. E. "S.P.C.K. archives with special reference to their value for the history of education (mainly 1699-c. 1740)." Archives, 3 (1957), 105-14.

2022. Teachers' Guild of Great Britain and Ireland Library. Catalogue of the Library, 3d issue. London, 1900. 211p.

2023. ———. Supplement to library catalogue, containing all additions from January 1900-January 1902. London, 1902. 32p.

2024. University College, Dublin, Library. List of research work in education and educational psychology presented at University College, Dublin, 1912-1968; a provisional list. Dublin: The College, 1969. 20l.

2025. Wandsworth Public Libraries. Education, a guide to current literature, comp. by E. W. Padwick. Wandsworth: Borough Council, 1963. 98p. + Index.
Classified by subjects and types of material.

2026. Warwick, County, County Council, Education Committee. Catalogue of books in the Students' Library. Warwick, 1921. 234p.

HIGHER EDUCATION

2027. Allen, P. S. "Early documents connected with the Library of Merton College." Library, ser.4, 4 (1924), 249-76.

Describes number of documents on history, administration and beginnings of library's collections.

2028. Anderson, P. J. Collections towards a bibliography of the Universities of Aberdeen. Edinburgh: Bibliographical Society, 1907. 159p. (Publications of the Edinburgh Bibliographical Society, v.8)
Copies located in British and Irish libraries.

2029. Birmingham, University, Library. Handlist to the University collection. Birmingham, 1967. 37*l*.
Relates to history of University of Birmingham.

2030. Blakiston, N. "The archives of Eton College." Archives, 5 (1962), 123-30.
History and present status.

2031. Cambridge, University. The archives of the University of Cambridge; an historical introduction, by Heather E. Peek and Catherine P. Hall. Cambridge: Univ. Pr., 1962. 89p.
Survey of internal records of Cambridge, from Middle Ages to present day.

2032. ———. Catalogue of Cambridge portraits; 1. The University collection, by J. W. Goodison. Cambridge: Univ. Pr., 1955. 212p. + 32 plates.
Arranged in groups under divisions of university where located; detailed descriptions.

2033. ———, Corpus Christi College Library. A collection of letters, statutes, and other documents, from the MS. Library of Corp. Christ. Coll., illustrative of the history of the University of Cambridge during the period of the Reformation, from A.D. MD. to A.D. MDLXVII, by John Lamb. London: John W. Parker, 1838. 402p.

2034. ———, Emmanuel College Library. Emmanuel College archive; hand list of books and papers relating to the history of the College now deposited in the College Library comp. by H. S. Bennett. Cambridge, 1956. Unpaged.

2035. ———, Library. Catalogue of the books and papers for the most part relating to the University, Town, and County of Cambridge, bequeathed to the University by John Willis Clark, by A. T. Bartholomew. Cambridge: Univ. Pr., 1912. 282p.
A collection of about 10,000 books, pamphlets, etc., relating to University of Cambridge and its area.

2036. Cordeaux, E. H., and Merry, D. H. A bibliography of printed works relating to the University of Oxford. Oxford: Clarendon, 1968. 809p.
Works not in the Bodleian Library are located in 29 other Oxford, British, American, and French libraries; records 8,868 items.

2037. Harvey, John H. "Winchester College muniments: an introduction with a summary index." Archives, 5 (1962), 201-16.
Summary of Sheila J. Elliott's Descriptive list of Winchester College muniments, 1960.

2038. Oxford, University, All Souls' College. Catalogue of the archives in the muniment rooms of All Souls' College, prep. by Charles Trice Martin. London: Spottiswoode, 1877. 467p.

2039. ———, Bodleian Library. "Early Oxford College manuscripts." Bodleian quarterly record, 1 (1914-16), 157-62.
Oxford College manuscripts written before A.D. 1200 listed.

2040. ——— ———. The history of the University of Oxford; guide to an exhibition held in 1953, prep. by I. G. Phillip. Oxford, 1953. 36p.

2041. ———, Merton College Library. Merton College catalogue of Mss. reproduced from the original calendar. n.p., 1961. 14v. (National Register of Archives)

2042. Sheffield, University, Library. University teaching methods; a select bibliography. Sheffield, 1972. 55p.

BLIND AND DEAF

2043. Manchester, University, Library for Deaf Education. Catalogue of the Library for Deaf Education, comp. by Charles W. E. Leigh. Manchester: Univ. Press, 1932. 143p.
In 2pts.: author index, subject index. Supplement, 1944. 14*l*.

2044. National Association of Teachers of the Deaf. The Arnold Library; catalogue of books in the Library, rev. ed., comp. by J. D. Rowan. Stoke on Trent: Hill & Ainsworth, 1907. 32p.
Collection now part of Library for Deaf Education, University of Manchester.

2045. National Library for the Blind. Catalogue of books. London, 1950-52. 2v.; Supplements, 1956, 1960, 1963.
Lists books in Braille; pt.1, fiction and juvenile; pt.2, nonfiction and foreign.

2046. ———. Catalogue of books in Moon type. London, 1952. 24p.

2047. Royal National Institute for the Blind. Catalogue of Braille books, Braille and letterpress periodicals, and letterpress books. London, 1957. 222p.; annual supplements, 1959- .

2048. ———. Catalogue of Braille books; pt.one: permanent stock. London, 1966. 98p.; supplements, 1967- .

Includes 600 entries; a Braille edition is published.

2049. ———. Catalogue of Braille books, pt.two: limited edition. London, 1967. 36p.

2050. ———. Students' Library. Catalogue of Braille books for loan. London, 1960. 258p.; supplements, 1962, 1964.

About 9,000 items.

2051. ———, Reference Library. Works on blindness and associated subjects: catalogue of the Reference Library. London, 1962. Various pagings. 2d supplement, 1967; 3d supplement, 1971.

2052. Royal National Institute for the Deaf Library. Hearing and spoken language; a select list of books. London: The Institute, 1964. 29p.

Subject arrangement.

2053. ———. Holdings of periodicals as at March 1962 (excluding sets of periodicals now extinct). London: The Institute, 1962. 18p.

Alphabetic list by titles, followed by alphabetic list by countries; shows holdings.

2054. Royal National Institute for the Deaf Reference Library. Works on blindness and associated subjects; catalogue of the Reference Library, Royal National Institute for the Deaf. London, 1962. Unpaged.

2055. Victoria University of Manchester Library. An annotated catalogue of books on the education of the deaf and cognate subjects, collected by Abraham Farrar and presented to the Arnold Library and the Library for Deaf Education in the Victoria University

of Manchester, comp. by A. Farrar. Stoke on Trent: Hill & Ainsworth, 1932. 30p.

Customs and Folklore

2056. Edinburgh, University, Library. The James Carmichaell collection of proverbs in Scots; from the original manuscript in the Edinburgh University Library, ed. by M. L. Anderson. Edinburgh: Univ. Pr., 1957. 149p.

2057. Exeter, University, Library. Folk-lore; a list of books in the University Library. Exeter, 1971. 65p.

Classified by geographical areas and types.

2058. Gypsy and Folk-lore Club Library. A catalogue of books and pamphlets. London, 1913. 24p.

2059. National Library of Scotland, Edinburgh. Catalogue of the Lauriston Castle chapbooks. Boston, Mass.: G. K. Hall, 1964. 273p.

Collection received by library in 1925; over 3,700 volumes, principally on Scottish literature, antiquities, and topography.

2060. Newcastle upon Tyne, University, Library. Chapbooks and garlands in the Robert White collection in the Library of King's College, Newcastle upon Tyne, by Desmond Sparling Bland. Newcastle upon Tyne, 1956. 40p. (King's College Library, publication, no.3)

Record of over 1,000 items, mainly printed in Newcastle, but examples also from Belfast, Glasgow, etc., up to 1800.

2061. ———. Newcastle chapbooks in the Newcastle upon Tyne Library, by Frances M. Thomson. Newcastle upon Tyne: Oriel, 1969. 109p.

Records 614 items; index of titles.

Science

General

2062. Aberdeen, University, Library. Catalogue of the books in the Library, Marischal College, 1874, by J. Fyfe. Aberdeen, 1874. 314p.

Books relating to botany, agriculture, chemistry, geology, law, medicine, mineralogy, and natural history.

2063. ———. Cruickshank Science Library subject catalogue. Aberdeen: Univ. Pr., 1921. 337p. (University of Aberdeen studies, no.82)

Dewey classification arrangement, with subject and author indexes.

2064. ———. Science and the Renaissance; an annotated bibliography of the sixteenth-century books relating to the sciences in the Library of the University of Aberdeen, by W. P. D. Wightman. Edinburgh and London: Oliver & Boyd, 1962. 293p.

Describes in detail 760 works.

2065. ———. Subject catalogue of the Science Library in Marischal College, by P. J. Anderson. Aberdeen: Univ. Pr., 1906. 319p. (Aberdeen University studies, no.23)

Arranged by Dewey classification, with detailed indexes.

2066. Birmingham Public Libraries, Bloomsbury Library. Some recent books on the pure sciences. Birmingham, 1971. 6p.

2067. Birmingham, University, Library, Science Information Office. Major information services currently available in the United Kingdom, 3d ed. Birmingham, 1972. 6l.

2068. Cambridge, University, Library. Items in an exhibition connected with the early history of the Royal Society. Cambridge, 1960. 3p.

2069. Edinburgh Museum of Science and Art Library. General catalogue of the books in the Library of the Museum, 2d edition. Glasgow: H. M. Stationery Office, 1899. 434p.

2070. Essex, University, Library. Physical sciences and mathematical studies; a guide to the bibliographical and reference materials held by the Library, 2 ed., by B. J. C. Wintour. Colchester, 1970. 165p.

Arranged by broad fields, with index.

2071. Glasgow, University, Hunterian Library. The scientific Renaissance: an exhibition of books printed mainly in the sixteenth century, held in the Hunterian Library, University of Glasgow. Glasgow, 1968. 29p.

Records 73 items, annotated.

2072. Great Britain, Patent Office Library. Subject list of works on general science, physics, sound, music, light, microscopy, and philosophical instruments in the Library of the Patent Office. London: H. M. Stationery Office, 1903. 184p.

2073. Gunther, R. T. Oxford and the history of science; with an appendix on scientific collections in college libraries; inaugural lecture, 1934. London, 1934. 49p. Reprinted in author's: Early science in Oxford, 2 (1937), 325-36.

2074. Jeffreys, Alan. "Manuscript sources for the history of science." Archives, 7 (1965), 75-79.

Notes on principal repositories of documents relating to history of science.

2075. Linnean Society of London Library. Catalogue of the manuscripts in the Library of the Linnean Society of London, by Warren R. Dawson. pt.1. The Smith papers (the correspondence and miscellaneous papers of Sir James Edward Smith). London: The Society, 1934. 114p.

Papers of society's first president.

2076. ———. Catalogue of the printed books and pamphlets in the Library of the Linnean Society of London. London: The Society, 1925. 860p.

Author-title catalog.

2077. Linnean Society of London. List of current periodicals in the Library, comp. by Sandra Raphael. London: Burlington House, 1964. 22p.

Alphabetical list, without data on holdings.

2078. Manchester, University, Library. An exhibition of notable books on science and medicine held in the Arts Library. Manchester, 1962. 63p.

Records 221 items, 15th to 18th century.

2079. National Lending Library for Science and Technology. Index of conference proceedings received by the NLL. Boston Spa: 1965- .

Issued periodically.

2080. ———. List of books received from the U.S.S.R. and translated books. Boston Spa: no.1- . 1957- .

Lists about 300 titles monthly.

2081. Newcastle upon Tyne, University, Library. 500 years of science: an alphabetical list of books included in the exhibition from March to April 1966, all drawn from the stock of the University Library, Newcastle upon Tyne. Newcastle upon Tyne, 1966. 4p.

2082. Nottingham and Nottinghamshire Technical Information Service. NANTIS handbook and directory of resources, 1969, 4th ed., comp. by M. J. Stacey. Nottingham: NANTIS, 1969. 56p.

Collections held by 95 firms and associations, members of NANTIS.

2083. Oxford, University, Bodleian Library. Bibliotheca Radcliviana, 1749-1949: catalogue of an exhibition held in the Bodleian Library and the Radcliffe Science Library to commemorate the bicentenary of the opening of the Radcliffe Library on 13 April 1749. Oxford, 1949. 48p. + 18 plates.

2084. ——— ———. Exhibition of scientific Mss. and printed books at the Bodleian Library, British Association meeting, October 1926. Oxford, 1926. 22p.

2085. ———, Radcliffe Science Library. Catalogue of books added, 1873-1926. Oxford, 1874-1927. 54v. in 3.

2086. Royal Dublin Society. Catalogue of the Library: 1. Catalogue, 1731-1839, by J. F. Jones; 2. Supplement, 1839-1849, by J. F. Jones; 3. Supplement, 1849-1859, by E. R. P. Colles. Dublin: Univ. Pr., 1860. 3pts.

Primarily science library.

2087. ———. General catalogue of the Library to June, 1895; not including scientific periodicals and the publications of learned societies. Dublin: University Press, 1896. 768p.

2088. ———. General catalogue of the Library, v.II, from July, 1895, to June, 1900; not including scientific periodicals and the publications of learned societies. Dublin: H. M. Stationery Office, 1902. 357p.

2089. Royal Military College of Science Library. Periodical holdings. Shrivenham, 1970. Unpaged.

2090. Royal Society of London. Catalogue of scientific papers, 1800-1900; subject index. Cambridge: Univ. Pr., 1908-14. 3v. in 4.

v.1, pure mathematics; v.2, Mechanics; v.3, Physics; pt.1, Generalities, heat, light, sound, pt.2, Electricity and magnetism. Locations noted in British and Irish libraries.

2091. ———. Catalogue of the scientific books in the Library of the Royal Society. London: Richard and John E. Taylor, 1839. 776p.

2092. ———. Catalogue of the scientific books in the Library of the Royal Society; transactions, journals, observations and reports, surveys, museums. London: Spottiswoode, 1881. 262p.

2093. ———. Catalogue of the scientific books in the Library of the Royal Society; general catalogue. London: Spottiswoode, 1883. 1,199p.

Alphabetical by authors.

2094. ———. Catalogue of the scientific books in the Library of the Royal Society. London: Richard and John E. Taylor, 1889. 776p.

2095. ———. Catalogue of transactions, journals, etc. London, 1871. 164p.

2096. ———. Some account of the 'Classified papers' in the archives, with an index of authors, comp. by A. H. Church. Oxford: Hart, 1907. 38p.

"Notes on a series of guard-books in the Library of the Royal Society," original papers, letters and memoranda, extracts from published works, and some broadsides and prospectuses.

2097. ———. Some account of the 'Letters and Papers' of the period 1741-1806 in the Archives with an index of authors, comp. by A. H. Church. Oxford: Hart, 1908. 73p.

2098. Science Museum Library. Catalogue of books and periodicals published in the Netherlands in foreign languages on science, technology, medicine & agriculture, etc., in the Science Museum Library, London. Amsterdam: Graphic Export Centre, 1954. 46p.

pt.1, scientific periodicals; pt.2, books.

2099. ———. Catalogue of the Library of the South-Eastern Union of Scientific Societies, now incorporated in the Science Library, Science Museum, South Kensington. London, 1939. 27p.

2100. ———. Weekly list of accessions to the library. London, 1931- . no.1- .

Each issue includes bibliographies, new periodicals, books, and pamphlets.

2101. Scientific and Learned Societies of Great Britain, a handbook compiled from official sources, 61st ed. London: Allen & Unwin, 1964. 222p.

Includes brief data on libraries.

2102. Singer, Dorothea Waley. "Hand-list of scientific Mss. in the British Isles dating from before the sixteenth century." Bibliographical Society transactions, 15 (1917-19), 185-99.

Describes and locates 42 items.

2103. Southampton University Library. Scientific and technical information, a practical guide. Southampton, 1971. 40p.

2104. Stafford County Library. Scientific and technical catalogue. Stafford: Staffordshire Education Committee, 1954. 206p.

Arranged by subjects with author index.

2105. Thorndike, Lynn, and Kibre, Pearl. A catalogue of incipits of medieval scientific writings in Latin, rev. and augmented ed. London: Mediaeval Academy of America, 1963. 1,938 cols.

Locates originals in numerous libraries and other collections in Britain, U.S., Continental Europe, etc.

2106. Thornton, John L., and Tully, R. I. J. Scientific books, libraries and collectors: a study of bibliography and the book trade in relation to science, 2d ed. London: Library Association, 1962. 406p.

"Scientific libraries of to-day," p.306-17, discusses resources of major scientific libraries in Britain and abroad.

2107. University College of Wales Library. A guide to the abstracting and current awareness services in the physical sciences. Aberystwyth: 1970. 7p. (Handlist, no.7)

2108. ———. A guide to the resources available in science: general. Aberystwyth, 1970. 9p. (Handlist, no.8)

2109. Victoria and Albert Museum, Science and Art Dept. Catalogue of the Science Library in the South Kensington museum. London: H. M. Stationery Office, 1891. 501p.

Periodicals, Scientific and Technical

2110. Aslib. Scientific and technical periodicals received from the U.S.S.R. London: Association of Special Libraries and Information Bureaux, 1942. 9l. (Aslib war-time guides to British sources of specialised information, no.4)

Entries for 334 titles.

2111. ——— Library. Periodicals held in the ASLIB Library as at 1st October 1971. London: Aslib, 1971. 16p.

2112. ———, Lancashire and Cheshire Branch. List of technical, scientific & commercial periodicals taken by certain libraries in Manchester. Manchester: Aslib, 1936. 45l.

Holdings reported for 9 libraries.

2113. Battersea College of Technology Library. Index of journals. Battersea, 1965. 241p.

Alphabetical list showing holdings.

2114. Birmingham Public Libraries. Periodicals in the Commercial and Patents Library. Birmingham, 1966. 33l.

Does not record holdings.

2115. ———. Periodicals in the Technical Library, Ratcliff Place, 1953. Birmingham, 1953. 20p.

2116. Birmingham, University, Library. Catalogue of serials in the Library of the Mason Science Library, Birmingham; transactions of societies, journals, magazines, reviews, reports, by S. Allport. Birmingham: W. G. Moore and Co., 1883. 58p.

Now part of Birmingham University Library.

2117. Bradford Institute of Technology Library. List of periodicals in stock. Bradford, 1965. 52l.

Holdings shown.

2118. Bradford Scientific, Technical and Commercial Services. Union list of periodical holdings. Bradford: BRASTACS, 1962. 71l.

Lists holdings of 15 libraries.

2119. British Aluminum Company, Research Laboratories, Group Technical Intelligence Service. List of group periodical holdings. Gerrards Cross, Bucks.: 1968. Unpaged.

Locations in 11 libraries.

2120. British Council, Science Library. List of current periodical holdings. London: British Council, 1965. 39p.

2121. British Museum, Dept. of Printed Books. List of scientific and technical periodicals received from the USSR, 1933-42. London: The Museum, 1943. 10p.

2122. British Museum (Natural History). List of serial publications in the Library of the Department of Entomology, 2d ed. London, 1962. 144*l*.
    Lists 1,300 titles.

2123. ———. List of serial publications in the British Museum (Natural History) Library. London, 1968. 1,164p.
    Alphabetical listing with holdings noted for about 12,500 entries.

2124. ———. List of serial publications in the libraries of the Departments of Zoology and Entomology. London, 1967. 281p. (Publication, no.664)

2125. ——— Library. Place-numbers of the societies and other corporate bodies issuing serial publications, and of the independent periodical publications, 3d ed. London, 1956. 296p.
    Listed in the order in which the publications are shelved in the library, with detailed index.

2126. Chelsea College of Science and Technology Library. List of current periodicals. Chelsea: College of Science and Technology, 1966. 43*l*.
    Alphabetical list, with holdings shown.

2127. Commercial and Technical Library Service. List of scientific and technical journals available for use in West London, 2d ed. London: Acton Public Libraries, 1962. 231p.

2128. Dudley Technical College Library. Periodicals list, 1971-1972. Dudley, n.d. 10p.

2129. Electrical Research Association. Library periodicals holdings, February 1971. Leatherhead, Surrey, 1971. 25p.

2130. Glasgow, University, Library. A select list of serials in the field of general science, 1967-68. Glasgow, 1968. 28p.
    Exact holdings shown.

2131. ———. A select list of serials in the field of geology, 1967-68. Glasgow, 1968. 90p.
    Exact holdings shown.

2132. ———. A select list of serials in the field of physics, 1967-68. Glasgow, 1967. 21p.
    Exact holdings shown.

2133. Great Britain, Admiralty, Admiralty Centre for Scientific Information and Liaison Library. Scientific and technical periodicals held by Admiralty. London, 1962. 48p.

2134. ———, Dept. of Scientific and Industrial Research, Lending Library Unit. List of irregular serials received from Eastern Europe and the USSR. London, 1959. 90p.

2135. ——— ———. List of scientific and technical periodicals in D.S.I.R. libraries. London, 1963. 185p.
    Records locations and holdings of 5,000 periodicals. Previous edition, 1960.

2136. ——— ———. A list of scientific periodicals in Glamorgan and Monmouthshire. London, 1952. 38p.
    Holdings of 12 libraries reported.

2137. ——— ———, Lending Library Unit. Titles of periodicals from the U.S.S.R. and "cover to cover" translations. London, 1960. 82p.
    Section A lists about 450 Russian periodicals; Section B about 220 cover-to-cover translations.

2138. ———, Ministry of Technology, Headquarters Library Service. List of current periodicals. London, 1970. 111p.
    Union list, noting holdings.

2139. ———, Patent Office Library. Class list and index of the periodical publications in the Patent Office Library, 2d ed. London: H. M. Stationery Office, 1906. 298p.

2140. ——— ———. Periodical publications in the Patent Office Library; list of current titles, 3d ed. London: H. M. Stationery Office, 1965. 436p.
    In 5 sections: British Patent Office publications; overseas patent specifications; overseas patent and trademark indexes, abstracts and periodicals; international patent indexes; scientific and technical periodicals. Lists 9,000 titles.

2141. ——— ———. Subject list of the periodical publications in the Patent Office Library. London: H. M. Stationery Office, 1924. 298p.
    Subjects alphabetically arranged; holdings indicated.

2142. Hawker Siddeley Group Libraries. Union list of periodicals, ed. by J. Burkett. Slough: Hawker Siddeley Nuclear Power Co., 1959. 34p.
    Locates files in 8 libraries.

2143. Hertfordshire Special Libraries Group. Duplicated union list of periodicals. [Hertford?] 1955. Unpaged.

Periodicals listed are primarily in fields of science and technology.

2144. Lewisham Public Libraries. Scientific and technical periodicals; a catalogue of the holdings of the Scientific and Technical Reference Library. London, 1964. 40p.

2145. Library Association, Reference and Special Libraries Section, Northern Group. Union list of scientific and technical periodicals in Northern libraries. Middlesbrough, 1955. 39p.

Nearly 2,500 periodicals are shown, and extent of holdings for 29 libraries in Northumberland, Durham, Cumberland, and Westmorland.

2146. Library Association, Reference, Special and Information Section, Northern Group. Union list of scientific & technical periodicals in Northern libraries, 2d ed. by T. D. Wilson and A. Wallace. London, 1963. 79p.

Locations in numerous libraries.

2147. ——— ———, Western Group. A union-catalogue of current scientific and technical periodicals in some Group libraries, 2d ed. Bristol, 1962. 273p.

Reports holdings of 72 libraries; 3,903 entries.

2148. Lincoln Public Libraries. Pool of technical periodicals. Lincoln, 1953. Unpaged.

Locates 194 periodicals in 17 libraries.

2149. Liverpool, University, Library. Finding list of scientific, medical & technical periodicals. Liverpool, 1966- .

Issued periodically.

2150. London, University, Imperial College of Science and Technology. Periodical and serial holdings, 1970. London, 1970. 141p.

Alphabetical list.

2151. ———, John Innes Institute Library. List of periodical holdings. London, 1969. 14p.

In field of general science.

2152. Loughborough University of Technology Library. Periodical holdings list. Loughborough, 1970. 169 + 88 p.

Alphabetical list, current and noncurrent; includes index of societies and institutions sponsoring the titles recorded.

2153. ———. Subject guide to periodicals. Loughborough, 1970. 159p.

Arranged alphabetically by subject; lists abstracting, indexing, and other journals; notes only titles and locations.

2154. Luton Public Libraries. Technical periodicals available in the Luton area, 5th ed. Luton, 1968. 103p. (Technical bulletin, no.60)

Locates files in 21 libraries.

2155. Manchester Literary and Philosophical Society. List of the current scientific serial publications received by the principal libraries of Manchester, comp. by C. W. E. Leigh. Manchester, 1898. 52p.

Lists 741 periodicals, with locations in 9 libraries.

2156. Manchester Public Libraries. Current abstracts & indexes in the Technical and Commercial Library. Manchester: Central Library, 1963. 42p.

Records 267 annotated entries, with holdings.

2157. National Lending Library for Science and Technology. Current serials received by the NLL, March, 1971. London: H. M. Stationery Office, 1971. 540p.

Records about 36,000 titles, but no data on holdings.

2158. ———. A KWIC index to the English language abstracting and indexing publications currently being received by the National Lending Library, 3d ed. Boston Spa, 1969. 24p.

Contains about 1,200 entries, arranged by subject key-words.

2159. ———. KWIC index to some of the review serials in the English language held at the N.L.L. Boston Spa, 1969. 21l.

2160. ———. List of current serials received from Asia. Boston Spa, Yorks., 1967. 48p.

Records about 2,800 titles, grouped by countries.

2161. ———. List of irregular serials received from the USSR and Bulgaria. Boston Spa, 1961. 111p.

Holdings listed.

2162. ———. List of scientific and technical periodicals received from China. Boston Spa, 1964. 54p.

2163. National Library of Ireland. List of scientific and technical periodicals in Dublin libraries. Dublin: Published by the Stationery Off., 1929. 147p.

Holdings shown for 18 libraries.

2164. National Reference Library of Science and Invention. Current Japanese journals containing articles on pure chemistry, by G. J. Sassoon. London, 1971. 22p.

2165. ———. Periodical publications in the National Reference Library of Science and Invention. London: British Museum, 1969-70. 3pts.

pt.1, List of non-Slavonic titles in the Bayswater Division; pt.2, List of Slavonic and East European titles in the Bayswater Division; pt.3, List of current titles in the Holborn Division.

2166. Nottingham, University, Science Library. List of periodicals and serials. Nottingham, 1970. 138*l*.

Alphabetical list, with holdings of titles in science, medicine, architecture, chemistry, agriculture, mycology, and geology.

2167. Oxford, University, Bodleian Library. Union list of serials in the science area, Oxford. Stage II (Incorporating Stage I). Oxford, 1970. 598p.

Records some 15,000 entries, with locations in about 50 Oxford libraries.

2168. ———, Dept. of Agricultural Science. List of periodicals, etc. held in the Library. London, 1969. 21*l*.

2169. ———, Dept. of Botany Library. List of periodicals held in the Library. Oxford, 1961. 22p.

2170. ———, Dept. of Forestry Library. List of periodicals and serial publications in the Library of the Department of Forestry, University of Oxford, 2d ed. Oxford: The Department, 1961. 284p.

International list, geographically arranged; title index.

2171. ——— ———. List of periodicals and serials in the Forestry Library, University of Oxford, 3d ed. rev. and ed. by J. S. Howse. Oxford, 1968. 187p.

Arranged under names of countries or places where published, with title index; notes holdings.

2172. ———, Radcliffe Library. Provisional catalogue of transactions of societies, periodicals, and memoirs available for the use of professors and students. Oxford, 1866. Unpaged.

Copies located in Oxford libraries. 2d ed., 1871; 3d ed., 1877; 4th ed., 1887.

2173. Plant Protection Limited. Serials in Jealott's Hill Library. Bracknell, Berks.: Jealott's Hill Research Station, 1971. Unpaged.

2174. Science Museum Library. Current periodicals in the Science Museum; a hand list, 9th ed., comp. by H. D. Phippen. London: H. M. Stationery Office, 1965. 196p.

Records complete holdings.

2175. Sheffield Polytechnic Library Service. Polyjournals. Sheffield, 1971. 35p.

2176. Sheffield, University, Dept. of Glass Technology, Joint Library of Glass Technology. List of periodicals. Sheffield: Department and Society of Glass Technology, 1969. 40*l*.

2177. Swansea, University College, Library. Scientific and technical periodicals; a short-title catalogue of holdings, 2d ed. Swansea, 1971. 132p.

Alphabetic list with holdings.

2178. Union list of scientific and medical periodicals in the Aberdeen area. Aberdeen: Univ. Pr., 1966. 233*l*.

Reports holdings of 14 special, college, and university libraries; exact holdings shown.

2179. World list of scientific periodicals published in the years 1900-1960, 4th ed., ed. by Peter Brown and George Burder Stratton. London: Butterworth, 1963-65. 3v.

Locates holdings in numerous British and Irish libraries; about 60,000 titles.

2180. World list of scientific periodicals. New periodical titles, 1960-1968. London: Butterworth, 1970. 603 + 128 + 9p.

2181. Yorkshire Regional Library System. A finding list of technical periodicals indexed in the British technology index and available through the libraries of the Yorkshire Regional Library System, comp. by William R. and Margaret M. Flint. Sheffield: Central Library, 1963. 15*l*.

Locates files in numerous libraries.

Mathematics

2182. Admiralty Centre for Scientific Information and Liaison, Library. Catalogue of books held by the Admiralty Research Organisation. pt.3, Mathematics. London; Dep., of Research Programmes and Planning, 1960. 60p.

2183. Birmingham, University, Institute of Education Library. Mathematics and statistics, 2d ed. Supplement. Birmingham, 1965. 5p. (Booklist, no.1)

2184. Cambridge, University, Library. Union catalogue of scientific departmental libraries in the University. I: Libraries in the Faculty of Mathematics. Cambridge: Scientific Periodicals Library, 1970. 300p.

Alphabetical listing of books, monographs, and technical reports.

2185. Karpinski, Louis C. Bibliography of mathematical works printed in America through 1850. Ann Arbor: Univ. of Mich. Pr., London: Oxford Univ. Pr., 1940. 697p.

Locates copies mainly in American libraries, but includes British Museum.

2186. London, University, Library. Union list of periodicals on mathematics and allied subjects in London libraries, 2d ed. London, 1968. 139p.

Locates files of 971 titles in numerous libraries.

2187. Mathematical Association. Catalogue of current mathematical journals, etc., with the names of the libraries in which they may be found. London: G. Bell, 1913. 39p.

182 titles arranged by country of publication; holdings in 43 libraries in Great Britain and Ireland, and 6 in South Africa; title, society, and geographical indexes included.

2188. ———Library. A first list of books & pamphlets in the Library of the Mathematical Association. London: The Association, 1926. 47p.

Classified list of works acquired before 1924. Second to fourth lists include material received from 1924 to 1935. London, 1929-36. 3pts.

2189. Newcastle upon Tyne City Libraries. Catalogue of the books and tracts on pure mathematics in the Central Library, comp. by Basil Anderton and R. T. Richardson. Newcastle upon Tyne: Andrew Reid & Co., 1901. 49p.

List arranged alphabetically by authors.

2190. St. Andrews, University, Library. Catalogue of mathematical books. St. Andrews: Joseph Cook & Son, 1883. 22p.

2191. Sheffield, University, Library. Mathematical applications in the biological and social sciences—a select bibliography of works in the University Library. Sheffield, 1972. 24p.

2192. ——— ———, Information Service. Reference and information sources in applied mathematics and physics. Sheffield: 1971. 24p.

2193. Simpkins, Diana M. "Early editions of Euclid in England." Annals of science, 22 (1966), 225-49.

STC and Wing numbers added to individual titles discussed.

2194. Southampton, University, Institute of Education Library. Aspects of modern mathematics; a select list of books for teachers. Southampton, 1963. 32p.

List of books held by Southampton Institute of Education Library.

2195. Thomas-Stanford, Charles. Early editions of Euclid's Elements. London: Bibliographical Society, 1926. 64p. + 12 plates.

Records locations in British and European libraries.

2196. University College of Wales Library. A guide to the resources available in mathematics. Aberystwyth, 1970. 6p. (Handlist, no.9)

Astronomy

2197. Birmingham, University, Library. The Lunar Society; an exhibition in connection with the bicentenary celebrations of the Lunar Society of Birmingham; catalogue compiled by D. W. Evans. Birmingham, 1966. 42p.

Records 221 items relating to society founded about 1766 for scientific study.

2198. British Astronomical Association Library. Catalogue of the Library of the British Astronomical Association. London: The Association, 1936. 93p.

2199. ———. Catalogue of the Library of the British Astronomical Association. London: The Association, 1954. 47p.

2200. Great Britain, Royal Observatory, Edinburgh, Library. Catalogue of the Crawford Library of the Royal Observatory, Edinburgh. Edinburgh: Published by authority of Her Majesty's Government, 1890. 497p.

Author catalog.

2201. ———. List of journals from the U.S.S.R. Edinburgh, 1963. 11l.

Includes journals, mostly astronomical, published since 1930, held by Library.

2202. Johnson, Francis Rarick. Astronomical thought in Renaissance England; a study of the English scientific writings from 1500 to 1645. Baltimore, Md.: Johns Hopkins, 1937. 357p.

Includes "A chronological list of books dealing with astronomy printed in England to 1640," p.301-35, with STC numbers.

2203. Kemp, D. Alasdair. "The Crawford Library of the Royal Observatory, Edinburgh." Isis, 54 (1963), 481-83.

Brief history and description of resources.

2204. O'Connor, J. G., and Meadows, A. J. Library provision in astronomy and space science. Leicester: Leicester Univ., 1970. 43 + 26p.

"General description of the coverage and organization of the libraries of major 'astronomical' centres in the U.K. both in universities and government establishments."

2205. Oxford, University, Bodleian Library. An Islamic book of constellations [the Book of fixed stars]. Oxford, 1965. 10p. + 23 plates. (Bodleian picture books, no.13)

2206. Royal Astronomical Society. Catalogue of the Grove-Hills Library. London, 1924. 48p.

2207. ———. Catalogue of the Library. London, 1886-1925. 3pts.

Basic volume, to 1884, includes about 9,000 volumes.

2208. Saxl, Fritz, and Meier, Hans. Catalogue of astrological and mythological illuminated manuscripts of the Latin middle ages. London: Warburg Institute, Univ. of London, 1953-66. 4v.

v.3, pts.1-2, records locations in English libraries.

2209. Science Museum. Historic astronomical books. London: H. M. Stationery Office, 1954. 29p. (Science Museum book exhibition, no.3)

2210. Willetts, Pamela J. "A reconstructed astronomical manuscript from Christ Church Library, Canterbury." British Museum quarterly, 30 (1965), 22-30.

A 12th-century manuscript acquired by British Museum.

2211. Winder, Marianne. "A bibliography of German astrological works printed between 1465 and 1600, with locations of those extant in London libraries." Annals of science, 22 (1966), 191-220.

Records 243 titles, with locations in British Museum, Wellcome Historical Medical Library, and Warburg Institute.

Physics

2212. Anthony, L. J., and Gosset, M. Harwell. "Atomic Energy Research Establishment Library." Library Association record, 63 (1961), 42-44.

A general description.

2213. Birkbeck College Library. M.S.C. nuclear and particle physics; recommended booklist, 1971-72. London, 1971. Unpaged. (Library publication, no.41)

2214. ———. Physics; recommended book list, 1971-72. London, 1971. 2l. (Library publication, no.39)

2215. British Optical Association Library. "Catalogue, Clifford's Inn Hall Library." In: British Optical Association year book, 1930, p.305-512.

Author-title list with subject index.

2216. ———. Catalogue, comp. and edited by Margaret Mitchell. London: Council of the British Optical Association, 1932-57. 3v.

2217. Great Britain, Patent Office Library. Subject list of works on general physics (including measuring, calculating and mathematical instruments, and meteorology). London: H. M. Stationery Office, 1914. 196p.

2218. Islington Libraries. Physics books, 1961-1967, comp. by Gertrude Watts. London, 1969. 70p.

2219. National Reference Library of Science and Invention. A guide to the literature on spectral data, by A. Clarke. London, 1971. 11p. (Occasional publications)

2220. Sheffield, University, Library, Information Service. Physics, mathematics and chemistry journals in the University Library; a handlist. Sheffield, 1968. Unpaged.

Lists 770 titles, with holdings.

2221. United Kingdom Atomic Energy Authority, Atomic Energy Research Establishment Library. Information bulletin, List no.1046-   . Harwell, Berks.: Harwell, 1966-   .

Issued periodically.

2222. ——— ———. Recent additions to the Library, List no.235-   , Nov. 1966-   . Harwell, Berks.: 1966-   .

Issued periodically.

2223. ———, Atomic Weapons Research Establishment. List of periodicals held in AWRE Library, March 1961. Aldermaston, Berks.: AWRE, 1961. Unpaged.

Alphabetic list with holdings.

2224. ———, Development and Engineering Group. Union list of periodicals and serials in libraries serving the Development and Engineering and Production Groups, comp. by M. A. Roche and J. C. Hartas. Risley, 1960. 46p. (DEG Information Series 229 [R])

Entries for 850 titles; holdings shown for 7 libraries.

2225. ———, Reactor Group. Union list of periodicals and serials in libraries serving the Reactor, Production, and Engineering Groups and Authority Health & Safety Branch (Safeguards Division), comp. by P. A. Dodds and J. C. Hartas. Risley, 1963. 63p. (TRG Information Series 290 [R])

Entries for 1,250 titles; holdings shown for 8 libraries.

2226. ———, Research Group Library. Periodicals held by A.E.R.E. Library. Harwell, Berks., 1964. 67p.

2227. University College of Wales Library. A guide to the resources available in physics, geophysics & astrophysics. Aberystwyth, 1970. 6p. (Handlist, no.10)

Chemistry and Chemical Technology

2228. Chemical Abstracts Service. Access; key to the source literature of the chemical sciences. Columbus, Ohio: American Chemical Society, 1969. 1,370p.

Lists about 21,000 titles, showing holdings of 397 libraries in 28 countries; includes 5 English libraries and 1 Irish; quarterly supplements issued.

2229. Chemical Society Library. A catalogue of the Library of the Chemical Society, arranged according to authors, with a subject index. London: Gurney and Jackson, 1903. 324p.

2230. ———. Periodicals in the Chemical Society library. London: The Society, 1960. 48p.

About 1,600 titles listed.

2231. Colvilles Limited Technical Offices. Catalogue of the Maclay Library. Motherwell, n.d. 101p.

Special library relating to chemistry, engineering, metallurgy, and related subjects.

2232. Glasgow, University, Library. Catalogue of the Ferguson collection of books, mainly relating to alchemy, chemistry, witchcraft, and gipsies, in the Library of the University of Glasgow, comp. by Katherine R. Thomson and Mary M. Service, ed. by William Ross Cunningham. Glasgow: Robert Maclehose, 1943. 2v. (Glasgow University publications) Supplement, 1955. Glasgow: R. Maclehose, 1955. 8p.

2233. Great Britain, Patent Office Library. Subject list of works on certain chemical industries. London: H. M. Stationery Office, 1901. 100p.

2234. ———. Subject list of works on chemical technology (including oils, fats, soaps, candles, and perfumery: paints, varnishes, gums, resins, india rubber: paper and leather industries), in the Library of the Patent Office. London: H. M. Stationery Office, 1911. 176p.

2235. ———. Subject list of works on chemistry and chemical technology. London: H. M. Stationery Office, 1901. 106p.

2236. ———. Subject list of works on chemistry (including alchemy, electrochemistry and radioactivity), in the Library of the Patent Office. London: H. M. Stationery Office, 1911. 218p.

2237. Newcastle upon Tyne City Libraries. Classified list of books on chemical technology, metallurgy and assaying, by B. Anderton. Newcastle upon Tyne, 1903. 18p. 2d ed. 1927. 32p.

2238. OXO Library. Biochemistry and biology. London: 1969. 14l. (Subject list, no.7)
Based on library's holdings.

2239. Peddie, Robert Alexander. "English books on alchemy." Notes and queries, ser.8, 11 (1897), 363-64, 464-65.
Locations in British Museum.

2240. Science Museum. A hundred alchemical books: exhibition catalogue. London: H. M. Stationery Office, 1952. 32p. (Science Museum book exhibitions series, no.1)

2241. ——— Library. Books on the chemical and allied industries; a subject catalogue of books in the Science Library, comp. by L. R. Day. London: H. M. Stationery Office, 1961. 118p. Supplement, 1961. 10p.
Short-title list of 3,500 items published since 1930.

2242. Singer, Dorothea Waley. Catalogue of Latin and vernacular alchemical manuscripts in Great Britain and Ireland dating from the XVI century. Brussels: Maurice Lamertin, 1928-31. 3v.
Locates manuscripts described.

2243. Warwick, University, Library, Science Division. A guide to sources of information in chemistry. Coventry, 1968. 29p.

Geology

2244. Birkbeck College Library. Geomorphology; select list of books in the College Library, comp. by J. Rose and A. Cooban. London, 1970. 14l. (Library publication, no.19)

2245. British Museum (Natural History), Dept. of Mineralogy. Catalogue of the books in the Department of mineralogy, by L. Fletcher. London: The Museum 1881. 105p.

2246. Edinburgh Geological Society. Catalogue of the Library of the Edinburgh Geological Society. Edinburgh: Robert Symon, 1887. 31p.

2247. Edinburgh, University Library. Edinburgh and geology; an exhibition on the occasion of the centenary of the foundation of the Chair of Geology in the

University of Edinburgh. Edinburgh, 1971. Unpaged.

Listing of 50 rare books by Werner, Hutton, Lyell, etc.

2248. Geological Society of London Library. Catalogue of the books and maps in the Library of the Geological Society of London. London: R. and J. E. Taylor, 1846. 225p.

2249. ———. Supplemental catalogue of the books, maps, sections and drawings in the Library of the Geological Society of London. London: Taylor and Francis, 1856. 181p. Supplements, 1856, 1863.

2250. ———. Catalogue of the Library of the Geological Society of London, comp. by James Dallas. London: Taylor and Francis, 1881. 618p.

2251. ———. Geological literature added to the Geological Society's Library. London, 1895-1935. 19v.

Additions to the library 1894-1934.

2252. ———. List of periodicals currently taken in the Library, comp. by Ann M. Paddick. London, 1962. 20p.

Alphabetical list; does not show holdings; records 550 titles.

2253. Geologists' Association Library. Catalogue of the Library. London: University College, 1879. 79p.

2254. Industrial Diamond Information Bureau Library. List of books and pamphlets in special library of Industrial Diamond Information Bureau. London: Industrial Distributors (Sales) Ltd., 1952. 214p.

2255. London, University, Imperial College, Lyon Playfair Library. Libraries for the geologist in and around London, 2d ed., comp. by Joan E. Hardy. London, 1971. Unpaged.

Brief descriptions of resources of 40 libraries for geological research.

2256. ———, University College Library. Catalogue of the geological books in the Library of University College, London, including the Library of the Geologists' Association, which is incorporated in the College Library, by W. Bonser. London: Edward Stanford, 1927. 102p.

Classified list of 1,198 items, with index.

2257. Manchester Geological Society Library. Catalogue of the Library of the Manchester Geological Society, comp. by C. S. D. Rabbitt. Manchester: Geological Society, 1891. 71p.

2258. Museum of Practical Geology Library. A catalogue of the Library of the Museum of Practical Geology and Geological Survey, comp. by Henry White and T. W. Newton. London: H. M. Stationery Office, 1878. 602p.

2259. Museum of Practical Geology and Royal School of Mines. A catalogue of the Library of the Museum of Practical Geology and Royal School of Mines, comp. by Henry White and T. W. Newton. London: H. M. Stationery Office, 1877. 3v.

Nongeological books recorded are now in Science Library; others in Geological Museum Library.

2260. Nash, Joan. "Periodicals in the Geologists' Association and University College Libraries." Proceedings of the Geologists' Association, 74 (1964), 467-82. Reprinted.

Alphabetical list, with holdings and list of geological surveys, arranged by countries.

2261. National Institute of Oceanography. List of serial holdings. Wormley, 1960. 34l.

2262. National Museum of Wales. A source-book of geological, geomorphological and soil maps for Wales and the Welsh borders, 1800-1966, by Douglas A. Bassett. Cardiff, 1967. 239p.

With bibliography.

2263. Reading, University, Library. The history and development of geological cartography; catalogue of the exhibition of geological maps in the University Library, by N. E. Butcher. Reading: The University, 1967. Unpaged.

2264. Royal Geological Society of Cornwall Library. A catalogue of the Library of the Royal Geological Society of Cornwall, comp. by William Ambrose Taylor. Plymouth: W. Brendon and Son, 1882. 160p.

2265. Royal Meteorological Society. Bibliography of meteorological literature; prepared by the Royal Meteorological Society with the collaboration of the Meteorological Office. London, 1922-50. 6v.

Locations in libraries of the Meteorological Office and the Royal Meteorological Society.

2266. ———. Catalogue of journals and shelf location. London, 1962. 14l. Supplements 1-2. 1963-64.

2267. ——— Library. Catalogue of the Library of the Royal Meteorological Society, comp. by J. S. Harding. London: E. Stanford, 1891. 214p.

2268. Wigan and District Mining and Technical College Library. A bibliography of books in the College Library on geology, mining, and related subjects published before 1840, by M. M. Hadcraft. Wigan: The College, 1971. 28p.

Microscopy

2269. Quekett Microscopical Club Library. Catalogue of the books in the Library of the Quekett Microscopical Club. London: The Club, 1904. 72p.

2270. Royal Microscopical Society Library. Catalogue of the printed books and pamphlets in the Library of the Royal Microscopical Society. London: The Society, 1929. 177p.

Author catalog.

Biological Sciences

2271. Armagh Natural History and Philosophical Society. New catalogue of the Library of the Armagh Natural History and Philosophical Society, comp. by E. L. Fischer. Armagh: McWatters, 1888. 31p.

2272. Birkbeck College Library. Chordate biology; handlist of books on chordate biology in the College Library, comp. by P. Woudhuysen. London, 1970. 85l. (Library publication, no.3)

2273. Birmingham Natural History and Microscopical Society Library. Catalogue of Library. Birmingham, 1892. 60p.

2274. Birmingham Natural History and Philosophical Society Library. Library catalogue. Walsall, 1954. 24p.

2275. Brighton and Sussex Natural History and Philosophical Society. Catalogue of books in the library of the Brighton and Sussex Natural History and Philosophical Society, etc. Brighton, 1895. 41p.

Name changed to Hove Natural History and Philosophical Society.

2276. British Association for the Advancement of Science. Directory of natural history and other field study societies in Great Britain, including societies for archaeology, astronomy, meteorology, geology and cognate subjects, ed. by Averil Lysaght. London, 1959. 217p.

Brief data on associated libraries.

2277. British Museum (Natural History) Library. Catalogue of the books, manuscripts, maps and drawings in the British Museum (Natural History) Library. London, 1903-15. 5v. Supplement, v.6-8. London: The Museum, 1922-40. 3v. Reprinted, v.1-6. 1964.

2278. ———. The history of the collections contained in the Natural History Departments of the British Museum. London, 1904. 442p.

Section 1, "The Libraries," p.1-76, gives history and lists important books, manuscripts, and drawings and current serial publications.

2279. ———. An index to the authors (other than Linnaeus) mentioned in the catalogue of the works of Linnaeus preserved in the Libraries of the British Museum. London, 1936. 60p.

2280. ———. List of accessions to the Museum Library. London, 1955- .

2281. ———. A short history of the libraries and list of Mss. and original drawings in the British Museum (Natural History), by F. C. Sawyer. London, 1971. 204p. (Bulletin of the British Museum (Natural History) historical series, v.4, no.2)

Alphabetical list of manuscripts and drawings.

2282. Edwards, P. I. "List of libraries in the field of pure and applied biology." Biological journal of the Linnean Society, 3 (1971), 173-88.

Data on collections, publications, services, etc., for 75 British libraries.

2283. Freshwater Biological Association Library. List of serial publications held by the Library of the Freshwater Biological Association. Ambleside, 1970. 31p.

2284. India Office Library. The East India Company and natural history: an exhibition of water-colours, manuscripts, rare books and other material illustrating the interest of the East India Company and its servants in the natural history of India and the East Indies. London, 1970. 22p.

A catalog.

2285. ———. Natural history drawings in the India Office Library, by Mildred Archer. London: H. M. Stationery Office, 1962. 116p. + 25 plates.

Catalog of about 5,000 drawings of plants and animals from India and Southeast Asia, drawn mostly by Indian artists, from 18th to 20th century.

2286. Marine Biological Association of the United Kingdom Library. Serial publications held in the Library. Plymouth, 1969. 100p.

2287. Oxford, University, Radcliffe Science Library. Catalogue of books on natural science in the Radcliffe Library at the Oxford University Museum up to December 1872. Oxford, 1877. 566p. Catalogue of books added, 1870-1927. Oxford, 1871-1928.

2288. OXO Library. Microbiology and bacteriology. London, 1968. 16p. (Subject list, no.6)

Books listed were in library's stock on 1 March 1968.

2289. Sheffield, University, Library, Information Service. Biological, chemical and dental journals in the University Library: a handlist. Sheffield: The Library, 1968. Unpaged.

Records 671 titles, with holdings.

2290. Woolhope Naturalists' Field Club. Catalogue of the Library of the Woolhope Naturalists' Field Club, comp. by F. C. Morgan. Hereford, 1941. 92p.

Anthropology

2291. Gaskin, L. J. P. "Anthropological and ethnological libraries." Library Association record, 4th ser., 1 (1934), 193-99.

Locates and describes libraries in Britain, Continental Europe, and United States.

2292. Horniman Museum. Guide to the collections in the Horniman Museum and Library, 4th ed. London: County Council, 1936. 128p.

Collections relating to anthropology and ethnology.

2293. ———— Library. Horniman Museum and Library; a handbook to the Library (1905) with supplement (1912). London: County Council, 1912. 90 + 81p.

Classified catalog with author index of library devoted largely to anthropology, ethnology, and zoology.

2294. Royal Anthropological Institute of Great Britain and Ireland Library. Anthropological index to current periodicals in the Library of the Royal Anthropological Institute. London: 1963- . v.1- .

Index preceded by list of current periodicals in Institute's Library.

2295. ————. Survey of anthropological journals and monograph series in libraries in the United Kingdom. London, 1955. 17p.

Reports holdings of 35 libraries.

2296. ————. Survey of anthropological journals and monograph series in libraries in the United Kingdom. London, 1957. 17p.

Botany

2297. Aberdeen, University, Library. "Books on botanical subjects bequeathed to the University Library by Professor Trail," by Annie Milne Davidson. Aberdeen, 1923. 56p. In: James William Helenus

Trail, a memorial volume. (Aberdeen Univ. studies, no.91)

2298. Birmingham Botanical and Horticultural Society. Catalogue of the Library. Birmingham, 1893. 16p.

2299. Cardiff Public Libraries. Catalogue of early works on botany, agriculture and horticulture. Cardiff, 1919. 24p.

2300. Edinburgh Museum of Science and Art, Science and Art Dept. List of books etc. relating to botany and forestry, including the Cleghorn Memorial Library, in the Library of the Museum. Edinburgh: H. M. Stationery Office, 1897. 199p.

Classified list.

2301. Gunther, R. T. "Goodyer's library." In his: Early British botanists. Oxford: Univ. Pr., 1922, p.197-232.

Catalogue of collection of botanical works presented to Magdalen College, Oxford, in 1664.

2302. London, University, Library. Botanical periodicals in London libraries. London, 1954. 25p.

Locates 417 periodicals in 17 libraries.

2303. National Library of Scotland. Botanical illustration: a loan exhibition. Edinburgh, 1964. 40p. + 12 plates.

Shows history of botanical illustration since mid-17th century; includes index of lenders, institutional and private.

2304. Oxford, University, Botany School. Library guide. Oxford, 1966. 17p.

Includes "List of periodicals and serial publications held."

2305. Royal Botanic Gardens, Kew. Catalogue of the Library of the Royal Botanic Gardens, Kew. London: H. M. Stationery Office, 1899. 2pts. 790l. Additions received, 1898-1915. London: 1899-1916. 18 parts. Supplement; additions received or incorporated in the years 1898-1915. London: H. M. Stationery Office, 1919. 433l.

2306. ————. Periodicals listed by first title-page, with references from alternative titles. London, 1971. 118p.

Alphabetical list of holdings.

Zoology

GENERAL

2307. British Museum (Natural History), Dept. of Zoology. Catalogue of the books in the Department of

Zoology, 3d ed., prep. by J. E. Harting. London: The Museum, 1884. 399p.

Records 5,309 works in 8,586 volumes.

2308. Library Association, Reference and Special Libraries Section, South Eastern Group. Library resources in the Greater London area. no.6, zoological libraries, comp. by A. C. Townsend and G. B. Stratton. London, 1957. 21p.

Describes collections of 6 libraries: British Museum (Natural History), Zoological Society, Commonwealth Institute of Entomology, Horniman Museum, Linnean Society, and Royal Entomological Society.

2309. Oxford, University, Bodleian Library. Zoological illustration. Oxford, 1951. 8p. + 24 plates. (Bodleian picture book, no.4)

2310. Zoological Society of London Library. Catalogue of the Library of the Zoological Society of London, 5th ed., ed. by F. H. Waterhouse. London: Taylor and Francis, 1902. 856p.

2311. ———. List of the periodicals and serials in the Library of the Zoological Society of London. London, 1949. 186p.

2312. ———. List of serials with title abbreviations pertaining to 1970 literature. London, 1971. Unpaged.

Records about 6,000 titles with locations in various libraries.

AVIFAUNA

2313. John Rylands Library. "Exhibition: illustrated bird books." Bulletin of the John Rylands Library, 51 (1969), 263-64.

Description and citation of rare works.

2314. National Book League. British birds and their books; catalogue of an exhibition, arr. by Raymond Irwin. London: Pub. for National Book League by the Cambridge Univ. Pr., 1952. 38p.

Lenders of exhibited items identified, public and private collections.

2315. Newcastle upon Tyne, University, Library. An exhibition of fine bird books, 1555-1900, from the Library of the Natural History Society of Northumberland, Durham and Newcastle upon Tyne. Newcastle upon Tyne, 1966. 5p.

2316. Royal College of Physicians Library. Bird books (some landmarks in the literature and iconography of birds in the Library). London, 1967. Unpaged.

ENTOMOLOGY

2317. Birkbeck College Library. Entomology; handlist of books on entomology in the College Library, comp. by P. Woudhuysen. London: 1970. 59*l*. (Library publication, no.2)

2318. Entomological Society of London. Catalogue of the Library of the Entomological Society of London, ed. by G. C. Champion and others. London, 1893. 291p. Supplementary catalogue. London, 1900. 147p.

Author catalogs.

2319. South London Entomological and Natural History Society. A catalogue of books in the Library of the South London Entomological and Natural History Society. Arbroath: T. Buncle & Co., 1960. p.104-75. (Reprinted from the Proceedings of the South London Entomological and Natural History Society for 1959)

LEPIDOPTERA

2320. Lisney, Arthur A. A bibliography of British lepidoptera, 1608-1799. London: Chiswick, 1960. 315p.

Arranged under names of scientists; copies located in British, American, and other libraries; 419 entries.

Medicine

General

2321. Bunch, Antonia J. "Scotland's special libraries: Scottish Hospital Centre Library." SLA news, no.89 (1969), 229-32.

National center in Edinburgh concerned with literature on hospital planning.

2322. Drummond, H. J. H. "Early medical and scientific societies of North-East Scotland." Bibliotheck, 1 (1957), 31-33.

Descriptions of records preserved in University of Aberdeen Library.

2323. Finlayson, C. P. "Records of medical and scientific societies in Scotland." Bibliotheck, 1 (1958), 14-19. Additions, 4 (1963), 38-39.

Describes, under names of societies, records preserved in University of Edinburgh Library.

2324. Heberden Society Library. The Library of the Heberden Society; a clinical and scientific society founded 1936 for the advancement of the study of rheumatic diseases, catalogue. London, 1960. 39p.

Library housed at the Ciba Foundation, London.

2325. Jolley, L., and Bell, M. D. "Medical libraries of Scotland." Bulletin of the Medical Library Association, 43 (1955), 356-65.

Review of resources and services of 7 principal medical libraries of Scotland.

2326. Jolley, L. "The records of the Royal College of Physicians of Edinburgh." Bibliotheck, 1 (1958), 20-27.

Records covering nearly 3 centuries, preserved by College.

2327. LeFanu, W. R. A list of medical libraries and information bureaux in the British Isles. London: Aslib, 1946. 28p. (Reprinted from Journal of documentation, no.3)

Gives size of collections and number of current periodicals, and adds an index of special collections.

2328. Library Association, Medical Section. Directory of medical libraries in the British Isles, 3d ed. London: The Association, 1969. 128p.

Lists 398 libraries with brief data on resources.

2329. Ogilvie, James D. "The Aberdeen doctors and the National Covenant." Edinburgh Bibliographical Society publications, 11 (1921), 73-86.

List of 11 editions, with copies located in Aberdeen University Library and private collection, of document printed 1638-63.

2330. Oxford Regional Hospital Board. Report of a survey of hospital medical libraries, by Margaret I. Williams. Oxford, 1967. Unpaged.

Includes individual descriptions of hospital libraries, with notes on resources and services.

2331. Poynter, F. N. L. "The Wellcome Historical Medical Library." Book collector, 4 (1955), 285-90.

History and general description of major collection in its field.

2332. Woosnam, R. "The Library of the North Staffordshire Medical Institute for Postgraduate Studies." Open access, 15 (Spring 1967), 12-13.

Brief description of collections.

History

2333. Aberdeen Medical Society. An account of the Aberdeen Medical Society, containing the laws, regulations, etc., also, a catalogue of the Library. Aberdeen, 1796. 40p. 3d ed. 1803. 56p.

2334. Cambridge, University, Library. An exhibition of books and manuscripts illustrating the history of obstetrics and gynaecology; a catalogue of an exhibition. Cambridge, 1968. 24*l*.

2335. Devon and Exeter Medico-Chirurgical Society and Exeter Memorial Library. Medical art and history in Exeter; an exhibition of books, documents and pictures. Exeter: Royal Albert Memorial Museum, 1955. 37p.

Copies of items exhibited located in 6 libraries.

2336. Royal College of Physicians of London. Catalogue of an exhibition of medical records in the Library of the Royal College of Physicians of London. London: British Records Association, 1958. 40p.

Describes 63 items, with locations.

2337. ———. Catalogue of engraved portraits in the Royal College of Physicians of London, by A. H. Driver. London, 1952. 219p.

2338. Sheffield, University, Library. List of books on the history of medicine [in Sheffield University Library]. Sheffield, 1959. 10p.

2339. Wellcome Historical Medical Library. Chinese medicine; an exhibition illustrating the traditional system of medicine of the Chinese people. London, 1966. 35p. + 25 plates.

2340. ———. The history of cardiology. London, 1970. 36p. (Exhibition catalogue, no.6)

2341. ———. Medicine and surgery in the Great War (1914-1918). London, 1968. 48p. + 32 plates.

2342. ———. Medicine in 1815; an exhibition to commemorate the 150th anniversary of the end of the Napoleonic Wars; 15 April to 31 December 1965. London, 1965. 43p. (Exhibition catalogue, no.2)

2343. ———. Psychiatry and mental health in Britain; a historical exhibition, 4th March-9th July 1963. London, 1963. 39p. (Exhibition guide, no.1)

Rare Books and Manuscripts

2344. Chapman, C. B. "A comment on holdings in old medicine and science in the St. John's College Library." American Oxonian, 51 (1964), 115-23.

2345. Davis, G. R. C. Medieval cartularies of Great Britain; a short catalogue. London: Longmans, Green, 1958. 182p.

Includes index of present owners.

2346. Exeter Cathedral Library. A catalogue of the medical books and manuscripts, including a selection of the scientific works in Exeter Cathedral Library, comp. by M. P. Crighton. Birmingham, 1934. 38 + 6p.

Works relating to history of medicine; lists 202 items.

2347. Gibson, Strickland. "An exhibition of manuscripts and printed books relating to medicine, surgery, and physiology." Bodleian Library record, 2 (1945), 160-68.

General description of works drawn from Bodleian Library collection.

2348. John Rylands Library. "Pre-1700 medical books in the Rylands Library." John Rylands Library bulletin, 54 (1971), 2-6.

General description.

2349. MacKinney, Loren. Medical illustrations in medieval manuscripts. London: Wellcome Historical Medical Library, 1965. 263p., including 96 figures.

Includes calendar of miniatures in medical manuscripts found in 168 libraries throughout world.

2350. Manchester, University, Library. Catalogue of medical books, 1480-1700, comp. by Ethel M Parkinson and A. Lumb. Manchester: Univ. Pr., 1972. 399p.

2351. Marsden, W. A. "Early books on surgery." British Museum quarterly, 11 (1937), 85-87.

Describes 3 early editions of works of Ambroise Paré, 16th century French surgeon, acquired by British Museum.

2352. Medical Society Library. Manuscripta medica; a descriptive catalogue of the manuscripts in the Library of the Medical Society of London, by Warren R. Dawson. London: J. Bale & Co., 1932. 140p.

2353. Medico-Chururgical Society of Aberdeen Library. The Library of the Medico-Chirurgical Society of Aberdeen, by Mabel D. Allardyce. Aberdeen: Univ. Pr., 1934. 80p.

History of library and listing of rare books.

2354. Newcastle upon Tyne, University, Library. One hundred medical works exhibited in the Library of King's College. Newcastle upon Tyne, during the meeting of the British Medical Association. Newcastle upon Tyne, 1957. 27p. (King's College Library publication, no.4)

Exhibition catalog.

2355. Osler, William. Incunabula medica; a study of the earliest printed medical books, 1460-1480. Oxford: Univ. Pr., 1923. 137p. + 16 facsimiles.

Contains 217 main entries; references to British Museum and other locations and citations to standard bibliographies of incunabula.

2356. Oxford, University, Bodleian Library. Catalogue of an exhibition of books on medicine, surgery, and physiology, Bodleian Library, Oxford. Oxford: Univ. Pr., 1947. 31p.

2357. Poynter, F. N. L. "Notes on a late-sixteenth-century ophthalmic work in English." Library, ser.5, 2 (1947), 173-79.

Bibliography of Jacques Gillemeaus' A worthy treatise of the eyes, c. 1587; copies located in several English libraries.

2358. Reading, University, Library. The Cole Library of early medicine and zoology: catalogue of books and pamphlets. pt.1. 1472 to 1800, by Nellie B. Eales. Reading: Alden Pr. for the Library, 1969. 425p. (Publications, no.1)

Listing of 2,108 titles in chronological order, with subject and author indexes.

2359. Royal College of Physicians of London. A descriptive catalogue of the legal and other documents in the archives of the Royal College of Physicians in London, comp. by Horace M. Barlow. London, 1924. 313*l*.

2360. —— Library. "Catalogue of Oriental manuscripts in the Library of the Royal College of Physicians," by A. S. Tritton. Journal of the Royal Asiatic Society, 1951, p.182-92.

Describes 63 Arabic, Persian, and Turkish manuscripts.

2361. —— ——. "List of fifteenth century books in the Library of the Royal College of Physicians, Edinburgh," by T. H. Graham. Publications of the Edinburgh Bibliographical Society, 9 (1904-13), 179-81.

2362. Royal College of Surgeons of England. Catalogue of manuscripts in the Library of the Royal College of Surgeons of England, by Victor G. Plarr. London, 1928. 76p.

2363. ——. English books printed before 1701 in the Library of the Royal College of Surgeons of England, by W. R. LeFanu. Edinburgh: E. & S. Livingstone, 1963. 28p.

Lists 637 STC and Wing editions, 37 of which are unrecorded or variant issues.

2364. Russell, Kenneth F. British anatomy, 1525-1800; a bibliography. Melbourne: Melbourne Univ. Pr., 1963. 254p. + 52 plates.

Locations in numerous British and foreign libraries.

2365. ——. "A check list of medical books published in English before 1600." Bulletin of the history of medicine, 21 (1947), 922-58.

Enumerates 150 separate works in about 380 editions; STC numbers added.

2366. Sheffield, University, Library. An annotated check-list of medical books printed before 1700, and held in Sheffield University Library, by Raymond J. Prytherch. Sheffield, 1968. 89*l*.

2367. Singer, Dorothea Waley, and Anderson, Annie. Catalogue of Latin and vernacular plague texts in Great Britain and Eire in manuscripts written before the sixteenth century. London: Heinemann Medical Books, 1950. 279p. (Académie Internationale d'histoire des sciences, Collection de travaux, no.5)

2368. Singer, Dorothea Waley. "Survey of medical manuscripts in the British Isles dating from before the sixteenth century." Proceedings of the Royal Society of Medicine, 13 (1919), 96-107.

Describes 34 items, with locations.

2369. Wellcome Historical Medical Library. A catalogue of Arabic manuscripts on medicine and science in the Wellcome Historical Medical Library, by A. Z. Iskandar. London, 1967. 256p. + 35 plates. (Library catalogue series, no.4)

2370. ——. A catalogue of incunabula in the Wellcome Historical Medical Library, by F. N. L. Poynter. London: Oxford Univ. Pr. 1954. 160p. + 12 plates.

Records 610 works and 22 fragments, alphabetical by authors or titles.

2371. ——. A catalogue of printed books in the Wellcome Historical Medical Library. I. Books printed before 1641, by F. N. L. Poynter. London, 1962. 408p. (Library catalogue series, no.1)

Describes 6,973 works, many of extreme rarity.

2372. ——. A catalogue of printed books in the Wellcome Historical Medical Library. II. Books printed between 1641 and 1850; A-E. London: 1966. 540p. v.III: F-L. In press. (Library catalogue series, no.3)

2373. ——. Catalogue of Western manuscripts on medicine and science in the Wellcome Historical Library, by S. A. J. Moorat. v.I: Mss. written before A.D. 1650. London, 1962. 679p. (Library catalogue series, no.2)

Describes about 800 manuscripts, containing 1,500 individual works.

Library Catalogs

2374. Aberdeen, University, Library. Medical Library subject catalogue. Aberdeen: Univ. Pr., 1923. 167p.

Dewey classification arrangement, with subject and author indexes.

2375. Birmingham Royal School of Medicine. Catalogue of the museum and library. Birmingham, 1832. 44 + 22p.

2376. Faculty of Physicians and Surgeons of Glasgow Library. Catalogue of books in the Library of the Faculty of Physicians and Surgeons of Glasgow. Glasgow: Bell and Bain, 1842. 359p. v.1.

2377. Great Britain, Army Medical Dept. Library. A catalogue of the Library of the Army Medical Department. London: Richard Taylor, 1833. 269p.

2378. King Edward's Hospital Fund for London, Division of Hospital Facilities. Catalogue of Reference Library, 2d ed. London: The Hospital, 1953. 86p.
List of 1,156 works.

2379. Leeds School of Medicine Library. Catalogue of books in the Library of the Leeds School of Medicine and Leeds and West-Riding Medico-Chirurgical Society. Leeds: Walker and Laycock, 1892. 94p. Appendix, 1895. 15p.

2380. Lewis's Medical & Scientific Lending Library. Catalogue of Lewis's Medical & Scientific Lending Library, new ed. London: H. R. Lewis, 1938. 2v.
pt.1, authors and titles; pt.2, classified index of subjects and authors.

2381. Lewis's Medical, Scientific and Technical Lending Library. Catalogue , new ed. London, 1965. 2v.
In 2pts., authors and titles; classified index of subjects. Library founded in 1848.

2382. Liverpool Medical Institution Library. Catalogue of the books in the Liverpool Medical Institution Library (to the end of the nineteenth century). Liverpool, The Institution, 1968. 569p.
Alphabetical listing by authors for about 11,000 entries.

2383. London, University, London School of Hygiene and Tropical Medicine. Dictionary catalogue. Boston, Mass.: G. K. Hall, 1965. 7v.
Reproduces 90,000 cards, representing author and subject entries for 40,000 monographs, pamphlets, and nonserial reports in the library.

2384. ———, University College. Catalogue of books in the Medical and Biological Libraries at University College, London. London: Taylor and Francis, 1887. 411p.

2385. Manchester Medical Society Library. Catalogue of the Library of the Manchester Medical Society. Manchester: The Society, 1890. 1,304p.

2386. Manchester Public Libraries. Recent books on medicine and nursing; a select list of publications in the Manchester Public Libraries. Manchester, 1945. 48l.

2387. Medical and Chirurgical Society of London Library. A catalogue of the Library of the Medical and Chirurgical Society of London, with a supplement. London: Richard and Arthur Taylor, 1816. 494p. Second part. 1819. 375p. Later editions: London: John Scott, 1844. 728p. London, The Society, 1856. 762p.

2388. Medical Society of Edinburgh Library. Catalogue of the Library of the Medical Society of Edinburgh. Edinburgh, The Society, 1845. 306p.

2389. ———. Catalogue raisonné; or classified arrangement of the books in the Library of the Medical Society of Edinburgh. Edinburgh: The Society, 1837. 342p.

2390. Medical Society of London Library. A catalogue of books contained in the Library of the Medical Society of London, instituted A.D.1773. London: The Society, 1803. 226p.

2391. ———. A catalogue of books contained in the Library of the Medical Society of London, instituted A.D. 1773. London: The Society, 1829. 346p. Appendix, 1846. 14p. Appendix, 1856. 81p.

2392. Ophthalmological Society Library. Catalogue of the Library of the Ophthalmological Society of the United Kingdom. pt.I, authors. pt.II, Subjects. 4th ed. London: Adlard and Son, 1901. 146p.

2393. Oxford, University, Radcliffe College Library. Catalogue of the works in medicine and natural history contained in the Radcliffe Library. London: S. Collingwood, 1835. 330p.
Arranged in broad subject categories.

2394. Queen's University, Medical Library. Interim short-title list of first part of Samuel Simms collection. Belfast, 1965. 56l.
Catalogue of a general medical collection.

2395. Royal College of Obstetricians and Gynaecologists Library. Catalogue of the Library up to 1850, comp. by W. J. Bishop. Manchester, 1956. 74p.
Alphabetical by authors.

2396. ———. Short-title catalogue of books printed before 1851 in the Library of the Royal College of Obstetricians and Gynaecologists, 2d ed., ed. by John L. Thornton. London, 1968. 90p. + 16 plates.

2397. Royal College of Physicians of Edinburgh Library. Catalogue of the Library of the Royal College of Physicians of Edinburgh. Edinburgh: Thomas Constable, 1849. 322p.

2398. ———. Catalogue of the Library of the Royal College of Physicians of Edinburgh. Edinburgh: R. and R. Clark, 1863. 757p.

2399. Royal College of Physicians of London Library. Bibliothecae Collegii Regalis Medicorum Londinensis. Catalogus. London, 1757. 349p.

2400. ———. Catalogue of the Library. London: Spottiswoode, 1912. 1,354p.
    An author-title catalog.

2401. Royal College of Surgeons in Ireland. Catalogue of the Library, 1852-1872, 1872-1876, 1876-1892. Dublin: Alexander Thom for H. M. S. Stationery Office, 1872-92. 3v.

2402. Royal College of Surgeons of Edinburgh Library. Catalogue of the Library of the Royal College of Surgeons of Edinburgh. Edinburgh, 1863. 65p.

2403. Royal College of Surgeons of England. Index to the catalogue of the Library of the Royal College of Surgeons of England. London: Taylor and Francis, 1853. 124p.

2404. Royal Medical and Chirurgical Society of London. Catalogue of the Library. London, 1879. 3v. Supplements, 1880-86. 5pts.
    Alphabetical list of authors, followed by society transactions, lists of journals, etc.

2405. Royal Medical Society Library. Catalogue of the Library of the Royal Medical Society. Edinburgh: Darien, 1896. 129p.

2406. Royal Medico-Psychological Association. Catalogue of Library of the Royal Medico-Psychological Association. London, 1928. 37p.

2407. St. Bartholomew's Hospital and College Library. Catalogue of the Library of St. Bartholomew's Hospital and College. London: Jas. Truscott, 1893. 450p.

2408. St. Mary's Hospital, Radford Library. Catalogue of the Radford Library, St. Mary's Hospital, Manchester, by Charles J. Cullingworth. Manchester: William Alcock, 1877. 258p.

2409. York Medical Society Library. Catalogue. York, 1961. 106p.
    Alphabetical list by authors.

Periodicals

2410. Charing Cross Hospital Medical School Library. Catalogue of journals, reports, yearbooks, etc. London, 1970. 18p.

2411. "Current medical periodicals of the British Empire." The Medical year book, ed. by Charles R. Hewitt. London: W. Heinemann, 1924, p.510-15. 2d annual issue, 1925, p.545-50.
    Files are located in medical libraries in London.

2412. Guy's Hospital, Wills Library. Union list of periodicals taken in the Wills Library and in departments of the Hospital and Medical School. London, 1965. 48l.

2413. Institute of Cancer Research, Royal Cancer Hospital Library. A list of the periodicals contained in the Library of the Institute of Cancer Research, 3d ed. London: Chester Beatty Research Institute, 1962. Unpaged.
    Lists 616 titles with holdings and subject index.

2414. Institute of Diseases of the Chest. A list of the periodicals filed in the Library, 2d ed. London, 1966. Unpaged.
    Lists 536 titles, with data on holdings.

2415. Institute of Psychiatry Library. Periodical holdings and checklist of other serials currently received. London: The Institute, 1970. 33l.

2416. Leeds, University, Medical and Dental Libraries. Periodicals currently received. Leeds, 1969. 14l.

2417. LeFanu, William R. British periodicals of medicine; a chronological list. Baltimore, Md.: Johns Hopkins, 1938. 93p. (Reprinted from Bulletin of the Institute of the History of Medicine, Oct.-Nov. 1937 and June 1938)
    Lists 1,362 titles in 2 groups: pre-1900 and post-1900; files located in at least one of 7 British libraries.

2418. Leiper, R. T., and others. Periodicals of medicine and the allied sciences in British libraries, including the sciences of agriculture, anatomy, anthropology, bacteriology, biology, botany, chemistry, ethnology, general science, physics, physiology, zoology. London: British Medical Association, 1923. 193p.
    Geographical groupings; records holdings in 21 London and 16 provincial libraries.

2419. London, University. List of current medical periodicals taken by the London medical schools and institutes and the University of London. London, 1957. Unpaged.
    Reports holdings of 24 institutions.

2420. ———, British Post-Graduate Medical Federation. Union list of the periodicals in the libraries of the Post-Graduate Medical School, Institutes of Cancer Research, Child Health, Dental Surgery, Dermatology, Diseases of the Chest, Laryngology and Otology, Neurology, Ophthalmology, Orthopaedics, Psychiatry, comp. by D. J. Campbell. London, 1955. 46p.

2421. ———, Institute of Diseases of the Chest Library. A list of the periodicals filed in the Library, September, 1966, 2d ed., comp. by Yvonne M. Bray and others. London, 1966. Unpaged.

In 2 pts.: thoracic medicine and surgery; general medicine, surgery and allied subjects. Lists 536 items.

2422. ———, Institute of Psychiatry Library. List of journals in the Library. London, 1961. 22p.

Lists 342 titles.

2423. ——— ———. List of serials. London, 1968. 8p.

Classified by subjects.

2424. ———, Library. List of journals in medical and allied sciences. London, 1962. 38p.

Handlist of periodicals in medicine and allied sciences published in 20th century.

2425. ———, London School of Hygiene and Tropical Medicine. Dictionary catalogue: serials. Boston, Mass.: G. K. Hall, 1965. 286p. (v.7 of Dictionary catalogue of the London School of Hygiene and Tropical Medicine, Univ. of London)

2426. ———, ———. Hand-list of periodicals in the Library, 2d ed. London, 1933. 44p.

2427. May & Baker, Ltd. Library. Periodicals currently taken and holdings, 8th ed. Dagenham, 1967. Unpaged.

Records 472 titles relating to medicine, pharmacology, etc.

2428. Medical Research Council. Union list of periodicals in MRC libraries. London, 1968. 60p.

Alphabetical list, showing holdings in 44 libraries.

2429. Medical Research Council of Ireland. List of medical periodicals available in Dublin libraries. Dublin, 1938. 65l.

2430. National Lending Library for Science and Technology. A select list of medical serials held in the N.L.L. Boston Spa, Yorks., 1964. 72p.

Lists 5,590 titles; holdings not shown.

2431. Oxford Joint Medical Libraries Committee. Union list of periodicals held in the medical libraries of the Oxford hospital region, 1971. Oxford, 1971. 28l.

2432. Royal College of Physicians of Ireland Library. List of medical periodicals preserved in the libraries of Ireland. Dublin: Hanna and Neale, 1911. 19p.

Section 1 shows entries for foreign medical periodicals in 12 libraries; section 2 lists medical periodicals in United Kingdom located in 2 libraries.

2433. Royal College of Physicians of London Library. A list of serial publications in the Library. London: The College, 1950. 24p.

2434. Royal College of Surgeons of England Library. List of the transactions, periodicals and memoirs in the Library of the Royal College of Surgeons of England, 2d ed., comp. by W. A. Fusedale. London: Taylor and Francis, 1931. 169p.

Alphabetical list of holdings.

2435. Royal Society of Medicine Library. List of the periodicals in the Library. London: The Society, 1938. 162p.

Shows holdings.

2436. St. Bartholomew's Hospital Library. List of current medical periodicals taken by London medical schools and institutes and the University of London. London, 1957. 90p.

Shows holdings for 24 libraries; revision of 1954 list.

2437. Sheffield, University, Library, Information Service. Comprehensive list of medical & psychological serials in Sheffield libraries other than the Main University Library. Sheffield: The Library, 1970. Unpaged.

Records 1,127 titles, with holdings, in numerous libraries.

2438. ——— ———. Medical journals in the University Library; a handlist. Sheffield: The Library, 1968. Unpaged.

Lists 586 titles, with holdings.

2439. Society for Cultural Relations with the U.S.S.R., Medical Committee. English index to Soviet medical periodicals available in London libraries, together with a location list of the periodicals indexed, ed. by Donovan T. Richnell; v.1, 1945-1947. London: H. K. Lewis & Co., 1950. 93p. (no more published)

Locates files of 18 journals in 4 London libraries.

2440. Tavistock Institute of Human Relations, Joint Library. List of periodicals. London, 1968. 17p.

Library dealing with psychiatry and related subjects.

2441. United Oxford Hospitals. List of medical periodicals taken in the United Oxford Hospitals. Oxford, 1964. 29l.

Locations in 35 departmental libraries or collections in the U.O.H. hospitals and related institutions and research units.

2442. Wales, University, Welsh Natoinal School of Medicine Libraries. List of periodicals in the general and departmental libraries. Cardiff, Wales, 1954. 26p.

Holdings given for general and 9 departmental libraries.

2443. Wellcome Foundation. Periodicals in the Wellcome Foundation; a union list. London, 1961. 169l.

Alphabetical list noting holdings of 10 libraries associated with the foundation.

Dentistry

2444. British Dental Association. A list of works on dentistry, published between the years 1536 and 1882; with a catalogue of the periodical literature relating to the profession, from 1839 to 1882, by Oakley Coles. London, 1883. 35p.

2445. ———— Library. Catalogue of dental and allied works published since 1945. London: The Association, 1956. 21p.

Classified list.

2446. ———— ————. Catalogue of the rare book room, comp. by H. A. Cufflin. London: The Association, 1964. 28p.

2447. Cohen, R. "Rare books in the British Dental Association." British dental journal, 118 (1965), 280-81.

Veterinary Medicine

2448. British Museum, Dept. of Printed Books. Exhibition at British Museum, Bloomsbury, of manuscripts and early English printed books dealing with veterinary medicine; a catalogue. (Eleventh International Veterinary Congress, London . . . 1930.) London: H. & W. Brown, 1930. Unpaged.

Lists 17 printed books and 18 manuscripts.

2449. Catton, R. "The historical collection in the Library of the Royal Veterinary College." Veterinary record, 77 (1965), 503-6.

History and brief description of collection.

2450. ————. "Some association copies in the historical collection in the Royal Veterinary College Library." British veterinary journal, 120 (1964), 583-86.

2451. London, University, Royal Veterinary College Library. A catalogue of the books, pamphlets and periodicals up to 1850 in the Library. London, 1965. 48p. (Supplement to Veterinary record, May 1, 1965)

Periodical list notes holdings.

2452. Royal College of Veterinary Surgeons Memorial Library. Catalogue of modern works, 1900-1954, with a section showing periodicals and reports, 2d ed. London, R.C.V.S., 1955. 98p. Supplement, 1955-56. 16p.; Supplement 2, 1957-58. 1960. 14p.

2453. ————. Catalogue of the Central Library for animal diseases; text-books published since 1900. London, 1936. 46p.

2454. ————. Catalogue of the historical collection; books published before 1850. London, 1953. 36p.

Pharmacology

2455. Aberdeen, University, Library. Subject catalogue of the Phillips Library of Pharmacology and Therapeutics, by P. J. Anderson. Aberdeen: Univ. Pr., 1911. 240p. (Aberdeen University studies, no.47)

Arranged by Dewey Decimal Classification.

2456. Brunn, A. L. How to find out in pharmacy; a guide to sources of pharmaceutical information. Oxford: Pergamon, 1969. 130p.

Includes a list of libraries with special collections and large general medical libraries, American and British.

2457. Chelsea Physic Garden. Catalogue of the Library at the Chelsea Physic Garden. London: C. F. Roworth, 1956. 35p.

Library relating to medical botany, established in 1633.

2458. Edinburgh, University, Library. Some early herbals and pharmacopoeias exhibited in Edinburgh University Library. May-June 1950. Edinburgh, 1950. 19p.

Historical essay, followed by listing of 54 herbals, works on domestic medicine, and pharmacopoeias.

2459. London, University, School of Pharmacy. Library guide, with some notes for preparing dissertations, rev. ed., comp. by Magda Pasztor and Jenny Hopkins. London, 1967. 31p.

2460. Pharmaceutical Society of Great Britain Library. Catalogue, 10th ed., comp. by John William Knapman. London: The Society, 1911. 560p.

Dictionary catalog.

2461. ———. Catalogue of the Library of the Pharmaceutical Society of Great Britain, North British Branch, Edinburgh, 11th ed. London: The Society, 1911. 85p.

2462. Pharmaceutical Society of Great Britain. Holdings of periodicals currently received. London, 1969. 17p.

2463. Rohde, Eleanour Sinclair. The Old English herbals. New York: Longmans, Green, 1922. 243p.

Records locations of manuscript and printed herbals in British and American collections from 9th century to 1678.

2464. Society of Apothecaries. Catalogue of the Library of the Society of Apothecaries, by William Bramley Taylor. London: Taylor and Francis, 1913. 106p.

Library dating from early 17th century.

2465. Society of Herbalists. A selection from the library. London, n.d. 67p.

Lists 555 items in classified arrangement.

Technology

General

2466. Ardern, L. L. "The Manchester College of Technology Library and its assistance to industry." Aslib proceedings, 7 (1955), 136-42.
Includes description of resources.

2467. Attwood, L. V. "The British Standards Institution Library." Aslib proceedings, 7 (1955), 31-36.
Description of library's resources relating to technical standards.

2468. Birmingham, University, Library. Nineteenth century industry collection; handlist. Birmingham, 1967. Unpaged. (Catalogue of the manuscript collections, no.3)
Describes 24 boxes of records relating to Midland area industries.

2469. British Scientific Instrument Research Association. Catalogue of books in the Library, 1960, comp. by J. E. Taylor. Chislehurst, Kent, 1960. 2v.
v.1, classified list; v.2, subject and author indexes.

2470. Courtaulds Limited. Union catalogue of books held by the Technical Libraries of the company at Coventry; subject catalogue, including holdings up to the end of 1954, 1955-1959, 1960. Coventry: Technical Information Bureau, n.d. 3v.

2471. Coventry Public Libraries. Metrication-decimalisation: a bibliography. Coventry, 1967. 19p.

2472. Ealing Public Library. Dictionaries technical and translating. London: CICRIS Commercial and Technical Library Service, 1959. 106p.
Lists 709 titles held by Ealing Central Library.

2473. Ferguson, John. Bibliographical notes on histories of inventions and books of secrets. Glasgow: Glasgow Univ. Pr., 1894-1915. 8pts. in 1v.

Ferguson collection is now in Glasgow University Library.

2474. Great Britain, Ministry of Technology Library Services. Book list. London, 1968-   .
Issued periodically.

2475. Lewisham Technical Reference Library. Metrins: a guide to metrication information and sources. London, 1971. 27p.

2476. Manchester Public Libraries. Technical translating dictionaries. Manchester, 1962. 34p.
Lists 373 titles, grouped by languages and subjects.

2477. Newcastle upon Tyne City Libraries. Catalogue of books on the useful arts (class 600 of Dewey's Decimal Classification) in the Central Library. Newcastle upon Tyne, 1903. 287p. Supplement, ed. by B. Anderton. Newcastle upon Tyne, 1914. 209p.

2478. Page, B. S. "The facilities of the Leeds University Libraries for the study of technology." Aslib proceedings 3 (1951), 131-36.
General review by subject areas.

2479. Rural Industries Bureau. Library catalogue, index and rules. London: The Bureau, 1938. 48l.

2480. Science Museum Library, London. Technical glossaries and dictionaries. London, 1952. 82p. (Science Library, Bibliographical Series, no.707)
First published 1947. (Science Library, Bibliographical Series, no.632) Supplements 1-4, 1945-50. About 1,300 items listed.

2481. Wigan and District Mining and Technical College Library. Industrial training; a reading list for training officers, 2d ed., comp. by Kenneth B. Swallow and M. M. Hadcroft. Wigan, 1969. 54p.

2482. ——— ———. Metrication. Wigan: The College, 1969. 39p.

Patents

2483. Great Britain, Patent Office Library. Catalogue of the Library of the Patent Office, arranged alphabetically in two volumes. London: Commissioners of Patents' Sale Dept., 1881-83. 2v.
v.1, authors; v.2, subjects.

2484. ———. Catalogue of the Library of the Patent Office. London: H. M. Stationery Office, 1898. 1,007p. (v.1, authors. No more published.)

2485. ———. Subject list of works of reference, biography, bibliography, the auxiliary historical sciences, etc., in the Library of the Patent Office. London: H. M. Stationery Office, 1908. 336p.

2486. ———. Subject list of works on the law of industrial property (patents, designs and trade marks) and copyright. London: H. M. Stationery Office, 1909. 84p.

2487. Manchester Public Libraries. Patents: a brief guide to the patents collection in the Technical Library, by J. E. Wild. Manchester, 1966. 4p.

2488. Sheffield City Libraries. Patent holdings in British public libraries. Sheffield, 1970. Unpaged.

Engineering

GENERAL

2489. Associated Engineering Limited, Information and Library Section. Periodicals taken and held in the Library. Warwickshire, n.d. 37p.
Includes statement of holdings.

2490. Aston, University, Library. Engineering; a guide to publications and sources information. Birmingham, 1971. 47p.

2491. Cambridge, University, Dept. of Engineering Library. Catalogue of periodicals. Cambridge, 1969. 36p.
Alphabetical list of holdings.

2492. ———. KWIC index to engineering book titles; a subject guide, comp. by K. A. Knell. Cambridge: The Department, 1968. 214p.
Lists Engineering Library's holdings.

2493. ———. List of periodicals and list of report series. Cambridge, 1967. 52 + 9p.
Notes holdings.

2494. Great Britain, Institution of Royal Engineers. Catalogue of the Royal Engineers Corps Library at the

Horse Guards, Whitehall, London. Chatham, 1992. 521p.

2495. ———, Ministry of Technology, National Engineering Laboratory Library, Journals taken by the Library. Glasgow, 1966. 21p.

2496. Institution of Civil Engineers. Catalogue of the Library of the Institution of Civil Engineers. London, 1895. 3v.

2497. Institution of Production Engineers, Hazleton Memorial Library. Hazleton Memorial Library catalogue. London, 1955. 202p. Supplement. London, 1958. 35p.
Library devoted to engineering subjects.

2498. ——— Library. Materials handling; a list of books published since 1950, together with a list of societies and associations and a list of films. London: The Institution, 1958. 27p.

2499. ——— ———. Quality control. 1, a list of books in the Hazleton Memorial Library. 2, a list of journal articles: a selection, 1957-59. London, 1959. 19p.

2500. Royal Engineers. Catalogue of books, maps, and plans, in the General Corps libraries of the Royal Engineers. London: Faithfull & Co., 1866. 316l.

2501. Royal Society Library. A catalogue of the civil and mechanical engineering designs, 1741-1792, of John Smeaton, F.R.S., preserved in the Library of the Royal Society, ed. by H. W. Dickinson and A. A. Gomme. London, 1950. 186p. (Newcomen Society, Extra publication, no.5)

2502. Science Museum Library. Books on engineering; a subject catalogue of books in the Science Library; short-title list of books published 1930 and onwards on mechanical, civil, electrical, marine, sanitary, and other branches of engineering, with engineering aspects of transport. London: H. M. Stationery Office, 1957. 183p.
Classified catalog with author index; lists about 6,000 books.

2503. Warwick, University, Library, Science Division. A guide to sources of information in engineering sciences and physics. Coventry: The Library, 1968. 28p.

ELECTRICAL

2504. Admiralty Center for Scientific Information and Liaison Library. A bibliography of literature relating to semi-conductors, comp. by H. L. R. Hinkley. London, 1954. 189p.

Contains 1,208 entries.

2505. Aslib Electronics Group. Union list of periodicals on electronics and related subjects, comp. by Rosemary England. London, 1961. 62p.

Holdings reported for 59 special libraries; about 1,500 titles listed.

2506. Aston, University, Library. Electrical engineering; a guide to publications and sources of information. Birmingham, 1971. 19p.

2507. British Electrical and Allied Industries Research Association Library. Catalogue of books and periodicals in E.R.A. Library, June 1945. London: The Association, 1945. 97p.

Classified list with author index.

2508. British Institution of Electronic and Radio Engineers. Library services and technical information for the radio and electronics engineer. London, 1958. 72p.

2509. Central Electricity Authority. Catalogue of the Central Library, December 1956. London: Bankside House, 1957. 157p.

2510. Central Electricity Generating Board. Union list of periodicals held by the Libraries of CEGB Headquarters. London: The Libraries, 1970. 104p.

Alphabetical list with locations in CEGB Libraries in London, Gloucestershire, Surrey, and Hants.

2511. Glasgow Public Libraries. A selected list of books on hydro-power and the future of the Highlands, ed. by George C. Emslie. Glasgow: Mitchell Library, 1952. 9p.

2512. Great Britain, Ministry of Supply, Radar Research Establishment. R.R.E. Library catalogue of books. Malvern, Worcs, 1955. 135p.

2513. ———, Patent Office Library. Subject list of works on electricity, magnetism, and electro-technics. London: H. M. Stationery Office, 1904. 286p.

2514. ———, Post Office Telecommunications Headquarter, Research Department Library. Subject and author catalogue of books added to the Library since May 1958. London: The Department, 1969. 146p.

2515. ———, Royal Radar Establishment Library. List of periodicals held in the Library of the Royal Radar Establishment. Great Malvern, Worcs., 1961. 50p.

2516. Imperial War Museum Library. Radar: a list of selected references. London, 1967. 8p. (Booklist, no.1230)

2517. Institution of Electrical Engineers. Catalogue of the Lending Library, 1956. London, 1956. 202p.

2518. ———. Catalogue of the Lending Library, 1959. London: 1960. 223p.

In 2 sections: alphabetical by authors and classified by subjects.

2519. Royal Radar Establishment Library. Catalogue of periodicals, 1970. Malvern, Worcs., 1970. 32l.

Alphabetical list of holdings.

2520. Society of Telegraph Engineers. Catalogue of books and papers relating to electricity, magnetism, the electric telegraph, etc., including the Ronalds Library, comp. by Francis Ronalds. London: E. & F. N. Spon, 1880. 564p.

COMPUTERS

2521. Kingston upon Hull City Libraries. Computers, a checklist. Kingston upon Hull, 1970. 18p.

Publications on computers and computer applications held in Central Library, Kingston upon Hull.

2522. University College of Wales Library. A guide to the resources available in computer science & statistics. Aberystwyth, 1970. 5p. (Handlist, no.11)

MECHANICAL

2523. Glasgow Corporation Public Libraries. Scotland's locomotive builders; an exhibition illustrative of the development of the locomotive industry in Scotland. Glasgow: Mitchell Library, 1971. 14p.

Includes brief description of the North British Locomotive Company collection received by Mitchell Library in 1962.

2524. Great Britain, Patent Office Library. Subject list of works on heat and heat engines (excluding marine engineering). London: H. M. Stationery Office, 1905. 200p.

2525. Institute of the Motor Industry Library. Library catalogue. London, 1948. 1v. (loose-leaf)

Classified order.

2526. Institution of Mechanical Engineers. Library catalogue; subject index of papers in the Proceedings 1847-1890. Westminster, 1890. 220 + 32p.

2527. ——— Library. A list of periodicals and other regular serials holdings in the Library of the Institute

of Mechanical Engineers as at April 1969. London:
The Institute, 1969. 130p.

Alphabetical list with holdings.

2528. Luton Public Libraries. Automobile engineering
and allied subjects, comp. by J. Loosely. Luton, 1962.
183p. (Technical bulletin, no.59)

Subject catalogue of all relevant items in Luton
Public Libraries.

2529. ———. Automobile engineering. Luton, 1971.
26p. (Technical bulletin, no.70. Supplement: Nov.
1969-June 1971)

Lists of works dealing with various types of motor
vehicles.

2530. Matthew Hall Libraries. Technical books and
data. London: Matthew Hall & Co., n.d. 434p.

Library deals with various aspects of mechanical
engineering.

2531. Rotherham Public Library. Books on private
motor cars, three wheeler motor cars, commercial
motor vehicles, motor bicycles, scooters and mopeds in
the stock of the Central Lending Library. Rotherham,
1963. 20p.

2532. Science Museum Library. Historic books on
machines. London: The Museum, 1953. 28p. (Book
exhibitions, no.2)

Exhibition drawn from collections of Science
Museum, British Museum, Patent Office Library, and
Tower of London.

2533. Stephenson Locomotive Society Library. Library catalogue, 1955. London: The Society, 1955. 54p.

2534. ———. Stephenson Locomotive Society's Library: list of principal additions, 1958-65. London,
1966. 10p.

2535. Westminster Public Libraries. Motor car manuals, prep. by R. H. Millward. London, 1963. 12p.

Manuals, handbooks, and similar publications
held by Westminster Public Libraries.

BUILDING

2536. Building Societies Institute. Library catalogue.
London, 1961. 28p.

2537. Cement and Concrete Association Library. A
bibliography of bibliographies on cement and concrete: an arrangement of all the published bibliographies compiled by the Library of the Cement and
Concrete Association during the period 1946-1967.
London: The Association, 1968. 3, 8p.

2538. ———. Bibliography of cement and concrete,
list of books and papers contained in libraries in the
London area, comp. by A. G. N. Bagwell. London:
The Association, 1952. 96p.

Locates copies in 12 libraries.

2539. ———. Catalogue of text and reference books in
the Library of the Cement and Concrete Association,
2d ed. London: The Association, 1949. 44p.

2540. ———. Catalogue of text and reference books
in the Library of the Cement and Concrete Association. London: The Association, 1959. 109p. Supplements, 1960-62. 3pts.

2541. ———. Design of concrete mixes; selected
articles, papers and books dealing with the subject of
design of concrete mixes many of which are held by
the Cement and Concrete Association. London: The
Association, 1951. 23p.

2542. ———. Non-destructive testing of concrete;
articles, papers and books dealing with the subject of
non-destructive testing of concrete, which are held by
the Cement and Concrete Association. London: The
Association, 1951. 5p.

2543. ———. Pozzolana cement; articles, papers and
books dealing with the subject of Pozzolana cement
held by the Cement and Concrete Association.
London: The Association, 1951. 10p.

2544. ———. Steam curing of concrete; articles,
papers and books dealing with the subject of steam
curing of concrete held by the Cement and Concrete
Association. London: The Association, 1951. 9p.

2545. Great Britain, Ministry of Public Building &
Works Library. Metric bibliography; a selection of the
more important material of interest to the construction
industry, 3d ed. London, 1970. 36p.

2546. McVittie, Thomas. "Scotland's special libraries:
Ministry of Public Building and Works Library,
Edinburgh." SLA news, no.94 (1969), 417-19.

Library of some 10,000 books, 25,000 pamphlets,
and 150 current periodicals on construction industry.

2547. Newcastle upon Tyne City Libraries. Classified
list of books on building and ship building (class 690 of
Dewey's Decimal Classification) in the Central Library,
by B. Anderton. Newcastle upon Tyne, 1903. 16p.

2548. Polytechnic of the South Bank, Faculty of Construction Technology and Design, and Brixton School
of Building. List of current periodicals. London, 1970.
23*l*.

2549. Sheffield City Libraries. Catalogue of books in the Central Libraries on the building and allied trades. Sheffield: Leng, 1924. 36p.

2550. Sheffield, University, Library. Reference and information sources in building science. Sheffield, 1971. 20p.

2551. Victoria and Albert Museum. A list of books and pamphlets in the National Art Library . . . on construction, engineering, and machinery, comp. by R. H. S. Smith. London: H. M. Stationery Office, 1889. 68p.

MINING

2552. Birmingham Assay Office Library. Catalogue of the books in the Library at the Assay Office, Birmingham, by A. Westwood. Birmingham, 1914. 308p.

2553. Birkbeck College Library. Crystallography: handlist of books in the College Library, 2d ed., comp. by P. Woudhuysen. London, 1971. 24p. (Library publication, no.1)

2554. Bluhm, R. K. A bibliography of the Somerset coalfield. London, 1968. 205*l*. (Thesis, Library Association Fellowship)
Contains 863 entries with locations in 8 libraries.

2555. Great Britain, Patent Office Library. Subject list of works on mineral industries in the Library of the Patent Office. pt.1, geological sciences—coal mining; pt.2, iron manufacture, alloys and metallography; pt.3, metallurgy, non-ferrous and general, assaying, and fuel combustion. London: H. M. Stationery Office, 1912. 3pts.

2556. ———. Subject list of works on peat, destructive distillation, artificial lighting, mineral oils and waxes, gas lighting and acetylene. London: H. M. Stationery Office, 1911. 108p.

2557. ———. Subject list of works on the mineral industries and allied sciences, in the Library of the Patent Office. London: H. M. Stationery Office, 1903. 302p.

2558. Hickman, F. Symposium on the nature and scope of fuel and power library and information services in the United Kingdom. London: Aslib, 1953. 28p.
Notes on resources and services of 32 libraries.

2559. Midland Institute of Mining Engineers Library, Catalogue of Library; subject-matter index of papers, and of articles on mining and allied subjects contained in the books, transactions, etc., in the library, on December 31st, 1915, comp. by F. Oxley. Sheffield: Loxley Bros., 1916. 232p.

2560. Newcastle upon Tyne City Libraries. Schedule of old deeds and documents relating to mines in the Lordship of the Manor of Winlaton. Newcastle upon Tyne, 1952. 11*l*.
Calendar of deeds deposited in Newcastle upon Tyne Central Reference Library.

2561. Newcastle upon Tyne, Institute of Mining Engineers Library. Index of recent books and articles on coal mining and allied subjects contained in the publications added to the Library, no.1-57, July 1946-Sept. 1951. Newcastle upon Tyne, 1946-51. Continued as Index of current literature on coal mining and allied subjects. London, 1951-56, and new series, London, 1963-66.

2562. ———. Periodicals and serial publications received in the Library, October 1963- . London, 1963-

Issued periodically.

2563. Science Museum Library. Historic books on mining and kindred subjects, by Robert Annan. London: H. M. Stationery Office, 1968. 33p.
Based on Science Museum and Institution of Mining and Metallurgy collections.

2564. Sheffield City Libraries. Catalogue of books in the Central Libraries on the gas industry. Sheffield: Leng, 1926. 22p.

2565. ———. National Coal Board; deeds relating to lands near former collieries in Silkstone deposited in the Sheffield City Libraries. Sheffield, n.d. 28*l*.

2566. ———. Records of South Yorkshire colliery companies deposited by the National Coal Board at Sheffield City Libraries. Sheffield, n.d. 30*l*.

2567. South Staffordshire & Warwickshire Institute of Mining Engineers. Catalogue of the Institute Library housed at the University, Edgbaston, Birmingham, by J. G. Garrett. Birmingham, 1930. 36p.

2568. Wigan Public Library. Index catalogue of books and papers relating to mining, metallurgy and manufactures, by Henry Tennyson Folkard. Southport: Robert Johnson, 1880. 158p.

2569. ———. Jubilee exhibition of early mining literature; annotated catalogue, comp. by Arthur J. Hawkes. Wigan, 1928. 38p.

METALLURGICAL

2570. Birch, Alan. "The Haigh Ironworks, 1789-1856; a nobleman's enterprise during the Industrial Revolution." Bulletin of the John Rylands Library, 35 (1953), 316-33. Reprinted. 1953. 20p.

Based on Crawford manuscripts deposited in John Rylands Library.

2571. Birmingham Public Libraries. The manufacture of non-ferrous seamless tubes; a bibliography, 2d ed., comp. by Irene A. Clarke. Birmingham, 1971. 38p.

2572. British Cast Iron Research Association. Periodicals held in the Library. Alvechurch, Birmingham, 1970. Unpaged.

2573. Brown-Firth Research Laboratories. The Brown-Firth Research Laboratories, founded 1908 [a description of their work, with a list of publications by the staff, a catalogue of the library, and illustrations]. Sheffield, 1937. 70p.

Library relating to steel technology and industry.

2574. Great Britain, House of Commons Library. The British iron and steel industry, 3d ed. London, 1959. 23p. (Bibliography, no.2)

Contains 152 references.

2575. Institute of Welding Library. Classified catalogue of the Library, 2d ed., comp. by C. Brayden. London: The Institute, 1944. 180p.

2576. Iron and Steel Institute. Abridged catalogue of the Library of the Iron and Steel Institute. London, 1914. 101p.

Classified list.

2577. Sheffield City Libraries. Cutlery, a bibliography. Sheffield: Libraries, Art Galleries, and Museums Committee, 1960. 30p. Supplement, 1960-68. n.d. 5l.

PETROLEUM

2578. Asiatic Petroleum Co., S.T.A. Dept. Library catalogue. London: Asiatic Petroleum, 1945. 52l.

Classified listing of works in field of petroleum technology.

2579. Burmah Oil Trading, Ltd. Library. List of periodicals taken at Burmah House. London: 1971. 11l.

2580. Institute of Petroleum. Library catalogue. London, 1956. 87p.

Classified arrangement, with author index.

2581. ——— Library. Periodicals in the Institute of Petroleum Library. London, 1969. 11p.

2582. Shell International Petroleum Company. Periodicals holding list. London: The Company's Library and Information Services, 1971. 42p.

AERONAUTICAL

2583. Aslib, Aeronautical Group. Union list of periodicals of aeronautics and allied subjects. n.p., 1953. 13l.

Alphabetically arranged, showing holdings for 17 English libraries.

2584. Bristol Aeroplane Company. Library catalogue. Bristol, 1946. 209p. Supplement, 1952. 160p. Supplement, 1957. 135p.

Dictionary arrangement in main work and supplements.

2585. Coventry City Libraries. Aeronautics; technical and general: books in the Coventry Libraries on the theory of flight, practical flying, aeronautical engineering . . . and on gliders and gliding, comp. by Harry Sargeant. Coventry, 1932. 27p.

2586. Great Britain, Ministry of Aviation Central Library. Book list. London, 1965- . Issued periodically.

Continuation of "List of accessions (accessions list)" published by Central Library of the Ministry of Supply.

2587. ———, Ministry of Aviation, Royal Radar Establishment Library. Catalogue of books, part 8, radio-communication. Great Malvern, Worcestershire, 1961. 7p.

2588. ——— ———, Technical Information and Library Services. Catalogue of periodicals held by the Ministry of Aviation Central Library, comp. by Joan M. Harding. London: The Library, 1965. 96p.

Alphabetical list noting holdings.

2589. ———, Royal Aircraft Establishment (Farnborough). Catalogue of periodicals held by the Main Library, Royal Aircraft Establishment. London: Ministry of Supply, 1958. 49p.

Alphabetical list noting specific holdings.

2590. ——— ———. Catalogue of periodicals, comp. by D. I. Raitt. London, 1969. 80p.

Alphabetical list of holdings and subject index.

2591. Higham, R. "Aeronautical history—some offbeat British archives." American archivist, 26 (1963), 63-65.

Notes on various society, government, and private collections relevant to aeronautical history.

2592. Imperial War Museum Library. A bibliography of aeronautics. London, 1961. 19p.

Three pts.: pt.1, 1900-60; pt.2, First World War; pt.3, Second World War and after.

2593. ———. Lighter-than-air craft; a bibliography of selected titles. London, 1970. 13p. (Booklist, no.1332)

2594. Rolls-Royce, Aero Engine Division, Library & Information Services. Quality & reliability—a list of items available from the Library. Derby, 1968. 104p.

Records 564 items.

2595. Royal Aeronautical Society Library. A list of the books, periodicals, and pamphlets in the Library of the Royal Aeronautical Society. London, 1941. 276p.

Classified catalog: library is in 2 sections: books of historical interest and modern scientific and technical works.

CERAMIC

2596. Brierley Hill Public Libraries. Check list of books and pamphlets on glass and glass-making in the Reference Library special collection. Brierley Hill, Staffs., 1962. 26p.

2597. British Ceramic Research Association. Mellor Memorial Library. List of periodical holdings. Stoke on Trent, 1969. 14*l*.

2598. Central School of Science & Technology, Stoke on Trent. Catalogue of the Ceramic Library. Stoke on Trent, 1925. 228p. Supplement, 1930. 95p.

Includes the Solon Library, the Ceramic Society Library, and the Library of the Pottery Department of the School. Name of institution changed to North Staffordshire Technical College.

2599. Derby Borough Libraries. Derby porcelain, 1750-1971; a select list of books and manuscripts, Derby Borough Libraries. Derby, 1971. 21p.

2600. Great Britain, Patent Office Library. Subject list of works on the silicate industry (ceramics and glass). London: H. M. Stationery Office, 1914. 88p.

2601. "The literature of ceramics in West Midland libraries." Open access, 18 (Winter 1970), 1-6.

Review of holdings of Staffordshire County Library, Stoke on Trent Public Libraries, and North Staffordshire College of Technology.

2602. Manchester Public Libraries. Catalogue of books on ceramics, glassware, ornamental metal work, enamels, and jade; in the Free Reference Library, comp. by F. Bentley Nicholson. Manchester, 1908. 20p. (Occasional lists, no.8)

2603. North Staffordshire Technical College. Catalogue of the Ceramic Library, supplement. Stoke on Trent, 1925-30. 2pts.

2604. Society of Glass Technology. List of books, pamphlets, & periodicals in the Library. Sheffield: J. W. Northend, 1922. 16p.

2605. Stoke on Trent Public Library. The history and collecting of British pottery and porcelain; a select book list, comp. by Norman Emery. Stoke on Trent: Horace Marks Reference Library and Information Service, Central Library, 1963. 16p.

2606. Victoria and Albert Museum. National Art Library . . . classed catalogue of printed books: ceramics, ed. by W. H. J. Weale. London: H. M. Stationery Office, 1895. 353p.

2607. Walton, S. M. "The Library of the British Ceramic Research Association." Open access, 15 (Spring 1967), 14-15.

Brief description of resources.

PLASTICS

2608. British Plastics Federation. List of books on plastics in the Library. London, 1958. 23p. Supplements 1-5. 1959-63.

Main list contains 500 entries.

2609. Science Museum Library. Bibliography of plastics. London, 1933. Unpaged. (Bibliographical series, no.82)

Classified arrangement, with Library's call numbers added.

Textiles

2610. Aslib. Aslib guides to sources of information in Great Britain, no.4: Textiles & allied interests. London: Aslib, 1949. 43p.

Listing of relevant libraries and organizations.

2611. ———. Textile Group. Union list of holdings of textile periodicals, 3d ed. London: Aslib, 1962. 37p.

Entries for about 500 titles, with locations in 27 libraries.

2612. Cotton Board Library. Catalogue of periodicals, 1962. Manchester: The Board, 1962. 37p.

About 600 titles, arranged under countries, with record of holdings.

2613. Cotton, Silk and Man-Made Fibres Research Association. Catalogue of periodicals in the Shirley

Institute Library. Manchester: Shirley Institute, 1964. 158p.

2614. Great Britain, Patent Office Library. Subject list of works on the textile industries and wearing apparel, including the culture and chemical technology of textile fibres. London: H. M. Stationery Office, 1919. 334p.

2615. Leeds, University, Brotherton Library. Gott papers. Leeds, 1968. 20*l*.

Papers relating to wool industry in Leeds, 1780-1867, and to Gott family in late 18th and 19th centuries.

2616. ———. Schedule of papers from the Leeds White Cloth Hall collection. Leeds, n.d. 49p.

Papers relating to the Leeds cloth market from mid-18th to end of 19th century.

2617. Linen Industry Research Association Library. Library catalogue, 1920-1933. Belfast: M'Caw, Stevenson and Orr, 1934. 101p.

2618. National Book League. The literature of fashion; an exhibition arranged by James Laver for the National Book League. London: Cambridge Univ. Pr., 1947. 64p.

Catalogue of an exhibition presented by the National Book League; identifies owners of 265 items shown, in public and private collections.

2619. Potter, Esther. "English knitting and crochet books of the nineteenth century." Library, ser.5, 10(1955), 25-40, 103-19.

Locates copies in British Museum, Victoria and Albert Museum, etc.

2620. Shirley Institute Library. Catalogue of the Shirley Institute Library. Didsbury, Manchester: The Institute, 1931. 246p.

Library relating to textile technology, chemistry, and other scientific subjects.

2621. Shoreditch Public Libraries. The clothing industry; a catalogue of the books in the special collection of the Shoreditch Public Libraries. London, 1955. 15p.

2622. Silk Centre Library. Catalogue of Silk Centre Library. London, 1953? 24p.

2623. The Textile Institute. Year book of the Textile Institute and library catalogue. Manchester, 1951-52. 190p. (no.4)

Library catalogue (by authors), p.83-138.

Food Technology

2624. Aslib. Guides to sources of information in Great Britain, no.3: Beverages and food. London, 1949. 45p.

Listing of relevant libraries and organizations.

2625. Borough Polytechnic Library. Bakery & food science literature. London, 1965. 11p.

2626. British Food Manufacturing Industries Research Association. Periodicals in the Library. Leatherhead, Surrey, 1970. 18p.

2627. Distillers Research Department Library. Catalogued books in the Library of the Distillers Research Department, Great Burgh, Epsom. Epsom, 1944. 77*l*.

Classified by subjects.

2628. Great Britain, Patent Office Library. Subject list of works on domestic economy, etc. London: H. M. Stationery Office, 1902. 136p.

2629. Guildhall Library. "A handlist of cookery books and books about food in Guildhall Library." Guildhall miscellany, no.9 (July, 1958), 52-59.

2630. Heinz, H. J., Co., Company Library and Information Service. Journal holdings list. London: The Company, 1961. Unpaged.

Library dealing with food technology.

2631. Lambeth Public Libraries, Reference Services. Food technology—a select bibliography. London: The Libraries, 1967. 30p.

Classified list of books and pamphlets concerning food technology, in London Borough of Lambeth Public Libraries.

2632. Mathias, Peter. "Historical records of the brewing industry." Archives, no.33 (1965), 2-10.

Traces nature and present locations of records.

2633. Milk Marketing Board Library. Complete catalogue of periodicals, 1967-68. London, 1968. 61*l*.

Alphabetical list by titles with country index.

2634. National Institute for Research in Dairying Library. List of journals and periodicals in the Library of the National Institute for Research in Dairying. Shinfield, n.d. 25p.

Institution affiliated with University of Reading.

2635. Oxford, Arnold Whitaker. Notes from a collector's catalogue. London: John and Edward Bumpus, 1909. 116p.

Includes list of English books on cookery and carving, p.39-107, with locations in 4 English libraries.

2636. OXO Library. Food science and technology. London, 1969. 19*l*. (Subject list no.5, June 1969)

Books listed were in library stock on 30 June 1969; grouped by subjects.

2637. Reading, University, National College of Food Technology Library. Food science and technology, a select list of books. Surrey, 1968. 80p. + index.

Classified listing.

2638. Wine & Food Society Library. Bibliotheca gastronomica: a catalogue of books and documents on gastronomy [published before 1861, and in the Library of the Wine & Food Society], comp. by André L. Simon. London: The Society, 1953. 197p.

Records 1,644 entries up to 1861.

Leather and Footwear

2639. Northampton Public Libraries. Catalogue of the leather and footwear collections in the Northampton Central Reference Library and the Library of the Northampton Central College of Further Education, comp. by David Powell and Victor A. Hatley. Northampton: Public Libraries, Museums and Art Gallery Committee, 1968. 53p.

Classified listing.

2640. Shoreditch Public Libraries. The boots, shoes, garment trades, and the clothing industry; a list of works published since 1947 held by Shoreditch Public Libraries. London, 1953. Unpaged.

Manufactures—Miscellaneous

2641. Aslib. Aslib guides to sources of information in Great Britain, no.1: the paper industry. London, 1948. 11p.

Listing of relevant libraries and organizations.

2642. ———, Furniture Group. Union list of periodicals dealing with furniture, timber, woodworking and allied subjects. London: Aslib, 1958. 13*l*.

Locates holdings in 14 libraries.

2643. Clockmakers' Company of London. A catalogue of books, manuscripts, specimens of clocks, watches and watchwork, paintings, prints, etc., in the Library and Museum of the Worshipful Company of Clockmakers deposited in the Free Library of the Corporation of the City of London. London: E. J. Francis, 1875. 103p.

2644. ——— Library. Catalogue of the Library of the Worshipful Company of Clockmakers of London, preserved in the Guildhall Library, London, 2d ed. London: Blades, East & Blades, 1898. 205p.

2645. ——— ———. Catalogue of the Library of the Worshipful Company of Clockmakers of London in the Guildhall Library, London, 3d ed. London: The Company, 1951. 79p.

2646. Hollaender, A. E. J. "The archives of the Worshipful Company of Gunmakers of the City of London." Archives, no.8 (1952), 8-19.

Records deposited in the Guildhall Library (Muniment Room).

2647. Research Association of British Paint, Colour and Varnish Manufacturers Library. Library catalogue, books and journals. Teddington, Middlesex: The Association, 1934. 93p.

2648. Research Association of British Rubber and Tyre Manufacturers Library. Library catalogue. Cambridge: Heffer, 1927. 210p.

Dictionary arrangement.

2649. Shoreditch Public Libraries. Furniture and allied trades; a catalogue of the books in the special collection. London, 1950. 53p.

In 3 sections: timber, woodworking, and furniture.

2650. Timber Development Association. T. D. A. Library catalogue, 4th ed. London, 1953. 69p.

Agriculture

GENERAL

2651. Agricultural Research Council, Food Research Institute Library. List of periodicals held in the Library. Norwich: The Institute, 1968. 15*l*.

2652. The Alpine Garden Society Library. Catalogue of the Alpine Garden Society Library; a descriptive list of books, pamphlets and other documents available to members of the Society, 4th ed., comp. by K. G. Lazenby. Farnborough: The Society, 1959. 22p.

List of 401 items.

2653. Aslib. Aslib guides to sources of information in Great Britain, no.2: Agriculture & allied interests. London, 1949. 63p. + index.

Listing of relevant libraries and organizations.

2654. Bath and West and Southern Counties Society for the Encouragement of Agriculture, Arts, Manufacture and Commerce Library. Catalogue of the Library, comp. by Peter Pagan and Philip Bryant. Bath, 1964. 86p.

2655. Birmingham and Midland Counties Gardeners' Mutual Improvement Association. Catalogue of books in the Library. Birmingham, 1896. 12p.

2656. Bristol, University, Dept. of Agriculture and Horticulture Library. Catalogue of periodicals, 4th ed. Bristol, 1971. 89p.
Alphabetical list of holdings.

2657. British Museum. Guide to an exhibition of manuscripts and printed books illustrating the history of agriculture. London: W. Clowes, 1927. 30p.

2658. Buttress, Frederick A. Agricultural periodicals of the British Isles, 1681-1900, and their location. Cambridge: Univ. of Cambridge, School of Agriculture, 1950. 16p.
Alphabetically arranged; locations in 16 British collections.

2659. Chatham Public Libraries. Catalogue of books on gardening. London, 1963. 81p.
Classified list of books available in Chatham Public Libraries.

2660. Farmers' Club Library. The Farmers' Club Library; a classified list of books, 2d ed. London, 1945. 44p.

2661. Fussell, George Edwin. More old English farming books from Tull to the Board of Agriculture, 1731-1793. London: C. Lockwood, 1950. 186p.
Checklist, with locations of copies.

2662. Great Britain, Ministry of Agriculture, Fisheries and Food Libraries. Accessions list. London, 1966- .
Issued periodically.

2663. ——— ———. Selective index to current periodical literature. London, 1966- .
Issued periodically.

2664. ——— ———. Union list of periodicals held in the Ministry's Libraries. London: The Ministry's Main Library, 1962. 136p.
Locates files in 22 libraries.

2665. ———, Ministry of Agriculture and Fisheries Library. Chronological list of early agricultural works in the Library of the Ministry of Agriculture and Fisheries, by George E. Fussell. London, 1930. 43p.
Contains 359 entries, 1533-1860.

2666. ——— ———. A selected and classified list of books relating to agriculture, horticulture, etc. in the library of the Ministry of Agriculture and Fisheries, 3d ed. London: H. M. Stationery Office, 1954. 87p. (Bulletin series, no.78)

2667. ———, Ministry of Agriculture, Research Division Library. Catalogue of pamphlets and books relating to cotton in the Library of the Research Division, Ministry of Agriculture. London, 1950. 69p.
Records all pamphlets and books directly relating to cotton in Ministry's Library.

2668. ———, Patent Office Library. Subject list of works on agriculture. London: H. M. Stationery Office, 1905. 424p.

2669. ———, Public Record Office. A classified list of agrarian surveys in the Public Record Office, by Hubert Hall. London, 1922. 23p. (Reprinted from Economica, no.4)

2670. International Association of Agricultural Libraries and Documentalists. World directory of agricultural libraries & documentation centres, ed. by D. H. Boalch. Harpenden, Herts., 1960. 280p.
Lists 2,531 agricultural libraries and documentation centres in 100 countries; items 1291-1436 relate to United Kingdom.

2671. Lancashire County Library. Agriculture and connected subjects, including gardening. Preston: 1928-30. 2pts. (Bibliography, no.5)

2672. Library Association. Library resources in the Greater London area: 5. Agricultural libraries. London, 1956. 20p.

2673. National Institute of Agricultural Engineering. Periodical holdings. Bedford, 1968. 38p.

2674. National Library of Wales. Agricultural books, 1924-38. Aberystwyth, 1926-39. 12pts. (Reprinted from the Welsh journal of agriculture, v.2-15. 1926-39)

2675. ———. A hand-list of books on agriculture, 3d ed. Aberystwyth, 1926. 44p.

2676. Newcastle upon Tyne City Libraries. Some books on agriculture in the Central Public Library, Newcastle upon Tyne. Newcastle upon Tyne, 1923. 8p.

2677. Oxford, University, Agricultural Economics Research Institute Library. List of annual publications currently received in the Library. Oxford, 1964. 13*l.*

2678. ——— ———. List of periodicals (other than annuals) currently received in the Library. Oxford, 1965. 26*l.* Supplements 1-2. 1965-66.

2679. ———, Bodleian Library. English rural life in the Middle Ages. Oxford, 1965. 10p. + 49 plates. (Bodleian picture books, no.14)

2680. Reading, University, Library. Accessions of historical farm records up to March 1970. Reading: The University, 1970. 20*l*.

Records collected by Museum of English Rural Life and deposited in Reading University Library.

2681. Rothamsted Experimental Station Library. Catalogue of serial publications in the Library of Rothamsted Experimental Station, 1953, ed. by D. H. Boalch, Harpenden, Herts., 1954. 356p.

Includes 4,700 titles (1,600 current) broadly relating to agriculture.

2682. ———. Catalogue of the printed books on agriculture published between 1471 and 1840, with notes on their authors, by Mary S. Aslin. Rothamsted, 1926. 331p.

Collection of historical works on agriculture acquired by library at Harpenden.

2683. ———. Current serials catalogue. Rothamsted, 1971. Unpaged.

Notes holdings.

2684. ———. Library catalogue of printed books and pamphlets on agriculture published between 1471 and 1840, 2d ed. Aberdeen: Univ. Pr., 1940. 293p.

2685. Royal Agricultural Society of England. Catalogue of the Library. London, 1918. 386p.

Author catalog.

2686. ———. Survey of agricultural libraries in England and Scotland. Aug. 1957. London, 1957. 75p.

Summary of resources and services of 46 libraries, each treated individually.

2687. Royal Highland and Agricultural Society of Scotland. Catalogue of the Library. Edinburgh, 1953. 526p.

Dictionary catalog.

2688. Royal Horticultural Society. Exhibition of manuscripts, books, drawings, portraits, medals, and congratulatory addresses on the occasion of the Society's 150th anniversary celebrations. London: Spottiswoode, 1954. 64p.

Exhibits drawn from society's valuable collection of books, manuscripts, and original drawings.

2689. ——— Library. The Lindley Library; catalogue of books, pamphlets, manuscripts and drawings. London: The Society, 1927. 488p.

Author catalog.

2690. Southampton University Library. Catalogue of the Walter Frank Perkins Agricultural Library, comp. by A. Anderson. Southampton, 1961. 291p.

Contains 2,009 entries, arranged by authors and titles; addenda of "Books printed in England and Scotland up to 1700," periodicals, and Board of Agriculture County reports.

2691. Tea Bureau. Library catalogue. London, 1951. 25p.

Classified list of works relating to tea.

FLORICULTURE

2692. National Book League. Flower books and their illustrators, an exhibition arranged for the National Book League, by Wilfrid Blunt. London: Cambridge Univ. Pr., 1950. 58p.

Locates copies in British and French public and private collections.

2693. Society of Herbalists Library. An exhibition of flower books from the Library of the Society of Herbalists. [A catalogue], comp. by Wilfrid Blunt and W. T. Stearn. London: Arts Council, 1953. 47p.

FORESTRY

2694. Great Britain, Forestry Commission. Library catalogue of books. London, 1971. 176p.

Classified listing with author index; library located at Farnham, Surrey.

2695. Oxford, University, Dept. of Forestry Library. Basic library list for forestry, 3d ed., ed. by E. F. Hemmings. Oxford, 1963. 56p.

ANIMAL HUSBANDRY

2696. Agricultural Research Council, Institute of Animal Physiology. List of periodicals held in the Library. Babraham, Cambridge, 1968. 28*l*.

Alphabetical list of holdings.

2697. ———, Meat Research Institute Library. List of periodicals held in the Library. Langford, Bristol: The Institute, 1971. 17p,

2698. Animal Diseases Research Association Library. Holdings of periodicals. Edinburgh, 1971. 5*l*.

2699. Goldie, F. J. "The Library of the Commonwealth Bureau of Animal Breeding and Genetics." Library Association record, 65 (1963), 374-77.

Edinburgh library; describes resources and services.

2700. Institute of Animal Physiology, Agricultural Research Council. List of periodicals held in the

Library. Babraham, Cambridge, 1971. 31*l*.
    Includes record of holdings.

2701. Newbury Public Library. A catalogue of the exhibition of dog books illustrated by Cecil Aldin, from the Hubbard collection, comp. by Clifford L. B. Hubbard. Bakewell: C. L. B. Hubbard, 1969. Unpaged.

2702. Stockport Public Libraries. Dogs: from Afghans to Yorkshire terriers. Stockport, 1964. 28p. (Handlist, no.6)
    Listing of books in special collection, Stockport Public Libraries.

APICULTURE

2703. Scottish Beekeepers' Association. Catalogue of the Moir Library. Edinburgh, 1950. 193p.
    Record of 2,054 books and 700 volumes of periodicals relating to beekeeping; classified by subject with author index. In 1939 the library was transferred to the care of the Edinburgh Public Library.

FISHING

2704. Fleetwood Corporation, Public Libraries Committee. A select list of books on the fishing industry in Fleetwood Public Libraries, comp. by Margaret A. Butcher. Fleetwood, 1964. 10p.

Fine Arts

General

2705. Allan, D. G. C. "The archives of the Royal Society of Arts, 1754-1847." Archives, 4 (1960), 220-25.

2706. Bristol Public Libraries, Reference Library. Reference Library catalogue, Fine Arts Section (Useful Arts Section—Sociology Section), ed. by E. R. Norris Mathews. Bristol, 1909-13. 3pts.

2707. Chatham Public Libraries. Catalogue of books on art. Chatham, 1962. 78p. Supplement, list of art books added to stock since 1st April, 1962. 13p.

Classified by subjects; records books held by Chatham Public Libraries.

2708. Chelsea School of Art Library. The almost complete periodical holdings of the Library. Chelsea, 1971. 13l.

2709. Collison, R. L. W. "Fine arts libraries and collections in Britain." Journal of documentation, 6 (1950), 57-69. Reprinted, 1950.

Review of resources of principal libraries in field.

2710. Coventry Libraries, Art Gallery and Museums Dept. Union list of periodicals. Coventry, 1967. Unpaged.

Titles located in 15 libraries.

2711. Dunfermline Carnegie Public Libraries. A catalogue of the art books in the Central Library. Dunfermline, 1924. 40p.

2712. Great Britain, Patent Office Library. Subject list of works on fine and graphic arts (excluding photomechanical printing and photography). London: H. M. Stationery Office, 1914. 228p.

2713. ——— ———. Subject list of works on the fine and graphic arts (including photography). London: H. M. Stationery Office, 1904. 374p.

2714. ———, Science and Art Dept. of the Committee of Council on Education, South Kensington. The first proofs of the universal catalogue of books on art, compiled for the use of the national art library and the schools of art in the United Kingdom. London: Chapman and Hall, 1870. 2v. Supplement, 1877. 655p. Reprinted, 1964. 3v.

Locates copies in 8 British and Irish libraries; contains 80,000 entries.

2715. Lancashire County Library. A catalogue of books on fine arts, sports and pastimes, comp. by E. Cockerlyne. Preston, 1930. 135p.

2716. Liverpool Free Public Library. Ex bibliotheca Hugh Frederick Hornby; catalogue of the art library bequeathed by H. F. Hornby . . . to the Free Public Library of the City of Liverpool, comp. by H. E. Curran and C. Robertson. Liverpool, 1906. 648p.

Collection illustrating history and progress of graphic arts in all periods.

2717. London, University, Library. Catalogue of books on archaeology and art and cognate works belonging to the Preedy Memorial Library and other collections in the University Library. London: The University, 1935-37. 437p. (4pts.)

Section I, archeology and ancient art; section II, art. Index. 1937. Supplement, 1937. 28p.

2718. Newcastle upon Tyne City Libraries. Catalogue of books on the fine arts, viz: architecture, sculpture, carving, coins, pottery, metal work, drawing, decoration, painting, engraving, photography, music, comp. by T. A. Onions. Newcastle upon Tyne, 1900. 144p.

2719. ———. Fine arts catalog; books in the Central Public Library on gardening and town planning, architecture, sculpture carving, numismatics, pottery, art metal work, drawing and decoration, painting, engraving, photography, comp. by Edward Pearson, ed. by Basil Anderton. Newcastle upon Tyne: Andrew Dickson, 1934. 226p.

2720. Oxford, University, Bodleian Library. Portraits of the sixteenth and early seventeenth centuries. Oxford: Univ. Pr., 1952. 7p. + 21p. of illustrations. (Bodleian picture book, no.6)

2721. Royal Academy of Arts Library. A catalogue of books added to the Library of the Royal Academy of Arts, London, between 1877 and 1900. London: W. Clowes, 1901. 197p.

2722. Royal Society of Arts. Catalogue of the Library of the Royal Society of Arts (lending section). London, n.d. 162p.

2723. Sampson, A. A. Art libraries: a survey of their administration, content and services in colleges and institutions concerned with the visual arts in the United Kingdom, 1968-9. London, 1969. 8p.

2724. Victoria and Albert Museum. Catalogue of the Educational Division of the South Kensington Museum, 9th ed. London: H. M. Stationery Office, 1876. 618p. Supplement, 1876. 55p.

2725. ———. Catalogue to the exhibition catalogues. Boston, Mass.: G. K. Hall. 1v. Announced for publication, 1973.

2726. Victoria and Albert Museum, Science and Art Dept. Dyce collection; a catalogue of the paintings, miniatures, drawings, engravings, rings, and miscellaneous objects bequeathed by the Reverend Alexander Dyce. London: H. M. Stationery Office, 1874. 326p.

2727. Victoria and Albert Museum. A list of books and pamphlets in the National Art Library . . . containing biographies of artists and of others connected with the history of art. London: H. M. Stationery Office, 1887. 261p.

2728. ———. A list of books and pamphlets in the National Art Gallery . . . on drawing, geometry, and perspective. London. H. M. Stationery Office, 1888. 92p.

2729. ———. List of books in the National Art Library . . . on anatomy, human and comparative. London: H. M. Stationery Office, 1886. 24p.

2730. ———. National Art Library catalogue, Victoria and Albert Museum (London). Boston: G. K. Hall. 10v. Announced for publication, 1973.

2731. ——— Library. "Recently acquired manuscripts together with some acquired before 1890 and now re-cataloged," comp. by J. I. Whalley. Monthly list, Sept. 1971, p.79-90.

Architecture

2732. Abel, Lola L. A bibliography of some 18th century books on architecture (British Palladians). (1715-1780). London, 1950. 166l. (Thesis, School of Librarianship, Univ. of London)
Copies located in 4 English libraries; lists and describes 137 items.

2733. Architectural Association Library. Catalogue of the books in the Library of the Architectural Association. London: Langley & Son, 1895. 160p.

2734. Barnet Public Libraries. Barnet Library Services. Books on architecture. London: Barnet London Borough Council, n.d. 22p.

2735. British Museum. Giovanni Battista Piranesi; his predecessors and his heritage; catalogue of an exhibition. London, 1968. 53p.

2736. Elton Hall. Architectural drawings in the Library of Elton Hall [Peterborough] by Sir John Vanbrugh and Sir Edward Lovett Pearce, ed. by Howard Colvin and Maurice Craig. [A catalogue, with reproductions.] London, 1964. 40p. + 82 plates.
Drawings of Vanbrugh (1644-1726) and Pearce (d. 1733) preserved in Elton Hall, Huntingdonshire.

2737. Great Britain, Historical Manuscripts Commission. Architectural history & the fine & applied arts: sources in the National Register of Archives. London: Quality House, 1969-71. 3pts.
Notes and describes "all references to art and architectural history in the lists of manuscript accumulations which comprise the National Register of Archives."

2738. ———, Patent Office Library. Subject list of works on architecture and building construction. London: H. M. Stationery Office, 1903. 164p.

2739. Guppy, Henry, and Vine, Guthrie. A classified catalogue of the works on architecture and the allied arts in the principal libraries of Manchester and Salford, with alphabetical author list and subject index. Manchester: Univ. Pr., 1909. 310p.
Classified by subjects with author index; records holdings of 11 libraries.

2740. Institution of Naval Architects Library. Catalogue of the Scott collection of books, manuscripts, prints and drawings, comp. by Betty M. Cooper. London: The Institution, 1954. 192p.

Chronological listing of items, 1532-1896, relating to naval architecture; author, title, and subject indexes.

2741. ———. Library catalogue. London, 1920. 49p.

2742. ———. Library catalogue. London: The Institution, 1930. 44p.

2743. Manchester Architectural Committee. A classified catalogue of the works on architecture and the allied arts in the principal libraries of Manchester and Salford, with alphabetical author list and subject index, ed. by Henry Guppy and Guthrie Vine. Manchester: Univ. Pr., 1909. 310p.

2744. Oxford, University, Bodleian Library. Architectural drawings in the Bodleian Library. Oxford, 1952. 7p. (Bodleian picture book, no.7)

2745. ———, Worcester College Library. A catalogue of architectural drawings of the 18th and 19th centuries in the Library of Worcester College, Oxford (the greater part belong to the collection bequeathed by George Clarke); comp. by H. M. Colvin. Oxford: Clarendon, 1964. 69p. + 130 plates.

2746. Royal Institute of British Architects. Catalogue of the drawings collection of the Royal Institute of British Architects. Farnborough: Gregg, 1969. 44p. + 28l.

2747. ——— Library. Catalogue of the Royal Institute of British Architects Library. London: The Institute, 1937-38. 2v.

Supplementing the catalogue are monthly lists of accessions in Royal Institute of British Architects journal to January, 1946. RIBA Library bulletin (v.1, no.1, Nov. 1946- quarterly) lists under subjects periodical articles on architecture, art, building, town and country planning, gardens, and rural preservation, with list of accessions to the library. Cumulated in RIBA annual review of periodical articles.

2748. ——— ———. Index of architects of several countries & many periods (except English mediaeval) in nearly 60 old and new selected indexes & indexed specialist works, incorporating some earlier indexes; with references to volumes and pages. London: The Institute, 1957. 66p.

2749. Stanley-Morgan, R. "Architectural library facilities in the provinces; a report." Royal Institute of British Architects journal, 70 (Jan. 1963), 24-29.

Account of library resources available in various types of libraries in Britain and Ireland.

2750. Victoria and Albert Museum. A list of books and pamphlets in the National Art Library . . . illustrating architecture of the Renaissance and later periods, to the close of the 18th century, ed. by R. H. S. Smith. London: H.M. Stationery Office, 1888. 66p.

Urban and Regional Planning

2751. Birmingham, University, Centre for Urban and Regional Studies. West Midland Group handlist; guide to the papers of the West Midland Group on post-war reconstruction and planning. Birmingham: The University, 1969. 35p. (Occasional paper, no.6)

Papers, correspondence, maps, and charts presented to University of Birmingham Library.

2752. ———, Library. Bournville Village Trust, West Midlands Group on post-war planning and reconstruction; a handlist to the papers and maps. Birmingham, 1969. 30 + 9l. (Catalogues of the manuscript collections, no.19)

Post-World War II documents.

2753. Great Britain, Ministry of Housing and Local Government Library. New towns, 1898-1956. London, n.d. 30p. Appendix I, Oct. 1955-July 1956. 4p.; Appendix II, Aug. 1956-Oct. 1959. 17p.; Appendix III, Nov. 1959-Aug. 1963. 20p.; Appendix IV, Sept. 1963-Dec. 1964. 6p.

Lists references relating to city planning.

2754. ———, Ministry of Town and Country Planning. Northumberland and Tyneside: a bibliography, by W. C. Donkin and E. F. Patterson. London: H.M. Stationery Office, 1946. 101p.

Books listed are located in 13 libraries.

2755. Greater London Council, Dept. of Planning & Transportation. Directory of GLC library resources, comp. by Linda Conroy. London: The Council, 1971. Unpaged.

Includes data on 14 libraries, with details of special collections.

2756. Harris, Eileen. Records of town planning before 1947, held by the Berkshire County Council. London, 1960. 28l. (Diploma in Archive Administration, Univ. of London)

2757. Manchester Public Libraries, Arts Library. Town and country planning: a selection of books available in the Arts Library. Manchester: The Libraries, 1967. 30p. (Arts Library booklists, 1)

2758. Salford, University, Library. Planning surveys in the British Isles; a list of town, county and regional surveys in the Library of the University of Salford. Salford, 1970. 15p.

Arranged by places.

Sculpture

2759. Victoria and Albert Museum. A list of works on sculpture in the National Art Library, 2d ed. London: H. M. Stationery Office, 1886. 154p.

Numismatics

2760. British Museum. Catalogue of British seal-dies in the British Museum, by A. B. Tonnocky. London, 1952. 212p. + 32 plates.

Lists 953 items.

2761. ———, Dept. of Manuscripts. Catalogue of seals in the Department of Manuscripts in the British Museum, by W. de G. Birch. London: The Museum, 1887-1900. 6v.

Covers all classes of seals in the department, attached or detached.

2762. ——— ———. Descriptive catalogue of impressions from ancient Scottish seals . . . from A.D. 1094 . . . to the Commonwealth, by Henry Laing. Edinburgh, 1850. 232p.

2763. ——— ———. Supplemental descriptive catalogue of ancient Scottish seals from A.D. 1150 to the eighteenth century, by Henry Laing. Edinburgh: Edmonston and Douglas, 1866. 237p.

2764. Great Britain, Public Record Office. Guide to seals in the Public Record Office, 2d ed. London: H. M. Stationery Office, 1968. 66p. (Public Record Office handbooks, no.1)

2765. Imperial War Museum Library. The Victoria cross; a selected list of general works in the Imperial War Museum Library. London, n.d. 3l. (Booklist, no.1226)

2766. Ranger, Felicity. A catalogue of medieval seals contained in six accumulations in the Archives Department of Leicester Museum. London, 1960. 485l. (Diploma in Archive Administration, Univ. of London)

Based on Leicester Borough records, Rothley Temple collection, Wyggeston Hospital records, Ferrers collection, Market Harborough Town Estate records, and Shangton records.

2767. Taylor, Frank. "Ecclesiastical, monastic and local seals (12th-17th cent.) from the Hatton Wood mss. in the John Rylands Library." Bulletin of the John Rylands Library, 30 (1947), 247-70. Reprinted, 1947. 26p.

Descriptions of 18 examples.

2768. Victoria and Albert Museum. A list of books and pamphlets in the National Art Library . . . illustrating seals, ed. by R. H. S. Smith. London: Eyre and Spottiswoode, 1888. 46p.

2769. ———. A list of books and pamphlets in the National Art Library . . . on coins and medals, comp. by R. H. S. Smith. London: H. M. Stationery Office, 1889. 88p.

Costume

2770. Victoria and Albert Museum. Costume; a general bibliography, by Pegaret Anthony and Janet Arnold. London: Costume Society and Victoria & Albert Museum, 1966. 49p. Reprinted, 1968.

Classified list.

2771. ———. A list of works on costume in the National Art Library, by Robert Henry Soden Smith. London: H. M. Stationery Office, 1881. 70p.

2772. ——— Library. Costume: an index to the more important material in the Library, with annotations & shelfmarks, together with a guide to other documentary material in the Museum, rev. ed., by C. H. Gibbs-Smith. London: The Museum, 1936. Unpaged.

Catalog of one of world's leading collections on costume.

Decorative Arts

2773. Chester Beatty Library. Chinese jade books in the Chester Beatty Library, described, and the Chinese texts translated, by William Watson . . . the Manchu texts translated by Dr. J. L. Mish. Dublin: Hodges, Figgis, 1963. 47p. + 10 plates.

Describes "what is probably the largest collection of the jade books of the Chinese imperial court ever formed."

2774. Great Britain, Patent Office Library. Subject list of works on enamelling, art metalwork, furniture, costume and hair dressing and working. London: H. M. Stationery Office, 1914. 70p.

2775. Victoria and Albert Museum. A list of books and pamphlets in the National Art Library . . . illustrating gems, ed. by R. H. S. Smith. London: H. M. Stationery Office, 1886. 27p.

2776. ———. A list of books and pamphlets in the National Art Library . . . illustrating glass. London: H. M. Stationery Office, 1887. 47p.

2777. ———. A list of books and pamphlets in the National Art Library . . . illustrating textile fabrics . . . lace and needlework, by R. H. S. Smith. London: Eyre and Spottiswoode, 1888. 85p.

2778. ———. A list of books and pamphlets, in the National Art Library, on pottery and porcelain, 2d ed., ed. by R. H. S. Smith. London: H. M. Stationery Office, 1885. 147p.

2779. ———. A list of books and photographs in the National Art Library illustrating armour and weapons. London: H. M. Stationery Office, 1883. 65p.

2780. ———. A list of books, photographs, etc., in the National Art Library, illustrating metal work, by R. H. S. Smith. London: H. M. Stationery Office, 1883. 141p.

2781. ———. A list of the books and pamphlets in the National Art Library . . . illustrating gold and silver-smiths' work and jewelry, 2d ed., ed. by R. H. S. Smith. London: H. M. Stationery Office, 1887. 91p.

2782. ———. A list of works on furniture in the National Art Library, South Kensington Museum, 2d ed. London: H. M. Stationery Office, 1885. 64p.

2783. ———. A list of works on ornament in the National Art Library, 2d ed., by R. H. S. Smith. London: H. M. Stationery Office, 1883. 102p.

2784. Worch, Dorothy Elaine. Woven silks from the end of the Renaissance to 1800: a bibliography of material in the Victoria and Albert Museum Library. London, 1957. 104*l*. (Diploma in Librarianship, Univ. of London)

Painting

2785. Oxford, University, Bodleian Library. A descriptive catalogue of the Persian paintings in the Bodleian Library, by B. W. Robinson. Oxford: Clarendon, 1958. 219p.

2786. ———, Christ Church Library. Pictures by the old masters in the Library of Christ Church, Oxford; a brief catalogue, with historical and critical notes upon the pictures in the collection, by Tancred Borenius. London: Oxford Univ. Pr., 1916. 117p.

2787. Victoria and Albert Museum. A list of works on painting in the National Art Library, 2d ed., ed. by R. H. S. Smith. London: H. M. Stationery Office, 1883. 157p.

2788. ——— Library. Painting and drawings: a selection of illustrated monographs on artists, arranged alphabetically, with annotations and shelf marks, 2d ed., comp. by C. H. Gibbs-Smith. London: H. M. Stationery Office, 1939. 43*l*.

2789. Wigan Public Library. Painters and painting; a list of books relating to painters and painting preserved in the Reference Department of the Wigan Free Public Library, by Henry Tennyson Folkard. Wigan: James Starr, 1904. 89p.

2790. Willetts, Pamela J. "Letters of J. M. W. Turner." British Museum quarterly, 22 (1960), 59-62.

Describes collection of over 80 autograph letters and documents of Joseph Mallord William Turner (1775-1851), the painter, received by British Museum.

Engraving

2791. Corbett, Margery, and Norton, Michael. Engraving in England in the sixteenth and seventeenth centuries; a descriptive catalogue with introductions; pt.III: the reign of Charles I. Cambridge: Univ. Pr., 1964. 397p. + 214 plates.

Arranged by names of engravers; copies located in British, American, and Continental libraries; includes STC and Wing numbers.

2792. Hind, Arthur M. Engraving in England in the sixteenth and seventeenth centuries; a descriptive catalogue with introductions: pt.I, Tudor period. Cambridge: Univ. Pr., 1952. 334p. + 156 plates.

Copies located in British, American, and Continental libraries and collections.

2793. ———. Engraving in England in the sixteenth and seventeenth centuries; a descriptive catalogue with introductions: pt.II, the reign of James I. Cambridge: Univ. Pr., 1955. 413p. + 252 plates.

Locations in British, American, and Continental libraries and collections.

2794. Rose, James Anderson. A collection of engraved portraits; catalogued and exhibited by James Anderson Rose, at the opening of the new library and museum of the Corporation of London . . . 1872. London: M. Ward, 1874-1894. 2v. in 3.

2795. Victoria and Albert Museum. A catalogue of engraved national portraits in the National Art Library. London: H. M. Stationery Office, 1895. 523p.

2796. ———. J. A. McNeil Whistler: etchings, etc., in the National Art Library, Victoria and Albert Museum, with a bibliography by M. Hardie, 2d ed. London: H. M. Stationery Office, 1908. 32p.

Prints and Drawings

2797. Bermondsey Public Libraries. Catalogue of prints and drawings in the Bermondsey Public Libraries illustrating Bermondsey past and present, comp. by James D. Stewart. London: Libraries Committee, 1927. 72p.

2798. British Museum, Dept. of Prints and Drawings. Catalogue of engraved British portraits preserved in the Department of Prints and Drawings in the British Museum, by Freeman O'Donoghue. London: The Museum, 1908-25. 6v.

2799. Guildhall Library. Selected prints and drawings from the collection in the Library: pt.I, the city. London: The Library Committee, 1964. 72p.

A sampling of 60,000 items in one of largest print collections in world.

2800. ———. Selected prints and drawings from the collection in the Library: pt.II, the metropolitan boroughs, 1965. London: The Library Committee, 1965. 104p.

2801. ———. Selected prints and drawings from the collection in the Library: pt.III, the environs of the metropolis and the home counties. London: The Library Committee, 1969. 64p.

2802. India Office Library, Commonwealth Office. British drawings in the India Office Library, by Mildred Archer. v.1, amateur artists. London: H. M. Stationery Office, 1969. 364p. + 56 plates.

2803. Newcastle upon Tyne City Libraries. Catalogue of the Bewick collection—Pease bequest, by Basil Anderton and W. H. Gibson. Newcastle upon Tyne: Public Libraries Committee, 1904. 110p.

Relates to pencil and water-color drawings, woodblock prints, etc.

Philately

2804. Aberdeen, University, Library. Rough list of specimens of philatelic literature, mostly of an early date, from the Aberdeen University Library, shown to the Aberdeen and North of Scotland Philatelic Society, etc., comp. by P. J. Anderson. Aberdeen, 1911. 34p.

2805. ———. Second rough list of specimens of philatelic literature from the Aberdeen University Library, comp. by P. J. Anderson. Aberdeen, 1923. 47p.

2806. Bath Municipal Libraries and Victoria Art Gallery. Philately: a catalogue of the Library of the Bath Philatelic Society and books in Bath Reference Library. Bath: The Libraries, 1967. 28p.

2807. Bibliotheca Lindesiana. A bibliography of the writings general, special and periodical forming the literature of philately. Aberdeen: Univ. Pr., 1911. 924 cols. (v.7 of library's catalog)

2808. Herts Philatelic Society. Catalogue of handbooks, journals, etc., in the Library of the Herts Philatelic Society on 31st March, 1913, 2d ed. London, 1913. 63p.

2809. Junior Philatelic Society. Catalogue of the Lending Library, incorporating the "Crouch" bequest. London, 1937. 32p.

Japanese Art

2810. Bristol Museum and Library. Japanese prints. Bristol, 1965. 118p.

Exhibition catalog, with illustrations.

2811. British Museum, Dept. of Oriental Antiquities. The work of Hokusai; woodcuts, illustrated books, drawings and paintings; a catalogue of an exhibition held on the occasion of the centenary of his death. London: The Museum, 1948. 32p.

Lists 208 items.

2812. Victoria and Albert Museum. Japanese colour prints; catalogue of prints of Utagawa Toyokuni I. in the National Art Library, Victoria and Albert Museum, comp. by E. F. Strange. London: H. M. Stationery Office, 1908. 18p.

2813. ———, National Art Gallery. Japanese art. I. Japanese books and albums of prints in colour, by E. F. Strange. London: H. M. Stationery Office, 1893. 94p.

2814. ——— ———. Japanese art. II. Books relating to Japanese art, by E. F. Strange. London: H. M. Stationery Office, 1898. 44p.

Photography

2815. Birmingham Public Libraries. The Stone collection of photographs in the Birmingham Reference Library. Birmingham, 1971. 4p.

Collection of 22,000 photographs, 2,500 lantern slides, and 1,400 negatives representing all areas of world.

2816. Cardiff Public Libraries. Catalogue of books on photography. Cardiff, 1909. 24p.

2817. Finsbury Central Library. Photography periodicals. London, 1962. 11p.

2818. McNeil, R. J. "The Shell Photographic Library." Aslib proceedings, 18 (1966), 128-37.

Describes collection of about 22,500 photographs dealing with activities of the Shell petroleum companies.

2819. Nunn, G. W. A. British sources of photographs and pictures. London: Cassell, 1952. 220p.

Annotated lists of photographs and photographic agencies; libraries, museums, and art galleries; and special sources. Detailed subject index.

2820. Royal Photographic Society of Great Britain Library. Library catalogue; pt.1, Author catalogue; pt.2, Subject catalogue, 3d ed. London: The Society, 1939-52. Supplements, 1939-52. 3pts.

2821. ———. Periodicals catalogue. London: The Society, 1955. 20p.

Lists 750 titles, with holdings.

2822. Victoria and Albert Museum Library. "A collection of catalogues issued in the 19th century by dealers in photographic prints." Monthly list, Dec. 1969, p.39-43.

2823. ———. Historical notes on an exhibition of early photography. London: H. M. Stationery Office, 1939. 4p.

Theatre

2824. Armstrong, Norma. The Edinburgh stage, 1715-1820: a bibliography. London, 1968. 4v. (Thesis, Library Association Fellowship)

Based on collections of National Library of Scotland, Edinburgh Public Libraries, and City Archives of Edinburgh.

2825. Arnott, James Fullarton, and Robinson, John William. English theatrical literature, 1559-1900, a bibliography: incorporating Robert W. Lowe's A bibliographical account of English theatrical literature published in 1888. London: Society for Theatre Research, 1970. 486p.

Records 4,506 items, locating copies in numerous British and American libraries.

2826. British Museum. Register of playbills, programmes, and theatre cuttings. 1951. Manuscript. 54l.

Arranged by place-names, with subheadings by theaters; 18th to 20th centuries.

2827. Gilder, Rosamond, and Freedley, George. Theatre collections in libraries and museums; an international handbook. London: Stevens & Brown, 1936. 182p.

Describes important collections of theatrical material in libraries and museums throughout world.

2828. Guildhall Library. "A select list of printed items in Guildhall Library, relating to pageants, entertainments and other special occasions in the City of London." Guildhall miscellany, 2 (1964), 257-69.

2829. Howard, Diana. London theatres and music halls, 1850-1950. London: Library Association, 1970. 291p.

p.277-80, "Location of material: directory of collections."

2830. International Federation of Library Associations, International Section for Performing Arts Libraries and Museums. Performing arts libraries and museums of the world, 2d ed. Paris: Éditions du Centre national de la recherche scientifique, 1967. 801p.

A directory of 310 institutions in 30 countries, noting nature of holdings, services, and other data.

2831. International Theatre Exhibition. Designs and models for the modern stage [with: List of works on the art of the theatre in the Victoria and Albert Museum Library]. London, 1922. 60p.

2832. Leach, Elizabeth. "Playbills and programmes." Manchester review, 11 (1966), 7-22.

Discussion of theater materials in Manchester Public Libraries' Arts Library.

2833. Library Association, Reference and Special Libraries Section, South Eastern Group. Theatre collections: a symposium, ed. by A. M. C. Kahn. London, 1955. 29p. (Library resources in the Greater London area, no.4)

Deals with holdings of national, public, special, and private libraries.

2834. National Book League. British theatre, 1530-1900; an exhibition of books, prints, drawings, manuscripts and playbills, arr. by Ifan Kyrle Fletcher. London: Cambridge Univ. Pr. for the National Book League, 1950. 72p.

Locates copies in public and private collections, British, Irish, Continental, and American.

2835. Price, Cecil. "Eighteenth century playbills of the English theatre in Wales." National Library of Wales journal, 6 (1950), 260-72.

Union list of extant playbills in British and American libraries.

2836. Shakespeare Memorial Library. Items of interest to theatre research workers. Stratford on Avon, 1957. 4*l*.

2837. Society for Theatre Research Library. Library catalogue, 1953. London: The Society, 1953. 37p.

Classified by subjects.

2838. Society of Antiquaries. Catalogue of a collection of works on pageantry bequeathed to the Society of Antiquaries by Frederick William Fairholt. London, 1869. 40p.

2839. Stratman, Carl J. American theatrical periodicals, 1789-1967; a bibliographical guide. Durham, N.C.: Duke University Press, 1970. 133p.

Entries for 685 titles; holdings shown for British Museum and for American and Canadian libraries.

2840. ———. A bibliography of British dramatic periodicals, 1720-1960. N.Y.: New York Public Library, 1962. 58p.

Lists 674 titles in U.S. and British libraries; limited to periodicals printed in England, Scotland, and Ireland in English.

2841. Toole-Stoole, Raymond. Circuses and allied arts; a world bibliography 1500-1957, based mainly on circus literature in the British Museum, the Library of Congress, the Bibliothèque Nationale and on his own collection. Derby: England Harper, 1958-71. 4v.

Records 13,086 items.

Motion Pictures and Television

2842. Aslib, Film Librarians Group. The directory of film and TV production libraries, 1963-4, including recorded music libraries, 2d ed. London, 1963. 36p.

Includes data on film archives.

2843. British Broadcasting Library. Books about broadcasting, revised edition 1958. London: BBC, 1958. 49p. Supplement, 1961.

2844. British Film Institute Library. Catalogue. London, 1948. 67p.

2845. British Film Institute, National Film Archive. A bibliography of the Lending Library. London, 1965. 65p.

2846. ———. Catalogue. London, 1951-60. 2v.

In 2pts.: pt.1, silent news films, 1895-1933; pt.2, silent nonfiction films, 1895-1934; chronologically arranged.

2847. ———. National Film Archive catalogue. London, 1965- .

Issued periodically.

Sports and Games

2848. Barnet Public Libraries. Reading about chess. London, 1969? Unpaged.

Based on Barnet Public Libraries holdings.

2849. Bristol Central Reference Library. Caving periodicals in the central collection of caving publications; a catalogue of the caving periodicals held by Bristol Central Reference Library, and a selected short title catalogue of books, comp. by K. and R. Mansfield. Bristol, 1968. 14p.

2850. British Museum. A descriptive catalogue of playing and other cards in the British Museum, by William Hughes Willshire. London, 1876. 360p. Supplement, 1877. 87p.

2851. Camping Club of Great Britain and Ireland. Library catalogue. London, 1927. 12p.

Books relating to boating, camping, natural history, foreign travel, guide books and maps.

2852. ———. Library catalogue, 1950. London, 1953. 19p.

2853. DeSomogyi, Joseph. "The Arabic chess manuscripts in the John Rylands Library." Bulletin of the John Rylands Library, 41 (1959), 430-45. Reprinted.

2854. Eccles Public Libraries. Chess; a union list of books, comp. and edited by A. Jones. Eccles: 1956. Unpaged.

Union list of books in 6 public libraries in Eccles area.

2855. Fly-fishers' Club. Library catalogue, 1935, prep. by Eric Taverner & Douglas Service. London: Seeley, Service & Co., 1935. 38p.

2856. Guildhall Library. "A handlist of books in the Guildhall Library on the art of fencing." Guildhall miscellany, 2 (1963), 227-29.

2857. Heyl, Edgar. A contribution to conjuring bibliography, English language, 1580 to 1850. Baltimore, Md., 1963. 62p.

Lists 360 items, with locations of copies in British Museum and American libraries.

2858. National Book League. Cricket; a catalogue of an exhibition of books, manuscripts and pictorial records presented by the National Book League with the co-operation of the Marylebone Cricket Club, arr. by Diana Rait Kerr. Cambridge: Univ. Pr., 1950. 120p.

Locations in public and private collections.

2859. Newcastle upon Tyne City Libraries. Hand list of books in the Central Lending Library on sports and games with a selection on gymnastics and athletics. Newcastle upon Tyne, 1927. 46p.

Music

GENERAL

2860. British Museum. Catalogue of an exhibition of music held in the King's Library, October, 1953. London, 1953. 52p.

2861. Burbridge, Eleanor. "A survey of music library resources in Yorkshire." Brio: journal of the United Kingdom Branch of the International Association of Music Libraries, 4 (Autumn 1967), 5-9.

General description of holdings of special, county, and public libraries in Yorkshire.

2862. Deakin, Andrew. Outlines of musical bibliography; a catalogue of early music and musical works printed or otherwise produced in the British Isles. pt.I: Early English music and musical works preserved in m.s., c. 700-c. 1650. Birmingham, 1899. 112p.

2863. Dove, Jack. Music libraries, including a comprehensive bibliography of music literature and a select bibliography of music scores published since 1957; original edition by Lionel Roy McColvin and Harold Reeves. London: André Deutsch, 1965. 2v.

v.1, p.85-156 lists British public libraries, British university and special libraries, and overseas libraries, with data on resources.

2864. Hutchings, A. "The seventeenth-century music in Durham Cathedral Library." Durham University journal, 55 (Dec. 1963), 23-30.

Descriptive essay.

2865. International Association of Music Libraries, Commission of Research Libraries. Directory of music research libraries, including contributors to the International inventory of musical sources (RISM). Iowa City: Univ. of Iowa, 1970. 235p.

pt.2, p.158-89, lists British and Irish libraries with data on collections and services.

2866. King, A. Hyatt. "A collection of musical programmes." British Museum quarterly, 33 (1969), 91-92.

Description of large collection of English and European material acquired by British Museum.

2867. ———. "The Hirsch music library." British Museum quarterly, 15 (1952), 11-13.

Describes major German private library of music, consisting of some 16,000 items, acquired by British Museum.

2868. ———. "The Royal Music Library; some account of its provenance and associations." Book collector, 7 (1958), 241-52.

Description of some of the volumes in the "King's Music Library" accumulated over several centuries by British royalty and deposited in the British Museum in 1911 by George V.

2869. ———. Some British collectors of music, c. 1600-1900. Cambridge: Univ. Pr., 1963. 178p.

Includes account of Royal Music Library and other collections; list of present locations of collections conserved in whole or part, p.145-47.

2870. ———, and Neighbour, O. W. "Printed music from the collection of Alfred Cortot." British Museum quarterly, 30 (1966), 8-16.

Listing of items published over period of two and half centuries, received by British Museum.

2871. Long, Maureen W. Music in British libraries; a directory of resources. London: Library Association, 1971. 183p.

Lists 468 libraries, with data on collections and services.

2872. Manchester Public Libraries. The Henry Watson Music Library; a survey of its resources, 2d ed., by L. W. Duck. Manchester, 1964. 14p.

Library of over 105,000 volumes and 300,000 pieces of sheet music.

2873. Oxford, University, Bodleian Library. English music; guide to an exhibition held in 1955, comp. by Jack A. Westrup and others. Oxford, 1955. 40p. + 8 plates.

2874. ———. Music in the Bodleian Library; a selection of manuscripts, printed music, and treatises exhibited, ed. by M. M. Moon. Oxford, 1963. 24p.

2875. Shaw, H. Watkins, and Wilkins, K. F. "Some West Midland music libraries." Open access, 19 (Autumn 1970), 1-6.

Discussion of resources of St. Michael's College, University of Birmingham, and Birmingham School of Music.

2876. Smith, William C. A bibliography of the musical works published by John Walsh during the years 1695-1720. London: Bibliographical Society at the Univ. Pr., Oxford, 1948. 215p. + 38 plates.

Lists 622 works, with locations. Reprinted with additions and corrections. 1968. 215p.

2877. ———, and Humphries, Charles. A bibliography of the musical works published by the firm of John Walsh during the years 1721-1766. London: Bibliographical Society, 1968. 351p.

Records 1,564 items, with locations of copies.

2878. Steele, Robert. The earliest English music printing; a description and bibliography of English printed music to the close of the sixteenth century. London: Printed for the Bibliographical Society at the Chiswick Pr., 1903. 108p. + 49 plates. (Bibliographical Society illustrated monographs, no.11)

Copies located in various English libraries.

2879. York, University, Library. Music reference materials in the J. B. Morrell Library. York, 1972? 24p. (Library guide, no.9)

MUSICOLOGY

2880. British Museum, Dept. of Manuscripts. A guide to the manuscripts and printed books illustrating the progress of musical notation, exhibited in the Department of Manuscripts and the King's Library. London: The Museum, 1885. 20p.

2881. ———, Dept. of Printed Books. Four hundred years of music printing, by A. H. King. London: The Museum, 1964. 48p. + 20 plates.

Survey based on British Museum holdings.

2882. Cudworth, Charles. "Richard, Viscount Fitzwilliam, and the French baroque music in the Fitzwilliam Museum, Cambridge." Fontes artis musicae, 1 (Jan.-April 1966), 27-31.

2883. Deutsch, Otto Erich. "The editions of Morley's Introduction." Library, ser.4, 23 (1942), 127-29.

Thomas Morley's A plaine and easie introduction to practicall musicke, 1597-1608; copies located in several British libraries.

2884. Farmer, Henry George. The sources of Arabian music: a bibliography of Arabic mss. which deal with the theory, practice and history of Arabic music. Glasgow: Jackson, Son & Co., 1939. 97p. (Records of the Glasgow Bibliographical Society, v.13)

Items located in 5 British and various foreign libraries.

2885. Oxford, University, Bodleian Library. A checklist of books on music published before 1800 in the Bodleian, by M. M. Moon. Oxford, 1965. 82l.

2886. Wigan Public Library. Music and musicians; a list of books and pamphlets relating to the history, biography, theory and practice of music, preserved in the reference and lending departments. Wigan, 1903. 44p.

LIBRARY CATALOGS

2887. American Library, Music Section. Catalogue of scores in the Music Section of the American Library. London: U. S. Information Service, 1950. 40p.

Library transferred to University of London.

2888. Anderson's College. Catalogue of the musical library of the late Wm. Euing, Esq. Glasgow: W. M. Ferguson, 1878. 256p.

Collection now held by University of Glasgow Library.

2889. Bristol Public Libraries. Catalogue of music scores. Bristol, 1959. 305p.

2890. British Broadcasting Corporation, Music Library. Catalogue of holdings. London: BBC, 1965-67. 9v.

Reference guide to what is claimed to be world's largest collection of performing editions; 289,000 entries.

2891. British catalogue of music; a record of music and books about music recently published in Great Britain, based upon the material deposited at the Copyright Receipt Office of the British Museum. London: Council of the British National Bibliography, Ltd., British Museum, 1957-   . Annual.

2892. British Museum. Catalogue of music; recent acquisitions of old music (printed before the year 1800). London: W. Clowes, 1899. 225p.

2893. ——— Catalogue of the King's Music Library, by W. Barclay Squire. London, 1927-29. 3pts.

pt.1, Handel mss.; pt.2, miscellaneous manuscripts; pt.3, printed music and musical literature.

2894. ———. Hand-list of music published in some British and foreign periodicals between 1787 and 1848 now in the British Museum. London, 1962. 80p. Reprinted, 1965.

Supplements The catalogue of printed music published between 1487 and 1800 in the British Museum, 1912.

2895. ——, Dept. of Printed Books. Catalogue of music; recent acquisitions of old music (printed before the year 1800). London: W. Clowes, 1899. 225p.

2896. —— ——. Catalogue of printed books in the British Museum. Accessions, third series—pt.291B. Books in the Hirsch Library, with supplementary list of music. London: The Museum, 1959. 542p.

2897. —— ——. Catalogue of printed music in the British Museum; accessions, pt.53—music in the Hirsch Library. London: The Museum, 1951. 438p.

pt.1, music printed before 1800; pt.2, music printed since 1800.

2898. —— ——. Catalogue of printed music published between 1487 and 1800 now in the British Museum, by W. Barclay Squire. London: The Museum, 1912. 2v. 1st supplement. 1912. 34p. 2d supplement, by William C. Smith, 1940. 85p.

2899. —— ——, Hirsch Library. Books in the Hirsch Library, with supplementary list of music. London: The Museum, 1959. 542p. (Catalogue of printed music in the British Museum, Accessions, 3d series, pt.29)
More than 11,500 items.

2900. British union-catalogue of early music printed before the year 1801; a record of the holdings of over one hundred libraries throughout the British Isles, ed. by Edith B. Schnapper. London: Butterworth, 1957. 2v.

2901. Cambridge, University, Fitzwilliam Museum Library. Catalogue of the music in the Fitzwilliam Museum, Cambridge, by J. A. Fuller-Maitland and A. H. Mann. London: C. J. Clay, 1893. 298p.

Lists and describes 496 titles; in 2pts.: manuscripts and printed music.

2902. ——, Libraries. Summary catalogue of books on theoretical music printed before 1801, in the libraries of Cambridge University [and colleges], by Christopher Hogwood. Cambridge, 1964. 103*l.*
Reproduced from catalog cards.

2903. Chelsea Public Libraries. Catalogue of music and the literature of music in the Lending Department, 5th ed. London, 1926. 54p.

2904. Dagenham Public Libraries. Catalogue of music; a complete catalogue of the scores, miniature scores and books dealing with the theory, history and criticism of music, in the Dagenham Public Libraries, comp. by W. C. Pugsley and G. Atkinson, rev. by W. C. Pugsley and C. H. Tripp. Dagenham, 1964. 515p.

2905. Durham Cathedral Library. A catalogue of the printed music and books on music in Durham Cathedral Library, by R. Alec Harman. London: Oxford Univ. Pr., 1968. 136p.

Records 682 items, 17th and 18th centuries; many secular items included.

2906. Edinburgh Public Library. Catalogue of music and musical literature in the Central Lending and Reference Departments. Edinburgh: Public Library Committee, 1907. 48p.

2907. Edinburgh, University, Faculty of Music, Reid Library. Catalogue of manuscripts, printed music and books on music up to 1850 in the Library of the Music Department at the University of Edinburgh (Reid Library), ed. by Hans Gál. Edinburgh: Oliver & Boyd, 1941. 78p.

2908. Essex County Library. Music catalogue. Chelmsford, 1964. 3v.

2909. Finsbury Public Libraries. Classified catalogue of music and the literature of music. London, 1925. 234p.

2910. Guildhall Library. Gresham Music Library, a catalogue of the printed books and manuscripts deposited in Guildhall Library. London: Corp. of London, 1965. 93p.

Primarily 18th-century works belonging to Gresham College, in 2 groups: printed works and manuscripts.

2911. Hampstead Public Libraries. Catalogue of music and of literature relating to music at the central and branch libraries. Hampstead, 1920. 84p.

2912. Liverpool Public Libraries. Catalogue of music in the Liverpool Public Libraries, comp. by J. A. Carr. Liverpool: Libraries, Museums and Arts Committee, 1933. 374p.
Records collection of 12,580 items.

2913. ——. Catalogue of the Music Library. Liverpool: Central Public Libraries, 1954. 572p.

Dictionary catalogue of music in English; covers musical scores and books on music; "believed to be the largest printed dictionary catalogue of music in English."

2914. Manchester Public Libraries. A catalogue of the ancient and modern books of music, mss, etc., etc., compiled from the general catalogue . . . of "The Henry Watson Music Library." Manchester, 1905. 19p.

2915. Newcastle upon Tyne City Libraries, Music Section. Handlist of miniature scores. Newcastle upon Tyne, 1953. 34p.

2916. ———— ————. Supplementary handlist, no.1-2; miniature scores, piano scores, vocal scores. Newcastle upon Tyne, 1955-56. 2pts.

2917. Oxford, University, Christ Church Library. Catalogue of music in the Library of Christ Church, Oxford, by G. E. R. Arkwright. London: Oxford Univ. Pr., 1915-23. 2v.

    pt.I, works of ascertained authorship; pt.II, ms. works of unknown authorship. i. vocal.

2918. ————. Catalogue of the printed music published prior to 1801 now in the Library of Christ Church, Oxford, ed. by Aloys Hiff. London: Oxford Univ. Pr., 1919. 76p.

2919. Plainsong & Mediaeval Music Society. Catalogue of the Society's Library. Burham, Bucks.: Nashdom Abbey, 1928. 39p.

2920. Royal Academy of Music, Angelina Goetz Library. A catalogue of the Angelina Goetz Library, presented to the Royal Academy of Music . . . 1904, comp. and ed. by A. Rosenkranz. London: Novello & Co., [1904?] 224p.

2921. Royal College of Music Library. Catalogue of printed music in the Library of the Royal College of Music, London, by Wm. Barclay Squire. London: The College, 1909. 368p.

2922. Royal National Institute for the Blind. Catalogue of Braille music and theoretical works in the Manuscript Music Library. London, 1959. 51p. 1st supplement, 1960. 25p.

2923. Sacred Harmonic Society Library. Catalogue of the Library of the Sacred Harmonic Society, new ed. London: The Society, 1872. 399p. Supplement. 1882. 40p.

    Arranged by types of music in 3 groups: printed music, manuscripts, and musical literature; lists 2,923 items.

2924. St. Marylebone Public Library. Catalogue of music and musical literature. London: Vail & Co., 1930. 85p.

2925. Squire, William Barclay. Musik-Katalog der Bibliothek der Westminster-Abtei in London. Leipzig: Breitkopf & Härtel, 1903. 45p. (Beilage zu den Monatsheften für Musikgeschichte, Jahrgang 35. 1903)

MANUSCRIPTS

2926. British Museum. Catalogue of the manuscript music in the British Museum. London, 1842. 105p.

2927. ————. Handlist of music manuscripts acquired 1908-67, by Pamela J. Willetts. London, 1970. 112p.

2928. ————, Dept. of Manuscripts. Catalogue of manuscript music in the British Museum, by Augustus Hughes-Hughes. London: The Museum, 1906-9. 3 vol. Reprinted. London, 1964-66. 3v.

    v.1, Sacred vocal music; v.2, secular vocal music; v.3, instrumental music, treatises, etc.

2929. ———— ————. Catalogue of the [39] musical manuscripts deposited on loan in the British Museum by the Royal Philharmonic Society of London. London: The Museum, 1914. 16p.

2930. Cambridge, University, Libraries. Source inventory of manuscripts of attributed music up to 1800 in Cambridge [University and College] libraries, comp. by R. M. Andrewes. Cambridge, 1969. 6v.

    Reproduced from manuscript record; alphabetical by composers.

2931. ————, Peterhouse College Library. Catalogue of the musical manuscripts at Peterhouse, Cambridge, comp. by Anselm Hughes. Cambridge: Univ. Pr., 1953. 75p.

    Description of 19 items.

2932. Crum, M. C. "Working papers of twentieth-century British composers." Bodleian Library record, 8 (1968), 101-3.

    Describes Bodleian Library's collection of papers of modern British composers.

2933. Farmer, Henry G. "The Arabic musical manuscripts in the Bodleian Library; a descriptive catalogue." Journal of the Royal Asiatic Society, 1925, p.639-54. Reprinted. 18p.

2934. Frere, W. H. Bibliotheca musicoliturgica: a descriptive handlist of musical and Latin-liturgical manuscripts of the Middle Ages preserved in the libraries of Great Britain and Ireland. London: Plainsong and Mediaeval Music Society, 1894-1932. 2v. Reprinted. 1966.

2935. Oxford, University, Bodleian Library. Early Bodleian music; introduction to the study of some of the oldest Latin musical manuscripts in the Bodleian Library, by E. W. B. Nicholson. London, 1913. xcivp. + 71 facsimiles.

2936. ———— ————. Medieval polyphony in the Bodleian Library, by Anselm Hughes. Oxford, 1951. 63p.

A catalogue of manuscripts.

2937. Royal College of Music. Catalogue of the manuscripts in the Library of the Royal College of Music, by William Barclay Squire . . . with additions by Rupert Erlebach. London, 1931. 568, 215*l*.

2938. St. Michael's College Library. The catalogue of manuscripts in the Library of St. Michael's College, Tenbury, comp. by Edmund H. Fellowes. Paris: Louise B. M. Dyer, 1934. 319p.

"The richest collection of music manuscripts in the British Isles after those in the British Museum, the Bodleian Library and the Cambridge University Library."

PERIODICALS

2939. London, University, Library. Union list of periodicals in music in the libraries of the University of London and some other London libraries. London, 1969. 56p.

Alphabetic list showing holdings in 21 libraries.

INSTRUMENTAL MUSIC

2940. Bradford Free Libraries and Art Museum. Catalogue of miniature and orchestral scores in the Central Lending Library. Bradford, 1956. 44p.

2941. British Broadcasting Corporation, Music Library. Chamber music catalogue; chamber music, violin and keyboard, cello and keyboard. London: BBC, 1965. Various paging.

Records 24,000 items.

2942. ————. Piano and organ catalogue. London: BBC, 1965. 2v.

2943. Brown, Howard Mayer. Instrumental music printed before 1600; a bibliography. London: Oxford Univ. Pr., 1965. 559p.

Locates copies in 189 libraries in 19 countries, the largest number in the British Museum, holding 126 items.

2944. Harris, K. G. E. A catalogue of miniature and full orchestral scores in Yorkshire libraries. Leeds: Library Association, Reference, Special and Information Section, Yorkshire Group, 1960. 200p.

About 4,000 items located in 35 public and university libraries.

2945. Hertfordshire County Library. Catalogue of sets of orchestral music. Hertford, 1969. 84p.

2946. Library Association, Reference, Special and Information Section, Yorkshire Group. A catalogue of miniature and full orchestral scores in Yorkshire libraries, by Keith G. E. Harris. Bradford, 1960. 200p.

Locations in 35 libraries.

2947. Liverpool Public Libraries. Catalogue of the Music Library; the piano, its music and literature. Liverpool, 1949. 103p.

2948. Manchester Public Libraries, Henry Watson Music Library. List of chamber music in the Library, comp. by John F. Russell. Manchester: The Libraries, 1913. 143p. (Music lists, no.2)

2949. ————. List of compositions for the organ and harmonium in the Henry Watson Music Library, comp. by John F. Russell. Manchester: The Libraries, 1913. 54p. (Music lists, no.5)

2950. ————. List of compositions for the pianoforte in the Library. Manchester: The Libraries, 1912. 71p. (Music lists, no.1)

2951. Newcastle upon Tyne City Libraries. Handlist of organ music. Newcastle upon Tyne, 1956. 20p.

2952. ————, Music Section. Handlist of piano scores. Newcastle upon Tyne: The Libraries, 1954. 53p.

2953. ———— ————. Handlist of piano scores, 2d ed. Newcastle upon Tyne: The Libraries, 1959. 126p.

2954. Westminster Public Libraries. The strong quartet, prep. by Miss J. Boothroyd. London, 1964. 12p.

Books held by Westminster's Central Music Library or British Museum.

VOCAL MUSIC

2955. British Broadcasting Corporation, Music Library. Choral and opera catalogue. London: BBC, 1967. 2v.

Lists 57,000 entries.

2956. ————. Song catalogue. London: BBC, 1966. 4v.

2957. British Museum, Dept. of Printed Books. Printed music in the Library of the Madrigal Society; an excerpt from part 59 of the catalogue of accessions of printed music. London: The Museum, 1955. p.251-66.

2958. Crum, M. C. "A seventeenth-century collection of music belonging to Thomas Hamond, a Suffolk landowner." Bodleian Library record, 6 (1957), 373-86.

Describes collection of vocal part-books, mainly copied in first half of 17th century, acquired by Bodleian Library in 1800.

2959. Day, Cyrus Lawrence, and Murrie, Eleanore Boswell. English song-books, 1651-1702; a bibliography with a first-line index of songs. London: Printed for the Bibliographical Society at the Univ. Pr., Oxford, 1940 (for 1937). 439p.

Describes 252 works, 1651-1730; copies located in British and American libraries.

2960. Hertfordshire County Library. Sets of choral music: a catalogue. Hertford, 1966. 184p. Supplement, no. 1- . 1970- .

2961. Leicestershire County Library. Choral music in the East Midlands; a union catalogue listing sets of vocal works in the libraries of Cambridgeshire, Derbyshire, Leicestershire, Lincolnshire, Northamptonshire, and Nottinghamshire, comp. by Jean Sewry and Kenneth H. Anderson. Leicester, 1970. 143p.

Includes holdings of 13 libraries.

2962. Newcastle upon Tyne City Libraries, Music Section. Handlist of songs. Newcastle upon Tyne: The Libraries, 1955. 49p.

2963. ———. Handlist of vocal scores. Newcastle upon Tyne, 1954. 40p.

2964. Nottinghamshire County Library. Choral music. Nottingham, 1957. 40p.

List of works held by library.

2965. Oxford, University, Bodleian Library. Early Bodleian music; sacred and secular songs, together with other ms. compositions in the Bodleian Library, by J. F. R. Stainer. London, 1901. 2v.

2966. ———. Manuscripts of Byzantine chant in Oxford, by N. G. Wilson and D. I. Stefanović. Oxford, 1963. 56p. + 4 plates.

Manuscripts in Bodleian and College Libraries.

2967. Willetts, Pamela J. "Sir Nicholas LeStrange's collection of masque music." British Museum quarterly, 29 (1965), 79-81.

Description of group of 17th-century masque tunes held by British Museum.

2968. Worcester County Council, Education Committee. Classified catalogue of the choral library. Worcester: Worcestershire County Library, 1964. 84p.

OPERA

2969. Central Music Library. A list of operas available for loan or reference at the Central Music Library. London, 1955. 43p. Supplement, 1957. 11p.

2970. Griffin, Jack Max. Scores of British operas composed and published during the period 1801-1850, in the Library of the British Museum. London, 1963. 139l. (Diploma in Librarianship, Univ. of London)

2971. Sadler's Wells Theatre. Catalogue of opera scores, libretti, books, etc. London, 1947. 3pts.

BALLADS

2972. Bibliotheca Lindesiana. Catalogue of a collection of English ballads of the XVIIth and XVIIIth centuries, printed for the most part in black letter. Aberdeen: Univ. Pr., 1890. 686p. Reprinted, N. Y.: Franklin, 1963.

1,466 entries; appendix lists items in Huth and Euing collections, the latter now in Glasgow University Library.

2973. Glasgow, University, Library. [A collection of English broadside ballads, formed by J. O. Halliwell, purchased by William Euing, presented by him to Anderson's College, Glasgow, and now forming part of the Library of the University of Glasgow.] 1575-[c. 1700]. 408pts.

Photocopies of the originals in Glasgow University Library.

2974. Halliwell-Phillipps, James Orchard. A catalogue of an unique collection of ancient English broadside ballads, with notes of the tunes and imprints. London: John Russell Smith, 1856. 141p.

Catalogue of the collection formed by J. O. Halliwell, purchased by William Euing, presented by him to Anderson's College, and now in the Library of the University of Glasgow.

2975. Hamer, Douglas. "Editions of Chevy Chase." Notes and queries, 164 (1933), 381-85, 398-40; 165 (1933), 418-20.

Checklist of 90 items, with locations of copies of famous ballad in British and American libraries.

2976. Hunt, Christopher. "Scottish ballads and music in the Robert White collection in the University Library, Newcastle upon Tyne." Bibliotheck, 5 (1968), 138-41.

Descriptions of 4 manuscripts.

2977. Sheffield, University, Library. Ballads in the Charles Harding Firth collection of the University of Sheffield, by Peter William Carnell. Sheffield, 1966. 3v.

RECORDED MUSIC

2978. Birmingham Public Libraries. Catalogue of gramophone records. Birmingham, 1966. 111p.

2979. Burnley, County Borough, Libraries Dept., Massey Music and Gramophone Record Library. List of orchestral works available for loan, 2d ed. Burnley: Central Library, 1970. 33p.

2980. Dagenham Public Libraries. Catalogue of gramophone records, ed. by W. C. Pugsley. Dagenham, 1961. 450p. Supplement 1. 1962. Supplement 2. 1962.

2981. Mansfield Public Library. Gramophone Record Library catalogue. Mansfield: 1958. Unpaged. Supplements, 1958-59.

2982. Motherwell and Wishaw Public Libraries. Gramophone Record Library catalogue. Motherwell, 1961. 118p.

2983. Saint Pancras Public Libraries. A catalogue of the collection of gramophone records. Saint Pancras, 1952. 64p.

MUSICAL INSTRUMENTS

2984. Tottenham Public Libraries. Electronic musical instruments: a bibliography. London, 1952. 31p.

2985. Victoria and Albert Museum Library. A bibliography of books on musical instruments in the Library of the Victoria and Albert Museum, comp. by M. I. Wilson. London, 1971. 45p. (Monthly list special supplement)
    Classified list.

2986. ———. List of accessions to the catalogue of the Library. Supplement: a bibliography of books on musical instruments in the Library, comp. by M. I. Wilson. London: H. M. Stationery Office, 1971. 50p.

Linguistics

2987. Alston, R. C., comp. A bibliography of the English language, from the invention of printing to the year 1800. Leeds: E. J. Arnold, 1965- . v.1- . In progress.

"Systematic record of writings on English, and on other languages in English, based on the collections of the principal libraries of the world." Planned in 20v., complete by 1972. Locations in numerous libraries.

2988. Bristol Public Libraries, Reference Library. The Stuckey Lean collection, ed. by Norris Mathews. Bristol: Libraries Committee, 1903. 268p.

A collection of philology, proverbs, etc., numbering about 5,000 books and pamphlets.

2989. Cambridge Philological Society Library. Catalogue. London: K. Paul, 1890. 78p.

2990. Canning House Library. Portuguese and Spanish dictionaries in the Canning House Library. London: Luso-Brazilian Council and Hispanic Council, 1971. 22p.

2991. CICRIS. Cicris union list of interlingual dictionaries; select list of foreign language dictionaries held by CICRIS members, comp. by staff of Ealing Reference Libraries, 2d ed. London: Co-operative Industrial and Commercial Reference and Information Service, 1971. 91p.

2992. Language Teaching Information Centre Reference Library. Books and materials for language teachers; contents of the Reference Library, Language Teaching Information Centre, rev. ed. York: Schools Council Modern Languages Project, 1970. 236p.

2993. Leeds, University, Institute of Education. Catalogue of the national collection of Greek and Latin school text-books (1800 onwards), by William B. Thompson and J. D. Ridge. Leeds, 1970. 119p.

pt.1: Dictionaries, grammars, vocabularies, notes and miscellanea, courses, composition manuals (prose and verse), reader selections.

2994. Liverpool Public Libraries. Select list of general dictionaries in the Picton Reference Library, William Brown Street: excluding special and technical dictionaries. Liverpool, 1950. 52p.

2995. London, University, Warburg Institute. A short-title list of subject dictionaries of the sixteenth, seventeenth, and eighteenth centuries as aids to the history of ideas, by Giorgio Tonelli. London, 1971. 64p.

Copies located, principally in British Museum and 10 Continental libraries.

2996. Manchester Public Libraries. The language laboratory: a bibliography, by John B. Hepworth. Manchester: The Libraries Committee, 1966. 29p.

2997. ———, English Dialect Library. Catalogue of the English Dialect Library, Free Reference Library, Manchester, by C. W. Sutton. Manchester, 1880-88. 2pts.

2998. Marsden, William. Bibliotheca Marsdenia philologica et orientalis; a catalogue of books and manuscripts collected with a view to the general comparison of languages, and the study of Oriental literature. London: J. L. Cox, 1827. 309p.

Collection now held by King's College Library, University of London.

2999. Newcastle upon Tyne, University, Library. Catalogue of the Heslop collection of dictionaries in the Library of King's College, Newcastle upon Tyne, by William S. Mitchell. Newcastle upon Tyne, 1955. 24p. (King's College Library publications, no.2)

3000. Oxford, University, Bodleian Library. Oxford English dictionary, 1884-1928; an exhibition of books illustrating the history of English dictionaries held in the Bodleian Library . . . to celebrate the completion of the Oxford English dictionary. Oxford, 1928. 20p.

3001. ——, Oriel College Library. A catalogue of the books in the Library of Oriel College connected with the studies of comparative philology and comparative mythology. Oxford, 1880. 32p. Addenda, 1885, 1891, 1903.

3002. Roberts, R. J. "Two early English-Spanish vocabularies." British Museum quarterly, 34 (1970), 86-91.

Descriptions of 16th-century works acquired by British Museum.

3003. Scheurweghs, Grace. "English grammars in Dutch and Dutch grammars in English in the Netherlands before 1800." English studies, 41 (1960), 129-67.

List of 12 grammars, with locations of copies in British and Dutch libraries.

Literature

General

3004. Belfast Library and Society for Promoting Knowledge. Catalogue of books in the Foreign Literature Section. London, 1914. 66p.

3005. Croft-Murry, Edward. "An exhibition of forgeries and deceptive copies; held in the Department of Prints and Drawings." British Museum quarterly, 24 (1961), 29-30.
Describes exhibition of items in fine arts, literature, music, etc., held in British Museum.

3006. Leeds, University, Brotherton Library. Inventory of the correspondence and other material bequeathed to the University by Jethro Bithell, 1878-1962, comp. by John S. Andrews, rev. ed. Leeds: The University, 1967. 39p.
Material relates mainly to Bithell's activities as anthologist of German, French, Belgian, and Flemish literature.

3007. ———. The Novello Clarke collection; a hand list. Leeds, 1955. 58p.
Collection of books, pamphlets, manuscripts, letters, and other material of a general literary nature.

3008. Sutton, Hilda Brenda. First editions of literary works by medical men in the eighteenth century. London, 1961. Unpaged. (Diploma in Librarianship, Univ. of London)
Copies located in 8 major medical and general libraries and various public libraries.

Classical

3009. Aberdeen, University, Library. Catalogue of the books in the Students' Classical Library. Aberdeen: Univ. Pr., 1900. 15p.

3010. Cambridge, University, Trinity College Library. The Wyse collection of classical pamphlets in the Library of Trinity College, Cambridge. Cambridge, 1915. 124p.

3011. John Rylands Library. Catalogue of an exhibition of the earliest printed editions of the principal Greek and Latin classics and of a few manuscripts. Manchester: Univ. Pr., 1926. 72p.

3012. ———. The John Rylands Library, Manchester; a brief historical description of the library and its contents, with catalogue of the selection of early printed Greek and Latin classics exhibited on the occasion of the visit of the Classical Association in October, MCMVI, by Henry Guppy. Manchester: Sherratt and Hughes, 1906. 89p.

3013. London, University, Institute of Classical Studies. A survey of classical periodicals; union catalogue of periodicals relevant to classical studies in certain British libraries, comp. by Joyce E. Southan. London, 1962. 181p. (Bulletin supplement, no.13)
Lists holdings of 51 libraries for 632 periodicals.

3014. ——— ———. A survey of periodicals relevant to Byzantine studies in several London libraries. London, 1968. 20p.
Locates files in 13 libraries.

3015. ———, King's College Library. Inventory of Professor P. J. Enk's classical library, as at 1st June 1960. London, 1960. 229p.
Collection now held by King's College Library.

3016. ——— ———. Inventory of Professor P. J. Enk's classical library . . . supplement, pamphlets and offprints. London, 1969. 83p.

3017. ——— ———. Subject index to list of pamphlets in the Enk library. London, 1972. 91p.
Classical literature.

3018. Newcastle upon Tyne City Libraries. Catalogue of books concerning the Greek and Latin classics in the Central Public Libraries, Newcastle upon Tyne, by Basil Anderton and T. E. Turnbull. Newcastle upon Tyne, 1912. 269p.

Classified arrangement with detailed index.

3019. Palmer, Henrietta. List of English editions and translations of Greek and Latin classics printed before 1641. London: Printed for the Bibliographical Society by Blades, East & Blades, 1911. 119p.

Copies located in British Museum, Bodleian, and Cambridge.

3020. Ryan, Michael J. "A list of Greek and Latin classics printed in Dublin down to 1800." Bibliographical Society of Ireland publications, 3, no.2 (1926), 1-8.

Checklist, 1692-1800, with locations of copies.

3021. Society for the Promotion of Hellenic and Roman Studies. A catalogue of books in the Library of the Society for the Promotion of Hellenic Studies. London, 1903. 98p.

3022. ———. A classified catalogue of the books, pamphlets and maps in the Library of the Society for the Promotion of Hellenic and Roman Studies. London: Macmillan, 1924. 336p.

Medieval

3023. Birkbeck College Library. Aucassin et Nicolette; handlist of books in the College Library, comp. by P. Woudhuysen. London, 1970. 2l. (Library publication, no.8)

3024. ———. Chanson de Roland; handlist of books in the College Library, comp. by P. Woudhuysen. London, 1970. 7l. (Library publication, no.6)

3025. ———. Roman de la Rose; select list of books and articles in the College Library, comp. by L. Polak and P. Woudhuysen. London, 1970. 4l. (Library publication, no.24)

Poetry

3026. Alden, John E. The muses mourn; a checklist of verse occasioned by the death of Charles II. Charlottesville: Bibliographical Society of the Univ. of Va., 1958. 62p.

Lists 143 poems, with locations of copies in 27 British and 54 U.S. libraries.

3027. Aubin, Robert Arnold. Topographical poetry in XVIIIth-century England. N.Y.: Modern Language Association of America, 1936. 419p.

Includes, p.297-391, bibliographies of hill poems, mine and cave poems, sea poems, estate poems, town poems, building poems, region poems, river poems, and journey poems, with locations of copies in British and American libraries.

3028. Birmingham Public Libraries, Reference Department. Catalogue of the war poetry collection. Birmingham, 1921. 60p.

3029. Birmingham, University, Library. Modern poetry collection. Birmingham: 1971. Unpaged. (Catalogues of the manuscript collections, no.32)

Lists 66 manuscripts.

3030. Bradner, Leicester. Musae Anglicanae; a history of Anglo-Latin poetry, 1500-1925. N.Y., London, 1940. 383p. (Modern Language Association of America, General series, no.10)

Includes "Chronological list of publications of Anglo-Latin poetry," p.346-73, with locations of rarer items in British, American, and French libraries.

3031. ———. "Musae Anglicanae; a supplemental list." Library, ser.5, 22 (1967), 93-103.

Anglo-Latin poetry printed from 1519 to 1926; copies located in 16 libraries, British, Irish, French, and American.

3032. British Museum, Dept. of Manuscripts. Poetry in the making: catalogue of an exhibition of poetry manuscripts in the British Museum, by Jenny Lewis. London: Turret Books, for the Arts Council of Great Britain and British Museum, 1967. 68p.

Annotated list of 129 items.

3033. Brown, Carleton, and Robbins, Rossell Hope. The index of middle English verse. N.Y.: Columbia Univ. Pr. for the Index Society, 1943. 785p.

Includes locations of "manuscripts in private possession," in Britain and abroad.

3034. Brown, Carleton. A register of middle English religious & didactic verse. Oxford: Univ. Pr., for the Bibliographical Society, 1916. 2v.

pt.1, list of manuscripts; pt.2, index of first lines and index of subjects and titles; describes holdings of individual libraries separately: Bodleian, Cambridge, British Museum, etc.

3035. Case, Arthur E. A bibliography of English poetical miscellanies, 1521-1750. Oxford: Univ. Pr. for the Bibliographical Society, 1935 (for 1929). 386p.

Locates copies in British and American libraries; lists 481 titles.

3036. Edmond, John Philip. "Elegies and other tracts issued on the death of Henry, Prince of Wales, 1612." Edinburgh Bibliographical Society proceedings, 6 (1906), 141-58.

Lists 44 items, with locations of copies.

3037. National Book League. English poetry; an illustrated catalogue of first and early editions, comp. by John Hayward. London: Cambridge Univ. Pr., 1950. 148p. + 356 facsimiles.

Locates copies in British and American libraries of 346 works from Chaucer to modern times.

3038. Oxford, University, Bodleian Library. Catalogue of early English poetry and other miscellaneous works illustrating the British drama, collected by E. Malone, and now preserved in the Bodleian Library, by B. Bandinel. Oxford, 1836. 52p.

3039. ——— ———. First-line index of English poetry, 1500-1800, in manuscripts of the Bodleian Library, Oxford, ed. by Margaret Crum. Oxford: Clarendon, 1969. 2v.

Lists Bodleian manuscripts in which poems are found.

3040. Ringler, William. "A bibliography and first-line index of English verse printed through 1500; a supplement to Brown and Robbins' Index of middle English verse." Papers of the Bibliographical Society of America, 49 (1955), 153-80.

Lists 98 works, with STC and Duff numbers.

3041. Stoddard, Roger E. A catalogue of books and pamphlets unrecorded in Oscar Wegelin's Early American poetry, 1650-1820. Providence, R. I.: Friends of the Library of Brown Univ., 1969. 84p.

Identifies 262 titles; copies located in British and American libraries.

3042. Williams, Franklin B. Index of dedications and commendatory verses in English books before 1641. London: Bibliographical Society, 1962. 256p.

Locates copies in British, American, and other libraries.

Drama

3043. Birley, Robert. "Additions from Eton College Library to the record of copies in Sir W. W. Greg's A bibliography of the English printed drama." Library, ser.5, 18 (1963), 228-29.

3044. Birmingham Public Libraries. List play sets in the Central Lending Library. Birmingham, 1967. 74p.

3045. Bristol Public Libraries. A guide to the play collection. Bristol, 1955. 51p.

3046. ———. Index of plays available in the Bristol Public Libraries. Bristol, 1950. 204p.

Includes collection of 1,700 volumes relating to Shakespeare.

3047. British Drama League Library. The Player's Library; the catalogue of the Library of the British Drama League, comp. by Margaret Burnham. London: Faber and Faber for British Drama League, 1950. 1,115p. Supplements 1-3, 1951-56. 3v.

Catalog of plays, of books on the theatre, and title indexes of plays. Supplement 3 includes section on French plays; basic work records about 7,000 volumes.

3048. British Museum, Dept. of Manuscripts. Catalogue of additions to the manuscripts: plays submitted to the Lord Chamberlain, 1824-1851: additional manuscripts 42865-43038. London: The Museum, 1964. 359p.

Records acting copies of plays produced in Great Britain during period indicated; collection is a continuation of Larpent collection held by Huntington Library.

3049. Camden, London Borough, Libraries & Arts Department. Play sets. (Inner London special collections) London, 1969. Unpaged.

Author list of play sets held by Camden Libraries, housed at Hampstead Central Library.

3050. East Riding County Library. Spotlight . . . a comprehensive list of plays in stock. Beverley, 1960-61. 2pts. Supplement, 1971. 30p.

pt.1, one-act plays; pt.2, full-length plays.

3051. Eastbourne Public Libraries. Play sets, 3rd ed. Eastbourne, 1966. 43p.

3052. Essex County Library. Drama catalogue. Chelmsford: Essex Education Committee, 1958. 172p.

List of over 4,000 plays.

3053. Greg, Walter Wilson. A bibliography of the English printed drama to the Restoration. London: Bibliographical Society, 1939-59. 4v.

Locations in English, European, and American libraries; detailed descriptions; chronological order.

3054. ———. A list of English plays written before 1643 and printed before 1700. London: Blades for the Bibliographical Society, 1900 (for 1899). 158p.

Locations in British Museum, Bodleian, etc.

3055. ———. A list of masques, pageants, etc., supplementary to A list of English plays. London: Bibliographical Society, 1902. cxxxip.

Locates copies in British Museum, Bodleian, etc.

3056. Harbage, Alfred Bennett. Annals of English drama, 975-1700: an analytical record of all plays, extant or lost, chronologically arranged and indexed by authors, titles, dramatic companies, etc., rev. by S. Schoenbaum. London: Methuen, 1964. 323p.

Locates copies.

3057. ———. "A census of Anglo-Latin plays." Publications of the Modern Language Association of America, 53 (1938), 624-29.

Locates copies, chiefly manuscripts, in British and American libraries.

3058. Hertfordshire County Library. A catalogue of play-reading sets. Hertford, 1970. 508p.

3059. Huntingdon and Peterborough County Library. Drama catalogue. Huntingdon, 1969. 89p.

3060. Lancashire County Library. Drama catalogue; a list of sets of plays and a selection of works on play production and other related subjects. Preston, 1962. 162p.

3061. Linton, Marion. "National Library of Scotland and Edinburgh University Library copies of plays in Greg's Bibliography of the printed drama." Studies in bibliography, 15 (1962), 91-104.

Listing in Greg's order, with locations.

3062. Loewenberg, A. Early Dutch librettos and plays with music in the British Museum. London: Aslib, 1947. 30p. Reprinted from Journal of documentation, 2, no.4 (March 1947).

3063. Manchester Public Libraries. Handlist of plays: sets available for loan from the Language and Literature Library, 3rd ed. Manchester, 1965. 106p.

3064. ———. Repertory plays; sets available for loan from Central Lending Library, 2d ed. Manchester: Manchester Libraries Committee, 1958. 108p.

3065. Newcastle upon Tyne City Libraries. Handlist of play sets. Newcastle upon Tyne, 1955. 42p.

3066. North East Lancashire Libraries. Sets of plays in the public libraries of Accrington, Bacup, Blackburn, Burnley, Darwen, Nelson, Rawtenstall, Rochdale, Royton, 5th ed. Rawtenstall, Rossendale, 1965. 43p.

3067. Nottinghamshire County Library. Plays for reading and production. Nottingham, 1951. 98p.

3068. ———. Plays for reading and production; a catalogue of the drama section. Nottingham, 1955. 109p.

3069. ———. Plays for reading and production: a catalogue of the drama section, new ed., 1958 supplement. Nottingham, 1958. 23p.

3070. Nottingham Public Libraries. List of plays. Nottingham, 1963. 121p.

3071. Oxford, University, Worcester College Library. A handlist of English plays and masques printed before 1750 in . . . Worcester College, Oxford. Oxford, 1929. 27p.

3072. ———. Plays added up to March 1948, including some previously omitted. Oxford, 1948. 7p.

Supplement to A handlist of English plays and masques printed before 1750.

3073. Religious Drama Society Library. A catalogue of selected plays, with books of general interest, ed. by Jessie Powell and Kathleen Bainbridge-Bell. London: The Society, 1951. 77p.

Classified by types.

3074. Schoenbaum, Samuel. "Plays, masques, etc., 1552-1659: a rough checklist for prospective editors." Research opportunities in Renaissance drama, 8 (1965), 20-45.

Locates manuscripts in British and American libraries.

3075. Sheffield City Libraries. Play catalogue. Sheffield: Libraries, Art Galleries and Museums Committee, 1959. 101p. Supplements, 1-4. 1960-63. 4pts.

Catalog of 7,000-volume collection.

3076. Stratman, Carl J. Bibliography of English printed tragedy, 1565-1900. Carbondale & Edwardsville: Southern Ill. Univ. Pr., 1966. 843p.

Contains 6,852 entries, with locations in 96 libraries, British and American.

3077. ———. Bibliography of medieval drama. Berkeley: Univ. of Calif. Pr., 1954. 423p.

Locations in 11 British and Irish and numerous American libraries.

3078. ———. "A survey of the Bodleian Library's holdings in the field of English printed tragedy." Bodleian Library record, 7 (1964), 133-43.

Includes statistics of Bodleian Library's holdings and list of authors for whom the Bodleian "has the first edition of all tragedies."

3079. Surrey County Library. Plays in sets in the Surrey County Library: a classified list. Esher, 1965. 303p.

3080. Warwickshire County Library. Sets of plays for reading & production, 3d ed. Warwick, 1955. 74p.

3081. Worcestershire County Library. Classified catalogue of the play set collection, Worcestershire County Library. Worcester, 1971. 103p.

Fiction

3082. Belfast Library and Society for Promoting Knowledge. Catalogue of prose fiction. Belfast, 1894. 76p. (Supplementary catalogue of general literature and of prose fiction to Dec. 1896. Belfast, 1897. 30p. Supplementary catalogue of books added 1897, 1899, 1900, 1903). Belfast: Northern Whig Office, 1898-1905. 4pts.

3083. Birmingham Library. Fiction, by Charles E. Scarse. Birmingham, 1896. 16p.
Title list of recent fiction added to library's permanent collection, 1891-95.

3084. Birmingham Public Libraries. Romanzi italiani; a select list of modern Italian novels in the Central Lending Library. Birmingham, 1956. Unpaged.

3085. Block, Andrews. The English novel, 1740-1850; a catalogue including prose romances, short stories, and translations of foreign fiction, 2d ed. London: Dawsons of Pall Mall, 1961. 349p.
Copies frequently located in British Museum, Bodleian, and other British and American libraries.

3086. British Museum, Dept. of Manuscripts. Catalogue of romances in the Department of Manuscripts. London: The Museum, 1883-1910. 3v. Reprinted, 1961-62. 3v.
Classical and medieval romances and legends; detailed analyses of individual works.

3087. Day, Robert Adams. "Bibliography of epistolary fiction, 1660-1740." In: Davys, Mary. Familiar letters betwixt a gentleman and a lady, 1725. Los Angeles: UCLA Library, 1955, p.1-10.
List of 186 items, with locations of copies in British Museum and Harvard University Library.

3088. Esdaile, Arundell. A list of English tales and prose romances printed before 1740; pt.I. 1475-1642; pt.II. 1643-1739. London: Printed for the Bibliographical Society by Blades, East & Blades, 1912. 329p.
Locates copies in British Museum, Bodleian, etc.

3089. Finsbury Public Libraries. Class guide to fiction, new and revised edition, by James Duff Brown. London, 1903. 155p.

3090. Henderson, James. "The gothic novel in Wales, 1790-1820." National Library of Wales journal, 11 (1960), 244-54.
Novels associated with Wales; copies located.

3091. Liverpool Public Libraries. Catalogue of fiction added to the lending libraries, 1958-1966. Liverpool: Brown, Picton and Hornby Libraries, 1967. 227p.

3092. McBurney, William Harlin. A check list of English prose fiction, 1700-1739. Cambridge, Mass.: Harvard Univ. Pr., 1960. 154p.
Locates copies of 391 works in 14 English, American, and French libraries.

3093. Mish, Charles C. English prose fiction, 1600-1700. Charlottesville: Bibliographical Society of the Univ. of Va., 1952. 3pts.
pt.1, 1600-1640; pt.2, 1641-1660; pt.3, 1661-1700. Includes STC and Wing numbers.

3094. National Committee on Regional Library Co-operation. Foreign fiction; a directory of collections within the regions. London: National Central Library, 1967. 4l. (Supplement to the N.C.L. Occasional newsletter, July 1967)
Lists areas of cooperation among participating libraries.

3095. Newcastle upon Tyne City Libraries. Catalogue of fiction (in English) in the Central Lending Library. Newcastle upon Tyne, 1906. 295p.

3096. O'Dell, Sterg. A chronological list of prose fiction in English printed in England and other countries, 1475-1640. Cambridge, Mass.: Technology Pr. of M.I.T., 1954. 147p. Reprinted, N.Y.: Kraus, 1969.
Copies located in numerous British, American, and other libraries.

3097. Ray, Gordon N. Bibliographical resources for the study of 19th century English fiction. Los Angeles: Univ. of Calif., School of Library Service, 1964. 31p.
Sampling of 130 books by major and secondary novelists. 20p. of text, 10p. of tables. "The first serious post-Sadleirian study of the factor of rarity, both copy-for-copy and in the original state, in novels between Sense and Sensibility and Dracula." Times literary supplement.

3098. Scottish Library Association. Scottish fiction reserve; a list of the authors included in the scheme, comp. by W. R. Aitken. n.p., 1955. 42l.

Lists "collecting libraries" alphabetically by authors.

3099. Swinton and Pendlebury Public Libraries. Social anthropology through the novel; a select list of works of fiction dealing with primitive peoples and native races in African countries, in Asia and in Latin America, including some novels of racial, cultural and religious conflict, 2d ed. Pendlebury, Swinton, 1962. Unpaged.

English

3100. Bole, Ruth Elizabeth Gertrude. Bibliography of literary material relating to the University of Durham in the University Library. London, 1948. 26l. (Diploma in Librarianship, Univ. of London)

3101. British Museum, Dept. of Prints and Drawings. Catalogue of prints and drawings in the British Museum: Division I, political and personal satires. London: The Museum, 1870- . v.1-11. Revised title: Catalogue of political and personal satires preserved in the Dept. of Prints and Drawings in the British Museum; v.1-4 prep. by F. G. Stevens, v.5-11 prep. by M. D. George. In progress.
   v.1-11 cover 1320-1832 period.

3102. Corns, A. R., and Sparke, A. A bibliography of unfinished books in the English language, with annotations. London: Quaritch, 1915. 225p. Reprinted, Detroit: Gale, 1968.
   Lists over 2,000 works, based largely on the British Museum Catalogue; not restricted to belles lettres.

3103. Edinburgh, University, Library. "Rhetoric and English literature"; an exhibition in commemoration of the two hundredth anniversary of the Regius Chair. Edinburgh, 1962. 14p.
   Lists 131 manuscripts and rare books.

3104. Hart, W. H. Index expurgatorius anglicanus: or a descriptive catalogue of the principal books printed or published in England, which have been suppressed, or burnt by the Common Hangman, or censured, or for which the authors, printers, or publishers have been prosecuted. London: John Russell Smith, 1872. 290p.
   Locations principally in British Museum.

3105. Havering Public Libraries. South Essex authors; a checklist issued for National Library Week, 1966. Romford: Central Library, 1966. 24p.

3106. Liverpool, University, Library. In memoriam William Noble; a catalogue of the books collected by the late William Noble . . . and bequeathed by him to the University Library. Liverpool: Univ. Pr., 1913. 182p.
   About 2,000 books, chiefly in field of English literature; includes many private press books.

3107. Manchester Public Libraries. Catalogue of the Alexander Ireland collection in the Free Reference Library, comp. by John Hibbert Swann. Manchester: Free Reference Library, 1898. 25p. (Occasional lists, no.5)
   Collection relates to Charles and Mary Lamb, William Hazlitt, Leigh Hunt, Thomas and Jane Welsh Carlyle, and Ralph Waldo Emerson.

3108. Merritt, Percival. "The Royal Primer." In: Bibliographical essays: a tribute to Wilberforce Eames. Cambridge, Mass.: Harvard Univ. Pr., 1924, p.35-60.
   "Check-list of Royal Primers," p.59-60, locates copies in British and American libraries.

3109. National Library of Scotland. English literature; an exhibition of manuscripts and of first and other early editions, comp. by William Park. Edinburgh, 1962. 33p.
   Notable for early Scottish verse; includes 4 Shakespeare first quartos.

3110. Oxford, University, Bodleian Library. Duke Humfrey and English humanism in the fifteenth century; catalogue of an exhibition held in the Bodleian Library, Oxford, comp. by Tilly de la Mare and Richard Hunt. Oxford, 1970. 77p.

3111. ———. English literature in the seventeenth century; guide to an exhibition held in 1957, comp. by John Buxton and D. G. Neill. Oxford, 1957. 167p.
   Books and manuscripts illustrative of outstanding works held by Bodleian Library; detailed descriptions of 234 selected titles.

3112. ———. A hand-list of the early English literature preserved in the Douce collection in the Bodleian Library, selected from the printed catalogue of that collection by J. O. Halliwell. London, 1860. 151p.
   Listing, by authors, of many early English rarities.

3113. ———. A hand-list of the early English literature preserved in the Malone collection in the Bodleian Library, selected from the printed catalogue of that collection by J. O. Halliwell. London, 1860. 96p.
   Listing, by authors, of early English rarities.

3114. Todd, William Burton. "The number, order, and authorship of the Hanover pamphlets attributed to Chesterfield." Papers of the Bibliographical Society of America, 44 (1950), 224-38.

Copies located in British Museum and various American libraries.

3115. Wigan Public Library. The foundations of glory; a victory exhibition of first or early editions . . . from Chaucer to Stevenson. Wigan, 1945. 15p.

3116. Williams, Franklin Burleigh, Jr. "Special presentation epistles before 1641; a preliminary check-list.' Library, ser.5, 7 (1952), 15-20.

List of works issued 1600-36, with copies located in British and American libraries; STC numbers added.

3117. Wise, Thomas James. The Ashley Library; a catalogue of printed books, manuscripts, and autograph letters collected by Thomas James Wise. London: printed for private circulation, 1922-36. 11v.

Records 2,000 items with descriptions; works of English poets and dramatists from Jacobean to modern times; acquired by British Museum.

American

3118. American Library. American literature catalogue. London: USIS, 1956. 100p.

Library transferred to University of London.

3119. National Central Library. American books in the humanities and social sciences 1970. London, 1971. 5pts.

Accessions list of books received by the library.

3120. Stepney Public Libraries. American writers and writing; a select list. London, 1962. Unpaged.

Selection of about 300 titles from 4,000-volume collection.

Celtic

3121. Aberdeen, University, Library. Catalogue of the books in the Celtic department, by Peter John Anderson. Aberdeen: Univ. Pr., 1897. 63p.

3122. ———. Scottish-Gaelic holdings, classified list, by Donald John MacLeod. Aberdeen, 1966. 109p.

Classified list of Gaelic publications held by Aberdeen University Library; in 2 divisions, secular and sacred.

3123. Advocates' Library. A descriptive catalogue of Gaelic manuscripts in the Advocates' Library, Edinburgh, and elsewhere in Scotland, by Donald MacKinnon. Edinburgh: T. & A. Constable, 1912. 348p.

Separate listings for manuscripts in Advocates' Library, Universities of Edinburgh and Glasgow, etc.

3124. Birmingham Public Libraries. Welsh books; a list of books in the Welsh language available in the Central Lending Library. Birmingham, 1959. 4p.

3125. Cork University Library [Irish manuscripts in Cork University Library] by Pádraig de Brún. Dublin, 1967. 2v.

In Gaelic.

3126. Dix, E. R. McC., and Cassedy, James. List of books, pamphlets, etc., printed wholly, or partly, in Irish, from the earliest period to 1820. Dublin: Hanna & Neale, 1913. 19p.

Locates copies in public and private collections.

3127. Great Britain, Historical Manuscripts Commission. Report on manuscripts in the Welsh language. [A descriptive catalogue.] London, 1898-1910. 2v. (Historical Manuscripts Commission, no.48)

v.1, pt.1. The Welsh manuscripts of Lord Mostyn, at Mostyn Hall, Co. Flint. 1898.

v.1, pts.2, 3. The first portion (The second portion) of the Welsh manuscripts at Peniarth, Towyn, Merioneth; the property of William Robert Maurice Wynne, 1899. 1905.

v.2, pt.1. Jesus College, Oxford, Free Library, Cardiff; Harod; Wrexham; Llanwrin; Merthyr; Aberdâr, 1902.

v.2, pt.2. Plas Llan Stephan; Free Library, Cardiff (cont.). 1903.

v.2, pt.3. Panton; Cwrtmawr. 1905.

v.2, pt.4. The British Museum. 1910.

3128. MacKechnie, John. Catalogue of Gaelic manuscripts in selected libraries in Great Britain and Ireland. Boston, Mass.: G. K. Hall. Announced for publication.

Includes description of every known Gaelic manuscript in National Library of Scotland, University Libraries of Aberdeen, Edinburgh and Glasgow, etc.

3129. National Library of Scotland. Celtica. Edinburgh, 1967. 56p.

Records 246 items, fully annotated, of material drawn from National Library of Scotland.

3130. National Library of Wales. Cornish manuscripts in the National Library of Wales, by W. Ll.

Davies, prep. for the Celtic Congress to be held at Truro, Cornwall . . . 1939. Aberystwyth, 1939. 18p.

French

3131. Hobson, A. R. A. "Unfamiliar libraries V: Waddesdon Manor." Book collector, 8 (1959), 131-39.

Consists largely of rare 18th-century French books and manuscripts.

3132. Nottingham, University, Library. Guides to bibliographical sources: French language and literature, prep. by D. A. Clarke. Nottingham, 1960? 22*l*. Supplement. 1965. 23-36*l*.

Limited to Nottingham University Library's holdings.

3133. Sutherland, D. M. Modern language libraries; a rapid survey of their resources in French. Oxford: Blackwell, 1963. 54p.

Worldwide survey, describing holdings of public and institutional libraries in field of French studies, with special emphasis on holdings of manuscripts and other source material.

German

3134. Birmingham, University, Library. A classified catalogue of the Karl Dammann Memorial Library [the German departmental library in the University]. Oxford: Hart, 1902. 49p.

3135. Leeds, University, Brotherton Library. Catalogue of an exhibition of German books and periodicals from the Library's collections, by E. Langstadt. Leeds, 1968. 54p.

Annotated list of 128 items selected from 2 special collections.

3136. Library of the German Language in Great Britain. Catalogue of books and periodicals in German. London, 1951. 63p.

Periodicals listed "are displayed in the Reference Room of the Westminster Public Library."

3137. London, University, Institute of Germanic Languages and Literatures. Union list of periodicals dealing with Germanic languages and literature in the University Library and in libraries of colleges and institutes of the University. London, 1956. 55p.

Lists 501 periodicals, giving holdings for 13 libraries.

3138. ———, Institute of Germanic Studies. Periodical holdings. London, 1970. 92p.

Lists 681 titles with holdings.

3139. ———, King's College Library. The Frida Mond collection at King's College; a descriptive catalogue, by Henry Gibson Atkins. London, 192—? 40p.

German collection, primarily concerned with Goethe.

3140. Manchester Goethe Society. Transactions . . . 1886-1893; being original papers and summaries of papers read before the Society, to which is added a classified catalogue of the Society's Library. Warrington, 1894. 213p.

3141. Oxford, University, Taylor Institution. Catalogue of the Fiedler collection; manuscript material and books up to and including 1850, by D. M. Sutherland. Oxford, 1962. 65p.

Emphasis is on 18th-century German literature, Goethe, Rilke, etc.

Greek (Modern)

3142. Camden Town Branch Library. Modern Greek. London Borough of Camden: Libraries & Arts Dept., 1969. Unpaged.

Catalog of books in modern Greek held by Camden Town Branch Library, London.

Hungarian

3143. Czigány, Lóránt. "The László Waltherr collection." British Museum quarterly, 33 (1969), 92-102.

Account of extensive Hungarian collection received by British Museum in 19th century.

3144. Hammersmith Public Libraries. Hungarian literature: a list of books available from the London Borough of Hammersmith Public Libraries, Metropolitan special collection. London, 1966. 41p.

Icelandic

3145. British Museum, Dept. of Printed Books. Catalogue of editions of Edda [in the British Museum] arranged chronologically; with an alphabetical list of editions, commentators, and works commenting upon Edda literature, comp. by T. W. Lidderdale. [In manuscript.] [1884.]

3146. ———. Catalogue of the books printed in Iceland from A.D. 1578 to 1880, in the Library of the British Museum, prep. by T. W. Lidderdale. London: W. Clowes, 1885. 30 cols.

3147. Edinburgh, University, Library. Icelandic sagas; an exhibition of books and manuscripts from the collections of the University Library and the National Library of Scotland. Edinburgh, 1971.

Catalog of 71 Icelandic manuscripts, printed editions, and critical works.

3148. Tupper, H. G. "Old Norse collection and its relevance for English studies." Library Association record, 51 (1949), 144-46.

Description of old Norse section of Brotherton Library, Leeds University.

Italian

3149. Cambridge Public Free Library. A catalogue of Italian books. Cambridge, 1952. 16p.

3150. Scott, Mary Augusta. Elizabethan translations from the Italian. Boston, Mass.: Houghton Mifflin, 1916. 558p.

Full bibliographical details on 466 works; copies frequently located in British Museum or elsewhere.

New Zealand

3151. Alcock, P. C. M. "New Zealand literature in United Kingdom university libraries: a pilot survey." New Zealand libraries, 31 (1968), 133-42.

Sampling of resources of British university libraries in New Zealand literature.

Norwegian

3152. British Museum, Dept. of Printed Books. Catalogue of Norwegian books, 1920- . London, 1954-

Issued periodically.

3153. Tveteraas, Harald L. "Norwegian books in British libraries." Norseman, 6 (1948), 349-59.

Review of holdings by types of libraries and by subject fields.

Romance Languages

3154. London, University, Library. Union list of periodicals in the Romance languages and literatures in British national, university and special libraries. London, 1964. 150p.

Locates files of about 750 titles in 60 libraries.

Scandinavian

3155. Evans, D. Wyn. "A short survey of Scandinavian libraries in Great Britain, together with a list of the sixteenth-century Danish and Icelandic books in the National Library of Scotland." Nordisk tidskrift för bok- och biblioteksväsen, 54 (1967), 81-85.

Includes list of Danish books, 1502-1600, and Icelandic books, 1578-1591.

Slavonic

3156. Auty, R., and Tyrrell, E. P. "A. H. Wratislaw's Slavonic books in the Library of Christ's College, Cambridge." Transactions of the Cambridge Bibliographical Society, 5 (1969), 36-46.

Lists 122 items.

3157. Barnicot, J. D. A. "The Slavonic manuscripts in the Bodleian." Bodleian Library record, 1 (1938), 30-33.

3158. ———, and Simmons, J. S. G. "Some unrecorded early-printed Slavonic books in English libraries." Oxford Slavonic papers, 2 (1951), 98-118.

Detailed descriptions of 18 works with locations in 5 English libraries.

3159. Birmingham, University, Centre for Russian and East European Studies, Alexander Baykov Library. Monthly list of accessions to Alexander Baykov Library. Birmingham, 1965- .

3160. ———, Library. List of books presented to the Alexander Baykov Library by Mr. E. Bishop. Birmingham, 1969. 47l.

3161. Cambridge, University, Libraries. An exhibition of Russian books of the eighteenth century from Cambridge libraries, arr. by A. G. Cross and E. P. Tyrrell, Cambridge, 1970. 16l.

Annotated list of 59 items.

3162. Christian, R. F., Sullivan, J., and Simmons, J. S. G. "Early-printed Russian books at St. Andrews and their background." Bibliotheck, 5 (1970), 215-31.

Spanish

3163. Cambridge, University, Library. Catalogue of the Maccoll collection and other Spanish books. Cambridge, 1910. 189p.

3164. ——— ———. An exhibition of Spanish books and books of Hispanic interest, comp. by E. M. Wilson. Cambridge, 1959. Unpaged.

3165. ——, Magdalene College Library. The Spanish books in the library of Samuel Pepys, by Stephen Gaselee, a catalogue. Oxford: Univ. Pr., 1921. 49p. (Supplement to the Bibliographical Society's Transactions, no.2)

List contains 185 items.

3166. Glasgow, University, Library. A select list of serials in the fields of Hispanic & Italian studies and theatre, 1967-68. Glasgow, 1967. 8p.

Exact holdings shown.

3167. National Library of Wales. Schedule of a collection of Spanish and Catalan books, mainly Shakespeareana, presented by Dr. Henry Thomas. Aberystwyth, 1941. 8l.

3168. Oxford, University, St. John's College Library. A catalogue of a portion of the Library [of Spanish literature] of H. Butler Clarke . . . now in the Library of St. John's College. n.p., 1906. 30p.

3169. Thomas, Henry. Early Spanish ballads in the British Museum. Cambridge: Stanley Morison, 1927. 3pts.

Descriptions and texts; 1. Romance del conde Dirlos; 2. Romance del conde Alarcos; 3. Romance de don Gayferos.

Swedish

3170. British Museum, Dept. of Printed Books. Catalogue of Swedish books acquired 1889- . London, 1951- .

Issued periodically.

3171. London, University, University College Library. Catalogue of Swedish books and books relating to Sweden in the Library of University College, London. London, 1952- .

Issued periodically.

Juvenile

3172. Barrow-in-Furness Free Public Library. Catalogue of the books in the Juvenile Lending Department, comp. by J. Frowde. Barrow-in-Furness: S. S. Lord, 1886. 35p.

3173. Bedford College of Education Library. Catalogue of the Hockliffe collection of early children's books, comp. by Doreen H. Boggis. Bedford, 1969. 155p.

Collection of about 800 books, grouped by types and subjects.

3174. Birmingham Library. Hand list of some of the children's books in the Birmingham Library. Birmingham, 1892. 19p.

3175. Bishop Lonsdale College of Education Library. Catalogue of the collection of early children's books, together with other books of special educational interest, in the Library of Bishop Lonsdale College of Education, by C. E. Saunders. Derby, 1968. 29p.

Classified list.

3176. British Museum. An exhibition of early English children's books: exhibition catalogue. London, 1968. 33p.

3177. Chelsea Public Libraries. Classified catalogue of books in the Children's Lending Department. London, 1929. 64p.

3178. Children's Book Club. Catalogue of the circulating library of the Children's Book Club, 3d ed. London: Harrods, 1938. 205p.

3179. Coventry City Libraries. The best children's books of 1963. Coventry, 1964. 15p.

3180. Dagenham Public Libraries. Biographies for children: a select list arranged under biographee, 2d ed., comp. by Keith S. Golland. Dagenham, 1962. 106p.

3181. Downton, Jane A., and Good, D. "The Spencer collection of early children's books and chapbooks in the Harris Public Library, Preston." YLG News, 14 (Feb. 1970), 11-14.

Description of collection of more than 600 early children's books and juvenile chapbooks.

3182. Edinburgh Public Libraries. Catalogue of books in the Juveniles' Library. Edinburgh: Edinburgh Public Library Committee, 1898. 94p.

3183. Glasgow Corporation Public Libraries. The special collection of children's books available in Glasgow Public Libraries. (Pre-1914.) Glasgow: Mitchell Library, 1965. 20p.

Alphabetical by authors.

3184. Hackney Public Libraries. Catalogue of the books in the Children's Department of the Central Public Library. Hackney, 1908. 104p.

3185. Hammersmith Public Libraries. Early children's books: a catalogue of the collection in the London Borough of Hammersmith Public Libraries. London: Central Library, 1965. 121p.

Author catalog with title and series index; records about 1,200 books.

3186. Harris Public Library. A catalogue of the Spencer collection of early children's books and chapbooks presented to the Harris Public Library, Preston, by Mr. J. H. Spencer, 1947, comp. by David Good. Preston, 1967. 307p.

Classified by subjects and types, with author-title indexes.

3187. Havering Public Libraries. Biographies for children: a select list, 4th ed., comp. by Keith S. Golland and ed. by R. W. Thompson. Havering, 1967. 123p.

3188. Library Association, Youth Libraries Group. "Collections of early children's books." Library Association record, 68 (1966), 261-62.

Lists collections in various locations, noting number of volumes, period covered, and special features.

3189. Manchester, University, Library. Books, manuscripts and illustrations presented to Manchester University Library by Alison Uttley. Manchester, n.d. 14l.

Papers and other materials of author of children's books.

3190. National Book League. Children's books of yesterday: a catalogue of an exhibition, comp. by Percy H. Muir. Cambridge: Pub. for the National Book League by Cambridge Univ. Pr., 1946. 211p. Reprinted, Detroit: Gale Research Co., 1970.

3191. National Library of Wales. Catalogue of old-time children's books, samplers, paintings, manuscripts, rare books, etc., in the Exhibition Gallery of the National Library. Aberystwyth, 1929. 55p.

3192. Newcastle upon Tyne City Libraries. Catalogue of the books in the Juvenile Lending Department, comp. by W. J. Haggerston. Newcastle upon Tyne, 1880. 23p.

3193. ———. Children's catalogue: books in the Central Public Libraries, Newcastle upon Tyne. Newcastle upon Tyne, 1920. 79p.

3194. Roberts, Julian. "The 1765 edition of Goody Two-shoes." British Museum quarterly, 29 (1965), 67-70.

Detailed description of work acquired by British Museum.

3195. Roscoe, Sydney. Newbery-Carnan-Power; a provisional check-list of books for the entertainment, instruction and education of children and young people, issued under the imprint of John Newbery and

his family in the period 1742-1802. London: Dawson's of Pall Mall, 1966. 83p.

Gives locations of all copies known to compiler; lists 397 titles.

3196. St. Bride Foundation Institute Library. An exhibition of a small collection of early children's books. London, 1938. 16p.

3197. Sandeman Public Library. Catalogue of the Juvenile Department, 2d ed. Perth, 1919. 45p.

3198. Sloane, William. Children's books in England & America in the seventeenth century; a history and a checklist. N.Y.: Columbia Univ. Pr., 1955. 251p.

Annotated checklist of 261 items, 1557-1710, with locations of copies in British and American libraries.

3199. Stone, Wilbur Macey. "The history of Little Goody Two-Shoes." American Antiquarian Society proceedings, n.s. 49 (1939), 333-70.

Checklists of British editions, 1765-1850, and American editions, 1774-1850, with locations of copies in British and American libraries and private collections.

3200. Victoria and Albert Museum Library. Victorian books exhibition, children's books; a list comprising exhibited books and additional works. London, 1967. 33 + 7 + 4l.

3201. Weiss, Harry Bishoff. "A preliminary check list of English and American editions of Little Red Riding Hood." In his: Little Red Riding Hood, a terror tale of the nursery. Trenton, N.J., 1939. p.15-60.

Lists 60 items, with locations of copies in British Museum and American libraries.

3202. Yates, W. E. "The Parker collection of early children's books in Birmingham Public Library." YLG news 14 (Feb. 1970), 9-10.

Description of collection of about 2,000 early children's books acquired by Birmingham Public Library in 1960.

Asian and African Languages and Literatures

GENERAL

3203. Beeston, A. F. L. "The Oriental manuscript collections of the Bodleian Library." Bodleian Library record, 5 (1954), 73-79.

Deals with history, catalogs, classification, and statistics of holdings.

3204. British Museum, Dept, of Oriental Printed Books and Manuscripts. The catalogues of the Oriental printed books and manuscripts, by Frank C. Francis.

London: The Trustees of the British Museum, 1959. 15p.

3205. Buchthal, Hugo, and Kurz, Otto. "A hand list of illuminated Oriental Christian manuscripts." London: Warburg Institute, 1942. 120p.

Locations in British and foreign libraries.

3206. Cambridge, University, King's College Library. Catalogue of the Oriental manuscripts in the Library of King's College, Cambridge. Cambridge, 1867. 27p. (Royal Asiatic Society publication)

3207. ———, Library. A descriptive catalogue of the Oriental mss. belonging to the late E. G. Browne, by Edward G. Browne. Cambridge: Univ. Pr., 1932. 325p.

Records 468 manuscripts deposited in University of Cambridge Library in 1926.

3208. Glasgow, University, Library. Catalogue of the James Robertson collection of works on Oriental literature and history. Glasgow, 1938-39. Unpaged.

3209. ———. "Catalogue of the Oriental mss. in the Library of the University of Glasgow," by J. Robson. In: Presentation volume to William Barron Stevenson, ed. by C. J. Mullo Weir. Glasgow, 1945, v.3, p.116-17. (Studia semitica et orientalia)

3210. John Rylands Library. "The Oriental manuscript collections in the John Rylands Library," by F. Taylor. Bulletin of the John Rylands Library, Manchester, 54 (1972), 449-78.

Summary arranged by languages.

3211. Pearson, J. D. Oriental manuscript collections in the libraries of Great Britain and Ireland. London: Royal Asiatic Society, 1954. 90p.

Summarizes holdings of libraries by languages and contains numerous citations to catalogs and other sources of information.

3212. Royal Asiatic Society Library. "Catalogue of the Arabic, Persian, Hindustani, and Turkish mss. in the Library of the Royal Asiatic Society," by Oliver Codrington. Journal of the Royal Asiatic Society, 1892. p.501-69.

Describes 455 manuscripts.

3213. ———. "Catalogue of the Tod collection of Indian manuscripts in the possession of the Royal Asiatic Society," by L. D. Barnett. Journal of the Royal Asiatic Society (1940), 129-78.

Describes 128 manuscripts.

3214. Selly Oak Colleges Library. Catalogue of the Mingana collection of manuscripts now in the posses-

sion of the trustees of the Woodbroke Settlement, Selly Oak, Birmingham. (v.1: Syriac and Garshūni manuscripts, by A. Mingana; v.2: Christian Arabic manuscripts and additional Syriac manuscripts; v.3: additional Christian Arabic and Syriac manuscripts; v.4: Islamic Arabic manuscripts.) Cambridge, 1933-50. 4v.

3215. Thompson, J. R. Fawcett. "The Rich manuscripts." British Museum quarterly, 27 (1963), 18-23.

Describes collection of more than 800 Arabic, Persian, Turkish, Syriac, and other manuscripts acquired by British Museum in 1825.

ARABIC

3216. Arberry, A. J. "Hand-list of Islamic manuscripts acquired by the India Office Library, 1936-38." Journal of the Royal Asiatic Society, July 1939, p.353-96.

Detailed descriptions of 75 items.

3217. ———. "Notes on Islamic manuscripts recently acquired by the India Office Library." Islamic culture, 13 (1939), 440-58.

3218. British Museum, Dept. of Oriental Printed Books and Manuscripts. Catalogue of Arabic books in the British Museum, by A. G. Ellis. London: The Museum, 1894-1935. 3v. v.1-2 reprinted, 1967.

v.3, Index, by A. S. Fulton.

3219. ———. Catalogus codicum manuscriptorum orientalium qui in Museo Britannico asservantur, pars secunda, codices arabicos complectens, by W. Cureton and C. Rieu. London, 1846-71. 2pts.

Describes 1,653 Arabic manuscripts, of which 57 are Christian.

3220. ———. A descriptive list of the Arabic manuscripts acquired by the Trustees of the British Museum since 1894, comp. by A. G. Ellis . . . and Edward Edwards. London: The Museum, 1912. 111p.

Indexes of titles of works, names of persons, and numerical index of manuscripts.

3221. ———. Supplement to the catalogue of the Arabic manuscripts in the British Museum, by Charles Rieu. London: The Museum, 1894. 935p.

Arranged by subject groupings, with indexes of titles, personal names, and subjects; describes 1,303 manuscripts.

3222. ———. Supplementary catalogue of Arabic printed books in the British Museum, comp. by

Alexander S. Fulton and A. G. Ellis. London: The Museum, 1926. 1,188 cols.

3223. ————. Second supplementary catalogue of Arabic printed books in the British Museum, 1927-1957, comp. by Alexander S. Fulton and Martin Lings. London: The Museum, 1959. 1,132 cols.

3224. Cambridge, University, Library. A hand-list of the Muhammadan manuscripts, including all those written in the Arabic character, preserved in the Library of the University of Cambridge, by Edward G. Browne. Cambridge: Univ. Pr., 1900. 440p. Supplements 1-2, 1922-52.

Includes descriptions of 1,422 manuscripts in Arabic, Persian, Turkish, Urdu, Pashto, Malay, and Panjabi.

3225. ———— ————. A supplementary hand-list of Muhammadan manuscripts, including all those written in the Arabic character, preserved in the Libraries of the University and Colleges of Cambridge, by Edward G. Browne. Cambridge: Univ. Pr., 1922. 348p.

Records 1,570 manuscripts in Cambridge's university and college libraries.

3226. ———— ————. A second supplementary hand-list of the Muhammadan manuscripts in the University and Colleges of Cambridge, by A. J. Arberry. Cambridge: Univ. Pr., 1952. 82p.

Describes 450 manuscripts in Arabic and Persian.

3227. ————, Trinity College Library. A descriptive catalogue of the Arabic, Persian, and Turkish manuscripts in the Library of Trinity College, Cambridge, by E. H. Palmer . . . with an appendix containing a catalogue of the Hebrew and Samaritan mss. in the same library, by William A. Wright. Cambridge: Deighton, Bell & Co., 1870. 235p.

3228. Chester Beatty Library. The Chester Beatty Library: a handlist of the Arabic manuscripts, by Arthur J. Arberry. Dublin: Hodges Figgis, 1955-66. 8v.

3229. Edinburgh, University, Library. A descriptive catalogue of the Arabic and Persian manuscripts in Edinburgh University Library, by Mohammed Ashraful Hukk, Hermann Ethé, and Edward Robertson. Edinburgh: Printed for the University by Stephen Austin, 1925. 454p.

Annotated listing of 429 works.

3230. India Office Library. A catalogue of the Arabic manuscripts in the Library of the India Office, by Otto Loth. London, 1877. 324p.

Describes 1,050 manuscripts possessed by library in 1876.

3231. ————. Catalogue of the Arabic manuscripts in the Library of the India Office, v.2. London: Oxford Univ. Pr., 1930-37. 3pts.

Continuation of 1877 catalog. In 3pts.: I. Qur'anic literature, by C. A. Storey; II. Sufism and ethics, by A. J. Arberry; III, Fiqh, by Reuben Levy.

3232. ————. Specimens of Arabic and Persian palaeography, selected and annotated by A. J. Arberry. London, 1939. 8p. + 48 facsims.

Plates 1-24 and 48 are in Arabic; the remainder are in Persian.

3233. John Rylands Library. Catalogue of Arabic papyri in the John Rylands Library, by D. S. Margoliouth. Manchester, 1933. 241p. + 40 facsimiles.

Describes 430 items.

3234. ————. Catalogue of the Arabic manuscripts in the John Rylands Library, by A. Mingana. Manchester, 1934. 1,192p.

Describes 818 manuscripts.

3235. Mingana, A. "Brief notes on some of the rarer or unique Arabic and Persian-Arabic manuscripts in the John Rylands Library." Bulletin of the John Rylands Library, 6 (1922), 522-30. Reprinted. 1922. 9p.

ARMENIAN

3236. British Museum, Dept. of Manuscripts. A catalogue of the Armenian manuscripts in the British Museum, by Francis Cornwallis Conybeare; to which is appended a catalogue of Georgian manuscripts in the British Museum, by J. Oliver Wardrop. London: The Museum, 1913. 410p.

Arranged by subject groups; lists 149 manuscripts.

3237. Chester Beatty Library. A catalogue of the Armenian manuscripts, with an introduction on the history of Armenian art, by Sirarpie der Nersessian. Dublin: Hodges Figgis, 1958. 2v.

3238. Oxford, University, Bodleian Library. Catalogue of the Armenian manuscripts in the Bodleian Library, by Sukias Baronian and F. C. Conybeare. Oxford: Clarendon, 1918. 254p.

Describes 124 manuscripts.

3239. Rice, David Talbot. "The illuminations of Armenian manuscript 10 in the John Rylands Library." Bulletin of the John Rylands Library, 43 (1961), 452-58. Reprinted.

ASSAMESE

3240. British Museum, Dept. of Oriental Printed Books and Manuscripts. Catalogue of Assamese books, by J. F. Blumhardt. London, 1906. 8 cols.

BATAK

3241. Voorhoeve, P. "Batak bark books." Bulletin of the John Rylands Library, 33 (1951), 283-98. Reprinted. 1951. 18p.
Includes an annotated list of bark books in John Rylands Library.

BENGALI

3242. British Museum, Dept. of Oriental Printed Books and Manuscripts. Catalogue of Bengali printed books in the Library of the British Museum, by J. F. Blumhardt. London: Longmans, 1886. 150p.

3243. ———. A supplementary catalogue of Bengali books in the Library of the British Museum acquired during the years 1886-1910, comp. by J. F. Blumhardt. London: The Museum, 1910. 470 cols.

3244. ———. Second supplementary catalogue of Bengali books in the Library of the British Museum acquired during the years 1911-1934, comp. by J. F. Blumhardt . . . and J. V. S. Wilkinson. London: The Museum, 1939. 678 cols.

3245. India Office Library. Catalogue of the Bengali and Assamese manuscripts, by James Fuller Blumhardt. London: Oxford Univ. Pr., 1924. 20p.
Describes 27 Bengali and 3 Assamese manuscripts.

3246. ———. Catalogue of the Library of the India Office, v.II pt.IV: Bengali, Oriya, and Assamese books, by J. F. Blumhardt. London: Eyre and Spottiswoode, 1905. 353p.

3247. ———. Catalogue of the Library of the India Office, v.II, pt.IV: supplement, 1906-1920. Bengali books, by J. F. Blumhardt. London: Eyre and Spottiswoode, 1923. 523p.

BURMESE

3248. British Museum, Dept. of Oriental Printed Books and Manuscripts. A catalogue of the Burmese books in the British Museum, by L. D. Barnett. London: The Museum, 1913. 346 cols.
Indexes of titles and subjects.

CHINESE

3249. British Museum. A guide to the Chinese and Japanese illustrated books exhibited in the King's Library. London: W. Clowes, 1887. 16p.

3250. ——— Dept. of Oriental Printed Books and Manuscripts. Catalogue of Chinese printed books, manuscripts and drawings in the Library of the British Museum, by Robert K. Douglas. London: Longmans, 1877. 344p.

3251. ——— ———. Descriptive catalogue of the Chinese manuscripts from Tunhuang in the British Museum, by Lionel Giles. London: The Museum, 1957. 334p.

3252. ——— ———. Les documents Chinois de la troisième expédition de Sir Aurel Stein en Asie Centrale, ed. by Henri Maspero. London: The Museum, 1953. 268p. + 40 plates.

3253. ——— ———. Supplementary catalogue of Chinese books and manuscripts in the British Museum, by R. K. Douglas. London: The Museum, 1903. 224p.

3254. ——— ———. Title index to the descriptive catalogue of Chinese manuscripts from Tunhuang in the British Museum, by E. D. Grinstead. London: The Museum, 1963. 41p.

3255. Cambridge, University, Library. A catalogue of the Wade collection of Chinese and Manchu books in the Library of the University of Cambridge, by Herbert A. Giles. Cambridge: Univ. Pr., 1898. 169p.

3256. ——— ———. Supplementary catalogue of the Wade collection of Chinese and Manchu books in the Library of the University of Cambridge, by Herbert A. Giles. Cambridge: Univ. Pr., 1915. 29p.

3257. Hughes, E. R. "The Bodleian Chinese collection." Bodleian quarterly record, 8 (1936), 227-33.
General description of collection started in 17th century.

3258. India Office Library. A catalogue of the Chinese translation of the Buddhist Tripitaka; the sacred canon of the Buddhists in China and Japan, comp. by Bunyiu Nanjio. Oxford: Clarendon, 1883. 480 cols.
Collection received by India Office Library.

3259. ———. Descriptive catalogue of the Chinese, Japanese, and Manchu books in the Library of the India Office, by James Summers. London, 1872. 70p.
Lists 170 books, a majority Chinese.

3260. Liu, Ts'un Yan. Chinese popular fiction in two London libraries: the British Museum, the Royal Asiatic Society. Hong Kong: Lung Men Bookstore, 1967. 375p.

pt.1 deals with popular Chinese fiction of the Ming and Ch'ing dynasties; pt.2 (in Chinese) consists of bibliographical notes. The Royal Asiatic Society collection is now at the University of Leeds.

3261. Oxford, University, Bodleian Library. A catalogue of Chinese works in the Bodleian Library, by J. Edkins. Oxford, 1876. 46p.

COPTIC

3262. Bonner, Gerald. "The Crum papers." British Museum quarterly, 28 (1964), 59-67.

Large collection of letters on Coptic studies, received from Walter Ewing Crum by British Museum.

3263. British Museum, Dept. of Oriental Printed Books and Manuscripts. Catalogue of the Coptic manuscripts in the British Museum, by W. E. Crum. London: The Museum, 1905. 623p.

Arranged in 3 main divisions according to principal Coptic dialects; detailed indexes; describes 1,252 codices and fragments.

3264. Cramer, Maria. "Some unpublished Coptic liturgical manuscripts in the John Rylands Library." Bulletin of the John Rylands Library, 50 (1968), 308-16. Reprinted.

Descriptive account.

3265. John Rylands Library. Catalogue of the Coptic manuscripts in the John Rylands Library, by W. E. Crum. Manchester, 1909. 273p. + 12 plates.

3266. ———. "New Coptic manuscripts in the John Rylands Library." Bulletin of the John Rylands Library, 5 (1920), 497-503. Reprinted, 1920. 7p.

3267. Till, W. C. "Die Nichtkatalogisierten Coptica der John Rylands Library." Das Antiquariat, Vienna, 8 (1952), nos. 13-18.

ETHIOPIC

3268. British Museum, Dept. of Oriental Printed Books and Manuscripts. Catalogue of the Ethiopic manuscripts in the British Museum acquired since the year 1847, by W. Wright. London: The Museum, 1877. 366p.

3269. ———. Catalogus codicum manuscriptorum qui in Museo Britannico asservantur, pars tertia, codices aethiopicos amplectens, by A. Dillman. London, 1847. 79p.

Describes 82 codices.

3270. Cambridge, University, Library. Catalogue of Ethiopian manuscripts in the Cambridge University Library, by Edward Ullendorf and Stephen G. Wright. Cambridge: Univ. Pr., 1961. 76p.

Describes 67 Biblical texts, service books, theology, homilies, and magical writings manuscripts.

3271. Oxford, University, Bodleian Library. Catalogue of Ethopian manuscripts in the Bodleian Library, by E. Ullendorff. Oxford, 1951. 32p.

Describes 66 additional manuscripts acquired by Bodleian since Dillman catalogue of 1848.

3272. ———. Catalogus codicum manuscriptorum Bibliothecae Bodleianae Oxoniensis. Pars VII: Codices Aethiopici, by A. Dillmann. Oxford, 1848. 87p.

Describes 35 Ethiopic manuscripts owned by the Bodleian in 1848.

GEORGIAN

3273. Blake, Robert P. "Catalogue of the Georgian manuscripts in the Cambridge University Library." Harvard theological review, 25 (1932), 207-24 + 8 plates.

Detailed descriptions of 11 manuscripts.

3274. British Museum, Dept. of Oriental Printed Books and Manuscripts. Catalogue of Georgian and other Caucasian printed books in the British Museum, comp. by David Marshall Lang. London: The Museum, 1962. 430 cols.

Over 3,000 entries with descriptions of books.

GUJARATI

3275. India Office Library. Catalogue of the Gujarati & Rajasthani manuscripts in the India Office Library, by James Fuller Blumhardt, revised and enlarged by Alfred Master. London: Oxford Univ. Pr., 1954. 167p.

HEBREW

3276. British Museum, Dept. of Oriental Printed Books and Manuscripts. Catalogue of Hebrew books in the British Museum acquired during the years 1868-1892. London: The Museum, 1894. 532p.

3277. ———. Catalogue of the Hebrew and Samaritan manuscripts in the British Museum, by G. Margoliouth. London: The Museum, 1899-1935. 4v. Reprinted, 1965.

Samaritan manuscripts not actually included, but are listed in earlier Descriptive list of Hebrew and Samaritan manuscripts, 1893; about 1,300 manuscripts are described in the 4 parts.

3278. ———. Catalogue of the Hebrew books in the British Museum, by Joseph Zedner. London: The Museum, 1867. Reprinted. 1964. 891p.

10,100 bound volumes, comprising works in all branches of Hebrew and rabbinical learning.

3279. ———. Descriptive list of the Hebrew and Samaritan mss in the British Museum, ed. by G. Margoliouth. London: The Museum, 1893. 134p.

3280. Cambridge, University, Girton College Library. Catalogue of the printed books and of the Semitic and Jewish mss. in the Mary Frere Hebrew Library at Girton College, Cambridge, by H. Loewe. Cambridge, 1916. 37p.

Includes descriptions of 46 Hebrew manuscripts.

3281. ———, Library. Catalogue of the Hebrew manuscripts preserved in the University Library, Cambridge, by S. M. Schiller-Szinessy. Cambridge, 1876. 248p. (v.1; no more published.)

In 2 sections: 1, the Holy Scriptures; 2, commentaries on the Bible.

3282. ——— ———. The oldest known literary documents of Yiddish literature, c. 1382, etc., ed. by L. Fuks. Leiden: E. Brill, 1957. 2pts.

Text of ms. codex C.Y. of Cambridge University Library.

3283. ———, Trinity College Library. Catalogue of the manuscripts in the Hebrew character collected and bequeathed to Trinity College Library by the late William Aldis Wright, by Herbert Löewe. Cambridge: Univ. Pr., 1926. 165p.

3284. Guildhall Library. Catalogue of Hebraica and Judaica in the Library of the corporation of the City of London, with a subject index by A. Lowry. London: The Corp., 1891. 231p.

Collection now on loan to University College, London.

3285. Jews' College. Catalogue of the Hebrew manuscripts in the Jews' College, London, comp. by Ad. Neubauer. Oxford: Hart, 1886. 64p. Reprinted, 1969, by Gregg International Publishers.

Collection now held in Library of Court of the Chief Rabbi, London.

3286. ———, Montefiore Library. Descriptive catalogue of the Hebrew mss. of the Montefiore Library, comp. by Hartwig Hirschfeld. London: Macmillan, 1904. 190. Reprinted, 1969, by Gregg International Publishers.

3287. John Rylands Library. Catalogue of an exhibition of Hebrew manuscripts and printed books, together with other items of Jewish interest. Manchester, 1958. 28p. + 17 plates.

3288. Metzger, Mendel. "The John Rylands Megillah and some other illustrated Megilloth of the XVth to XVIIth centuries." Bulletin of the John Rylands Library, 45 (1962), 148-84. Reprinted.

Descriptions of examples in John Rylands and other libraries.

3289. Oxford, University, Bodleian Library. Catalogue of the Hebrew manuscripts in the Bodleian Library and in the college libraries of Oxford, including mss. in other languages, which are written with Hebrew characters, or relating to the Hebrew language or literature; and a few Samaritan mss., comp. by Ad. Neubauer and A. E. Cowley. Oxford, 1886-1906. 2v.

Contains descriptions of 2,918 manuscripts.

3290. ———. A concise catalogue of the Hebrew printed books in the Bodleian Library, by A. E. Cowley. Oxford: Clarendon, 1929. 816p.

Dictionary catalog.

3291. Rosenau, Helen. "Notes on the illuminations of the Spanish Haggadah in the John Rylands Library." Bulletin of the John Rylands Library, 36 (1954), 468-83. Reprinted, 1954. 18p.

3292. Sassoon Library. Descriptive catalogue of the Hebrew and Samaritan manuscripts in the Sassoon Library, London. London, 1932. 2v.

Describes 1,153 manuscripts.

3293. Wallenstein, Meir. "Genizah fragments in the Chetham's Library, Manchester." Bulletin of the John Rylands Library, 50 (1967), 159-77. Reprinted.

HINDI

3294. British Museum, Dept. of Oriental Printed Books and Manuscripts. Catalogue of the Hindi, Panjabi, and Hindustani manuscripts in the Library of the British Museum, by J. F. Blumhardt. London: The Museum, 1899. 84 + 2 + 91 + 1p.

Separate catalogs for Hindi, Panjabi, and Hindustani manuscripts.

3295. ———. Catalogues of the Hindi, Panjabi, Sindhi, and Pushtu printed books in the Library of the

British Museum, by J. F. Blumhardt. London: Quaritch, 1893. 4pts.

3296. ———. A supplementary catalogue of Hindi books in the Library of the British Museum acquired during the years 1893-1912, by J. F. Blumhardt. London: The Museum, 1913. 470 cols.

3297. ———. A second supplementary catalogue of printed books in Hindi, Bihari (including Bhojpuria, Kaurmali and Maithili) and Pahari (including Nepali or Khaskura, Jaunsari, Mandeali, etc.) in the Library of the British Museum, comp. by L. D. Barnett, J. F. Blumhardt, and J. V. S. Wilkinson. London: The Museum, 1957. 1,678 cols.

3298. India Office Library. Catalogue of the Library of the India Office, v.II, pt.III: Hindi, Panjabi, Pushtu, and Sindhi books, by J. F. Blumhardt. London: Eyre and Spottiswoode, 1902. 4pts.

3299. ———. Short catalogue of Hindi manuscripts in the India Office Library, comp. by A. Master. London, n.d. 51*l*. + index.

HINDUSTANI

3300. British Museum, Dept. of Oriental Printed Books and Manuscripts. Catalogue of Hindustani printed books in the Library of the British Museum, by J. F. Blumhardt. London: Longmans, 1889. 458 cols.

3301. ———. A supplementary catalogue of Hindustani books in the Library of the British Museum acquired during the years 1889-1908, by J. F. Blumhardt. London: The Museum, 1909. 678 cols.

3302. India Office Library. Catalogue of the Hindustani manuscripts in the Library of the India Office, by J. F. Blumhardt. London: Oxford Univ. Pr., 1926. 171p.
Records 160 manuscripts.

3303. ———. Catalogue of the Library of the India Office, v.II, pt.II: Hindustani books, by J. F. Blumhardt. London: Eyre and Spottiswoode, 1900. 379p.

INDONESIAN

3304. Cambridge, University, Library. List of Indonesian manuscripts in the University Library, Cambridge, followed by notes about certain college manuscripts, by P. Voorhoeve. Cambridge and Leiden, 1950-54. 17*l*. Supplement. 1954. 3*l*.

3305. London, University, School of Oriental and African Studies. List of Indonesian manuscripts in the Library of the School of Oriental and African Studies, London, comp. by P. Voorhoeve. London, 1950. 18*l*.

IRANIAN

3306. Dhalla, M. N. "Iranian manuscripts in the Library of the India Office." Journal of the Royal Asiatic Society (April 1912), 387-98.
Descriptions of 27 examples.

JAPANESE

3307. British Museum, Dept. of Oriental Printed Books and Manuscripts. Catalogue of Japanese printed books and manuscripts in the British Museum acquired during the years 1899-1903, by Robert K. Douglas. London: The Museum, 1904. 98p.

3308. ———. Catalogue of Japanese printed books and manuscripts in the Library of the British Museum, by Robert Kennaway Douglas. London: The Museum, 1898. 399p.

3309. Cambridge, University, Library. Classified catalogue of modern Japanese books in the Cambridge University Library, by E. B. Ceadel. Cambridge: Heffer, 1962. 552p.
About 6,000 entries.

3310. Chibbett, D. G. "Japanese language collections in British libraries: a general survey." Journal of librarianship, 2 (1970), 175-89.
Reviews current position of British libraries with regard to book buying in Japan, discusses acquisition problems, etc.

3311. Gardner, K. B. "Illustrated manuscripts from Japan." British Museum quarterly, 23 (1961), 95-100.
Describes examples of Japanese works produced between 1600 and 1700, acquired by British Museum.

3312. ———. "Japanese illustrated books of the seventeenth century." British Museum quarterly, 21 (1957), 36-38.
Collection of 87 examples of Japanese block printing acquired by British Museum.

3313. Oxford, University, Bodleian Library. A catalogue of Japanese and Chinese books and manuscripts lately added to the Bodleian Library, by B. Nanjio. Oxford, 1881. 28 cols.

KANNADA

3314. British Museum, Dept. of Oriental Printed Books and Manuscripts. A catalogue of the Kannada,

Badaga, and Kurg books in the Library of the British Museum, comp. by L. D. Barnett. London: The Museum, 1910. 278 cols.

MALAY

3315. Oxford, University, Bodleian Library. Catalogue of Malay manuscripts and manuscripts relating to the Malay language in the Bodleian Library, by Richard Greentree and E. W. B. Nicholson. Oxford, 1910. 20 cols.

Describes 8 Malay manuscripts and 4 works on Malay language.

MALAYALAM

3316. British Museum, Dept. of Oriental Printed Books and Manuscripts. Catalogue of Malayalam books in the British Museum, ed. by Albertine Gaur. London: The Museum, 1971. 464p.

3317. India Office Library. A catalogue of the Malayalam manuscripts in the India Office Library, by Chelnat Achyuta Menon. London: Oxford Univ. Pr., 1954. 29p.

Describes 67 manuscripts, all except 2 on palm leaves.

MARATHI

3318. British Museum, Dept. of Oriental Printed Books and Manuscripts. Catalogue of Marathi and Gujarati printed books in the Library of the British Museum, by J. F. Blumhardt. London: Quaritch, 1892. 23 2+ 196 cols.

Separate catalog for each language.

3319. ———. Catalogue of the Marathi, Gujarati, Bengali, Assamese, Oriya, Pushtu, and Sindhi manuscripts in the Library of the British Museum, by J. F. Blumhardt. London: The Museum, 1905. 4pts. in 1v.

Separate catalogs of: 1. Marathi; 2. Gujarati; 3. Bengali, Assamese, and Oriya; and 4. Pushtu and Sindhi.

3320. ———. A supplementary catalogue of Marathi and Gujarati books in the British Museum, by J. F. Blumhardt. London: The Museum, 1915. 2pts.

Separate catalog for each language.

3321. India Office Library. Catalogue of the Library of the India Office, v.II, pt.V: Marathi and Gujarati books, by J. F. Blumhardt. London: Eyre and Spottiswoode, 1908. 320p.

3322. ———. Catalogue of the Marathi manuscripts in the India Office Library, by James Fuller Blumhardt and Sadashiv Govind Kanhere. Oxford: Clarendon, 1950. 125p.

Records 251 manuscripts.

MONGOLIAN

3323. Bawden, Charles Roskelly. "A first description of a collection of Mongol manuscripts in the University Library, Cambridge." Journal of the Royal Asiatic Society (Oct. 1957), p.151-60 + 4 plates.

Includes 34 texts in Mongolian and 1 in Tibetan.

ORIYA

3324. India Office Library. Catalogue of the Oriya manuscripts in the Library of the Indian Office, by James Fuller Blumhardt. London: Oxford Univ. Pr., 1924. 22p.

Describes 50 manuscripts, 48 of which are on palm leaf.

PALI

3325. India Office Library. Catalogue of Pali mss. in the India Office Library, by Hermann Oldenberg. London: H. Frowde, 1882, p.59-128. (Reprinted from Journal of the Pali Text Society for 1882)

Lists 111 titles.

3326. ———. Catalogue of the Mandalay mss. in the India Office Library, by V. Fausböll. Woking: Gresham Pr., 1897. 52p.

Pali and Burmese manuscripts.

PANJABI

3327. British Museum, Dept. of Oriental Printed Books and Manuscripts. Panjabi printed books in the British Museum; a supplementary catalogue, comp. by L. D. Barnett. London: The Museum, 1961. 121p.

Descriptions of about 1,100 Panjabi and Multani printed books acquired after 1893.

PASHTO

3328. British Museum, Dept. of Oriental Printed Books and Manuscripts. Catalogue of Pashto manuscripts in the libraries of the British Isles: Bodleian Library, the British Museum, Cambridge University Library, India Office Library, John Rylands Library, School of Oriental and African Studies, Trinity College, Dublin, by James Fuller Blumhardt and David Neil Mackenzie. London: The Museum and Commonwealth Relations Office, 1965. 147p.

PERSIAN

3329. British Museum, Dept. of Oriental Printed Books and Manuscripts. Catalogue of the Persian manuscripts in the British Museum, by Charles Rieu. London: The Museum, 1879-83. 3v. Reprinted, 1966.

Contains entries for 2,536 manuscripts.

3330. ———. A catalogue of the Persian printed books in the British Museum, comp. by Edward Edwards. London: The Museum, 1922. 968 cols.

3331. ———. Handlist of Persian manuscripts 1895-1966, by G. M. Meredith-Owens. London: The Museum, 1968. 126p.

Record of about 1,000 manuscripts acquired since 1895 list.

3332. ———. Persian illustrated manuscripts, by G. M. Meredith-Owens. London: The Museum, 1965. 32p. + 24 plates.

3333. ———. Supplement to the Catalogue of the Persian manuscripts in the British Museum, by Charles Rieu. London: The Museum, 1895. 308p.

Describes 425 manuscripts.

3334. Cambridge, University, Library. "Catalogue and description of 27 Bábí manuscripts" [in Cambridge University Library], by E. G. Browne. Journal of the Royal Asiatic Society of Great Britain and Ireland (1892), 433-706.

Persian and Arabic manuscripts relating to Muhammadan sect.

3335. ———. A catalogue of the Persian manuscripts in the Library at the University of Cambridge, by Edward G. Browne. Cambridge: Univ. Pr., 1896. 471p.

Includes 343 manuscripts.

3336. Chester Beatty Library. The Chester Beatty Library: a catalogue of the Persian manuscripts and miniatures. Dublin: Hodges Figgis, 1960. 89p. + 43 plates.

Manuscripts dating from the period 1450-1550.

3337. India Office Library. Catalogue of Persian manuscripts in the Library of the India Office, by Hermann Ethé. Oxford: Clarendon, 1903-37. 2v.

"Volume II, containing additional descriptions and indices . . . revised and completed by Edward Edwards." Describes about 3,200 items.

3338. ———. Catalogue of the Library of the India Office, v.II, pt.VI: Persian books, by A. J. Arberry. London: Secretary of State for India, 1937. 571p.

3339. ———. Catalogue of two collections of Persian and Arabic manuscripts preserved in the India Office Library, by E. Denison Ross and Edward G. Browne. London: Eyre and Spottiswoode, 1902. 189p.

Lists 280 titles; collections transferred to India Office Library by Royal Society.

3340. National Library of Wales. Catalogue of Oriental manuscripts, Persian, Arabic, and Hindustani, comp. by Herman Ethé. Aberystwyth, 1916. 30p.

Describes 24 manuscripts.

3341. Oxford, University, Bodleian Library. Catalogue of the Persian, Turkish, Hindustani, and Pushtu manuscripts in the Bodleian Library; begun by E. Sachau, continued, completed and edited by Hermann Ethé. (pt.III: additional Persian manuscripts, by A. F. L. Beeston.) Oxford, 1889-1954. 3v.

3342. ———. Mughal miniatures of the earlier periods. Oxford, 1953. 8p. + 24 plates. (Bodleian picture book, no.9)

Based on Bodleian collection; Persian manuscripts of 16th-17th centuries.

3343. Robinson, B. W. "Some illustrated Persian manuscripts in the John Rylands Library." Bulletin of the John Rylands Library, 34 (1951), 69-80. Reprinted, 1951. 14p.

Describes periods and styles of some 20 Persian manuscripts, illustrated with miniatures.

PRAKRIT

3344. Oxford, University, Bodleian Library. Catalogue of Prākrit manuscripts in the Bodleian Library, by Arthur B. Keith. Oxford, 1911. 53p.

SAMARITAN

3345. John Rylands Library. Catalogue of the Samaritan manuscripts in the John Rylands Library, Manchester, by Edward Robertson. Manchester: Univ. Pr., 1938-62. 2v.

SANSKRIT

3346. British Museum, Dept. of Oriental Printed Books and Manuscripts. Catalogue of Sanskrit and Pali books in the British Museum, by Ernst Haas. London: Trübner, 1876. 188p.

3347. ———. Catalogue of Sanskrit, Pali, and Prakrit books in the British Museum acquired during the years 1876-92, by Cecil Bendall. London: The Museum, 1893. 624 cols.

3348. ———. Catalogue of the Sanskrit manuscripts in the British Museum, by Cecil Bendall. London: The Museum, 1902. 261p.

Describes 559 manuscripts, in 2pts.: Vedic and Brahmanical literature and Buddhistic literature.

3349. ———. A supplementary catalogue of Sanskrit, Pali, and Prakrit books in the Library of the British Museum, acquired during the years 1892-1906, comp. by L. D. Barnett. London. The Museum, 1908. 1,096 cols.

3350. ———. A supplementary catalogue of the Sanskrit, Pali, and Prakrit books in the Library of the British Museum, acquired during the years 1906-1928, comp. by L. D. Barnett. London: The Museum, 1928. 1,694p.

3351. Cambridge, University, Library. Catalogue of the Buddhist Sanskrit manuscripts in the University Library, Cambridge, by Cecil Bendall. Cambridge: Univ. Pr., 1883, 225p.

Describes 248 manuscripts.

3352. ———, Trinity College Library. A catalogue of Sanskrit manuscripts in the Library of Trinity College, Cambridge, by Th. Aufrecht. Cambridge: Deighton, Bell & Co., 1869. 111p.

3353. Clauson, G. L. M. "Catalogue of the Stein collection of Sanskrit mss. from Kashmir." Journal of the Royal Asiatic Society (1912), 587-627.

Collection received by Indian Institute, Oxford, in 1911.

3354. India Office Library. Catalogue of a collection of Sanskrit manuscripts, by A. C. Burnell. London, 1869. 65p.

3355. ———. Catalogue of the India Office Library, v.II, pt.I: Sanskrit books, rev. ed., by Prana Northa and Jatindra B. Chaudhuri, rev. ed. London: H. M. Stationery Office, 1938-57. 4v.

3356. ———. Catalogue of the Sanskrit (and Prakrit) manuscripts in the Library of the India Office, by Julius Eggeling. ([v.1] pt.4. Sanskrit literature: philosophy and Tantra, by Enrst Windisch and Julius Eggeling. v.2. Arthur Borriedale Keith. With a supplement, Buddhist manuscripts, by F. W. Thomas.) London: Oxford, 1887-1935. 2v.

Describes 8,220 manuscripts.

3357. ———. Catalogue of two collections of Sanskrit manuscripts preserved in the India Office Library, comp. by C. H. Tawney and F. W. Thomas. London: Eyre and Spottiswoode, 1903. 60p.

3358. ———, Foreign and Commonwealth Office. Select accessions in Sanskrit, Pali and Prakrit. London: The Library. Currently issued.

3359. Oxford, University, Bodleian Library. Catalogi codicum manuscriptorum Bibliothecae Bodleianae para octava codices sanscriticos complectens, by Th. Aufrecht. Oxford, 1864. 575p.

Describes 854 Sanskrit manuscripts in Bodleian Library.

3360. ——— ———. A catalogue of photographs of Sanskrit mss. purchased for the administrators of the Max Müller memorial fund, by T. R. Gambier-Parry. London, 1930. 59p.

3361. ——— ———. Catalogue of Sanskrit manuscripts in the Bodleian Library; appendix to v.I (Th. Aufrecht's Catalogue), by Arthur B. Keith. Oxford: Clarendon 1909. 123p.

3362. ——— ———. Catalogue of Sanskrit manuscripts in the Bodleian Library, v.II, begun by Moriz Winternitz, continued and completed by Arthur B. Keith. Oxford: Clarendon, 1905. 350p.

Continues Aufrecht's 1864 catalog, adding items 855-1621.

3363. ——— ———. A catalogue of the Sanskrit manuscripts purchased for the administrators of the Max Müller memorial fund, by T. R. Gambier-Parry. Oxford, 1922. 62p.

3364. ———, Indian Institute Library. A catalogue of the Sanskrit and Prakrit mss. in the Indian Institute Library, by A. B. Keith. Oxford, 1903. 99p.

Describes 162 manuscripts since transferred to Bodleian Library.

3365. Royal Asiatic Society of Great Britain and Ireland Library. "Catalogue of Buddhist Sanskrit manuscripts in the possession of the Royal Asiatic Society," by E. B. Cowell and J. Eggeling. Journal of the Royal Asiatic Society (1876), 1-52.

3366. ———. A catalogue of South Indian Sanskrit manuscripts, especially those of the Whish collection, belonging to the Royal Asiatic Society of Great Britain and Ireland, comp. by M. Winternitz. London, 1902. 340p. (Asiatic Society monographs, v.2)

Describes 215 manuscripts.

3367. Thomas, F. W. "The Aufrecht collection." Journal of the Royal Asiatic Society (Oct. 1908), 1,029-63.

Collection of Sanskrit manuscripts, etc., acquired by India Office Library in 1904.

SAURASHTRA

3368. British Museum, Dept. of Oriental Printed Books and Manuscripts. Catalogue of Saurāshtra books in the Library of the British Museum, comp. by L. D. Barnett. London, The Museum, 1960. 12p.

SINHALESE

3369. British Museum, Dept. of Oriental Printed Books and Manuscripts. Catalogue of the Sinhalese manuscripts in the British Museum, by Don M. de Z. Wickremasinghe. London: The Museum, 1900. 199p.

3370. ———. Catalogue of the Sinhalese printed books in the Library of the British Museum, by Don Martino de Z. Wickremasinghe. London: The Museum, 1901. 308 cols.

SYRIAC

3371. British Museum, Dept. of Oriental Printed Books and Manuscripts. Catalogue of Syriac manuscripts in the British Museum, acquired since the year 1838, by W. Wright. London: The Museum, 1870-72. 3v. 1,352p.

pt.1, Biblical manuscripts and service books; pt.2, theology; pt.3, history, lives of saints, martyrdoms, and scientific literature. Descriptions of total of 1,036 manuscripts, including some of oldest dated books in existence.

3372. ———. Catalogue of Syriac printed books and related literature in the British Museum, comp. by Cyril Moss. London: The Museum, 1962. 1,174, 206, 272 cols.

More than 11,000 items, including periodical articles on Syriac studies in Western languages.

3373. ———. Catalogus codicum manuscriptorum orientalium qui in Museo Britannico asservantur; pars prima, codices syriacos et carshunicos amplectens, by Josiah Forshall and Friedrich Rosen. London: The Museum, 1838. 140p.

3374. ———. Descriptive list of Syriac and Karshuni mss. in the British Museum acquired since 1873, by G. Margoliouth. London: The Museum, 1899. 64p.

3375. Cambridge, University, Library. A catalogue of the Syriac manuscripts preserved in the Library of the University of Cambridge, by William Wright. Cambridge: Univ. Pr., 1901. 2v.

3376. Goodman, Alan Edward. "The Jenks collection of Syriac manuscripts in the University Library, Cam-

bridge." Journal of the Royal Asiatic Society (Oct. 1939), p.581-600.

3377. LeRoy, Jules. "Notes sur trois manuscrits syriaques de la John Rylands Library." Bulletin of the John Rylands Library, 47 (1964), 151-64. Reprinted.

3378. Oxford, University, Library. Catalogi codicum manuscriptorum Bibliothecae Bodleianae, pars sexta, codices syriacos, carshunicos, mendaeos, complectens, by R. Payne Smith. Oxford, 1864. 679p.

Describes 205 Syriac manuscripts owned by Bodleian in 1859.

TAMIL

3379. British Museum, Dept. of Oriental Printed Books and Manuscripts. A catalogue of the Tamil books in the Library of the British Museum, comp. by L. D. Barnett and G. U. Pope. London: The Museum, 1909. 590 cols.

3380. ———. A supplementary catalogue of the Tamil books in the Library of the British Museum, comp. by L. D. Barnett. London: The Museum, 1931. 696 cols.

TELUGU

3381. British Museum, Dept. of Oriental Printed Books and Manuscripts. A catalogue of the Telugu books in the Library of the British Museum, comp. by L. D. Barnett. London: The Museum, 1912. 444 cols.

THAI (SIAMESE)

3382. Cambridge, University, Library. A list of books by the King of Siam, H. M. Mahâ-Vajiravudh, or Râma the Sixth, presented to the Cambridge University Library, by Edward Walter Hutchinson. Cambridge, 1926. 16*l*.

Lists 79 works in Thai.

TIBETAN

3383. Chester Beatty Library. A catalogue of the Tibetan collection, by David L. Snellgrove; and a catalogue of the Mongolian collection, by C. R. Bawden. Dublin: Hodges Figgis, 1969. 110p.

3384. India Office Library. Catalogue of the Tibetan manuscripts from Tun-Huang in the India Office Library, by Louis de la Vallée Poussin. London: Oxford Univ. Pr., 1962. 299p.

Literary (mainly Buddhist) texts and documents; appendix on Chinese manuscripts.

3385. ———. Inventory of the Lhasa collection of Tibetan works amassed by Lieutenant-Colonel L. A. Waddell, 1903-4, and deposited in the India Office Library, comp. by F. W. Thomas. London, n.d. Unpaged. (Manuscript)

3386. Royal Asiatic Society Library. "List of the Tibetan mss. and printed books in the Library of the Royal Asiatic Society, by H. Wenzel." Journal of the Royal Asiatic Society of Great Britain and Ireland (1892), 570-79.

TURKISH

3387. British Museum. Turkish miniatures, by G. M. Meredith-Owens. London, 1969. 32p.

3388. ———, Dept. of Oriental Printed Books and Manuscripts. Catalogue of the Turkish manuscripts in the British Museum, by Charles Rieu. London: The Museum, 1888. 345p.

Contains separate section for Turki or Eastern Turkish manuscripts; lists total of 483 items.

3389. Cambridge, University, Library. A hand-list, arranged alphabetically under the titles of the Turkish and other printed and lithographed books presented by Mrs. E. J. W. Gibb to the Cambridge University Library, comp. by Edward G. Browne. Cambridge: Univ. Pr., 1906. 87p.

3390. Chester Beatty Library. The Chester Beatty Library. A catalogue of the Turkish manuscripts and miniatures, by V. Minorsky. Dublin: Hodges Figgis, 1958. 145p.

3391. Meredith-Owens, G. M. "A sixteenth-century illustrated Turkish manuscript in the John Rylands Library." Bulletin of the John Rylands Library, 48 (1966), 372-80 + 4 plates. Reprinted.

Geography and Maps

General

3392. Birkbeck College Library. Human geography; handlist of books in the College Library, comp. by N. McN. Jackson and others. London, 1970. 134p. (Library publication, no.12)

3393. ———. Urban geography; select list of books in the College Library, comp. by N. McN. Jackson and others. London, 1970. Unpaged. (Library publication, no.27)

3394. British Museum. Catalogue of maps, prints, drawings, etc. forming the geographical and topographical collection attached to the Library of his late Majesty King George the Third and presented by his Majesty King George the Fourth to the British Museum. London, 1829. 373p.

3395. ———. Catalogue of the printed maps, plans, and charts in the British Museum, comp. by R. K. Douglas. London, 1885. 2v.

Dictionary arrangement.

3396. ———, Dept. of Manuscripts. Catalogue of the manuscript maps, charts, and plans and of the topographical drawings in the British Museum, by John Holmes. London: The Museum, 1844-61. 3v. Reprinted, 1962.

Arranged geographically.

3397. ———, Dept. of Printed Books. Catalogue of printed maps, charts and plans; photolithographic edition complete to 1964. London: The Museum, 1967. 15v.

Updates 1885 catalog.

3398. ——— ———. World; an excerpt from the British Museum Catalogue of printed maps, charts and plans. London: The Museum, 1967. 240p.

3399. ——— ———, Map Room. Catalogue of printed maps, charts and plans . . . complete to 1964; corrections and additions. London: The Museum, 1968. 55p.

3400. British Records Association. Loan exhibition of maps and plans. London, 1938. 28p.

Annotated catalogue of 55 items, c. 1376-1938, with locations in public and private collections.

3401. DeVilliers, J. A. J. "Famous maps in the British Museum." Geographical journal, 44 (1914), 168-88.

Discussion of famous early maps held by British Museum.

3402. Edinburgh University Library. Some nineteenth-century travellers; an exhibition held in the Main Library. Edinburgh, 1970. 14p.

Lists 52 annotated titles in library's collections, by continents.

3403. Fordham, H. George. "Note on a series of early French atlases, 1594-1637, presented to the British Museum, 1920." Library, ser.4, 1 (1920), 145-52.

Descriptions of 5 early French atlases and fragments of other atlases received by British Museum.

3404. Geographical Association Library. Library catalogue of the Geographical Association. London: The Association, 1955-68. 4pts.

pt.1, Asia; pt.2, Africa; pt.3, Australia, New Zealand and the Oceans; pt.4, the Americas.

3405. Glasgow, University, Hunterian Library. Exploration and travel; an exhibition of books and manuscripts held in the Hunterian Library, University of Glasgow. Glasgow, 1967. 20p.

Exhibition of 60 works from Marco Polo to David Livingstone.

3406. Harris, C. D., and Fellman, J. D. A union list of geographical serials, 2d ed. Chicago: Univ. of Chicago, Dept. of Geography, 1950. 124p.

Lists over 1,000 titles; includes holdings of Royal Geographical Society and other British, American, and French libraries.

3407. Hereford Cathedral. The world map by Richard of Haldingham in Hereford Cathedral, circa A.D. 1285. London: Royal Geographical Society, 1954. 30p.

Famous 13th-century map preserved in Hereford Cathedral.

3408. ———. The world map in Hereford Cathedral, by A. L. Moir; the pictures in the Hereford Mappa mundi, by Malcolm Letts, 5th ed. Hereford, 1970. 40p.

Detailed analysis of famous 13th-century world map.

3409. International Geographical Union, Commission on Ancient Maps. Mappemondes A.D. 1200-1500, ed. by Marcel Destombes. Amsterdam: N. Israel, 1964. 322p. + 38 plates.

Catalog of more than 1,100 manuscript world maps contained in over 900 manuscripts; locations in British, Continental and American collections.

3410. Leeds, University, Brotherton Library. Travel books; early accounts of travels and voyages, topical and related works in the Brotherton collection. Leeds, 1963. 18*l*. Addenda, 1- . Leeds, 1965- .

3411. London, University, King's College, Map Library, Dept. of Geography. Atlas list. London: The Library, 1972. 19*l*.

"This list gives details of all atlases held in the map library."

3412. Manchester Public Libraries, Commercial Library & Information Department. National and economic atlases available in the Commercial Library. Manchester, 1968. 11p. (Business bibliographies, 5)

3413. Manchester, University. Catalogue of historical maps, arr. by Dudley L. Mills. Manchester, 1937. 95p.

World list, geographically arranged.

3414. National Maritime Museum Library, Greenwich. Catalogue of the Library. London: H. M. Stationery Office, 1968-71, 3v. in 5pts.

v.1, voyages and travel; v.2, in 2pts., biography; v.3, in 2pts., atlasses and cartography.

3415. Oxford, University, St. John's College Library. "Manuscript maps belonging to St. John's College," by H. M. Colvin. Oxoniensia (1950), 92-103.

3416. Robinson, A. H. W. Marine cartography in Britain; a history of the sea chart to 1855. Leicester: Leicester Univ. Pr., 1962. 222p. + 42 plates.

Detailed listing of charts in appendices; copies located in 11 British libraries.

3417. Royal Geographical Society. Catalogue of Map Room of the Royal Geographical Society. London: John Murray, 1882. 404p.

3418. ——— Library. Catalogue of the Library of the Royal Geographical Society. London. John Murray, 1865. 541p.

3419. ——— ———. Catalogue of the Library of the Royal Geographical Society, containing the titles of all works up to December, 1893, comp. by Hugh Robert Mill. London: The Society, 1895. 833p.

3420. ——— ———. Classified catalogue of the Library of the Royal Geographical Society, to December, 1870. London: John Murray, 1871. 478p.

3421. ——— ———. Current geographical periodicals: a hand-list and subject index of current periodicals in the Library of the Royal Geographical Society. London: The Society, 1961. 19p. (R.G.S. Library series, no.5)

Lists about 700 titles.

3422. ——— ———. New geographical literature and maps. London: The Society, 1951- .

Semiannual listing of new geographical literature and maps received by Royal Geographical Society.

3423. Royal Institution of Chartered Surveyors. Five centuries of maps & map-making; an exhibition. London, 1953. 128p.

3424. ——— Library. Lending Library catalogue, 19th ed. London: The Institution, 1955. 90p.

Library of 25,000 books (2,000 in lending library) on agriculture, topography, surveying, and law.

3425. Skelton, R. A. "King George III's maritime collection." British Museum quarterly, 18 (1953), 63-64.

Charts, atlases, and books owned by British Museum.

3426. ———. "The Royal map collections." British Museum quarterly, 26 (1962), 1-6.

Description and list of early maps and atlases received by British Museum.

3427. University College of Wales Library. A guide to the resources available in geography. Aberystwyth, 1970. 7p. (Handlist, no.12)

3428. Verner, Coolie. A carto-bibliographical study of The English pilot, the fourth book. Charlottesville: Univ. of Va. Pr., 1960. 87p.

Locates copies of The English pilot from 1689 and related works, in English and American libraries.

3429. York Gate Geographical and Colonial Library. Catalogue of the York Gate Library formed by Mr. S. William Silver; an index to the literature of geography, maritime and inland discovery, commerce and colonisation, by Edward Augustus Petherick, 2d ed. London: John Murray, 1886. cxxxii, 333p.

British Isles

GENERAL

3430. Chubb, Thomas. The printed maps in the atlases of Great Britain and Ireland, a bibliography, 1579-1870; and biographical notes on the map makers, engravers and publishers, by T. Chubb and others. London: Homeland Association, 1927. 479p.

All items described are in British Museum.

3431. Doig, Ronald P. "A bibliographical study of Gough's British topography." Edinburgh Bibliographical Society transactions, 4 (1963), 103-36.

Locates copies.

3432. Great Britain, Public Record Office. Maps and plans in the Public Record Office; I. British Isles c. 1410-1860. London: H. M. Stationery Office, 1967. 648p.

Contains 4,173 items.

3433. Huddy, Ernest John. Early printed topographical maps of the counties of England and Wales; a descriptive catalogue. London, 1960. 403l.

Lists and describes 240 maps with locations in British Museum, Royal Geographical Society, Cambridge, Bodleian, etc.

3434. Leeds, University, Brotherton Library. The Harold Whitaker collection of county atlases, roadbooks & maps presented to the University of Leeds; a catalogue, by Harold Whitaker. Leeds, 1947. 143p.

Geographical works relating mainly to England and Wales; arranged chronologically, 16th to 19th century.

3435. National Book League. Mirror of Britain; or, The history of British topography: catalogue of an exhibition. London, 1957. 91p.

Locates copies in public and private libraries.

3436. Oxford, University, Bodleian Library. A catalogue of the books, relating to British topography, and Saxon and Northern literature, bequeathed to the Bodleian Library in . . . MDCCXCIX, by Richard Gough, comp. by Bulkeley Bandinel. Oxford, 1814. 459p.

3437. ———. The large scale county maps of the British Isles, 1596-1850; a union list, by Elizabeth M. Rodger. Oxford, 1960. 52p.

A list of 832 items; copies located in various British and Irish libraries.

3438. ———. The map of Gt. Britain c. A.D. 1360 known as The Gough map, by E. J. S. Parsons. Oxford: Univ. Pr., 1959. 38p. + 2 maps.

3439. Royal Geographical Society. Early maps of the British Isles, A.D. 1000-A.D. 1579. London, 1961. 31p.

Contains 20 plates reproducing maps, each noting location.

3440. Skelton, R. A. County atlases of the British Isles, 1579-1850, a bibliography. London: Carta, 1970. 262p. + 40 plates.

"Locations are given selectively, or to distinguish variant states. Copies in the British Museum are usually recorded."

BEDFORDSHIRE

3441. Bedfordshire County Council. A catalogue of the maps in the Bedfordshire County muniments. Bedford, 1930. 47p.

BIRMINGHAM

3442. Birmingham Public Libraries. Birmingham before 1800; six maps in the Local Studies Library, Birmingham Reference Library. Birmingham: The Libraries, in association with Silk & Terry, Ltd., 1968. Unpaged.

BUCKINGHAMSHIRE

3443. Buckinghamshire Record Office. Catalogue of maps. Aylesbury, 1961. 59l. (Occasional publications, no.3)

Comprehensive catalog of maps, in county Record Office, preceding 1850.

3444. Buckinghamshire Record Society. A hand-list of Buckinghamshire estate maps, comp. by Elizabeth M. Elvey. Chalfont St. Giles, 1963. 60p.

3445. Price, Ursula E. "The maps of Buckinghamshire," Records of Buckinghamshire, 15 (1947-52), 107-33, 182-207, 250-69.

Locates copies.

CARDIGANSHIRE

3446. National Library of Wales. "The Printed maps of Cardiganshire, 1578-1900, in the National Library of Wales; a descriptive list with a tabular index," by M. Gwyneth Lewis. Ceredigion, 2 (1955), 244-76.

CHESHIRE

3447. Stockport Public Libraries. Cheshire maps in the Stockport local history collection. Stockport, 1962. 16p.

List of over 100 maps, 1577-1960.

CORNWALL

3448. Rodger, Elizabeth M. Printed maps of Cornwall, 1576-1800. London, 1956. Unpaged. (Diploma in Librarianship, Univ. of London)

Lists and describes 271 maps with locations in 7 English libraries.

DURHAM

3449. Durham, University, Library. Durham topographical prints up to 1800; an annotated bibliography, by Phyllis M. Benedikz. Durham: G. Bailes, 1968. 88p.

Copies located in 16 English libraries and museums.

3450. ———. Maps of Durham, 1576-1872, in the University Library, Durham, including some other maps of local interest; a catalogue, by Ruth M. Turner. Durham, 1954. 40p. (Durham University Library publications, no.1)

Annotated list of 153 items.

3451. ———. Maps of Durham, 1607-1872; a supplementary catalogue, by A. I. Doyle. Durham, 1960. 16p. (Durham University Library publications, no.1a)

EDINBURGH

3452. Cowan, William. The maps of Edinburgh, 1544-1929, 2d edition, revised, with census of copies in Edinburgh libraries, by Charles B. Boog Watson. Edinburgh: Public Libraries, 1932. 132p.

Copy in Public Library interleaved to show recent accessions.

ENGLAND

3453. Newcastle upon Tyne, University, Library. An exhibition of old maps of North East England, 1600-1865. Newcastle upon Tyne, 1967. 8l. (Publications, extra series, no.7)

3454. Wright, C. E. "Topographical drawings in the Department of Manuscripts, British Museum." Archives, 3 (1957), 78-87.

Relate particularly to English local history; general description of collection.

ESSEX

3455. Essex County Council. Catalogue of maps in the Essex Record Office, 1566-1855, ed. by F. G. Emmison. Chelmsford, 1947. 106p. (Essex Record Office publications, no.3) 1st supplement, 1952. 53p.; 2d supplement, 1964. 52p.; 3d supplement, 1968. 34p.

3456. Essex Record Office. County maps of Essex, 1576-1852: a handlist, comp. by F. G. Emmison. Colchester: Essex County Council, 1955. 20p.

HERTFORDSHIRE

3457. Fordham, Herbert George. Hertfordshire maps: a descriptive catalogue of the maps of the County, 1579-1900. Hertford: Stephen Austin, 1907. 181p. Supplement, 1914. 42p.

Occasional locations.

3458. Hertfordshire County Council. A catalogue of manuscript maps in the Hertfordshire Record Office, by Peter Walne. Hertford, 1969. 156p.

HUNTINGDONSHIRE

3459. Huntingdon County Record Office. Maps in the County Record Office, Huntingdon, comp. by P. G. M. Dickinson. Huntingdon: Huntingdon and Peterborough County Council, 1968. 72p.

3460. Lynam, Edward W. "Maps of the Fenland." In: Page, W., ed. Victoria history of the County of Huntingdon. London, 1926-36. v.3, p.291-306.

Lists 101 items from 1576; locates copies.

IRELAND

3461. Andrews, John. Ireland in maps, an introduction; with a catalogue of an exhibition mounted in the Library of Trinity College, Dublin, 1961, by the Geographical Society of Ireland in conjunction with the Ordnance Survey of Ireland. Dublin: Dolmen, 1961. 36p.

Materials covered deal with history from Ptolemy and Giraldus Cambrensis to current Ordnance Survey maps.

3462. Dunlop, Robert. "Sixteenth-century maps of Ireland." English historical review, 20 (1905), 309-37.

Catalog of maps of Ireland, printed or manuscript, preserved in British Museum, Public Record Office, Trinity College Library (Dublin), etc.

3463. National Library of Ireland. Catalogue of Irish topographical prints and original drawings, by Rosalind M. Elmes. Dublin: Stationery Office, 1943. 255p.

Based upon National Library of Ireland's holdings.

ISLE OF MAN

3464. Manx Museum. Early maps of the Isle of Man; a guide to the collection in the Manx Museum, by A. M. Cubbon. Douglas, 1954. 44p.

LEEDS

3465. Bonser, Kenneth J., and Nichols, Harold. Printed maps and plans of Leeds, 1711-1900. Leeds: Thoresby Society, 1960. 147p. + 12 plates.

Copies located in various collections.

3466. Leeds City Libraries. Surveyors and map makers; catalogue of an exhibition arranged by the Yorkshire Branch of the Royal Institution of Chartered Surveyors and Leeds City Libraries. Leeds: E. J. Arnold & Son, 1955. 52p.

Locates items exhibited in libraries and other collections.

LONDON

3467. British Museum, Dept. of Printed Books. London; an excerpt from the British Museum Catalogue of printed maps, charts and plans. London: The Museum, 1967. 104p.

3468. Crace, Frederick. A catalogue of maps, plans, and views of London, Westminster & Southwark collected and arranged by Frederick Crace; ed. by his son John Gregory Crace. London: Spottiswoode, 1878. 696p.

Collection purchased by British Museum in 1880.

3469. Darlington, Ida, and Howgego, James. Printed maps of London, circa 1553-1850. London: George Phillips & Son, 1964. 257p. + 16 plates.

Locations for 421 maps in 36 British and Continental libraries.

3470. Scouloudi, Irene. Panoramic views of London, 1600-1666; with some later adaptations; an annotated list. London: Library Committee of the Corporation of London, 1953. 87p.

Copies located in British Museum and other libraries.

MERIONETHSHIRE

3471. Lewis, M. Gwyneth. "The printed maps of Merioneth, 1578-1900, in the National Library of Wales; a descriptive list with a tabular index." Journal of the Merioneth Historical and Record Society, 1 (1951), 162-79.

Checklist of 57 items.

NEWCASTLE

3472. Welford, Richard. "Early Newcastle typography, 1639-1800." Archaeologia Aeliana, ser.3, 3 (1906), 1-134.

Includes list of imprints in chronological order, with locations in various libraries.

NORFOLK

3473. Chubb, Thomas, and Stephen, Geo. A. A descriptive list of the printed maps of Norfolk, 1574-1916, and a descriptive list of Norwich plans, 1541-1914. Norwich: Jarrold & Sons, 1928. 289p.

Locations, chiefly in the Norwich Public Library.

SCOTLAND

3474. Royal Scottish Geographical Society. The early maps of Scotland, with an account of the Ordnance Survey, by Harry R. G. Inglis and others. Edinburgh, 1934. 120p.

3475. ———. The early maps of Scotland, with an account of the Ordnance Survey, 2d ed., ed. by H. R. G. Inglis. Edinburgh, 1936. 171p.

Copies located in 13 British libraries.

3476. ———. Scotland on the map; an exhibition of maps held in the Kelvingrove Museum. Glasgow, 1956. 23p.

Annotated list of 131 items, with locations in public and private collections.

3477. Scottish Record Office. Descriptive list of plans in the Scottish Record Office, by Ian H. Adams. Edinburgh: H. M. Stationery Office, 1966-70. 2v.

Arranged by localities and by dates.

3478. Taylor, Alexander B. "Some additional early maps of Scotland." Scottish geographical magazine, 77 (1961), 37-43.

Supplements Royal Scottish Geographical Society's 1936 list, edited by Inglis.

SHEFFIELD

3479. Sheffield City Libraries.A guide to the Fairbank collection of maps, plans and surveyors' books and correspondence in the Reference Library. Sheffield, 1936. 22p.

SHROPSHIRE

3480. British Museum, Dept. of Manuscripts. Shropshire topographical manuscripts in the British Museum. (Extracted from the British Museum Class catalogue of mss.) London, 1890. 29p.

SOUTHAMPTON

3481. Southampton Corporation. Southampton maps from Elizabethan times. Southampton, 1964. 92p. +11 plates + 14 maps.

SURREY

3482. Royal Institution of Chartered Surveyors, Surrey County Branch. The story of Surrey in maps; catalogue of an exhibition. Kingston-upon-Thames, 1956. 63p.

Items exhibited located in public and private collections.

SUSSEX

3483. Gerard, Ethel. "Notes on some early printed maps of Sussex and their makers; with special reference to those in the Worthing Reference Library." Library, ser.3, 6 (1915), 252-75.

General summary, with references to locations.

WALES

3484. Cardiff Free Public Library and Museum. Beautiful Britain exhibition . . . handlist of manuscript tours in Wales, original drawings and sketch books, and illustrated works on the scenery of Wales in the Cardiff Public Library, ed. by Wyndham Morgan. Cardiff, 1933. 38p.

3485. Evans, David Glyn. Bibliography and location list of topographical prints of Wales and Monmouthshire located within the Principality. London, 1970. 843*l.* (Thesis, Library Association Fellowship)

Locations in 32 Libraries for 6,602 items.

WARWICKSHIRE

3486. Harvey, P. D. A., and Thorpe, Harry. The printed maps of Warwickshire, 1576-1900. Warwick: Records and Museum Committee of the Warwickshire County Council in collaboration with the University of Birmingham, 1959. 279p.

Based on collections listed on p.68-69, but without locations for individual items.

WORCESTER

3487. Smith, Brian S. "The Dougharty family of Worcester, estate surveyors and mapmakers, 1700-60." Worcestershire Historical Society. Miscellany II, n.s.5 (1967), 138-80. Reprinted.

Copies of maps located in public and private collections.

Non-British

3488. Blakiston, N. "Maps, plans and charts of Southeast Asia in the Public Record Office." Southeast Asian archives, 2 (July 1969), 21-64.

3489. British Museum, Dept. of Printed Books. Cartografía cubana del British Museum; catalogo cronológico de cartas, planos y mapas de los siglos xvi al xix, by Domingo de Figarola-Caneda, 2d ed.. Havana: Biblioteca Nacional, 1910. 21p.

3490. ——— ———, Map Room. Catalogue of maps: Quebec. London, 1908. 22*l.*

List of maps, plans, and views of Quebec Province and city, 1660 to 1908, extracted from British Museum's Catalogue of printed maps.

3491. Geographical Association Library. The Americas: a list of works added to the Geographical Association Library, 1958-1968. Sheffield: The Association, 1968. 32p.

3492. Stevens, Henry. Catalogue of American maps in the Library of the British Museum, Christmas 1856. London: Charles Whittingham, 1859. 17p.

3493. Wheat, James Clements, and Brun, Christian F. Maps and charts published in America before 1800; a bibliography. New Haven and London: Yale Univ. Pr., 1969. 215p.

Annotated list of 915 items; locations in British Museum, Public Record Office, and numerous American libraries.

3494. Wroth, Lawrence C. "The early cartography of the Pacific." Papers of the Bibliographical Society of America, 38 (1944), 87-268.

Lists principal maps from c. 150 to 1798, with locations in British Museum and other European and American libraries.

Mountaineering

3495. Alpine Club. Catalogue of books in the Library of the Alpine Club, by Henry Cockburn. Edinburgh: Univ. Pr., 1899. 223p.

Library relating to mountaineering and allied subjects.

3496. Harris Public Library, Museum and Art Gallery. The delectable mountains; a selection of books on mountains and mountaineering in the stock of the Harris Public Library, Preston. Preston: Preston & District Master Printers' Association, 1953. Unpaged.

3497. National Library of Scotland. Shelf-catalogue of the Lloyd collection of Alpine books. Boston, Mass.: G. K. Hall, 1964. 94p.

Approximately 2,000 titles, mainly in English, dating from late 16th to 20th century.

Genealogy and Heraldry

General

3498. Beddington and Wallington Public Library. Class 929; a hand-list of books on genealogy and heraldry collected under the South Eastern Regional Library System Subject Specialisation Scheme, together with other books pertaining to these subjects in the Library. Wallington, Surrey, 1961. 45p. + author index.

3499. Bond, Maurice. The records of Parliament; a guide for genealogists and local historians. Canterbury: Phillimore, 1964. 54p.

3500. British Museum, Dept. of Manuscripts. Catalogue of the heralds' visitations; with references to many other valuable genealogical and topographical manuscripts in the British Museum, 2d ed. London: J. Taylor, 1825. 128p.

3501. Camp, Anthony J. Willis and their whereabouts; being a thorough revision and extension of the previous work of the same name by B. G. Bouwens. Bridge Place, near Canterbury: Published for Society of Genealogists by Phillimore & Co., 1963. 137p.

Locations in county record offices, etc., arranged by places.

3502. Edinburgh Public Libraries. Scottish family histories: a list of books for consultation in the Reference Library, George IV Bridge, 3d ed. Edinburgh, 1958. 68p.

3503. Ferguson, Joan P. S. Scottish family histories held in Scottish libraries. Edinburgh: Scottish Central Library, 1960. 194p.

List of 2,000 works held in 77 Scottish public, county, university, and special libraries.

3504. Gardner, David E., and Smith, Frank. Genealogical research in England and Wales. Salt Lake City, Utah: Bookcraft, 1956-66. 3v.

Notes on principal genealogical sources for England and Wales (excluding Scotland and Ireland) from 1538 to present.

3505. Gatfield, George. Guide to printed books and manuscripts relating to English and foreign heraldry and genealogy. London: Mitchell and Hughes, 1892. 646p.

Includes heraldic treatises and collections, heraldic visitations, armorials, genealogical collections, parish registers, etc.

3506. Guildhall Library. A list of emigrants from England to America, 1718-1759; transcribed from microfilms of the original records at the Guildhall, London, by Jack and Marion Kaminkow. Baltimore, Md.: Magna Charta Book Co., 1964. 288p.

3507. ———. Parish registers: a handlist. London, 1964-67. 3pts.

pt.1, registers of Church of England parishes within the City of London; pt.2, register of Church of England parishes outside the City of London; pt.3, provisional guide to "foreign registers."

3508. ———. Parish registers, a handlist; pt.II, containing: I. Registers of C of E parishes outside the City of London; II. Non-parochial registers and registers of foreign denominations; III. Burial ground records, 2d ed. London: Library Committee of the Corporation of London, 1970. 25p.

3509. Kaminkow, Marion J. Genealogical manuscripts in British libraries; a descriptive guide. Baltimore, Md.: Magna Charta Book Co., 1967. 140p.

Lists holdings of 279 libraries, with notes on types of manuscripts and references to published guides or descriptions.

3510. Library Association, West Midlands Branch. Genealogy; a survey of the local genealogical material available in the public libraries of Herefordshire,

Shropshire, Staffordshire, Warwickshire and Worcestershire, comp. by Audred Hamsher Higgs and Donald Wright. Birmingham, 1966. 101*l*.

3511. Manchester Public Libraries. Reference library subject catalogue, ed. by G. E. Haslam. Section 929: genealogy. Manchester, 1956-58. 3v.

3512. Newcastle upon Tyne City Libraries. Catalogue of books and tracts on genealogy & heraldry in the Central Public Libraries, by Basil Anderton. Newcastle upon Tyne, 1910. 68p.

3513. Oxford, University, Bodleian Library. Index of persons in Oxfordshire deeds acquired by the Bodleian Library, 1878-1963, by W. O. Hassall. Oxford, 1966. 238p. (Oxfordshire record series, v.45)

3514. Sims, Richard. An index to the pedigrees and arms contained in the Heralds' Visitations and other genealogical manuscripts in the British Museum. London: John Russell Smith, 1849. 330p.

3515. ———. A manual for the genealogist, typographer, antiquary, and legal professor; consisting of descriptions of public records; parochial and other registers; wills; county and family histories; heraldic collections in public libraries, etc. London: John Russell Smith, 1856. 526p.

3516. Society of Genealogists. A catalogue of directories and poll books in the possession of the Society of Genealogists, ed. by J. M. Sims. London, 1964. 41*l*.

3517. ———. A catalogue of parish register copies in the possession of the Society of Genealogists, rev. ed. London, 1963. 70*l*.

3518. ———. A catalogue of parish register copies in the possession of the Society of Genealogists. London: 1969. 78*l*.

3519. ———. Catalogue of the parish registers in the possession of the Society of Genealogists, 2d ed. London: 1937. 80*l*.
Details of 3,533 parishes.

3520. ———. National index of parish register copies, comp. for the Society of Genealogists by Kathleen Blomfield and H. K. Percy-Smith. London, 1939. 90p.
Listing of all copies known to exist in public libraries, record and archeological societies, and private collections.

3521. ———. National index of parish registers. London, 1966- . v.1- . To be completed in 11 volumes.

To include all known copies in libraries and record repositories in England and Wales.

Heraldry

3522. Birmingham City Museum and Art Gallery. Catalogue of an heraldic exhibition at the City Museum & Art Gallery, Birmingham. Birmingham, 1936. 180p.
Lists 1,255 items, with names of lenders, from public and private collections.

3523. College of Arms. The records and collections of the College of Arms, by Anthony Richard Wagner. London: Burke's Peerage, 1952. 84p. + index.
Relate to coats of arms and heraldry.

3524. Heraldry Society. Library and slide collection catalogue. London, 1967. 68p.

3525. Oxford, University, Bodleian Library. The Bodleian Library heraldry; catalogue of an exhibition held in connection with the English Heraldry Society, 1967. Oxford, 1967. 60p. + 24 plates.
Lists and describes in detail 128 exhibits.

3526. Pollard, Alfred W. "The Franks collection of armorial book-stamps." Library, ser.2, 3 (1902), 115-34.
Describes collection of about 300 books, 16th-18th centuries, bearing armorial book-stamps on bindings; acquired by British Museum.

3527. Reid, David. "Notes on the heraldry of the Hunterian manuscripts in the University of Glasgow." Bibliotheck, 3 (1962), 151-64.
Descriptions of heraldic devices in 49 15th-16th-century manuscripts.

3528. Victoria and Albert Museum. A list of works on heraldry, or containing heraldic illustrations in the National Art Library, 3d ed. London: H. M. Stationery Office, 1901. 86p. + 16 plates.

3529. ———. National Art Library . . . classed catalogue of printed books: heraldry, ed. by G. H. Palmer. London: H. M. Stationery Office, 1901. 186p. + 16 plates.

3530. Wagner, Anthony Richard. Aspilogia: being materials of heraldry. I. A catalogue of English medieval rolls of arms. Oxford: Univ. Pr., 1950. 177p. (Harleian Society publications, no.100)
Copies located in British Museum, Bodleian Library, etc.

History

General

3531. Clark, G. K., and Elton, G. R. Guide to research facilities in history in the universities of Great Britain and Ireland, 2d ed. Cambridge: Univ. Pr., 1965. 55p.

Describes resources of 36 universities.

3532. Glasgow, University, Library, A select list of serials in the field of history, 1967-68. Glasgow, 1968. 86p.

Exact holdings shown.

3533. Historical Association. Library catalogue. London, 1967. 142p.

Subject and geographical arrangement, with index of authors.

3534. ———. Permanent exhibition of textbooks; acquisition list, August 1964-September 1966. London, 1966. 12p.

3535. Historical Society of Great Britain. Catalogue of the Library of the Royal Historical Society. London, 1915. 83p.

3536. Owens College Library. Catalogue of the Freeman Library presented to the Owens College, comp. by James Tait. Manchester: T. Sowler, 1894. 329p.

Historical library now held by Manchester University Library.

3537. York, University, Library. Select list of reference and bibliographical material on historical and geographical subjects. York, 1968. 53p. (Library guide, no.1)

World Wars I and II

3538. Acton Public Libraries. The Great War, 1914-1918; a list of books available at Acton Public Libraries, December, 1964, comp. by J. W. Thirsk. Acton, 1964. 12p.

3539. British Museum, Dept. of Printed Books. Subject index of the books relating to the European war 1914-1918 acquired by the British Museum, 1914-1920. London: The Museum, 1922. 196p.

3540. Great Britain, Public Record Office. The Second World War; a guide to documents in the Public Record Office. London: H. M. Stationery Office, 1972. 303p. (Public Record Office Handbook, no.15)

Arranged by ministries, departments, etc.

3541. Imperial War Museum Library. The East African theatre, 1940-1941; a bibliography of selected references to the naval, military and air operations in East Africa. London, 1970. 15l. (Booklist, no.1350)

3542. ———. Finland 1939-1940; a list of selected references. London, 1971. 4l. (Booklist, no.1353)

3543. ———. First World War, Gallipoli Campaign. [A catalogue of books available at the Library.] London, 1951. 12p.

3544. ———. The First World War, 1914-1918; Gallipoli and the Dardanelles, 1915; a list of selected references. London, n.d. 8p. (Booklist, no.1235)

3545. ———. The German occupation of the Netherlands. London, n.d. 3l. (Booklist, no.1315)

3546. ———. Germans against Hitler and the plot of 20th July 1944. London, n.d. 4l. (Booklist, no.1044)

3547. ———. Guide books to the Western Front, Belgium and France 1914-1918. (Booklist, no.1105)

3548. ———. Military operations—Soviet theatre, 1939-1945. London, 1954. 14p.

3549. ———. Personal experiences, 1914-1918; German accounts that have been translated into English. London, n.d. 5l. (Booklist, no.1017)

3550. ———. Second World War: airborne operations; excluding histories of operations in which airborne troops operated, i.e., Bruneval, Normandy, Arnhem, Rhine, etc. London, 1954. 11p.

3551. ———. Second World War; German occupation of the Channel Islands. London, n.d. 5p. (Booklist, no.1242)

3552. ———. Second World War military operations; the North African campaign. London, 1966. 6p.

3553. ———. Second World War, Pacific theatre: military operations. [A list of books available in the Library.] London, 1953. 11p.

3554. ———. Second World War; Yugoslavia; selected list of references. London, 1965. 13p. (Booklist, no.1236)

3555. ———. The Zeebrugge and Ostend raids, April-May, 1918; a list of selected references. London, 1961. 6l. (Booklist, no.1239)

Ancient

3556. Birkbeck College Library. Ancient history—Greece and Rome; handlist of books on Greek and Roman history of the classical period in the College Library, comp. by P. Woudhuysen. London, 1970. 112p. (Library publication, no.4)

3557. British Museum, Dept. of Egyptian and Assyrian Antiquities. Catalogue of the cuneiform tablets in the Kouyarjik collection of the British Museum, by C. Bezold. London, 1889-1914. 6v.

3558. Chester Beatty Library. Papyri from Panopolis in the Chester Beatty Library, Dublin, ed. by T. C. Skeat. Dublin: Hodges Figgis, 1964. 194p. (Chester Beatty monographs, no.10)

3559. Fish, T. "Some Sumerian tablets in the John Rylands Library." Bulletin of the John Rylands Library, 8 (1924), 406-11. Reprinted, 1924. 6p.
Descriptions of 9 tablets.

3560. John Rylands Library. Catalogue of the Demotic papyri in the John Rylands Library, Manchester, with facsimiles and complete translations, by F. Ll. Griffith. Manchester, 1909. 3v.

3561. ———. Catalogue of the Sumerian tablets in the John Rylands Library, by T. Fish and others. Manchester, 1932. 160p.

3562. ———. Sumerian tablets from Umma in the John Rylands Library, Manchester, transcribed, transliterated, and translated by C. L. Bedale. Manchester: Univ. Pr.; London: Longmans, Bernard Quaritch, 1915. 16p.

3563. Manchester Egyptian and Oriental Society. Books on Egyptology. Manchester: William Morris, 1913. 14p.
Locates copies in University of Manchester, John Rylands Library, Manchester Public Library, Manchester Museum, and Manchester Egyptian and Oriental Society.

3564. Oxford, University, Bodleian Library. A catalogue of late Babylonian tablets in the Bodleian Library, Oxford, by R. Campbell Thompson. London, 1927. 79l.

3565. ———. Worcester College Library. A catalogue of the books relating to classical archaeology and ancient history in the Library of Worcester College, Oxford. Oxford: Hall and Stacy, 1878-80. 77 + 12 + 8p.

3566. Reymond, Eve A. E. "Studies in the late Egyptian documents preserved in the John Rylands Library." Bulletin of the John Rylands Library, 46 (1963), 154-63; 48 (1966), 433-66; 40 (1967), 464-96.

British

GENERAL

3567. Birkbeck College Library. History; handlist of books on English history, 1460-1603, in the College Library, comp. by J. Cooper. London, 1970. 46p. (Library publication, no.5)

3568. Bock, Friedrich. "Some new documents illustrating the early years of the Hundred Years War (1353-1356)." Bulletin of the John Rylands Library, 15 (1931), 60-83. Reprinted, 1931. 42p.
Based on John Rylands Library manuscripts.

3569. Brighton Public Library. Regency England: a booklist. Brighton, 1971. 36p. + 4 plates.

3570. British Museum, Dept. of Printed Books, Thomason Collection. Catalogue of the pamphlets, books, newspapers, and manuscripts relating to the Civil War, the Commonwealth, and Restoration, collected by George Thomason, 1640-1661. London: The Museum, 1908. 2v. Reprinted, 1969.

3571. Davies, A. A student's guide to the manuscripts relating to English history in the seventeenth century in the Bodleian. London, 1922. 32p. (Helps for students of history, no.47)

3572. East Anglia, University, Library. Periodicals and sets relating to British history in Norfolk and Suffolk libraries; a finding list. Norwich, in conjunction with the Centre of East Anglian Studies, 1971. 143p.

In 2 sections: national printed sources and local printed sources: locations in 28 libraries.

3573. Hardy, Thomas Duffus. Descriptive catalogue of materials relating to the history of Great Britain and Ireland to the end of the reign of Henry VII. London: Longmans, Green, 1862-71. 3v. in 4 pts.

From the Roman period to A.D. 1327; includes many manuscript chronicles, etc., in British Museum.

3574. Hastings Public Library. The Norman Conquest. Hastings, 1966. 28p.

Selective book list.

3575. Lyde, R. G. "Jacobite leaflets and pamphlets." British Museum quarterly, 19 (1954), 31-32.

Describes collection of over 100 Jacobite and anti-Jacobite items, mainly published in Scotland, acquired by British Museum.

3576. Mullins, E. L. C. Texts and calendars; an analytical guide to serial publications. London: Royal Historical Society, 1958. 674p.

"Guide to printed texts and calendars relating to English and Welsh history issued in general collections or in series by a public body or private society before the end of March 1957; the volumes it describes are, with few exceptions, part of the library of the Royal Historical Society, London."

3577. National Book League. Restoration life and letters; an exhibition. London, 1960. 44p.

Classified short-title catalog.

3578. National Library of Scotland, Edinburgh. Shelf-catalogue of the Blaikie collection of Jacobite pamphlets, broadsides and proclamations. Boston: G. K. Hall, 1964. 42l.

Records 754 titles.

3579. Sheffield, University, Library. Unrecorded Civil War tracts, 1641-1649, held in Sheffield University Library, by Alison Hanbidge. Sheffield, 1970. 93l.

ARCHIVES AND MANUSCRIPTS

3580. Barnes, Thomas G. "The archives and archival problems of the Elizabethan and early Stuart Star Chamber." Journal of the Society of Archivists, 2 (1963), 345-60.

3581. Bibliotheca Lindesiana. A bibliography of royal proclamations of the Tudor and Stuart Sovereigns and of others published under authority, 1485-1714. Oxford: Clarendon, 1910. 2v. (v.5-6 of library's catalog)

v.1, England and Wales; v.2, Scotland and Ireland.

3582. ———. Hand list of a collection of broadside proclamations issued by authority of the Kings and Queens of Great Britain and Ireland. London, 1886. 132p.

Lists 697 items, 1549-1718.

3583. ———. Handlist of proclamations issued by Royal and other constitutional authorities, 1714-1910, George I to Edward VII, together with an index of names and places. Wigan: Roger and Rennick, 1913. 836 + 182p. (v.8 of Bibliotheca Lindesiana Catalogue)

3584. British Museum. The Hamilton papers; letters and papers illustrating the political relations of England and Scotland in the XVIth century, formerly in the possession of the Dukes of Hamilton, now in the British Museum, ed. by Joseph Bain. Edinburgh: H. M. General Register House, 1890-92. 2v.

3585. ———, Dept. of Manuscripts. Facsimiles of ancient charters in the British Museum. London: The Museum, 1873-78. 4v.

Contains facsimiles and transcripts of all charters written in England before the Conquest acquired by British Museum up to date of publication.

3586. ——— ———. Facsimiles of royal & other charters in the British Museum, v.I. William I-Richard I, ed. by George F. Warner and Henry J. Ellis. London: The Museum, 1903. 5p.+50 plates +19p. of indexes.

3587. ——— ———. Magna Carta, by G. R. C. Davis. London: The Museum, 1963. 31p. + 6 plates. Reprinted, 1965.

3588. British Records Association. List of record repositories in Great Britain. London, 1956. 46p. (Reports from Committee, no.5)

List of 155 repositories; no data on collections.

3589. Cambridge, University, Corpus Christi College Library. Guide to an exhibition of historical authorities illustrative of British history, compiled from the manuscripts of Corpus Christi College, Cambridge, by Geoffrey Butler. Cambridge: Univ. Pr., 1920. 16p.

3590. Collins, A. J. "The Lacock Abbey Magna Carta." British Museum quarterly, 16 (1951), 1-2.

Magna Carta of 1225 presented to British Museum in 1945.

3591. Fisher, H. A. L. "Manuscripts in the Bodleian and college libraries in Oxford bearing on English history from 1485 to 1547." Bulletin of the Institute of Historical Research, 1 (1923), 45-48.

3592. Great Britain, Historical Manuscripts Commission. Calendar of the Stuart papers belonging to His Majesty The King preserved at Windsor Castle. London: H. M. Stationery Office, 1902-23. 7v. (Report, no.56)

Papers formerly property of James III and his sons Charles Edward and Henry, Cardinal Duke of York.

3593. —— ——. Manuscripts and men. London: H. M. Stationery Office, 1969. 197p.

"An exhibition of manuscripts, portraits and pictures held at the National Portrait Gallery, London, June-August 1969, to mark the centenary of the Royal Commission on Historical Manuscripts, 1869-1969." Annotated list of 198 items with index of lenders.

3594. —— ——. "Materials for English diplomatic history, 1509-1783, calendared in the Reports of the Historical Manuscripts Commission, with references to similar materials in the British Museum." Eighteenth report of the Royal Commission on Historical Manuscripts, Appendix II, p.357-402, by F. G. Davenport. London: H. M. Stationery Office, 1917. 46p.

3595. —— ——. The Prime Ministers' papers, 1801-1902; a survey of the privately preserved papers of those statesmen who held the office of Prime Minister during the 19th century, by John Brooke. London: H. M. Stationery Office, 1968. 79p.

Locations in libraries and other depositories.

3596. —— ——. Record repositories in Great Britain; a list prepared by a joint committee of the Historical Manuscripts Commission and the British Records Association. London: H. M. Stationery Office, 1964. 44p.

3597. ——, Public Record Office. Calendar of Chancery rolls, supplementary close rolls, Welsh rolls, scutage rolls, preserved in the Public Record Office, A.D. 1277-1326. London: H. M. Stationery Office, 1912. 552p.

3598. —— ——. Calendar of Chancery warrants preserved in the Public Record Office . . . A.D. 1244-1326. London: H. M. Stationery Office, 1927. 753p.

Record of privy seals.

3599. —— ——. Calendar of Home Office papers of the reign of George III, 1760-1775, preserved in the Public Record Office, ed. by Joseph Redington and Richard Arthur Roberts. London: Longmans and others, 1878-99. 4v.

3600. —— ——. Calendar of Inquisitions post mortem and other analogous documents preserved in the Public Record Office. London: H. M. Stationery Office, 1904-70. 25v.

Series 1, v.1-15, covers period Henry III-Richard II; 2d series, v.1-3, reign of Henry VIII; calendar of miscellaneous inquisitions, v.1-7, Henry III-Henry V.

3601. —— ——. Calendar of memoranda rolls (Exchequer) preserved in the Public Record Office, Michaelmas 1326-Michaelmas 1327. London: H. M. Stationery Office, 1968. 523p.

3602. —— ——. Calendar of patent rolls preserved in the Public Record Office. London: H. M. Stationery Office, 1891-1966. 76v.

Covers period 1216-1572; patent grants including grants and leases of land, appointments to office, licences and pardons, and other royal acts.

3603. —— ——. Calendar of state papers, colonial series, preserved in Her Majesty's Public Record Office and elsewhere, ed. by W. Noël Sainsbury and others. London: Longmans, 1860-1969. 44v.

Covers East Indies, China and Japan, 1513-1624; East Indies, China and Persia, 1625-34; America and West Indies, 1574-1738.

3604. —— ——. Calendar of state papers, domestic series, preserved in the State Paper Department of Her Majesty's Public Record Office, ed. by Robert Lemon and others. London: Longmans and H. M. Stationery Office, 1856-1925. 91v.

Covers reigns of Edward VI through Anne, 1547-1704.

3605. —— ——. Calendar of state papers, foreign series, preserved in the State Paper Department of Her Majesty's Public Record Office, ed. by William B. Turnbull, Joseph Stevenson and others. London: Longmans and H. M. Stationery Office, 1861-1950. 23v.

Covers period 1547-1590.

3606. —— ——. Calendar of the charter rolls preserved in the Public Record Office. London: H. M. Stationery Office, 1903-27. 6v.

Covers period 1226-1516; charter rolls were royal grants of lands, liberties and privileges to corporations.

3607. ———— ————. Calendar of the close rolls preserved in the Public Record Office. London: H. M. Stationery Office, 1892-1963. 60v.

Covers period 1227-1509; the close rolls contain royal instructions for performance of various acts.

3608. ———— ————. Calendar of the Committee for Compounding with Delinquents, etc., 1643-1660, preserved in the State Paper Department of Her Majesty's Public Record Office, ed. by Mrs. Everett Green. London: H. M. Stationery Office, 1889-93. 5pts.

"Delinquents were those who took the Royalist side in the Civil War or were Papists or Recusants."

3609. ———— ————. Calendar of the fine rolls preserved in the Public Record Office. London: H. M. Stationery Office, 1911-63. 22v.

Covers period 1272-1509; fine rolls were payments for writs, grants, licences, pardons, etc. of various kinds, most of them under the Great Seal.

3610. ———— ————. Calendar of the liberate rolls preserved in the Public Record Office. London: H. M. Stationery Office: H. M. Stationery Office, 1916-64. 6v.

Covers period 1226-1272, reign of Henry III; liberate rolls were orders to officers of the Exchequer to make payments on behalf of the Crown.

3611. ———— ————. Calendar of the Treasury books, 1660-1718, preserved in the Public Record Office, prep. by William A. Shaw. London: H. M. Stationery Office, 1904-62. 32v. in 61pts.

3612. ———— ————. Calendar of Treasury books and papers, ed. by W. A. Shaw. London: H. M. Stationery Office, 1898-1903. 5v.

Covers period 1729-1745.

3613. ———— ————. Calendar of Treasury papers, 1556-1728, preserved in H. M. Public Record Office, prep. by Joseph Redington and W. A. Shaw. London: Longmans and H. M. Stationery Office, 1868-1889. 6v.

3614. ———— ————. Catalogue of manuscripts and other objects in the Museum of the Public Record Office, with brief descriptive and historical notes, 16th ed., comp. by J. H. Collingridge. London: H. M. Stationery Office, 1948. 91p.

Includes various types of documents, from 1199 to 1910, relating to British history.

3615. ———— ————. Catalogue of microfilm, 1967. London, 1967. 94p.

Lists over 5,200 rolls of microfilm reproductions of records currently available.

3616. ———— ————. Catalogue of the Library in the Public Record Office, 3d ed., comp. by T. Craib. London: H. M. Stationery Office, 1902. 573p. Supplement, 1902-8. London, 1909. 281p.

3617. ———— ————. Classes of departmental papers for 1906-1939. London: H. M. Stationery Office, 1966. 39p. (Public Record Office handbook, no.10)

3618. ———— ————. Descriptive list of Exchequer, Queen's remembrancer, port books; pt.I, 1565 to 1700. London, 1960. 566p.

Describes surviving books for Port of London and for each outport from 1565 to 1700—a total of 10,162 separate items.

3619. ———— ————. Diplomatic documents preserved in the Public Record Office. London, 1964-   .

In progress.

3620. ———— ————. Domesday commemoration, 1886; notes on the manuscripts, etc., exhibited at H. M. Record Office. London: Longmans, Green, 1886. 30p.

3621. ———— ————. Exhibition of notable wills. London, 1963. Unpaged.

Lists and describes 52 items, 1399-1818.

3622. ———— ————. Gascon rolls preserved in the Public Record Office, 1307-1317, ed. by Yves Renouard. London, 1962. 660p.

3623. ———— ————. Guide to the contents of the Public Record Office. London: H. M. Stationery Office, 1963-68. 3v.

v.1, legal records, etc.; v.2, state papers and departmental records; v.3, documents transferred, 1960-66.

3624. ———— ————. Guide to the manuscripts preserved in the Public Record Office, by M. S. Giuseppi. London, 1923-24. 2v.

v.1, legal records, etc.; v.2, state papers, etc.

3625. ———— ————. Guide to the various classes of documents preserved in the Public Record Office, by S. R. Scargill-Bird, 3d ed. London, 1908. 460p.

3626. ———— ————. The Hearth tax, 1662-1689; exhibition of records. London, 1962. Unpaged.

3627. ———— ————. Justices of the Peace, 1361-1961; exhibition of records. London, 1961. Unpaged.

List describes 55 items.

3628. ———— ————. Letters and papers, foreign and domestic of the reign of Henry VIII, preserved in the Public Record Office, the British Museum, and elsewhere. London: H. M. Stationery Office, 1864-1932. 22v. in 37pts.

3629. ———— ————. List and analysis of state papers, foreign series, Elizabeth I, preserved in the Public Record Office, ed. by Richard Bruce Wernham. London: H. M. Stationery Office, 1964-69. 2v.

Covers period 1589-91.

3630. ———— ————. List of Cabinet papers, 1880-1914. London: H. M. Stationery Office, 1964. 143p. (Public Record Office handbooks, no.4)

3631. ———— ————. List of Cabinet papers, 1915 and 1961. London: H. M. Stationery Office, 1966. 112p. (Public Record Office handbooks, no.9)

3632. ———— ————. List of Colonial Office confidential print to 1916. London: H. M. Stationery Office, 1961. 179p. (Public Record Office handbooks, no.8)

3633. ———— ————. List of documents relating to the Household and Wardrobe, John to Edward I. London: H. M. Stationery Office, 1964. 148p. (Public Record Office handbooks, no.7)

3634. ———— ————. List of papers of the Committee of Imperial Defence to 1914. London: H. M. Stationery Office, 1964. 46p. (Public Record Office handbooks, no.6)

3635. ———— ————. A list of wills, administrations, etc., in the Public Record Office, London, England, 12th-19th century. Baltimore, Md.: Magna Carta Book Co., 1968. 158p.

3636. ———— ————. Privy Council registers preserved in the Public Record Office; 1 June-31 October 1637. London, 1967- .

In progress.

3637. ———— ————. The records of the Cabinet Office to 1922. London: H. M. Stationery Office, 1966. 52p. (Public Record Office handbooks, no.11)

3638. ———— ————. The records of the Colonial and Dominions Offices, by R. B. Pough. London: H. M. Stationery Office, 1964. 119p. (Public Record Office handbooks, no.3)

3639. ———— ————. The records of the Foreign Office, 1782-1939. London: H. M. Stationery Office, 1969. 180p. (Handbooks, no.13)

3640. ———— ————. The records of the Forfeited Estates Commission. London: H. M. Stationery Office, 1968. 147p. (Public Record Office handbooks, no.12)

3641. ———— ————. Treaties: catalogue of an exhibition at the Public Record Office. London: H. M. Stationery Office, 1948. 46p.

Lists 52 representative treaty documents from 1197 to 1934.

3642. John Rylands Library. Court rolls, rentals, surveys, and analogous documents in the John Rylands Library, Manchester, by Frank Taylor. Manchester, 1948. 44p. (Reprinted from the Bulletin of the John Rylands Library)

3643. ————. Hand-list of charters, deeds, and similar documents in the possession of the John Rylands Library, by Robert Fawtier. Manchester: Univ. Pr., 1925. 159p.

Includes "Documents of which the provenance has been ascertained."

3644. ————. Hand-list of charters, deeds, and similar documents in the possession of the John Rylands Library; miscellaneous documents acquired by gift or purchase, by Moses Tyson. Manchester: Univ. Pr., 1935. 192p.

3645. ————. Hand-list of charters, deeds, and similar documents in the possession of the John Rylands Library; miscellaneous documents acquired by gift or purchase, by Frank Taylor. Manchester: Univ. Pr., 1937. 96p.

3646. ————. Hand-list of the Arderne deeds deposited in the John Rylands Library, by Frank Taylor. Manchester, 1955. 58l.

3647. ————. Hand-list of the Bagshawe muniments deposited in the John Rylands Library, by F. Taylor Manchester: Univ. Pr., 1955. 143p. (Reprinted from the Bulletin of the John Rylands Library with the addition of an index of persons and places, a reissue)

3648. ————. Hand-list of the Clowes deeds in the John Rylands Library, by F. Taylor. Manchester 1947. 116, 33l.

3649. ————. The Hatton Wood manuscripts in the John Rylands Library, by F. Taylor. Manchester: Univ. Pr., 1940. 25p. (Reprinted from the Bulletin of the John Rylands Library, 24, October 1940, no.2)

Collection of charters and deeds, transferred to University of Keele Library.

3650. Joint Committee of the Historical Manuscripts Commission and the British Records Association. Record repositories in Great Britain: a list prepared by a Joint Committee of the Historical Manuscripts Commission and the British Records Association, 2d ed. London: H. M. Stationery Office, 1966. 49p.

Directory of about 150 repositories, with data on facilities and services.

3651. London, University, Library. Catalogue of the collection of English, Scottish, and Irish proclamations in the University Library. (Goldsmiths' Library of Economic Literature) London: Univ. of London Pr., 1928. 99p.

List of 429 items, 1575-1797, with detailed annotations; copies located also in other British libraries.

3652. ———. Catalogue of the collections of proclamations and broadsides in the University Library (Goldsmiths' Library of Economic Literature). London: Univ. of London Pr., 1930. 201p.

Describes 679 items in detail; copies located in 15 British libraries.

3653. Madan, Falconer. "The Bodleian copies of the confirmations by Henry III of Magna Charta, with special reference to their seals." Bodleian quarterly record, 7 (1934), 512-14.

Description of 3 copies of Henry III confirmations of Magna Charta, 1216-17, in Bodleian Library.

3654. Oxford, University, Bodleian Library. Calendar of charters and rolls preserved in the Bodleian Library, ed. by W. H. Turner. Oxford: Clarendon, 1878. 849p.

Arranged under areas of Britain.

3655. ——— ———. Calendar of the Clarendon state papers, preserved in the Bodleian Library, ed. by O. Ogle and others. Oxford: Clarendon, 1872-1970. 5v.

Covers period 1523-1726; papers consist principally of Clarendon's correspondence as lord chancellor. and king's chief minister.

3656. ——— ———. The Crawford collection of early charters and documents now in the Bodleian Library, ed. by A. S. Napier and W. H. Stevenson. Oxford, 1895. 167p.

3657. ———, Christ Church. Calendar of the private Foreign Office correspondence of Robert, Third Marquess of Salisbury. 1878-1880, 1885-1886, 1887-1892, 1895-1900, prep. by J. F. A. Mason. Oxford, 1963. 2v.

Papers of Secretary of State for Foreign Affairs, 10,958 items, now arranged and deposited in Christ Church, Oxford.

3658. Routledge, Frederick James. "Manuscripts at Oxford relating to the late Tudors, 1547-1603." Transactions of the Royal Historical Society, 3d ser., 8 (1914), 119-59.

3659. Sawyer, P. H. Anglo-Saxon charters; an annotated list and bibliography. London: Royal Historical Society, 1968. 538p.

Records 1,875 items with locations.

3660. Skeat, T. C. "Letters from the reign of Henry VIII." British Museum quarterly, 21 (1957), 4-8.

Describes group of 43 16th-century letters addressed for most part to Henry, Lord Clifford (d. 1523) and his son Henry; in British Museum.

3661. Slatter, M. D. Lists of the records of the Court of Arches, deposited for temporary safe keeping in the Bodleian Library in 1941. Oxford, 1951. 26p.

BRITISH CORONATIONS

3662. British Museum. Coronation exhibition; manuscripts, printed books, prints, drawings and medals exhibited in the King's Library of the British Museum. London, 1902. 47p.

Annotated list of 87 items, 925-1838.

3663. ———. Coronation exhibition; manuscripts, printed books, medals, prints and drawings shown in the King's Library of the British Museum. London, 1937. 61p.

3664. Cambridge, University, Corpus Christi College. Coronation exhibition: a selection of Parker manuscripts illustrating the history of the English Coronation Order. Cambridge, 1937. 8p.

Annotated catalog of 21 items.

3665. Durham Cathedral Library. A coronation exhibition in Durham Cathedral Library, May to September, 1953. Durham, 1953. 16p.

3666. Glasgow, University, Hunterian Library. Splendours and miseries: an exhibition of festival books and commemorative albums; held in the Hunterian Library, University of Glasgow. Glasgow, 1967. 19p.

Records 47 items, annotated.

3667. National Book League. The Festival of Britain; exhibition of books arranged by the National Book League at the Victoria & Albert Museum, comp. by John Hadfield. London: Cambridge Univ. Pr., 1951. 192p.

Annotated list of 782 items, with locations in numerous British and American public and private collections.

Scottish

3668. Aberdeen, University, Library. Catalogue of the books in the Wilson Archaeological Library in Marischal College. Aberdeen: Univ. Pr., 1894. 18p.

3669. ———. Macbean collection; a catalogue of books, pamphlets, broadsides, portraits, etc., in the

Stuart and Jacobite collection gathered together by W. M. Macbean, comp. by Mabel D. Allardyce. Aberdeen: Univ. Pr., 1949. 307p. (Aberdeen University studies, no.126)

3670. British Records Association. Handlist of Scottish and Welsh record publications; the Scottish section by Peter Gouldesbrough and A. P. Kup; the Welsh section by Idwal Lewis. London, 1954. 34p. (Publications pamphlet, no.4)

3671. Edinburgh, University, Library. Calendar of the Laing charters, A.D. 854-1837, belonging to the University of Edinburgh, ed. by John Anderson. Edinburgh: James Thin, 1899. 1,053p.

Listing of over 3,000 charters, mainly Scottish, left to Edinburgh University by David Laing.

3672. ———. "Edinburgh manuscripts in the possession of the University of Edinburgh Library." Book of the Old Edinburgh Club, 31 (1962), 168-70.

List of manuscript material in the University Library relating to history of Edinburgh.

3673. ———. Franco-British historians conference: special exhibitions National Library of Scotland, General Register House, University Library. Edinburgh, 1954. 15p.

Listing of books and manuscripts on relations between France and Scotland, etc.

3674. Glasgow, University, Library. Catalogue of a collection of books and manuscripts relating to the Darien scheme presented to the University of Glasgow by Mr. J. J. Spencer. Glasgow: Jackson, Wylie, 1932. Unpaged. (Glasgow University publications)

3675. Great Britain, Public Record Office. Calendar of documents relating to Scotland preserved in Her Majesty's Public Record Office, London, ed. by Joseph Bain. Edinburgh: H. M. General Register House, 1881-88. 4v.

Covers period, 1108-1509.

3676. ———. Calendar of the state papers relating to Scotland preserved in the State Paper Department of Her Majesty's Public Record Office, by Markham John Thorpe. London: Longmans, 1858. 2v.

Relates to reigns of Henry VIII, Edward VI, Mary, and Elizabeth and to Mary Queen of Scots.

3677. Harvey, P. D. A. "Three Scottish documents of the sixteenth century." British Museum quarterly, 25 (1962), 79-82.

Describes letters from Henry VIII to James V, Queen Regent Mary of Guise, and James VI in British Museum.

3678. Imrie, John, and Simpson, Grant G. Local archives of Great Britain: XV. "Local and private archives of Scotland, pts.1-2." Archives, 3 (1958), 135-47, 219-30.

Summary of holdings of principal collections.

3679. Ogilvie, James D. "A bibliography of the Bishops' Wars, 1639-40." Glasgow Bibliographical Society records, 12 (1936), 21-40.

Ogilvie collection now in Glasgow University Library.

3680. Rosebery, Eva. "Unfamiliar libraries VII: Barnbougle Castle." Book collector, 11 (1962), 35-44.

Of special interest for Scottish books and manuscripts.

3681. Scotland, Public Record Office. The Border papers; calendar of letters and papers relating to the affairs of the borders of England and Scotland preserved in Her Majesty's Public Record Office, London, ed. by Joseph Bain. [1560-1603.] Edinburgh, 1894-96. 2v.

3682. ———. Calendar of documents relating to Scotland preserved in Her Majesty's Public Record Office, London, ed. by Joseph Bain. A.D. 1108-1272 (-1357-1509.) Edinburgh, 1881-88. 4v.

3683. ———. Calendar of the State Papers relating to Scotland and Mary Queen of Scots 1547-1603, preserved in the Public Record Office, the British Museum, and elsewhere in England, ed. by Joseph Bain. (v.3-9 edited by William K. Boyd; v.10 by W. K. Boyd and Henry W. Meikle; v.11 [etc.] by Annie I. Cameron.) Edinburgh: H. M. General Register House, 1898-1969. 13v. in 14pts.

3684. ———. A guide to the public records of Scotland deposited in H. M. General Register House, Edinburgh, by M. Livingstone. Edinburgh: H. M. General Register House, 1905. 233p.

Descriptive lists of various classes of public documents.

3685. ———. List of gifts and deposits, v.I. Edinburgh: H. M. Stationery Office, 1971. 122p.

Private archives, consisting mainly of family records, but also some business archives and miscellaneous documents.

3686. ———. Official guide to the documents exhibited in the Historical Museum of Register House, Edinburgh, prep. by H. M. Paton. Edinburgh: H. M. Stationery Office, 1949. 28p.

3687. ———. Official guide to the documents exhibited in the Historical Museum of the Register House, Edinburgh, 2d ed. Edinburgh, 1959. 30p.

3688. Scott, John. A bibliography of printed documents and books relating to the Scottish Company, commonly called the Darien Company, with additions and corrections by George P. Johnston. Edinburgh, 1906. 75p.

Some locations of copies.

3689. Terry, Charles Sanford. An index to the papers relating to Scotland, described or calendared in the Historical Mss. Commission's reports. Glasgow: James MacLehose and Sons, 1908. 62p.

Lists and describes 78 collections in various locations.

Welsh

3690. Breconshire County Libraries. Books on Wales at the Breconshire County Libraries. Brecon, 1960. 28p.

Excludes books written exclusively in Welsh and books classed as pure literature (poetry, plays, novels, etc.).

3691. British Museum, Dept. of Manuscripts. A catalogue of the manuscripts relating to Wales in the British Museum, comp. and ed. by Edward Owen. London, 1900-22. 4v. (Cymmrodorion record series, no.4)

3692. Cardiff Public Libraries. Catalogue of an exhibition of manuscripts, documents, maps, etc., illustrating the history and topography in Wales. Cardiff, 1931. 30p.

3693. ———. Catalogue of historical works and historical novels relating to Wales. Cardiff, 1909. 30p.

3694. ———. Catalogue of printed literature in the Welsh Department, by John Ballinger and James Ifano Jones. Cardiff: Free Libraries Committee, 1898. 559p.
  Classified arrangement.

3695. ———. Hand-list of early documents (before 1500) in the Manuscript Department of the Reference Library. Cardiff, 1926. 28p.

3696. ———. Welsh National Festival, 1931 . . . Welsh historical exhibition . . . descriptive handbook to the exhibition illustrating the history and topography of Wales. Cardiff, 1931. 15p.

3697. Evans, John R. "The Popish plot." National Library of Wales journal, 6 (1949), 43-50.

Lists 72 pamphlets, 1678-86, in National Library of Wales.

3698. Great Britain, Public Record Office. An exhibition of records relating to Wales. London, 1960. Unpaged.

3699. National Library of Wales. Bibliotheca Celtica; a register of publications relating to Wales and the Celtic peoples & languages. Aberystwyth, 1910- .

In 3 series: 1st, 1909-28; 2d, 1929-52; 3d, 1953- ; published irregularly, annually since 1954. Registers all books collected by library printed in Wales or on Welsh or Celtic subjects.

3700. ———. Calendars of deeds & documents, comp. by Francis Green. Aberystwyth, 1921-31. 3v.

v.I, the Coleman deeds; v.II, the Crosswood deeds; v.III, the Hawarden deeds.

3701. ———. A calendar of letters relating to North Wales, 1533-circa 1700; from the Llanfair-Brymodol, Gloddaeth, Crosse of Shaw Hill and Rhual collections in the National Library of Wales, ed. by B. E. Howells. Cardiff: Univ. of Wales Pr., 1967. 287p. + charts. (Board of Celtic Studies, Univ. of Wales. History and law series, no.23)

3702. ———. Calendar of Wynn (of Gwydir) papers, 1515-1690; in the National Library of Wales and elsewhere. Aberystwyth, 1926. 512p.

Papers of Sir John Wynn (1553-1626) and other members of Wynn family, nearly all of which are held by National Library of Wales.

3703. ———. Catalogue of tracts of the Civil War and Commonwealth Period relating to Wales and the Borders. Aberystwyth, 1911. 96p.

Chronological listing, 1640-61; records 264 pieces in the National Library of Wales.

3704. ———. Clenennau letters and papers in the Brogyntyn collection, calendared and ed. by T. Jones Pierce, pt.I. Aberystwyth, 1947. 160p. (National Library of Wales journal supplement, ser.IV, pt.1)

Letters and papers, 1584-1622.

3705. ———. A county list of manorial records and other manuscript material relating to the manors and lordships of Wales. Aberystwyth, 1936. 2v.

3706. ———. The custody of the local records of Wales. Aberystwyth, 1932. 26p.

3707. ———. Guide to the exhibition of manuscripts, books, prints, maps, broadsides, etc. Aberystwyth, 1932. 60p.

Principally Welsh books and books of Welsh interest, and fine printing.

3708. ———. List of annuals, newspapers, and periodicals relating to Wales and the Celtic peoples and languages filed in National Library for the year 1912. Aberystwyth, 1915. 52p. (Reprinted from Bibliotheca Celtica, 1912)

3709. Robinson, B. P. "Bodleian Welsh purchases, 1964-1967." Bodleian Library record, 8 (1969), 145-50.
Summary with listing of major items.

3710. St. David's College. List of books in the Welsh Library, by William Davies. Lampeter: Welsh Church Press and Printing Co., 1904. 26p. (Reprinted from the College and school magazine)

3711. ———. A second list of books in the Welsh Library, by William Davies. Lampeter: Welsh Church Press & Printing Co., 1905. 31p. (Reprinted from the College and school magazine)

Commonwealth

3712. Birkbeck College Library. Commonwealth history; select list of Commonwealth history library resources in the greater London area and Oxford, comp. by J. Cooper. London, 1970. 6p. (Library publication, no.18)

3713. Commonwealth Institute Library. The Commonwealth; selected reading lists for advanced studies. London: The Institute, 1969. 14p.

3714. Commonwealth Institute. Working Party on Library Holdings of Commonwealth Literature. A handbook of library holdings of Commonwealth literature in the United Kingdom, comp. and ed. by Gail Wilson. London, 1971. 41 + xviip.
Brief descriptions of holdings of 41 libraries.

3715. Hewitt, A. R. Guide to resources for Commonwealth studies in London, Oxford, and Cambridge; with bibliographical and other information. London: London University, published for the Institute of Commonwealth Studies, The Athlone Pr., 1957. 219p.
Brief descriptions of resources and services of individual institutions.

3716. Horne, A. J. "Development of the Commonwealth Institute Library." Library Association record, 68 (1966), 9-12.
General history and discussion of resources and services.

3717. London, University, Institute of Commonwealth Studies. Commonwealth studies; a guide to resources in London, Oxford & Cambridge, with other relevant information, by A. R. Hewitt. London, 1956. 135p.
Discussion of resources of individual libraries.

3718. ———, Institute of Commonwealth Studies Library. Select list of current periodicals. London, 1970. 15p.
Geographically arranged.

3719. Royal Colonial Institute. A select list of recent publications contained in the Library of the Royal Colonial Institute illustrating the constitutional relations between the various parts of the British Empire, comp. by Evans Lewin. Manchester, 1926. 31p.
Classified catalog.

3720. Royal Commonwealth Society. Biography catalogue of the Library of the Royal Commonwealth Society, by Donald H. Simpson. London, 1961. 511p.
Mainly biographies of persons associated in some way with Commonwealth nations; country and author indexes.

British Local History

GENERAL

3721. Emison, F. G. Archives and local history. London: Methuen, 1966. 122p.
Brief survey of various repositories in England and Wales, with detailed account of main groups of local records.

3722. Hassal, W. O. "Local history sources in the Bodleian Library." Amateur historian, 2 (1955), 130-32.

3723. Historical Association, Local History Committee. English local history hand-list: a select bibliography and list of sources for the study of local history, 4th ed., by F. W. Kuhlicke and F. G. Emmison. London: The Association, 1969. 84p.

3724. Hollaender, Albert E. J. "Local archives of Great Britain: XII. Guildhall Library." Archives, 2 (1955), 312-23.

3725. John Rylands Library. Hand-list of the Leycester of Toft muniments in the John Rylands Library, by F. Taylor. Manchester, 1951. 69l.

ABERDEEN

3726. Aberdeen Public Library. Catalogue of local collection to be found in the Reference Department, comp. by G. M. Fraser. Aberdeen: Central, 1914. 323p.
Publications relating to Aberdeenshire, Banffshire, and Kincardineshire, owned by Aberdeen Public Library.

3727. Aberdeen, University, Library. "A concise bibliography of the history of the City of Aberdeen and its institutions." Aberdeen Univ. Library bulletin, 1 (1913), 699-738.

Books listed are held by Aberdeen University Library.

3728. Johnstone, J. F. K., and Robertson, Alexander W. Bibliographia Aberdonensis; being an account of books relating to or printed in the shires of Aberdeen, Banff, Kincardine, or written by natives or residents or by officers, graduates, or alumni of the Universities of Aberdeen. Aberdeen: Third Spalding Club, 1929-30. 2v.

Locates copies in English and Scottish libraries; covers period 1472-1700.

3729. Johnstone, James Fowler Kellas. A concise bibliography of the history, topography, and institutions of the Shires of Aberdeen, Banff, and Kincardine. Aberdeen: Univ. of Aberdeen, 1914. 193p.

With few exceptions, all books listed were published in Aberdeen and may be consulted in University of Aberdeen Library.

ANTRIM

3730. Antrim County Library. A subject catalogue of books and some other material relating to County Antrim, 2d ed. Ballymena, 1969. 27p.

BATH

3731. Bath Public Libraries. Bath guides, directories and newspapers in the Reference Library, rev. ed. Bath, 1967. 24p.

3732. ———— and Victoria Art Gallery. Select list of books on Bath. Bath: The Libraries, 1972. 16p.

BEDFORD AND BEDFORDSHIRE

3733. Bedford County Records Committee. A handlist of the Bedfordshire County muniments, prepared by the County Records Committee. Bedford: County Council, 1925. 24p. 2d ed., 1931. 24p.; 3d ed., 1938.

3734. Bedfordshire County Council. Catalogue of the enclosure awards, supplementary catalogue of maps, and list of awards upon tithe, in the Bedfordshire County muniments. Bedford, 1939. 45p.

3735. ————. A hand list of the Bedfordshire County muniments; prepared by the County Records Committee. Bedford, 1938. 36p.

3736. Bedfordshire County Record Office. Guide to the Russell estate collections for Bedfordshire and Devon to 1910, deposited in the County Record Offices at Bedford and Exeter, prep. by Joyce Godber and Peter Kennedy. Bedford: Bedfordshire County Council, 1966. 32p.

3737. Bedfordshire County Records Committee. Guide to the Bedfordshire Record Office. Bedford: Bedfordshire County Council, 1957. 161p.

Includes catalog of over 400 maps.

3738. Conisbee, L. R. A Bedfordshire bibliography, with some comments and biographical notes. Bedfordshire: Historical Records Society, 1962. 333p.

Classified arrangement, with index of authors and editors; copies located in various libraries in area and British Museum.

3739. Godber, Joyce. "Local archives of Great Britain: I. The County Record Office at Bedford." Archives, no.1 (1949), 10-20.

BELFAST

3740. Belfast Public Library. Catalogue of books and bound mss. of the Irish historical, archaeological and antiquarian Library of the late Francis Joseph Bigger presented to the Belfast Public Library. Belfast: John Adams, 1930. 303p.

Includes about 3,000 books, pamphlets, and manuscripts of Irish interest.

3741. Stevenson, Noragh. Belfast before 1820; a bibliography of printed material. Belfast: Belfast Library and Society for Promoting Knowledge (Linen Hall Library), 1967. 60p.

Lists 618 items with locations in 11 Irish libraries.

BERKSHIRE

3742. Berkshire and Reading Committee of the National Register of Archives. Exhibition of documents relating to Berkshire and its boroughs, 1140-1901. Reading: Art Gallery, 1951. 43p.

List of 222 items with locations.

3743. Berkshire County Council. Guide to the Berkshire Record Office, prep. by Felix Hull. Reading, 1952. 117p.

3744. Berkshire Record Office. "A catalogue of inclosure maps in the Berkshire Record Office," ed. by Peter Walne. Berkshire archaeological journal, 54 (1954-55), 1-26. Reprinted. 28p.

3745. Reading Public Libraries. Local collection catalogue of books and maps relating to Berkshire. Reading, 1958. 259p.

Classified arrangement, with author-subject indexes; includes chronological list of Berkshire maps.

3746. ———. Local collections catalogue of books and maps relating to Berkshire. Supplement: books added 1956-1966. Reading: Central Public Library, 1967. 85p.

3747. Walne, Peter. "Local archives of Great Britain: XVIII. The Berkshire Record Office." Archives, 4 (1959), 65-74.

BEVERLEY

3748. Great Britain, Historical Manuscripts Commission. Report on the manuscripts of the Corporation of Beverley. London: H. M. Stationery Office, 1900. 227p. (Report, no.54)

A calendar.

BIRMINGHAM

3749. Andrews, Alfred. "Local archives of Great Britain: V. The Birmingham Reference Library." Archives, no.5 (1951), 11-21.

Describes resources of Manuscripts Section of Library.

3750. Birmingham Archaeological Society Library. Catalogue of the library of books, etc., belonging to the Society, prep. by H. New. Birmingham, 1927. 50p.

3751. Birmingham Library. Rough list of Birmingham books & pamphlets. Birmingham, 1881. 12p.

"Books and pamphlets relating to the Town and District," or printed in Birmingham.

3752. Birmingham Public Libraries. "List of manorial documents preserved in the Reference Library, Birmingham." Genealogists' magazine, 9 (1943), 308-12.

3753. ———, Central Reference Library. Birmingham books, etc., in the Birmingham Free Libraries, Reference Department. 1881. Birmingham, 1881. 40p.

3754. ——— ———. The Birmingham muniments; documents of an earlier date than 1800 relating to Birmingham preserved in the Birmingham Reference Library. Birmingham, 1926. 8p. (Reprinted from the Library Association record)

3755. ——— ———. Calendar of deeds and other documents relating to the Lloyd estates in Birmingham and Wednesbury, comp. from the originals deposited on permanent loan in the Birmingham Reference Library. Birmingham, 1936. 84l.

3756. ——— ———. Calendar of deeds and other documents relating to the Mynors estates in Birmingham, Sutton Coldfield, and Hartshorne, Derbyshire, compiled from the originals deposited on permanent loan in the Birmingham Reference Library. Birmingham, 1936. 29l.

3757. ——— ———. Calendar of deeds, maps, and other documents relating to the Colmore estates in Birmingham and elsewhere in the County of Warwick and in the Counties of Gloucester and Salop, compiled from the originals deposited on permanent loan in the Birmingham Reference Library. Birmingham, 1934. 290l.

3758. ——— ———. Calendar of deeds relating to estates of the Smallbrook family in Birmingham and in the Counties of Stafford, Warwick, Buckingham, and elsewhere, compiled from the originals deposited on permanent loan in the Birmingham Reference Library by Maj.-Gen. Sir Richard Howard-Vyse, etc. Birmingham, 1938. 23l.

3759. ——— ———. Calendar of the Hampton collection of manuscripts, being documents relating to the Pakington family and estates in the Counties of Worcester, Buckingham, and Pembroke, and elsewhere, compiled from the originals deposited on permanent loan in the Birmingham Reference Library, by the Rt. Hon. Herbert Stuart Pakington, D.S.O., 4th Baron Hampton. Birmingham, 1941. 543l.

3760. ——— Reference Dept. A catalogue of the Birmingham collection, including printed books and pamphlets, manuscripts, maps, views, portraits, etc., comp. by Walter Powell and Herbert M. Cashmore. Birmingham: Public Libraries Committee, 1918. 1,132p.

3761. ——— ———. A catalogue of the Birmingham collection . . . supplement, 1918-1931. Birmingham, 1931. 913p.

3762. Birmingham, University, Library. Bunce collection; letters and manuscripts. Birmingham, 1969. Unpaged. (Catalogues of the manuscript collections, no.23)

Miscellaneous collection, 1546-1896.

3763. Chubb, Leonard. "Manuscripts relating to Birmingham in the City Reference Library." Birmingham Archaeological Society transactions and proceedings, 55 (1931), 11-24.

General description.

3764. Norris, Dorothy May. "Materials for a history of Birmingham in the Reference Library." Birmingham Archaeological Society transactions and proceedings, 66 (1945-46), 156-66.

General discussion of local collection in Birmingham Public Libraries.

BOLTON

3765. Bolton Public Library. Bibliographia Boltoniensis; being a bibliography, with biographical details of Bolton authors, and the books written by them from 1550 to 1912; books about Bolton; and those printed and published in the Town from 1785 to date, by Archibald Sparke. Manchester: Univ. Pr., 1913. 211p.

All books in Bolton Reference Library unless otherwise indicated,

BRADFORD

3766. Bradford Historical and Antiquarian Society. Catalogue of the library, comp. by Keith G. E. Harris. Bradford, 1957. 114p.

Dictionary arrangement.

BRENTFORD

3767. Brentford and Chiswick Public Libraries and Museums. An introduction to the material in the public libraries illustrating the history and development of Brentford and Chiswick. Brentford, 1957. 21p.

BRISTOL

3768. Bristol and Gloucestershire Archaeological Society. A catalogue of books, pamphlets, and mss. in the Library of the Bristol & Gloucestershire Archaeological Society. Bristol, 1898. 36p.

Relates to local history of society's area.

3769. ———. Guide to the parish records of the City of Bristol and the County of Gloucester, ed. by Irvine Gray and Elizabeth Ralph. Bristol, 1963. 315p. (Publications of the Bristol and Gloucestershire Archaeological Society, Records Section, v.5)

3770. Bristol Archives Office. Guide to the Bristol Archives Office, City and County of Bristol, by Elizabeth Ralph. Bristol: Bristol Corp., 1971. 132p.

3771. Bristol Public Libraries, Reference Library. Bristol bibliography; a catalogue of the books, pamphlets, collecteana, etc., relating to Bristol, contained in the Central Reference Library, ed. by E. R. Norris Mathews, etc. Bristol: The Libraries, 1916. 404p.

3772. Ralph, Elizabeth, and Masters, Betty. "Local archives of Great Britain: XIV. The City of Bristol Record Office." Archives, 3 (1957), 88-96.

BRITTANY

3773. Cardiff Public Libraries. List of books on Brittany and Breton in the Celtic collections at the Central Library. Cardiff, 1935. 24p.

BROMLEY

3774. Alderton, H. "Baxter bequest." Library Association record, ser.4, 2 (1935), 108-10.

Local material in Bromley (Kent) Public Library.

3775. Bromley Public Library. A bibliography of printed material relating to Bromley, Hayes and Keston in the County of Kent, by Brian Burch. Bromley, 1964. 146p.

Locates copies in 16 libraries and collections.

CAERNARVONSHIRE

3776. Caernarvonshire Record Office. Guide to the Caernarvonshire Record Office, by W. Ogwen Williams. Caernarvon: Caernarvonshire County Records Joint Committee, 1952. 45p.

3777. National Library of Wales. A list of Caernarvonshire manuscripts and records in the National Library of Wales. Aberystwyth, 1936. 102l.

3778. Parry, Bryn R. "Local archives of Great Britain: XXVII. The Caernarvonshire Record Office." Archives, 7 (1965), 34-39.

CAMBRIDGE AND CAMBRIDGESHIRE

3779. Cambridge, University, St. Catharine's College Library. Catalogue of documents in the Muniment Room; the Master's Lodge; and the College Library, comp. by E. A. B. Bernard. Cambridge, 1930. 70l. Addendum, 1934. 19l.

Documents relating to Cambridge history.

3780. Cambridgeshire County Library. Cambridgeshire; an annotated list of the books, maps, prints, pamphlets, and other material in the Cambridgeshire County Library Local History Collection, comp. by P. R. Gifford. Cambridge: Cambridgeshire Education Committee, 1961. 57p.

CARDIGANSHIRE

3781. Janes, Glyn Lewis. A bibliography of Cardiganshire. London, 1966. 896l. (Thesis, Library Association Fellowship)

Items located in National Library of Wales and Cardiganshire Joint Library.

CHELMSFORD

3782. Chelmsford Public Library and Museum. Diamond jubilee 1906-1966. Prep. for Second National Library week in Chelmsford by Miss J. V. Dansie and ed. by E. O. Reeds. Chelmsford, 1967. 14p.

CHELSEA

3783. Kensington and Chelsea Public Libraries. A short guide to the Chelsea local history collection. London, 1967. 9p.

CHESTER

3784. Groombridge, Margaret J. Guide to the charters, plate and insignia of the City of Chester. Chester: Phillipson & Golder, 1950. 52p.

Includes descriptive list of 75 charters, letters patent, city records, coats of arms, seals, etc., 1176-1614.

3785. Taylor, Frank. "Selected Cheshire seals (12th-17th century) from the collections in the John Rylands Library." Bulletin of the John Rylands Library, 26 (1942), 393-412. Reprinted, 1942. 20p.

CHICHESTER

3786. Chichester County Record Office. A descriptive list of the archives of the City of Chichester. Chichester, 1949. 44*l*.

COCKINGTON

3787. Sparkes, M. M. Calendar of documents of the Malloch family of Cockington. London, 1959. 504*l*. (Diploma in Archive Administration, Univ. of London)

Records now deposited in Exeter City Library.

CORNWALL

3788. Rogers, Kenneth Herbert. Calendar of Wynell-Mayow records. London, 1958. 137*l*. (Diploma in Archive Administration, Univ. of London)

Now deposited in Cornwall County Record Office.

COVENTRY

3789. Coventry, Corporation. A calendar of the books, charters, letters patent, deeds, rolls, writs, and other writings in the cases and drawers of the new muniment-room of St. Mary's Hall, made and edited for the corporation of the City of Coventry, by John Cordy Jeaffreson. Coventry, 1896. 87p.

3790. ———, City Muniment Room, St. Mary's Hall. Supplementary catalogue of the books and mss. added to the collections since the publication of Mr. J. Cordy Jeaffreson's Catalogue of 1896. Coventry, 1931. 33p.

3791. ———, Public Relations Dept. Coventry city charters, by A. A. Dibben. Coventry, 1969. 39p,

Lists 58 items, with locations.

CUMBERLAND

3792. Carlisle, Public Library. Bibliotheca Jacksoniana; catalogue by James Pitcairn Hinds. Kendal: Carlisle Public Library Committee, 1909. 199p.

Records collection of books, prints, manuscripts, etc., relating to Cumberland, Westmoreland, and Lancashire-north-of-the-Sands.

3793. Durham, University, Durham Colleges, Dept. of Paleography and Diplomatic. Howard family documents; list of miscellaneous papers relating to Cumberland, formerly at Naworth Castle, now deposited in the Department of Paleography and Diplomatic, comp. by C. R. Hudleston. Durham, 1968. 125*l*.

3794. Jones, B. C. "Local archives of Great Britain: XXVIII. Cumberland, Westmorland and Carlisle Record Office, 1960-1965." Archives, 7 (1965), 80-86.

DARTFORD

3795. Knight, Roy. A bibliography of printed material relating to Dartford, in the County of Kent. London, 1969. 585*l*. (Library Association Fellowship thesis)

Contains 2,080 entries with locations in various libraries.

DENBIGHSHIRE

3796. Denbighshire County Library. Bibliography of the County. Ruthin, 1933-37. 3pts.

In 3pts.: biographical sources; historical and topographical sources; Denbighshire authors and their works.

3797. ———. Bibliography of the County. pt.2: Historical and typographical sources, 2d ed. Ruthin, 1951. 251p. Supplement, 1959. 56p.

DERBY AND DERBYSHIRE

3798. Derby Borough Libraries, Local History Dept. Family papers in the Local History Department, Derby Borough Libraries. Derby, 1971. 18p.

3799. ———. Leisure long ago; a select list of books and manuscripts relating to leisure in Derby and Derbyshire, Derby Borough Libraries. Derby, 1971. 21p.

3800. ———. Manuscript books in the local history collection (select list), Derby Borough Libraries. Derby, 1971. 20p.

3801. ———. Trade and industry in 19th century Derby; a select list of books and manuscripts, Derby Borough Libraries. Derby, 1971. 20p.

3802. Derby, County. Calendar of the records of the County of Derby, comp. by J. Charles Cox. London & Derby: Bemrose and Sons, 1899. 385p.

3803. Derby Public Libraries. Derbyshire: a select catalogue of books about the County, comp. by James Ormerod. Derby, 1930. 128p.

List of books, pamphlets, and manuscripts relating to Derbyshire in Derby Municipal Library.

3804. Derbyshire County Library. Derbyshire: a list of books about the County. Derby, 1953. 24p.

3805. Hall, T. Walter. A descriptive catalogue of early land-charters relating to lands in the County of Derby, with genealogies & notes. Sheffield: J. W. Northend, 1946. 18p.

3806. ———. A descriptive catalogue of land-charters & muniments relating to vills & burghs of North Derbyshire, with illustrations, genealogies & notes. Sheffield: J. W. Northend, 1939. 52p.

3807. Jeayes, Isaac Herbert. Descriptive catalogue of Derbyshire charters in public and private libraries and muniment rooms. London & Derby: Bemrose and Sons, 1906. 486p.

Record of 2,786 items; locations in public and private collections.

DEVON

3808. Bone, Margaret. Calendar of deeds of the Worth family of Washfield, Devon. London, 1956. 236l. (Diploma in Archive Administration, Univ. of London)

Records now deposited in Exeter City Library.

3809. Devon & Cornwall Record Society. Devon monastic land: calendar of particulars for grants, 1536-1558, ed. by Joyce Youings. Exeter, 1955. 154p.

3810. ———. Transcripts of parish registers, bishops' transcripts, etc., in the possession of the Society. Exeter, 1948. 11p.

3811. Devon Record Office. Brief guide: pt.1: Official and ecclesiastical. Devon, 1969? 75p.

3812. MacPherson, Sheila Jessie. Marwood Elton deeds and other documents. London, 1960. 199l. (Diploma in Archive Administration, Univ. of London)
In Devon Record Office.

3813. Torquay Public Libraries. The hundred of Heytor; a guide to the printed sources relating to South Devon, comp. by M. L. Ruse Smith. Torquay, 1967. 26p.

DONCASTER

3814. Doncaster, Corporation. A calendar to the records of the Borough of Doncaster. Doncaster, 1899-1903. 4v.

DORSET

3815. Dorset, County. Dorset records: being indexes, calendars and abstracts of records relating to the County of Dorset, also transcripts of Dorset Parish registers, ed. by E. A. and G. S. Fry. London: C. J. Clark, 1894-1912. 13v.

3816. Holmes, Margaret. "Local archives of Great Britain. XXIV. The Dorset Record Office." Archives, 7 (1966), 207-14.

DURHAM

3817. Durham County Council. Catalogue of the documents deposited in the Durham County Record Office by the 9th Marquess of Londonderry. Durham, 1969. 166p.

3818. Durham, University, Durham Colleges, Dept. of Palaeography and Diplomatic. List of documents relating to the Manor of Chester Deanery, deposited in the Department of Palaeography and Diplomatic, South Road, Durham, comp. by E. Peirce. Durham, 1967. 48l.

3819. ———, Library. Durham elections: a list of material relating to Parliamentary elections in Durham, 1675-1874, by H. R. Klieneberger. Durham, 1956. 47p. (Durham University Library publications, no.2)

3820. Gateshead Public Libraries. Cotesworth mss. Gateshead, 1971. 12l.

"A summary of a detailed list which may be consulted at the Central Library."

EASTBOURNE

3821. Eastbourne Public Libraries. Catalogue of the local collection, comprising books on Eastbourne and Sussex. Eastbourne, 1956. 36p.

Arranged by localities and subjects; list of 901 items held by Eastbourne Public Libraries.

EDINBURGH

3822. Edinburgh Public Libraries. Books on the history of Edinburgh, with a select list of historical and descriptive books on the city, by William Cowan. Edinburgh, 1929. 26p.

3823. ———. Edinburgh past and present; a select list of books, prints, and maps on the history and topography of Edinburgh. Aberdeen, 1948. 16p.

3824. ———. The Edinburgh scene; catalogue of prints and drawings in the Edinburgh Room, Central Public Library. Edinburgh: Public Libraries Committee, 1951. 270p.

Copy in Public Library annotated for later additions.

3825. Edinburgh Town Council, Public Libraries and Museums Committee. Edinburgh, 1767-1967; a select list of books. Edinburgh, 1967. 16p. (Occasional publications, no.7)

ESSEX

3826. Dagenham Public Libraries. A catalogue of the Essex & Dagenham collections. Dagenham, 1957. 113p.

Records 1,087 items.

3827. ———. Essex and Dagenham: a catalogue of books, pamphlets and maps, 2d ed., comp. by James Howson and Mrs. Alan Green. Dagenham, 1961 202p.

3828. Emmison, F. G. "Local archives of Great Britain: II. The Essex Record Office." Archives, no.2 (1949), 8-16.

3829. Essex County Council. Catalogue of Essex Parish records, 1240-1894, with supplement on nonconformist, charities, societies and school records, 1341-1903, 2d ed., prep. by F. G. Emmison. Essex, 1966. 269p. (Essex Record Office publications, no.7)

3830. ———. Essex Parish records, 1240-1894, prep. by E. J. Erith. Essex, 1950. 262p. (Essex Record Office publications, no.7)

3831. Essex Record Office. Farm and cottage inventories of mid-Essex, 1635-1749, ed. by Francis W. Steer. Chelmsford: 1950. 305p. (Publications, no.8)

3832. ———. Guide to the Essex Record Office, by F. G. Emmison, 2d ed. (revised to 1968). Chelmsford: Essex County Council, 1969. 251p. (Essex Record publications, no.51)

3833. ———. Record retrospect; the Essex Record Office, Essex County Council, 1964. 24p. (Essex Record Office publications, no.42)

3834. Leyton Public Libraries. Essex literature; catalogue of books published in or relating to the county, comp. by Zebedee Moon. Leyton, 1900. 11p.

Materials held by Leyton Public Library.

EXETER

3835. Great Britain, Historical Manuscripts Commission. Report on the records of the City of Exeter. London: H. M. Stationery Office, 1916. 536p. (Report, no.73)

FARNE ISLANDS

3836. Thompson, J. W. Farne Islands, Northumberland: a bibliography. London, 1967. 121*l*. (Thesis, Library Association Fellowship)

Locates copies of 436 entries in various libraries and collections.

FIFE

3837. Fife County Library. Books on local subjects. (In the County Library and Buckhaven, Dunfermline, and Kirkcaldy Public Libraries.) Kirkcaldy, 1962. 2pts.

Biographies, family histories, works on individual places, and general works located in 4 libraries.

3838. ——— and Kirkcaldy Public Library. Check list of books on local subjects. Kirkcaldy, 1957. 70p.

Arranged by places and subjects.

FLINTSHIRE

3839. Flint County Library. Bibliography of the County of Flint. (pt.1: Biographical sources), comp. by E. R. Harries. Mold, 1953. 70p.

3840. Flintshire Record Office. Guide to the Flintshire Record Office; Flintshire quarter sessions and other official records, prep. by M. Bevan-Evans. Mold, 1955. 108p.

3841. Veysey, A. G. "Local archives of Great Britain: XXXII. The Flintshire Record Office." Archives, 10 (1971), 38-46.

FULHAM

3842. Fulham Public Libraries. Reader's guide to recent additions, ed. by James E. Walker. London: Public Libraries Committee, 1927. 68p.

p.56-68, "Fulham: A list of books, pamphlets, and other material for the study of local history contained in the Public Libraries."

GAINSBOROUGH

3843. Gainsborough Public Libraries. Lindsey towns and villages: books, pamphlets, and other material, in the Gainsborough Public Library. Gainsborough, 1967. 15p.

3844. Gainsborough Public Library. Gainsborough local studies; a handlist of books and pamphlets, articles, illustrations, and maps, relating to the town and its past, based on the Local and Brace collections of the Gainsborough Public Library. Gainsborough, 1965. 25p.

GATESHEAD

3845. Gateshead Public Libraries. Gateshead archives, comp. by F. W. D. Manders. Gateshead, 1968. 30p.

3846. ———. A select list of the books and pamphlets in the local collection of the Reference Department relating to the history of Gateshead, etc. Gateshead, 1929. 14p.

GILLINGHAM

3847. Gillingham Public Libraries. Archives collection, Gillingham Public Archives. Gillingham, 1971. 13p.

3848. ———. Local history catalogue. Gillingham: Kent Education Committee, 1951. 20p. Supplement, 1955. 22p.

Records books on Kent, Medway Towns, Chatham, Gillingham, and Rochester.

GLAMORGANSHIRE

3849. Elsas, Madeleine. "Local archives of Great Britain: III. The County Record Office of Glamorgan." Archives, no.3 (1950), 7-16.

3850. Fonmon Castle Library. A catalogue of the Library at Fonmon Castle, Glamorgan, by Margaret Evans. Cardiff: Univ. College Library, 1969. 265p.

List of 1,135 items of general historical nature.

3851. Seaman, William Allan Lewis. Fonmon Castle collection; summary list. London, 1959. 66l. (Diploma in Archive Administration, Univ. of London)

Records deposited in Glamorgan Record Office.

3852. Sidaway, Margaret Anne. Records of Yniscedwyn estate. London, 1957. 283l. (Diploma in Archive Administration, Univ. of London)

Deposited in Glamorgan Record Office.

GLASGOW

3853. Glasgow Archaeological Society Library. Catalogue of the Library of the Glasgow Archaeological Society. Glasgow: The Society, 1919. 140p.

Records about 1,700 books and pamphlets; dictionary arrangement.

3854. Glasgow Corporation Public Libraries. Catalogue of the Andrew Bain memorial collection in the Mitchell Library. Glasgow, 1924. 180p.

Collection particularly rich in Glasgow and Scottish history.

3855. Glasgow, University, Library. Catalogue of the Wylie collection of books (mainly relating to Glasgow) bequeathed to the University of Glasgow, prep. by Wilson Steel. Glasgow: Jackson, Wylie, 1929. 26l.

GLOUCESTER AND GLOUCESTERSHIRE

3856. Blanchard, Susan Rosemary. Calendar of Dursley and Stroud apprentice indentures in the 17th and 18th centuries. London, 1958. 176l. (Diploma in Archive Administration, Univ. of London)

Records now in the Gloucester City Library and the Gloucester County Records Office.

3857. Gloucester City Libraries. Catalogue of the Gloucestershire collection; books, pamphlets, and documents in the Gloucester Public Library relating to the county, cities, towns and villages of Gloucestershire, comp. by Roland Austin. Gloucester, 1928. 1,236p.

Records 15,333 items.

3858. ———. The Dancey gift; catalogue of manuscripts, books, pamphlets, and prints relating to the City and County of Gloucester and other works of general literature deposited in the Gloucester Public Library. Gloucester, 1911. 55p.

3859. ———. Painswick House collection; catalogue of books, tracts, broadsides . . . relating to the County of Gloucester and the City of Bristol presented by F. A. Hyett, Esq., to the Gloucester Public Library, by Roland Austin. Gloucester, 1916. 185p.

3860. ———. Records relating to Gloucestershire parishes. Gloucester, 1960. 15p. (Local history pamphlets, no.3)
Summary listing.

3861. Gloucester, Corporation. Calendar of the records of the Corporation of Gloucester, comp. by W. H. Stevenson. Gloucester: J. Bellows, 1893. 562p.

3862. Gloucestershire County Council, County Records Committee. Gloucestershire quarter sessions archives, 1660-1889, and other official records; a descriptive catalogue compiled for the County Records Committee by I. E. Gray and A. T. Gaydon. Gloucester, 1958. 96p.

3863. Gloucestershire County Library. Catalogue of Gloucestershire books collected by Sir Francis Hyett of Painswick and placed in the Shire Hall [Gloucester], comp. by Roland Austin. Gloucester: Records Office, 1950. 39p.

3864. Gloucestershire Records Office. Royalist and Roundhead in Gloucestershire, 1640-1660; an exhibition arranged by the Gloucestershire Records Office and the Gloucester City Library, at the Wheatstone Hall, Gloucester, 18th to 27th July, 1960. Gloucester, 1960. 16p.

3865. ———. A short handlist of the contents of the Gloucestershire Records Office, Shire Hall, Gloucester. Gloucester, 1968. 13p.

3866. Gray, Irvine E. "Local archives of Great Britain: XXV. The Gloucestershire Records Office." Archives, 6 (1964), 178-85.

3867. Hyett, Francis Adams, and Bazeley, William. The bibliographers's manual of Gloucestershire literature; being a classified catalogue of books, pamphlets, broadsides, and other printed matter relating to the County of Gloucestershire or to the City of Bristol. Gloucester: J. Bellows, 1895-97. 3v.
Locates copies in 23 English libraries.

3868. Hyett, Francis Adams, and Austin, Roland. Supplement to the Bibliographer's manual of Gloucestershire literature; being a classified catalogue of biographical and genealogical literature relating to men and women connected by birth, office, or many years' residence with the County of Gloucester or the City of Bristol. Gloucester: J. Bellows, 1915-16. 2v.
Copies located in 25 public and private collections.

3869. Woodman, V. A. "Local archives of Great Britain: XXVI. Archives in the Gloucester City Library." Archives, 6 (1964), 225-28.

HACKNEY

3870. Tyssen Library, Hackney. Catalogue of the Tyssen Library; a collection of books, manuscripts, maps, plans, etc., relating to . . . Hackney and its vicinity; the catalogue, comp., by J. T. Whitehead. London, 1888. 92p.

HAMMERSMITH

3871. Given, Evelyn Barbara. Documents relating to land at the Creek, Hammersmith, 1659-1931; a calendar. London, 1956. 132*l*. (Diploma in Librarianship, Univ. of London)
In the Hammersmith Public Library.

3872. Taylor, Pamela. "Local archives of Great Britain: XXXI. The London Borough of Hammersmith Record Office." Archives, 9 (1970), 192-96.

HAMPSHIRE

3873. Hampshire Archivists' Group. Archives of Hampshire and the Isle of Wight. Winchester, 1965. 14p.

3874. ———. Poor law in Hampshire through the centuries; a guide to the records. Hampshire, 1970. 78p. (Publication, no.1)

HAMPSTEAD

3875. Hampstead Public Libraries. Catalogue of works of history and historical material contained in the Lending and Reference Depts, at the Central Library. West Norwood: Truslove & Bray, 1923. 168p.
Classified listing, with author-subject indexes.

HARROW

3876. Harrow Local Archives Committee. Harrow—from villages to borough. Catalogue of documents, maps, and views relating to Harrow and neighborhood, exhibited by the Harrow Local Archives Committee in conjunction with the Middlesex County Records Office and the Harrow Arts Council at the County Library, Grant Road, Wealdstone. Harrow, 1965. 60p.

HAVERFORDWEST

3877. National Library of Wales. Calendar of the records of the Borough of Haverfordwest 1539-1660, ed. by B. G. Charles. Cardiff: Univ. of Wales Pr., 1967. 274p.

Records of town and county of Haverfordwest, deposited in National Library of Wales in 1948.

HEREFORD AND HEREFORDSHIRE

3878. Herefordshire County Library. Local history collection. Herefordshire books: a select list of books in the local collection of the Herefordshire County Library. Hereford: County Library, Local History Section, 1955. 23*l*.

3879. MacRay, Will Dunn. Catalogue of and index to mss., papers, proclamations, and other documents selected from the municipal archives of the city of Hereford. Hereford: Wilson & Phillips, 1894. 40p.

HERNE BAY

3880. Kent County Library. A list of books and references concerning Herne Bay, Herne and Reculver. Herne Bay, 1951. 16p.

HERTFORD AND HERTFORDSHIRE

3881. British Records Association. Catalogue of exhibition of records, maps, etc., relating to Hertfordshire, 1932-1957. London, 1957. 23p.

Based on materials in Hertfordshire County Record Office.

3882. Hertfordshire County Museum. Catalogue of the Lewis Evans collection of books and pamphlets relating to Hertfordshire. St. Albans, 1906-8. 2pts. 154p.

3883. Hertfordshire Local History Council. Periodicals and transactions relating to Hertfordshire; a short guide and subject index, comp. by M. F. Thwaite. Hertford, 1959. 109p.

Locates files of Hertfordshire periodicals and transactions in libraries and museums.

3884. Hertfordshire Record Office. Quarter sessions and other records in the custody of the officials of the County, ed. by William LeHardy. Hertford: County Council, 1961. 283p. (Guide to the Hertfordshire Record Office, pt.1)

3885. LeHardy, William. "Local archives of Great Britain: IV. The Hertford County Record Office." Archives, no.4 (1950), 16-24.

HULL

3886. Kingston upon Hull City Libraries. Books on Hull and district; a select list. Kingston upon Hull, 1957. 11p.

3887. ———. A select list of books on Hull and district; a guide to the collections in the Local History Library, comp. by R. F. Drewery. Kingston upon Hull, 1968. 32p.

3888. Kingston upon Hull Corporation. Calendar of the ancient deeds, letters, miscellaneous old documents, etc., in the archives of the Corporation, calendared and indexed by L. M. Stanwell. Kingston upon Hull, 1951. 494p.

HUNTINGDONSHIRE

3889. Huntingdonshire County Council. Guide to the Huntingdonshire Record Office, prep. by G. H. Findlay. Huntingdon, 1958. 33p.

3890. Huntingdonshire County Library. Catalogue of the books and maps relating to Huntingdonshire in the County Library. Huntingdon: Gazeley House, 1950. 39p.

Classified by subject.

3891. ———. Catalogue of the Local History collection, 2d ed. Huntingdon, 1958. 59p.

HYTHE

3892. Hythe, Borough. Catalogue of documents. (Catalogue of documents belonging to the Corporation of Hythe 11th to 20th century; also churchwardens' accounts 1840 and subsequently, comp. by H. D. Dale and C. Chidell.) Hythe, 1937. Unpaged.

Lists 283 documents.

ILCHESTER

3893. Gorton, L. J. "The Holland House papers and their history." British Museum quarterly, 29 (1965), 71-78.

Ilchester and Holland family archives, 18th-20th centuries, form bulk of extensive collection received by British Museum.

INVERNESS

3894. Anderson, Peter J. A concise bibliography of the printed & mss. material on the history, topography & institutions of the Burgh Parish and Shire of Inverness. Aberdeen: Univ. Pr., 1917. 264p.

"With few exceptions, the books noted may be consulted in the Aberdeen University Library."

IPSWICH

3895. Charman, Derek. "Local archives of Great Britain: XVII. The Ipswich and East Suffolk Record Office." Archives, 4 (1959), 18-28.

ISLE OF ELY

3896. Isle of Ely County Library. Books on the Fenland in the Isle of Ely County Library. March, Isle of Ely: County Council of Isle of Ely Education Committee, 1954. 24p.

3897. ———. Hereward's Isle; books on the Fenland, 4th ed., comp. by W. E. Dring. March, Cambs.: County Council of Isle of Ely Education Committee, 1962. 39p.

ISLE OF MAN

3898. Cubbon, William. A bibliographical account of works relating to the Isle of Man. London: Oxford Univ. Pr., 1933-39. 2v.

Based primarily on Manx Museum Library's holdings.

ISLE OF PINES

3899. Ford, Worthington Chauncey. The Isle of Pines, 1668; an essay in bibliography. Boston, Mass.: Club of Odd Volumes, 1920. 117p.

Bibliography, p.91-109, records locations in British, American, and Continental libraries.

ISLE OF SHEPPEY

3900. Kent County Library. The Isle of Sheppey. Maidstone, 1956. 12p.

Includes "a select list of books relating to Sheppey in the Kent County Library."

KENT

3901. Hull, Felix. "Local archives of Great Britain: XI. The Kent Archives Office." Archives, no.13 (1955), 237-46.

History and description of holdings.

3902. Kent County Archives Office. Guide to the Kent County Archives Office, prep. by Felix Hull. Maidstone: Kent County Council, 1958. 290p. + 22 plates.

3903. ———. Guide to the Kent County Archives Office, 1st supplement, 1957-1968, prep. by Felix Hull. Maidstone: Kent County Council, 1971. 236p.

3904. Kent County Library. Local history catalogue, 1939. Maidstone, 1939. 107p.

Books on Kent in Kent County Library.

3905. Lambeth Palace Library. East Kent records; a calendar of some unpublished deeds and court rolls in the Library of Lambeth Palace, with appendices referring especially to the manors of Knowlton, Sandown, South Court and North Court, ed. by Irene Joseph Churchill. London, 1922. 1,224p. (Kent records, v.7)

KINGSTON UPON THAMES

3906. Kingston upon Thames Borough. Guide to the Borough archives. Kingston upon Thames: Kingston Borough Council, 1971. 136p.

KNUTSFORD

3907. John Rylands Library. Hand-list of the Legh of Booths charters in the John Rylands Library, by Frank Taylor. Manchester: John Rylands Library, 1950. 74p. (Reprinted from the Bulletin of the John Rylands Library, 32 (March 1950), 229-300)

List of 362 items relating to old Cheshire family of Legh of Norbury Booths Hall, near Knutsford, 13th to 19th century; collection transferred to University of Keele Library.

LAMBETH

3908. Lambeth Public Libraries. A short guide to the Surrey collection, by M. Y. Williams. London, 1965. 20p.

Analysis of local history collection of Lambeth Public Libraries.

LANARKSHIRE

3909. Miller, Andrew. A pilot scheme for a bibliography of Lanarkshire. London, 1967. 239*l*. (Library Association Fellowship thesis)

Locations for 1,294 items in 12 libraries.

LANCASHIRE

3910. Fishwick, Henry. The Lancashire library; a bibliographical account of books on topography, biography, history, science, and miscellaneous literature relating to the County Palatine, including an account of Lancashire tracts, pamphlets and sermons printed before the year 1720. London: George Routledge, 1875. 443p.

Frequently locates copies.

3911. France, R. Sharpe. "Local archives of Great Britain: VII. The Lancashire Record Office." Archives, no.7 (1952), 45-51.

Includes description of records held.

3912. Joint Committee on the Lancashire Bibliography. Lancashire acts of Parliament, 1266-1957, comp. by Sidney Horrocks. Central Library. Manchester, 1969. 350p.

3913. Lancashire County Council. A handlist of Lancashire enclosure acts and awards. Preston, 1946. 40p.

3914. Lancashire Record Office. Guide to the Lancashire Record Office, by R. Sharpe France, 2d ed. Preston: Lancashire County Council, 1962. 353p.

3915. Manchester Public Libraries, Book Service Dept. Author catalogue of the Lancashire and Cheshire Antiquarian Society Library in the Manchester Central Library, ed. by N. K. Firby. Manchester: The Libraries, 1968. Unpaged.

Lists 1,917 items.

3916. Wigan Public Libraries. Lancashire books; a list of books and pamphlets relating to the County Palatine of Lancaster preserved in the Reference Department of the Wigan Free Public Library, by T. H. Folkard. Wigan, 1898. 42p.

3917. ———. Lancashire printed books; a bibliography of all the books printed in Lancashire down to the year 1800, by Arthur John Hawkes. Wigan: J. Starr for the Public Libraries Committee, 1925. 155p.

Contains 1,055 annotated entries; based on holdings of Wigan Reference Library; copies located also in other public and private collections.

LANCASTER

3918. Lancaster, Corporation. A calendar of charters and records belonging to the Corporation of Lancaster, by John Brownbill. Lancaster, 1929. 44p.

LEEDS

3919. Leeds Public Libraries. Leeds and Yorkshire: a guide to the collections. Leeds: Libraries and Arts Committee, 1947. 30p.

Describes collection of 33,000 items in Leeds Central Library of books, manuscripts, maps, and prints relating to Leeds and Yorkshire.

3920. Osborne, George Godolphin, Duke of Leeds. The manuscripts of the Duke of Leeds, the Bridge-water Trust, Reading Corporation, the Inner Temple, etc., calendared by William Dunn Macray and others. London, 1888. 383p. (Historical Manuscripts Commission, 11th Report, Appendix, pt.7)

LEICESTER

3921. Lee, J. M. Leicestershire history: a handlist to printed sources in the libraries of Leicester. Leicester, 1958. 64p. (Vaughan College papers, no.4)

Locates copies in 8 Leicester libraries.

3922. Leicester Abbey Library. "Catalogue of the Library of Leicester Abbey, by Montague Rhodes James." Transactions of the Leicestershire Archaeological Society, 19 (1936-37), 111-61, 377-440.

3923. Leicester City Council. Records of the Borough of Leicester, v.VI. The Chamberlains' accounts, 1688-1835, ed. by G. A. Chinnery. Leicester: Leicester Univ. Pr., 1967. 581p.

3924. Leicester Museum and Art Gallery. A brief guide to the Muniment Room. Leicester: The Museum, 1949. 12p.

3925. ———, Dept of Archives. Handlist of Leicestershire Parish registers transcripts. Leicester, 1953. 44p.

3926. ——— ———. The records of the Corporation of Leicester. A handlist of the documents preserved at the Leicester Museum and Art Gallery. Leicester, 1956. 59p.

3927. Leicester Public Libraries. Catalogue of the books, pamphlets . . . relating to Leicester, comp. by C. V. Kirkby. Leicester: Thornley and Waddington, 1893. 94p.

3928. Leicester, University. Leicestershire history; a handlist of printed sources in the libraries of Leicester, by J. M. Lee. Leicester, 1958. 64p.

Copies located in 8 libraries.

LINCOLN AND LINCOLNSHIRE

3929. Finch, Mary. "Five years of the Lincolnshire Archives Office, 1958-1963." Lincolnshire historian, 2 (1964), 29-37.

3930. Lincoln, Corporation, Muniment Room. Catalogue of the Royal charters and other documents and list of books belonging to the Corporation of Lincoln, now preserved in the Muniment Room of the Corporation, by Walter De Gray Birch. 1906. 2pts.

3931. Lincoln Public Library. Bibliotheca Lincolniensis; a catalogue of the books, pamphlets, etc., relating to the City and County of Lincoln preserved in the Reference Department of the City of Lincoln Public Library, comp. by A. R. Corns. Lincoln: W. K. Morton, 1904. 276p.

3932. Varley, Joan. "Local archives of Great Britain: VI. The Lincolnshire Archives Committee." Archives, no.6 (1951), 5-16.

LIVERPOOL

3933. Liverpool Libraries, Museums & Arts Committee. Local History Library and Record Office. Liverpool, 1961. 52p.

Describes municipal archives and other local history materials.

3934. Liverpool Public Libraries, Reference Library. Liverpool prints and documents: catalogue of maps, plans, views, portraits, memoirs, literature, etc., in the Reference Library relating to Liverpool. Liverpool: Library, Museum & Arts Committee, 1908. 374p.

3935. Liverpool, University, Library. Catalogue of the Rathbone papers in the University Library, Liverpool, ed. by D. F. Cook. Liverpool: Univ. Pr., 1959-62. 2pts.

Papers relate mainly to business activities of Rathbone family in 18th and 19th centuries.

LONDON

3936. Baylis, Sheila M. An annotated catalogue of the part of the Stowe collection now in the London Section of the Greater London Record Office. London, 1966. Unpaged. (Thesis, Library Association fellowship)

Mainly 17th-18th-century documents concerning London properties.

3937. Darlington, Ida. "Local archives of Great Britain: XIII. The County of London Record Office." Archives, no.2 (1956), 477-86.

3938. Greater London Record Office. Guide to the Middlesex sessions records, 1549-1889. London, 1965. 98p.

3939. ———. A survey of the parish registers of the Diocese of London, Inner London area. London, 1968. 80p.

Arranged by localities.

3940. Guildhall Library. "Calamities, wonders and topics of the town, 1603-1902; some aspects of popular taste as reflected in a list of items in Guildhall Library." Guildhall miscellany, 2 (1968), 463-82.

3941. ———. Calendar of Coroner's rolls of the City of London, A.D. 1300-1378, ed. by Reginald R. Sharpe. London: Richard Clay & Sons, 1913. 324p.

3942. ———. Calendar of early Mayor's court rolls preserved among the archives of the Corporation of the City of London at the Guildhall, A.D. 1298-1307, ed. by A. H. Thomas. Cambridge, 1924. 304p.

3943. ———. Calendar of letters from the Mayor and Corporation of the City of London, circa A.D. 1350-1370, enrolled and preserved among the archives of the Corporation at the Guildhall, ed. by R. R. Sharpe. London: J. C. Francis, 1885. 185p.

3944. ———. Calendar of plea and memoranda rolls preserved among the archives of the Corporation of the City of London at the Guildhall, A.D. 1458-1482, ed. by Philip E. Jones. Cambridge: Univ. Pr., 1961. 217p.

3945. ———. Catalogue of the Guildhall Library. London, 1889. 1,137p.

3946. ———. Catalogue of the lending department of the Library of the Corporation . . . of London . . . , 2d ed. London: The Corp., 1911. 490p.

3947. ———. A catalogue of the Library of the Corporation of London . . . with an alphabetical list of authors annexed. London: The Corp., 1859. 658p.

3948. ———. The County of London: a select book list. London: Library Association, Reference and Special Libraries Section, South Eastern Group, 1959. 32p.

Includes 225 items on variety of aspects.

3949. ———. A guide to the records in the Corporation of London Records Office, and the Guildhall Library muniment room, by Philip E. Jones and Raymond Smith. London: English Universities Pr., 1951. 203p. + 6 plates.

3950. ———. A handlist of poll books and registers of electors in Guildhall Library, comp. by K. I. Garrett. London, 1970. 87p. + index.

3951. ———. Index to testamentary records in the Commissary Court of London, London Division, now preserved in the Guildhall Library. London. v.I. 1374-1488, ed. by Marc Fitch. London, 1969. 239p. (Historical Manuscripts Commission, JP12)

3952. ———. "A list of bills of mortality in the Corporation of London Records Office and a supplementary list of bills in Guildhall Library." Guildhall miscellany, 2 (1966), 367-68.

3953. ———. "A list of works in Guildhall Library relating to the plague in London, together with the bills of mortality, 1532?-1858." Guildhall miscellany, 2 (1965), 306-17.

3954. ———. London parks and pleasure haunts in the 18th and 19th centuries: a selection from the print collections of the Guildhall Library. London: Guildhall Art Gallery, 1958. 14p.

3955. ———. London rate assessments and inhabitants lists in Guildhall Library and the City Corporation of London Records Office, 2d ed. London: Library Committee of the Corporation of London, 1968. 63p.

Arranged by localities.

3956. ———. "A select list of printed works relating to the Great Fire of 1666 and the rebuilding of London, from the collections of the Guildhall Library." Guildhall miscellany, 2 (1966), 369-76.

3975. ———. Vestry minutes: a handlist of vestry minutes of City of London parishes, 2d ed. London, 1964. 31p.

3958. Kahl, William F. "A checklist of books, pamphlets, and broadsides on the London livery companies." Guildhall miscellany, 2 (1962), 99-126.

Copies located in 8 libraries—7 British, and Harvard University Library.

3959. ———. The development of London livery companies; an historical essay and a select bibliography. Boston, Mass.: Baker Library, Harvard Graduate School of Business Administration, 1960. 104p.

Classified list of books, pamphlets, and broadsides locates copies in Harvard University Library and 7 British libraries.

3960. Lambeth Palace Library. Estate documents at Lambeth Palace Library; a short catalogue, by Jane Sayers. Leicester: Univ. Pr., 1965. 87p.

3961. ———. Index of wills recorded in the Archiepiscopal registers at Lambeth Palace. London, 1919. 88p. (Reprinted from the Genealogist, n.s. v.34-35)

3962. London, Corporation of the City. Catalogue of plea and memoranda rolls preserved among the archives of the Corporation of the city of London at the Guildhall, A.D. 1437-1457, by Philip E. Jones. Cambridge: Univ. Pr., 1954. 229p.

3963. ——— Library. London possessory assizes; a calendar, ed. by Helena M. Chew and William Kellaway. London: London Record Society, 1965. 201p. (London Record Office publications, v.1)

Rolls preserved in Corporation of London Records Office.

3964. London County Council Library. Members' library catalogue. v.1, London history and topography. London: The Council, 1939. 142p.

Classified arrangement, with author-subject indexes.

3965. London County Council, London County Record Office. Guide to the records in the London County Record Office, by Ida Darlington. London: The Council, 1963. 63p.

pt.1 of series, "Records of the predecessors of the London County Council except the Board of Guardians."

3966. National Book League. London and its environs, 1971. London, 1971. 44p.

Catalog of an exhibition held by the National Book League with the British Council.

3967. Port of London Authority. The library and the picture collection of the Port of London Authority, by Bertram Stewart. London: Richards, 1955. 86p.

Survey of archives, books, and pictures preserved by the Authority.

3968. Sims, J. M. London and Middlesex published records, a handlist. London: Record Society, 1970. 66p. (London Record Society occasional publications, no.1)

3969. Society of Antiquaries of London. Catalogue of a collection of printed broadsides in the possession of the Society of Antiquaries of London, comp. by Robert Lemon. London, 1866. 228p.

Covers period 1513-1815.

3970. Society of Antiquaries of London Library. A catalogue of manuscripts in the Library of the Society of Antiquaries of London. London: Bensley and Son, 1816. 92p.

3971. ———. A catalogue of the printed books in the Library of the Society of Antiquaries of London. London: Bensley and Son, 1816. 260p.

3972. ———. Printed books in the Library of the Society of Antiquaries of London. London: The Society, 1887. 800p.

3973. ———. Printed books in the Library of the Society of Antiquaries of London; supplement, 1887-1899. London, 1899. 390p.

3974. Victoria and Albert Museum. The growth of London, A. D. 43-1964; catalogue of an exhibition at the Victoria & Albert Museum. London, 1964. 102p.

Chronologically arranged, from Roman London to 20th century; items exhibited located in various libraries and collections.

LONDONDERRY

3975. Carson, W. R. H. A bibliography of printed material relating to the County and Borough of Londonderry. London, 1967. 145*l*. (Thesis, Library Association fellowship)

Contains 1,791 entries, with locations in various British and Irish libraries.

LUDLOW

3976. Skipton, Anne Laetitia Daphne Kennedy. Descriptive list of some medieval deeds relating to Ludlow. London, 1956. 64*l*. (Diploma in Archive Administration, Univ. of London)

In Salop County Record office.

MAIDENHEAD

3977. Maidenhead, Corporation. A calendar of the ancient charters and documents of the Corporation of Maidenhead, comp. by J. W. Walker. Maidenhead, 1908. Unpaged.

Describes 203 documents.

MAIDSTONE

3978. Keen, Rosemary Ann. The Monckton collection: deeds, etc, of Maidstone and district, 1470-1932; presented to . . . Kent County Council. London, 1956. 83*l*. (Diploma in Archive Administration, Univ. of London)

MANCHESTER

3979. British Association for the Advancement of Science. An index to Manchester and its region, comp. by the Manchester and District Division of the Association of Assistant Librarians, ed. by M. J. Harkin. Manchester: Univ. Pr., 1964. 14p.

3980. Historical Association, Manchester Branch. Manchester manuscripts, 1- . Manchester, 1969- .
Issued periodically.

3981. Manchester Public Libraries. Index to the Owen mss. in the Free Reference Library, comp. by Ernest Axon. Manchester: Free Reference Library, 1900. 25p. (Occasional lists, no.6)

Collection relates to history and genealogy of Manchester area.

3982. ———. Manuscript diaries in Manchester libraries, comp. by R. V. Osbourn. Manchester, 1950. 15*l*.

Notes holdings of Manchester Public Libraries and Chetham's Library, Manchester.

3983. ———. Peterloo, Monday, 16th August 1819; a bibliography, comp. by Margaret E. Leighton. Manchester: Libraries Committee, 1969. 32p.

3984. ———, Archives Dept. A brief guide, Manchester, 1968. 6*l*.

MARGATE

3985. Margate Public Library. Catalogue of books, pamphlets and excerpts dealing with Margate, the Isle of Thanet and the County of Kent in the local collection, comp. by Archibald J. Gritten. Margate, 1934. 166p.

MEDBOURNE

3986. Thomson, Sheila Dorling. Some Medbourne deeds from the Peake (Nevill of Holt) manuscripts. London, 1955. 157*l*. (Diploma in Archive Administration, Univ. of London)

Records deposited in Leicester County Record Office.

MERIONETHSHIRE

3987. Merioneth County Council, County Records Committee. A calendar of the Merioneth quarter sessions rolls, ed. by Keith Williams-Jones. Dolgelley, 1965. 376p. (v.1, 1733-65)

MIDDLESEX

3988. Mercer, E. Doris. "Local archives of Great Britain: XXIV, The Middlesex County Records Office." Archives, no.6 (1963), 30-39.

MONMOUTHSHIRE

3989. Monmouthshire Record Office. Guide to the Monmouthshire Record Office, ed. by W. H. Baker. Newport: Monmouthshire Archives Committee, 1959. 126p.

3990. Newport Public Libraries. Museum and Art Gallery. John Frost and the Chartist movement in Monmouthshire; catalogue of Chartist literature, prints, and relics, etc., by John Warner and W. A. Gunn. Newport: Chartist Centenary Committee, 1939. 55p.

3991. —— ——. Old deeds and official records as a factor in the history of Monmouthshire. Newport, 1934. 23p.

NEWCASTLE UPON TYNE

3992. Cook, Michael. "Local archives of Great Britain: XXIII. Newcastle upon Tyne City Archives Office." Archives, no.5 (1962), 226-33.

3993. Newcastle upon Tyne City Libraries. Calendar of the Greenwell deeds in the Public Reference Library, by Joseph Walton. Newcastle upon Tyne, 1927. 237p.

Records 467 items from about 1137 to 1823, with detailed descriptions.

3994. ——. A catalogue of the Hexham Court rolls belonging to the Society [of Antiquaries] 1532-1832. Newcastle upon Tyne, 1950. 16p.

3995. ——. Delaval deeds: provisional summary of the contents of the boxes in the possession of the Central Reference Library, Newcastle upon Tyne. Newcastle upon Tyne, 1919. 208p.

3996. ——. Local catalogue of material concerning Newcastle and Northumberland, as represented in the Central Public Library, Newcastle upon Tyne, ed. by Basil Anderton. Newcastle upon Tyne: Public Libraries Committee, 1932. 626p.

Author and subject lists.

3997. ——. A short guide to the archives collection. Newcastle upon Tyne, 1961. 24p.

3998. Newcastle upon Tyne Society of Antiquaries. A catalogue of the Library belonging to the Society. Newcastle upon Tyne, 1896. 176p.

3999. Newcastle upon Tyne, University, Library. Allendale mss. in the University Library, Newcastle upon Tyne; a handlist. London: National Register of Archives, 1962. 22l.

In 2pts.: Hexham and Anick Grange manorial documents; Blackett-Beaumont lead mining records.

4000. —— ——. Blackett-Beaumont lead mining records; a list. Newcastle upon Tyne, 1962. 4p.

Records deposited in Newcastle upon Tyne University Library in 1935.

NEWPORT

4001. Parker, David F. An annotated bibliography of Newport (Monmouthshire). London, 1971. 422l. (Thesis, Library Association Fellowship)

Locates copies in several Welsh libraries.

NORFOLK

4002. Humphrey, Elizabeth. History collections in Norfolk and Suffolk libraries, a handbook. Norwich: Centre of East Anglian Studies, Univ. of East Anglia, 1971. 68p.

4003. Kennedy, Jean. "Local archives of Great Britain: XXX. The Norfolk and Norwich Record Office." Archives, no.8 (1967), 63-69.

NORTHAMPTONSHIRE

4004. Northamptonshire Archives Committee. Summary guide to the Northamptonshire Record Office, by P. I. King. Northampton: J. Stevenson Holt, 1954. 24p.

Includes description of 6 principal classes of holdings.

4005. Northamptonshire Record Office. Guide to the Northamptonshire & Rutland probate records, by P. I. King. Northampton, 1964. 14l.

NORTHUMBERLAND

4006. Donkin, W. C., and Patterson, E. F. Northumberland and Tyneside, a bibliography. London: H. M. Stationery Office, 1946. 101p.

Locates copies of 475 items in 13 libraries.

4007. Northumberland County, Office of the Clerk of the Peace. List of documents of public interest filed in the Office of the Clerk of the Peace for the County. Morpeth: Northumberland County, 1922. 90p.

4008. Taylor, H. A. Northumberland history; a brief guide to records and aids in Newcastle upon Tyne. Newcastle upon Tyne: Northumberland County Council, 1963. 59p.

Includes printed sources, calendars and lists, manuscripts, and other primary sources.

NORWICH

4009. Castle Museum. Revised catalogue of the records on the City of Norwich, as arranged in the Muniment Room, in the Castle Museum, comp. by William Hudson and John Cottingham Tingey. Norwich: Edward Burgess, 1898. 132p.

4010. Hepworth, Philip, and Grace, Mary. "Local archives of Great Britain: VIII. The Norwich Central Library." Archives, no.2 (1953), 86-93.

4011. Norwich. A calendar of Norwich deeds enrolled in the Court Rolls of that City, 1307-1341, comp. by

Mrs. Mackinnon, ed. by Walter Rye. Norwich, 1915. 248p.

4012. ———. The records of the City of Norwich, comp. and ed. by William Hudson (v.1) . . . and J. C. Tingey (v.2). Norwich, London: Jarrold & Sons, 1906-10. 2v.

4013. ———. A short calendar of the deeds relating to Norwich, enrolled in the Court Rolls of that City, 1285-1306, ed. by Walter Rye (with the assistance of William Hudson). Norwich, 1903. 136p.

4014. ———, Diocese, Consistory Court. Index of wills proved in the Consistory Court of Norwich, 1687-1750, and now preserved in the Norfolk and Norwich Record Office, comp. by Thomas F. Barton and M. A. Farrow. Norwich, 1965. 214p. (Norfolk Record Society publications, no.34)

4015. Norwich Public Library. Guide to the study of Norwich; a select bibliography of the principal books, pamphlets and articles on Norwich in the Norwich Public Library, by George A. Stephen. Norwich, 1914. 21p.

4016. ———. Guide to the study of Norwich: a select bibliography of the principal books, pamphlets, and articles on Norwich in the Norwich Public Library, by George A. Stephen. 2d ed. Norwich, 1919. 25p.

4017. ———. A short list of works relating to the biographies of Norfolk men & women, preserved in the Free Library, at Norwich, comp. by Walter Rye. Norwich, 1908. 34p.

NOTTINGHAM AND NOTTINGHAMSHIRE

4018. Nottingham Corporation. Historical records of Nottingham Corporation. Nottingham, n.d. 16p. + 20 plates.

4019. Nottingham Public Libraries. List of books in the Reference Library, no.14: Nottinghamshire collection, comp. under direction of J. Potter Briscoe. Nottingham, 1890. 95p.

Includes sections on directories and annuals, Robin Hood collection, Byron collection, and Kirke White collection.

4020. Nottinghamshire County Council, Records Committee. Guide to the Nottinghamshire County Records Office, prep. for the Records Committee, by P. A. Kennedy. Nottingham, 1960. 180p.

4021. Nottinghamshire County Library. Nottinghamshire; a catalogue of the County Library local history collection. Nottingham, 1961. 59p.

Arranged by subjects, towns and villages, and types of material.

4022. ———. Nottinghamshire: a catalogue of the County Library local history collection. 3d ed. Nottinghamshire, 1966. 119p.

OXFORD AND OXFORDSHIRE

4023. Cordeaux, E. H., and Merry, D. H. A bibliography of printed works relating to Oxfordshire (excluding the University and City of Oxford). Oxford: Clarendon Pr. for Oxford Historical Society, 1955. 411p. (Oxford Historical Society, n.s. v.11, 1949-50)

Based on Bodleian's holdings, the shelfmarks of which are given; supplemented by other libraries, inside and outside Oxfordshire; records 4,310 items.

4024. ——— ———. "A bibliography of printed works relating to Oxfordshire, 1955; addenda and corrigenda." Bodleian Library record, 6 (1958-60), 433-43, 558-71.

4025. Henderson (afterwards Gretton), May S. Sturge. "A pull calendar of the earliest extant Oxfordshire Quarter Sessions records in the County Hall, Oxford. Easter Sessions 1687 to Trinity Sessions 1689, inclusive." In her: Oxfordshire justices of the peace in the seventeenth century. Oxford, 1934. 134p. (Oxfordshire Record Society series, v.16)

4026. Oxford, University, Bodleian Library. Rough list of manuscript materials relating to the history of Oxford contained in the printed catalogues of the Bodleian and college libraries, by F. Madan. Oxford, 1887. 170p.

4027. ——— ———. Summary catalogue of manuscripts in the Bodleian Library relating to the City, County, and University of Oxford; accessions from 1916 to 1962, by P. S. Spokes. Oxford: Clarendon, 1964. 207p. (Oxford Historical Society, n.s. no.17)

4028. ———, Christ Church. A catalogue of manorial records at Christ Church. Oxford, 1953. 280p.

4029. ———, Magdalen College. The collection of Brockley deeds at Magdalen College, Oxford, comp. by William Dunn Macray and ed. by Richard Ussher. Buckingham, 1910. 152l. (Reprinted from the Buckingham advertiser)

4030. ———, New College. A catalogue of "manorial documents" preserved in the muniment room of New College, Oxford, comp. by T. F. Hobson. London, 1929. 71p. (Manorial Society's publications, no.16)

4031. Oxfordshire County Council. A handlist of inclosure acts and awards relating to the County of Oxford. Oxford, 1963. 61p.

Lists and describes 196 documents.

4032. ———. A handlist of plans sections and books of reference for the proposed railways in Oxfordshire, 1925-1936. Oxford, 1964. 23p.

4033. ———. Summary catalogue of the privately-deposited records in the Oxfordshire County Record Office. Oxford, 1966. 158p. (Record publication. no.4)

4034. Oxfordshire County Records Joint Committee. The Oxfordshire County Record Office and its records. Oxford, 1948. 15p. (Record publication, no.1)

PEMBROKESHIRE

4035. Cardiff Public Libraries. Catalogue of manuscripts, books, engravings, references, etc., relating to St. David, St. David's Day, St. David in romance, and the Cathedral Church of St. David's, Pembrokeshire, comp. by Wyndham Morgan. Cardiff: Libraries Committee, 1927. 41p.

PLYMOUTH

4036. Plymouth City Libraries, Plymouth records. A guide to the Archives Department of Plymouth City Libraries. Plymouth, 1962. 37p. (Plymouth records, no.1)

4037. Plymouth Corporation. Calendar of the Plymouth municipal records, by R. N. Worth. Plymouth, 1893. 308p.

4038. ———. Plymouth city charters, 1439-1935; a catalogue, by C. E. Welch, Plymouth, 1962. 44p. (Plymouth records, no.2)

4039. Welch, C. E. "Local archives of Great Britain: XXI. The Plymouth Archives Department." Archives, no.5 (1961), 100-5.

PORTSMOUTH

4040. Portsmouth Corporation. City of Portsmouth: records of the Corporation, 1936-1945, comp. by G. E. Barnett, ed. by V. Blanchard. Portsmouth, 1965. 357p. + 24 plates.

4041. ———. City of Portsmouth; records of the Corporation, 1945-1955, comp. by G. E. Barnett, ed. by V. Blanchard. Portsmouth, 1968. 340p.

PRESTON

4042. France, R. Sharpe. "The County Record Office, Preston." Transactions of the Historic Society of Lancashire and Cheshire, 92 (1940), 77-84. Reprinted, Liverpool, 1940.

Summary description of archives.

RICHMOND

4043. North Riding County Library. Around Richmond; a select list of books, articles and illustrations prepared on the occasion of the quatercentenary (1567-1967) of Richmond School. Northallerton, 1967. 43p.

ROCHESTER

4044. Oakley, Anne Mary. Rochester capitular archives title deeds, c. 1093-1540. London, 1960. 156*l*. (Diploma in Archive Administration, Univ. of London)

In Kent County Record Office.

4045. Rochester, Corporation of the City. The City of Rochester charters, by Philip M. Bartlett. Rochester, 1961. 101p.

ST. ANDREWS

4046. St. Andrews, University, Library. Collections towards a bibliography of St. Andrews, by J. H. Baxter. St. Andrews: W. C. Henderson & Son, Univ. Pr., 1926. 143p.

Contains 1,208 entries; "catalogue of local literature in the University Library."

ST. MARYLEBONE

4047. St. Marylebone Public Libraries Committee. Handlist to the Ashbridge collection on the history and topography of St. Marylebone, comp. by Ann Cox-Johnson. St. Marylebone, 1959. 215p.

Collection acquired by St. Marylebone Borough Council and housed in the Borough Library.

4048. St. Marylebone Public Libraries. The history of St. Marylebone; an exhibition of prints, maps, photographs, etc.; a catalogue. London, 1936. 18p.

4049. St. Marylebone Public Library. A list of the records of the Parish of St. Marylebone (1683-1900) in the Town Hall and of records relating to St. Marylebone (1726-1935) in St. Marylebone Public Library. St. Marylebone, 1952. 25p.

ST. PANCRAS

4050. St. Pancras Public Libraries. Catalogue of an exhibition . . . illustrating "Saint Pancras through the ages," comp. by Frederick Sinclair. London, 1938. 103p.

SANDWICH

4051. Sandwich. A classified list of the records lodged in the Guildhall of the Town and Port of Sandwich, comp. by Edith S. Scroggs. Sandwich, 1932. 38p.

SCARBOROUGH

4052. Scarborough, Corporation. Catalogue of ancient documents belonging to the Corporation of Scarborough, by I. H. Jeayes. Scarborough, 1915. Unpaged.

4053. ———. A descriptive catalogue of the records in the possession of the Corporation of Scarborough, by G. C. F. Foster. Scarborough, 1968. 35p.

SEAFORD

4054. Seaford, Corporation. Records of the Corporation of Seaford; a catalogue, ed. by Francis W. Steer. Lewes: Sussex County Council, 1959. 65p.

SELBORNE

4055. Oxford, University, Magdalen College. Calendar of charters and documents relating to Selborne and its priory, preserved in the muniment room of Magdalen College, Oxford, ed. by W. Dunn Macray. London: Simpkin & Co., 1891-94. 2v.

SHEFFIELD

4056. Freemantle, W. T. A bibliography of Sheffield and vicinity; section 1, to the end of 1700. Sheffield: Pawson and Brailsford, 1911. 285p.
   Locates items recorded in 15 libraries.

4057. Hall, T. Walter. A descriptive catalogue of ancient charters & instruments relating to lands near Sheffield in the counties of York, Derby, Nottingham & Lincoln, with genealogies and notes. Sheffield: J. W. Northend, 1935. 96p.
   Records chiefly in Sheffield City Libraries.

4058. ———. A descriptive catalogue of early charters relating to lands in & near Sheffield with illustrations, genealogies & notes. Sheffield: J. W. Northend, 1938. 41p. + 4 plates.

4059. ———. Sheffield, 1297-1554; a catalogue of the ancient charters belonging to the Twelve Capital Burgesses and Commonalty of the town and parish of Sheffield, usually known as the Church Burgesses; with abstracts of all Sheffield wills proved at York prior to 1554. Sheffield: J. W. Northend, 1913. 148p.

4060. ———. Sheffield, Hallamshire; a descriptive catalogue of Sheffield manorial records from the 8th year of Richard II to the Restoration. Sheffield: J. W. Northend, 1926. 237p.

4061. ———. Worsborough, Eckington and Sheffield; descriptive catalogue of the Edmunds collection including charters, court-rolls and estreats relating to Worsborough, Stainborough & Barnsley near Sheffield court-roll & parliamentary survey of the Manor of Eckington near Sheffield; deeds and wills relating to Sheffield. Sheffield: J. W. Northend, 1924. 323p.

4062. Lewis, N. B. "The abolitionist movement in Sheffield, 1823-1833; with letters from Southey, Wordsworth and others." Bulletin of the John Rylands Library, 18 (1934), 377-92. Reprinted. 1934. 18p.
   From original papers in the John Rylands Library.

4063. Newton, Surr Carl. A calendar of the Bright papers. London, 1959. 374*l*. (Diploma in Archive Administration, Univ. of London)
   Deposited in Sheffield Public Library.

4064. Sheffield City Libraries. Basic books on Sheffield history. Sheffield: Dept. of Local History and Archives, Central Library, 1962. 15p.
   Compiled in the Department of Local History and Archives, Sheffield Central Library.

4065. ———. Catalogue of the Arundel Castle manuscripts, being the muniments of his grace the Duke of York . . . relating to the Yorkshire, Nottingham and Derbyshire estates of the Dukes of Norfolk and their predecessors. Sheffield: Libraries and Arts Committee, 1965. 222p.

4066. ———. Catalogue of the charters, deeds, and manuscripts in the Public Reference Library at Sheffield, prep. by T. Walter Hall. Sheffield: J. W. Northend, 1912. 105p.

4067. ———. A catalogue of the portion of Edward Carpenter's library now in the Department of Local History in the Sheffield City Libraries. Sheffield, 1963. 222p.

4068. ———. Crewe muniments. Sheffield, 1954. 164p.
   Collection originating with Marchioness of

Crewe, now in Dept. of Local History and Archives, Sheffield City Libraries.

4069. ———. Descriptive catalogue of charters, copy court rolls and deeds, forming part of the Wheat collection at the Public Reference Library, Sheffield, also others from private collections, with abstracts of Sheffield wills proved at York from 1560 to 1566, and 285 genealogies deduced therefrom, comp. by T. Walter Hall. Sheffield, 1920. 279p.

4070. ———. Descriptive catalogue of the charters, rolls, deeds . . . and miscellaneous papers forming the Jackson collection, comp. by T. Walter Hall and A. Hermann Thomas. Sheffield: J. W. Northend, 1914. 420p.

4071. ———. Guide to the manuscript collections in the Sheffield City Libraries, prep. by Miss R. Meredith. Sheffield: Libraries, Art Galleries and Museums Committee, 1956. 115p. Supplements 1-2, 1962-67. 2v.

Includes family records, "solicitors' accumulations," other professional and business records, antiquaries' collections, etc.

4072. ———. Material for the history of Wincobank, Sheffield, 1523-1750, gathered from the Wheat collection . . . with abstracts of wills . . . and genealogies of the ancient family of Greaves, comp. by T. W. Hall. Sheffield, 1922. 35p.

4073. ———. Records of the Clark family of Noblethorpe Hall, Silkstone, relating to their colliery business and to the Noblethorpe estates. Sheffield, 1972. 44*l*.

4074. ———. Summary list of the papers of the 4th Earl Fitzwilliam, as listed (with some amendments) when first received at the Library. Sheffield, n.d. 34*l*.

4075. ———, Dept. of Local History and Archives. The Baxter papers, pt.1; a list of the contents of a solicitor's office, deposited in 1955 by the representatives of Messrs. Somerville and Baxter, solicitors of Doncaster, at Sheffield City Library, reproduced by the National Register of Archives from the original list. Sheffield, 1959. 110*l*. Supplement, 1965. 28*l*.

4076. ——— ———. A calendar of the Bright papers, Wentworth Woodhouse muniments; reproduced by the National Register of Archives from originals supplied by the Department of Local History and Archives, Central Library, Sheffield. Sheffield, 1960. 154*l*. + index.

4077. ——— ———. Handlist of the Wheat collection. Sheffield, 1955. 157*l*.

SHREWSBURY

4078. Hill, Marion Trenchard. Calendar of some sixteenth and seventeenth century deeds relating to Shrewsbury. London, 1958. 129*l*. (Diploma in Archive Administration, Univ. of London)

Deposited in Salop County Record Office.

4079. Shrewsbury, Corporation. Calendar of the muniments and records of the Borough of Shrewsbury. (Compiled by a Special Committee appointed by the Finance Committee of the Corporation) Shrewsbury, 1896. 136p.

4080. ———, Library, Museums and Arts Committee. A list of wills and marriage settlements in the local history collection of the Shrewsbury Public Library. Shrewsbury, 1958. Unpaged.

4081. ——— ———. Shrewsbury Free Public Library; index-catalogue of the Reference Department Local Section, and other works having some local connection, comp. by H. T. Beddows; with list of manuscripts comp. by W. G. D. Fletcher. Shrewsbury: W. B. Walker, 1903. 82p.

SHROPSHIRE

4082. Birmingham, University, Library. Shropshire biography; containing much curious and other information relating to many families either born in or connected with that county; collected from various sources and arranged by Edward Edwards; a handlist to the contents. Birmingham, 1969. 7*l*. (Catalogues of the manuscript collections, no.20)

4083. ———. Slaney family manuscripts; handlist of items relating to Shropshire. Birmingham, 1968. Unpaged. (Catalogues of the manuscript collections, no.14)

4084. Fletcher, W. G. D., and Auden, Miss. "Shropshire topographical and genealogical manuscripts preserved in the Bodleian Library." Transactions of the Shropshire Archaeological Society, 2d ser., 7 (1895), 79-93.

4085. Peele, E. C., and Cease, R. S. Shropshire Parish documents. Shrewsbury: W. B. Walker, 1903. 378p. + Index.

4086. Salop County Council. A guide to the Shropshire records, 1952. Shrewsbury: Wilding & Son, 1952. 172p.

Records available in County Record Office.

4087. Charles, B. G. "The records of Slebech." National Library of Wales journal, 5 (1948), 179-98.

Archival and manuscript records of Slebech deposited in National Library of Wales.

SOMERSET

4088. Somerset County Council, County Records Committee. A handlist of the records of the Board of Guardians in the County of Somerset preserved in the Somerset Record Office, Shire Hall, Taunton. Taunton: Harold King, Clerk of the County Council, 1949. 129p.

4089. ———. Interim handlist of Somerset Quarter Sessions documents and other official records preserved in the Somerset Record Office. Taunton, 1947. 68p.

4090. ———. Inventory of parochial documents in the Diocese of Bath and Wells and the County of Somerset, ed. by J. E. King, 1938. 400p.

4091. ———. Somerset in manuscript; notes on the main archive groups preserved in the Somerset Record Office, with a description of documents selected for exhibition. Taunton, 1959. 36p.

SOUTHAMPTON

4092. Great Britain, Historical Manuscripts Commission. The manuscripts of the Corporations of Southampton and King's Lynn. London: H. M. Stationery Office, 1887. 291p. (Report, no.18)

4093. Southampton Corporation. Southampton records I; guide to the records of the Corporation and absorbed authorities in the Civic Record Office. Southampton, 1964. 56p.

4094. Southampton Public Libraries. Southampton's history; a guide to the printed resources. Southampton, 1968. 20p.

Based on Central Library's local history collection.

SOUTHPORT

4095. Southport Public Libraries. Works by Southport authors; a list of books, pamphlets, etc., in the Reference Department of the Atkinson Public Library, comp. by Vera M. Latham. Southport, 1958. 100p.

Alphabetical arrangement by authors and titles.

SOUTHWARK

4096. Greater London Record Office. A survey of the parish registers of the Diocese of Southwark, Inner London area. London, 1970. 66p.

Arranged by localities.

STAFFORD AND STAFFORDSHIRE

4097. Birmingham Public Libraries, Central Reference Library. Calendar of deeds chiefly relating to estates in Wigginton and Tamworth in the County of Stafford, comp. from the originals presented to the Birmingham Reference Library by Messrs. Tunbridge and Co., etc. [Birmingham,] 1940. 12*l*.

4098. Jeayes, Isaac Herbert. Descriptive catalogue of the charters and muniments (of Burton Abbey) belonging to the Marquis of Anglesey, sometimes preserved at Beaudesert but now at Plas Newydd, Isle of Anglesey. Derby, 1937. 219p. (Collections for a history of Staffordshire, 1937)

4099. Kidson, Ruth Monica. Manorial documents and deeds relating to Abbots Bromley, County of Stafford, deposited by the Marquis of Anglesey in the William Salt Library, Stafford. London, 1954. 156*l*. (Diploma in Archive Administration, Univ. of London)

4100. Ridley, Marian Rosemary Catherine. County Record Office, Stafford, Hatherton collection, Persehowse papers. London, 1958. 51*l*. (Diploma in Archive Administration, Univ. of London)

Records deposited in Stafford County Record Office.

4101. Stafford Free Public Library. Staffordshire; a list of books in Stafford Public Library. Stafford, 1953. 14p.

Local history.

4102. Stitt, F. B. "Local archives of Great Britain: XIX. Record Office work in Staffordshire." Archives, no.4 (1960), 204-13.

4103. Stoke on Trent Public Free Library. Current bibliography of published material relating to North Staffordshire and South Cheshire. Stoke on Trent, 1964- . v.1- .

Quarterly classified lists.

STAMFORD

4104. Stamford Public Library. List of books (in date sequence) forming Local History Reference collection, 3d ed. Stamford, 1969. 26 + 2*l*.

4105. Ipswich and East Suffolk Record Office, Parish Records Survey. Report of the survey in the County of East Suffolk and in the Archdeaconries of Ipswich and Suffolk in the Diocese of St. Edmondsbury and Ipswich. Ipswich, 1963. 35p.

4106. Suffolk Institute of Archaeology and Natural History. Catalogue of books in the Library at the Athenaeum, Bury Saint Edmund's. Bury St. Edmund's, 1933. 30p.

4107. Baker, Keith Howard. Records of Boards of Guardians and Joint Poor Law. Committees in the custody of Surrey County Council in the Surrey Record Office, County Hall, Kingston upon Thames. London, 1962. 151p. (Diploma in Archive Administration, Univ. of London)

4108. Cowe, Francis Mitchell. Descriptive list of documents . . . the property of the Clayton family in Surrey. London, 1957. 22 + (67)*l*. (Diploma in Archive Administration, Univ. of London)
Deposited in Surrey County Record Office.

4109. Guildford Public Library, Reference Dept. Catalogue of works in the Library relating to the County of Surrey. Guildford: The Library, 1957. 55p. + index. Supplement, 1968. 42p. + index.
Classified listing.

4110. Minet Public Library. A catalogue of the collection of works relating to the County of Surrey contained in the Minet Public Library, comp. by William Minet and Charles J. Courteney. Aberdeen: Univ. Pr., 1901. 148p. Supplements, 1910, 1912, 1923.

4111. Surrey County Council, Records and Ancient Monuments Committee. Guide to Surrey records, comp. by Miss D. L. Powell, ed. by Hilary Jenkinson. Kingston and London, 1928-35. 7v.
Includes abstract of parish records; abstract of the court rolls of the manorial records; inventory of the Borough records; records of schools and other endowed institutions; quarter sessions records; quarter sessions records, order book, and session rolls, 1659-1661; and quarter sessions, records, order books, and session rolls, 1661-1663.

4112. Surrey Librarians Group. Surrey people: a union list of directories and allied material held in the libraries of Surrey. Esher: Surrey County Library, 1965. 125p.

4113. Williams, M. Y. A short guide to the Surrey collection. London Borough of Lambeth, 1965. 20p.
Guide to Minet Public Library collection, covering Surrey County, Battersea, Wandsworth, Lambeth, Camberwell, Southwark, Bermondsey, and Rotherhithe.

4114. Chapman, Brenda Rosalie. Legal papers on the Ashdown Forest case (1876-1882): a descriptive list. London, 1960. 43*l*. (Diploma in Archive Administration, Univ. of London)
In East Sussex Record Office.

4115. East and West Sussex County Councils. A descriptive report on the quarter sessions, other official, and ecclesiastical records in the custody of the County Councils of East and West Sussex with a guide to the development and historical interest of the archives. Lewes and Chichester, 1954. 212p. (Record publication, no.2)

4116. Sussex Archaeological Society. A calendar of the deeds & other documents in the possession of the Sussex Archaeological Society, by E. H. W. Dunkin. Lewes: South Counties Pr., 1889. 72p. (Reprinted from the Sussex archaeological collections, v.37)
Records 458 items, 1443-1755.

4117. Sussex Record Society. A catalogue of Sussex estate and tithe award maps, comp. by Francis W. Steer. Lewes, 1962. 240p.

4118. East Sussex County Council. The Ashburnham archives; a catalogue, ed. by Francis W. Steer. Lewes, 1958. 144p.
Documents relating to Ashburnham family, 16th to 20th century.

4119. ———. The Danny archives; a catalogue, ed. by Judith A. Wooldridge. Lewes, 1966. 174p.
Records associated with Danny House, near Hurstpierpont.

4120. ———. The Glynde Place archives; a catalogue, ed. by Richard F. Dell. Lewes, 1964. 312p.

4121. ———. The records of Rye Corporation; a catalogue, ed. by Richard F. Dell. Lewes, 1962. 323p.

4122. ———. The Shiffner archives; a catalogue, ed. by Francis W. Steer. Lewis, 1959. 126p.
Records associated with Shiffner's family, deposited in East Sussex Record Office.

4123. ———. Winchelsea Corporation records; a catalogue, ed. by Richard F. Dell. Lewes, 1963. 105p.

Classified list of 2,315 items, deposited in East Sussex County Record Office.

4124. Wooldridge, Judith A. The Hickstead Place archives; a catalogue. London, 1962. 254p. (Diploma in Archive Administration, Univ. of London)

Archives held by East Sussex Record Office.

SUSSEX, WEST

4125. West Sussex County Council. Arundel Castle archives; interim handlists, nos. 1-12, ed. by Francis W. Steer. Chichester, 1968. 258p.

4126. ———. The Cowdray archives; a catalogue, ed. by A. A. Dibben. Chichester, 1960-64. 2v.

Records associated with Cowdray House in Eastbourne, West Sussex Parish.

4127. ———. The Crookshank collection in the West Sussex Record Office; a catalogue, ed. by Francis W. Steer. Chichester, 1960. 41p.

Lists 437 items received by bequest from Arthur Chichester Crookshank, 1889-1958; includes rare books, local history, etc.

4128. ———. A descriptive report on the Quarter Sessions, other official and ecclesiastical records in the custody of the County Councils of West and East Sussex, with a guide to the development and historical interest of the archives. Chichester: West Sussex County Council; Lewes: East Sussex County Council, 1954. 212p.

4129. ———. The Goodwood Estate archives; a catalogue, ed. by Francis W. Steer and J. E. Amanda Venables. Chichester, 1970. 309p. (v.1)

4130. ———. The Greatham archives; a catalogue, ed. by A. A. Dibben. Chichester, 1962. 22p.

Records associated with Greatham, West Sussex Parish.

4131. ———. The Lavington Estate archives; a catalogue of the Lavington papers in the West Sussex Record Office, ed. by Francis W. Steer. Chichester, 1964. 127p.

4132. ———. Local history in West Sussex; a guide to sources, by Kim C. Leslie and Timothy J. McCann. Chichester, 1971. 30p.

Locations in 12 libraries.

4133. ———. The Maxse papers; a catalogue, ed. by Francis W. Steer. Chichester, 1964. 36p.

Archives of Maxse family for 18th to 20th centuries.

4134. ———. The Petworth House archives; a catalogue, ed. by Francis W. Steer and Noel H. Osborne. Chichester, 1968. 207p.

Catalog of records collected and accumulated by Percy, Seymour, and Wyndham families at Petworth House.

4135. ———. Sussex poor law records; a catalogue, ed. by Jane M. Coleman. Chichester, 1960. 72p.

4136. ———. The probate records of West Sussex, deposited in the County Record Office at Chichester. Chichester, 1950. Unpaged.

SWANSEA

4137. Swansea Corporation, Public Libraries Committee, Festival of Britain, 1951. The Association of Bookmen of Swansea & West Wales in cooperation with the Swansea Public Libraries Committee presents: "Literary Swansea"—an exhibition of books about Swansea and by Swansea authors . . . A catalogue. Swansea, 1951. 25p.

TAMWORTH

4138. Tamworth Borough Records. Being a catalog of civic records with appendices, by Henry Wood. Tamworth, 1952. 75p.

TAUNTON

4139. Taunton, Archdeaconry, Archdeacon's Court. Calendar of wills and administrations in the Court of the Archdeacon of Taunton; pts.I and II, wills . . . 1537-1799. (pt.III, administrations, 1596-1799, and pt.IV, calendar of wills in the Royal Peculiar of Ilminster, 1690-1857), ed. by Edward Alexander Fry. London: British Record Society, 1912-21. 2v. (Index Library, v.45, 45a)

TUNBRIDGE WELLS

4140. Tunbridge Wells Public Library. Local history catalogue. Mount Pleasant, 1966. 12p.

WALSALL

4141. Sims, Reginald William. Borough of Walsall; calendar of deeds and documents belonging to the Corporation of Walsall; with a list added of the charters relating to Walsall, referred to in the Walsall chartulary. Walsall & Kirby, 1882. 70p.

4142. Walthamstow. Calendar of deeds relating to Walthamstow (1584 to 1855) 1595 to 1890. (1541 to 1682), by Stephen J. Barns. Walthamstow, 1923-35. 3pts. (Walthamstow Antiquarian Society, Official publication, nos. 11, 21, 33)

WARRINGTON

4143. Warrington Public Library. Digging up the past in Warrington and district, ed. by G. A. Carter. Warrington, 1964. 12p.

WARWICKSHIRE

4144. Wood, Anthony. "Local archives of Great Britain: X. The Warwick County Record Office and the preservation of records in Warwickshire." Archives, no.2 (1954), 192-204.

WATERFORD

4145. Newcastle upon Tyne City Libraries. Waterford charters; a calendar of documents in the possession of the Central Reference Library, Newcastle upon Tyne. Newcastle upon Tyne, n.d. 43l.

WESTMINSTER

4146. Smith, John Edward. A catalogue of Westminster records deposited at the Town Hall, Caxton Street, in the custody of the Vestry of St. Margaret & St. John. London: Wightman & Co., 1900. 260p.

WIGAN

4147. Wigan Public Libraries. Calendar of the Standish deeds, 1230-1575, preserved in the Wigan Public Library; together with abstracts made by . . . Thomas West in 1770 of 228 deeds not now in the collection, by Thomas Cruddas Porteus. Wigan: T. Wall, 1933. 156p. (Reprinted from the Wigan observer)

Lists and describes 469 items.

4148. ———. Wigan bibliography; a local catalogue of Wigan-printed books and pamphlets and the works of authors connected with Wigan and the district, collected and preserved in the Wigan Free Public Library, by H. T. Folkard. Wigan, 1886. 27p.

WILTSHIRE

4149. Wilts County Library. Catalogue of books about or connected with Wiltshire, comp. by G. F. Webb. Wilts, 1933. 34p.

Based on County Library's collection.

4150. Wiltshire Archaeological and Natural History Society. Catalogue of the collection of drawings, prints, and maps in the Library of the Wiltshire Archaeological and Natural History Society at Devizes, comp. by W. Howard Bell and E. H. Goddard Devizes: C. H. Woodward, 1898. 158p.

4151. ———. Catalogue of the printed books, pamphlets, mss., and maps in the Library of the Wiltshire Archaeological and Natural History Society's Museum at Devizes, comp. by W. Howard Bell and E. H. Goddard. Devizes, 1894. 100p.

4152. ———, Records Branch. List of Wiltshire borough records earlier in date than 1836, ed. by Maurice G. Rathbone. Devizes: The Society, 1951. 108p.

4153. Wiltshire County Council. Guide to county, council, parish, poor law and other official records in the Wiltshire County Record Office, comp. by Pamela Stewart. Wilts, 1961. 131p.

4154. ———. Guide to the records in the custody of the Clerk of the Peace for Wiltshire, comp. by Maurice G. Rathbone. Trowbridge, 1959. 41p.

WINDSOR

4155. Windsor Castle. The manuscripts of St. George's Chapel, Windsor Castle, ed. by John Neale Dalton. Windsor: Dean and Canons of St. George's Chapel, 1957. 629p.

A catalogue.

4156. Windsor, Corporation. Records at the Guildhall and Kipling Memorial Building (Handlist of the records of the Royal Borough of New Windsor), comp. by Shelagh M. Bond. Windsor, 1959. 12p.

WOLVERHAMPTON

4157. Mander, Gerald Poynton. Early Wolverhampton books and printers, with a note on some playbills. Wolverhampton: Whitehead Brothers, 1922. 42p.

Lists 95 items, 1724-1801, locating copies in public and private collections.

WORCESTERSHIRE

4158. Barnard, E. A. B. "Some original documents concerning Worcestershire, and the Great Rebellion." Transactions of the Worcestershire Archaeological Society, 5 (1927-28), 69-91. Reprinted, 1929.

Materials preserved in the Birmingham Reference Library.

4159. Cashmore, H. M. "Worcestershire mss. at Birmingham Reference Library." Worcestershire Archaeological Society transactions, n.s. 15 (1938), 78-80.

General discussion.

4160. Sargeant, E. H. "Local archives of Great Britain: XXII. The Worcestershire Record Office." Archives, no.5 (1962), 151-59.

4161. Society of Antiquaries. List of the printed papers and miscellanea with index; and of the pedigrees and portraits, in the Prattinton collections of Worcestershire history, in the possession of the Society of Antiquaries, by E. A. B. Barnard. London, 1932. 162*l*.

4162. Worcestershire Archaeological Society Library. Subject catalogue, comp. by R. Mary Sargeant, 1966. Worcester, 1966. 41p.

Arranged by Dewey classification.

4163. Worcestershire Historical Society. Bibliography of Worcestershire, by J. R. Burton and F. S. Pearson. Oxford, 1898-1907. 3v.

v.1, Acts of Parliament relating to the county; v.2, classified catalogue of books and other printed matter relating to the county; v.3, the botany of Worcestershire; copies of items in v.2 located in 7 English libraries.

4164. ———. Original charters relating to the City of Worcester, in the possession of the Dean and Chapter, and by them preserved in the Cathedral Library, ed. by J. Harvey Bloom. Oxford: James Parker & Co., 1909. 215p.

4165. ———. Worcestershire County Records; Division I. Documents relating to Quarter Sessions. Calendar of the Quarter Sessions papers. vol.I. 1591-1643, comp. by J. W. Willis Bund. Worcester, 1900. 2pts. 952p.

WYTHENSHAWE

4166. Manchester Public Libraries. Wythenshawe, a bibliography, comp. by William H. Shercliff. Manchester, 1955. 12p.

YORK AND YORKSHIRE

4167. Bradford Free Libraries and Art Museum. Catalogue of the books and pamphlets relating to Yorkshire in the Central Reference Library. Bradford, 1892. 89p.

4168. Gurney, Norah K. M. "The Borthwick Institute of Historical Research." Archives, no.7 (1966), 157-62.

Collection consists of archives of diocese and province of York; associated with University of York.

4169. Leeds, University, Brotherton Library. Manuscripts collected by John Wilson, of Broomhead (1719-1783) in the Brotherton Library. Leeds, 1967. 6*l*.

Collection relating largely to Yorkshire.

4170. Scarborough Public Libraries. Yorkshire in fiction. Scarborough, 1958. 11p.

4171. Sheffield, University, Library, Information Service. Sheffield University theses relating to Yorkshire and Derbyshire, 1920-1970, comp. by J. Hall and R. Wells. Sheffield, 1971. 10p.

4172. York, Corporation. Catalogue of the charters, house books, freemen's rolls, chamberlains', etc., accounts, and other books, deeds, and old documents, belonging to the Corporation of York; together with report on their renovation, comp. by William Giles. York, 1909. 159p.

4173. York Public Library. List of books in the local collection relating to the City and County of York. York, 1912. 171p.

4174. York, University, Borthwick Institute of Historical Research. A brief guide to Yorkshire Record Offices. York, 1968. 41*l*.

4175. Yorkshire Archaeological Society Library. Catalogue of manuscripts and deeds in the Library of the Yorkshire Archaeological Society at 10, Park Place, Leeds, 2d ed., comp. by E. W. Crossley. Leeds, 1931. 109p. Supplements, 1931-43. 3pts.

4176. Yorkshire Archaeological Society. Catalogue of manuscripts in the Library of the Yorkshire Archaeological Society, comp. by W. T. Lancaster. Leeds: J. Whitehead, 1912. 52p.

4177. ———. Catalogue of the maps and plans in the Library of the Yorkshire Archaeological Society, Leeds, comp. by G. E. Kirk. Wakefield: Printed for the Society by the West Yorkshire Printing Co., 1937. 26p.

4178. ———. Catalogue of the printed books and pamphlets in the Library, comp. by G. E. Kirk. Wakefield: West Yorkshire Printing Co., 1935-36. 2pts.

Library located in Leeds; emphasis on British history.

Irish

4179. Belfast Library and Society for Promoting Knowledge (Linen Hall Library). Catalogue of the books in the Irish section. Belfast: H. MacBride, 1917. 268p.

Records over 5,000 volumes of Irish interest; dictionary arrangement.

4180. Belfast Public Libraries. Finding list of books added to the stock of the Irish and local history collection before 1956. Belfast, 1964. 2v.

In 2 sections: author and title entries alphabetically; classified subject listing.

4181. Cambridge, University, Library. A catalogue of the Bradshaw collection of Irish books in the University Library, Cambridge, London: Quaritch, 1916. 3v.

Records 8,743 numbered items; v.1, books printed in Dublin by known printers, 1602-1882; v.2, books printed in Dublin of which the printer is not known, etc.; v.3, index.

4182. ———. The Henry Bradshaw Irish collection, presented in 1870 and 1886. Cambridge, 1909. 1,095p. (Cambridge University Library bulletin extra series)

Extensive collection of Irish books and papers assembled by Henry Bradshaw and acquired by Cambridge University Library.

4183. Darwin, Kenneth. "The Public Record Office of Northern Ireland." Archives, no.6 (1963), 108-16.

History and analysis of holdings.

4184. Dix, E. R. McC. "The case of Ireland's being bound by the acts of Parliament in England stated, by William Molyneux of Dublin, Esq.; list of editions." Irish book lover, 5 (1914), 116-18.

Locates copies of 12 editions, 1698-1897.

4185. Dublin, Corporation. Calendar of Ancient Records of Dublin, in the possession of the Municipal Corporation of that City. [v.1-11 edited by John T. Gilbert. v.III [etc.] edited by Lady Gilbert and J. F. Weldrick.] Dublin: Joseph Dollard, 1889-98. 7v.

4186. ———. Catalogue of the books and manuscripts comprising the library of the late Sir John T. Gilbert, comp. by Douglas Hyde and D. J. O'Donoghue. Dublin: Browne and Nolan, 1918. 962p.

Collection particularly rich in Irish history, including many rare books and manuscripts.

4187. Galway County Libraries. A bibliography of the County Galway, by Mary Kavanagh. Galway, 1965. 187p.

Copies located in National Library of Ireland, Galway County Libraries, etc.; subject arrangement of 1,669 items.

4188. Galway, Wardenship. Report on documents relating to the wardenship of Galway, ed. by Edward MacLysaght [containing a calendar, prepared on behalf of the English Historical Manuscripts Commission, by H. F. Berry; additions to the calendar, edited by E. MacLysaght, and an appendix of documents, preserved in the archives of the diocese of Kerry, relating to the wardenship of Galway, ed. by D. A. Reidy]. Dublin, 1944. 249p. (Analecta Hibernica, no.14)

4189. Great Britain, Public Record Office. Calendar of documents relating to Ireland, preserved in Her Majesty's Public Record Office, London, ed. by H. S. Sweetman and Gustavus Frederick Handcock. London: Longmans, 1881-86. 5v.

Covers period 1293-1307.

4190. ———. Calendar of the state papers relating to Ireland preserved in the State Paper Department of Her Majesty's Public Record Office, ed. by Hans Claude Hamilton and others. London: Longmans and H. M. Stationery Office, 1860-1912. 27v.

Covers period 1509-1670.

4191. Hayes, Richard J. Manuscript sources for the history of Irish civilization. Boston, Mass.: G. K. Hall, 1965. 11v.

v.1-4, persons; v.5-6, subjects; v.7-8, places; v.9-10, dates; v.11, lists of manuscripts; locations in numerous depositories.

4192. Imperial War Museum Library. Ireland, 1914-1921; a selected list of references. London, 1966. 11l. (Bibliography, no.PH. 851)

4193. Ireland, Public Record Office. Calendar of the Justiciary rolls or proceedings in the Court of the Justiciar of Ireland, preserved in the Public Record Office of Ireland, ed. by James Mills. London: H. M. Stationery Office, 1905-14. 2v.

Covers reign of Edward I, 1295-1307.

4194. ———. A guide to the records deposited in the Public Record Office of Ireland, by Herbert Wood. Dublin: H. M. Stationery Office, 1919. 334p.

4195. ———. A short guide to the Public Record Office of Ireland, by Margaret Griffith. Dublin: Stationery Office, 1964. 16p. (Reprinted from Irish historical studies, v.8, no.29)

4196. Limerick County Library. A bibliography of Limerick history and antiquities, by Roisin de Nais. Limerick, n.d. 61p.

List of 581 items, with locations in British Museum, National Library of Ireland, and Limerick County and Municipal Libraries.

4197. Murray, Robert H. A short guide to the principal classes of documents preserved in the Public Record Office, Dublin. London: Society for Promoting Christian Knowledge, 1919. 64p.

4198. National Library of Ireland. Bibliography of Irish history, 1870-1911, by James Carty. Dublin: Stationery Office, 1940. 319p.

Contains more than 2,700 numbered references.

4199. ———. Books on Ireland. Dublin: Cultural Relations Committee of Ireland, 1953. 45p.

Selective list compiled by National Library of Ireland.

4200. ———. Catalogue of engraved Irish portraits, mainly in the Joly collection, and of original drawings, by Rosalind M. Elmes. Dublin: Stationery Office, 1937. 279p.

Arranged alphabetically by subjects of portraits.

4201. ———. Catalogue of Irish manuscripts in the National Library of Ireland, by N. Sheaghdha. Dublin: Institute for Advanced Studies, 1961-68. Fasc. 1-2.

4202. ———. Manuscript sources for the history of Irish civilization, ed. by Richard J. Hayes. Boston, Mass.: G. K. Hall, 1965. 11v.

Union catalog, containing 310,000 entries, of manuscripts relating to Ireland and Irishmen, 5th-20th centuries, from collections in 678 libraries and archives in 30 countries and more than 600 private collections.

4203. ———. Sources for the history of Irish civilization, articles in Irish periodicals, National Library of Ireland (Dublin). Boston, Mass.: G. K. Hall, 1970. 9v.

Covers period 1800-1969.

4204. O'Neill, James J. "The volunteers of 1782." Irish book lover, 6 (1915), 123-24, 144-45.

List of contemporary pamphlets in Royal Irish Academy, Halliday collection.

4205. Oxford, University, Bodleian Library. The Carte manuscripts in the Bodleian Library, Oxford, by C. W. Russell and J. P. Prendergast. London: H. M. Stationery Office, 1871. 236p.

Early 18th-century papers relating to Irish affairs, etc.

4206. Queen's University, Institute of Irish Studies. A guide to sources of research material in Irish studies. Belfast, 1968. 11l.

4207. Royal Irish Academy. Catalogue of Irish manuscripts in the Royal Irish Academy. Dublin, 1926-58. 27 fascicules + 2v. index.

4208. Wigan Public Library. Ireland and the Irish; catalogue of works relating to Ireland in the Reference Department of the Wigan Free Public Library, by Henry Tennyson Folkard. Wigan: R. Platt, 1896. 20p.

European

FRENCH

4209. British Museum, Dept. of Printed Books. List of the contents of the three collections of books, pamphlets and journals in the British Museum relating to the French Revolution, comp. by G. K. Fortescue. London: The Museum, 1899. 48p.

The 3 collections contain 48,579 books, pamphlets, and sets or volumes of periodicals. Fully listed in the general catalog.

4210. Manchester, University, Library. The Renaissance in France. Manchester, 1968. 55p.

Exhibition catalog, with annotated listing of 126 items, manuscript and printed, of 15th and 16th centuries.

4211. ———. Seventeenth-century France; catalogue of an exhibition held in Manchester University Library and in John Rylands Library, by Margaret M. Wright. Manchester, 1971. 35p.

Annotated list of 127 items.

4212. National Book League. Versailles, the Chateau and its history in books and pictures; catalogue of an exhibition arranged for the National Book League by Desmond Flower. London, 1953. 75p.

Locates copies in French and British public and private collections.

4213. National Central Library. French books on history, 1970. London, 1971. 22p.

Accession list of books received by the library.

4214. National Library of Scotland. France: an exhibition of books and manuscripts. Edinburgh: H. M. Stationery Office, 1969. 19p.

Lists 277 items, drawn from National Library's collections, illustrating Scotland's relations with France.

4215. Rose, R. B. "The French Revolution and the grain supply; nationalization pamphlets in the John Rylands Library." Bulletin of the John Rylands Library, 39 (1956), 171-87. Reprinted, 1956. 19p.

4216. ————. "The Revolutionary Committees of the Paris Sections in 1793; a manuscript in the John Rylands Library." Bulletin of the John Rylands Library, 35 (1952), 88-110. Reprinted, 1952. 25p.

4217. Taylor, A. C. Bibliography of published theses on French subjects deposited in university libraries of the United Kingdom, 1905-1950. Oxford: Blackwell, published for the Society for French Studies, 1964. 45p.

4218. Victoria University Library. The Renaissance in France. Manchester, 1968. 55p.
   Exhibition catalog of French literature.

GERMAN

4219. Wiener Library. After Hitler: Germany, 1945-1963. London: Vallentine, Mitchell, 1963. 261p. (Catalogue series, no.4)
   Lists 2,694 entries; Jewish viewpoint; based on Wiener Library's holdings.

4220. ————. Books on persecution, terror and resistance in Nazi Germany. London, 1949. 51p. (Catalogue series, no.1) Supplement. 1953. 23p.
   Contains 519 classified entries with index.

4221. ————. From Weimar to Hitler: Germany 1918-1933, 2d ed. London: Vallentine, Mitchell, 1964. 269p. 1st ed,, 1951. 100p. (Catalogue series, no.2)
   Contains 2,990 entries; Jewish point of view.

4222. ————. German Jewry; its history, life and culture. London: Vallentine, Mitchell, 1958. 279p. (Catalogue series, no.3)
   Based on Wiener Library's holdings.

4223. ————. Persecution and resistance under the Nazis, 2d ed. London: Vallentine, Mitchell, 1960. 208p. (Catalogue series, no.1)
   Based on Wiener Library's holdings.

GYPSIES

4224. Leeds, University, Brotherton Library. Catalogue of the Romany collection formed by D. U. McGregor Phillips, LL.D., and presented to the University of Leeds, comp. by David Masson. Edinburgh: Thomas Nelson, 1962. 227p.
   Lists printed books, music, typescripts, manuscripts, drawings and paintings, photographs, sound records, etc., a total of 1,234 items.

4225. Liverpool, University, Library. In memoriam Robert Andrew Scott Macfie; a catalogue of the Gypsy books collected by the late Robert Andrew Scott Macfie, prep. by Dora E. Yates. Liverpool, 1936. 178p.
   Alphabetical by authors.

ITALIAN

4226. British Museum. Risorgimento collection; accessions to the general catalogue of printed books. London, 1971. 78 cols.
   Listing of collection of about 600 books and pamphlets relating to Italian Risorgimento.

4227. ————, Dept. of Manuscripts. Catalogo di manoscritti Italiani esistenti nel Museo Britannico di Londra, by Alessandro Palma di Cesnola. Torino: Tipografia L. Roux e. c., 1890. 209p.

4228. Michel, Ersilio. "I manoscritti del 'British Museum' relativi alla storia di Corsica." Archivio storico di Corsica, 6, no.3 (1930), 1-18.
   General discussion.

4229. National Library of Scotland. Italy: an exhibition of books and manuscripts. Edinburgh: H. M. Stationery Office, 1966. 13p.
   Lists 120 items, 12th to 19th century, drawn from National Library's collections, illustrating Scotland's relations with Italy.

4230. Turner, Olga. A brief survey of the documents relating to Sardinia, its history and its kings, to be found in the Department of Manuscripts of the British Museum. Florence: Sansoni, 1959. p.365-95. (Reprinted from Studi storico in onore di Francesco Loddo Canepa)

NORWEGIAN

4231. National Library of Scotland. Norway in books and manuscripts. Edinburgh: H. M. Stationery Office, 1963. 10p.
   An exhibition catalog, compiled by D. W. Evans; lists 148 items drawn from National Library of Scotland.

4232. Royal Norwegian Embassy Library. Catalogue of the Royal Norwegian Embassy Library. London, 1968. 112p.
   Main parts of library consists of books, Norwegian and English, on Norwegian subjects; Dewey classification arrangement.

POLISH

4233. National Library of Scotland. Poland: an exhibition mainly of printed books. Edinburgh, 1965. 11p. (National exhibitions, 3)

List of 111 items, drawn from National Library, illustrating Scotland's relations with Poland.

4234. Polish Library. Bibliography of books in Polish or relating to Poland published outside Poland since September 1st 1939, comp. by J. Zabielska. London, 1953-59. 2v.

A catalog.

PORTUGUESE

4235. British Museum, Dept. of Manuscripts. Catálogo dos manuscritos portugueses ou relativos a Portugal existentes no Museu Britânico, by Conde de Tovar. Lisbon: Academia das Ciéncias de Lisboa, 1932. 407p.

4236. Francisco de la Figanière, Frederico. Catalogo dos manuscriptos portuguezes existentes no Museu Britannico. Lisbon: Na Imprensa Nacional, 1853. 416p.

Grouped under individual collections.

4237. Lima, Oliveira. Relação dos manuscriptos portuguezes e estrangeiros de interesse para o Brazil, existentes no Museu Britannico de Londres, comp. by Oliveira Lima. Rio de Janeiro: Edição do Instituto historico e geographico brazileiro, 1903. 139p. (Revista trimensal, v.65, pt.2)

RUMANIAN

4238. Tappe, E. D. Documents concerning Rumanian history (1427-1601), collected from British archives. London: Mouton, 1964. 162p.

Detailed descriptions of 218 documents in the Public Record Office, British Museum, and other public and private collections.

RUSSIAN AND EAST EUROPEAN

4239. Birmingham Public Libraries. A selection of books on Russia available for consultation in the Birmingham Reference Library. Birmingham, 1944. 29p.

4240. Birmingham, University, Library. Russian and East European library materials at the University of Birmingham, a reader's guide. Birmingham, 1972. 31p.

Includes select list of 118 works of reference.

4241. Burtsev, Vladimir. "Russian documents in the British Museum." Slavonic review, 4 (1926), 669-85.

Discussion of groups of documents.

4242. Loewenson, Leo. "Russian documents in the British Museum." Slavonic and East European review, 14 (1936), 380-88, 661-69.

Discussion of 16th- and 17th-century documents.

4243. SCONUL, Slavonic and East Europe Group. Directory of libraries and special collections of Eastern Europe and the USSR, ed. by G. Walker. London: Crosby, Lockwood, 1971. 159p.

Data on collections and services.

4244. Walker, Gregory. "Library resources in Britain for East European studies." Cahiers du monde russe et soviétique, 12 (1971), 339-46.

Description of library holdings in United Kingdom significant for study of Soviet Union and Eastern Europe.

SCANDINAVIAN

4245. Evans, D. W. "Inscriptions and bookplates from the Thorkelin collection in the National Library of Scotland." Bibliotheck, 4 (1965), 247-48.

Scandinavian collection, principally 18th century.

4246. National Library of Scotland. Scandinavia. Edinburgh, 1970. 55p. (Catalogues of exhibitions held at the National Library of Scotland, Edinburgh, no.12)

Lists 342 items by subjects and types.

4247. Viking Society for Northern Research. List of books belonging to the club, comp. by Jon Stefánsson. Coventry, 1907. 23p.

SLAVIC

4248. London, University, School of Slavonic and East European Studies Library. Acquisitions to the Library. London, no.2- . 1950- .

Issued periodically.

4249. ———. A guide to the Library. London, 1971. 5l.

General description of resources.

4250. ———. A selected list of books in the Library. London, 1942. 47p.

SPANISH

4251. British Museum, Dept. of Manuscripts. Catálogo de documentos sevillanos que se conservan en el Museo Británico, by Francisco Aguilar Piñal. Seville: Imprenta Municipal, 1965. 35p.

4252. ———. Manuscritos canarios del Muséo Británico; [a catalogue] by Eloy Benito Ruano. Madrid, 1955. 27p. (Offprint from Annuario de estudios atlanticos, 1955, no.1)

4253. Canning House Library, Hispanic Council, London. Canning House Library. Boston, Mass.: G. K. Hall, 1967. 4v.
v.1-2, author catalog; v.3-4, subject catalog. Library devoted to materials relating to Portuguese- and Spanish-speaking countries.

4254. Cardiff Public Libraries. List of books on Spain & Portugal in the Central Library. Cardiff: Public Libraries Committee, 1932. 92p.
Arranged under broad subject headings.

4255. Institute of Spain Library. [A catalogue of books in the Library of the Institute.] London, 1946. 41p.
Library relating to Spanish culture, history, and literature.

4256. Thornton, A. P. "The G.R.G. Conway manuscript collection in the Library of the University of Aberdeen." Hispanic American historical review, 36 (1956), 345-47.

SWEDISH

4257. Tapsell, Alan. A guide to the materials for Swedish historical research in Great Britain. Stockholm: Kungl. Boktryckeriet P. A. Norstedt & Söner, 1958. 264p.
Analyses of holdings of individual institutions: Public Record Office, British Museum, university libraries, etc.

Asian

GENERAL

4258. Collison, Robert Lewis. Directory of libraries and special collections on Asia and North Africa. London: Crosby Lockwood, 1970. 123p.
Descriptions of 164 libraries in British Isles and their holdings, arranged by locations of libraries.

4259. Conference on the Acquisition of Library Materials from Asia. Report of conference on the acquisition of library materials from Asia, 30 June 1967. London: School of Oriental and African Studies, 1967. 38l.

4260. London, University, School of Oriental and African Studies. Union catalogue of Asian publications, ed. by D. E. Hall. London: Mansell, 1971. 4v.

Author catalogue of about 66,000 entries, covering systematically or partially the holdings of 64 British libraries.

4261. ———, School of Oriental and African Studies Library. Catalogue of books printed between 1500 and 1599 in the Library of the School of Oriental and African Studies, University of London, a bibliography, by Lesley Eleanor Forbes. London, 1967. 182l.

4262. ——— ———. Catalogue of books printed between 1500 and 1599 in the Library of the School of Oriental and African Studies, prelim. ed., ed. by Lesley Eleanor Forbes. London, 1968. 193p.

4263. ——— ———. Catalogue of periodicals and series. Boston, Mass.: G. K. Hall, 1963. 177p.

4264. ——— ———. The Far East and South-East Asia; a cumulated list of periodical articles, May 1954-April 1956. London, 1955-56. 2pts.

4265. ——— ———. Cumulated list of periodical articles [on the Far East and South East Asia] May 1956-April 1957. London, 1958. 123p.

4266. ——— ———. Cumulated list of periodical articles [on the Far East and South East Asia] May 1957-April 1958. London, 1959. 126p.

4267. ——— ———. Library catalogue. Boston, Mass.: G. K. Hall, 1963. 28v.
Reproduction of 554,000 cards, comprehensive of all aspects of Asia, Oceania, and Africa.

4268. ——— ———. Library catalogue; first supplement. Boston, Mass.: G. K. Hall, 1968. 16v.
Reproduces 191,000 cards.

4269. ——— ———. Library guide. London, 1969. 78p.
Describes holdings under various divisions of 300,000-volume Library.

4270. ——— ———. List of titles added to the catalogue. no.1- . 28 May-23 June, 1951- . London, 1951- .
Issued periodically.

4271. ——— ———. Monthly list of periodical articles on the Far East and South-East Asia. London, 1963-65. 27 nos.

4272. Royal Asiatic Society Library. Catalogue of printed books published before 1832 in the Library of the Royal Asiatic Society. London, 1940. 541p.
Dictionary arrangement.

4273. Royal Asiatic Society of Great Britain and Ireland. Catalogue of the Library. London, 1893. 537p.

4274. Wainwright, Mary Doreen, and Matthews, Noel. A guide to Western manuscripts and documents in the British Isles relating to South and South East Asia. London: Oxford Univ. Pr., 1965. 532p.

Descriptions of holdings of libraries, arranged by locations.

BURMESE

4275. India Office Library. Catalogue of Burmese printed books in the India Office Library, by Kenneth Whitbread. London: H. M. Stationery Office, 1969. 231p.

CHINESE

4276. British Museum. Guide to an exhibition of paintings, manuscripts, and other archaeological objects collected by Sir Aurel Stein in Chinese Turkestan. London, 1914.

INDIAN

4277. Cambridge, University, Library. Handlist of Hardinge papers at the University Library, Cambridge, by N. J. Hancock. Cambridge, 1968. 107p.

Relate to British Empire in India, 1858-1947, and English history, 1815-1901.

4278. Commonwealth Institute Library. Selected reading lists for advanced study: India. London: The Institute, 1969. 22p.

4279. Datta, Rajeshwari. "The India Office Library; its history, resources, and functions." Library quarterly, 36 (1966), 99-148.

4280. East-India Company. A catalogue of the Library of the Hon. East-India Company. London: J. & H. Cox for the Company, 1845. 324p. Supplemental catalogue, 1851. 237p. Reprinted. N.Y.: B. Franklin, 1969. 2v.

Arranged by subjects and languages; collection now in India Office Library.

4281. India House Library. A short catalogue. London: Office of the High Commissioner for India, 1933. 533p.

"Cover all branches of learning, in their application to India"; arranged by subjects, with author and subject index.

4282. India Office Library. Catalogue of European printed books. Boston, Mass.: G. K. Hall, 1964. 10v.

Contains 110,000 entries, covering about 90,000 volumes; last volume is periodical catalog.

4283. ———. Catalogue of manuscripts in European languages belonging to the Library of the India Office. London: H. M. Stationery Office, 1916-37. 2v.

4284. ———. Catalogue of the Library of the India Office, v.1. London: Eyre and Spottiswoode, 1888. 567p. Index, v.1, 1888. 207p. Supplements, v.1-2, 1895-1909. Accessions, 1-18. 1911-26.

4285. ———. A guide to lists and catalogues of the India Office Records, by Joan C. Lancaster, 2d ed. London, 1966. 26p.

4286. ———. A guide to the India Office Library, with a note on the India Office Records, by S. C. Sutton, Librarian, Keeper of the Records, 2d ed. London: H. M. Stationery Office, 1967. 122p.

4287. ———. Index of post-1937 European manuscript accessions. Boston, Mass.: G. K. Hall, 1964. 156p.

4288. ———, Foreign & Commonwealth Office. Monthly list of accessions in European languages. London: The Library. Currently issued.

4289. India Office Map Room. A catalogue of manuscript and printed reports, field books, memoirs, maps, etc., of the Indian surveys deposited in the Map Room of the India Office. London: H. M. Secretary of State for India, 1878. 672p.

4290. India Office Records. Catalogue of the home miscellaneous series of the India Office Records, by Samuel Charles Hill. London: H. M. Stationery Office, 1927. 682p.

Describes 803 groups of records, with detailed index.

4291. ———. A guide to the India Office Records, 1600-1858, by William Foster. London: H. M. Stationery Office, 1966. 130p.

4292. Khan, Shafaat Ahmad. Sources for the history of British India in the seventeenth century. Oxford: Univ. Pr., 1926. 395p.

Individual sections list chronologically documents in British Museum, Public Record Office, Bodleian Library. India Office, Guildhall Library, and Lambeth Palace Library.

4293. Lancaster, Joan C. "The India Office Records." Archives, 9 (1970), 130-41.

General description and summary.

4294. Mountfort, Molly Cecilia. A catalogue of the Viceregal papers of the eighth Earl of Elgin. London, 1957. 119*l*. (Diploma in Archive Administration, Univ. of London)

Records now deposited in the India Office Library.

4295. Taylor, F. "Manuscript materials on modern Indian history in the John Rylands Library." Indian archives, 16 (1965-66), 23-28.

KOREAN

4296. Imperial War Museum Library. The war in Korea, 1950-1953; a list of selected references. London, 1962. 2pts.

MALAYSIAN

4297. Great Britain, Commonwealth Institute Library. Malaysia & Singapore; selected reading lists for advanced study. London, 1969. 17p.

Based on Institute library's holdings.

PAKISTANI

4298. Great Britain, Commonwealth Institute Library. Selected reading lists for advanced study: Pakistan & Ceylon. London: The Institute, 1970. 22p.

PERSIAN

4299. India Office Library. Report on the India Office records relating to Persia and the Persian Gulf, by F. C. Danvers. London: Eyre and Spottiswoode, 1889? 79p.

SOUTH ASIAN

4300. Cambridge, University, Centre of South Asian Studies. Guide to South Asian material in the libraries of London, Oxford & Cambridge, 2d ed., by Rajeshwari Datta. Cambridge, 1966. 18*l*.

Describes resources of 39 libraries.

4301. Hull, University, Brynmor Jones Library. Recent accessions in the field of Southeast Asian studies. Hull, 1970-

TURKISH

4302. British Museum. The literature of the Turkish people; catalogue of an exhibition. London, 1967. 11p.

African

GENERAL

4303. Blake, E. C. "Sources for African studies, 12: British Library of Political and Economic Science." Library materials on Africa, 5 (July 1967), 10-13.

Analysis of library's extensive holdings, chiefly in social sciences.

4304. Bowyer, T. H. "Sources for African studies, 11: Birmingham University Library." Library materials on Africa, 4 (April 1967), 5-7.

Description of library's resources, concentrating on history and social sciences.

4305. Cambridge, University, African Studies Centre. Bibliography of African bibliographies, comp. by Anthea Garling. Cambridge, 1968. 138p.

Locates copies of about 900 items in 9 Cambridge University libraries.

4306. Edinburgh, University, Library. A miscellany of Africana; an exhibition on the occasion of the first conference of the African Studies Association of the United Kingdom to be held in Scotland. Edinburgh, 1966. 14p.

Annotated listing of 103 items.

4307. Jones, Ruth. "The Library of the International African Ihstitute." Library materials on Africa, 4 (July 1966), 17-19.

Review of library's holdings (periodicals, pamphlets, reports, bibliographical files, etc.) concerned with African social and cultural studies.

4308. Leonard, Mrs. J. M. "Sources for African studies, 15: Selly Oak Colleges, Birmingham." Library materials on Africa, 7 (Nov. 1969), 48-49.

Brief description of resources.

4309. London, University, School of Oriental and African Studies. Bibliography of African law; pt.1: East Africa. London, 1961. 83p.

Indicates locations in School of Oriental and African Studies, University of London.

4310. ———. A guide to manuscripts and documents in the British Isles relating to Africa, comp. by Noel Matthews and M. Doreen Wainwright, ed. by J. D. Pearson. London: Oxford Univ. Pr., 1971. 321p.

4311. "Materials on Africa in the United Kingdom." Unesco bulletin for libraries, 21 (1967), 49-50.

Listing of geographical and subject specializations among British libraries.

4312. Oxford, University, Rhodes House Library. Manuscript collections of Africana in Rhodes House Library, Oxford, comp. by Louis B. Frewer. Oxford: Bodleian Library, 1968. 100p.

Lists 1,258 groups of material.

4313. Standing Conference on Library Materials on Africa. "Debates and proceedings of legislative (and legislative advisory) bodies in Africa," by Miriam Alman. Library materials on Africa, 4 (July 1966), 1-37.

Files located in 14 British and American libraries.

4314. ———. The Scolma directory of libraries and special collections on Africa, by Robert Collison, 2d ed., 1967. London: Crosby Lockwood, 1967. 92p.

Brief descriptions of resources and services of 160 individual institutions and collections in British Isles.

4315. Theal, George McCall. Catalogue of books and pamphlets relating to Africa south of the Zambesi, in the English, Dutch, French and Portuguese languages in the collection of G. M. Theal; to which have been added several hundred titles of volumes in those languages and in German in the Library of the British Museum, London, the South African Public Library, Capetown, and a few others; with notes upon those published before 1872, etc. Capetown: Cape Times, 1912. 408p.

4316. United Africa Company. Catalogue of books in the Public Relations Department Library at United Africa House, London. London, 1966. 74p.

ETHIOPIAN

4317. British Museum. Exhibition of books, manuscripts and antiquities from Ethiopia, King's Library. London, 1963. 19p.

GHANAIAN

4318. Commonwealth Institute Library. Ghana, Sierra Leone, the Gambia. London: The Institute, 1968. 16p.

Selected list for advanced study, compiled in the Commonwealth Institute Library.

KENYAN

4319. Commonwealth Institute Library. Kenya, Tanzania, Uganda. London, 1968. 25p. (Selected reading lists for advanced study)

Compiled in Commonwealth Institute Library.

4320. ———. Selected reading lists for advanced study: Kenya, Tanzania, Uganda. London: The Institute, 1971. 27p.

MALAWIAN

4321. Commonwealth Institute Library. Selected reading lists for advanced study: Malawi, Rhodesia, Zambia. London: The Institute, 1969. 15p.

Based on Institute's holdings.

MATACONG ISLAND

4322. Birmingham, University, Library. Catalogue of the Matacong Island (West Africa) papers. Birmingham, 1970. Unpaged. (Catalogues of the manuscript collections, no.26)

Calendar of 239 late-19th-century items relating to Matacong.

NIGERIAN

4323. Commonwealth Institute Library. Nigeria; selected reading lists for advanced study. London, 1970. 21p.

Based on Institute Library's holdings.

American

GENERAL

4324. Andrews, C. M. Guide to the materials for American history to 1783, in the Public Record Office of Great Britain. Washington: Carnegie Institution, 1912-14. 2v.

4325. Calderón Quijano, José Antonio. Guía de los documentos, mapas y planos sobre historia de América y España moderna en la Biblioteca Nacional de París, Museo Británico y Public Record Office de Londres. Seville, 1962. 70p. (Publicaciones de la Escuela de estudios hispano-americanos de Sevilla, no.142)

4326. Corson, James C. "Some American books at Abbotsford." Bibliotheck, 4 (1963), 44-65.

Descriptions of 64 works contained in Sir Walter Scott's library at Abbotsford.

4327. Crick, B. R., and Alman, Miriam. A guide to manuscripts relating to America in Great Britain and Ireland. London: Published for the British Association for American Studies by the Oxford Univ. Pr., 1961. 667p.

Geographical arrangement for locations of collections, followed by analyses of holdings of individual institutions; complements Andrews, Andrews and Davenport, and Paullin and Paxon works (nos.4324, 4338, 4345).

4328. Edinburgh, University, Library. "A miscellany of Americana"; an exhibition on the occasion of the first conference of the British Association of American Studies to be held in Scotland, Edinburgh, 8-11 April 1963. Edinburgh, 1963. 13p.

Listing of 92 manuscripts and "rare and curious items of Americana in the Edinburgh University and New College Libraries."

4329. Griffin, Grace Gardner. A guide to manuscripts relating to American history in British depositories reproduced for the Division of Manuscripts of the Library of Congress. Washington: Library of Congress, 1946. 313p.

Records listed under original repositories: Public Record Office, British Museum, etc.

4330. Higham, C. S. S. The colonial entry-books; a brief guide to the colonial records in the Public Record Office before 1696. London: Society for Promoting Christian Knowledge, 1921. 48p.

Descriptions of records relating to British colonies in America and elsewhere.

4331. Lambeth Palace Library. The Fulham papers in the Lambeth Palace Library; American colonial section calendar and indexes, by William Wilson Manross. Oxford: Clarendon, 1965. 524p.

Relate to Church of England in America.

4332. ———. The New World; a catalogue of an exhibition of books, maps, manuscripts and documents held at Lambeth Palace Library, together with transcripts of five unpublished documents in the Library relating to the early history of the American continent. Westminster: Church Information Board, 1957. 94p.

4333. London, University, Institute of Historical Research. Union list of American historical periodicals in United Kingdom libraries, comp. by H. Hale Bellot. London, 1959. 41p.

Lists holdings of numerous libraries in 2 groups, national and regional.

4334. Manchester, University, Dept. of American Studies. Select list of American historical materials in Manchester libraries. Manchester, 1956. 47*l*.

Records materials in Manchester Public Reference Library, John Rylands Library, and University of Manchester Library.

4335. Wigan Public Library. Souvenir of the Columbus quincentenary exhibition, being a descriptive guide to the exhibition of rare books relating to America opened in the Wigan Library, comp. by

Arthur J. Hawkes. Wigan: Public Libraries Committee, 1944. 12p.

CANADIAN

4336. Birmingham, University, Library. French-Canadian studies; a select bibliography of books in the Library of the University of Birmingham, comp. by Cedric Paul Roger May. Birmingham, 1967. 37*l*.

4337. Commonwealth Institute Library. Selected reading lists for advanced study: Canada. London: The Institute, 1971. 25p.

Based on Commonwealth Institute Library's holdings.

UNITED STATES

4338. Andrews, C. M., and Davenport, F. G. Guide to the manuscript materials for the history of the United States to 1783, in the British Museum, in minor London archives, and in libraries of Oxford and Cambridge. Washington, D.C.: Carnegie Institute of Washington, 1908. 499p.

4339. Baer, Elizabeth. Seventeenth century Maryland; a bibliography. Baltimore, Md.: John Work Garrett Library, 1949. 219p. + about 200 plates.

Detailed descriptions; copies located in British and American libraries.

4340. Cumming, W. P. The discoveries of John Lederer. Charlottesville: Univ. of Va. Pr., 1958. 148p.

Reprint of 1670 translation of Lederer's discoveries in "Three several marches from Virginia to the West of Carolina"; 29 copies recorded, 6 in British Museum.

4341. Kellaway, William. "The archives of the New England Company." Archives, no.12 (1954), 175-82.

Society created in 1649; surviving records deposited in Guildhall Library in 1953.

4342. Liverpool Public Libraries. United States of America; select list of books in the Picton Reference Library. Liverpool, 1951. 54p.

Classified by subjects.

4343. London, University, Institute of United States Studies. Current periodicals of American interest catalogued by the Library of Congress August 1969-July 1970. London, 1970. 12p.

Grouped by subjects, noting holdings.

4344. Manchester, University, Dept. of American Studies. The American Civil War, 1861-1865; a select list of titles in Manchester libraries. Manchester, 1956. 91*l.*

Locations in Manchester Public Reference Library, John Rylands Library, University of Manchester Library, and in private collection.

4345. Paullin, Charles O., and Paxson, Frederic C. Guide to materials in London archives for the history of the United States since 1783. Washington, D.C.: Carnegie Institution of Washington, 1914. 642p.

4346. Royal Institution of Great Britain. Report on American manuscripts in the Royal Institution of Great Britain. London: H. M. Stationery Office, 1904-9. 4v. (Historical Manuscript Commission report, no.59)

Relates to period 1747-88; consists principally of headquarters papers of successive British commanders during American Revolution.

4347. Scotland, Public Record Office. Material relating to the U.S.A. and Canada in the Scottish Record Office. Edinburgh: H. M. General Register House, 1965? 6*l.* (List, no.2)

4348. ———. Source list of manuscripts relating to the U.S.A. and Canada in private archives preserved in the Scottish Record Office. London: P. & D. Swift, 1970. 112*l.* (Special series, v.3)

4349. Virginia State Library. The British Public Record Office; history, description, record groups, finding aids, and materials for American history, with special reference to Virginia. Richmond, 1960. 178p.

MEXICAN

4350. Bonner, A. R. "Mexican pamphlets in the Bodleian Library." Bodleian Library record, 8 (1970), 205-13.

About 1,750 items, 18th- and 19th-century imprints, acquired by Bodleian Library.

4351. Great Britain, Public Record Office. Guia de documentos para la historia de México existentes en la Public Record Office de Londres, 1827-1830, by Gloria Grajales. Mexico City: Comisión de historia de I.P.G.H., Comité interamericano de archivos, 1967. 50p.

4352. Street, John. "The G. R. G. Conway collection in Cambridge University Library: a checklist." Hispanic American historical review, 37 (1957), 60-81.

A collection, based on transcripts from the National Library of Mexico, relating to Mexican history.

CARIBBEAN AND WEST INDIAN

4353. Bell, Herbert C., and Parker, David W. Guide to British West Indian archive materials, in London and in the Islands, for the history of the United States. Washington, D.C.: Carnegie Institution, 1926. 435p. (Carnegie Institution of Washington publications, no.372)

Detailed listing of Colonial Office papers, geographically arranged.

4354. British Museum. List of documents relating to the Bahama Islands in the British Museum and Record Office, London. Nassau: Nassau Guardian, 1910. 63p.

4355. Commonwealth Institute Library. Selected reading lists for advanced study, the Caribbean. London: The Institute, 1970. 18p.

Based on Institute Library's holdings.

4356. Great Britain, Public Record Office. "Records relating to Caribbean countries in the Public Record Office, London," by D. B. Wardle. In: Caribbean Archives Conference Report (1965), 471-98.

4357. West India Committee Library. Catalogue of the Library of the West India Committee. London: The Committee, 1941. 125p.

Relates to West Indian subjects, sugar industry, slavery and emancipation, etc.

LATIN AMERICAN

4358. British union catalogue of Latin Americana: new Latin American titles, ed. by Bernard Naylor. London: Univ. of London, Institute of Latin American Studies, Oct. 1968- , v.1- . 10 nos. per year.

4359. Essex, University, Library. U.K. Brazilian book exhibition arranged by the National Book Institute of Brazil and Essex University Library. Colchester: The University, 1969. 217p.

A catalog.

4360. International Colloquium on Luso-Brazilian Studies, 1966. Europe informed; an exhibition of early books which acquainted Europe with the East. Cambridge, Mass.: Harvard College Library, 1966. 192p.

Lists and describes 247 works; copies located in numerous libraries, American, British, etc.

4361. London, University, Institute of Latin American Studies. Guide to Latin American collections in London libraries, ed. by Bernard Naylor. London, 1967. 20p.

Brief reviews of resources of 28 libraries.

4362. Walford, A. J. "Latin Americana in British libraries and archives." Inter-American Bibliographical and Library Association publications, 1 (1951), 174-77.

4363. Whitehead, H. G. "A collection of Latin American pamphlets." British Museum quarterly, 34 (1969), 1-10.

Description and partial listing of over 500 pamphlets and broadsides, nearly all 19th century and from the River Plate countries, acquired by British Museum.

Oceanic and Polar

AUSTRALIAN AND NEW ZEALAND

4364. Commonwealth Institute Library. Selected reading lists for advanced study; Australia. London: The Institute, 1969. 21p.

4365. ———. Selected reading lists for advanced study; New Zealand. London: The Institute, 1970. 16p.

Based on library's holdings.

POLAR

4366. King, H. G. R. The libraries and literature of cold and cold regions; the Library of the Scott Polar Institute. Special Libraries Association, Geography and Map Division bulletin, 61 (Sept. 1965), 7-12.

Describes resources of Scott Polar Research Institute Library, Cambridge.

4367. National Library of Scotland, Edinburgh. Shelf-catalogue of the Wordie collection of Polar exploration. Boston, Mass.: G. K. Hall, 1964. 191p.

Printed books, pamphlets, journals, reports, and miscellaneous papers, received by library in 1959.

4368. Savours, Ann. "The manuscript collection of the Scott Polar Research Institute, Cambridge." Archives, no.4 (1959), 102-8.

Description of special collections and listing of individual items, such as ships' logs.

4369. Scott Polar Research Institute Library. Periodicals and serial publications in the Library of the Scott Polar Research Institute. Cambridge, 1964. 22p.

Individual Bibliography, Biography, and Criticism

Acton, John Emerich Edward Dalberg, 1834-1902

4370. Cambridge, University, Library. Acton collection (Germany, Spain, political philosophy, papacy, etc.) Cambridge, 1908-10. 4v. (Cambridge University Library bulletin, extra series)
Collection associated with Lord Acton.

Aeschylus, 525-456 B.C.

4371. British Museum, Dept. of Printed Books. Catalogue of printed books: Aeschylus. London: The Museum, 1883. 24 cols.

4372. Cambridge, University, King's College Library. A hand-list of books connected with Aeschylus, principally from the Library of the late Dr. Walter Headlam, now in the Library of King's College, Cambridge, comp. by A. R. Benten. Cambridge: Univ. Pr., 1910. 20p.

Aesop, c. 620-560 B.C.

4373. British Museum, Dept. of Printed Books. Aesop. London: W. Clowes, 1883. 17p.

Albert, Prince Consort of England, 1819-61

4374. British Museum. The Prince Consort Albert of Saxe-Coburg, 1819-1861; an exhibition to commemorate the centenary of his death, December 14, 1861; King's Library, 1961-62. London, 1961. 20p.

Alexeïff, Alexandre, 1901-

4375. National Library of Scotland. Alexandre Alexeïff. Edinburgh, 1967. 15p.
Exhibition of book illustrations of Alexeïff; 19 titles described.

Amyraut, Moïse, 1596-1664

4376. Dr. Williams's Library. Amyraldus; a list of the works by Moïse Amyraut in Dr. Williams's Library. London: Dr. Williams's Trust, 1958. 16p. (Occasional paper, no.4)
List of 17th-century editions.

Andersen, Hans Christian, 1805-75

4377. National Book League. Hans Christian Andersen, 1805-2nd April-1955; catalogue of a jubilee exhibition held at the National Book League, org. by Elias Bredsdorff. London, Copenhagen, 1955. 89p.
List of 286 items, with locations in British, Danish, and American public and private collections.

Anselm, Saint, 1033-1109

4378. Cook, David Frederick. The first 200 years in print of St. Anselm, Archbishop of Canterbury; a survey of works attributed to him, 1474-1675, bibliography. London, 1955. 104l. (Diploma in Librarianship, Univ. of London)
Copies located in British and foreign libraries.

Arber, Edward, 1836-1912

4379. Birmingham, University, Library. Catalogue of the Edward Arber papers. Birmingham, 1968. 26l. + index. (Catalogues of the manuscript collections, no.4)
Records 1,127 items relating to Edward and other members of Arber family.

Aristophanes, 448?-?380 B.C.

4380. British Museum, Dept. of Printed Books. Aristophanes. An excerpt from the General catalogue of printed books in the British Museum. London: W. Clowes, 1933. 46 cols.

Aristotle, 384-22 B.C.

4381. British Museum, Dept. of Printed Books. Aristotle; an excerpt from the General catalogue of printed books in the British Museum. London, 1933. 170 cols.

Armstrong, Martin, 1882-

4382. Bristol Public Libraries. Martin Armstrong, poet and novelist; a bibliography. Bristol, 1937. 4p.

Arnold, Matthew, 1822-88

4383. Davis, Arthur Kyle. Matthew Arnold's letters, a descriptive checklist. Charlottesville: University of Va. Pr., 1968. 429p.

Appendix B: "The holders of autograph letters, with the number of letters held by each," locates items in British and American collections.

Arnold-Forster, Hugh Oakeley, 1855-1909

4384. Hudson, J. P. "The Arnold-Forster papers." British Museum quarterly, 24 (1961), 12-14.

Papers of Hugh Oakeley Arnold-Forster, Unionist statesman and Secretary of State for War in Balfour's administration, received by British Museum.

Arthur, legendary king of Britain, fl. 520

4385. Flintshire County Library. The legend of King Arthur: a list of books in the Flintshire County Library, comp. by E. R. Harries. Hawarden, 1963. 184p.

Ascham, Roger, 1515-68

4386. Thomas, Beryl E. A bibliography of the works of Roger Ascham. London, 1949. 131*l*. (Diploma in Librarianship, Univ. of London)

Notes locations of copies examined and STC numbers.

Auchinleck, Claude John Eyre, 1884-

4387. Manchester, University, Library. The papers of Field Marshal Sir Claude Auchinleck; list and index. Manchester: n.d. 104p. + index.

Lists 1,353 items.

Austen, Jane, 1775-1817

4388. Keynes, Geoffrey. Jane Austen: a bibliography. London: Printed for the Nonesuch Pr., 1929. 289p.

Copies located in British Museum, Bodleian, and Cambridge University Libraries.

Bacon, Francis, 1561-1626

4389. British Museum, Dept. of Printed Books. Catalogue of printed books: Bacon. London, 1884. 24 cols.

4390. Gibson, R. W. Francis Bacon, a bibliography of his works and of Baconiana to the year 1750. Oxford: Scrivener, 1950. 369p.

Annotated list of 680 items; list of "Libraries consulted," p.331-32.

Bagshawe, Samuel, 1713-62

4391. Hayes, James. "The military papers of Colonel Samuel Bagshawe (1713-62)." Bulletin of the John Rylands Library, 39 (1957), 356-89. Reprinted.

General survey of collection in John Rylands Library.

Baker, Slade, fl. late 18th century

4392. Birmingham, University, Library. Catalogue of the correspondence of Slade Baker, solicitor of Bewdley. Birmingham, 1971. 17*l*. + index. (Catalogues of the collections, no.31)

Calendar of 983 items, 18th-19th centuries.

Bale, John, 1495-1563

4393. Davies, W. T. "A bibliography of John Bale." Oxford Bibliographical Society, Proceedings & papers, 5 (1939), 201-79.

Bibliography, p.247-79, supplies detailed bibliographical descriptions of Bale's works, with copies located in British and American libraries.

4394. McCusker, Helen. John Bale, dramatist and antiquary. Bryn Mawr, Pa., 1942. 142p.

Identifies 40 manuscripts as extant in Trinity College Library, Dublin, and in several English libraries.

Ballantyne, Robert Michael, 1825-94

4395. Quayle, Eric. R. M. Ballantyne: a bibliography of first editions. London: Dawsons of Pall Mall, 1968. 128p.

Notes British Museum copies.

Banks, Joseph, 1743-1820

4396. British Museum (Natural History). The Banks letters; a calendar of the manuscript correspondence of Sir Joseph Banks preserved in the British Museum, the British Museum (Natural History) and other collections in Great Britain, ed. by Warren R. Dawson. London, 1958. 965p.

4397. Lysaght, A. M. Joseph Banks in Newfoundland and Labrador, 1766; his diary, manuscripts and collections. London: Faber & Faber, 1971. 512p.

Manuscripts and other items located in British and American collections.

Bantock, Granville, 1868-1946

4398. Birmingham, University, Library. Catalogue of the Granville Bantock collection. Birmingham: 1971. Unpaged.

Barling, Edith, d.1961

4399. Birmingham, University, Library. Edith Barling album. Birmingham, 1968. 6l. (Catalogues of the manuscript collections, no.5)

Calendar of 83 items, 19th-20th century.

Baskerville, John, 1706-75

4400. Birmingham Public Libraries, Central Reference Library. Literature and other miscellaneous items relating to John Baskerville in the Reference Library, Birmingham. Birmingham: City of Birmingham School of Printing, 1937. 12p.

4401. Gaskell, Philip. John Baskerville: a bibliography. Cambridge: Univ. Pr., 1959. 72p. + 12 plates.

In 2 parts: Specimens, proposals and other ephemera, mentioning all types used and locations of all known copies; and books, of which only one copy each is cited.

4402. Straus, Ralph, and Dent, Robert K. John Baskerville, a memoir. Cambridge: Printed at the Univ. Pr. for Chatto and Windus, London, 1907. 144p. + 14 plates.

Copies located in 6 libraries.

Bate, George, 1608-69

4403. Madan, Francis Falconer. "A bibliography of George Bate's Elenchus motuum nuperorum in Anglia." Library, ser.5, 6 (1951), 189-99.

Lists 21 items, locating copies of Bate's Short history of the Civil War, 1649-61, in British Museum, Bodleian, and Cambridge.

Bax, Arnold Edward Trevor, 1883-1953

4404. Willetts, Pamela J. "Autograph music manu-

scripts of Sir Arnold Bax." British Museum quarterly, 23 (1961), 43-45.

Describes autograph music manuscripts of Sir Arnold Edward Trevor Bax (1883-1953), Master of the Queen's Music, acquired by British Museum.

Baxter, Richard, 1615-91

4405. Dr. Williams's Library. The Baxter treatises; a catalogue of the Richard Baxter papers (other than the letters) in Dr. Williams's Library, comp. by Roger Thomas. London: Dr. Williams's Trust, 1959. 31p. (Occasional paper, no.8)

Items relating chiefly to Baxter's Reliquiae Baxterianae in 17th century.

Bayard family

4406. Birmingham, University, Library. Bayard family manuscripts catalogue. Birmingham, 1970. Unpaged. (Catalogues of the manuscript collections, no.29)

Lists 196 items for period 1584-1925.

Beazley, Charles Raymond, 1868-1955

4407. Birmingham, University, Library. The papers and manuscripts of Sir C. Raymond Beazley. Birmingham, 1969. 20l. (Catalogues of the manuscript collections, no.17)

Bede, Saint, 673-735

4408. Kemp, J. A. The Venerable Bede; editions of his works printed before 1700 a.d., bibliography. London, 1953. 32l. (Diploma in Librarianship, Univ. of London)

Copies located in British Museum, Bodleian, Cambridge, and Continental libraries.

4409. Laistner, M. L. W., and King, H. H. A handlist of Bede manuscripts. Ithaca, N. Y.: Cornell Univ. Pr., 1943. 168p.

Locations in British and foreign collections.

Beethoven, Ludwig van, 1770-1827

4410. British Museum. Beethoven, 1770-1827; catalogue of an exhibition held in the King's Library, by A. Hyatt King. London, 1970. Unpaged.

4411. ———, Dept. of Manuscripts. Beethoven and England; an account of sources in the British Museum, by Pamela J. Willetts. London: The Museum, 1970. 76p. + 17 plates.

4412. ———— ————. Ludwig van Beethoven; autograph miscellany, from circa 1786 to 1799, British Museum additional manuscript 29801, ff. 39-162, ed. by Joseph Kerman. London: The Museum, 1970. 2v.

v.1, facsimile; v.2, music.

4413. Exeter, University, Library. Beethoven and England, 1793-1855; catalogue of a bi-centenary exhibition at the University Library, March 2-25, 1970. Exeter: The University, 1970. 47p.

4414. Tyson, Alan. The authentic English editions of Beethoven. London: Faber & Faber, 1963. 152p. + 12 plates.

Copies located in British Museum, Bodleian, Cambridge, and Royal College of Music; covers period 1799 to 1827.

Bellay, Joachim du, 1522-60

4415. Birkbeck College Library. Du Bellay: handlist of books by and about Joachim du Bellay in the College Library, comp. by P. Woudhuysen. London, 1970. 5l. (Library publication, no.10)

Bembo, Pietro, 1470-1547

4416. British Museum. Pietro Bembo's library as represented particularly in the British Museum, rev. ed., by Cecil H. Clough. London, 1971. 16p. + 4 plates.

4417. Clough, Cecil H. "Pietro Bembo's library represented in the British Museum." British Museum quarterly, 30 (1965), 3-17. Reprinted, 1966. 15p.

Account of library amassed by Venetian cardinal Pietro Bembo (Lucrezia Borgia's lover) and its dispersal among institutions and private collectors; appendix lists his "Epistolario" in the British Museum.

Bennett, Arnold, 1867-1931

4418. Hepburn, James G. "Arnold Bennett manuscripts and rare books; a list of holdings." English fiction in transition, 1, no.2 (1958), 23-29.

List of libraries with data on holdings of manuscripts, etc.; includes British Museum and various American libraries.

Bentham, Jeremy, 1748-1832

4419. London, University, University College. Report on the Bentham mss. at University College, London, with catalogue. London: Reynell, n.d. 20p.

Analysis of Jeremy Bentham manuscript collection now held by University of London.

4420. ————, University College Library. Catalogue of the manuscripts of Jeremy Bentham in the Library at University College, London, comp. by A. Taylor Milne. London, 1937. 147p.

4421. ———— ————. Catalogue of the manuscripts of Jeremy Bentham in the Library of University College, London, comp. by A. Taylor Milne, 2d ed. London: Athlone, 1962. 104p.

Papers arranged by subject and date, with suitable indexes.

Bentley, Richard, 1662-1742

4422. Bartholomew, A. T. Richard Bentley, D. D.; a bibliography of his works and of all the literature called forth by his acts or his writings. Cambridge: Bowes and Bowes, 1908. 115p.

Rare works are located in British Museum and Cambridge libraries.

Berkeley, George, 1685-1753

4423. Cambridge, University, King's College Library. A catalogue of the works of George Berkeley forming part of the library bequeathed by John Maynard, Baron Keynes of Tilton, to King's College, Cambridge. Cambridge, 1951. 38l.

Philosophical works.

4424. Dublin, University, Trinity College Library. Catalogue of manuscripts, books, and Berkleiana exhibited in the Library of Trinity College, Dublin, on the occasion of the commemoration of the bicentenary of the death of George Berkeley. Dublin: Univ. Pr., 1953. 37p.

Annotated list of 137 exhibits.

4425. Jessop, T. E. A bibliography of George Berkeley, by T. E. Jessop, with an inventory of Berkeley's manuscript remains, by A. A. Luce. London: Oxford Univ. Pr., 1934. 99p.

"Inventory" records manuscripts in British Museum, Trinity College in Dublin, and National Library of Ireland.

Berlioz, Hector, 1803-69

4426. Hopkinson, Cecil. A bibliography of the musical and literary works of Hector Berlioz, 1803-1869, with histories of French music publishers concerned. Edinburgh: Edinburgh Bibliographical Society, 1951. 205p.

Includes list of manuscripts, published and unpublished, with their locations.

4427. National Library of Scotland. Hector Berlioz, 1803-1869. Edinburgh, 1969. 23p.

Records 79 items, manuscript and printed, drawn from National Library's collections.

Bernard, Saint, 1091-1153

4428. Morson, John. "Some manuscripts of the life of St. Bernard." Bulletin of the John Rylands Library, 37 (1955), 476-502. Reprinted. 1955. 29p.

Based on manuscripts in John Rylands Library, British Museum, Bodleian, Lambeth Palace Library, Cambridge, etc.

Bewick, Thomas, 1753-1828

4429. Bain, Iain. Thomas Bewick; engraver, of New-castle, 1753-1828; a check-list of his correspondence and other papers. London: 1970. 46p. (Reprinted from the Private library with addenda)

Locations cited.

4430. Roscoe, Syney. Thomas Bewick; a bibliography raisonné of editions of the General history of quad-rupeds, The history of British birds, and the Fables of Aesop issued in his lifetime. London: Oxford Univ. Pr., 1953. 198p.

Copies located in major English libraries.

Blake, William, 1757-1827

4431. Georgian House. William Blake, 1757-1827; notes for a catalogue of the Blake Library at the Georgian House, Merstham, by Kerrison Preston. Cambridge: Golden Head, 1962. 48p.

Books by and about Blake, pictures, catalogs, etc., in Blake Library.

4432. Keynes, Geoffrey, and Wolf, Edwin, 2d. William Blake's illuminated books: a census. N. Y.: Grolier Club, 1953. 125p.

Describes 156 copies of 20 books and tracts, 40 of which are located in British collections.

4433. Lowery, Margaret Ruth. "A census of copies of William Blake's Poetical sketches, 1783." Library, ser.4, 17 (1936), 354-60.

Copies located in British and American collections.

4434. National Library of Scotland. William Blake; a loan exhibition. Edinburgh, 1969. 34p. (Catalogue, no.11)

4435. Westminster City Libraries. William Blake; catalogue of the Preston Blake library, presented by Kerrison Preston in 1967, comp. by Phyllis Goff. London, 1969. 127p.

Records 700 entries relating to Blake.

4436. Wright, C. E. "William Blake's notebook." British Museum quarterly, 21 (1958), 88-90.

Quarto manuscript of Blake's writings and sketches, acquired by British Museum.

Blathwayt, William, c. 1649-1717

4437. Smith, Brian S. "Blathwayt of Dyrham Park archives." Archives, no.5 (1962), 224-25.

Papers of William Blathwayt, secretary at war, secretary of state to William III in Flanders, etc., now deposited in Gloucestershire Records Office and elsewhere.

Boehme, Jacob, 1575-1624

4438. British Museum, Dept. of Printed Books. Jacob Boehme; an extract from the Catalogue of printed books, etc. London: W. Clowes, 1921. 13p.

Borrow, George Henry, 1803-81

4439. Wise, Thomas J. A bibliography of the writings in prose and verse of George Henry Borrow. London: Richard Clay, 1914. 316p. Reprinted. London: Dawsons of Pall Mall, 1966.

Locates copies, principally in British Museum.

Boughton, Rutland, 1878-1960

4440. Willetts, Pamela J. "The Rutland Boughton collection." British Museum quarterly, 28 (1964), 67-75.

Description and list of autograph music manu-scripts of Boughton received by British Museum.

Boyle, Robert, 1627-91

4441. Fulton, John F. A bibliography of the Honour-able Robert Boyle, Fellow of the Royal Society. Oxford, 1932-33. 2pts. (Oxford Bibliographical Society proceedings and papers, v.3, pts.1, 3.)

Locates copies.

4442. ———. A bibliography of the Honourable Robert Boyle, Fellow of the Royal Society, 2d ed. Oxford: Clarendon, 1961. 218p.

Locations in numerous British, American, and other libraries; lists 541 items by and about Boyle, pioneer chemist.

4443. Maddison, R. E. W. "A tentative index of the correspondence of the Honourable Robert Boyle, F.R.S." Notes and records of the Royal Society of London, 13 (1958), 128-201.

Locates items in Royal Society, British Museum, Guildhall Library, Bodleian Library, etc.

Bright, Timothy, 1550-1615

4444. Keynes, Geoffrey. Dr. Timothie Bright, 1550-1615; a survey of his life with a bibliography of his writings. London: Wellcome Historical Medical Library, 1962. 47p.

Locates copies in British and American libraries and private collections.

Brontë family

4445. Brontë Society, Brontë Parsonage Museum. Catalogue of the Bonnell collection in the Brontë Parsonage Museum. Haworth: The Society, 1932. 90p.

List of 336 items relating to Brontë family.

4446. Brontë Society Museum and Library. Catalogue of the Museum and Library, comp. by J. Alex. Symington. Haworth: The Society, 1927. 200p.

Books and manuscripts relating to Brontë family.

4447. Manchester Public Libraries. Brontë collection, Public Library, Moss Side, Manchester. List of additions, 1907-1916, by John Albert Green. Manchester, 1916. 24p.

4448. ———. Catalogue of the Gleave Brontë collection at the Moss Side Free Library, Manchester, by John Albert Green. Moss Side, 1907. 32p.

Works by and about Charlotte, Emily, and other members of Brontë family.

4449. Wise, Thomas J. A bibliography of the writings in prose and verse of the members of the Brontë family. London: Richard Clay, 1917. 256p.

Locates some copies in British Museum.

4450. ———. A Brontë library; a catalogue of printed books, manuscripts, and autograph letters by the members of the Brontë family. London, 1929. 82p.

Collection now in British Museum.

Brown, Ford Madox, 1821-93

4451. Liverpool Free Public Library, Museum, and Walker Art Gallery. Ford Madox Brown, 1821-1893; exhibition organised by the Walker Art Gallery. Liverpool, 1964. 35p.

Browne, Thomas, 1605-82

4452. Keynes, Geoffrey. A bibliography of Sir Thomas Browne, Kt., M.D. Cambridge: Univ. Pr., 1924. 255p.

Copies of 506 works located in British, Irish, and Continental libraries.

4453. Norwich Public Libraries. Sir Thomas Browne; a catalogue of works by and about Sir Thomas Browne in the Norwich Public Libraries, by Mary Alexander. Norwich: Public Libraries Committee, 1925. 4p.

4454. Williams, Charles. The bibliography of the Religio Medici, 2d ed. Norwich, 1907. 20p.

Lists editions, 1642-1906, with locations of copies.

Browning, Elizabeth Barrett, 1806-61

4455. St. Marylebone Public Libraries. Elizabeth Barrett Browning, 1806-1861; catalogue of the centenary exhibition held at the St. Marylebone Central Public Library, ed. by Lachlan Phil Kelley. London, 1961. 21p.

4456. Wise, Thomas J. A bibliography of the writings in prose and verse of Elizabeth Barrett Browning. London: Richard Clay, 1918. 249p.

Locates copies in British Museum.

Browning, Robert, 1812-89

4457. British Museum, Dept. of Printed Books. Robert Browning; an excerpt from the General catalogue of printed books in the British Museum. London: The Museum, 1939. 28 cols.

4458. Carter, John W., and Pollard, Graham. "Census of copies of the Reading Sonnets." In their: An enquiry into the nature of certain nineteenth century pamphlets. London, 1934, p.361-68.

Lists 36 copies with locations.

Bruno, Giordano, 1548?-1600

4459. Hayward, John. "First editions of Giordano Bruno; location of additional copies." Book collector, 5 (1956), 381-82.

4460. ———. "The location of copies of the first editions of Giordano Bruno." Book collector, 5 (1956), 152-57.

Contains 26 entries for Bruno's writings published before his death in 1600. Copies located in British, European, and American libraries.

Bry, Théodore de, 1528-98

4461. Bibliotheca Lindesiana. Grands et petits voyages of DeBry, by Ludovic, Earl of Crawford and Bakarres. London: Bernard Quaritch, 1884. 215p. + 33 plates.

Buckler, Edward, 1610-1706

4462. Mead, Herman Ralph. "Three issues of A buckler against the fear of death." Library, ser.4, 21 (1940), 199-206.

Work by Edward Buckler, poet and minister, first issued in 1640; copies located in British and American libraries.

Bunyan, John, 1628-88

4463. Bedford Public Library. Catalogue of the John Bunyan Library. Bedford: Borough of Bedford Public Library, 1938. 42p.

Works by and about Bunyan in Bedford Public Library; more than 800 items listed.

4464. British Museum. Catalogue of printed books: Bunyan. London, 1884. 38 cols.

4465. ———, Dept. of Printed Books. John Bunyan; an excerpt from the General catalogue of printed books in the British Museum. London, 1939. 74 cols.

4466. Bunyan, John. The Pilgrim's progress, ed. by James Blanton Wharey, 2d ed. Oxford: Clarendon, 1960. 365p.

"Introduction," p.xxi-cxvi, locates copies of early editions of the Pilgrim's progress in British and American libraries.

4467. Bunyan Meeting Library and Museum. Catalogue of the Bunyan Meeting Library and Museum, Bedford, by Cyril Hargreaves and Margaret Greenshields. Bedford: Bunyan Meeting, 1956. 43p.

Books by or relating to John Bunyan.

4468. "First editions of John Bunyan's Pilgrim's progress." Publishers' weekly, 114 (1928), 2063-65.

Locates 11 known copies in public and private collections.

4469. Harrison, Frank Mott. A bibliography of the works of John Bunyan. Oxford: Oxford Univ. Pr. for the Bibliographical Society, 1932 (for 1930). 83p. (Bibliographical Society supplement, no.6)

Copies of 57 items located in British and American libraries.

4470. Nixon, H. M. "Bunyan editions from the library of Sir Leicester Harmsworth." British Museum quarterly, 15 (1952), 17-18.

Extensive collection of early and rare editions of John Bunyan's works, acquired by British Museum.

Burke, Edmund, 1729-97

4471. Todd, William B. A bibliography of Edmund Burke. London: Rupert Hart-Davis, 1964. 312p. (Soho bibliographies, no.17)

Copies located in British, Irish, and American libraries.

Burney, Fanny, 1752-1840

4472. Wright, C. E. "The Barrett collection of Burney papers." British Museum quarterly, 18 (1953), 41-43.

Describes collection of Fanny Burney manuscripts and letters acquired by British Museum.

Burns, Robert, 1759-96

4473. British Museum, Dept. of Printed Books. Robert Burns; an excerpt from the General catalogue of printed books in the British Museum. London: The Museum, 1939. 40 cols.

4474. Cuthbertson, David. Manuscripts of Robert Burns, the property of Edinburgh University; a description, with some notes and comments. Edinburgh, 1921. 23p. (Reprinted from the Kilmarnock standard)

Narrative account.

4475. Dunfermline Public Libraries. The Murison Burns collection; a catalogue of the books and pamphlets presented by Sir Alexander Gibb to the City and Royal Burgh of Dunfermline, comp. by Nancie Campbell. Dunfermline, 1953. 140p.

Books by or about Robert Burns.

4476. Edinburgh Public Libraries. Robert Burns; exhibition manuscripts, letters, books and relics of the poet, his family and associates. Edinburgh, 1953. 17p.

4477. Edinburgh, University, Library. Burns bicentenary exhibition. Edinburgh, 1959. Unpaged.

Listing of 110 manuscripts, printed editions, and pictures.

4478. Glasgow Public Libraries. Catalogue of the Robert Burns collection in the Mitchell Library, Glasgow, ed. by Anthony G. Hepburn. Glasgow, 1959. 217p.

Short-title list of more than 3,500 items, believed to be most comprehensive collection of its kind in world, by and about Burns.

4479. ———. A selected list of books on and by Robert Burns, ed. by William Aitkenhead. Glasgow, 1956. 13p.

Locations noted in branches of Glasgow Public Libraries.

4480. MacKie Burnsiana Library. Catalogue, comp. by David Sneddon. Kilmarnock: Standard Print., 1909. 170p.

Burton, Richard Francis, 1821-90

4481. Penzer, Norman M. An annotated bibliography of Sir Richard Francis Burton. London, 1923. 351p. Reprinted, London: Dawsons of Pall Mall, 1967.

Occasional copies located.

Burton, Robert, 1577-1640

4482. Gibson, Strickland, and Needham, F. R. D. "Two lists of Burton's books." Oxford Bibliographical Society, Proceedings and papers, 1 (1922-1926), 222-46.

Two lists of Robert Burton's library as distributed between the Bodleian and Christ Church Library, Oxford.

4483. Oxford, University, Bodleian Library. "Lists of Burton's library. Two lists of Robert Burton's library as distributed between (a) the Bodleian Library (b) the Library of His College, Christ Church," ed. by S. Gibson and F. R. D. Needham. Proceedings and papers, Oxford Bibliographical Society, 1 (1925), 222-46.

Butler, Samuel, 1835-1902

4484. Cambridge, University, St. John's College Library. The Samuel Butler collection at Saint John's College, Cambridge; a catalogue and a commentary, by Henry Festing Jones and A. T. Bartholomew. Cambridge: Heffer, 1921. 59p.

Byron, George Gordon, 1788-1824

4485. British Museum, Dept. of Printed Books. Byron; an excerpt from the General catalogue of printed books in the British Museum. London: The Museum, 1939. 78 cols.

4486. First Edition Club. Bibliographical catalogue of first editions, proof copies & manuscripts of books by Lord Byron exhibited at the fourth exhibition held by the First Edition Club, January 1925. London, 1925. 97p.

Locates copies of items shown; full bibliographical descriptions.

4487. Nottingham Public Libraries. The Roe-Byron collection, Newstead Abbey. Nottingham: Corporation of Nottingham, 1937. 188p.

Classified listing of extensive collection relating to George Gordon, Lord Byron.

Carlier, Antoine Guillaume, 1869-

4488. Birmingham, University, Library. Carlier collection catalogue. Birmingham, 1970. 21l. (Catalogues of the manuscript collections, no.30)

Lists 1,364 items; correspondence of Antoine Guillaume Carlier and family.

Carlyle, Thomas, 1795-1881

4489. Edinburgh, University, Library. Carlyle and Edinburgh; exhibition of Carlyleana in Edinburgh University Library. Edinburgh, 1970. Unpaged.

Listing with annotations of 58 items.

4490. Sanders, Charles Richard. "Carlyle's letters to Ruskin: a finding list with some unpublished letters and comments." Bulletin of the John Rylands Library, 41 (1958), 208-38. Reprinted.

Carpenter, Edward, 1844-1929

4491. Sheffield City Libraries. A bibliography of Edward Carpenter; a catalogue of books, manuscripts, letters, etc., by and about Edward Carpenter in the Carpenter collection in the Department of Local History of the Central Library, Sheffield, with some entries from other sources. Sheffield, 1949. 100p.

Carroll, Lewis (Charles Lutwidge Dodgson), 1832-98

4492. Weaver, Warren. "The first edition of Alice's adventures in wonderland; a census." Papers of the Bibliographical Society of America, 65 (1971), 1-40.

Detailed descriptions of variant versions, with locations in public and private collections.

4493. Williams, Sidney Herbert. A bibliography of the writings of Lewis Carroll (Charles Lutwidge Dodgson). London: Bookman's journal, 1924, 142p.

Copies located in public and private collections.

4494. ———, and Madan, Falconer. The Lewis Carroll handbook; being a new version of A handbook of the literature of the Rev. C. L. Dodgson. Folkestone and London: Dawsons of Pall Mall, 1970. 307p.

Occasional copies located.

Cavendish, Margaret, 1623-73

4495. Colquhoun, Jean. A bibliography of Margaret Cavendish, Duchess of Newcastle (1623-1673). London, 1950. 68*l.* (Diploma in Librarianship, Univ. of London)

Locates copies in British Museum, Oxford, and Cambridge libraries.

Caxton, William, 1422?-91

4496. British Museum, Dept. of Printed Books. William Caxton; an excerpt from the General catalogue of printed books. London: The Museum, 1926. 8p.

Cervantes, Miguel de, 1547-1616

4497. Birmingham Public Libraries, Central Reference Library. Brief hand-list of the Cervantes collection, presented to the Birmingham Free Library, Reference Department, by W. Bragge. Birmingham, 1874. 15p.

4498. British Museum, Dept. of Printed Books. Catalogue of printed books: Cervantes. London: W. Clowes, 1908. 72 cols.

4499. ———. Cervantes, an excerpt from the General catalogue of printed books in the British Museum. London: W. Clowes, 1942. 94 cols.

4500. Thomas, Henry. "The Cervantes collection in the British Museum." Library, n. s. 9 (1908), 429-43.

Summary review, with notes on particular rarities.

Chamberlain, Austen, 1863-1937

4501. Birmingham, University, Library. Handlist to the papers of Austen Chamberlain [in Birmingham University Library]. Birmingham, 1965. Unpaged.

Chamberlain, Joseph, 1836-1914

4502. Birmingham, University, Library. Handlist to the papers of Joseph Chamberlain. Birmingham, 1965. Unpaged.

4503. ———. Joseph, Mary, and Austen Chamberlain; handlist of miscellaneous items [in Birmingham University Library]. Birmingham, 1970. Unpaged.

Chamberlain, Neville, 1869-1940

4504. Birmingham, University, Library. Handlist to the papers of Neville Chamberlain. Birmingham, 1971. Unpaged.

Charles II, 1630-85

4505. Devon Record Office. Charles II and the Restoration; an exhibition to commemorate the tercentenary of the restoration of the monarchy, held in the Chapter House, Exeter. Exeter: The Office, 1960. 54p.

4506. Horrox, William Arthur. A bibliography of the literature relating to the escape and preservation of King Charles II after the battle of Worcester, 3 September, 1651, exclusive of mss., plays, novels. Aberdeen: Aberdeen Univ. Press, 1924. 64p.

Locates copies examined.

Chatterton, Thomas, 1752-70

4507. Bristol Museum and Library. A catalogue of the autograph manuscripts and other remains of Thomas Chatterton now in the Bristol Museum, edited by W. R. Barker. Bristol, 1907. 54p.

4508. Hyett, Francis Adams, and Bazeley, W. Chattertoniana; being a classified catalogue of books, pamphlets, magazine articles & other printed matter relating to the life or works of Chatterton, or to the Rowley controversy. Gloucester: J. Bellows, 1914. 43p.

Locates copies.

Chaucer, Geoffrey, 1340?-1400

4509. British Museum, Dept. of Printed Books. Chaucer; an excerpt from the General catalogue of printed books in the British Museum. London, 1943. 46 cols.

4510. Hetherington, John R. Chaucer, 1532-1602; notes and facsimile texts designed to facilitate the identification of defective copies of the black-letter folio editions of 1532, 1542, c. 1550, 1561, 1598 and 1602. Birmingham, 1964. 21p.

Locates copies and adds STC numbers.

4511. McCormick, William, and Heseltine, Janet E. The manuscripts of Chaucer's Canterbury tales; a critical description of their contents. Oxford: Clarendon, 1933. 561p.

Describes 57 complete and 28 defective manuscripts in British collections.

4512. Vine, Guthrie. "The miller's tale: a study of an unrecorded fragment of a manuscript in the John Rylands Library in relation to the first printed text." Bulletin of the John Rylands Library, 17 (1933), 333-47. Reprinted. 1933. 17p.

Chesterton, Gilbert Keith, 1874-1936

4513. Manchester Public Libraries. G. K. Chesterton, 1874-1936; manuscripts, drawings, cartoons, and first editions. Manchester, 1956. 33p.

Catalogue of an exhibition.

Churchill, Winston, 1874-1965

4514. Imperial War Museum Library. Sir Winston Churchill; a bibliography of references selected from the collection in the Reference Library. London, 1961. 10p.

Cicero, Marcus Tullius, 106-43 B.C.

4515. British Museum, Dept. of Printed Books. Cicero, an excerpt from the General catalogue of printed books in the British Museum. London: W. Clowes, 1944. 196 cols.

Clare, John, 1793-1864

4516. Northampton Public Library. Catalogue of the John Clare collection in the Northampton Public Library, with notes to the poems in manuscript. Northampton: Public Libraries, Museums and Art Gallery Committee, 1964. 72p.

Listing of 87 items by and about Clare and Clare's library of 440 volumes.

4517. Peterborough Natural History, Scientific, and Archaeological Society. Catalogue of the centenary exhibition of portraits, books, manuscripts . . . belonging to or connected with John Clare, ed. by Charles Dack. Peterborough, 1893. 28p.

Cleveland, John, 1613-58

4518. Morris, Brian. "The editions of Cleveland's poems, 1647-1687." Library, ser.5, 19 (1964), 90-111.

Editions of John Cleveland's works listed and described, accompanied by Wing numbers or exact locations.

4519. ———. John Cleveland (1613-1658); a bibliography of his poems. Oxford: Univ. Pr. for London Bibliographical Society, 1967. 60p.

Compiler sought to locate 12 copies of each edition or issue, 6 in America and the remainder in Britain or Europe; Wing numbers included.

Cobbett, William, 1762-1835

4520. Pearl, Morris Leonard. William Cobbett; a bibliographical account of his life and times. London: Oxford Univ. Pr., 1953. 266p.

Locates copies.

Cobden, Richard, 1804-65

4521. West Sussex County Council. The Cobden papers; a catalogue, ed. by Francis W. Steer. Chichester, 1964. 125p.

Papers relating to Richard Cobden (1804-65) and other members of Cobden family.

Cole, William, 1714-82

4522. British Museum, Dept. of Manuscripts. Index to the contents of the Cole manuscripts in the British Museum, by George J. Gray. Cambridge: Bowes and Bowes, 1912. 170p.

Manuscripts of Rev. William Cole, 1714-82.

Coleridge, Samuel Taylor, 1772-1834

4523. British Museum, Dept. of Printed Books. Coleridge; an excerpt from the General catalogue of printed books in the British Museum. London, 1947. 36 cols.

4524. Skeat, T. C. "Note-books and marginalia of S. T. Coleridge." British Museum quarterly, 16 (1952), 91-93.

Extensive collection of Coleridge material acquired by British Museum.

4525. University College of the South West of England. S. T. Coleridge . . . centenary exhibition. Exeter, 1934. 19p.

Now Exeter University Library.

4526. Wise, Thomas J. A bibliography of the writings in prose and verse of Samuel Taylor Coleridge. London: Bibliographical Society, 1913. 316p.

Occasional references to locations in British Museum.

Collins, William, 1721-59

4527. Winchester College Library. William Collins. Winchester: Wykeham Press, 1959. 14p.

Exhibition catalog.

Columbus, Christopher, 1451-1506

4528. British Museum, Dept. of Printed Books. Colombo (Cristoforo); from the Catalogue of printed books, 1888, cols. 55-63. London, 1888.

4529. Lazare, E. "Census of printed editions before 1500 of Christopher Columbus's Letter on the discovery of America." Antiquarian bookman, 11 Oct., 1952, p.955-57.

Locates 17 copies, in British, Continental, and U.S. libraries.

Congreve, William, 1670-1729

4530. Hodges, John C. The library of William Congreve. N.Y.: New York Public Library, 1955. 116p.

Records 659 entries, with locations in British, American, and French libraries.

Conrad, Joseph, 1857-1924

4531. Polish Library. The Joseph Conrad collection in the Polish Library in London; catalogue (nos.1-399), comp. by Jadwiga Nowak. London, 1970. 59p.

Records 399 items by and about Conrad.

Cook, James, 1728-79

4532. British Museum, Dept. of Printed Books. Captain James Cook—after two hundred years, by R. A. Skelton. London, 1969. 32p. + 24 plates.

Cowen, Joseph, 1831-1900

4533. Newcastle upon Tyne City Libraries. The Cowen collection: a calendar of the papers of Joseph Cowen (1829-1900) in the possession of the Central Reference Library, Newcastle upon Tyne. Newcastle upon Tyne, 1952. 2v.

Cowper, William, 1731-1800

4534. Povey, K. "Handlist of manuscripts in the Cowper and Newton Museum, Olney, Bucks." Transactions of the Cambridge Bibliographical Society, 4 (1965), 107-27. Reprinted.

Listing of manuscripts relating to William Cowper, John Newton, and other literary figures.

4535. Russell, Norma Hull. A bibliography of William Cowper to 1837. Oxford: Oxford Bibliographical Society, 1963. 339p.

Full bibliographical treatment of 338 Cowper works; copies located in numerous British, Irish, American, and Canadian libraries.

Crabbe, George, 1754-1832

4536. East Suffolk County Library. George Crabbe, 1754-1832, bicentenary celebrations: exhibition of works and manuscripts held at the Moot Hall, Alde-

burgh. Aldeburgh: Aldeburgh Festival Committee in Cooperation with Suffolk Institute of Archaeology, 1954. 43p.

4537. Matthews, David Anthony. Notes toward a bibliography of George Crabbe, 1754-1832. London, 1954. 25l. (Diploma in Librarianship, Univ. of London)

Locates copies in 6 English libraries.

Cross, Richard, d. 1760

4538. Pedicord, Harry William. "Course of plays, 1740-2: an early diary of Richard Cross, prompter to the theatres." Bulletin of the John Rylands Library, 40 (1958), 432-72. Reprinted.

Manuscript in John Rylands Library.

Daillé, Jean, 1594-1670

4539. Dr. Williams's Library. Dallaeus; a list of the works by Jean Daillé in Dr. Williams's Library. London: Dr. Williams's Trust, 1958. 12p. (Occasional paper, no.7)

Lists works by Daillé published 1594-1670.

Dale, Robert William, 1829-95

4540. Birmingham, University, Library. Handlist to the letters of R. W. Dale. Birmingham, 1968. 6l. (Catalogues of the manuscript collections, no.7)

Letters from John Bright, John Morley, and Henry Mace; 75 items for period 1862-91.

Dalton, John, 1766-1844

4541. Smyth, Albert Leslie. John Dalton, 1766-1844; a bibliography of works by and about him. Manchester: Univ. Pr., 1966. 114p.

Copies located in 13 British libraries and Library of Congress; checklist of 771 items.

Daniel, Samuel, 1562-1619

4542. Sellers, H. "A bibliography of the works of Samuel Daniel, 1585-1623." Oxford, Bibliographical Society proceedings and papers, 2 (1927), 29-54.

Works of English historian, poet, and essayist, with locations of copies in English and American libraries.

Dante Alighieri, 1265-1321

4543. Birkbeck College Library. Dante: handlist of books in the College Library, ed. by P. Woudhuysen. London, 1971. 21p. (Library publication, no.15)

4544. British Museum, Dept. of Printed Books. Catalogue of printed books: Dante Alighieri. London: The Museum, 1887. 58 cols.

4545. ————. Dante; an excerpt from the General catalogue of printed books in the British Museum. London: The Museum, 1952. 234 cols.

4546. John Rylands Library. Catalogue of an exhibition of the works of Dante Alighieri, shown in the Main Library from March to October, MCMIX, comp. by Henry Guppy. Manchester, 1909. 55p.

4547. Liverpool, University, Library. The Dante collection of the late Canon John T. Mitchell. Liverpool, 1948. Unpaged.
Works by and about Dante.

4548. London, University, University College. Catalogue of the exhibition of books, manuscripts, pictures and medals, arranged in celebration of the sexcentenary of the death of Dante, at University College, London. London: Langley & Sons, 1921. 12p.

4549. ———— Library. Catalogue of the Dante collection in the Library of University College, London, by R. W. Chambers. Oxford: Printed for University College, London, 1910. 152p.
Lists about 1,500 items.

4550. Speight, Kathleen. "The John Rylands Library Dante collection." Bulletin of the John Rylands Library, 44 (1961), 175-212. Reprinted.
General survey of manuscripts and printed works relating to Dante, 14th to 20th centuries.

Darwin, Charles, 1809-82

4551. Cambridge, University, Botany School. Catalogue of the library of Charles Darwin now in the Botany School, Cambridge, comp. by H. W. Rutherford. Cambridge: Univ. Pr., 1908. 91p.

4552. ————, Christ's College. Darwin centenary; the portraits, prints and writings of Charles Robert Darwin, exhibited at Christ's College, Cambridge. Cambridge: Univ. Pr., 1909. 47p.

4553. ————, Library. Darwin Library. List of books received in the University Library, March-May 1961. Cambridge, 1961. 29l.

4554. ———— ————. Handlist of Darwin papers at the University Library, Cambridge, by N. J. Hancock. Cambridge: Univ. Pr., for the University Library, 1960. 72p.

Dawson, William Harbutt, 1860-1948

4555. Birmingham, University, Library. Catalogue of the W. H. Dawson papers. Birmingham, 1970. 152l.

Defoe, Daniel, 1659?-1731

4556. Brigham, Clarence S. Bibliography of American editions of Robinson Crusoe to 1830. Worcester, Mass.: American Antiquarian Society, 1958, p.137-83. (Reprinted from the Proceedings of the American Antiquarian Society, Oct. 1937)
Copies located in British Museum and various American libraries and private collections.

4557. British Museum, Dept. of Printed Books. Daniel Defoe; an excerpt from the General catalogue of printed books in the British Museum. London, 1953. 122 cols.

4558. Faxon, David F. "Defoe: a specimen of a catalogue of English verse, 1701-1750." Library, ser.5, 20 (1965), 277-97.
Full bibliographical descriptions of 142 poetical works by or attributed to Daniel Defoe; copies located in 38 British and American libraries.

4559. Moore, John Robert. A checklist of the writings of Daniel Defoe. Bloomington: Ind. Univ. Pr., 1960. 254p. (Indiana University humanities series, no.47)
Records 547 items; locates copies in numerous British and American libraries and private collections.

4560. Stoke Newington Public Libraries. Daniel Defoe, 1660-1731; commemoration in Stoke Newington of the tercentenary of his birth; an exhibition of books, pamphlets, views and portraits and other items. Stoke Newington: Stoke Newington Borough Council, 1960. 40p.
Lists 389 items by and about Defoe.

De la Mare, Walter John, 1873-1956

4561. National Book League. Walter de la Mare; a checklist prepared on the occasion of an exhibition of his books and mss. at the National Book League, comp. by Leonard Clark. London: Published for the National Book League at the Cambridge Univ. Pr., 1956. 55p.
Locates copies in Bodleian Library and private collections.

De Quincey, Thomas, 1785-1859

4562. Manchester Public Libraries. Thomas De Quincey; a bibliography based upon the De Quincey collection in the Moss Side Library, by John Albert Green. Manchester, 1908. 110p.

Dickens, Charles, 1812-70

4563. Bath Public Libraries. Charles Dickens; list of

works, criticisms, etc., Dickensiana, biography and illustrations in books and periodicals in the Libraries. Bath, 1926. 4p.

4564. British Museum, Dept. of Printed Books. Charles Dickens; an excerpt from the General catalogue of printed books. London: The Museum, 1926. 29p.

4565. ———. Dickens; an excerpt from the General catalogue of printed books in the British Museum. London: The Museum, 1960. 72p., 144 cols. Reprinted, 1965.

4566. Dickens' Birthplace Museum. List of books, prints . . . memorials exhibited at Dickens' Birthplace Museum, comp. by Alfred A. Searle. Portsmouth: W. H. Barrell, 1914. 71p.

4567. Harvey, P. D. A. "Charles Dickens as playwright." British Museum quarterly, 24 (1961), 22-25.

Describes manuscripts of 3 Dickens plays in British Museum.

4568. Kitton, Frederick George. The minor writings of Charles Dickens; a bibliography and sketch. London: E. Stock, 1900. 260p.

Collection presented to Guildhall Library in 1908.

4569. Tyson, Moses. "A review and other writings by Charles Dickens, edited from the original manuscripts in the John Rylands Library." Bulletin of the John Rylands Library, 18 (1934), 177-96. Reprinted, 1934. 22p.

4570. Victoria and Albert Museum. Dickens exhibition. London: H. M. Stationery Office, 1912. 63p. (Victoria and Albert Museum guides)

Drawn from the museum's rich collection of original manuscripts, first editions, and other Dickens material.

4571. Wellcome Historical Medical Library. Dickens and medicine; an exhibition of books, manuscripts and prints to mark the centenary of his death: with an introduction and bibliography. London, 1970. 32p. (Exhibition catalogue, no.5)

4572. Wilson, R. A. "Translations of the works of Charles Dickens." British Museum quarterly, 14 (1940), 59-60.

Description of collection received by British Museum.

Dickinson, Patric, 1914-

4573. Birmingham, University, Library. Patric Dickinson collection. Birmingham, 1972. Unpaged. (Catalogues of the manuscript collections, no.33)

Dobson, Austin, 1840-1921

4574. Dobson, Alban. A bibliography of the first editions of published and privately printed books and pamphlets by Austin Dobson. London: First Edition Club, 1925. 88p.

References to British Museum copies.

4575. Ealing Public Libraries. Austin Dobson; the special collection in Central Library Reference Department. Ealing, 1962. 16p.

Listing of books by and books from library of Austin Dobson.

4576. London, University, Library. Catalogue of the collection of the works of Austin Dobson (1840-1921), comp. by Alban T. A. Dobson. London: The University, 1960. 62p.

Catalog of special collection in University of London library; lists 340 printed items, plus miscellaneous manuscripts, letters, notebooks, etc.

Dohnányi, Ernst von, 1877-1960

4577. Willetts, Pamela J. "The Dohnányi collection." British Museum quarterly, 25 (1962), 3-11.

Description with listing of collection of Ernst von Dohnányi works acquired by British Museum.

Donne, John, 1573-1631

4578. Keynes, Geoffrey Langdon. Bibliography of the works of Dr. John Donne, Dean of St. Paul's. Cambridge, 1914. 167p. (Baskerville Club publications, no.2)

4579. ———. A bibliography of Dr. John Donne, 2d ed. Cambridge: Univ. Pr., 1932. 195p.

4580. ———. A bibliography of Dr. John Donne, Dean of Saint Paul's, 3d ed. Cambridge: Univ. Pr., 1958. 285p.

Copies of 151 items located in British, American, and other libraries; STC and Wing numbers added.

Douglas, Eleanor, d. 1652

4581. Hindle, C. J. A bibliography of the printed pamphlets and broadsides of Lady Eleanor Douglas, the seventeenth-century prophetess. Edinburgh: Edinburgh Bibliographical Society, 1936. 34p. (Reprinted from Edinburgh Bibliographical Society transactions, 1 (1936), pt.1)

Listing of 53 items, with locations.

Douglas, James, 1675-1742

4582. Glasgow, University, Hunterian Library. "An annotated catalogue of the manuscripts and drawings of James Douglas (1675-1742) . . . preserved by his pupil, William Hunter, known as the Blackburn collection, the Hunterian Library, University of Glasgow." In: Thomas, K. Bryn. James Douglas of the Pouch and his pupil William Hunter. London: Pitman Medical Publishing Co., 1964, p.85-193.

Douglas was Scottish anatomist, obstetrician, and physician.

Drake, Francis, 1540?-96

4583. British Museum, Dept. of Printed Books, Map Room. Sir Francis Drake's voyage round the world, 1577-1580; two contemporary maps, 2d ed. London: The Museum, 1931. 11p.

Drayton, Michael, 1563-1631

4584. Elton, Oliver. "Bibliography" [of Michael Drayton] In his: Michael Drayton, a critical study. London: Archibald Constable, 1905, p.157-205.

Locates copies in English libraries.

4585. Juel-Jensen, Bent. "Bibliography of the early editions of the writing of Michael Drayton." In: Hebel, John W., ed. The works of Michael Drayton. Oxford, 1961, v.5, p.265-306.

Locates copies in British and American libraries.

Drinkwater, John, 1882-1937

4586. Birmingham, University, Library. John Drinkwater; a small collection of ms. poems presented by J. S. Vinden. Birmingham, 1968. Unpaged. (Catalogues of the manuscript collections, no.8)

Dryden, John, 1631-1700

4587. British Museum, Dept. of Printed Books. Catalogue of printed books: Dryden (John). London: W. Clowes, 1886. 24 cols.

4588. Macdonald, Hugh. John Dryden: a bibliography of early editions and of Drydeniana. Oxford: Clarendon, 1939. 358p.

Frequent references to locations in British Museum, Cambridge, and Bodleian libraries.

Dugdale, William, 1605-86

4589. Maddison, Francis, and others. Sir William Dugdale, 1605-1685: a list of his printed works and of his portraits, with notes on his life and the manuscript sources. Warwick: Records and Museum Committee of the Warwickshire County Council, 1953. 92p.

Manuscript and portrait sources listed and described in appendices.

4590. Warwickshire County Museum. Exhibition of the life and works of Sir William Dugdale, 1605-1686, historian of Warwickshire; description of the exhibits, produced as a supplement to Sir William Dugdale, 1605-1686. A list of his printed works and of his portraits, with notes on his life and the manuscript sources (Warwick, 1953) and containing additions and corrections to that publication, by Francis Maddison and others. Warwick, 1953. 49p.

Records 168 items; copies located.

D'Urfey, Thomas, 1653-1723

4591. Biswanger, Raymond Adam, Jr. "Thomas D'Urfey's Richmond heiress, (1693): a bibliographical study." Studies in bibliography, 5 (1952), 169-78.

Copies located in British and American libraries.

Durham, James, 1622-58

4592. Christie, George. "A bibliography of James Durham, 1622-1658." Edinburgh Bibliographical Society publications, 11 (1918), 35-46.

Locates copies of 11 works by Durham.

Edgeworth, Maria, 1767-1849

4593. Birmingham, University, Library. Catalogue of the Maria Edgeworth letters. Birmingham, 1969. 7l. (Catalogues of the manuscript collections, no.21)

Calendar of 50 letters, 1820-48.

4594. Colvin, Christina Edgeworth. "Maria Edgeworth's literary manuscripts in the Bodleian Library." Bodleian Library record, 8 (1970), 196-201.

4595. Slade, Bertha Coolidge. Maria Edgeworth, 1767-1849; a bibliographical tribute. London: Constable, 1937. 253p.

Detailed bibliographical descriptions; copies located in British, American, and French libraries.

Eliot, Thomas Stearns, 1888-1965

4596. Cambridge, University, King's College Library. A preliminary hand-list of the literary manuscripts in the T. S. Eliot collection bequeathed to King's College, Cambridge, by John Davy Hayward in 1965. Cambridge, 1936. 26l.

Elliott, Ebenezer, 1781-1849

4597. Sheffield City Libraries and Rotherham Public Libraries. "A bibliography of Ebenezer Elliott." In: Ebenezer Elliott, the corn-law rhymer, 1781-1849; a commemorative brochure. Sheffield, 1950, p.21-35.
Locates copies of poetry, prose, and manuscripts.

Elyot, Thomas, 1490 ?-1546

4598. Freeman, Eric James. Bibliography of Sir Thomas Elyot (1490?-1546). London, 1962. 205p. (Diploma in Librarianship, Univ. of London)
Locates copies of works in numerous British and American libraries.

4599. Lehmberg, Stanford E. "Editions of Elyot's works." In his: Sir Thomas Elyot, Tudor humanist. Austin: Univ. of Tex. Pr., 1960, p.197-98.
Checklist, 1522-45, with STC numbers and locations of copies.

Erasmus, Desiderius, 1466 ?-1536

4600. Allison, A. F., and Nixon, H. M. "Three sixteenth-century English translations of Erasmus in a contemporary binding." British Museum quarterly, 23 (1961), 59-63.
Describes 3 rare works, printed 1530-36, acquired by British Museum.

4601. Devereux, E. J. A checklist of English translations of Erasmus to 1700. Oxford: Oxford Bibliographical Society, 1968. 40p. (Occasional publication, no.3)
Copies located in British, American, Canadian, and Dutch libraries.

Evelyn, John, 1620-1706

4602. Keynes, Geoffrey Langdon. John Evelyn; a study in bibliophily & a bibliography of his writings. Cambridge: Univ. Pr., 1937. 308p. + 24 plates.
Contains full bibliographical details for 186 entries, with locations in British and American libraries.

4603. ———. John Evelyn; a study in bibliophily with a bibliography of his writings, 2d ed. Oxford: Clarendon, 1968. 313p.
Contains full bibliographical details for 186 entries, with locations in British and American libraries.

Everard, Thomas, 1560-1633

4604. Allison, Antony Francis. "An early seventeenth-century translator, Thomas Everard, S. J.; a study of the bibliographical evidence." Biographical studies, 2 (1954), 188-215.
Locates copies in British and American libraries.

Eyton, Frances, fl. mid-19th century

4605. Birmingham, University, Library. Catalogue of the Eyton letters. Birmingham, 1968. Unpaged. (Catalogues of the manuscript collections, no.9)
Lists 226 items; letters to Elizabeth Frances Eyton and other members of Eyton family, mainly 19th century.

Faraday, Michael, 1791-1867

4606. Jeffreys, Alan E. Michael Faraday; a list of his lectures and published writings. London, 1958. Unpaged. (Diploma in Librarianship, Univ. of London)
Chronological listing, 1816-1932; locates periodicals cited in bibliography.

Farjeon, Eleanor, 1881-

4607. Camden Public Libraries. Eleanor Farjeon; a handlist of the collection of her works in the Camden Public Libraries. London Borough of Camden: Central Library, 1968. Unpaged.
Annotated list of 117 items.

Farquar, George, 1678-1707

4608. Gibb, Ian Pashley. A bibliography of the works of George Farquar (1678-1707). London, 1952. 239*l.* (Diploma in Librarianship, Univ. of London)
Locates copies in various libraries.

Fergusson, Robert, 1750-74

4609. Fairley, John A. Bibliography of Robert Fergusson. Glasgow: J. Maclehose, 1915. 49p.
Lists 93 items, 1769-1914, with locations of copies examined.

4610. Law, Alexander. "The inscribed copies of the first edition (1773) of the poems of Robert Fergusson." Transactions of the Edinburgh Bibliographical Society, 3 (1954), 125-35.
Copies traced and located as far as known.

Fiedler, Hermann Georg, 1862-1945

4611. Birmingham, University, Library. Catalogue of Fiedler-Harding letters. Birmingham, 1969. Unpaged. (Catalogues of the manuscript collections, no.24)
Lists 92 items, 1888-1909, relating to H. G. Fiedler, Charles Harding, etc.

Field, John, 1782-1837

4612. Neighbour, O. W. "Early editions of John Field." British Museum quarterly, 19 (1954), 1-2.

Works of British composer (1782-1837) held by British Museum.

Fielding, Henry, 1707-54

4613. Jones, Brian P. Fielding in France, a bibliography of editions and critical references, 1733-1847. London, 1962. 164*l*. (Diploma in Librarianship, Univ. of London)

Locates copies in British, French, and American libraries.

Fisher, Saint John, 1469-1534

4614. Steiner, J. H. A bibliography of the works of Saint John Fisher, Cardinal Bishop of Rochester, 1469-1534. London, 1952. 85*l*. (Diploma in Librarianship, Univ. of London)

Copies located in British Museum, Cambridge, Bodleian, and Durham University.

Fitzwilliam, William Wentworth, 1748-1833

4615. Sheffield City Libraries. Wentworth Woodhouse manuscripts; handlist of correspondence of William Wentworth Fitzwilliam, 4th Earl Fitzwilliam (d. 1833). London: National Register of Archives, 1971. 2pts. in 4v.

Covers period 1748-1832; records deposited in Sheffield City Libraries.

Fletcher, Giles, 1549 ?-1611

4616. Berry, Lloyd Eason. "Giles Fletcher, the elder: a bibliography." Cambridge Bibliographical Society transactions, 3 (1961), 200-15.

Locates copies of 11 printed works, 1571-1678, and manuscripts.

Fletcher, John, 1579-1625

4617. Bowers, Fredson Thayer. "A bibliographical history of the Fletcher-Betterton play, The prophetess, 1690." Library, ser.5, 16 (1961), 169-75.

Copies located in British and American libraries.

Foulis, Andrew, 1712-75

4618. Glasgow, University, Hunterian Museum. Robert and Andrew Foulis; an exhibition in the Hunterian Museum to commemorate the silver jubilee of the British Records Association. Glasgow, 1958. 106*l*.

Fox, Charles James, 1749-1806

4619. Aldridge, H. R. "The Charles James Fox papers." British Museum quarterly, 18 (1953), 39-41.

Papers of famous Whig leader received by British Museum.

Francis of Assisi, Saint, 1182-1226

4620. British Museum, Dept. of Manuscripts. Septingentenary of St. Francis, October, 1926; notes on the exhibition of Franciscan manuscripts in the British Museum, by A. G. Little. London: The Museum, 1926. 8p.

Fuller, Thomas, 1608-61

4621. Gibson, Strickland. A bibliography of the works of Thomas Fuller, D.D. Oxford: Univ. Pr., 1936. 99p. (Reprinted from Proceedings of the Oxford Bibliographical Society, 4 (1934-35), 63-161)

Detailed bibliographical descriptions with locations in various libraries.

4622. Manchester Public Libraries, Reference Library. The Fuller collection in the Free Reference Library. Manchester: H. Blacklock, 1891. 10p.

Collection relating to Thomas Fuller, D.D., 1608-61.

Galen, fl. 2d century, A.D.

4623. Durling, Richard Jasper. A bibliography of sixteenth-century editions of Galen (excluding Omnia opera). London, 1959. 573*l*. (Diploma in Librarianship, Univ. of London)

Contains 462 entries; locates copies in 24 British, Continental, and American libraries.

4624. ———. "A chronological census of Renaissance editions and translations of Galen." Journal of the Warburg and Courtauld Institutes, 24 (1961), 230-305.

Census lists some 660 items; locates copies in numerous British, Irish, Continental, American, and Canadian libraries.

4625. ———. "Unsigned editions of Galen and Hippocrates (1527): further light on an elusive printer." Library, 16 (1961), 55-57.

Editions probably produced by a French printer, Simon DuBois; copies located in British and American libraries.

Galsworthy, John, 1867-1933

4626. Birmingham, University, Library. Galsworthy centenary exhibition, catalogue, comp. by D. W. Evans. Birmingham, 1967. 16p.

Records 289 items.

4627. ———. John Galsworthy: catalogue of the collection, comp. by D. W. Evans. Birmingham, 1967. 88p.

Records 2,049 entries; "the collection contains almost everything of importance for the study of John Galsworthy's life and work."

Gandhi, Mohandas, 1869-1948

4628. India Office Library. Gandhi and the British Raj: an exhibition of documents, photographs and other material to illustrate the relations between Mahatma and the British authorities. London, 1969. 23 + 4 pages.

Gaskell, Elizabeth Cleghorn, 1810-65

4629. Waller, Ross D. "Letters addressed to Mrs. Gaskell by celebrated contemporaries; now in the possession of the John Rylands Library." Bulletin of the John Rylands Library, 19 (1935), 102-69. Reprinted, 1935. 70p.

Gibbon, Edward, 1737-94

4630. Historical Society of Great Britain—Royal Historical. Society. Proceedings of the Gibbon Commemoration, 1794-1894. London, 1895. 52p.

Catalog of the exhibition of manuscripts, books, portraits, and relics at the British Museum, 1894.

4631. Norton, Jane Elizabeth. A bibliography of the works of Edward Gibbon. Oxford: Univ. Pr., 1940. 256p. Reprinted, 1970.

List of 160 items, mainly before 1838, with locations of copies in English, American, and Continental libraries.

4632. Royal Historical Society. "Catalogue of the exhibition of manuscripts, books . . . at the British Museum, November, 1894." In: Proceedings of the Gibbon commemoration, 1794-1894. London, 1895, p.36-52.

Items relating to Edward Gibbon, 1737-94.

Gilbert, William Schwenck, 1836-1911

4633. Gransden, K. W., and Willetts, Pamela J. "Papers of W. S. Gilbert." British Museum quarterly, 21 (1958), 67-69.

Description of manuscripts—letters, diaries, plays, libretti, etc.—of Sir William S. Gilbert acquired by British Museum.

Gill, Eric, 1882-1940

4634. West Sussex County Council. The Eric Gill memorial collection, a catalogue, ed. by Noel H. Osborne. Chichester, 1967. 26p.

Records 255 items, deposited in West Sussex Record Office, County Hall, Chichester, by or relating to Gill, author and artist.

Gissing, George Robert, 1857-1903

4635. National Book League. The rediscovery of George Gissing; a reader's guide, by John Spiers and Pierre Coustillas. London, 1971. 163p.

Locates copies in British and American public and private collections.

Gladstone, William Ewart, 1809-98

4636. British Museum, Dept. of Manuscripts. The Gladstone papers; additional manuscripts 44086-44835. London: The Museum, 1953. 400p.

4637. "Contributions to a bibliography of the Right Hon. W. E. Gladstone." Notes and queries, ser.8, 2 (1892), 461-63, 501-3; 3 (1893), 1-3, 41-43.

Covers period 1827-92; locates copies, mainly in British Museum.

4638. Saint Deniol's Library. Materials for the study of the Rt. Hon. W. E. Gladstone and his times at St. Deniol's Library. Hawarden, Chester, 1969. 8p.

Godfrey, Edward Smith, 1769-1843

4639. Walker, Marjorie. Papers of Edward Smith Godfrey, 1806-1843. London, 1962. 144p. (Diploma in Archive Administration, Univ. of London)

Descriptive list of papers of Godfrey, clerk of the peace for Nottinghamshire; deposited in Nottinghamshire County Records Office.

Godwin, Francis, 1562-1633

4640. Lawton, H. W. "Bishop [Francis] Godwin's Man in the moone." Review of English studies, 7 (1931), 23-55.

Locates copies of work first published in 1638, in British Museum and Bibliothèque Nationale.

Goethe, Johann Wolfgang von, 1749-1832

4641. British Museum, Dept. of Printed Books. Catalogue of printed books: Goethe. London: W. Clowes, 1888. 82 cols.

Goldsmith, Oliver, 1728-74

4642. Cassedy, James. "Skeffington Gibbon in the Goldsmith country." Irish book lever, 22 (1934), 58-62.
Checklist, 1829-64, with locations of copies.

4643. Dix, E. R. McC. "The works of Oliver Goldsmith; handlist of Dublin editions before 1801." Bibliographical Society of Ireland publications, 3 (1928), 93-101.
Checklist, 1762-1800, with locations of copies.

4644. Friedman, Arthur. "Two notes on Goldsmith: 1. The first edition of Goldsmith's Life of Bolinbroke. 2. The 1772 edition of Goldsmith's Traveller." Studies in bibliography, 13 (1960), 232-35.
Copies located in British and American libraries.

4645. Todd, William Burton. "The first editions of The good natur'd man and She stoops to conquer." Studies in bibliography, 11 (1958), 133-42.
Copies located in British and American libraries.

4646. ———. "The 'private issues' of The deserted village." Studies in bibliography, 6 (1954), 25-44.
Copies located in British and American libraries.

Goodman, Scholefield

4647. Birmingham, University, Library. Scholefield Goodman collection catalogue. Birmingham, 1970. Unpaged. (Catalogues of the manuscript collections, no.28)
Documents, business records, correspondence, etc., relating to Goodman family, 18th to 20th centuries.

Gordon, Charles George, 1833-85

4648. Lewis, Jenny. "The Gordon papers." British Museum quarterly, 28 (1964), 75-82.
Extensive collection of papers of General "Chinese" Gordon received by British Museum.

Gosse, Edmund William, 1849-1928

4649. Leeds, University, Brotherton Library. A catalogue of the Gosse correspondence in the Brotherton collection, consisting mainly of letters written to Sir Edmund Gosse in the period from 1867 to 1928. Leeds, 1950. 80p. (Library publications, no.3)

Grace, William Gilbert, 1848-1915

4650. Gloucester Public Library. W. G. Grace centenary, 1848-1948; a list of selected items relating to W. G. Grace and Gloucestershire cricket. (From the Gloucestershire collection in Gloucester City Library) Gloucester, 1948. 8p.

Grainger, Percy, 1882-1961

4651. Willetts, Pamela J. "The Percy Grainger collection." British Museum quarterly, 27 (1963-64), 65-71.
Description and listing of Grainger autograph manuscripts acquired by British Museum.

Gray, Thomas, 1716-71

4652. Northup, Clark Sutherland. A bibliography of Thomas Gray. New Haven, Conn.: Yale Univ. Pr., 1917. 296p.
Locations in 24 British, American, and Continental libraries.

Greene, Robert, 1560?-92

4653. Johnson, Francis Rarick. "The editions of Robert Greene's Three parts of 'Conny-catching,' a bibliographical analysis." Library, ser.5, 9 (1954), 17-24.
Four editions, 1591-92, described and copies located in 3 English libraries and Huntington Library (San Marino, Calif.).

4654. Miller, Edwin Haviland. "The editions of Robert Greene's A quip for an upstart courtier." Studies in bibliography, 6 (1953), 107-16.
Copies located in British and American libraries.

4655. Parr, Johnstone. Instructions to editors of the works of Robert Greene. Stratford on Avon: Shakespeare Institute, Univ. of Birmingham, 1959. 31l.
Lists editions, copies, and locations of Greene works.

Guazzo, Stefano, 1530-93

4656. Lievsay, John Leon. Stefano Guazzo and the English renaissance 1575-1675. Chapel Hill: Univ. of N.C. Pr., 1961. 344p.
"Bibliographical finding list of Guazzo's works," p.277-303, records 126 items with copies located in British, American, and Continental libraries.

Handel, George Frederick, 1685-1759

4657. British Museum. Handel's Messiah; catalogue

of an exhibition held May-July, 1951, comp. by Alexander Hyatt King. London, 1951. 16p.

4658. ——— Dept. of Printed Books. Handel and his autographs, by A. Hyatt King. London: The Museum, 1967. 32p. + 20 plates.

4659. Hopkinson, Cecil. "Handel and France; editions published there during his lifetime." Edinburgh Bibliographical Society transactions, 3 (1957), 223-48.

Copies located in British and Continental libraries.

4660. National Library of Scotland. George Frederick Handel, 1685-1759; catalogue of an exhibition, comp. by William C. Smith. Edinburgh, 1948. 20p.

Records 51 items, manuscripts and early printed works.

4661. Smith, William C., and Humpries, Charles. Handel, a descriptive catalogue of the early editions, 2d ed. with supplement. Oxford: Blackwell, 1970. 378p.

Locations in public and private collections.

Hardy, Thomas, 1840-1928

4662. Dorset County Library. Thomas Hardy catalogue; a list of the books by and about Thomas Hardy, O.M., (1840-1928) in Dorset County Library, comp. by Kenneth Carter. Dorset: County Council, 1968. 37p.

4663. Ealing Central Library. Thomas Hardy, 1840-1928; a list of books by and about Thomas Hardy available at Ealing Public Libraries, comp. by J. W. Thirsk. London, 1968. 8p.

4664. Purdy, Richard Little. Thomas Hardy; a bibliographical study. Oxford: Clarendon, 1954. 388p. Reprinted. 1968.

Many manuscripts located.

Harington, Sir John, 1561-1612

4665. Kirkwood, A. E. M. "The metamorphosis of Ajax and its sequels." Library, ser.4, 12 (1931), 208-34.

Late 16th-century work by Sir John Harington; copies located in British Museum.

Harvey, William, 1578-1657

4666. Keynes, Geoffrey Langdon. A bibliography of the writings of Dr. William Harvey, 1578-1657, 2d ed. Cambridge: Univ. Pr., 1953. 80p.

Registers holdings of 26 libraries, European and American; records 46 copies of 1628 edition of De moto cordis.

4667. ———. A bibliography of the writings of William Harvey. Cambridge: Univ. Pr., 1928. 67p.

4668. Royal College of Physicians of London. William Harvey, 1578-1656; an exhibition of books and manuscripts illustrating his life and work, comp. by L. M. Payne. London, 1957. 25p.

Annotated catalog of 39 items drawn from college's collection.

Hauptmann, Gerhart, 1862-1946

4669. London, University, Institute of Germanic Studies. Gerhart Hauptmann exhibition; catalogue prepared by H. F. Garten. London, 1962. 20p.

Hawkins, John, 1761-1841

4670. West Sussex County Council. The Hawkins papers; a catalogue, ed. by Francis W. Steer. Chichester, 1962. 36p.

Papers relating to John Hawkins, 1761-1841, a founder of the Royal Horticultural Society.

Hayward, John, 1564?-1627

4671. Plomer, Henry Robert. "Examination of some existing copies of Hayward's 'Life and raigne of Henrie IV.'" Library, ser.3, 3 (1902), 13-23.

Copies of John Hayward's 1599 work located in several libraries.

Hazlitt, William, 1778-1830

4672. Keynes, Geoffrey Langdon. Bibliography of William Hazlitt. London: Nonesuch, 1931. 135p.

Locates rare copies of 138 items, 1805-1930.

Henry the Navigator, 1394-1460

4673. British Museum. Prince Henry the Navigator and Portuguese maritime enterprise; catalogue of an exhibition at the British Museum, comp. by R. A. Skelton. London, 1960. 166p.

Detailed descriptions of 326 items.

Herrick, Robert, 1591-1674

4674. Cox, Edwin Marion. "Notes on the bibliography of Herrick." Library, ser.3, 8 (1917), 105-19.

Early editions of Robert Herrick's works located in several libraries.

Heywood, Thomas, 1574?-1641

4675. Clark, Arthur Melville. "A bibliography of

Thomas Heywood." Oxford Bibliographical Society, Proceedings and papers, 1 (1924), 97-153.

Comprehensive bibliography of 17th-century playwright and literary light; locations in British Museum, Bodleian, etc.

Hobbes, Thomas, 1588-1679

4676. Cambridge, University, King's College Library. A catalogue of first and early editions of the works of Thomas Hobbes forming part of the library bequeathed by John Maynard, Baron Keynes of Tilton, to King's College, Cambridge, by A. N. L. Munby. Cambridge, 1949. 42*l*.

4677. MacDonald, Hugh, and Hargreaves, Joan Mary. Thomas Hobbes: a bibliography. London: Bibliographical Society, 1952. 84p.

Aims to include all editions of Hobbes' works to 1725, collected editions since then, and translations to 1700. Copies located in British Museum, Bodleian, Cambridge, and Dr. Williams's Library, or elsewhere, if not held by one of these 4.

Home, John, 1722-1808

4678. Lefèvre, Jean M. "John Home: a check list of editions." Bibliotheck, 3 (1961), 121-38.

Works of Home, "the Scottish Shakespeare"; 152 items listed, with locations in 10 British, American, and French libraries.

4679. Simpson, Jean Mary. John Home. London, 1957. Unpaged. (Diploma in Librarianship, Univ. of London)

Lists 168 items, with locations of copies in British and American libraries.

4680. Stratman, Carl J., and Hepburn, A. G. "John Home: a check list continued." Bibliotheck, 3 (1962), 222-28.

Supplements Lefèvre's list; copies located in 17 British and American libraries.

Homer

4681. British Museum, Dept. of Printed Books. Catalogue of printed books: Homer. London: W. Clowes, 1890. 110 cols.

Hooke, Robert, 1635-1703

4682. Keynes, Geoffrey. A bibliography of Dr. Robert Hooke. Oxford: Clarendon, 1960. 115p.

Copies located in British, American, and other libraries.

Housman, Alfred Edward, 1859-1936

4683. London, University, University College. A. E. Housman: catalogue of an exhibition on the centenary of his birth, by John Carter and J. W. Scott. London, 1959. 35p.

Howard, John, 1726?-90

4684. Baumgartner, Leona. "John Howard (1726-1790), hospital and prison reformer; a bibliography." Bulletin of the history of medicine, 7 (1939), 486-626. Reprinted.

Copies located in British, American, and other libraries.

Hugo, Victor, 1802-85

4685. Manchester, University, Library. Victor Hugo (1802-1885): an exhibition of autograph letters, manuscripts, prints, and books. Manchester: The University, 1965. 32p.

Hume, David, 1711-76

4686. Edinburgh, University. David Hume; University of Edinburgh 250th anniversary of the birth of David Hume, 1711-1961; a record of the commemoration. Edinburgh: Univ. Pr., 1961. 39p.

p.29-39, "The Hume exhibition; a catalogue of the exhibits, by C. P. Finlayson.

4687. Johnston, George P. "The first edition of Hume of Godscroft's History." Edinburgh Bibliographical Society publications, 4 (1901), 149-71.

List of manuscripts and printed editions of The history, with locations of copies.

Humphrey, Herbert Alfred, 1868-1951

4688. London, University, Imperial College. Herbert Alfred Humphrey; list of his papers in the Imperial College Archives, comp. by Jeanne Pingree and Denis Smith. London, 1971. 37p.

Humphrey was a leading British engineer.

Hunter, John, 1728-93

4689. LeFanu, W. R. John Hunter: a list of his books. Cambridge: Univ. Pr., 1946. 31*l*.

Locates copies in 25 British, Irish, Continental, and American libraries.

4690. Royal College of Surgeons of England. List of books, manuscripts, portraits, etc., relating to John Hunter in the Royal College. London, 1891. 8p.

Hunter, William, 1861-1937

4691. Glasgow, University, Hunterian Library. William Hunter: an exhibition of books and manuscripts. Glasgow, 1965. 24p.

Annotated list of 82 works by or relating to famous Scottish physician.

Hutton, Edward, 1875-

4692. Rhodes, Dennis Everard. The writings of Edward Hutton. London: Hollis & Carter, 1955. 64p.

Lists 225 items, 1898-1954, with locations of copies.

Huxley, Thomas Henry, 1825-95

4693. London, University, Imperial College of Science and Technology. Thomas Henry Huxley, a list of his scientific notebooks, drawings and other papers, preserved in the College Archives, comp. by Jeanne Pingree. London, 1968. 94p.

4694. ———. Thomas Henry Huxley, list of his correspondence with Miss Henrietta Anne Heathorn, later Mrs. Huxley, 1847-1854, comp. by Jeanne Pingree. London, 1969. 36p.

Correspondence preserved in the Imperial College archives.

4695. ———. The Huxley papers; a descriptive catalogue of the correspondence, manuscripts, and miscellaneous papers of the Rt. Hon. Thomas Henry Huxley . . . preserved in the Imperial College of Science and Technology, London, by Warren R. Dawson. London: Macmillan, 1946. 201p.

James I, king of England, 1566-1625

4696. Craigie, James. "The Latin folio of King James's prose works." Edinburgh Bibliographical Society transactions, 3 (1952-54), 19-30, 155.

Locates 14 copies in Scottish and English libraries.

4697. Glasgow, University, Hunterian Library. James VI and I: an exhibition to commemorate the quarter-centenary of the birth of James Charles Stuart, successively King of Scotland and of Great Britain and Ireland, held in the Hunterian Library, University of Glasgow. Glasgow, 1966. 20p.

Records 57 items, annotated.

Jenner, Edward, 1749-1823

4698. LeFanu, W. R. A bio-bibliography of Edward Jenner, 1749-1823. London: Harvey and Blythe, 1951. 176p.

Copies located in numerous British, American, Continental, and Australian libraries.

4699. Wellcome Historical Medical Museum. Catalogue of an exhibition of books, manuscripts and relics commemorating the bicentenary of Edward Jenner, 17 May 1749-26 January 1923. London: Geoffrey Cumberlege, 1949. 36p.

Johnson, Richard, 1734-93

4700. Weedon, Margaret J. P. Richard Johnson and the successors of John Newbery; an account of the work done by R. Johnson from 1769 to 1793 for T. Carnan, F. Newbery, jun. and F. Power and Co. at No. 65, St. Paul's Church-yard; and for F. Newbery and his widow and successor E. Newbery at the Corner of St. Paul's Church-yard. London, 1948. 94l. Diploma in Librarianship, Univ. of London)

Notes location of copies in public and private collections.

4701. ———. "Richard Johnson and the successors of John Newbery." Library, ser.5, 4 (1949), 25-63.

Checklist of 91 items by Johnson, with copies located in British Museum, Bodleian, Library of Congress, etc.

Johnson, Samuel, 1709-84

4702. Birmingham Library. Catalogue of an exhibition of books in the Birmingham Library to celebrate the 250th anniversary of the birth of Dr. Samuel Johnson, September 14th-October 3rd, 1959. Birmingham, 1959. 12p.

Annotated list of 50 items.

4703. Birmingham Reference Library. Dr. Samuel Johnson, 1709-1784; celebrations in Birmingham of the 250th anniversary of his birth; an exhibition of books, manuscripts, views, and portraits arranged jointly by the Reference Library and the Museum and Art Gallery. Birmingham, 1959. 28p.

4704. Chapman, R. W., and Hazen, Allen T. "Johnsonian bibliography; a supplement to Courtney." Oxford Bibliographical Society proceedings and papers, 5 (1939), 117-66.

Some locations in English and American libraries.

4705. Fleeman, J. D. A preliminary handlist of documents & manuscripts of Samuel Johnson. Oxford: Oxford Bibliographical Society, Bodleian Library, 1967. 51p. (Oxford Bibliographical Society occasional publications, no.2)

Locations in British and American libraries; chronological list of 218 items.

4706. Hazen, Allen Tracy. Samuel Johnson's prefaces & dedications. New Haven, Conn.: Yale Univ. Pr., 1937. 257p.

Locates copies in British and American libraries.

4707. Kolli, Gwin J., and Sledd, James H. "The Reynolds copy of Johnson's Dictionary." Bulletin of the John Rylands Library, 37 (1955), 446-75. Reprinted, 1955. 32p.

Copy in John Rylands Library.

4708. Oxford Bibliographical Society. A preliminary handlist of documents & manuscripts of Samuel Johnson, by J. D. Fleeman. Oxford: The Society, Bodleian Library, 1967. 51p. (Occasional publications, no.2)

Copies located, if known, in British and American libraries.

4709. Oxford, University, Bodleian Library. "A Johnson exhibition." Bodleian quarterly record, 7 (1934), 466-71.

Listing of manuscripts and printed books in Bodleian Library relating to Samuel Johnson.

4710. Taylor, Frank. "Johnsoniana from the Bagshawe muniments in the John Rylands Library: Sir James Caldwell, Dr. Hawkesworth, Dr. Johnson, and Boswell's use of the 'Caldwell minute.'" Bulletin of the John Rylands Library, 35 (1952), 211-47. Reprinted, 1952. 39p.

4711. Tyson, Moses. "Unpublished manuscripts, papers and letters of Dr. Johnson, Mrs. Thrale, and their friends, in the John Rylands Library." Bulletin of the John Rylands Library, 15 (1931), 467-88.

4712. Wright, J. D. "Some unpublished letters to and from Dr. Johnson; from the originals now in the possession of the John Rylands Library." Bulletin of the John Rylands Library, 16 (1932), 32-76. Reprinted, 1932. 55p.

Jollie, Thomas, 1629-1703

4713. Dr. Williams's Library. Thomas Jollie's papers; a list of the papers in Dr. Williams's Library. London: Dr. Williams's Trust, 1956. Unpaged. (Occasional paper, no.3)

List of 58 items relating to Jollie.

Jonson, Ben, 1573?-1637

4714. Simpson, Percy. "The Ben Jonson exhibition." Bodleian quarterly record, 8 (1935-37), 405-11.

Description, with listing of major items, of works drawn from Bodleian Library collection.

Junius

4715. Birmingham, University, Library. Junius collection. Birmingham, 1968. Unpaged. (Catalogues of the manuscript collections, no.10)

"Collections for Junius Letters."

4716. Bowyer, T. H. A bibliographical examination of the earliest editions of the letters of Junius. Charlottesville: Univ. of Va. Pr., 1957. 147p.

Locates copies in England, Eire, and United States.

4717. ———. The letters of Junius; a bibliographical examination of the earliest editions, 1769-1775. London, 1952. 109l. (Diploma in Librarianship, Univ. of London)

Copies located in British and American libraries.

Kingsley, Charles, 1819-75

4718. Parrish, Morris L., and Mann, B. K. Charles Kingsley and Thomas Hughes; first editions (with a few exceptions) in the Library at Dormy House. London: Constable, 1936. 165p.

Kipling, Rudyard, 1865-1936

4719. British Museum, Dept. of Printed Books. Catalogue of printed books: Rudyard Kipling London: W. Clowes, 1949. 154p.

4720. Hanson, Laurence. "The Kipling bequest." British Museum quarterly, 14 (1940), 93-95.

Comprehensive collection of 1,200 volumes of Kipling's works received by British Museum.

Kirkman, Francis, 1652-80

4721. Gibson, Strickland. A bibliography of Francis Kirkman, with his prefaces, dedications and commendations (1652-80). Oxford: Univ. Pr., 1949. 152p. (Oxford Bibliographical Society publications, n.s. v.1, fasc. ii, 1947)

Full bibliographical descriptions of 41 works by Kirkman, issued 1652-77; copies located in British and American libraries.

Lahontan, Baron de, 1666-1750

4722. Paltsits, Victor Hugo. A bibliography of the writings of Baron Lahontan. Chicago: McClurg, 1905. lii-xciiip. (Reprinted from Lahontan's New voyages to North America, London, 1703, ed. by Reuben G. Thwaites)

Copies located in British Museum, Bibliothèque Nationale, and American and Canadian libraries.

Laing, David, 1793-1878

4723. Edinburgh, University. Report on the Laing manuscripts preserved in the University of Edinburgh. London: H. M. Stationery Office, 1914-25. 2v. (Historical Manuscript Commission report, no.72)

Manuscripts associated with David Laing, covering period 1827-71.

Lamb, Charles, 1775-1834

4724. Foxon, David Fairweather. "The chapbook editions of the Lambs' Tales from Shakespeare." Book collector, 6 (1957), 41-53.

Copies located in British Museum and Folger Library.

4725. Skeat, T. C. "Letters of Charles and Mary Lamb and Coleridge." British Museum quarterly, 26 (1962), 17-21.

Description of collection received by British Museum.

Lanchester, Frederick William, 1868-1946

4726. Baxter, E. G. Catalogue of the private papers of F. W. Lanchester in the Library of Lanchester College of Technology, Coventry. London, 1966. 155*l*. (Thesis, Library Association Fellowship)

Lanchester was pioneer in aeronautics and automobile engineering.

Landor, Walter Savage, 1775-1864

4727. Lyde, R. G. "A Landor gift." British Museum quarterly, 22 (1960), 7-8.

Describes collection of books, many containing manuscript notes, belonging to Walter Savage Landor, received by British Museum.

4728. Wise, Thomas James, and Wheeler, Stephen. A bibliography of the writings in prose and verse of Walter Savage Landor. London: Blades for the Bibliographical Society, 1919. 426p.

Some copies located in British Museum.

Laurence, John, 1668-1732

4729. Gilmour, John S. L. "The Rev. John Laurence (1668-1732); the man and his books." Huntia, a yearbook of botanical and horticultural bibliography, 2 (1965), 117-37.

Locates copies of early editions of 14 horticultural and religious works in English and American libraries.

Lawes, Henry, 1596-1662

4730. British Museum, Dept. of Manuscripts. The Henry Lawes manuscript, by Pamela Willetts. London: The Museum, 1969. 85p. + 23 plates.

Lawrence, David Herbert, 1885-1930

4731. Edwards, Lucy I. D. H. Lawrence: a finding list; holdings in the City, County and University libraries of Nottingham. Nottingham: Nottinghamshire County Council, 1968. 125p.

Copies located in Nottinghamshire County Library, Nottingham City Library, and University of Nottingham Library.

4732. Nottingham, University, Library. D. H. Lawrence after thirty years, 1930-60, ed. by V. de S. Pinto. Nottingham: The University, 1960. 56p.

Catalog of exhibition of first editions, manuscripts, letters, and memorabilia; majority of 306 items lent by private collector, George L. Lazarus.

Lawrence, Thomas Edward, 1885-1935

4733. Imperial War Museum Library. Colonel T. E. Lawrence; a short list of references. London, 1966. 7p. (Bibliography, no.1076)

Lawson, John, d. 1711

4734. Kirkham, E. Bruce. "The first English editions of John Lawson's 'Voyage to Carolina': a bibliographical study." Papers of the Bibliographical Society of America, 61 (1967), 258-65.

Copies located in British and American libraries.

Lee, Nathaniel, 1653?-92

4735. McLeod, A. L. "A Nathaniel Lee bibliography, 1670-1960." Seventeenth & eighteenth century theatre research, 1 (Nov. 1962), 27-39.

Locates some copies of collected works, plays, poems, etc., in British and American libraries.

Lewis, Matthew Gregory, 1775-1818

4736. Todd, William Burton. "The early editions and issues of The monk, with a bibliography." Studies in bibliography, 2 (1949), 3-24.

Copies located in British Museum and various American libraries of work by Matthew Gregory Lewis.

Lilburne, John, 1614?-57

4737. Peacock, Edward. "John Lilburne, a bibliography." Notes and queries, ser.7, 5 (1888), 122-23, 162-63, 242-43, 342-43, 423-24, 502-3.

Checklist, 1638-59, with copies located in various English libraries.

4738. Wolfe, Don M. "List of pamphlets by and about Lilburne." In his: Milton in the Puritan Revolution. N.Y.: T. Nelson, 1941, p.469-80.

Locates copies, in British and American libraries, of pamphlets by and about John Lilburne.

Lincoln, Abraham, 1809-65

4739. London, University, Libraries. Abraham Lincoln sesquicentennial, 1959: exhibit catalogue (a display of Lincolniana from the Justin G. Turner collection at London University Library). London: U. S. Information Service, 1959. 16p.

Linnaeus, Carolus, 1707-78

4740. British Museum. Catalogue of the works of Linnaeus and publications more immediately relating thereto preserved in the Libraries of the British Museum, Bloomsbury, and the British Museum, Natural History, South Kensington. London, 1907. 27p.

4741. British Museum (Natural History). A catalogue of the works of Linnaeus (and publications more immediately relating thereto) preserved in the Libraries of the British Museum (Bloomsbury) and the British Museum (Natural History) (South Kensington), 2d ed. London, 1933. 246 + 68p.

Contains 3,874 entries.

Livingstone, David, 1813-73

4742. Bonner, Gerald. "Some letters of David Livingstone." British Museum quarterly, 23 (1961), 38-43.

Describes collection of 71 letters of Livingstone, missionary and explorer, covering period 1844-72, acquired by British Museum.

Locke, John, 1632-1704

4743. Long, P. "The Mellon donation of additional manuscripts of John Locke from the Lovelace collection." Bodleian Library record, 7 (1964), 185-93.

Descriptions of items received by Bodleian Library.

4744. Oxford, University, Bodleian Library. A summary description of the Lovelace collection of the papers of John Locke in the Bodleian Library, by P.

Long. Oxford, 1959. 64p. (Publications of the Oxford Bibliographical Society, n.s. v.8)

Manuscripts and letters classified by subjects and fully described.

Loftus, Robert, 1773-1850

4745. Ainsworth, John. "The papers of Lord Robert Loftus." Archives, no.4 (1960), 170-73.

Correspondence and other papers of Bishop Loftus, now preserved in National Library of Ireland.

Long, Robert Ballard, 1771-1825

4746. McGuffie, T. H. "Report on the military papers of Lt.-Gen. Robert Ballard Long (1771-1825) in the Royal United Service Institution Library." University of London, Institute of Historical Research, Bulletin, 20 (May-Nov. 1941), 106-10.

Lope de Vega, 1562-1635

4747. British Museum, Dept. of Printed Books. Lope de Vega, 1562-1635; catalogue of an exhibition held in the King's Library, September 1962, comp. by H. G. Whitehead. London, 1962. 39p.

4748. Whitehead, H. G. "Lope de Vega, 1562-1635; an exhibition held in the King's Library." British Museum quarterly, 25 (1962), 70-74.

Describes exhibition in British Museum of works of Lope de Vega and other early Spanish dramatists.

Lovelace, Richard, 1618-58

4749. Ker, C. Sylvia. A bibliography of Richard Lovelace. London, 1949. 102l. (Diploma in Librarianship, Univ. of London)

Locates copies examined and adds Wing numbers.

Lower, Richard, 1631-91

4750. Fulton, John F. "A bibliography of Richard Lower and John Mayow." Oxford Bibliographical Society, Proceedings and papers, 4 (1934-35), 1-62.

Bibliographies of works of two Oxford physiologists, Richard Lower (1631-91) and John Mayow (1643-79), with locations of copies.

Lupset, Thomas, 1495?-1530

4751. Gee, John Archer. "Bibliography and canon of Lupset's works." In his: The life and works of Thomas Lupset. New Haven, Conn. and London: Yale Univ. Pr., 1928, p.157-74.

Locates copies in British and American libraries.

Luther, Martin, 1483-1546

4752. Bibliotheca Lindesiana. Catalogue of a collection of fifteen hundred tracts by Martin Luther and his contemporaries, 1511-1598. Aberdeen: Univ. Pr., 1903. 280p.

4753. British Museum. Luther exhibition, 1883, in the Grenville library; printed books, manuscripts, portraits, and medals illustrating the life of Martin Luther, 2d ed. London: W. Clowes, 1883. 57p.

4754. ———, Dept. of Printed Books. Catalogue of printed books: Luther, Martin. London: The Museum, 1894. 215p.

4755. ——— ———. Luther exhibition, 1883, in the Grenville library; printed books, manuscripts, portraits and medals, illustrating the life of Martin Luther, with biographical sketch, arr. by G. Bullen. London: The Museum, 1883. 42p.

4756. Edinburgh, University, Library. Martin Luther, 1517-1967; an exhibition to commemorate the 450th anniversary of the publication of Luther's 95 Theses, held in New College Library (Theological Section of Edinburgh University Library), October-December, 1917. Edinburgh, 1916. 16p.

List of 35 first or early editions of Luther's writings.

Lyttleton, George, 1709-73

4757. Todd, William Burton. "Multiple editions of Lyttleton's The court-secret, 1741." Papers of the Bibliographical Society of America, 47 (1953), 380-81.

Copies located in British Museum and various American libraries.

MacDiarmid, Hugh, 1892-

4758. National Library of Scotland. Hugh MacDiarmid. Edinburgh, 1967. 39p. (Exhibition catalogue, no.7)

MacDonald, George, 1824-1905

4759. Hutton, Muriel. "Unfamiliar libraries XIII: The George MacDonald collection, Brander Library, Huntly." Book collector, 17 (1968), 13-25.

Describes collection of books and manuscripts relating to George MacDonald in Brander Library at Huntly.

Mackenzie, George, 1636-91

4760. Ferguson, F. S. "A bibliography of the works of Sir George Mackenzie, Lord Advocate, founder of the Advocates' Library." Edinburgh Bibliographical Society transactions, 1 (1936), 1-60.

Detailed bibliographical descriptions of 26 18th-century editions of works of Mackenzie, founder of National Library of Scotland; copies located.

Maimonides, 1135-1204

4761. Stern, S. M. "Autographs of Maimonides in the Bodleian Library." Bodleian Library record, 5 (1955), 180-202.

Malory, Thomas, fl. 1470

4762. Vinaver, Eugène. "A note on the earliest printed texts of Malory's Morte Darthur." Bulletin of the John Rylands Library, 23 (1939), 102-6. Reprinted, 1939. 5p.

Comparison of 2 surviving copies of Caxton's edition, in John Rylands Library and Pierpont Morgan Library.

Mandeville, John, d. 1372

4763. Bennett, Josephine Waters. The rediscovery of Sir John Mandeville. N.Y., 1954.

"Appendix II, The editions," p.335-85, lists editions in various languages, with copies located in British, American, and Continental libraries.

Markham, Gervase, 1568?-1637

4764. Poynter, F. N. L. A bibliography of Gervase Markham, 1568?-1637. Oxford: Oxford Bibliographical Society, 1962. 218p. (Oxford Bibliographical Society publications, n.s. v.11)

Detailed bibliographical descriptions with numerous library locations, British and foreign, of Markham's voluminous writings—verse, drama, literary works in prose, and works of information and instruction.

Marot, Clément, 1495?-1544

4765. Birkbeck College Library. Marot: handlist of books by and about Clément Marot in the College Library, comp. by P. Woudhuysen. London, 1970. 4l. (Library publication, no.9)

Marston, John, 1575?-1634

4766. Brettle, Robert E. "Bibliographical notes on some Marston quartos and early collected editions." Library, ser.4, 8 (1927), 336-48.

Descriptions and locations of copies of John Marston's plays, 1604-1652.

Martineau, Harriet, 1802-76

4767. Birmingham, University, Library. Catalogue of the Harriet Martineau papers, by D. W. Evans. Birmingham, 1969. 82*l.*

Calendar of 1,417 items.

Mary, Queen of Scots, 1542-87

4768. Scott, John. A bibliography of works relating to Mary, Queen of Scots, 1544-1700. Edinburgh: Edinburgh Bibliographical Society, 1896. 96 + 6p. + 20 facsimiles. (Edinburgh Bibliographical Society publications, no.2)

Lists 289 items, with locations of copies in Scottish libraries and British Museum.

Mason, William, 1724-97

4769. Gaskell, Philip. The first editions of William Mason. Cambridge: Bowes and Bowes, 1951. 41p. (Cambridge Bibliographical Society monograph, no.1)

Copies located in 6 British libraries.

Mather, Cotton, 1663-1728

4770. Holmes, Thomas James. Cotton Mather; a bibliography of his works. Cambridge, Mass.: Harvard Univ. Pr., 1940. 3v.

Locations in numerous British and American libraries.

Mather, Increase, 1639-1723

4771. Holmes, Thomas James. Increase Mather; a bibliography of his works. Cleveland, Ohio: Printed at Harvard Univ. Pr. for William Gwinn Mather, 1931. 2v.

Locates copies in numerous British and American libraries and private collections.

Mather family

4772. Holmes, Thomas James. The minor Mathers; a list of their works. Cambridge, Mass.: Harvard Univ. Pr., 1940. 218p.

Locations in numerous British and American libraries.

Maxwell, Alexander, fl. mid-19th century

4773. Birmingham, University, Library. Maxwell letters, handlist. Birmingham, 1968. 5*l.* (Catalogues of the manuscript collections, no.11)

Letters of Alexander Maxwell and other members of Maxwell family, c. 1840-1909.

Mead, Richard, 1673-1754

4774. Ferguson, Valerie Anne. A bibliography of the works of Richard Mead, M.D., F.R.S. (1673-1754). London, 1959. 53*l.* (Diploma in Librarianship, Univ. of London)

Copies located in 5 London libraries and U.S. National Library of Medicine.

Medici family

4775. Grandsen, K. W. "The Medici papers." British Museum quarterly, 20 (1955), 28-30.

Describes 118 lots of Medici family papers, 16th and 17th centuries, acquired by British Museum.

Medina, José Toribio, 1852-1930

4776. British Museum, Dept. of Printed Books. José Toribio Medina, 1852-1930; centenary exhibition; a catalogue. London: The Museum, 1952. 11p.

Meredith, George, 1828-1909

4777. Forman, Maurice Buxton. A bibliography of the writings in prose and verse of George Meredith. Edinburgh: Dunedin Pr. for the Bibliographical Society, 1922. 324p.

References to British Museum copies.

4778. ———. Meredithiana, being a supplement to the bibliography of Meredith. Edinburgh, 1924. 315p.

Meynell, Alice, 1847-1922

4779. National Book League. Alice Meynell, 1847-1922: Catalogue of the centenary exhibition of books, manuscripts, letters and portraits, comp. by Francis Meynell. London, 1948. 45p.

Miller, Thomas, 1807-74

4780. Gainsborough Public Libraries. Thomas Miller (1807-74): a list of his works, and books about him, in the local collection, comp. by J. S. English. Gainsborough: 1966. 4p. (Local history handbooks, no.1) 2d ed. Gainsborough, 1970. 5p.

Milton, John, 1608-74

4781. Ayer, Robert W. "A suppressed edition of Milton's Defensio secunda, (1654)." Papers of the Bibliographical Society of America, 55 (1961), 75-87.

Copies located in Bodleian and several American libraries.

4782. British Museum, Dept. of Printed Books. Catalogue of printed books: Milton (John). London: W. Clowes, 1892. 56 cols.

4783. Cambridge, University, Christ's College Library. Early editions of Milton's works in Christ's College Library. Cambridge: Univ. Pr., 1921. 8p. (Reprinted from Christ's College magazine)

4784. ———. Milton tercentenary; the portraits, prints, and writings of John Milton exhibited at Christ's College, Cambridge, 1908, by George C. Williamson. 2d ed. Cambridge: Univ. Pr., 1908. 168p. Reprinted, 1968.

Catalog of 768 items.

4785. Grolier Club. Catalogue of an exhibition commemorative of the tercentenary of the birth of John Milton, 1608-1908, including original editions of his poetical and prose works, together with three hundred and twenty-seven engraved portraits. N.Y., 1909. 116p.

Copies cited in Christ's College, Cambridge, and Marsh's Library, Dublin.

4786. John Rylands Library. Catalogue of an exhibition of the original editions of the principal works of John Milton, arranged in celebration of the tercentenary of his birth. Manchester, 1908. 24p.

4787. Madan, Francis Falconer. "A revised bibliography of Salmasius' Defensio regia and Milton's Pro populo Anglicano defensio." Library, ser.5, 9 (1954), 101-21.

Copies located in British and Continental libraries.

4788. Pershing, James H. "The different states of the first edition of Paradise lost." Library, ser.4, 22 (1941), 34-66.

Locates copies in 15 British and American libraries.

4789. Stoke Newington Public Library. Milton tercentenary; catalogue of exhibits and programme of entertainment. Stoke Newington, 1908. 55p.

Drawn principally from collection owned by Wynne E. Baxter.

Mitchel, William, 1670?-1739

4790. Johnston, George P. "William Mitchel, the Tincklarian doctor, a bibliography, 1711-39." Edinburgh Bibliographical Society publications, 11 (1921), 113-37.

List of 81 items, with locations of copies.

Montagu, Mary Wortley, 1689-1762

4791. Halsband, Robert. "Lady Mary Wortley Montagu as a friend of Continental writers." Bulletin of the John Rylands Library, 39 (1956), 57-74. Reprinted, 1956. 20p.

Based in part on Bagshawe records in John Rylands Library.

Montesquieu, Charles de Secondat, 1689-1755

4792. Howard, Alison K. "Montesquieu, Voltaire and Rousseau in eighteenth century Scotland; a check list of editions and translations of their works published in Scotland to 1801." Bibliotheck, 2 (1959?), 40-63.

Locates copies in 19 British, American, and French libraries.

Montgomery, Bernard Law, 1887-

4793. Imperial War Museum Library. Field Marshal Montgomery. London, 1962. 5p. (Booklist and photographs list, no.1203)

More, Thomas, 1478-1535

4794. Gibson, Reginald W. St. Thomas More: A preliminary bibliography of his works and of Moreana to the year 1750; with a bibliography of Utopiana compiled by R. W. Gibson and J. Max Patrick. New Haven, Conn., and London: Yale Univ. Pr., 1961. 499p.

Copies of 877 items located in numerous British American, and other libraries.

4795. Guildhall Library. The Alfred Cock memorial: catalogue of books, portraits, etc., of or relating to Sir Thomas More, collected by the late Alfred Cock, purchased and presented to the Corporation of London as a gift to the Guildhall Library. London: The Library Committee, 1903. 28p.

4796. ———. "A handlist of printed books in Guildhall Library by or relating to Sir Thomas More." Guildhall miscellany, 4 (1971), 44-60.

4797. Oxford, University, Bodleian Library. An exhibition in commemoration of the canonization of Sir Thomas More and Bishop John Fisher, including works of Robert Southwell and the Oxford recusants, 1535-1660. Oxford, 1935. 7p.

Morley, John, 1838-1923

4798. India Office Library, Commonwealth Relations Office. A catalogue of the Morley collection; the private papers of John Viscount Morley of Blackburn (1838-1923), Secretary of State for India in Council,

1905-1910 and March-May 1911, by Molly C. Poulter. London, 1965. 2v.

Collection received by India Office Library in 1959.

Morris, William, 1834-96

4799. Flower, R. "The William Morris manuscripts." British Museum quarterly, 14 (1940), 8-12.

Description of extensive collection received by British Museum.

Motteux, Peter Anthony, 1663?-1718

4800. Cunningham, R. N. "A bibliography of the writings of Peter Anthony Motteux." Oxford Bibliographical Society, Proceedings and papers, 3 (1933), 317-37, 368.

Writings of Motteux described bibliographically, with locations of copies in British and American libraries.

Mottram, Ralph Hale, 1883-

4801. Birmingham, University, Library. R. H. Mottram letters. Birmingham, 1967. 4l. (Catalogues of the manuscript collections, no.2)

Autograph letters to Gilbert H. Fabes, concerned with bibliography of Mottram's works.

Mozart, Wolfgang Amadeus, 1756-91

4802. British Museum. Mozart in the British Museum. London, 1956. 27p.

Includes "A select list of items in the British Museum."

Musket, David

4803. National Manuscript Commission. Musket correspondence. London, 1970. 25l.

Papers of David Musket, pioneer metallurgist, relating to iron and steel making, preserved in Gloucestershire County Records Office, Shire Hall, Gloucester.

Napoleon Bonaparte, 1769-1821

4804. British Museum. Catalogue of the Napoleon Library. London, 1858. 56p.

Catalog of Napoleonic and French Revolution collection owned by Joshua Bates and presented to British Museum by A. H. Bleeck, compiler of catalog.

4805. ———, Dept. of Printed Books. Catalogue of printed books: Napoleon. London, 1892. 96 cols.

Nashe, Thomas, 1567-1601

4806. McKerrow, Ronald Brunlees. "Note on copies of the early editions of Nashe's works." In: The works of Thomas Nashe. Oxford, 1910, v.5, p.204-7.

Checklist with locations of copies.

Nelson, Horatio, 1758-1805

4807. British Museum. A guide to the manuscripts, printed books, prints, and medals exhibited on the occasion of the Nelson centenary. London, 1905. 107p. + 8 plates.

4808. Norwich Public Library. Horatio, Viscount Nelson; a catalogue of the books, pamphlets, articles, and engravings relating to Nelson in the Norwich Public Library. Norwich: Public Library Committee, 1915. 19p.

Newman, John Henry, 1801-90

4809. Birmingham Library. The mind of John Henry Cardinal Newman; catalogue of an exhibition of his books and manuscripts, drawn from the Library of the Oratory, Birmingham and from the Birmingham Library, comp. by Hamish Swanston. Birmingham: Newman Association (Birmingham Circle), 1961. 30p.

Newton, Isaac, 1642-1727

4810. Cambridge, University, King's College Library. A catalogue of the manuscripts and printed books in the Sir Isaac Newton collection forming part of the library bequeathed by John Maynard, Baron Keynes of Tilton to King's College, by A. N. L. Mumby. Cambridge, 1936-49. 192p.

4811. ———, Library. A catalogue of the Portsmouth collection of books and papers, written by or belonging to Sir Isaac Newton, the scientific portion of which has been presented by the Earl of Portsmouth to the University of Cambridge. Cambridge: Univ. Pr., 1888. 56p.

Collection now in University Library.

4812. ———, Trinity College Library. Library of Sir Isaac Newton; presentation by the Pilgrim Trust to Trinity College, Cambridge, 30 October, 1943. Cambridge: Univ. Pr., 1944. 23p.

4813. Mackenzie, A. G. "Newton: Commercium epistolicum." Durham philobiblon, 2 (March 1958), 14-16.

Locates copies of various editions and states.

4814. Macomber, Henry P. A census of copies of the 1687 first edition and the 1726 presentation issue of Newton's Principia. Babson Park, Mass.: Babson Institute Library, 1953. 32p. (Reprint from Papers of the Bibliographical Society of America, 47 (1953), 292-300)

Locates 189 copies of 1687 edition and 34 copies of 1729 issue in British, American, and Continental libraries.

Nightingale, Florence, 1820-1910

4815. Bishop, W. J., and Goldie, Sue. A bio-bibliography of Florence Nightingale. London: Dawsons of Pall Mall for the International Council of Nurses, 1962. 160p.

Records 150 items, with detailed descriptions; frequently locates copies.

Nugent, George, 1757-1849

4816. McGuffie, T. H. "Report on the military papers of Field-Marshal Sir George Nugent, Bart. (1757-1849), in the Royal United Service Institution Library." University of London Institute of Historical Research, Bulletin, 21 (1948), 225-32.

Oldham, John, 1653-83

4817. Brooks, Harold F. "A bibliography of John Oldham, the Restoration satirist." Oxford Bibliographical Society, Proceedings and papers, 5 (1936), 1-38.

Describes and locates copies of editions of Oldham's works, 1677-1805, and lists manuscripts held by Bodleian and British Museum.

Onions, Charles Talbut, 1873-1965

4818. Birmingham, University, Library. Catalogue of the C. T. Onions letters. Birmingham, 1970. Unpaged. (Catalogues of the manuscript collections, no.27)

Principally letters to Onions on philological matters; 476 items.

Osborne, Francis, 1593-1659

4819. Madan, Francis F. "Some notes on the bibliography of Francis Osborne," Oxford Bibliographical Society publications, n.s. 4 (1952), 55-60.

List of 17 editions of Osborne's Advice to a son and other works, 1656-59, with copies located.

Ott, Johann Heinrich, 1617-82

4820. Huguenot Society Library. A calendar of the correspondence of J. H. Ott, 1658-1671, in the Library of the Huguenot Society of London, ed. by Leonard Forster. Frome: Butler & Tanner, 1960. 58p. (Publications of the Huguenot Society of London, v.46)

Collection now in Huguenot Library, University College, London.

Ottley family

4821. Jones, Evans D. "The Ottley papers." National Library of Wales journal, 4 (1945), 61-74.

Description of collection of over 4,000 papers of the Ottley family for the period 1679-1740.

Owen, Robert, 1771-1858

4822. Cardiff Public Libraries. Robert Owen and his works: (a list of books, pamphlets and periodicals by and relating to R. Owen in the Welsh Department [of the Cardiff Public Library]). Cardiff, 1902. (Extracted from the Public library journal, v.3, pt.6. March 1902.)

4823. London, University, Library. Robert Owen, 1771-1858; catalogue of an exhibition of printed books held in the Library of the University of London, comp. by Margaret B. Canney. London, 1959. 40p.

Annotated list of 121 items.

4824. National Library of Wales. A bibliography of Robert Owen, the Socialist, 1771-1858. Aberystwyth, 1914. 54p.

4825. ———. A bibliography of Robert Owen, the Socialist, 1771-1858, 2d ed., comp. by A. J. Hawkes. Aberystwyth, 1925. 90p.

Records 597 items of books, pamphlets, periodical articles, and manuscripts.

Palmer, Roundell, 1812-95

4826. Lambeth Palace Library. Catalogue of the papers of Roundell Palmer (1812-1895), first Earl of Selborne, by E. G. W. Bill. London, 1967. 56p.

Peele, George, 1558?-1597?

4827. Larsen, Thorleif. "A bibliography of the writings of George Peele." Modern philology, 32 (1934), 143-56.

Locates copies in British and American libraries.

Penn, William, 1644-1718

4828. Goodbody, Olive C., and Pollard, M. "The first

edition of William Penn's Great case of liberty of conscience, 1670." Library, ser.5, 16 (1964), 146-49.

Locates 4 extant copies in English, Irish, and American libraries.

Pennecuik, Alexander, 1652-1722

4829. Brown, William. "Writings of Alexander Pennecuik, M.D., and Alexander Pennecuik, merchant." Edinburgh Bibliographical Society publications, 6 (1906), 117-31.

Locates copies in British Museum and Scottish libraries.

Pepys, Samuel, 1633-1703

4830. Cambridge, University, Magdalene College Library. Bibliotheca Pepysiana; a descriptive catalogue of the library of Samuel Pepys. London: Sidgwick & Jackson, 1914-40. 4v.

pt.1, "Sea" manuscripts; pt.2, early printed books to 1558; pt.3, medieval manuscripts; pt.4, shorthand books.

4831. ———— ————. Report on the Pepys manuscripts, preserved at Magdalene College, Cambridge; a calendar, by E. K. Purnell. London: H. M. Stationery Office, 1911. 379p. (Historical Manuscripts Commission, no.70)

4832. ————, Magdalene College, Pepysian Library. A catalogue of the engraved portraits in the library of Samuel Pepys, F.R.S., now belonging to Magdalene College, comp. by John Charrington. Cambridge: Univ. Pr., 1936. 203p.

4833. ———— ———— ————. A descriptive catalogue of the naval manuscripts in the Pepysian Library at Magdalene College, Cambridge, ed. by J. R. Tanner. London: Navy Records Society, 1903-23. 4v. (The Society's publications, v.26-27, 36, 57)

4834. ———— ———— ————. The Pepys Library, by Francis McD. C. Turner. Cambridge, 1951. 18p.

Petty, William, 1623-87

4835. Keynes, Geoffrey Langdon. A bibliography of Sir William Petty, F.R.S., and of Observations on the bills of mortality by John Graunt, F.R.S. Oxford: Clarendon, 1971. 103p.

Locates copies in 20 libraries.

Plat, Hugh, 1552?-1611?

4836. Juel-Jensen, Bent. "Some uncollected authors

XIX: Sir Hugh Plat, ?1552-?1611." Book collector, 8 (1959), 60-68.

Checklist of 52 items, with copies located in British and American libraries.

Playfair, Lyon, 1818-98

4837. London, University, Imperial College. List of the papers and correspondence of Lyon Playfair, first Baron Playfair of St. Andrews, in the Imperial College Archives, by Jeanne Pingree. London, 1967. 122p.

Materials relating to Playfair, famous scientist, preserved in Imperial College Archives.

Pope, Alexander, 1688-1744

4838. Griffith, Reginald Harvey. Alexander Pope, a bibliography. Austin: Univ. of Tex. Pr., 1922-27. 2v.

Locates some copies in British and American libraries.

4839. Guerinot, J. V. Pamphlet attacks on Alexander Pope, 1711-1744; a descriptive bibliography. London: Methuen, 1969. 360p.

Locations principally in U.S. libraries, but occasional references to copies in British libraries.

4840. Todd, William Burton. "Concealed Pope editions." Book collector, 5 (1956), 48-52.

Study of 4 poems published 1731-37; 73 copies located in 12 British and American libraries.

Potter, Beatrix, 1866-1943

4841. National Book League. The Linder collection of the works and drawings of Beatrix Potter. London: The League and the Trustees of the Linder Collection, 1971. 65p. + 16 plates.

Collection of 280 original drawings and paintings by Beatrix Potter and first editions of her books, now housed in the National Book League Library.

Priestley, Joseph, 1733-1804

4842. Birmingham, University, Library. Calendar of Joseph Priestley letters. Birmingham, 1969. Unpaged. (Catalogues of the manuscript collections, no.22)

Calendar of 9 Priestley letters, 1767-1802.

4843. ————. Priestley album letters. Birmingham, 1968. 7l. (Catalogue of the manuscripts, no.12)

Collection relating to Sir William Overend Priestley and Mrs. Eliza Priestley, 1875-1907.

4844. Crook, Ronald E. A bibliography of Joseph Priestley, 1733-1804. London: Library Association, 1966. 202p. (Library Association bibliographies, no.6)

Copies located in numerous British, Irish, Canadian, American, and other libraries.

4845. Guildhall Library. "A handlist of books in Guildhall Library relating to Joseph Priestley." Guildhall miscellany, 3 (1971), 287-300.

Proust, Marcel, 1871-1922

4846. Painter, George D. "Proust's letters to Sydney and Violet Schiff." British Museum quarterly, 32 (1968), 65-74.

Discussion and detailed description of 24 Proust letters acquired by British Museum.

Prynne, William, 1600-69

4847. Fry, Mary Isobel, and Davies, Godfrey. "William Prynne in the Huntington Library." Huntington Library quarterly, 20 (1956), 53-93.

Catalog, with additional locations of copies; includes STC numbers.

Ptolemaeus, Claudius, fl. 2d century A.D.

4848. British Museum, Dept. of Printed Books. Catalogue of printed books: Ptolemaeus (Claudius). London: W. Clowes, 1895. 20 cols.

Pugin family

4849. Victoria and Albert Museum Library. "Recently acquired manuscripts on the Pugin family and others, and items acquired pre-1890 now re-catalogued." Monthly list (Dec. 1970), p.53-65.

Purcell, Henry, 1659?-95

4850. British Museum. Henry Purcell, 1659(?)-1695, George Frederick Handel, 1685-1759; catalogue of a commemorative exhibition, May-August 1959. London, 1959. 47p.

4851. Shaw, H. Watkins. "A collection of musical manuscripts in the autograph of Henry Purcell and other English composers, c. 1665-85." Library, ser.5, 14 (1959), 126-31.

Describes and lists small collection held by Music Library of the Barber Institute of Fine Arts, University of Birmingham.

Quarles, Francis, 1592-1644

4852. Horden, John. Francis Quarles (1592-1644); a bibliography of his works to the year 1800. Oxford:

Univ. Pr., 1953. 83p. (Oxford Bibliographical Society publications, n.s. v.2, 1948).

Full bibliographical description of various editions of works of 17th-century poet; copies located in British and American libraries.

Rabelais, François, 1494?-1553

4853. Birkbeck College Library. Rebelais: handlist of books by and about François Rabelais in the College Library, comp. by P. Woudhuysen. London: 1970. 13l. (Library publication, no.7)

4854. Cambridge, University, St. John's College Library. Hand-list to the Rabelais collection given by the late Mr. W. F. Smith to the St. John's College Library, Cambridge. Cambridge, 1920. 12p.

Raffles, Sir Thomas Stamford, 1781-1826

4855. India Office Library. Sir Thomas Stamford Raffles; with an account of the Raffles-Minto manuscript collection presented to the India Office Library on 17 July 1969 by the Malaysia-Singapore Commercial Association, by John Bastin. Liverpool: Ocean Steam Ship Company, 1969. 22p. + plates.

Raffles was founder of Singapore.

Raleigh, Sir Walter, 1552?-1618

4856. British Museum, Dept. of Printed Books. Raleigh-Hakluyt quatercentenary exhibition: Sir Walter Raleigh and Richard Hakluyt, an exhibition held in the King's Library, British Museum. London: The Museum, 1952. 34p.

Drawn from Departments of Manuscripts, Printed Books, Prints and Drawings, and British and Mediaeval Antiquities.

Ramsay, Allan, 1686-1758

4857. Arts Council of Great Britain, Scottish Committee. Allan Ramsay and his circle; an exhibition. 1962. Unpaged.

Listing of 28 works with locations of copies in 8 Scottish libraries.

4858. Martin, Burns. "A bibliography of the writings of Allan Ramsay." Glasgow Bibliographical Society records, 10 (1931), 1-114. Reprinted, 1931. 114p.

Locates copies of 411 items, 1713-1899, in numerous British and American libraries.

Ramsay family

4859. Gouldesbrough, P. "The Dalhousie muniments

in the Scottish Record Office." Archives, no.5 (1961), 65-74.

Description of records of 2 notable Scottish families, Ramsays and Maules, 1848-56, including papers of Lord Dalhousie, Governor General of India.

Rastrick, John Urpeth, 1780-1856

4860. London, University, Library. The Rastrick papers; being letters, papers, and diaries of John Urpeth Rastrick, civil engineer (1780-1856), now in the University of London Library, a hand-list, comp. by T. D. Rogers. London, 1968. 75*l*.

Ray, John, 1627 ?-1705

4861. Keynes, Geoffrey Langdon. John Ray, a bibliography. London: Faber & Faber, 1951. 163p.

Detailed bibliographical descriptions of 106 works, with locations in 21 libraries.

4862. ———. John Ray, F.R.S.; a handlist of his works. Cambridge: Univ. Pr., 1944. 23*l*.

Copies located in 16 British and Irish libraries.

Reid, Forrest, 1876-1947

4863. Belfast Public Libraries. Forrest Reid; an exhibition of books and manuscripts held in the Museum and Art Gallery. Belfast: City and County Borough of Belfast Libraries Museums and Arts Committee, 1954. 35p.

Records 183 items.

Reynolds, Joshua, 1723-92

4864. Hilles, Frederick Whiley. "A bibliography of Sir Joshua's writings." In his: The literary career of Sir Joshua Reynolds. Cambridge: Univ. Pr., 1936, p.277-300.

Lists 28 items, 1759-98, with locations of copies in British, American, and other libraries.

Richard III, 1452-85

4865. Birmingham Public Libraries. Discovering Richard III; a select list of books available in the Birmingham Public Libraries. Birmingham, 1967. 4p.

Richardson, Samuel, 1689-1761

4866. Sale, William Merritt, Jr., Samuel Richardson; a bibliographical record of his literary career with historical notes. New Haven, Conn.: Yale Univ. Pr., 1936. 141p. Reprinted, Archon Books, 1965.

Locates copies in British and American libraries.

Rigaud, Stephen Peter, d. 1839

4867. Oxford, University, Bodleian Library. "Inventory of Rigaud papers in Bodleian Library, Oxford, England." Smithsonian miscellaneous collections, 48 (8 Sept. 1905), 229-30.

Papers of Stephen Peter Rigaud (d. 1839), scientist.

Robin Hood

4868. Gable, J. Harris. Bibliography of Robin Hood. Lincoln, Nebraska, 1939. 163p.

Records 1,028 items, locating copies in British Museum, Bodleian, Bibliothèque Nationale, and 5 American libraries.

4869. Nottingham Public Libraries and Natural History Museum. Robin Hood literature in the Nottingham Public Libraries; list compiled by Violet M. Walker. Nottingham, 1933. 12p.

Robinson, Henry Crabb, 1775-1867

4870. Dr. Williams's Library. Index to the Henry Crabb Robinson letters in Dr. Williams's Library, comp. by Inez Elliott. London: Dr. Williams's Trust, 1960. 36p. (Occasional paper, no.10)

Robinson correspondence, diaries, and memoirs are in library's manuscript collection.

Rochester, John Wilmot, 1647-80

4871. Todd, William Burton. "The 1680 editions of Rochester's Poems, with notes on earlier texts." Papers of the Bibliographical Society of America, 47 (1953), 43-58.

Locates copies in British Museum and Bodleian Library.

Rogers, Samuel, 1763-1855

4872. Smith, Simon Nowell- . "Samuel Rogers. Human life, 1819." Book collector, 14 (1965), 362-65.

Copies located in British Museum and Bodleian Library.

Rosenberg, Isaac, 1890-1918

4873. Leeds, University. Isaac Rosenberg, 1890-1918; a catalogue of an exhibition held at Leeds University May-June 1959, together with the text of unpublished material. Leeds: Univ. of Leeds with Partridge Pr., 1959. 36p.

Rossetti, Dante Gabriel, 1828-82

4874. Hampstead Public Libraries. Catalogue of the Rossetti centenary exhibition at the Central Public Library. Hampstead, 1928. 32p.

Based primarily on holdings of Hampstead Central Library.

Ruskin, John, 1819-1900

4875. Dearden, James S. "John Ruskin, the collector; with a catalogue of the illuminated and other manuscripts formerly in his collection." Library, ser.5, 21 (1966), 124-54.

Lists 87 items with provenances, including present locations, if they can be traced.

4876. Ruskin Museum Library. A descriptive catalogue of the Library and Print Room of the Ruskin Museum, Sheffield, by William White. Orpington & London: George Allen, 1890. 95p.

4877. Skelton, Robin. "John Ruskin: the final years; a survey of the Ruskin correspondence in the John Rylands Library." Bulletin of the John Rylands Library, 37 (1955), 562-86. Reprinted, 1955. 27p.

Correspondence with or relating to several individuals during 1874-1903 period.

Russell, George William (AE), 1867-1935

4878. Denson, Alan. Printed writings of George W. Russell (AE): a bibliography with notes on his pictures and portraits. Evanston, Ill.: Northwestern Univ. Pr., 1962. 255p.

Locates copies of some printed works and manuscripts.

Rye, Walter, 1843-1929

4879. Norwich Public Library. Walter Rye; memoir, bibliography, and catalogue of his Norfolk manuscripts in the Norwich Public Libraries, by Geo. A. Stephen. Norwich, 1929. 32p.

Savile, Henry, 1568-1617

4880. Watson, Andrew G. The manuscripts of Henry Savile of Banke. London: Bibliographical Society, 1969. 102p.

Lists 298 items relating to Savile, with locations if known.

Scarlatti, Domenico, 1685-1757

4881. Hopkinson, Cecil. "Eighteenth-century editions of the keyboard compositions of Domenico Scarlatti (1685-1757)." Edinburgh Bibliographical Society transactions, 3 (1952), 47-71.

Copies located in British and Continental libraries.

Schiff, Sydney, 1869?-1944

4882. Borrie, M. A. F. "The Schiff papers." British Museum quarterly, 31 (1966), 24-27.

Collection of 950 letters to novelist Sydney Schiff (pseud. "Stephen Hudson") and his wife, received by British Museum.

Schilders, Richard, d.c. 1634

4883. Wilson, John Dover. "Richard Schilders and the English Puritans." Transactions of the Bibliographical Society, 11 (1911), 65-134.

List of 51 items, 1579-1616; copies located in British Museum, etc.

Scipio Le Squyer, 1620-59

4884. Taylor, Frank. "The books and manuscripts of Scipio Le Squyer, Deputy Chamberlain of the Exchequer (1620-59)." Bulletin of the John Rylands Library, 25 (1941), 137-64.

Based on documents in John Rylands Library.

Scot, Michael, 1175?-1234?

4885. Ferguson, John. "Bibliographical notes on the works of Michael Scot." Glasgow Bibliographical Society records, 9 (1931), 75-100.

List of 56 items with locations of copies in Scottish and English libraries.

Scott, John, 1710-82

4886. Russell, Norma Hull. "Some uncollected authors XL: John Scott of Amwell, 1710-1782." Book collector, 14 (1965), 350-60.

Copies of Scott's poems, literary criticisms, etc., located in English and American libraries.

Scott, Sir Walter, 1771-1832

4887. Birmingham Public Libraries. Sir Walter Scott (1771-1832), a bi-centenary book list. Birmingham, 1971. 4p.

4888. British Museum, Dept. of Printed Books. Catalogue of printed books, Scott (Sir Walter). London: W. Clowes, 1896. 48 cols.

4889. Dyson, Gillian. The manuscripts and proof sheets of Scott's "Waverley novels." London, 1956. 53*l.* (Diploma in Librarianship, Univ. of London)

Traces present locations as far as known.

4890. Edinburgh, University, Library. Catalogue of the Sir Walter Scott exhibition from a private collection (Dr. J. C. Corson's) held in the Upper Library Hall. Edinburgh, 1953. 28p.

Listing of 128 first and early editions.

4891. National Gallery of Scotland. Catalogue of the Sir Walter Scott exhibition in the National Gallery of Scotland, Edinburgh. Edinburgh: T. and A. Constable, 1932. 70p.

Original portraits, engravings, books, manuscripts, and relics, drawn from various identified collections, public and private.

4892. ———. Sir Walter Scott 1771-1971; a bicentenary exhibition. Edinburgh: H. M. Stationery Office, 1971. 60p.

Organized by the Court of Sessions, the Faculty of Advocates, and National Library of Scotland; exhibit items drawn from various libraries.

4893. Ruff, William. "A bibliography of the poetical works of Sir Walter Scott, 1796-1832." Edinburgh Bibliographical Society transactions, 1 (1937), 99-239. "Additions and corrections," ibid., 1 (1938), 279-81.

Detailed descriptions with occasional location of copies.

Sedley, Sir Charles, 1639 ?-1701

4894. Pinto, Vivian de Sola. "A bibliography of works by or ascribed to Sir Charles Sedley." In: The poetical and dramatic works of Sir Charles Sedley. London, 1928, v.2, p.235-61.

Locates copies.

Selden, John, 1584-1654

4895. Barratt, D. M. "The library of John Selden and its later history." Bodleian quarterly record, 3 (1951), 128-42, 208-13, 256-74.

Library received by Bodleian shortly after death of John Selden in 1654; account includes calendar of literary and miscellaneous manuscripts in collection.

Servetus, Michael, 1511-53

4896. Fulton, John F. Michael Servetus, humanist and martyr; with a bibliography of his works and census of known copies, by Madeline E. Stanton. N. Y.: Herbert Reichner, 1953. 98p. + 28 illustrations.

Locations in numerous British, Continental, and North American libraries.

Settle, Elkanah, 1648-1724

4897. Dunkin, Paul Shaner. "Issues of The fairy queen, 1692." Library, ser.4, 26 (1946), 297-304.

Operatic adaptation of A midsummer night's dream, attributed to Elkanah Settle, printed 1692-93; copies located.

4898. Guildhall Library. "A list of works in Guildhall Library by, or relating to, Elkanah Settle, 1648-1724." Guildhall miscellany, 2 (1967), 418-23.

Settle was last of line of "City poets," who prepared various City pageants.

Seward, Anna, 1742-1809

4899. Birmingham, University, Library. Anna Seward letters, handlist. Birmingham, 1968. 3p. (Catalogues of the manuscript collections, no.13)

Small collection for period 1764-1804.

Shakespeare, William, 1564-1616

4900. Bartlett, Henrietta C. "First editions of Shakespeare's quartos." Library, ser.4, 16 (1935), 166-72.

Includes census of copies in British and American libraries.

4901. ———. Mr. William Shakespeare; original and early editions of his quartos and folios; his source books and those containing contemporary notices. New Haven, Conn.: Yale Univ. Pr., 1922. 217p.

Copies located in British and American libraries.

4902. ———, and Pollard, Alfred W. A census of Shakespeare's plays in quarto, 1594-1709. New Haven., Conn.: Yale Univ. Pr., 1939. 165p.

Copies located and described in British and American libraries; 1,222 numbered items.

4903. Birmingham Library. Eighteenth century attitudes to Shakespeare; the catalogue of an exhibition of books in the Birmingham Library to celebrate the 400th anniversary of the birth of William Shakespeare. Birmingham, 1964. 16p.

Drawn from the Birmingham Library supplemented by the Shakespeare Memorial Library, Birmingham.

4904. Birmingham Public Libraries. Birmingham Shakespeare Library: a brief description. Birmingham, 1971. 8p.

4905. ———. Catalogue of the Shakespeare Memorial Library, Birmingham, by J. D. Mullins. Birmingham: Josiah Allen, 1872-76. 5pts.

4906. ———. Cornmarket acting versions of Shakespeare's plays from the Restoration to the death of David Garrick. London: Cornmarket, n.d. Unpaged.

"Seventy-eight rare texts from the Birmingham Shakespeare Library reprinted to celebrate the hundredth anniversary of the opening of the Library." Second series adds 51 titles.

4907. ———. An index to the Shakespeare Memorial Library, by A. Capel Shaw. Birmingham: Percival Jones, 1900-3. 3pts.

4908. ———. A Shakespeare bibliography; the catalogue of the Birmingham Shakespeare Library, comp. and ed. by Waveney R. N. Fredrick. London: Mansell, 1971. 7v.

Contains more than 100,000 entries; largest existing collection of printed material relating exclusively to Shakespeare's life and work.

4909. ———, Shakespeare Memorial Library. Shakespeare exhibition to celebrate the four hundredth anniversary of his birth and the centenary of the Library. Birmingham, 1964. 59p.

Records 304 exhibits under various categories.

4910. Boase, T. S. R. "An extra-illustrated second folio of Shakespeare." British Museum quarterly, 20 (1955), 4-8.

Illustrations added in early 19th century, including 6 water colors by Blake, acquired by British Museum.

4911. British Museum. British Museum Shakespeare exhibition, 1923; guide to the mss. & printed books exhibited in celebration of the tercentenary of the first folio Shakespeare, by A. W. Pollard and H. Sellers. London, 1923. 77p.

4912. ———, Dept. of Printed Books. Catalogue of printed books: Shakespeare (William). London: W. Clowes, 1897. 232 cols.

4913. ——— ———. Shakespeare; an excerpt from the General catalogue of printed books in the British Museum. London: The Museum, 1964. 517 cols.

4914. ——— ———, King's Library. William Shakespeare, 1564-1616, and Christopher Marlowe, 1564-1593; an exhibition of books, manuscripts, and other illustrative material held in the King's Library of the British Museum. London: The Museum, 1964. 16p.

4915. Cambridge, University, Trinity College Library. Catalogue of the books presented by Edward Capell to the Library of Trinity College in Cambridge, comp. by W. W. Greg. Cambridge: Univ. Pr., 1903. 172p.

Collection of Shakespeareana.

4916. Cardiff Public Libraries. Catalogue of the exhibition of Shakespeareana, held at the Cardiff Public Library in commemoration of the 1st folio tercentenary (1623-1923). Cardiff: Educational Publication Co., 1923. 52p.

4917. Clifton Shakespeare Society Library. Catalogue of the Library. Bristol: H. Hill, 1881. 41p.

4918. Edinburgh, University, Library. Shakespeare; an exhibition of printed books to mark the quatercentenary of his birth, drawn from the resources of the National Library of Scotland and of the Library of the University of Edinburgh. Edinburgh, 1964. 40p. (Exhibition catalogue, no.3)

Annotated listing of 141 items, with locations.

4919. Eton College Library. A descriptive catalogue of the early editions of the works of Shakespeare preserved in the Library of Eton College, comp. by Walter W. Greg. Oxford: Univ. Pr., 1909. 27p.

4920. Fox, L. "Local archives of Great Britain; XX. Shakespeare's Birthplace Library, Stratford-upon-Avon." Archives, no.5 (1961), 90-99.

4921. ———, and others. "Shakespeare in the library, a symposium." Open access, 10 (Jan. 1962), 1-11.

Discussion of Shakespeare collections held be Shakespeare's Birthplace and Royal Shakespeary Theatre, Stratford on Avon; Birmingham University Shakespeare Institute Library at Stratford; and Shakespeare Memorial Library, Birmingham Public Libraries.

4922. Great Britain, Public Record Office. Shakespeare in the public records. London, 1964. 40p. (Public Record Office handbooks, no.5)

Lists "known documents in the Public Records which relate directly to William Shakespeare or to his literary work."

4923. Hastings Public Library. A Shakespeare booklist; published in commemoration of the quatercentenary of the birth of William Shakespeare. Hastings, 1964. Unpaged.

4924. Jaggard, W. Shakespeare bibliography: a dictionary of every known issue of the writings of our national poet and of recorded opinion thereon in the English language. Stratford on Avon: Shakespeare Pr., 1911. 729p.

Records 36,000 references; gives locations in British, American, and other libraries.

4925. John Rylands Library. Catalogue of an exhibition of the works of Shakespeare, his sources, and the writings of his principal contemporaries, with an introductory sketch, and sixteen facsimiles; tercentenary of the death of Shakespeare, 1616 April 23, 1916. Manchester: Univ. Pr., 1916. 169p. + 16 plates.

Based on John Rylands Library collection.

4926. Lee, Sidney. "Notes and additions to the census of copies of the Shakespeare First Folio." Library, ser.2, 7 (1906), 113-39.

Supplement to census published as supplement to Oxford facsimile of Shakespeare First Folio (1902), which enumerated all copies then known to Sidney Lee.

4927. National Library of Wales. Shakespeare tercentenary, 1916; annotated catalogue of books, etc., exhibited at the University College of Wales, Aberystwyth. Aberystwyth, 1916. 20p.

4928. Newcastle upon Tyne City Libraries. William Shakespeare; select catalogue of books in Newcastle upon Tyne City Libraries. Newcastle upon Tyne, 1952. 36p.

Classified by subjects or types of material.

4929. Oxford, University, Bodleian Library. A catalogue of the Shakespeare exhibition held in the Bodleian Library. Oxford, 1916. 99p.

Full bibliographical descriptions of 132 items drawn from Bodleian collection.

4930. ———. Specimens of Shakespeareana in the Bodleian Library. Oxford, 1927. 68p.

4931. ———. William Shakespeare, 1564-1964; a catalogue of the quatercentenary exhibition in the Divinity School. Oxford, 1964. 83p.

4932. Payne, W. R. N. "The Shakespeare Memorial Library." Library world, 65 (1964), 255-56.

Review of resources of 38,000-volume library relating to Shakespeare in Birmingham; includes all folios and numerous other rarities.

4933. ———. "Shakespeare Memorial Library, Birmingham." Library Association record, 60 (1958), 120-22.

History and description of resources of library established in 1864.

4934. Shakespeare Library and Museum. A catalogue of the books, manuscripts, works of art, antiquities, and relics, illustrative of the life and works of Shake-speare, and of the history of Stratford-upon-Avon; which are preserved in the Shakespeare Library and Museum in Henley Street. London: Shakespeare Fund, 1868. 183p.

4935. Shakespeare Memorial Library. Illustrated catalogue of the pictures, etc., in the Shakespeare Memorial at Stratford Upon Avon. 3d ed. Stratford on Avon: John Morgan, 1903. 100p.

4936. Shakespeare's Birthplace. Catalogue of the books, manuscripts, works of art, antiquities, and relics exhibited in Shakespeare's Birthplace, comp. by Frederick C. Wellstood, new ed. Stratford on Avon, 1944. 180p.

4937. ———. List of manorial documents preserved in the Record Room of the Shakespeare Birthplace Trust, Stratford-upon-Avon, comp. by Frederick C. Wellstood. Frome & London: Butler & Tanner, 1942, p.259-63. (Reprinted from the Genealogists' magazine)

4938. ———. Shakespeare tercentenary commemoration, 1616-1916; catalogue of an exhibition of original documents of the XVIth & XVIIth centuries preserved in Stratford-upon-Avon, illustrating Shakespeare's life in the town, with appended lists of facsimiles belonging to the Trustees of contemporary Shakespearean documents which are preserved elsewhere, comp. by Frederick C. Wellstood. Stratford on Avon: Edward Fox, 1916. 50p.

4939. Shattuck, Charles H. The Shakespeare prompt-books: a descriptive catalogue. Urbana & London: Univ. of Ill. Pr., 1965. 553p.

About 2,000 entries; copies located in several hundred British, American, and other libraries.

4940. Southwark Public Libraries. Shakespeare first folio tercentenary 1623-1923, Southwark commemoration exhibition catalogue and catalogue of the Harvard-Shakespeare memorial donation. London, 1923. 36p.

4941. Victoria and Albert Museum. Shakespeare exhibition, 1916, 2d ed. London: H. M. Stationery Office, 1916. 20p.

Shaw, George Bernard, 1856-1950

4942. Birmingham Public Libraries. George Bernard Shaw centenary exhibition, 1956. Birmingham, 1956. 22p.

Catalog.

4943. Brown, Alison M. "The George Bernard Shaw papers." British Museum quarterly, 24 (1961), 14-21.

Description of extensive collection bequeathed by Shaw to British Museum.

Shelley, Percy Bysshe, 1792-1822

4944. Guildhall Library. Hand-list of manuscripts, letters, printed books, & personal relics of Percy Bysshe Shelley and his circle, exhibited, comp. by Charles Welch. London: Blades, East & Blades, 1893. 27p.

4945. Oxford, University, Bodleian Library. The Shelley collection; conditions [of presentation] proposed by Lady Shelley and accepted by the Bodleian Curators on June 11, 1892. Oxford, 1893. 3p.

Includes list of manuscripts, printed books, and portraits comprised in collection.

4946. ———. The Shelley correspondence in the Bodleian Library, edited by R. H. Hill, with a list of other Shelley manuscripts and relics in the Library. Oxford, 1926. 48p.

Sheridan, Frances, 1724-66

4947. Russell, Norma Hull. "Some uncollected authors, XXXVIII: Frances Sheridan, 1724-1766." Book collector, 13 (1964), 196-205.

Editions of Mrs. Sheridan's novels, plays, poems, etc., located in English and American libraries.

Shuttleworth, Sir J. P. Kay, 1804-77

4948. St. Mark and St. John, College, Library. A handlist of the papers in the deed box of Sir J. P. Kay Shuttleworth (1804-1877), by B. C. Bloomfield. Manchester, 1961. 66p. (Occasional papers, no.2)

Collection now held by Manchester University Library.

Siddons, Sarah, 1755-1831

4949. Burnim, Kalman A. "The letters of Sarah and William Siddons to Hester Lynch Piozzi in the John Rylands Library." Bulletin of the John Rylands Library, 52 (1969), 46-95.

Sidney, Philip, 1554-86

4950. Juel-Jensen, Bent. "Some uncollected author-XXXIV: Sir Philip Sidney, 1554-1586." Book collector, 11 (1962), 468-79.

Copies of Sidney's Arcadia and other works located in British and American libraries.

4951. Oxford, University, Bodleian Library. Sir Philip Sidney, 1554-1586; list of exhibits. Oxford, 1954. 1v. Unpaged.

Simons, Menno, c. 1496-1561

4952. Horst, Irvin B. A bibliography of Menno Simons, ca. 1496-1561, Dutch reformer, with a census of known copies. Nieuwkoop: B. De Graaf, 1962. 157p.

Lists 166 items, locating copies in British Museum, 14 Continental and 38 American libraries.

Sitwell, Edith, 1887-1964

4953. Lewis, Jenny. "Edith Sitwell letters." British Museum quarterly, 30 (1965), 17-22.

Description of over 200 items received by British Museum.

Smart, Christopher, 1722-71

4954. Gray, George John. "A bibliography of the writings of Christopher Smart." Transactions of the Bibliographical Society, 6 (1901-2), 269-303.

Checklist of 57 items, 1740-51, with some copies located.

Smith, Adam, 1723-90

4955. Bonar, James. A catalogue of the library of Adam Smith. London: Macmillan, 1894. 126p.

4956. ———. A catalogue of the library of Adam Smith, author of the "Moral Sentiments" and "The Wealth of Nations," 2d ed. London: Macmillan, 1932. 218p.

Locates copies in libraries.

4957. Mizuta, Hiroshi. Adam Smith's Library, a supplement to Bonar's Catalogue, with a checklist of the whole Library. Cambridge: Univ. Pr. for the Royal Economic Society, 1967. 153p.

Locates copies in 23 public and private libraries, British, American, Japanese, etc.

Smith, Sir Jarrit, 1692-1783

4958. Ratcliffe, F. A. Ashton Court: the papers of Jarrit Smith. London, 1962. 207l. (Diploma in Archive Administration, Univ. of London)

Calendar of records in Bristol Archives Office relating to Sir Jarrit Smith (1692-1783), Bristol businessman.

Smith, William, 1769-1839

4959. Eyles, Joan M. "William Smith (1769-1839): a bibliography of his published writings, maps and geological sections, printed and lithographed." Journal of the Society for the Bibliography of Natural History, 5 (1969), 87-109.

Copies located in 6 English libraries.

Southey, Robert, 1774-1843

4960. Wright, C. E. "Manuscripts and papers of Robert Southey." British Museum quarterly, 19 (1954), 32-33.

Describes collection of literary manuscripts and letters received by British Museum.

Southwell, Robert, 1561?-95

4961. Janelle, Pierre. "Bibliography." In his: Robert Southwell the writer; a study in religious inspiration. N.Y., 1935, p.306-23.

Locates copies of Southwell writings, manuscript and printed, in British and French libraries.

4962. Macdonald, James Harold. The poems and prose writings of Robert Southwell, S. J.: a bibliographical study. Oxford: Printed for the Roxburghe Club, 1937. 161p.

Locates copies.

Spenser, Edmund, 1552?-99

4963. Johnson, Francis R. A critical bibliography of the works of Edmund Spenser printed before 1700. Baltimore, Md.: Johns Hopkins, 1933. 61p.

Describes in detail 23 works in 66 libraries, British and American.

Stanley, Thomas, 1625-78

4964. Flower, Margaret Cameron. "Thomas Stanley (1625-1678); a bibliography of his writings in prose and verse (1647-1743)." Transactions of the Cambridge Bibliographical Society, 1 (1950), 139-72.

Copies of 68 items located in British and American libraries.

Steele, Richard, 1672-1729

4965. Blanchard, Rae. "The Christian hero by Richard Steele: a bibliography." Library, ser.4, 10 (1929), 61-72.

Detailed descriptions of editions, 1701-1820, with locations in English and American libraries.

Sterne, Laurence, 1713-68

4966. Oates, J. C. T. "Notes on the bibliography of Sterne." Cambridge Bibliographical Society transactions, 2 (1955), 155-69.

Locates copies examined.

Stevenson, Robert Louis, 1850-94

4967. Edinburgh Public Library. Robert Louis Stevenson, 1850-1894, catalogue of the Stevenson collection in the Edinburgh Room, Central Library. Edinburgh, 1950. 37p.

In 2 parts: books by Stevenson; books about Stevenson.

Stukeley, William, 1687-1765

4968. Long, P. "The Keiller collection of Stukeley papers." Bodleian Library record, 5 (1956), 256-61.

Describes collection of manuscripts of William Stukeley, archaeologist and antiquarian presented to Bodleian Library.

Suetonius, Caius, fl. 2d century A.D.

4969. Briggs, Geoffrey Hugh. Suetonius; a bibliography of editions of the text of the Vitae Caesarum of Caius Suetonius Tranquillus published between the years 1470-1570. London, 1950. 79l. (Diploma in Librarianship, Univ. of London)

Locates copies examined.

Swift, Jonathan, 1667-1745

4970. Cambridge, University. A catalogue of printed books and manuscripts by Jonathan Swift, D.D., exhibited in the Old Schools in the University of Cambridge, to commemorate the 200th anniversary of his death, October 19, 1745, comp. by John D. Hayward. Cambridge: Univ. Pr., 1945. 45p.

Copies located in private and public collections.

4971. Craig, Maurice James. "Short catalogue of the exhibition held in the Royal College of Physicians in Ireland." In: St. Patrick's Hospital. The legacy of Swift, a bi-centenary record. Dublin, 1948, p.49-70.

4972. Dublin, University, Trinity College Library. Catalogue of the exhibition held in the Library . . . to commemorate the bicentenary of the death of Jonathan Swift. Dublin: Univ. Pr. by Ponsonby and Gibbs, 1945. 16p.

4973. Ehrenpreis, Irvin, and Clifford, James L. "Swiftiana in Rylands English ms. 659 and related documents." Bulletin of the John Rylands Library, 37 (1955), 368-92. Reprinted, 1955. 27p.

4974. Teerink, H. A bibliography of the writings in prose and verse of Jonathan Swift, D.D. The Hague: Nijhoff, 1937. 434p.

4975. ———. A bibliography of the writings of Jonathan Swift, 2d ed., ed. by Arthur H. Scouten. Philadelphia: Univ. of Pa. Pr., 1963. 453p.

Copies located in British, Irish, American, and other libraries.

Synge, John Millington, 1871-1909

4976. Dublin, University, Trinity College Library. John Millington Synge, 1871-1909: a catalogue of an exhibition held . . . on the occasion of the fiftieth anniversary of his death, comp. by Ian MacPhail, with the help of M. Pollard. Dublin: Dolmen, 1959. 38p.

4977. ———. The Synge manuscripts in the Library of Trinity College, Dublin; a catalogue on the occasion of the Synge centenary exhibition, 1971. Dublin, 1971. 55p.

Taylor, Jeremy, 1613-67

4978. Gathorne-Hardy, Robert, and Williams, William Proctor. A bibliography of the writings of Jeremy Taylor to 1700, with a section of Tayloriana. De Kalb: Northern Ill. Univ. Pr., 1971. 159p.

Locations in numerous British and American libraries.

Tennyson, Alfred, 1809-92

4979. Lincoln City Libraries, Museum and Art Gallery Committee. Tennyson collection: Usher Gallery, Lincoln, with foreword and annotations by Sir Charles Tennyson. Lincoln, 1963. 34p. + 5 plates.

Permanent exhibition; catalog of 394 items, including manuscripts, proofs, portraits, printed editions, books from Tennyson's library, etc.

4980. Ricks, Christopher. "The Tennyson manuscripts at Trinity College, Cambridge." Times literary supplement, August 21, 1969, p.918-22.

4981. Tennyson Research Centre Library. Tennyson in Lincoln: a catalogue of the collections in the Research Centre, comp. by Nancie Campbell. Lincoln: Tennyson Society, 1971. 203p. v.1.

4982. Tennyson Research Centre, Tennyson Society. Tennyson research bulletin, no.1, Oct. 1967- . Lincoln, 1967- .

Issued periodically.

4983. Wise, Thomas J. A bibliography of the writings of Alfred, Lord Tennyson. London, 1908. 209p. Reprinted, London: Dawsons of Pall Mall, 1967.

Occasional locations in British Museum.

Thomas à Kempis, 1380-1471

4984. Evans, Albert Owen. "Thomas à Kempis and Wales." Welsh Bibliographical Society journal, 4 (1932), 5-32.

Checklist of 22 items, 1679-1908; copies located.

Thomas, Dylan, 1914-53

4985. Gransden, K. W. "Early poems of Dylan Thomas." British Museum quarterly, 19 (1954), 50-51.

Describes manuscripts received by British Museum.

4986. Swansea Public Libraries. Exhibition two Swansea poets: Dylan Thomas & Vernon Watkins; 3rd-12th July, 1969, catalogue. Swansea: Public Libraries Committee, 1969. 15l.

Thomas, Edward, 1878-1917

4987. Oxford, University, Bodleian Library. Edward Thomas, 1878-1917; an exhibition held in the Divinity School, Oxford, 1968. Oxford, 1968. 38p.

Annotated list of 99 items, drawn mainly from Bodleian Library collection.

Thompson, Francis Joseph, 1859-1907

4988. Harris Public Library. Catalogue of the "Francis Thompson" collection, presented to the Harris Public Library by Mr. J. H. Spencer, 26th October, 1950; with a supplementary list of "Thompsoniana" already in the stock of the Harris Reference Library. Preston, 1959? 24p.

4989. ———, Museum, and Art Gallery. Francis Thompson centenary, 1859-1959; catalogue of manuscripts, letters and books in the Harris Public Library, Preston, based on the collection presented by Mr. J. H. Spencer in 1950. Preston, 1959. 77p.

Thompson, Silvanus Phillips, 1851-1916

4990. London, University, Imperial College. List of the papers and correspondence of Silvanus Phillips Thompson, F.R.S., preserved in the Imperial College Archives. London, 1967. 61p.

Thompson was Professor of Applied Physics and Electrical Engineering, Finsbury Technical College, 1885-1916.

Thompson, Thomas Perronet, 1783-1869

4991. Leeds, University, Brotherton Library. Inventory of the correspondence of Thomas Perronet Thompson (1783-1869) & members of his family & related material. Leeds, 1971. 32p.

General Thompson was politician, reformer, and one-time governor of Sierra Leone.

Thomson, James, 1700-1748

4992. Rodgers, Francis. James Thomson (1700-48); a bibliography of his minor work to the year 1800. London, 1952. 125*l.* (Diploma in Librarianship, Univ. of London)

Notes copies seen in various libraries.

Toland, John, 1670-1722

4993. Dienemann, W. A bibliography of John Toland (1670-1722). London, 1953. 116*l.* (Diploma in Librarianship, Univ. of London)

Copies located.

Tyndale, William, 1492?-1536

4994. Gloucester Public Library. 400th anniversary of the martyrdom of William Tyndale. Gloucester, 1936. 14p.

"A list of the material available in the Public Library of the city of Gloucester concerning William Tyndale (otherwise known as William Huchyns), reformer, translator, martyr, died 6 October 1536."

Unwin, William Cawthorne, 1838-1933

4995. London, University, Imperial College. List of the papers and correspondence of William Cawthorne Unwin, F.R.S., preserved in the Imperial College Archives. London, 1966. 31p.

Unwin was professor of engineering in Central Technical College, a predecessor of Imperial College.

Vancouver, George, 1757-98

4996. Richmond Public Library. A list of books, prints, maps, etc., relating to Captain George Vancouver . . . contained in the Vancouver collection. Richmond, Surrey, 1936. 9*l.*

Vaughan Williams, Ralph, 1872-1958

4997. DeLaMare, Judith Mary. Bibliography of the published musical works of Ralph Vaughan Williams in the Library of the British Museum up to 1st May,

1949. London, 1949. 2v. (Diploma in Librarianship, Univ. of London)

4998. Willetts, Pamela J. "The Ralph Vaughan Williams collection." British Museum quarterly, 24 (1961), 3-11.

Description, with detailed listing, of Williams collection acquired by British Museum.

Vergil, 70-19 B.C.

4999. British Museum, Dept. of Printed Books. Catalogue of printed books: Virgilius Maro (Publius). London, 1882. 74 cols.

5000. Copinger, W. A. "Incunabula Virgiliana; a list of editions of Virgil printed during the 15th century." Bibliographical Society transactions, 2 (1893-94), 123-226.

Detailed bibliographical descriptions with locations of copies.

Vesalius, Andreas, 1514-64

5001. Glasgow, University, Hunterian Library. An exhibition of books and manuscripts held in the Hunterian Library, University of Glasgow, to commemorate the quatercentenary of the death of Andreas Vesalius. Glasgow, 1964. 19p.

Records 73 items, annotated.

Wallace the Minstrel (Blind Harry), fl. 1470-92

5002. Miller, J. F. "Blind Harry Wallace." Glasgow Bibliographical Society records, 3 (1914), 1-25.

Bibliography, 1488-1910, with locations of copies, of works relating to Henry the Minstrel (Blind Harry).

Walpole, Horace, 1717-97

5003. Hazen, Allen T. A bibliography of Horace Walpole. New Haven, Conn.: Yale Univ. Pr., 1948. 189p.

Copies located in British, American, and other libraries.

5004. Malcolmson, A. P. W. "Some new Walpoliana from the Caledon papers, Public Record Office of Northern Ireland." Irish booklore, 1 (1971), 157-64.

Letters of Horace Walpole.

Walpole, Robert, 1676-1745

5005. Cambridge, University, Library. A handlist of the Cholmondeley-Houghton mss., Sir Robert Walpole's archive, by G. A. Chinnery. Cambridge, 1953. 30p.

Walton, Izaak, 1593-1683

5006. Butt, J. E. "A bibliography of Izaak Walton's Lives." Oxford Bibliographical Society, Proceedings and papers, 2 (1930), 327-40.

Detailed bibliographical descriptions of 18 17th-century editions, with some locations.

5007. Oliver, Peter. A new chronicle of The compleat angler. N.Y. and London: Paisley Pr., Williams & Norgate, 1936. 301p.

Copies located of 284 items, 1653-1935, in British Museum and in American libraries.

Watt, James, 1736-1819

5008. Birmingham Board of Education, Science Museum. Catalogue of the Watt centenary exhibition. Birmingham, 1919. 45p.

Includes exhibits from the Boulton and Watt collection in the Birmingham Reference Library.

Watts, Isaac, 1674-1748

5009. Stoke Newington Public Libraries. Catalogue of exhibition to commemorate the bi-centenary of Dr. Isaac Watts, 1674-1748. London, 1948. 31p.

Catalogue of 167 items by or about Watts; owners identified.

5010. Stone, Wilbur Macey. The divine and moral songs of Isaac Watts; an essay and a tentative list of editions. N.Y., 1918. 93p.

Lists British and American editions, with locations of copies in British, Irish, and American libraries.

Wells, Herbert George, 1866-1946

5011. Birmingham Public Libraries. Books by and about H. G. Wells, 1866-1946, in the Birmingham Public Libraries. Birmingham, 1966. 4p.

5012. Ealing Public Libraries. H. G. Wells, 1866-1946; a centenary booklist, comp. by James W. Thirsk. London Borough of Ealing, 1966. 15p.

Locates copies in 17 libraries.

5013. Spade House. Centenary of H. G. Wells, 1866-1966: Spade House, Folkestone, comp. by James E. Brydone. Folkestone, 1966. 16p.

Wesley, John, 1703-91

5014. Baker, Frank. A union catalogue of the publi-

cations of John and Charles Wesley. Durham, N.C.: Divinity School, Duke Univ., 1966. 230p.

Copies located in numerous British, American, Canadian, and other libraries.

White, Gilbert, 1720-93

5015. British Museum (Natural History). Gilbert White of Selborne; an exhibition commemorating the 250th anniversary of his birth. London, 1970. 272p.

5016. Ealing Public Libraries. Selborne Society Library; a catalogue of mss., books and periodicals devoted to Gilbert White and natural history. London Borough of Ealing, 1958. 34p.

Society's library is now deposited in Ealing Public Libraries.

Whitman, Walt, 1819-92

5017. Bolton Public Libraries. A catalogue of works by and relating to Walt Whitman in the Reference Library, Bolton. Bolton: The Libraries Committee, 1955. 52p.

Includes books, manuscripts, letters, portraits, association items.

5018. ———. Collection of Whitmaniana in the Reference Library, Bolton, by Archibald Sparke. Bolton: The Libraries Committee, 1931. 28p.

Collection of books by and about Walt Whitman.

Whittington, Robert, fl. 1490-1548

5019. Bennett, H. S. "A check-list of Robert Whittington's Grammars." Library, ser.5, 7 (1952), 1-14.

Locates copies of 1515-32 editions in British and American libraries.

Wilberforce, William, 1759-1833

5020. Kingston upon Hull Public Libraries. William Wilberforce, 1759-1833; a catalogue of the books and pamphlets on William Wilberforce and slavery in the Reference Library of Kingston upon Hull Public Libraries; issued on the occasion of the bicentenary of his birth with particular reference to his part in the abolition of the slave trade and emancipation of the slaves in the British Colonies. Kingston upon Hull, 1959. 36p.

Wilde, Jane Francesca, 1826-96

5021. Coleman, James. "Bibliography of Lady Wilde,

née Jane Francesca Elgee." Irish book lover, 20 (1932), 60.

Locates copies.

Wilde, Oscar, 1856-1900

5022. Dublin, University, Trinity College Library. Catalogue of an exhibition of books and manuscripts in commemoration of the centenary of the birth of Oscar Wilde, 1954. Dublin: Univ. Pr., Trinity College, 1954. 24p.

Wilkes, John, 1727-97

5023. Guildhall Library. "A select list of works in Guildhall Library by, or relating to, John Wilkes." Guildhall miscellany, 3 (1969), 75-84.

Williams, David, 1738-1816

5024. Williams, David. "A bibliography of the printed work of David Williams, 1738-1816." National Library of Wales journal, 10 (1957), 121-36.

List of 35 items, 1771-1810, with locations of copies.

Willis, Thomas, 1621-75

5025. Wing, H. J. R. A bibliography of Dr. Thomas Willis (1621-1675). London, 1962. 127l. (Diploma in Librarianship, Univ. of London)

Works by and about English physician; copies located in 11 libraries.

Wilson, H. J., 1833-1914

5026. Sheffield City Libraries. Catalogue of the papers of H. J. Wilson, M.P., and Mrs. M. A. Rawson deposited in Sheffield City Library at various dates. Sheffield, n.d. 20l.

Wilson was radical and nonconformist Liberal M.P. 1885-1912.

Wise, Thomas James, 1859-1937

5027. Guildhall Library. "A handlist of books in Guildhall Library associated with Thomas J. Wise." Guildhall miscellany, 2 (1962), 165-69. "Additional items," 2 (1965), 305-6.

Lists forgeries, counterfeits, and piracies.

Withering family

5028. Birmingham, University, Library. Catalogue of the Withering collection. Birmingham, 1972. Unpaged.

Relates to William Withering of Birmingham and family, 16th to 19th centuries.

5029. ———. William Withering letters, handlist. Birmingham, 1968. Unpaged. (Catalogues of the manuscript collections, no.16)

Lists 20 late-18th-century items.

Wordsworth, William, 1770-1850

5030. Dove Cottage, Local Committee of Management. The official catalogue of Dove Cottage, Grasmere, the home of Wordsworth . . . and of DeQuincey. Ambleside: G. Middleton, 1911. 39p.

Worthington, John, 1618-71

5031. Christie, Richard Copley. A bibliography of the works written and edited by Dr. John Worthington. Manchester: Chetham Society, 1888. 88p.

Worthington was Master of Jesus College, Cambridge, Vice-Chancellor of the University of Cambridge, etc.; copies located, principally in British Museum.

Wright, Thomas, 1561-1623

5032. Rogers, David Morrison. "A bibliography of the published works of Thomas Wright (1561-1623)." Biographical studies, 1 (1952), 262-80.

Lists 14 items, with locations of copies and STC numbers.

Wycliffe, John, 1320?-1384

5033. British Museum. Wycliffe exhibition in the King's Library, arr. by E. M. Thompson. London: W. Clowes, 1884. 68p.

Xenophon, 434?-355 B.C.?

5034. British Museum, Dept. of Printed Books. Catalogue of printed books: Xenophon. London: The Museum, 1883. 28 cols.

Yeats, William Butler, 1865-1939

5035. Dublin, University, Trinity College Library, Friends of the Library of Trinity College. W. B. Yeats: manuscripts and printed books exhibited in the Library of Trinity College, Dublin, 1956; catalogue comp. by R. O. Dougan. Dublin, 1956. 50p.

Lists 154 items, with additional section of portraits and illustrations; chronological arrangement.

5036. Newcastle upon Tyne, University, Library. William Butler Yeats, 1865-1939: catalogue of an exhibition. Newcastle upon Tyne, 1969. 19*l*.

Young, Arthur, 1741-1820

5037. Gazley, John G. "Arthur Young, agriculturalist and traveller, 1741-1820; some biographical sources." Bulletin of the John Rylands Library, 37 (1955), 393-428. Reprinted, 1955. 38p.

Based in part of Bagshawe collection deposited in John Rylands Library.

5038. ———. "The Reverend Arthur Young, 1769-1827: traveller in Russia and farmer in the Crimea." Bulletin of the John Rylands Library, 38 (1956), 360-405. Reprinted, 1956. 48p.

Largely based on Bagshawe records in John Rylands Library.

Young, Francis Brett, 1884-1954

5039. Birmingham, University, Library. Catalogue of the Francis Brett Young manuscript collection, by D. W. Evans. Birmingham, 1968. 120*l*.

Index

gold work, 2781; handwriting, 871; heraldry, 3528-29; illuminated manuscripts, 796-98; illustrated books, 1369-72; incunabula, 1149; Japanese art, 2812-14; London history, 3974; manuscripts, 2731; metal work, 2780; miniature books, 1312; musical instruments, 2985-86; ornament, 2783; painting and drawings, 2787-88; photography, 2822-23; portraits, 2795; pottery and porcelain, 2778; printers' marks, 920; printing, 921; Pugin family, 4849; Science Library, 2109; sculpture, 2759; seals, 2768; Shakespeare, William, 4941; textiles, 2777; theatre art, 2831; Whistler etchings, 2796

Victoria Cross, 2765

Victoria University Library: French Renaissance, 4218

Victorian literature, 1370, 1372

Viking Society for Northern Research, 4247

Vinaver, Eugène, 4762

Vincent, Benjamin, 195

Vincent, Charles W., 1690-91

Vinden, J. S., 4586

Vine, Guthrie, 1169, 2739, 2743, 4512

Virginia history, 4349

Vocal music, 2955-68

Voltaire, 4792

Voorhoeve, P., 3304-5

Vosper, Robert, 1313

Waddesdon Manor Library, 3131

Wagner, Anthony Richard, 3523, 3530

Wagner, Henry Raup, 1740

Wainwright, Mary Doreen, 4274

Wales, A. P., 122

Wales National School of Medicine Libraries: periodicals, 2442

Wales, University College, Library: periodicals, 536

Walford, A. J., 5, 4362

Walker, Benjamin, 620

Walker, Gregory, 4243-44

Walker, J. W., 3977

Walker, James E., 3842

Walker, John S., 116

Walker, Marjorie, 4639

Walker, T. MacCallum, 123

Walker, Violet M., 4869

Walker, Violet W., 1511, 4869

Wallace, A., 2146

Wallace the Minstrel, 5002

Wallenstein, Meir, 3293

Waller, Ross D., 4629

Wallington Public Library, 7

Walne, Peter, 3458, 3744, 3747

Walpole, Horace, 355, 5003-4

Walpole, Robert, 5005

Walsall Corporation: records, 4141

Walsh, John, 2876-77

Walters Art Gallery: calligraphy, 874

Walthamstow Antiquarian Society: records, 4142

Waltherr, László, 3143

Walton, Izaak, 5006-7

Walton, Joseph, 3993

Walton, S. M., 2607

Wandsworth Public Libraries, 294; education, 2025

Ward, William S., 537

Wardle, D. B., 4356

Wardrop, J. Oliver, 3236

Warner, George F., 653, 655, 698, 751, 801, 3586

Warner, John, 3990

Warrington Public Library: local history, 4143

Warwick County Council, Education Committee Library, 2026

Warwick County Record Office, 4144

Warwick, University, Library: chemistry, 2243; engineering and physics, 2503; periodicals, 538

Warwickshire County Library: plays, 3080

Warwickshire County Museum, Dugdale, William, 4590

Waterhouse, F. H., 2310

Waterloo, University, Library: government publications, 40

Watford College of Technology: printing, 923

Watford Public Libraries; printing, 924

Watkins, Vernon, 4986

Watson, Andrew C., 836, 4880

Watson, Charles, B. B., 3452

Watson, Edward John McCartney, 1586

Watson, Henry, 2872, 2914

Watson, William, 2773

Watt, James, 5008

Watts, G. H., 1222

Watts, Gertrude, 2218

Watts, Isaac, 5009-10

Way, D. J., 1880

Weale, W. H. James, 1320, 1355, 1358, 2606

Weaver, Warren, 4492

Webb, G. F., 4149

Weedon Margaret J. P., 4700-1

Wegelin, Oscar, 3041

Weil, Ernst, 968

Weiss, Harry Bishoff, 3201

Welch, C. E., 1618, 4039

Welch, Charles, 4944

Weldrick, J. F., 4185

Welfare and social activities, 1944-57

Welford, Richard, 3472

Wellcome Historical Medical Library, 2331; Arabic

THE
HOWARD UNIVERSITY
BIBLIOGRAPHY OF AFRICAN
AND
AFRO-AMERICAN
RELIGIOUS STUDIES